ANTHOLOGY OF SCORES TO

A HISTORY

OF MUSIC IN WESTERN CULTURE

Volume II: The Classical Era through the Twentieth Century

Second Edition

MARK EVAN BONDS
Department of Music
University of North Carolina at Chapel Hill

PEARSON

Prentice Hall

Upper Saddle River, New Jersey 07458

Library of Congress Cataloging-in-Publication Data

Bonds, Mark Evan.
  A history of music in Western culture / Mark Evan Bonds.—2nd ed.
    p. cm.
  Includes bibliographical references and index.
  ISBN 0-13-193104-0 (main textbooks)
  1. Music—History and criticism. I. Title.

ML160.B75 2006
780'.9—dc22

2004043171

President, Humanities/Social Sciences:
  Yolanda de Rooy
**AVP/Director of Production and
Manufacturing:** Barbara Kittle
Editor-in-Chief: Sarah Touborg
Acquisitions Editor: Christopher T. Johnson
Editorial Assistant: Evette Dickerson
Marketing Manager: Sheryl Adams
Marketing Assistant: Cherron Gardner

Managing Editor: Lisa Iarkowski
Production Editor: Joseph Scordato
Production Assistant: Marlene Gassler
Permissions Supervisor: Ron Fox
Manufacturing Manager: Nick Skilitis
Manufacturing Buyer: Ben Smith
Creative Design Director: Leslie Osher
Interior and Cover Design: Laura Gardner

Credits and acknowledgments borrowed from other sources and reproduced, with permission,
in this textbook appear on pages 592–594.

This book was set in 9/11 Times Roman by A-R Editions, Inc. and was printed and bound by
The Courier Companies. The cover was printed by Phoenix Color Corp.

10 9 8 7 6 5 4 3 2 1
ISBN 0-13-193112-1

CONTENTS

PART FOUR
THE CLASSICAL ERA

99 Symphony in B Major, first movement
(ca. 1740)
Georg Matthias Monn (1717–1750)

CD7 Track 1 p. 323

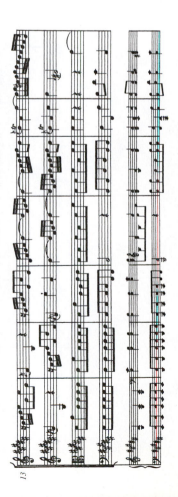

Note: The keyboard part (cembalo) represents the editor's realization of the original figured bass.

No. 99 Monn: Symphony in B Major

Monn's Symphony in B Major exhibits elements of both Baroque and Classical styles. The repetition of the opening four-measure phrase creates a kind of antiphonal effect, and the sequential writing that follows (m. 9) is typical of the Baroque. The bass line, however, is decidedly un-Baroque, in that it provides harmonic underpinning but very little in the way of an independent voice. With its steady drum-like rhythm and repetition of single notes for up to two measures, the bass line also helps create a relatively slow harmonic rhythm.

Formally, the movement represents an early manifestation of sonata form. The exposition (m. 1–31) sets out two different themes in the tonic (1P and 2P, the latter beginning in m. 9), another within the transition from the tonic to the secondary key area (T, beginning in m. 19), and another (1S, m. 26) in the secondary key area, F# major, the dominant of B. The development (m. 32–58) begins with 1P but now in the dominant. The development then circulates through a series of harmonies, none of which establishes an area of clear stability. From m. 39 until the end of the development, a variant of the musical idea 2P predominates. At m. 59, the recapitulation begins with the return of the opening theme (1P) in its original key. At m. 67 we hear what is recognizably 2P, but in a different form. Beginning in m. 79, we hear a variant of the transitional theme (T), which now remains in the tonic, leading to a restatement of 1S (m. 86), likewise in the tonic. The movement ends with the recapitulation and has no coda.

The first movement of Monn's Symphony in B Major.

Section	Exposition				Development		Recapitulation			
Themes	‖:1P	2P	T	1S	:‖: 1P	2P	1P	2P	T	1S .‖
Measure	1	9	19	26	32	39	59	67	79	86
Key	I		V		V	ii (unstable)	I			

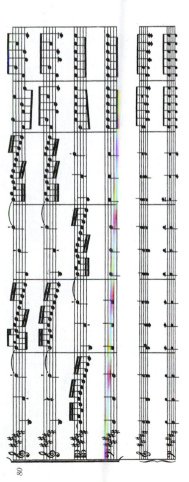

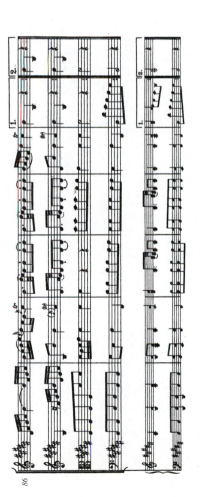

74

80

86

No. 99 Monn: Symphony in B Major

100 Sonata in D Major, K. 492 (ca. 1750?)

Domenico Scarlatti (1685–1757)

CD7 Track 4 · p. 324

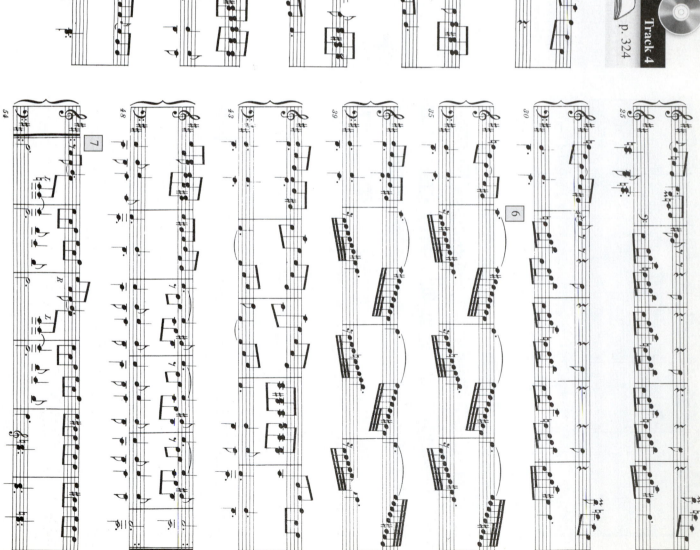

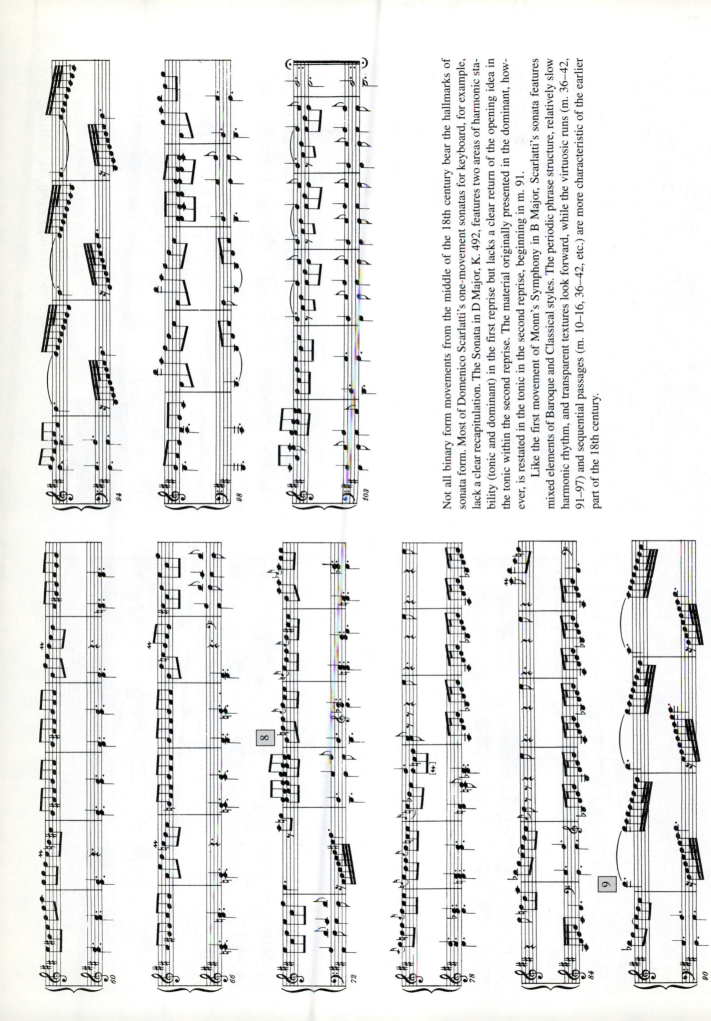

Not all binary form movements from the middle of the 18th century bear the hallmarks of sonata form. Most of Domenico Scarlatti's one-movement sonatas for keyboard, for example, lack a clear recapitulation. The Sonata in D Major, K. 492, features two areas of harmonic stability (tonic and dominant) in the first reprise but lacks a clear return of the opening idea in the tonic within the second reprise. The material originally presented in the dominant, however, is restated in the tonic in the second reprise, beginning in m. 91.

Like the first movement of Monn's Symphony in B Major, Scarlatti's sonata features mixed elements of Baroque and Classical styles. The periodic phrase structure, relatively slow harmonic rhythm, and transparent textures look forward, while the virtuosic runs (m. 36–42, 91–97) and sequential passages (m. 10–16, 36–42, etc.) are more characteristic of the earlier part of the 18th century.

No. 100 Scarlatti: Sonata in D Major, K. 492

■ **5**

101 Symphony in D Major, Op. 3, No. 2,
first movement (ca. 1752–1755)
Johann Stamitz (1717–1757)

CD7 Track 10   p. 324

Timpano
2 Clarini in D.
2 Corni in D.
2 Oboi. (vel Flauti.)
Violino I.
Violino II.
Viola.
Basso.
Klavierauszug.)

Presto.

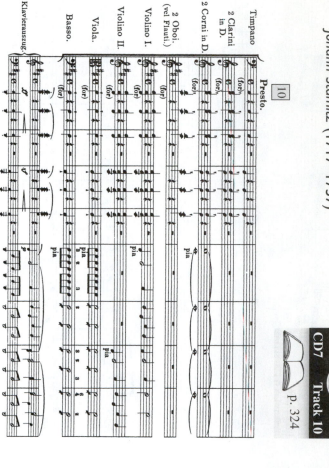

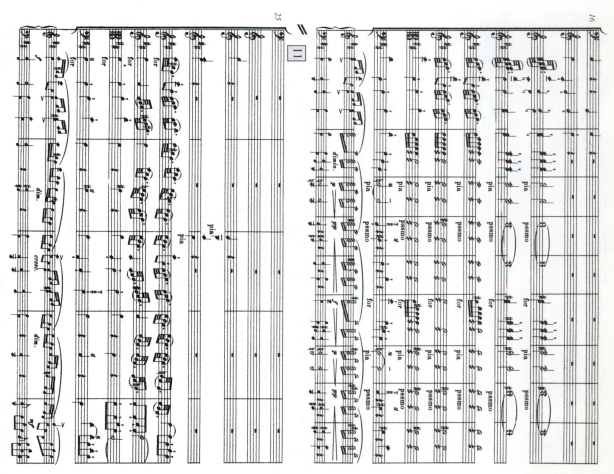

*) Timpani, Clarini und Oboi fehlen in der Pariser Ausgabe. Der erste Satz ist mit Allegro comodo bezeichnet. Bässe und Viola haben Takt 5–12 und in den Parallelstellen ausgehaltene Töne statt der Achtel.

Note: The keyboard reduction (Klavierauszug) is for rehearsal purposes only and is not part of Stamitz's original score.

No. 101 Stamitz: Symphony in D Major, Op. 3, No. 2

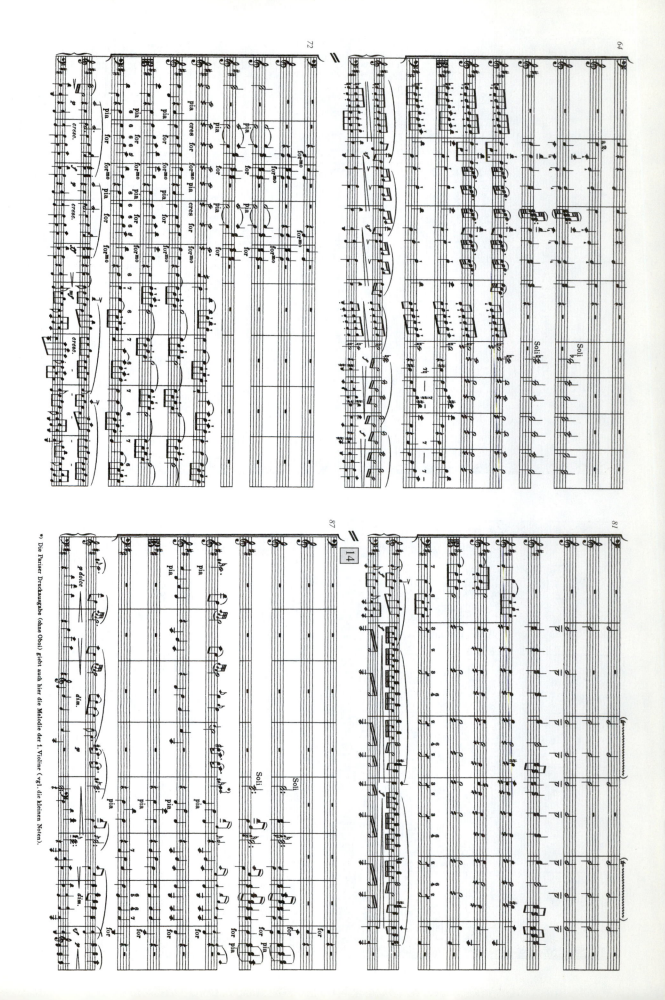

8   ■   No. 101 Stamitz: Symphony in D Major, Op. 3, No. 2

*) Die Pariser Druckausgabe (ohne Oboi) giebt auch hier die Melodie der 1. Violine (vgl. die kleinen Noten).

No. 101 Stamitz: Symphony in D Major, Op. 3, No. 2

9

Binary form is not the only historical antecedent to sonata form. Another is the ritornello structure of the typical Baroque aria or concerto. Like sonata form, the ritornello structure features a modulation from a primary to a secondary key area, followed by a period of harmonic instability and a return to the tonic at the end. Thus the first movement of Stamitz's Symphony in D Major, Op. 3, No. 2, although it more closely follows a ritornello structure, can also be analyzed in terms of sonata form. Consistent with ritornello structure, two statements of the opening theme in the tonic (m. 5, m. 103) flank a middle statement of the same theme in the dominant (m. 53), with contrasting material in between. Following the pattern of sonata form, the opening section of the movement progresses from tonic to dominant; the music then moves to a different key area (m. 77) before returning to the tonic (m. 87). The return of the opening theme (m. 103) does not coincide with the return of the tonic, however, and in this sense, the recapitulation is diffused. Many movements from the mid-18th century feature such mixed elements of old (ritornello) and new (sonata) forms, however. Even in the later decades of the 18th century, composers frequently departed from the standard conventions of sonata form.

The relationship of ritornello structure and sonata form in the first movement of Stamitz's Symphony in D Major, Op. 3, No. 2.

Ritornello Structure	Rit. I					Rit. II					Rit. III	
Sonata form	"Exposition"					"Development"					"Recapitulation"	
Themes	1P	2P	1T	2T	1S	2S	1P	2P	2T	1S	2S	1P	2P
Measure	5	13	18	29	37	44	53	61	77	87	94	103	111
Key	I					V	V		IV	I			

This material is reprinted from J.C. Bach, *Twelve Keyboard Sonatas, Set 1 (Opus V)*, Oxford University Press.

102 Sonata in D Major, Op. 5, No. 2, first movement (1766)
Johann Christian Bach (1735–1782)

CD7 Track 16
P. 325

Allegro di molto

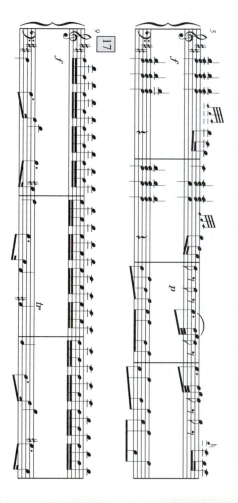

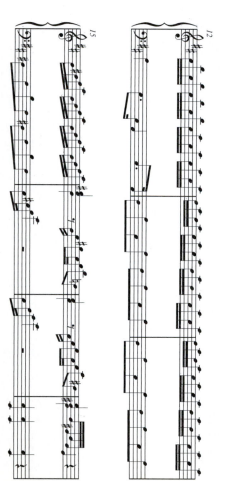

No. 102 J. C. Bach: Sonata in D Major, Op. 5, No. 2

11

No. 102 J. C. Bach: Sonata in D Major, Op. 5, No. 2

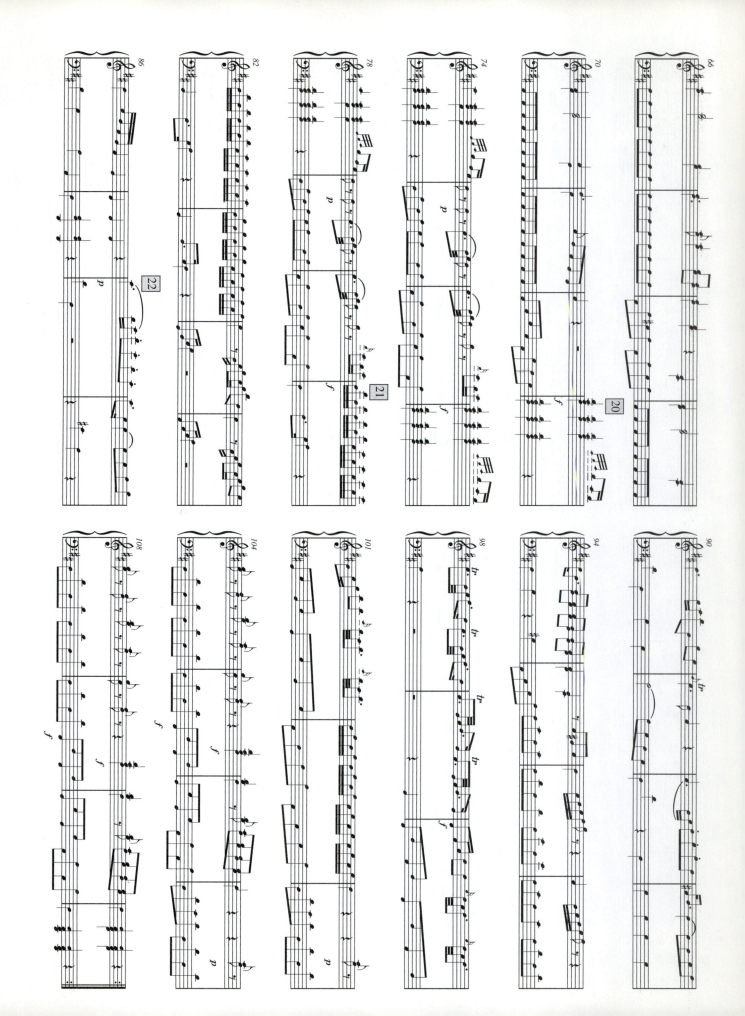

103 Fantasia in C minor (finale of Keyboard Sonata, Wq. 63/6) (1753)
Carl Philipp Emanuel Bach (1714–1788)

CD7 Track 23 p. 328

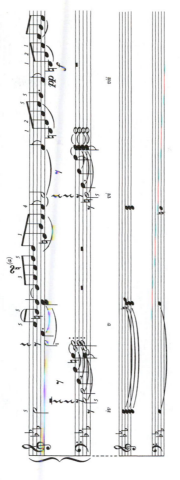

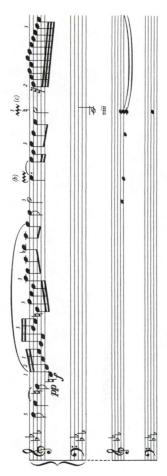

1) The two phrase-marks are printed thus in the source; but possibly they should end and begin one note later, on the C.

Note: The "Harmonic Skeleton" has been added by the editor of the score and is not part of C. P. E. Bach's original composition.

By the 1760s, sonata form had established itself as the structural framework for the first movements of most instrumental works, and for some slow movements and many finales as well. Except for concertos, the influence of ritornello structure had largely disappeared. The opening movement of Johann Christian Bach's Keyboard Sonata in D Major, Op. 5, No. 2, first published in 1766, is typical for its time, and not just from the standpoint of form. The simple, straightforward melodies, textures, and rhythms create a movement that is unpretentious in the best sense of the word. The first movement of this sonata offered what 18th-century critics perceived to be a natural form of expression that was unforced, without overt displays of contrapuntal, rhythmic, or textural artifice.

The sharp contrast between this movement by J. C. Bach and a work like his father Johann Sebastian Bach's "Goldberg" Variations, written only 25 years earlier, illustrates the generation gap that divided Classical from Baroque style. In the opening air of the "Goldberg" Variations, the theme is in the bass and remains there through all subsequent variations, while the melody in the soprano is of only momentary significance. In the opening measures of the son's work, in contrast, the lowest voice consists of repeated figurations on a series of triadic harmonies. This Alberti bass—so called because it was a favorite device of an otherwise obscure Italian composer named Domenico Alberti (1710–ca. 1740)—provides harmonic support for the melody in the upper voice but is not itself very engaging. The frequent repetition of the same broken chord necessarily leads to a harmonic rhythm slower than that typically found in music from the Baroque era. J. C. Bach's sonata also avoids the kind of sequential repetition so basic to much of his father's music.

Typically for music of the 1760s, the dimensions of J. C. Bach's movement are relatively small. The exposition presents only one theme in the primary key area (1P, m. 1–8), and the transitional theme (T) suggests a move away from the tonic as early as its second measure (with the A♯ in the bass at the end of m. 10) before cadencing clearly on V/V in m. 18. The first theme in the secondary key area (1S, beginning in m. 19) presents a strong contrast to the opening theme, and the exposition as a whole ends with a clearly articulated cadence (m. 42). During the development, the themes appear in fragments. The end of 1S, for example, appears at the beginning of the development in m. 43, and the beginning of T can be heard in m. 48. In m. 60 the harmony reaches what later theorists would call a "point of furthest remove" from the tonic, in this case B minor. The music then gathers itself for a retransition back to the tonic and the opening theme, which arrives with great emphasis at m. 77, the beginning of the recapitulation. In typical sonata form fashion, the themes are presented in the same order as in the exposition, but this time all in the tonic, and with only small variations and embellishments.

Performance notes: The fortepiano recorded here is a modern-day copy of an instrument built by Stein of Vienna in 1786, very similar to the one shown in the illustration textbook on p. 336.

No. 103 C. P. E. Bach: Fantasia in C minor

(h) *Bebung* (see Intro. p. 3)

2) Thus in the source. The dotted semibreve A in the r.h. is probably *not* a misprint of a dotted minim, but a way of securing a delayed entry of the *p* r.h. phrase that follows.

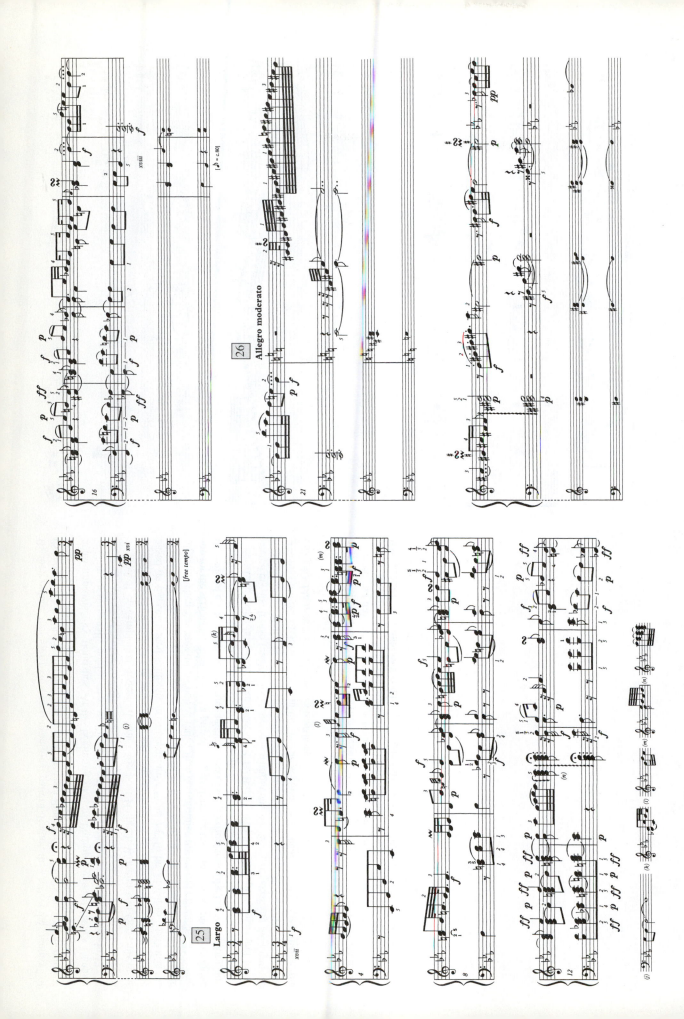

No. 103 C. P. E. Bach: Fantasia in C minor

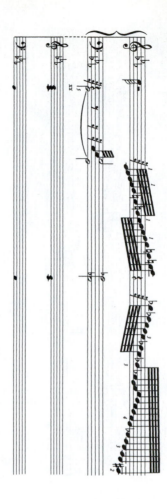

By their nature, fantasias follow no conventional pattern. Rather, they reflect the "fantasy" of the composer and/or performer. The typical fantasia thus often features no central musical idea and is instead characterized by a multiplicity of ideas, often linked by rhapsodic, quasi-improvisatory flourishes. At the beginning of Carl Philipp Emanuel Bach's Fantasia in C minor (originally published as the finale to a three-movement keyboard sonata in 1753), we hear a series of broken arpeggios and seemingly aimless passagework. The music conveys a mood of contemplation. Indeed, it struck the poet Heinrich Wilhelm von Gerstenberg as grappling with issues of life and death, inspiring him to set an elaborate text to this music based on the celebrated soliloquy in Shakespeare's *Hamlet* ("To be, or not to be: that is the question…"). Gerstenberg later set a second text to it as well, this one based on the dramatic moment when Socrates drinks poison rather than compromise his ethical principles. One reason for the serious reaction this work provoked is its dramatic trajectory: it begins with a mood of resigned contemplation, becomes agitated, recedes to a lyrical tone (the Largo section), and concludes with agitated force (Allegro moderato).

Like many fantasias of the time, C. P. E. Bach's is full of abrupt changes and unexpected events. It also features long stretches without any bar lines, emphasizing the rhythmic freedom with which it is to be performed. The notated meter at the opening—allegro moderato—seems almost irrelevant. Only in the middle section do we hear a recognizable theme in a recognizable meter; but this proves transitory.

Performance notes: The clavichord, unlike the harpsichord, allows the performer to inflect a note even after striking a key, applying pressure through the finger to create added vibration, an effect not unlike a string player's vibrato. This device, known as *Bebung* (from the German *beben*, meaning "to shake or quiver") is explictly notated through what look like a series of four staccato marks above a single note and is particularly audible in this recording at m. 19–21 of the middle Largo section.

104 **Piano Sonata in C minor**, Hob. XVI:20,
first movement (1771)
Joseph Haydn (1732–1809)

No. 104 Haydn: Piano Sonata in C minor, Hob. XVI:20

No. 104 Haydn: Piano Sonata in C minor, Hob. XVI:20

Haydn's Sonata in C minor, Hob. XVI:20, published in 1771, reflects the increasing size and complexity of sonata-form movements in the 1770s. Compared to Bach's Sonata in D Major, Op. 5, No. 2, Haydn's sonata is longer, more varied musically and emotionally, and technically more demanding of the performer.

The first eight measures of the sonata also illustrate Haydn's ability to create irregular patterns even within the constraints of periodic phrase structure. The opening two measures present a standard tonic to dominant progression, leading the listener familiar with this kind of pattern to expect the next two measures to lead back from the dominant to the tonic, completing a closed unit. But Haydn delays the half-cadence (a cadence on the dominant) by repeating the turning figure sequentially to create an antecedent phrase of four rather than two measures. The next two measures (5–6) reiterate the tonic, but this time in a lower register—register will be a very important compositional element in this movement—and after a surprise flourish in m. 6, the music returns to the tonic in m. 8. This initial point of harmonic and rhythmic closure, however, is not very strong. The composer does not yet want the music to come to a complete stop, so he creates the expectation of continuity by placing the tonic cadence on the third beat of the measure rather than on the downbeat, and also by leaving it harmonically "empty"—that is, as unharmonized octave Cs. We may be at the end of a sentence, Haydn is telling us, or even of a paragraph, but certainly not the end of a chapter or an entire work. In one sense, then, this opening eight-measure unit fulfills all our expectations about melodic and rhythmic structure. The first four measures take us from the tonic to the dominant, and the second four bring us back to the tonic. Haydn, however, has manipulated the inner workings of this larger progression in ways that are full of small surprises.

105 : String Quartet in C Major, Op. 33, No. 3 (1781)
Haydn

CD7 Track 32 p. 337

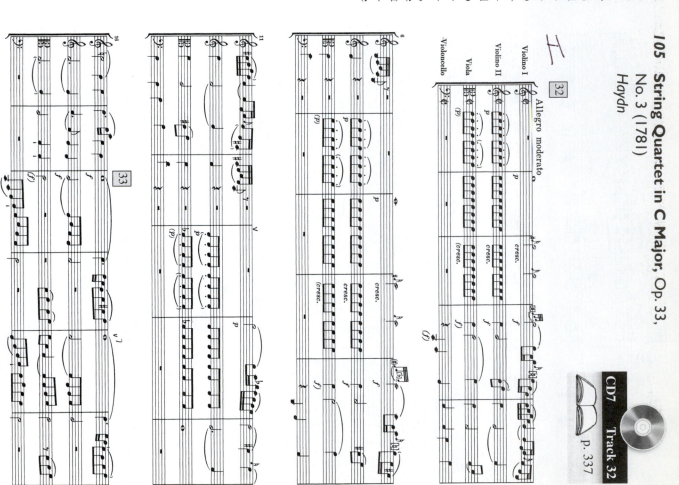

No. 105 Haydn: String Quartet in C Major, Op. 33, No. 3

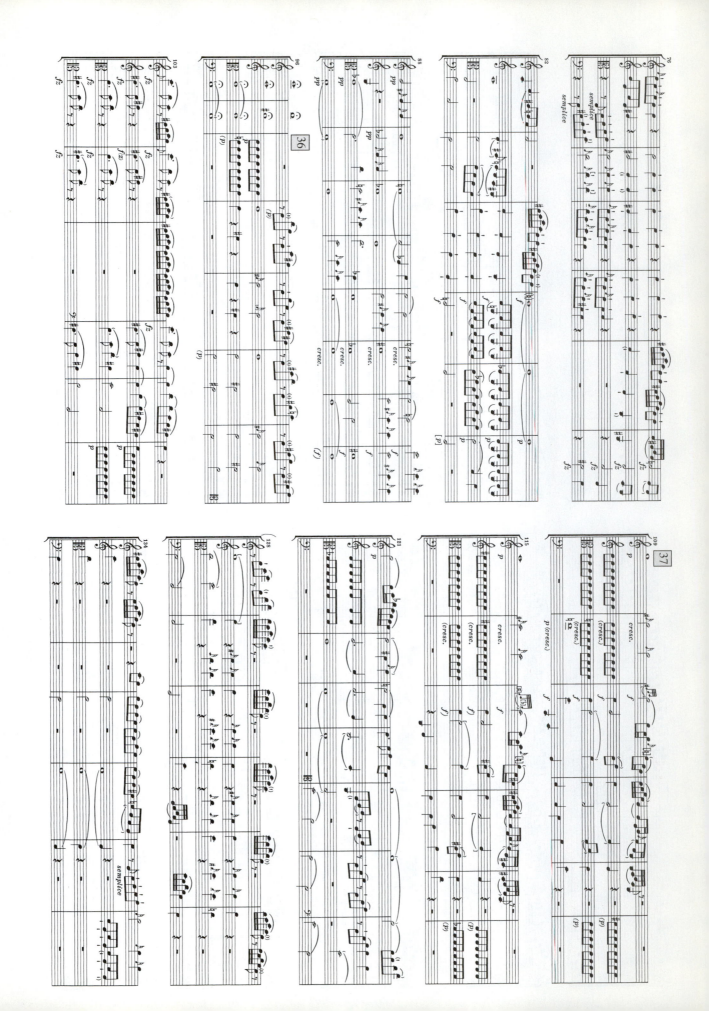

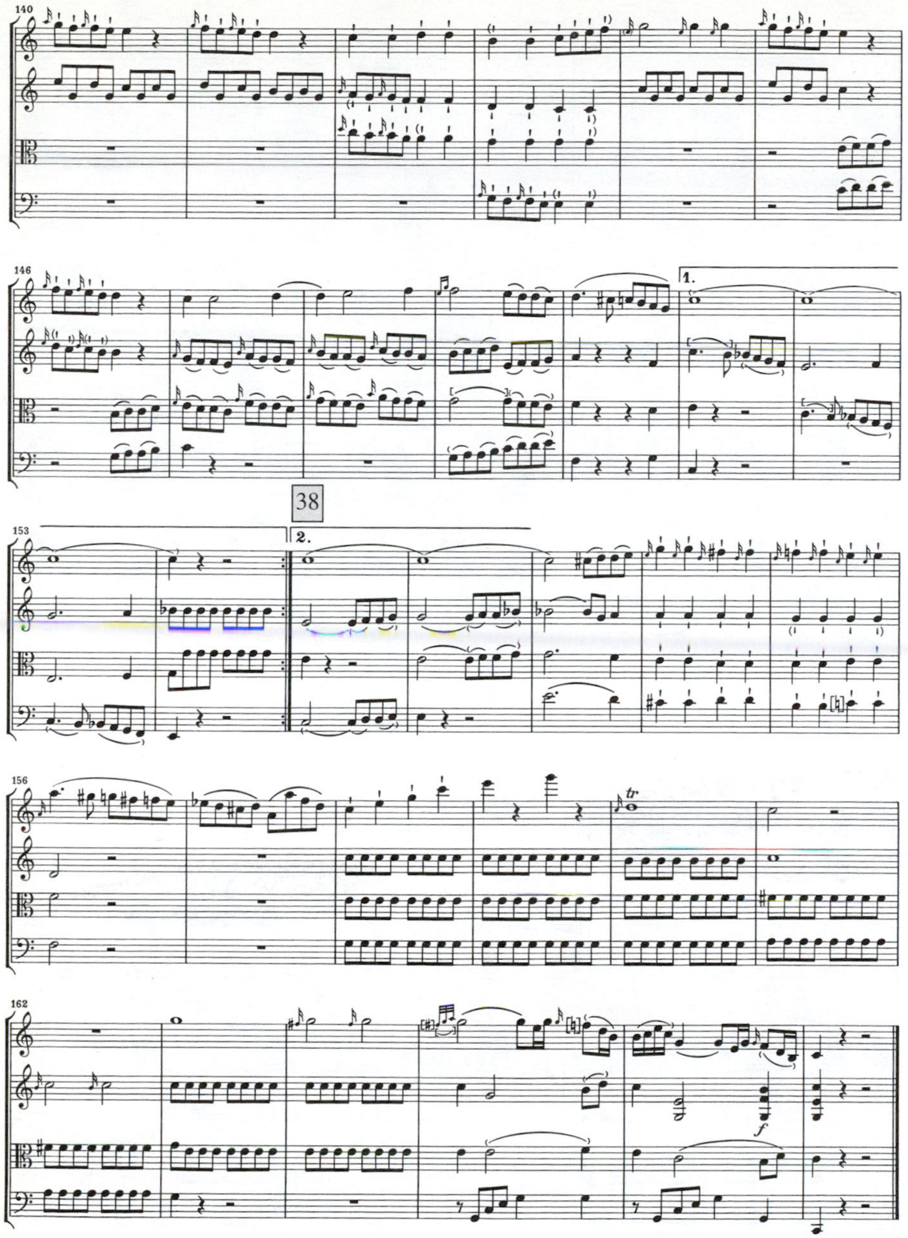

II.

Scherzo
Allegretto
sotto voce

Fine

Da Capo fin al Segno

No. 105 Haydn: String Quartet in C Major, Op. 33, No. 3

23

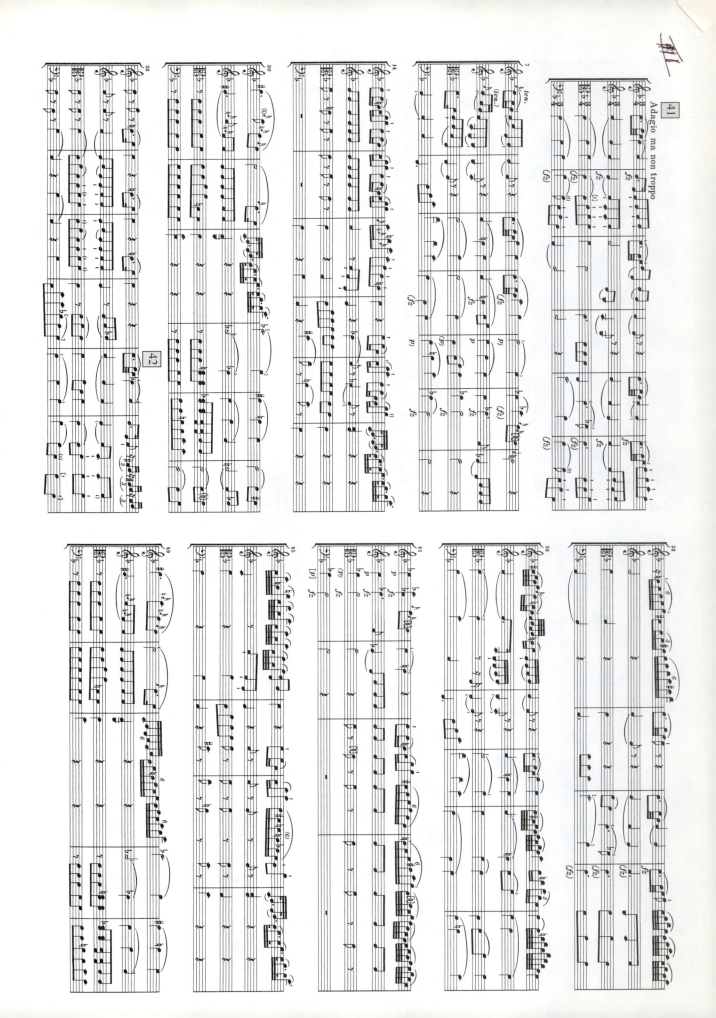

No. 105 Haydn: String Quartet in C Major, Op. 33, No. 3

(Finale)
Rondo
Presto

No. 105 Haydn: String Quartet in C Major, Op. 33, No. 3

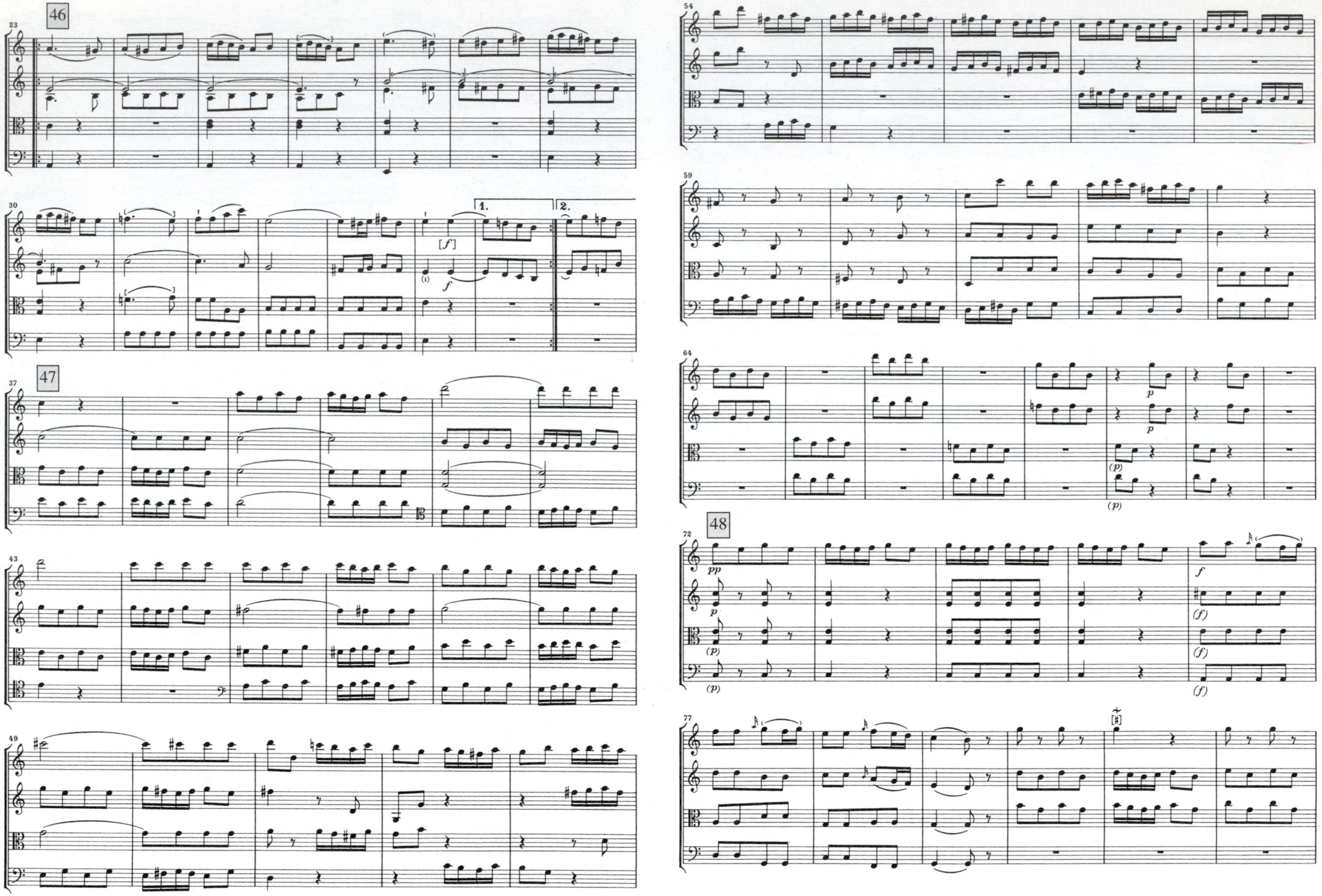
46
47
48
1.
2.
[f]
f
pp
p
(p)
(f)

No. 105 Haydn: String Quartet in C Major, Op. 33, No. 3

The first movement of Haydn's String Quartet in C Major, Op. 33, No. 3 illustrates the characteristic textural richness of his quartets. The repeated notes in the second violin and viola parts in the opening measures seem at first to be preparing us for the entry of a more engaging melodic line, which does indeed begin to emerge in the first violin in m. 2. Yet the surprising changes of pitch in this seemingly innocuous pulsing figure give it a growing significance: the C and E in the opening measures shift to F and D in m. 7, and B♭ and D in m. 13. What appears to be a subordinate figure, completely static in its pitch and rhythm, gradually emerges as a motivic idea in its own right, blurring the boundary between melody and accompaniment. That boundary is similarly ambiguous in the interaction between the first violin and the cello figure from m. 18 to 26. Are the two parts exchanging the melody from measure to measure, or is the cello figure merely accompanying the longer note values of the violin's melody? What these examples illustrate is the truly obligatory nature of the obbligato accompaniment in this quartet. Blending counterpoint with homophony, Haydn has created a texture in which accompaniment and melody are inextricably linked.

The lively second movement of this quartet, which Haydn labeled "scherzo," follows the typical structure of a minuet, with m. 1–34 constituting the minuet proper; m. 35 to 51 make up the trio. (Why Haydn chose to call this movement and its counterparts in the other quartets in Op. 33 scherzos rather than minuets is not clear; he returned to the designation "minuet" in his later quartets.)

The slow third movement is a sonata form with varied reprise. In this variant of sonata form, the exposition is not repeated note for note, but instead written out and changed in subtle ways. The varied reprise in this particular movement begins with the return to the tonic in m. 30 and a restatement of the opening theme with new melodic embellishments, especially in the first violin. The modulation to the dominant, confirmed in m. 14 in the first statement of the exposition, is repeated in the second statement in m. 43, again with an elaboration in the first violin part. The effect is similar to that of a da capo aria, in which the singer was expected to embellish a reprise the second time through. In this case, however, Haydn specified the embellishments rather than leaving them up to the performer. After a short development section (m. 59–64), the music returns to the tonic (m. 65) at the onset of the recapitulation, which repeats the themes of the exposition, but this time all in the tonic.

The last movement, a rondo, illustrates one of Haydn's favorite devices in this form—to incorporate thematic material from the opening refrain (the A section) within a contrasting episode. The A section (m. 1–22) and the B section (m. 23–26) are clearly distinct. The material in m. 37 to 72, however, which leads back to a second statement of A, is as long as the A and B sections combined and is based on material from A. By manipulating harmonies and fragmenting the thematic material into increasingly small units, Haydn makes the return to A at m. 72 a significant event even though it offers no thematic contrast to what precedes it. What, then, is the formal status of the material in m. 37–72? Because it is based on thematic material from A, it could be considered a statement of A within a typical rondo structure. Functionally, however, it is more like an extended retransition—a return to the opening idea—or even (in sonata-form terms) a development section.

Performance notes: The ensemble in this recording plays on period instruments—that is, instruments with gut strings (not wire, as on modern-day instruments), a lower bridge, a shorter fingerboard, and a lower tension on the strings in general. All of this produces a more mellow, less aggressive quality of sound.

*) Besser e¹?

106 **Symphony No. 103 in E♭ Major,**
first movement (1795)
Haydn

CD7 Track 51 p. 344

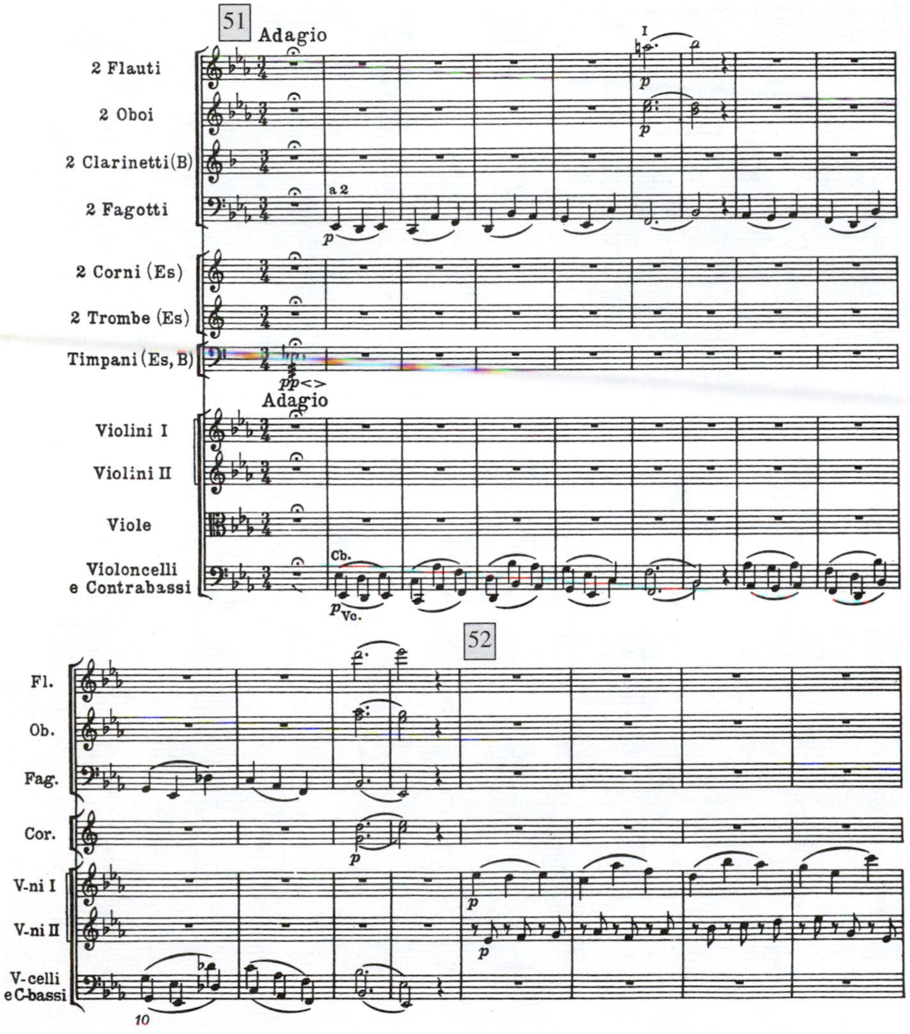

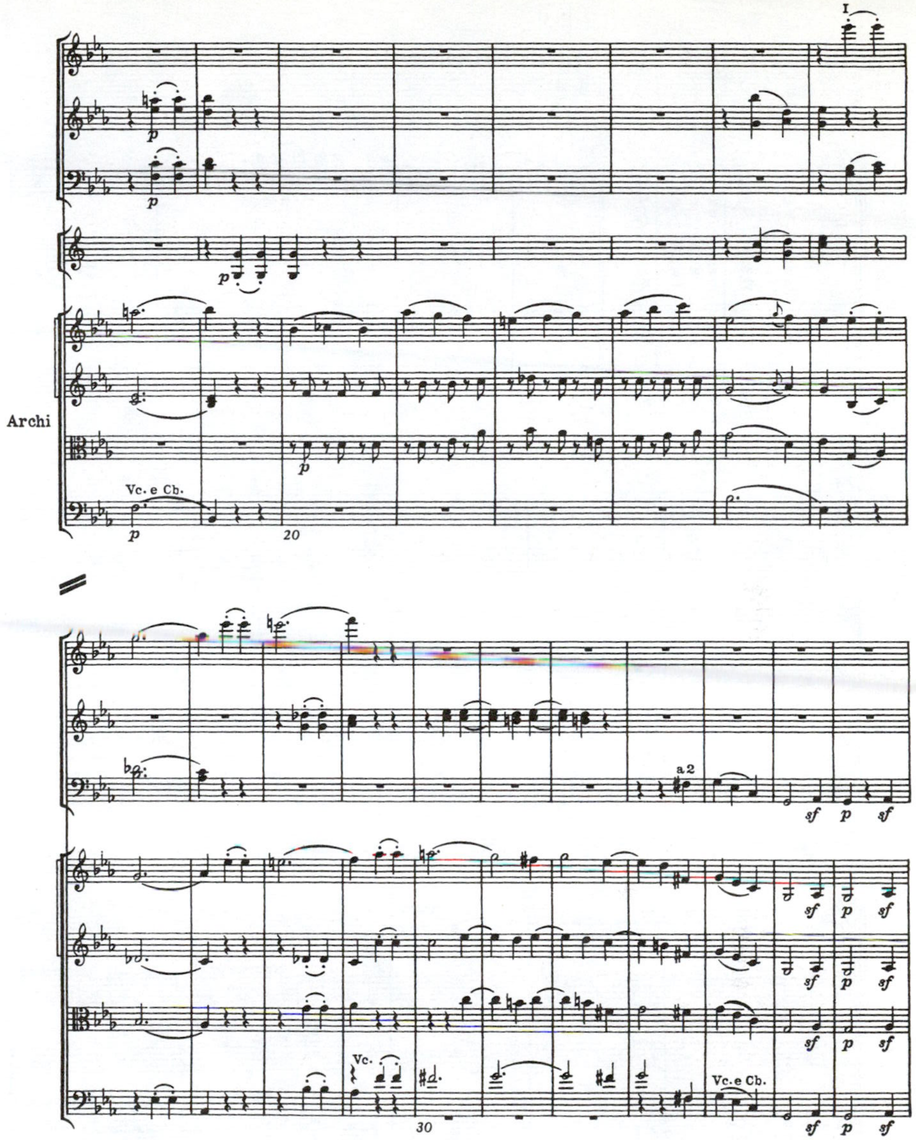

51 Adagio

2 Flauti
2 Oboi
2 Clarinetti (B)
2 Fagotti
2 Corni (Es)
2 Trombe (Es)
Timpani (Es, B)
Violini I
Violini II
Viole
Violoncelli e Contrabassi

Adagio

52

Fl.
Ob.
Fag.
Cor.
V-ni I
V-ni II
V-celli e C-bassi

Archi

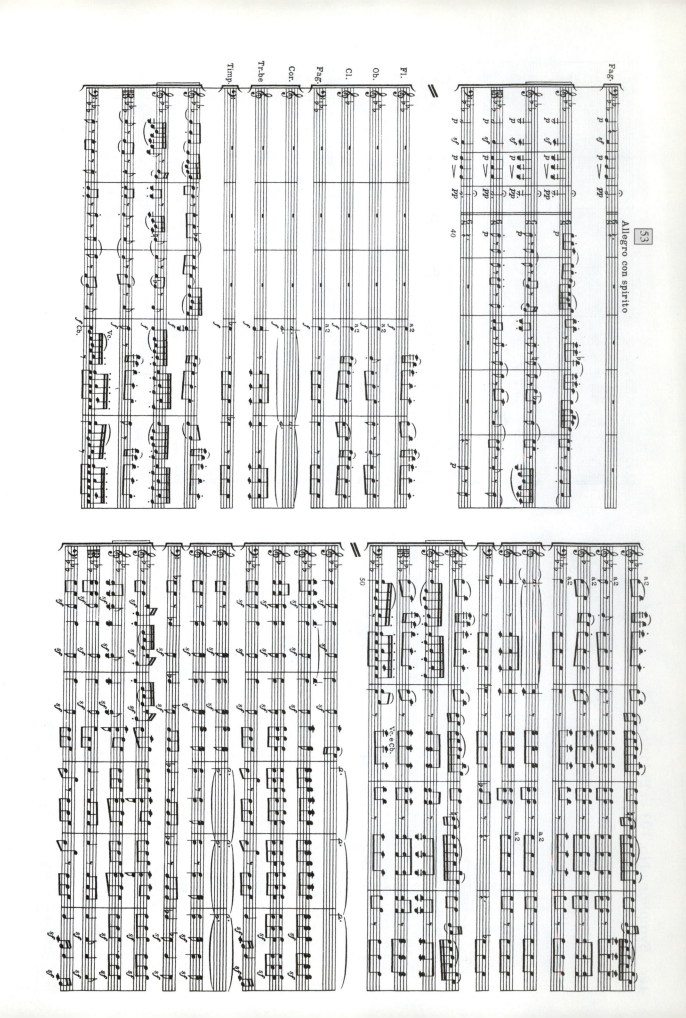

No. 106 Haydn: Symphony No. 103 in E♭ Major

No. 106 Haydn: Symphony No. 103 in E♭ Major

No. 106 Haydn: Symphony No. 103 in E♭ Major

No. 106 Haydn: Symphony No. 103 in E♭ Major

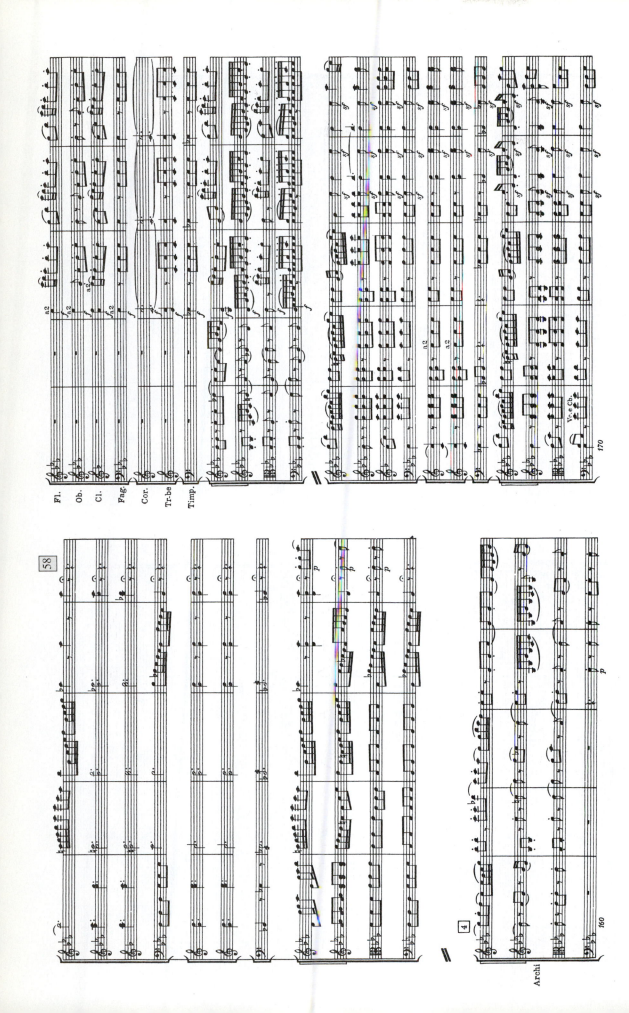

No. 106 Haydn: Symphony No. 103 in E♭ Major

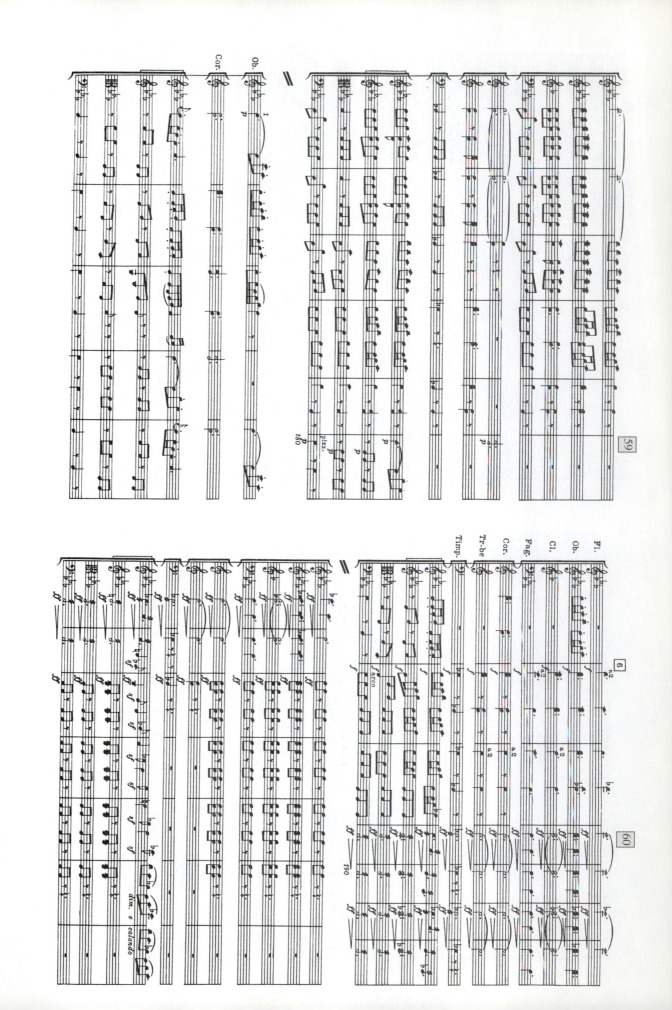

No. 106 Haydn: Symphony No. 103 in E♭ Major

The powerful, sudden, and wholly unexpected drumroll that opens Haydn's Symphony No. 103 in E♭ Major illustrates what critics of his time had in mind when they wrote of the sublime in music. It would have struck contemporary listeners as loud, bizarre, and portentous—surely a signal announcing some great event—but what kind of event? It gets our attention but not necessarily our sympathy. The musical idea that follows is dark, fragmented, and difficult to grasp, like a painting of a scene shrouded in mist. Only later will we realize that what we are hearing at this point is a premonition of themes to come.

The opening theme in the low strings reinforces the mysterious air of this slow introduction. The first two measures sound very much like the opening of the *Dies irae* ("Day of wrath") from the plainchant Mass for the Dead (see Example 12-2 in the Textbook, p. 344). The slow introduction ends with a curious insistence on the notes G and A♭ (m. 35–39). But what sounds dark and ominous at the end of the slow introduction is immediately transformed into a bright and airy theme at the beginning of the Allegro con spirito that follows. Progressions like this—from somber to bright, dark to light, obscurity to clarity—are another manifestation of what 18th-century critics considered sublime. The sudden deflection from the dominant of C minor to E♭ Major is likewise another portent of things to come, this time of the many other sudden and unexpected modulations that abound in this sonata-form first movement, not to mention the unexpected return of the slow movement's opening in the coda of the first movement at m. 202.

107 Piano Concerto in D Major, K. 107, No. 1, first movement (1772)
Wolfgang Amadeus Mozart (1756–1791)

CD7 Track 63 p. 350

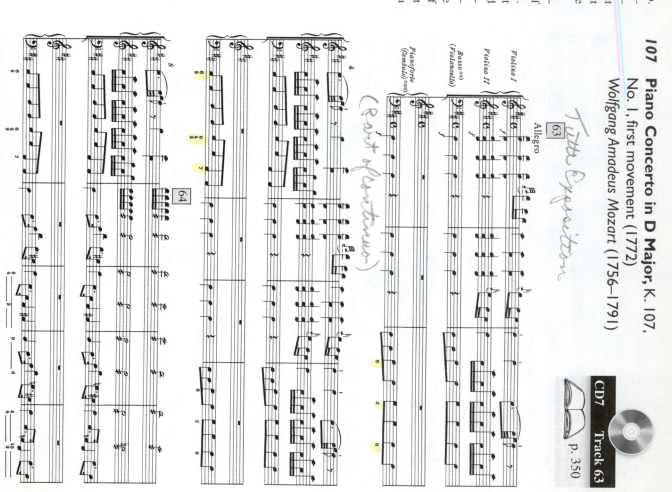

*) Zu Entstehungszeit und -ort vgl. Vorwort, S. XVII.
**) Zum Begriff des „Basso" vgl. Vorwort, S. XIX.
***) Vgl. Vorwort, S. XIX. — Klavierstimme und Generalbaß-Bezifferung sind durchweg von Leopold Mozart geschrieben; hierüber sowie über den etwaigen weiteren Anteil Leopolds im Originalmanuskript vgl. Vorwort, S. XVII.

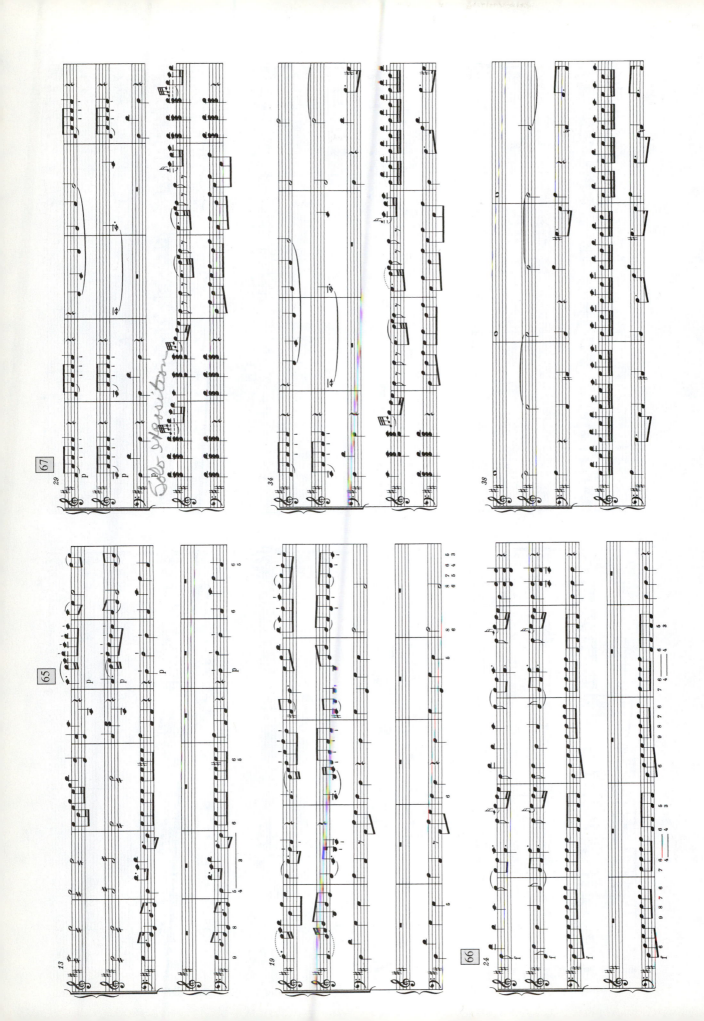

No. 107 Mozart: Piano Concerto in D Major, K. 107, No. 1

No. 107 Mozart: Piano Concerto in D Major, K. 107, No. 1

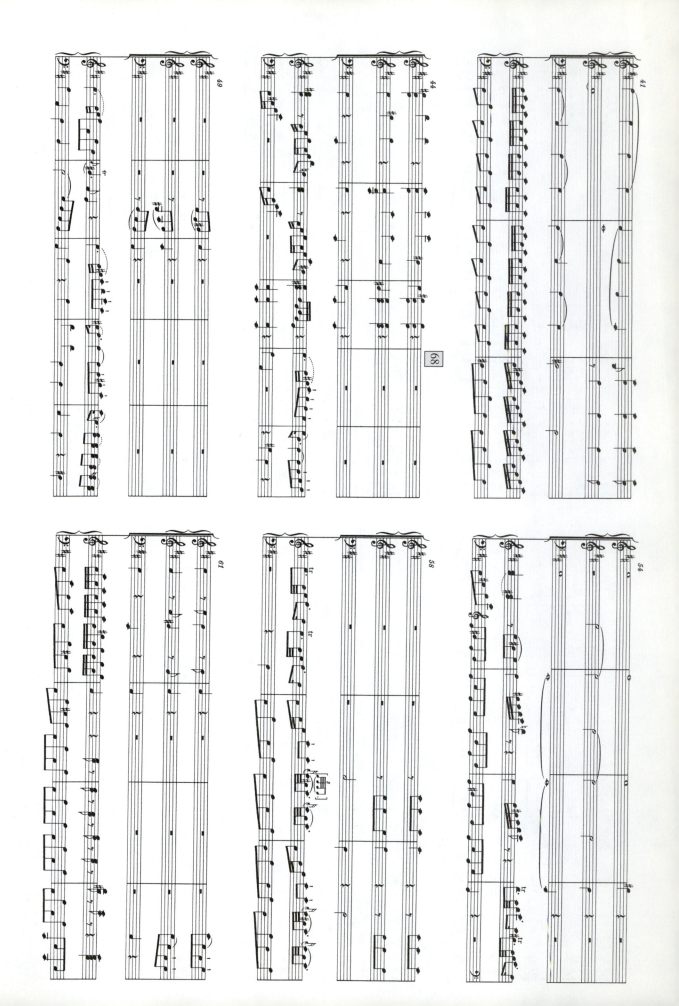

No. 107 Mozart: Piano Concerto in D Major, K. 107, No. I

*) Diese Ausführung auch in den folgenden Takten (vgl. Takt 88 ff., Violine I, II).

No. 107 Mozart: Piano Concerto in D Major, K. 107, No. 1

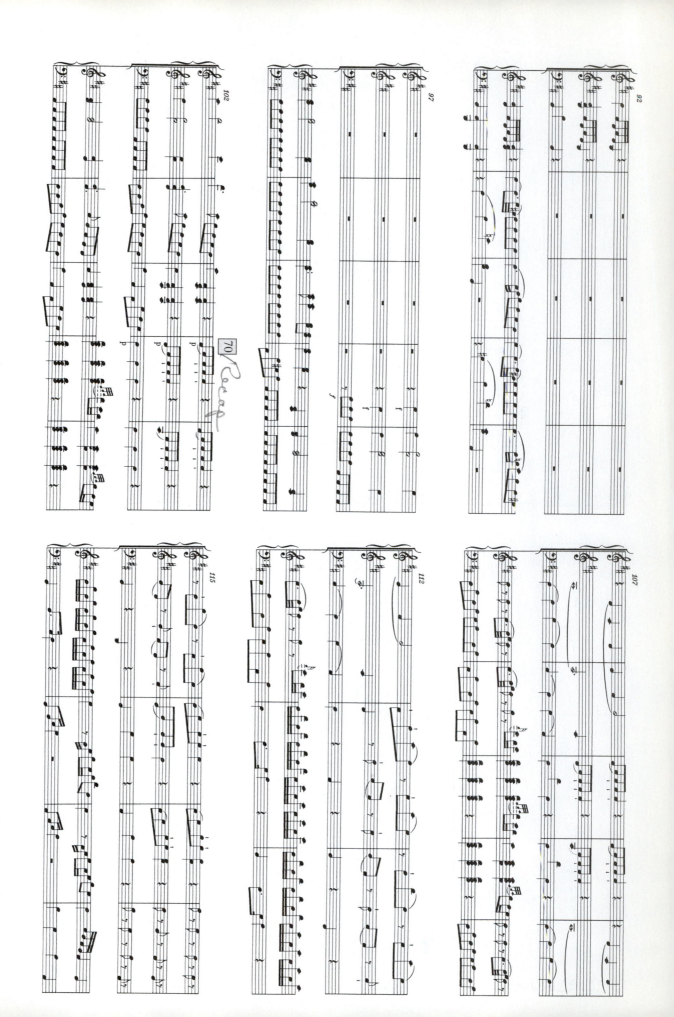

No. 107 Mozart: Piano Concerto in D Major, K. 107, No. 1

*) Zur originalen Notierung der Takte 147 f. im Klavier vgl. Krit. Bricht.

43

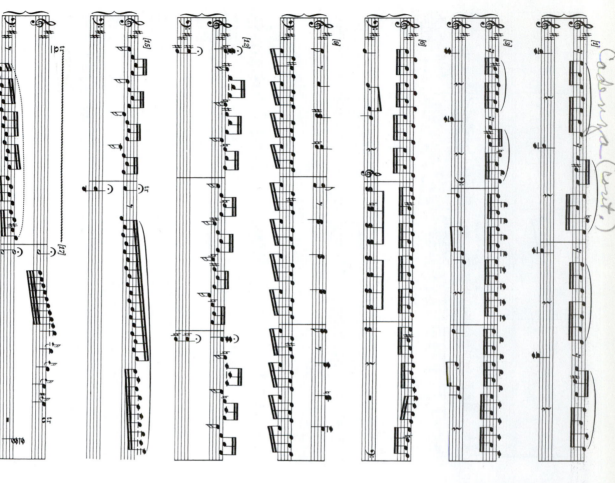

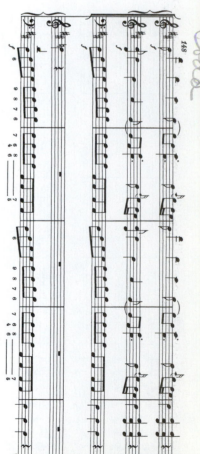

The first movement of this concerto is based on the opening movement of Johann Christian Bach's Keyboard Sonata in D Major, Op. 5, No. 2 (Anthology 2#102). Mozart's reworking of this movement illustrates the relationship between sonata form and double-exposition concerto form. For the first eight measures, Mozart closely follows Bach's sonata, adding additional accompaniment in the inner voices (second violins and violas) but making no structural changes. At the beginning of the transition (m. 9), however, when the sonata modulates to the dominant, the concerto stays in the tonic. Mozart then abbreviates much of what J. C. Bach had presented in the secondary key area, adding a cadential figure of his own (m. 24–28) to close out the tutti exposition. All this time the soloist has been playing as a member of the basso continuo, filling in harmonies according to Mozart's figured bass.

The soloist assumes an altogether different function in the solo exposition, which begins at m. 29. Now the melody moves to the piano, the accompaniment moves to the strings, and the basso continuo drops out altogether. In the solo exposition Mozart also follows J. C. Bach's sonata much more closely, modulating to the dominant on the transitional theme (m. 37–46) and staying there to introduce all the themes J. C. Bach had presented in the secondary key area. (In retrospect, we can now see why Mozart abbreviated the tutti exposition: the music would have stayed in the tonic for far too long in proportion to the movement as a whole.)

The first movement of this concerto can also be analyzed in terms of ritornello structure, a form that Mozart never wholly abandoned in his concertos. As in a Baroque concerto, the movement as a whole consists of alternating tutti and solo sections. The contrasting tutti and solo sections are easy to identify in the score with a quick look at the keyboard part: figured-bass notation—indicating that the solo instrument is acting as part of the basso continuo—signals a tutti section; the absence of figured bass notation signals a solo section.

108 Piano Concerto in E♭ Major, K. 271,
first movement (1777)
Mozart

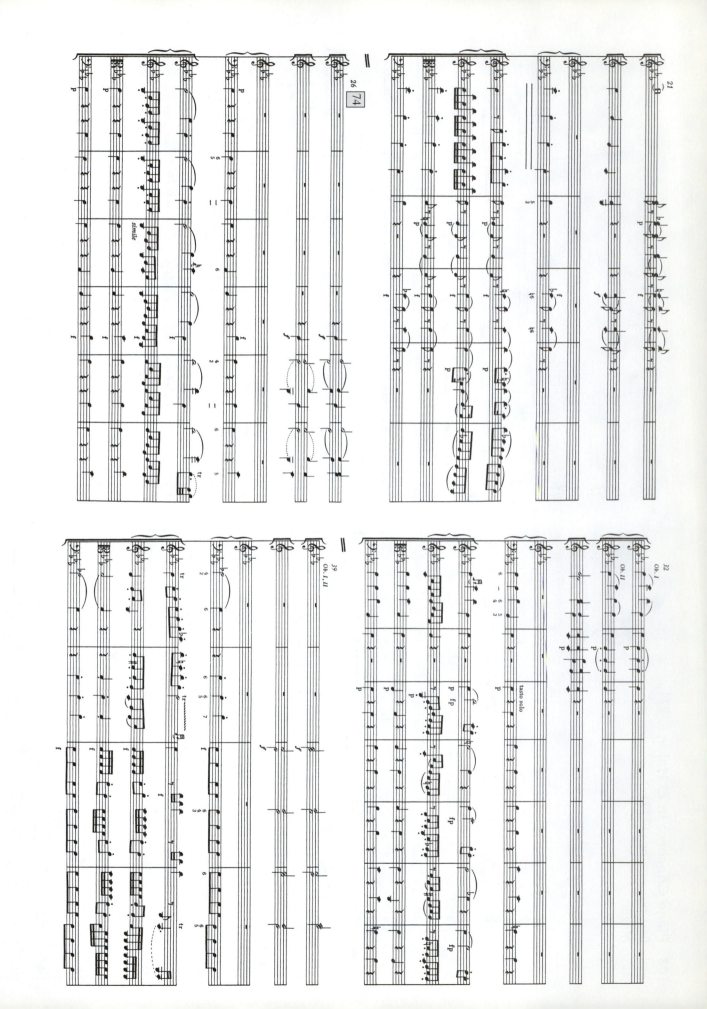

No. 108 Mozart: Piano Concerto in E♭ Major, K. 271

■ No. 108 Mozart: Piano Concerto in E♭ Major, K. 271

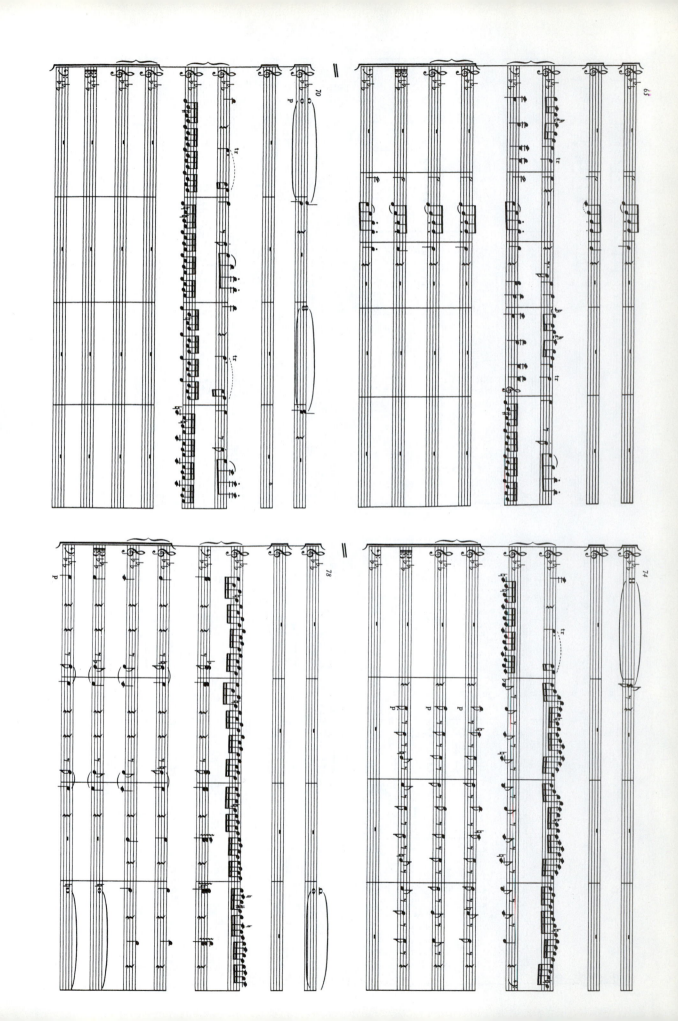

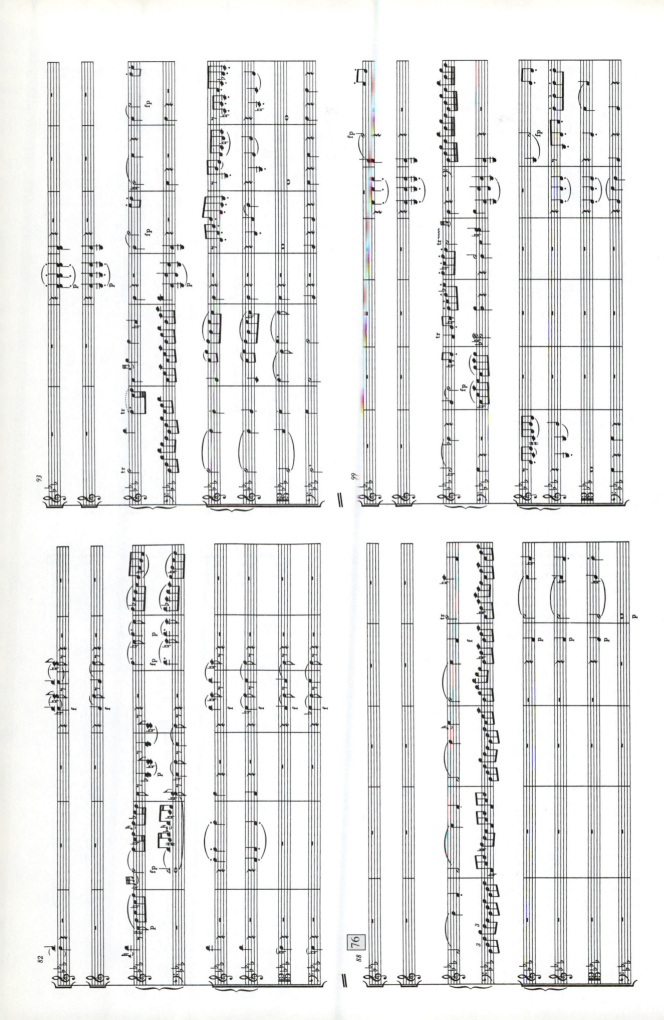

No. 108 Mozart: Piano Concerto in E♭ Major, K. 271

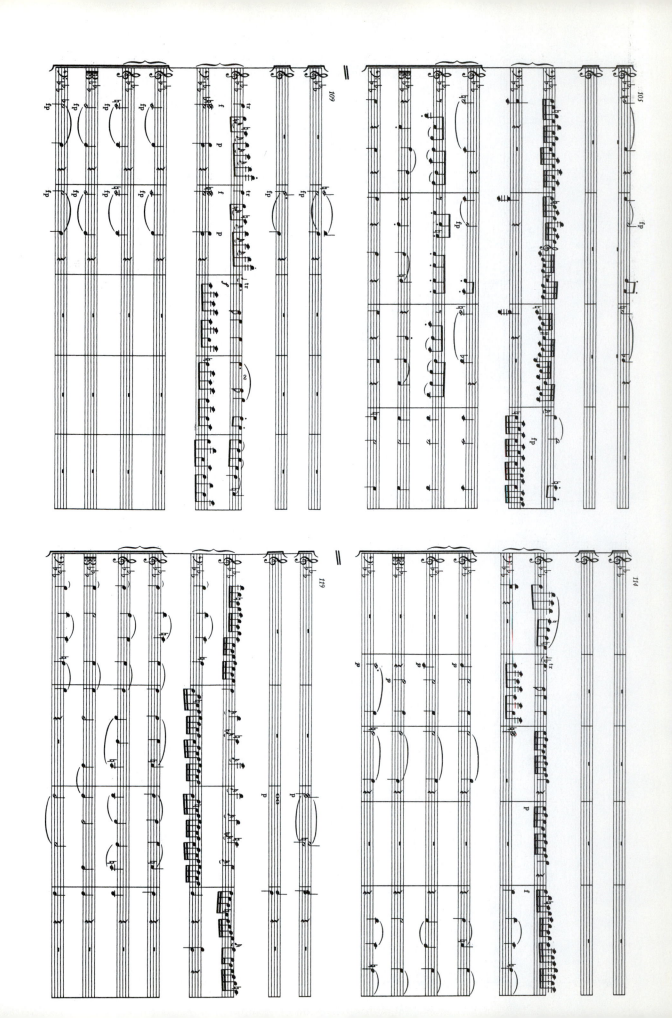

No. 108 · Mozart: Piano Concerto in E♭ Major, K. 271

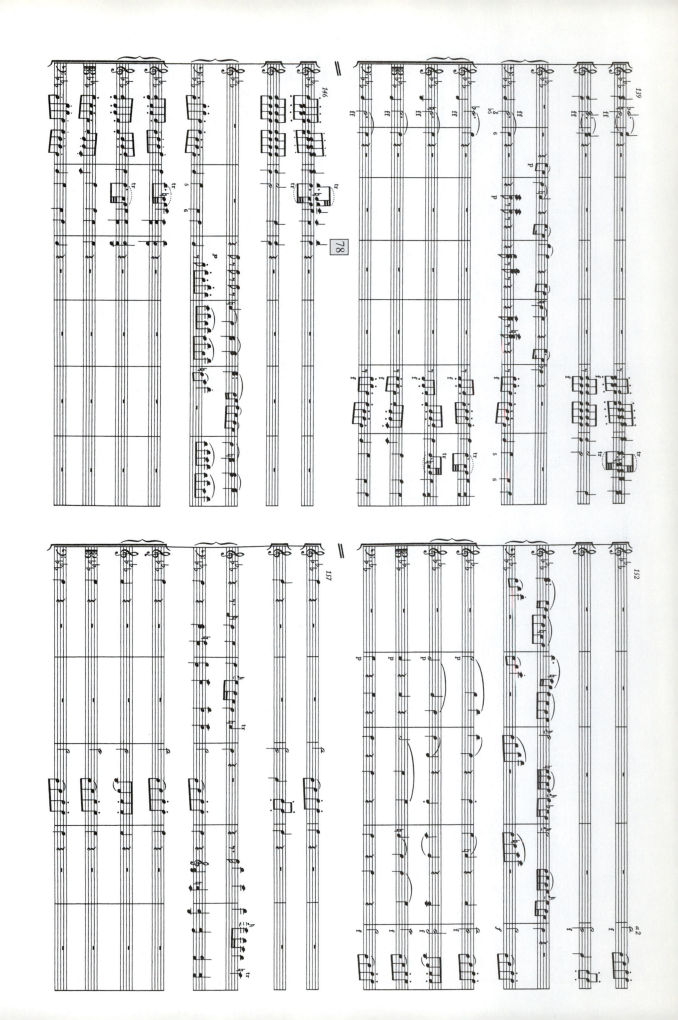

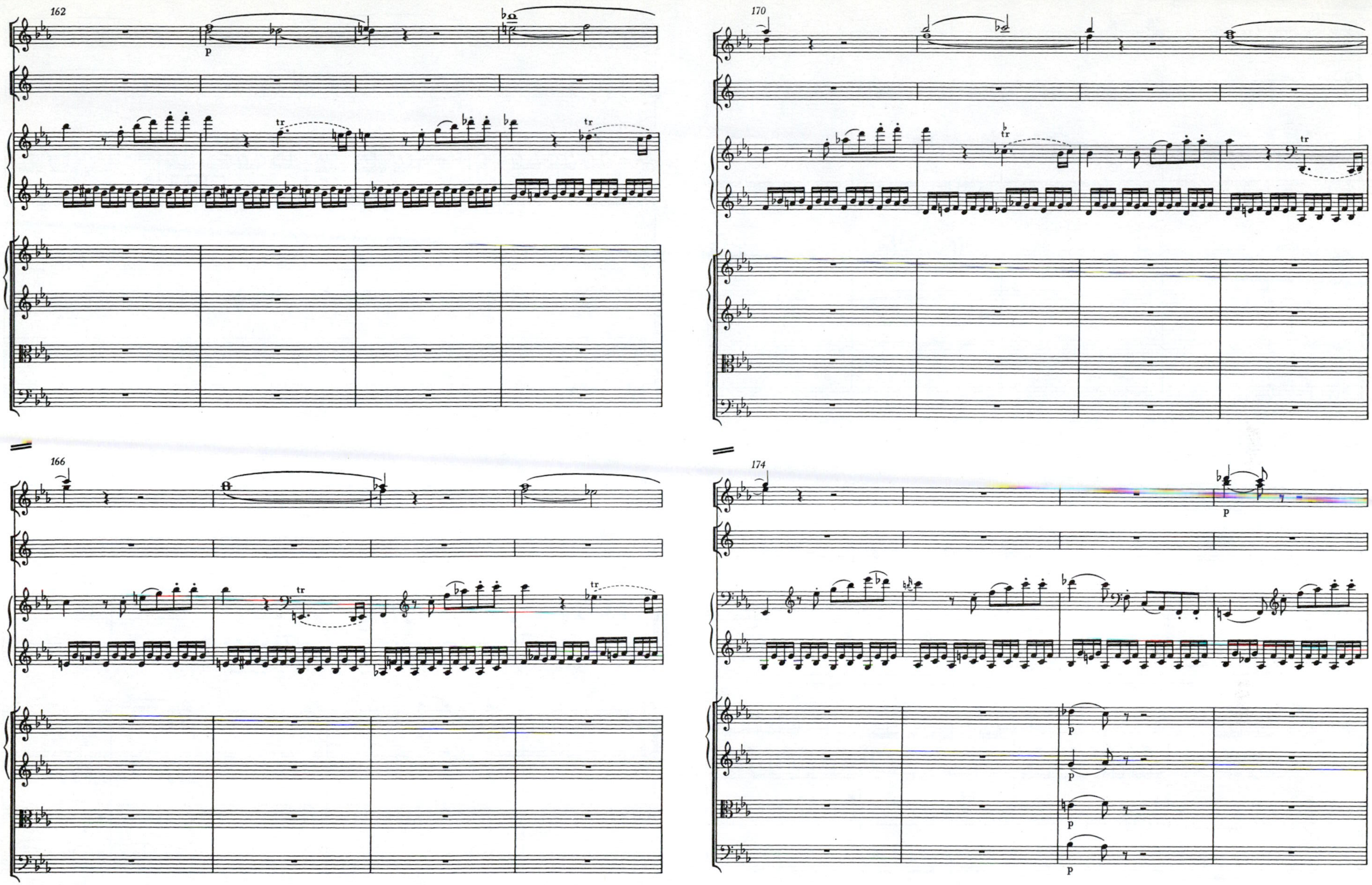
162
p
tr
170
166
174

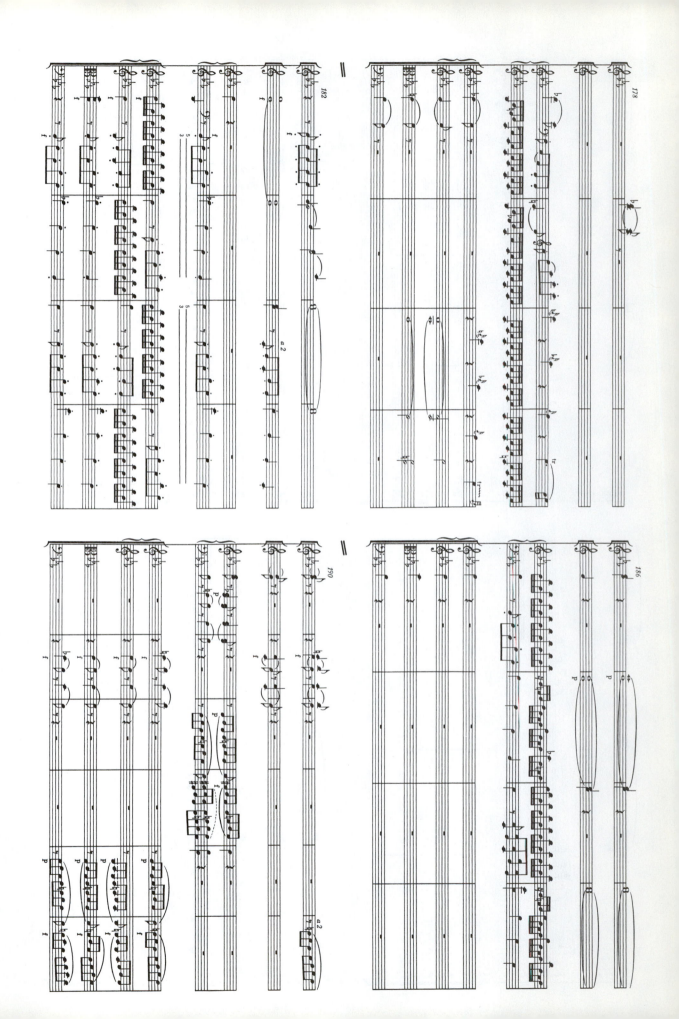

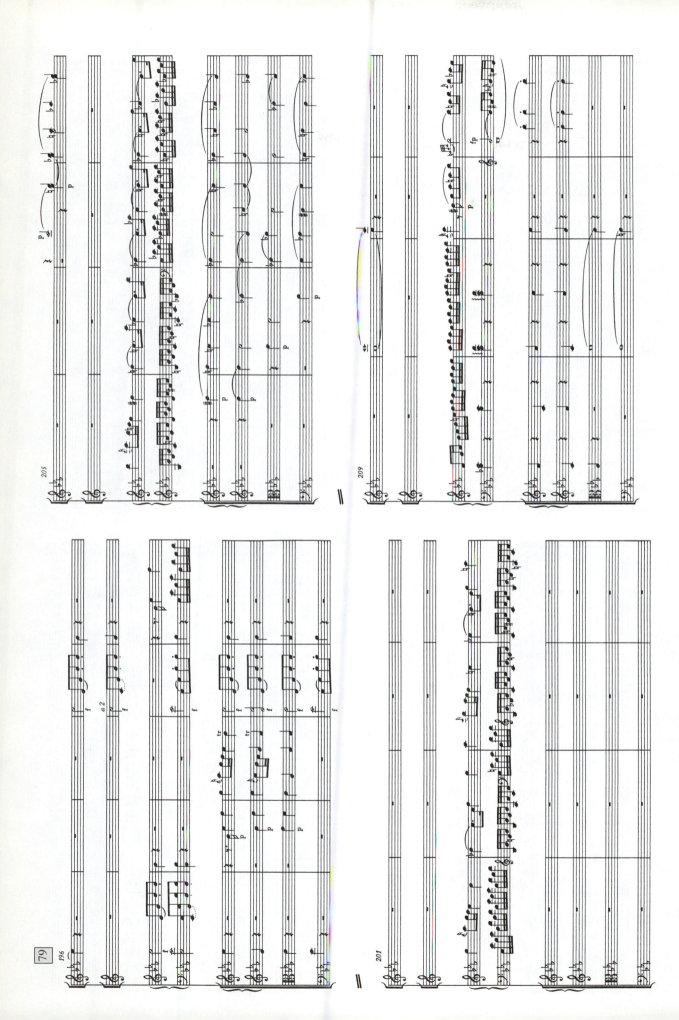

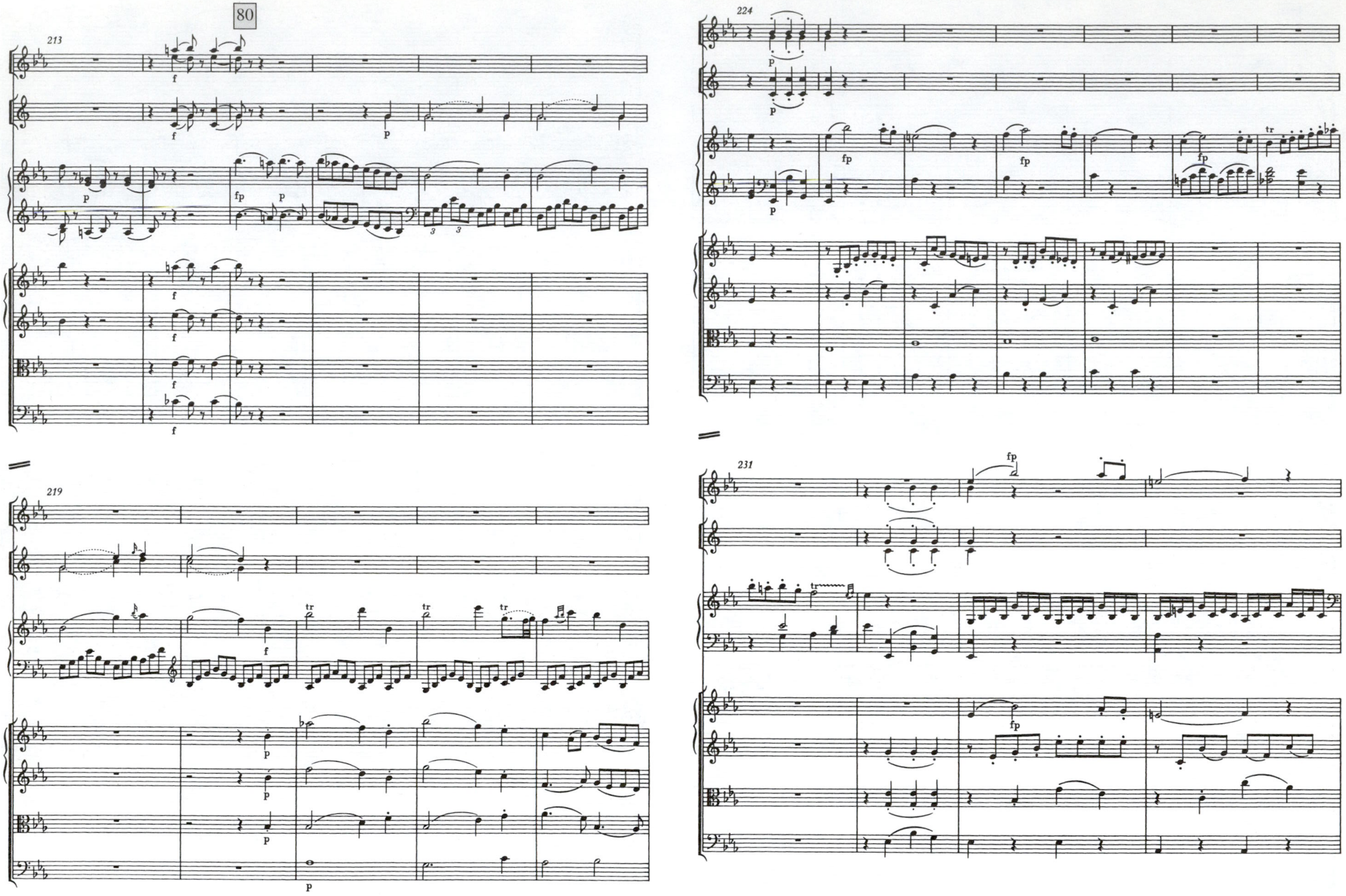
80
213
219
224
231
f
p
fp
tr
3

No. 108 Mozart: Piano Concerto in E♭ Major, K. 271

No. 108 Mozart: Piano Concerto in Eb Major, K. 271

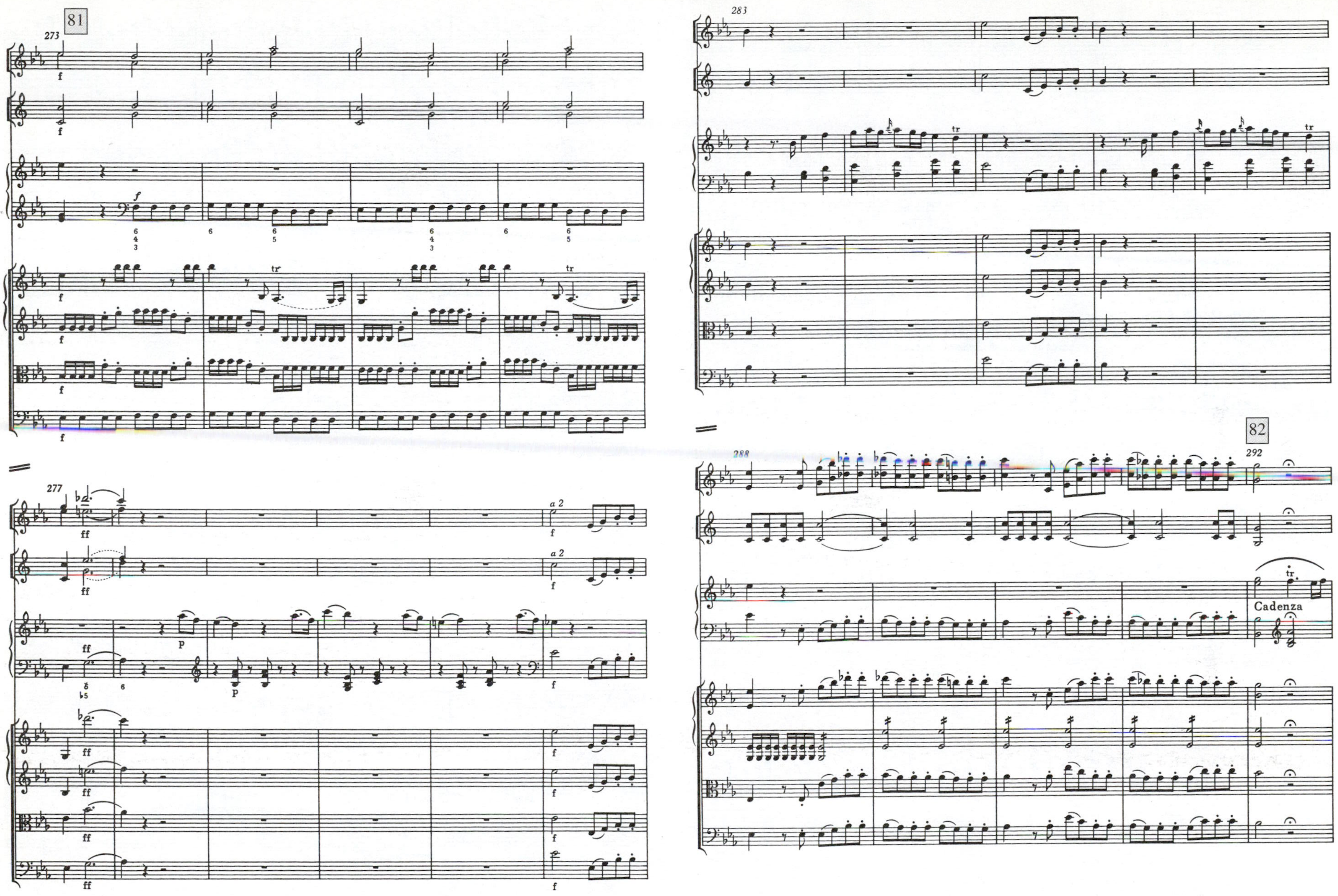
81
273
f
6
4
3
5
tr
277
ff
p
a 2
283
82
288
292
Cadenza

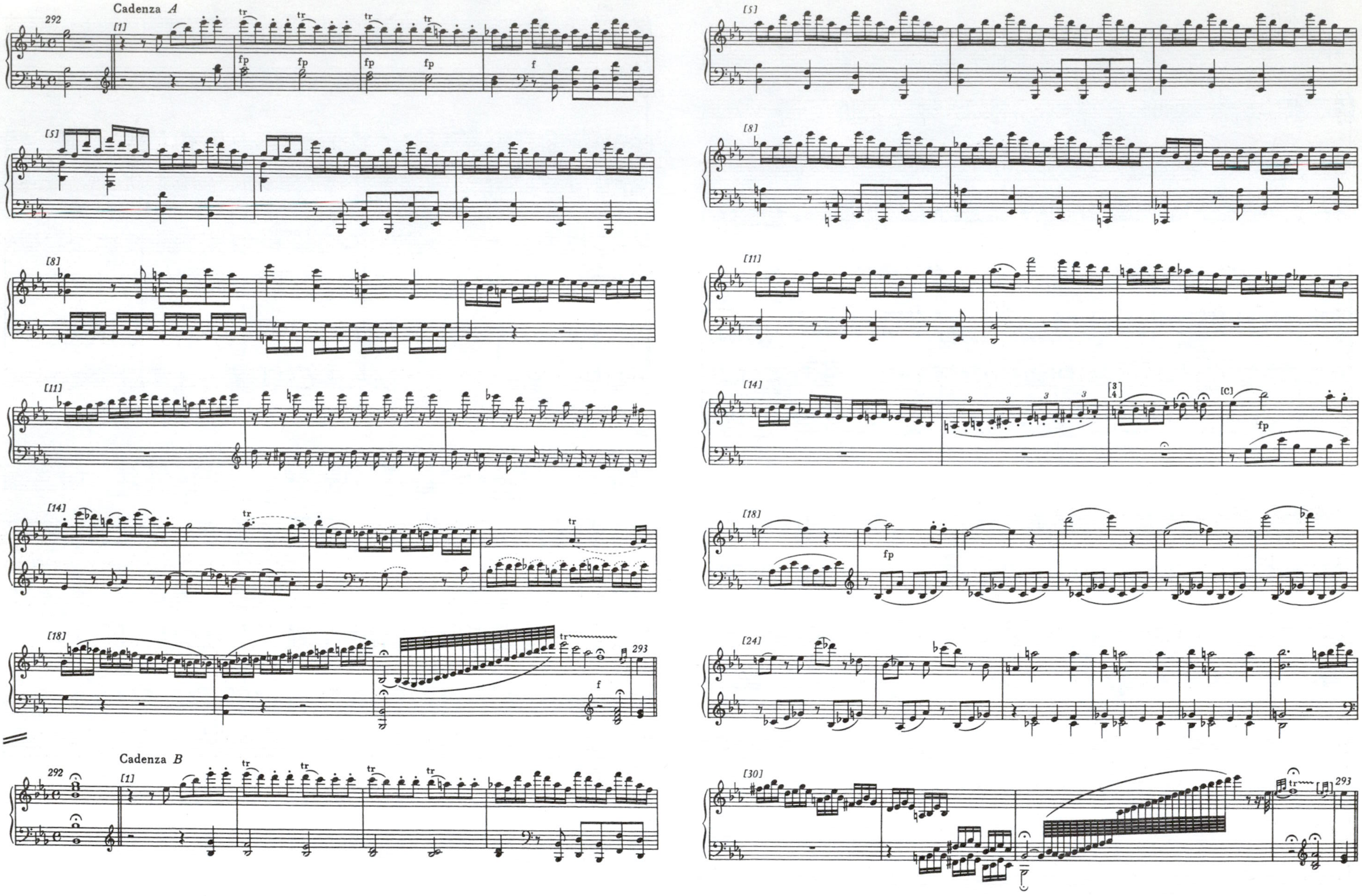
292
Cadenza A
[1]
[5]
[8]
[11]
[14]
[18]
293
Cadenza B
[24]
[30]

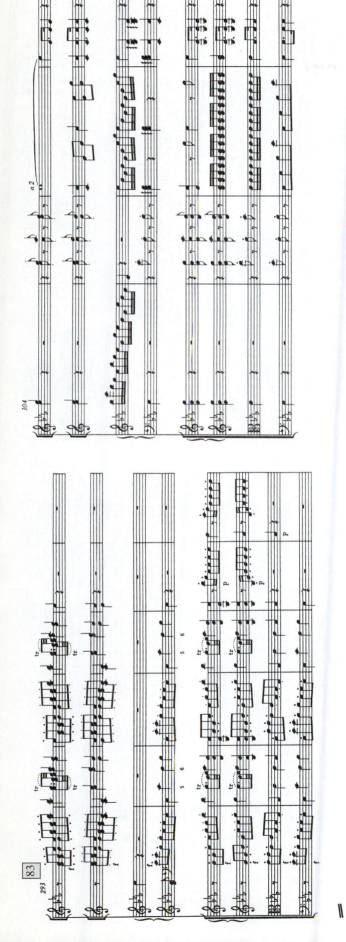

The overlapping patterns of double-exposition concerto form and ritornello structure are evident in all of Mozart's concertos, including the Piano Concerto in E♭ Major, K. 271. The very opening of the first movement reminds us (yet again) that composers were constantly playing with conventions, for here the soloist enters quite unexpectedly as a soloist almost at once (m. 2–7) before receding back into the framework of the basso continuo. (The subsequent marking of *tasto solo* indicates that the soloist is to play only the note indicated, not any harmony above it, until the resumption of the figured bass markings in m. 12.)

From a thematic point of view, Mozart's Piano Concerto K. 271 is tightly organized: almost every idea relates in some fashion to the opening theme (see the diagram in the Textbook, p. 351).

Performance notes: This recording uses a relatively small orchestra playing on period instruments. The transparency of the ensemble's sound allows the period fortepiano to stand out with special clarity, even in those passages in which the keyboard player functions as a member of the basso continuo. Mozart notated two cadenzas for this first movement; the soloist here has chosen the second of these ("B"). The use of the soft pedal on the fortepiano, operated by a lever underneath the keyboard pushed to the side by the player's knee, is particularly evident at m. 17–28 within this cadenza.

No. 108 Mozart: Piano Concerto in E♭ Major, K. 271

109 **La serva padrona:** "Aspettare e non venire" (1733)

Giovanni Battista Pergolesi (1710–1736)

INTERMEZZO PRIMO

(Una camera: Uberto e Vespone, più tardi Serpina)
(*Zimmer: Uberto und Vespone, später Serpina*)
(*Une chambre: Pandolphe et Scapin, plus tard Zerbine*)

84 ARIA
Allegro

CD7 Track 84
p. 355

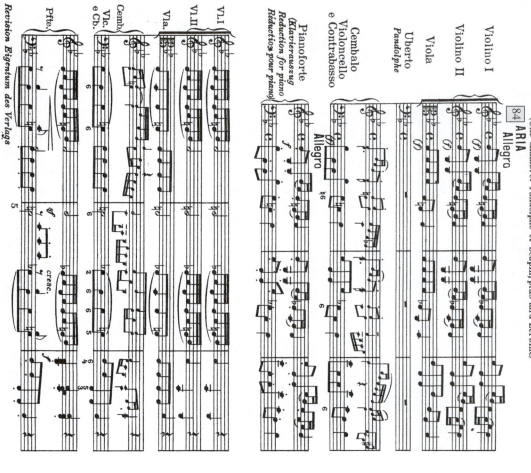

Violino I
Violino II
Viola
Uberto *Pandolphe*
Cembalo Violoncello e Contrabasso
Pianoforte (*Klavierauszug Reduction for piano Réduction pour piano*)

Vl.I
Vl.II
Vla.
Cemb. Vlc. e Cb.
Pfte.

85

Uberto-Pandolphe

A - spet - ta - re,
Muß man war - - ten,
Long-temps at-ten - - - dre,

è non ve - ni - re,
und darf nicht kla - gen,
Sans voir ve - nir,

Vl.I
Vl.II
Vla.
U. P.
Cemb. Vlc. e Cb.
Pfte.

sta - rea let - - - to,
liegt man schlaf - - los,
Au lit sè - ten - - dre,

e non dor-mi - re
wenn Sor-gen na - gen,
Ne point dor-mir,

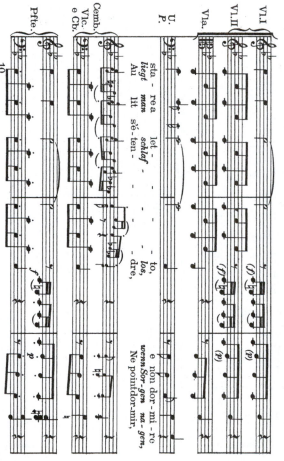

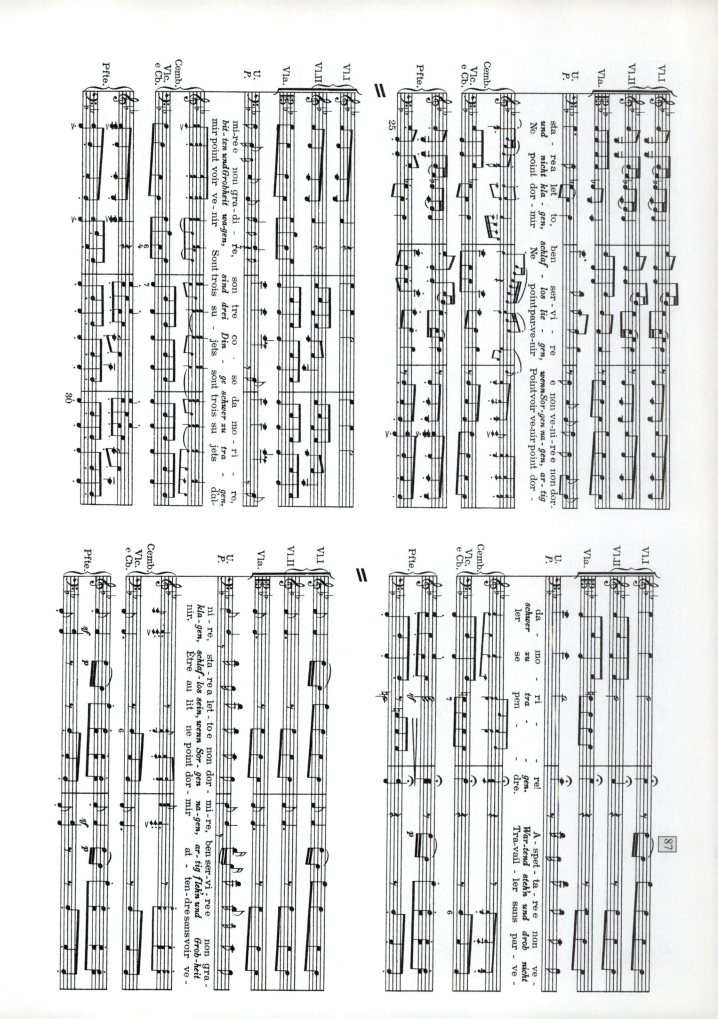

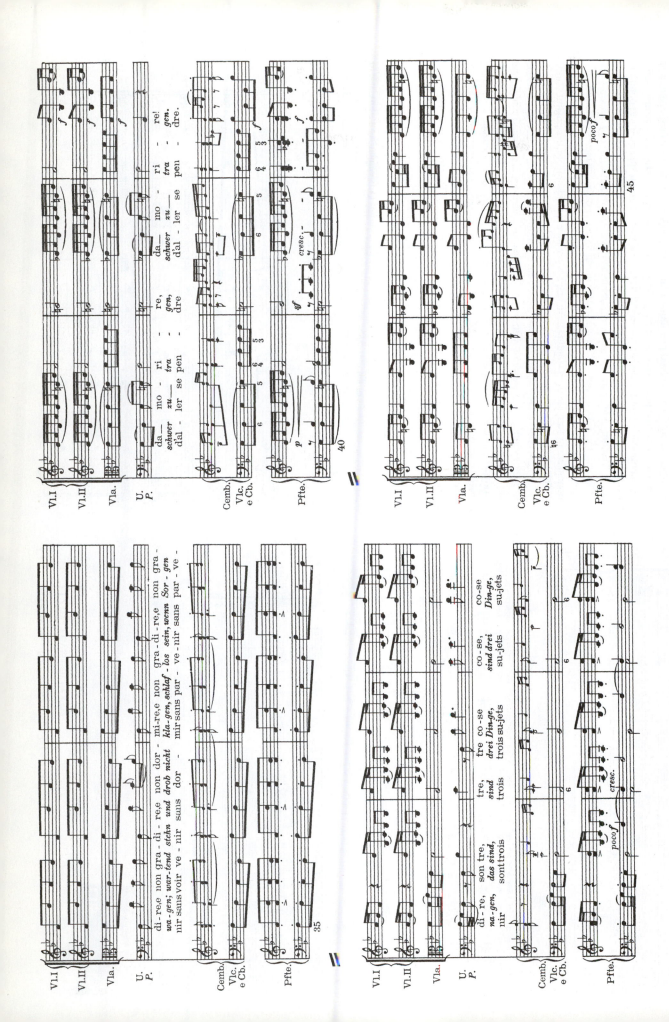

No. 109 Pergolesi: *La serva padrona*

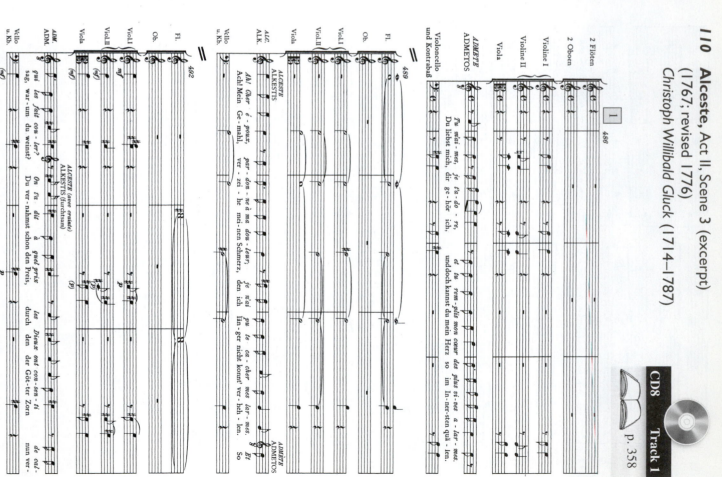

The origins of *opera buffa*—comic opera—lie in the tradition of the intermezzo, a work intended for performance between the acts of a larger (serious) opera. Giovanni Battista Pergolesi's intermezzo *La serva padrona* ("The Maidservant as Mistress") was first performed in Naples between the acts of an *opera seria* also written by Pergolesi. Over time, this intermezzo and others like it, became so well known that they were performed alone rather than between the acts of larger works, thus giving rise to *opera buffa* as a separate genre.

La serva padrona tells the story of a maidservant who, through guile and cunning, becomes mistress of the household in which she had been employed. In contrast to the elaborate cast of characters found in many *opere serie* of the time, Pergolesi's intermezzo makes do with only two singers, Uberto (a bass), the master of the house, and Serpina (a soprano), the maidservant. (The character of Vespone, a manservant, is entirely mute and limited to mime.) In his opening aria, "Aspettare e non venire," Uberto expresses impatience with Serpina for failing to bring him his morning hot chocolate. Devoid of elaborate runs or opportunities for embellishment, the aria typifies what audiences of the time considered a more natural style. The music features a relatively slow harmonic rhythm and predominantly homophonic textures with frequent unisons in the strings. The vocal line consists of short melodic phrases organized around the principles of phrase structure. The work as a whole points toward the lighter style of the mid-18th century.

Aspettare e non venire,
Stare a letto e non dormire,
Ben servire e non gradire,
Son tre cose da morire.

To wait and have no one come,
To lie in bed and not to sleep,
To serve well and not give satisfaction,
Are three things that can make one die.

110 Alceste, Act II, Scene 3 (excerpt)
(1767; revised 1776)
Christoph Willibald Gluck (1714–1787)

CD8 Track 1

p. 358

66

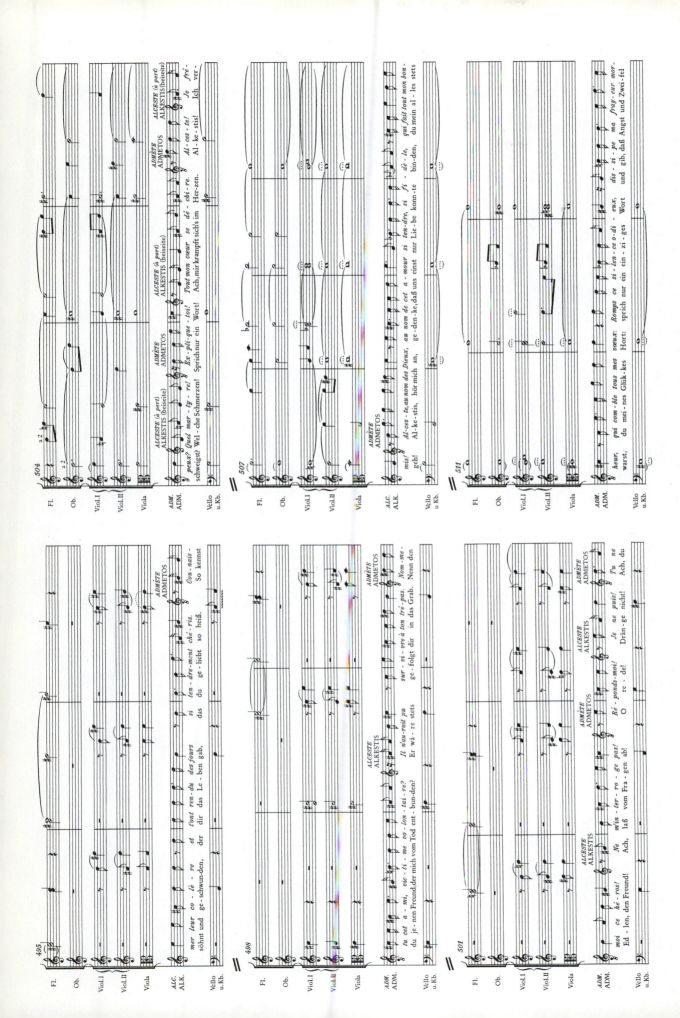

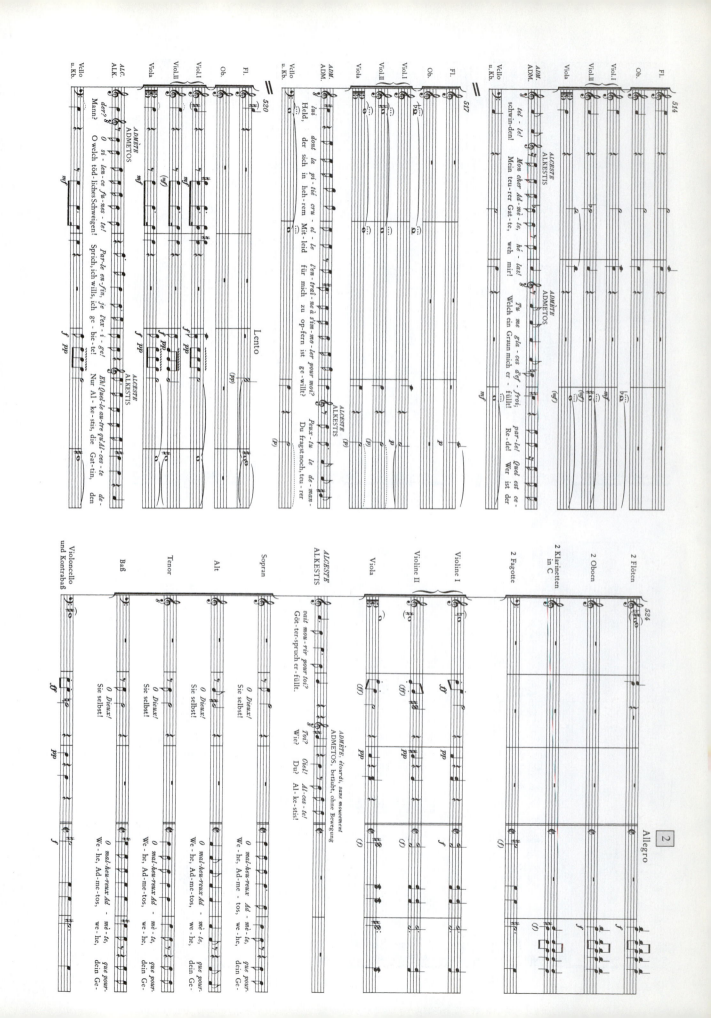

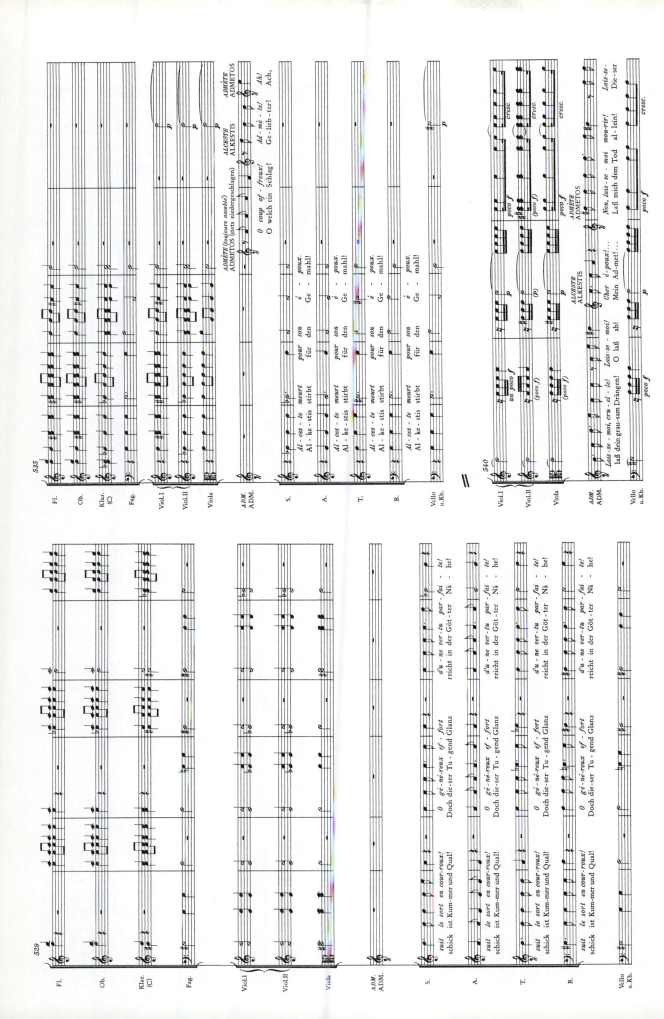

No. 110 Gluck: Alceste

543
Viol.I
Viol.II
Viola
ADM.
ADM.
moi suc-com - ber à ma dou-leur mor - tel - le, à des tour-ments que je ne puis souf-
bren - nen-de Schmerz wird mir das Herz ver - sen - gen, mich wird die Qual bald der Ver-nich - tung
Vcllo
u. Kb.
ff
546
p
ALCESTE
ALKESTIS
frir. Cal - me cet - te dou - leur, ce dés - es - poir ex - trê - me. Vis! Con - ser - ve des jours si
weihn. O be - zäh - me den Gram, stil - le des Her - zens Bren - nen. Leb'! Ich fle - he dich an, bei
550
3
mf
ADMÈTE
ADMETOS
ALC.
ALK.
cher à mon a - mour. Tu veux mou - rir, tu veux me quit - ter sans re - tour?
uns - rer Lie - be Glück. Du suchst den Tod, fliehst mich, keh - rest nim - mer zu - rück?
553
f
ressenti
Et tu veux que je vi - ve? Et tu dis que tu m'ai - mes! Qui t'a don - né le droit de
Und du willst, daß ich le - be, willst es Lie - be noch nen - nen? Wer gab dir denn das Recht, dich
556
dis - po - ser de toi? Les ser - ments de l'A - mour et ceux de l'Hy - me -
selbst dem Tod zu weihn? Sind die Schwü - re der Lie - be und der Treu - e
558
né - e ne te tien - nent - ils pas à mes loix en - chaî - né - e? Tes
Pflich - ten da - zu da, daß in Will - kür wir selbst sie ver - nich - ten? Ge -

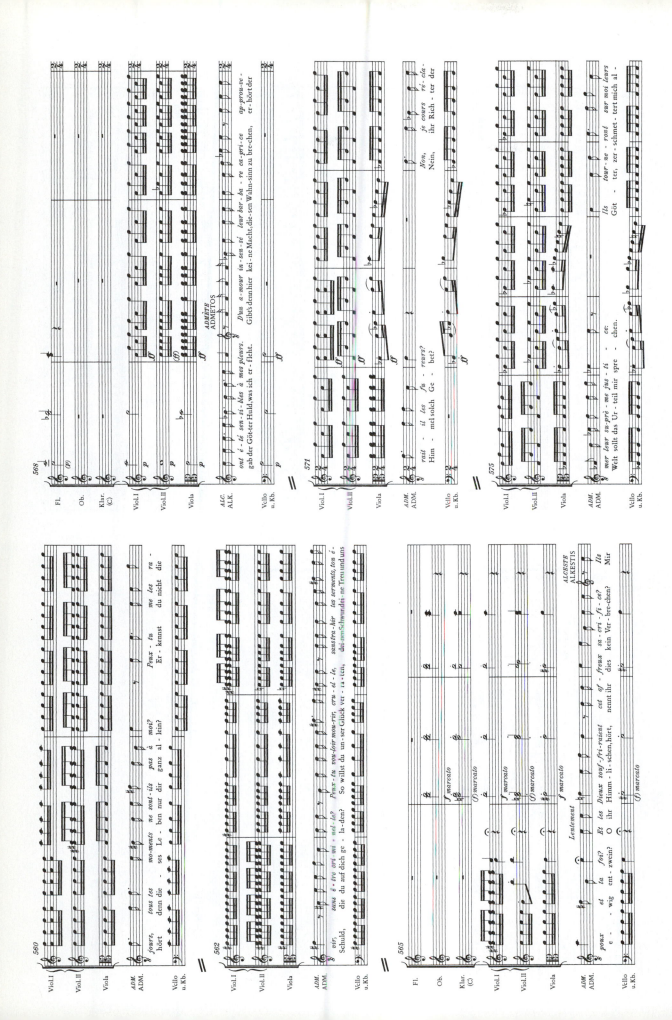

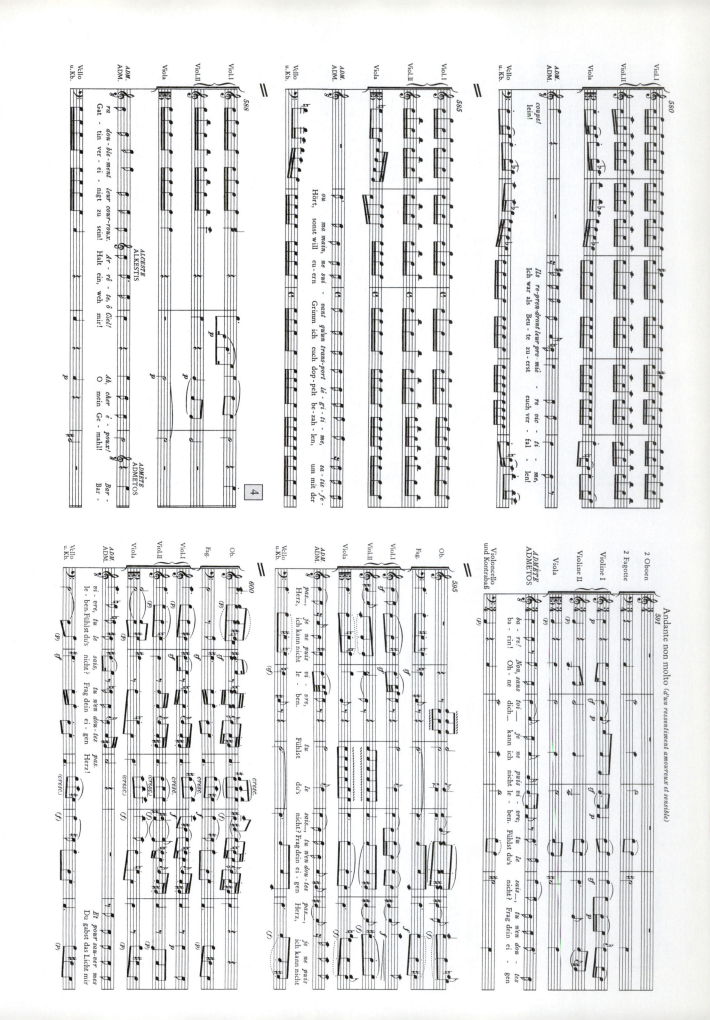

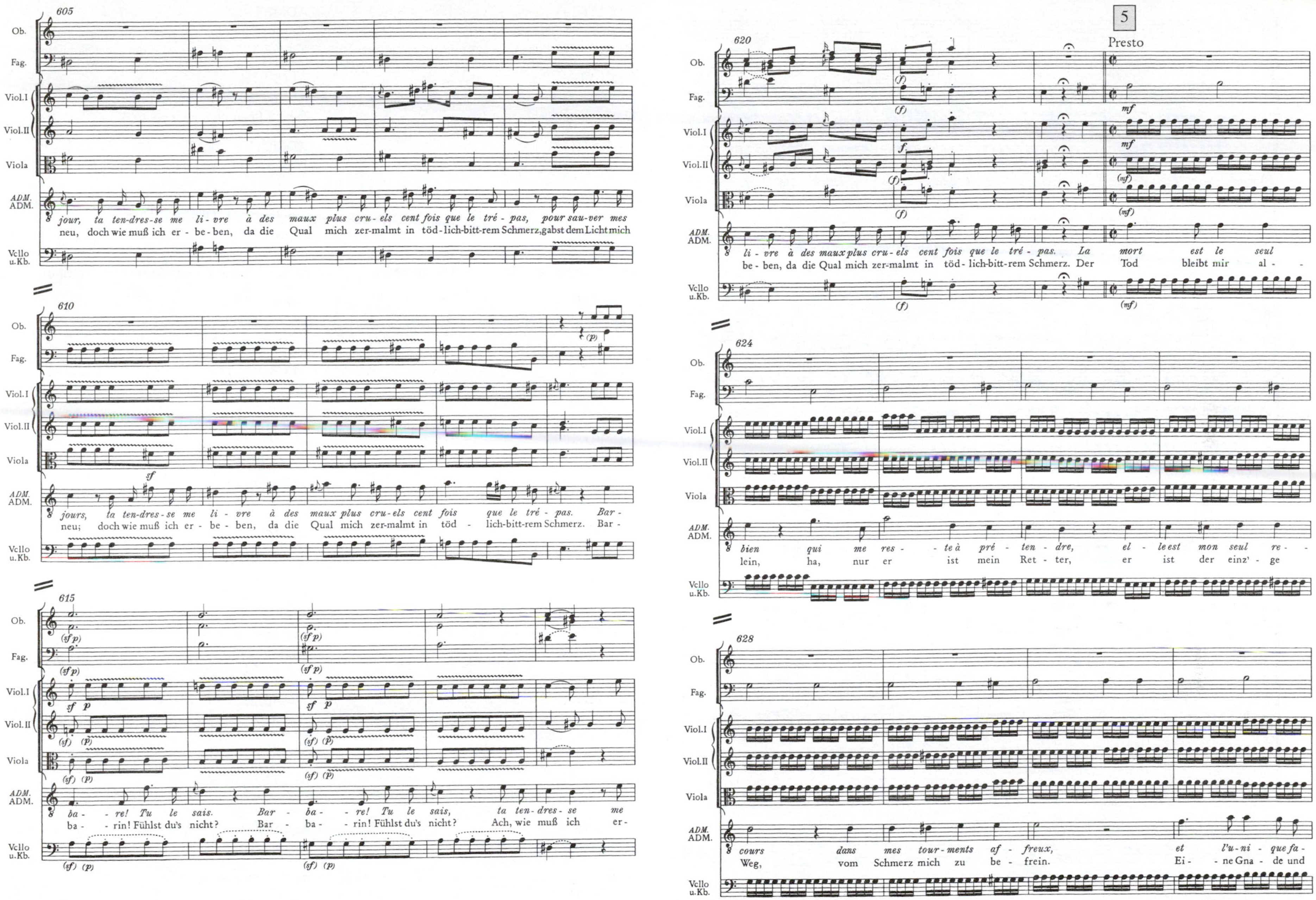
605
Ob.
Fag.
Viol.I
Viol.II
Viola
ADM.
ADM.
jour, ta ten-dres-se me li-vre à des maux plus cru-els cent fois que le tré-pas, pour sau-ver mes
neu, doch wie muß ich er-be-ben, da die Qual mich zer-malmt in töd-lich-bitt-rem Schmerz, gabst dem Licht mich
Vello
u.Kb.
610
jours, ta ten-dres-se me li-vre à des maux plus cru-els cent fois que le tré-pas. Bar-
neu; doch wie muß ich er-be-ben, da die Qual mich zer-malmt in töd-lich-bitt-rem Schmerz. Bar-
615
ba-re! Tu le sais. Bar-ba-re! Tu le sais, ta ten-dres-se me
ba-rin! Fühlst du's nicht? Bar-ba-rin! Fühlst du's nicht? Ach, wie muß ich er-
620
5
Presto
li-vre à des maux plus cru-els cent fois que le tré-pas. La mort est le seul
be-ben, da die Qual mich zer-malmt in töd-lich-bitt-rem Schmerz. Der Tod bleibt mir al-
624
bien qui me res-te à pré-ten-dre, el-le est mon seul re-
lein, ha, nur er ist mein Ret-ter, er ist der einz'-ge
628
cours dans mes tour-ments af-freux, et l'u-ni-que fa-
Weg, vom Schmerz mich zu be-frein. Ei-ne Gna-de und

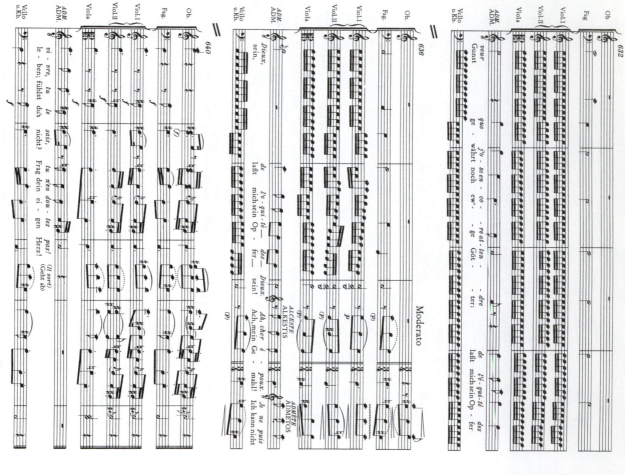

ADMÈTE	ADMETUS
Tu m'aimes, je t'adore,	You love me, I adore you
et tu remplis mon cœur des plus vives alarmes.	Yet you fill my heart with the greatest anxiety.
ALCESTE	ALCESTE
Ah! Cher époux, pardonne à ma douleur;	Ah, my husband, pardon my anguish,
je n'ai pu te cacher mes larmes.	Which I can no longer conceal.
ADMÈTE	ADMETUS
Et qui les fait couler?	Why do you weep?
ALCESTE	ALCESTE
On t'a dit à quel prix les Dieux ont consenti	You have heard the sacrifice demanded by the
de calmer leur colère	gods
et t'ont rendu des jours si tendrement chéris.	to calm their anger
	So that you may return to your cherished life.
ADMÈTE	ADMETUS
Connais-tu cet ami, victime volontaire?	Do you then know the friend who has
	volunteered?
ALCESTE	ALCESTE
Il n'aurait pu survivre à ton trépas.	That person could never have survived your
	death.
ADMÈTE	ADMETUS
Nomme-moi ce héros!	Name the noble friend!
ALCESTE	ALCESTE
Ne m'interroge pas!	Do not ask!
ADMÈTE	ADMETUS
Réponds-moi!	Respond!
ALCESTE	ALCESTE
Je ne puis!	I cannot!
ADMÈTE	ADMETUS
Tu ne peux?	You cannot?
ALCESTE	ALCESTE (aside)
Quel martyre!	What pains!
ADMÈTE	ADMETUS
Aleste!	Aleste!
ALCESTE	ALCESTE (aside)
Je frémis!	I tremble!
ADMÈTE	ADMETUS
Explique-toi!	Speak!
ALCESTE	ALCESTE (aside)
Tout mon cœur se déchire.	My heart aches!
ADMÈTE	ADMETUS
Aleste, au nom des Dieux,	Aleste, in the name of the gods, listen to me:
au nom de cet amour si tendre, si fidèle,	In the name of the tender, faithful love

qui fait tout mon bonheur, qui comble tous mes
vœux:
Romps ce silence odieux,
dissipe ma frayeur mortelle!

ALCESTE
Mon cher Admète, hélas!

ADMÈTE
Tu me glaces d'effroi;
parle! Quel est celui
dont la pitié cruelle l'entraîne à s'immoler pour
moi?

ALCESTE
Peux-tu le demander?

ADMÈTE
O silence funeste!
Parle enfin, je l'exige!

ALCESTE
Eh! Quelle autre qu'Alceste
devait mourir pour toi?

ADMÈTE
Toi? Ciel! Alceste!

[CHOEUR]
O Dieux!

[CHOEUR]
O malheureux Admète,
que poursuit le sort en courroux!
O généreux effort
d'une vertu parfaite!
Alceste meurt pour son époux.

ADMÈTE
O coup affreux!

ALCESTE
Admète!

ADMÈTE
Ah! Laisse-moi, cruelle! Laisse-moi!

ALCESTE
Cher époux!

ADMÈTE
Non, laisse-moi mourir!
Laisse-moi succomber à ma douleur mortelle,
à des tourments que je ne puis souffrir.

ALCESTE
Calme cette douleur, ce désespoir extrême.
Vis! Conserve des jours si cher à mon amour.

ADMÈTE
Tu veux mourir, tu veux
me quitter sans retour?
Et tu veux que je vive? Et tu dis que tu m'aimes!
Qui t'a donné le droit de disposer de toi?
Les serments de l'Amour et ceux de l'Hymenée,
ne te
tiennent-ils pas à mes loix enchaînée?
Tes jours, tous tes moments ne sont-ils pas à moi?
Peux-tu me les ravir, sans être criminelle?
Peux-tu vouloir mourir, cruelle,
sans trahir tes serments, ton époux et ta foi?

Et les Dieux souffriraient cet affreux sacrifice?

ALCESTE
Ils ont été sensibles à mes pleurs.

ADMÈTE
D'un amour insensé leur barbare caprice
approuverait-il les fureurs?
Non, je cours réclamer leur suprême justice:
Ils tourneront sur moi leurs coups!
Ils reprendront leur première victime,
ou ma main, ne suivant qu'un transport légitime,
satisfera doublement leur courroux.

ALCESTE
Arrête, ô Ciel!
Ah, cher époux!

ADMÈTE
Barbare!
Non, sans toi je ne puis vivre;
tu le sais, tu n'en doutes pas,
Et pour sauver mes jour,
ta tendresse me livre à des maux plus
cruels cent fois que le trépas.
La mort est le seul bien qui me reste à prétendre,
elle est mon seul recours dans mes tourments
affreux,
et l'unique faveur que j'ose encore attendre
de l'équité des Dieux.

ALCESTE
Ah, cher époux.

ADMÈTE
Je ne puis vivre, tu le sais,
tu n'en doutes pas!

That gives me all my happiness, answers all my
prayers:
Say but a word,
And then my mortal terror shall disappear!

ALCESTE
My dear Admetus, alas!

ADMETUS
You fill me with terror!
Speak! Who is the one
Would sacrifice himself for me?

ALCESTE
Can you ask?

ADMETUS
Oh deadly silence!
Speak, I command it!

ALCESTE
Who other than Alceste
Could die for you?

ADMETUS
You? Heavens! Alceste!

[CHORUS]
O gods!

[CHORUS]
Woe to Admetus,
Your fate is pain and torment!
Oh noble gesture
Of perfect virtue!
Alceste dies for her spouse.

ADMETUS
Oh dreadful blow!

ALCESTE
Admetus!

ADMETUS
Ah! Leave me, cruel one, leave me!

ALCESTE
Dear husband!

ADMETUS
No, let me die!
Let me die of mortal pain,
Of torments I cannot bear.

ALCESTE
Calm your anguish, this extreme despair.
Live! Preserve this life so dear to my love.

ADMETUS
You wish to die, to leave me,
Never to return?
So that I can live, do you call that love?
Who gave you the right to choose death?
Do not the pledges and oaths of love and marriage

Keep you bound to me?
Do the days of your life belong to you alone?
Can you lawfully take them from me?
Can you wish to die, cruel one,
Without betraying your oaths, your spouse, and
your loyalty?
And could the gods tolerate this terrible sacrifice?

ALCESTE
They have been moved by my tears.

ADMETUS
Could their barbarous capriciousness approve the
frenzies of an insane love?
No, I shall pursue their supreme justice;
They shall redirect their blows toward me;
They shall reclaim their original victim,
Or my own hand, following a rightful path,
Shall doubly satisfy their wrath.

ALCESTE
Stop, oh heavens!
Oh my husband!

ADMETUS
Barbarous one!
No, without you I cannot live,
You know it, you cannot doubt it.
And to save me,
Your tenderness brings me misfortunes,
A hundred times worse than death.
Death is the only good that remains for me,
It is my only recourse in my horrible torments,

And the only grace I can dare attain
From the justice of the gods

ALCESTE
Ah, dear husband!

ADMETUS
I cannot live, you know it,
You cannot doubt it.

In *Alceste*, Gluck sought to create an opera that was more faithful to the principles of drama than to the demands of singers. This meant pruning away virtuosic passages, eliminating da capo arias (with their embellished repeats and textual repetition), diminishing the distinction between aria and recitative in general, and giving greater prominence to the chorus, as in the dramas of ancient Greece.

The subject-matter of the libretto of *Alceste* is very much in the tradition of *opera seria*. The story is based on a Greek legend revolving around Queen Alceste's extraordinary devotion to her husband, King Admetus. When the dying Admetus learns from an oracle that he will be saved if another mortal agrees to die in his place, Alceste resolves to sacrifice herself for him. Admetus recovers and Alceste is summoned to the underworld, but Hercules, with the blessing of Apollo, brings her back and she is restored to life.

In this excerpt, Admetus learns that Alceste is the one who will die for him and he pleads with her to change her mind. Here, Gluck skillfully weaves together accompanied recitative, chorus, aria, and duet into a musically continuous dramatic sequence:

• *Accompanied recitative* (m. 486–524). In the opening dialogue, Admète (French for Admetus) pleads with Alceste to reveal who has agreed to die for him. She resists but in the end admits that she herself is the victim.

• *Chorus* (m. 525–538). At the climactic moment when Alceste reveals that she is to be the sacrificial victim, the Chorus interjects with an outcry of "O Dieux!" ("O ye gods!"). This is in keeping with principles of ancient Greek tragedy, in which the chorus reflects the perspective of the community as a whole, transcending that of any individual character. After Admète registers his own astonishment, the chorus sings a lament for Admète and praises Alceste for her courage and love toward her husband.

• *Accompanied recitative* (m. 538–590). The dialogue resumes. Admète admonishes Alceste, telling her that she will be breaking her marriage vows by abandoning him if she dies and leaves him alone. He calls on the gods to intercede. Alceste answers these protestations calmly, ending the dialogue (in m. 589–590) with the pleading phrase *Ah, cher époux* ("Ah, dear husband").

• *Aria* (m. 591–638). Without fanfare or ritornello, the accompanied recitative flows into an aria, sung by Admète, who proclaims his love for Alceste and tells her that he cannot live without her. The aria adheres to no conventional structure, following instead to the sense of the text. In m. 623, for example, when Admète declares that death is his only salvation, the music shifts abruptly from andante and 3/4 time to alla breve presto.

• *Interruption* (m. 638–639). Just before the end of Admète's aria, Alceste interrupts with a simple but dramatic repetition of her earlier plea, *Ah, cher époux.*

• *Return of aria's opening section* (m. 639–644). The tempo shifts to moderato, the meter back to 3/4, and Admète closes by repeating the key phrase from the opening part of his aria just before leaving the stage: *Je ne puis vivre, tu le sais, tu n'en doutes pas* ("I cannot live [without you], you know it, you have no doubt of that").

By returning to earlier material at the end of the aria, Gluck is to some extent following the conventions of the da capo aria, including even the exit convention. But the differences here are more revealing than the similarities: the return is extremely brief, and virtuosity for its own sake plays no role at all. The repetition reinforces the text, reminding us that in spite of Admète's desire to die, his overwhelming emotion is one of grief at the thought of losing Alceste.

III Don Giovanni, K. 527, Act I, Scenes 1–5 (1787)
Mozart

CD8 p. 361 Track 6

Act I.
Nº 1 Introduction.

Scene — A Garden, Night.
Leporello, in a cloak, discovered watching before the house of Donna Anna; then Donna Anna and Don Giovanni, afterwards the Commandant.

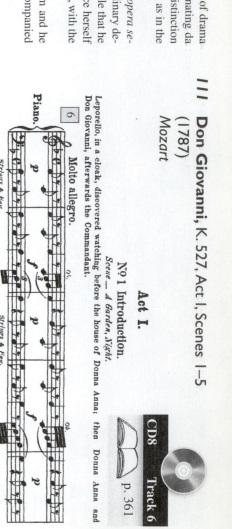

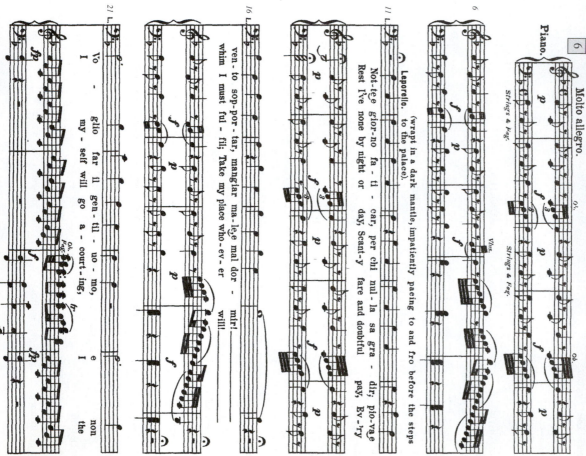

Note: This is a piano reduction of Mozart's original version for voices and orchestra.

No. III Mozart: *Don Giovanni*

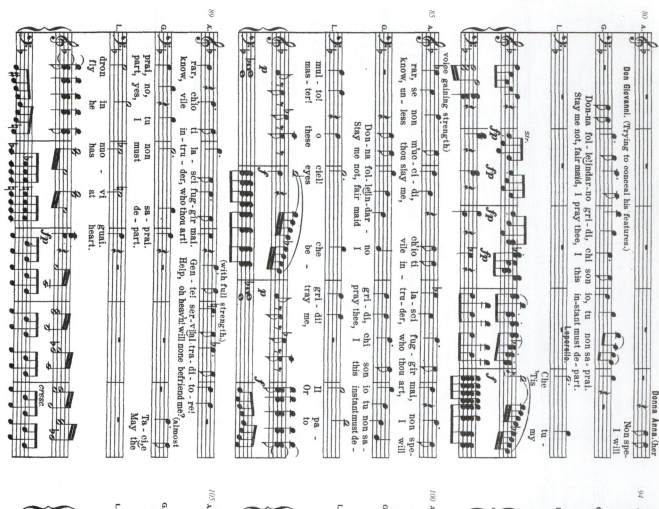

No. 111 Mozart: *Don Giovanni*

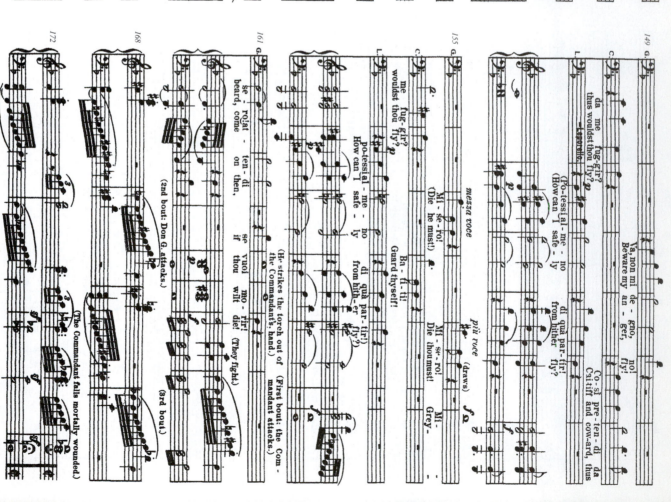

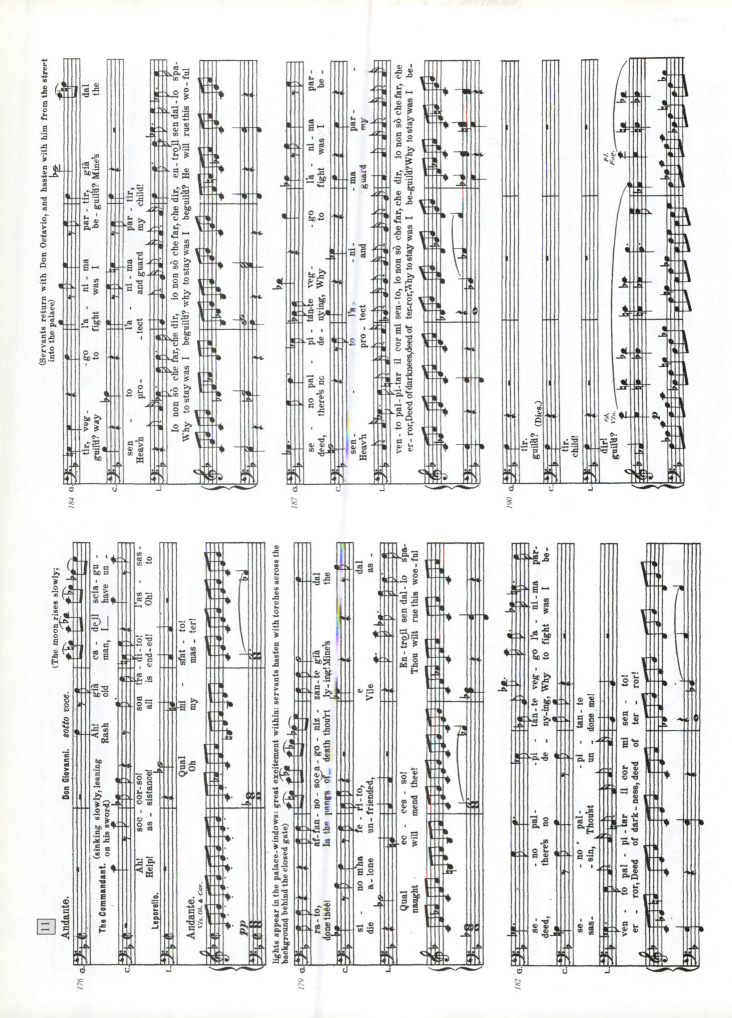

No. III Mozart: *Don Giovanni*

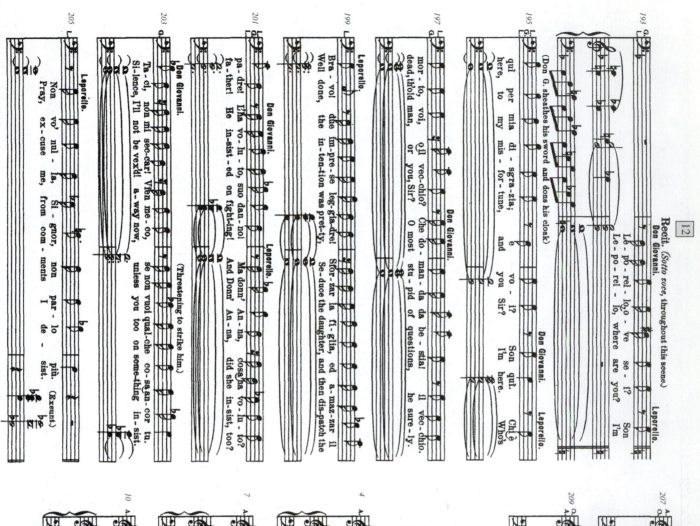

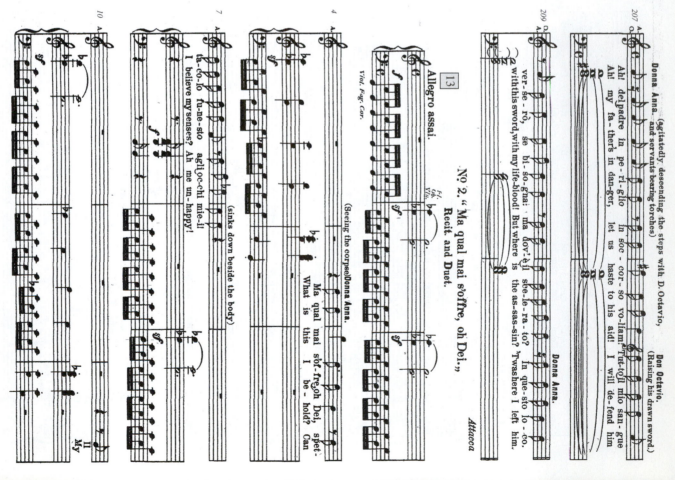

No. III Mozart: Don Giovanni

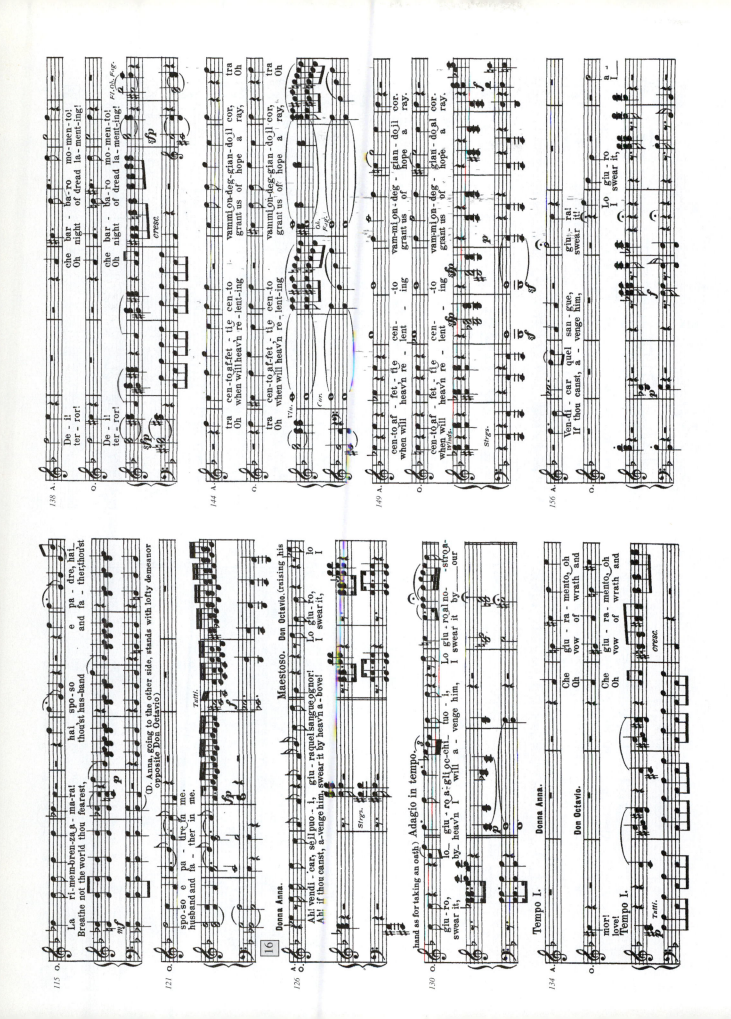

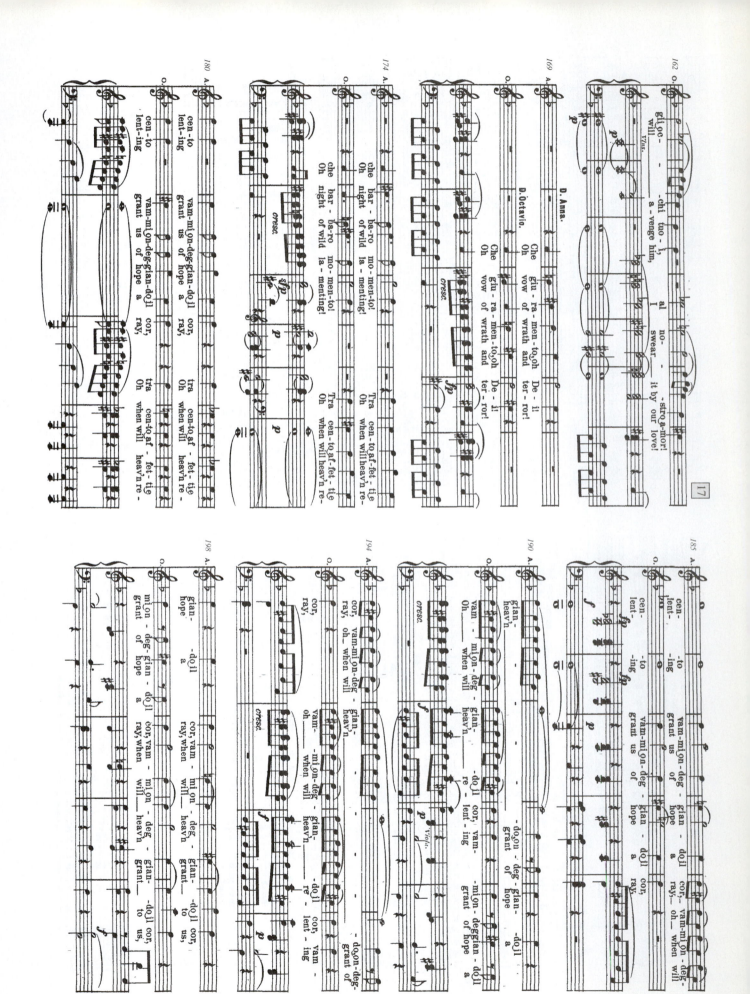

No. III Mozart: *Don Giovanni*

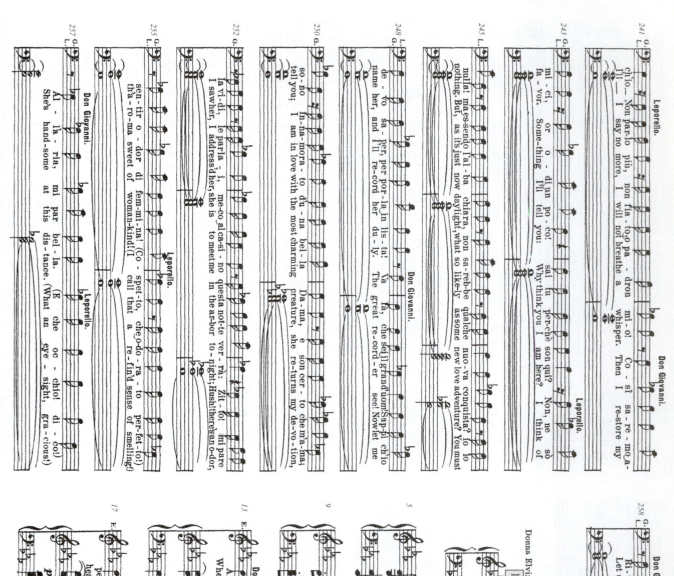
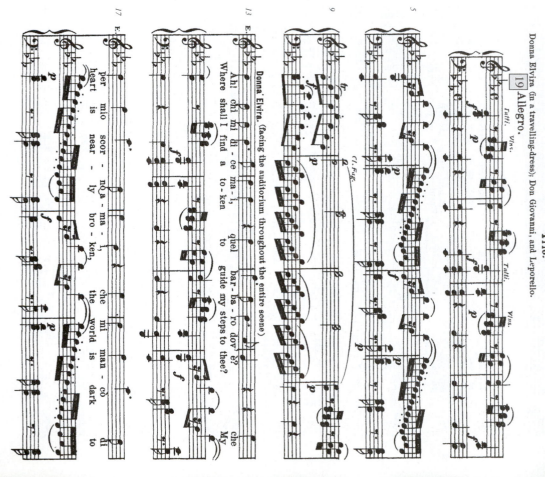

Donna Elvira (in-

Don Giovanni. (starting back;
mezza voce)

Recit.

Leporello. (aside)

la? Stel-le! che ve-do! O bel-la! Don-na El-vi-ra! Don Gio-
voice! She? oh! con-fu-sion! How charming! Don-na El-vi-ra! Don Gio-

(dignantly)

Leporello. (aside)

van-ni!
van-ni!
sei qui? mostro! fel-lon! ni-do d'in-ganni! Che ti-to-li cruscan-ti!
You here? She? Monster of baseness! Falsest of men! (Now compliments are passing!)

cen-to.
jole her.

Don Giovanni.

Via, ca-ra Donna El-
El-vi-ra dear, I

man-co ma-le che lo co-no-sce be-ne.
Waste of words,she by this time ought to know him.)

vi-ra,
pray you,
cal-ma-te que-sta col-le-ra!
re-strain that voice im-pet-u-ous!
sen-ti-te, la-
now lis-ten, and

Donna Elvira.

scia-te-mi par-lar!
I will tell you all.
Co-sa ptoi di-re do-po-a-zion si ne-ra? In ca-sa
What can you say that will ex-cuse your falsehood? First you be-

Donna Elvira.

mi-a en-tri fur-ti-va-men-te, a for-za d'ar-te, di giu-ramen-ti,e
sought me se-cret-ly to re-ceive you, with vows of fond-ness, oaths of de-vo-tion,

di lu-sin-ghe ar-ri-vi
love e-ter-nal pro-fess-ing,
a se-dur-rell cor mi-o;
I be-lieved that you loved me,
mfm-na-
in your

Donna Elvira.

Gli vo' ca-va-
His love can ne'er
re il cor, gli vo' ca-va-
re-turn,his love can ne'er

p

(Don Giovanni clears his throat several times,to attract

gli
his

Don Giovanni clears his throat several times,to attract
-re il cor,
re-turn,

Donna Elvira's notice; she does not hear him,but grows more and more excited. Finally his patience

il re-

vo'
love
cavar
can ne'er
il cor,
re-turn,
ca-
can
var
ne'er

cresc.

f

22

D.Elvira.

(raising
his hat)

gives way, and he steps up to Don Giovanni.
Donna Elvira boldly,but politely.)

Don Giovanni.

Si-gno-ri-nal
Fair Se-ño-ra!
Si-gno-ri-nal
Fair Se-ño-ra!
Ohiè
That

cor!
turn!

p

cresc.

p

92

97

101

104

109

111

114

116

118

120

122

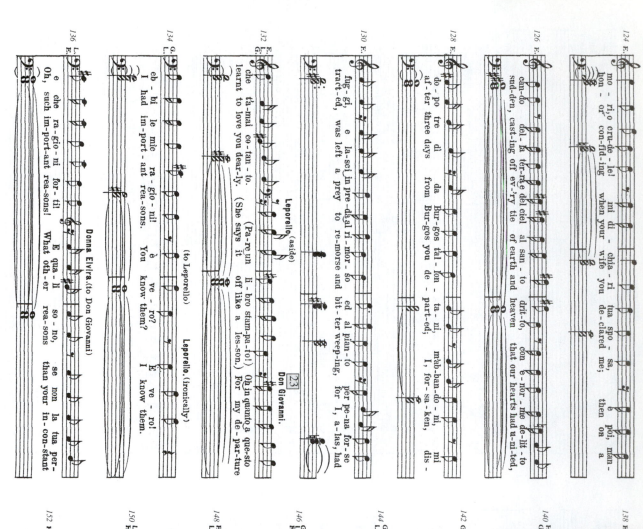

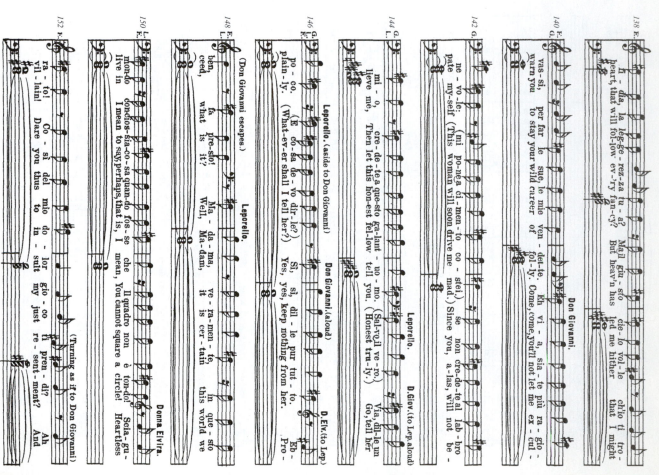

No. III Mozart: Don Giovanni

The plot of *Don Giovanni* is based on the legend of Don Juan, a nobleman and notorious libertine. Lorenzo Da Ponte's libretto is both comic and serious, pitting men against women and nobles against commoners. The title character is at once malevolent and alluring, a man who openly flaunts conventional morality, pursuing instead his own pleasure under the guise of "liberty." At the beginning of the opera he slays the Commendatore (Commandant), the father of Donna Anna, a woman who has just fought off the Don's attempted assault. At the end of the opera, the statue of the Commendatore consigns the unrepentant Don to the flames of Hell.

The overture and first three scenes of *Don Giovanni*, which together constitute some twenty minutes of continuous music and seamless dramatic action, demonstrate the way Mozart integrates *buffa* and *seria* elements. True to the principles of Gluck's operatic creed, Mozart uses the overture to set the tone of the opera as a whole, with its unpredictable juxtaposition of tragedy and farce. When the curtain rises we find Leporello, the servant of Don Giovanni, standing guard outside a nobleman's house while his master attempts to seduce yet another woman. Even before Leporello sings a single note, the music announces that he is a commoner: the opening theme, which Leporello picks up when he begins his aria-monologue, bounces back and forth between tonic and dominant. There is nothing sophisticated about this theme. It is harmonically, rhythmically, and melodically simple, almost to the point of simple-mindedness. Leporello is complaining to himself about the wicked ways of his master while at the same time longing to be a "gentleman" himself. With its relentlessly syllabic text underlay and vehement repetitions of "No, no, no," the aria sounds appropriately comical.

But as in the overture, the juxtaposition of comedy and tragedy occurs without warning. Leporello's monologue segues into a frantic duet between two members of an altogether different class: the noblewoman Donna Anna and the nobleman Don Giovanni. Donna Anna pursues the unknown man (Don Giovanni), who attempts to escape unrecognized. Almost at once, the duet becomes a trio as Leporello joins their agitated exchange with more of his melodically simple line, this time commenting on the action and predicting that his master's philandering will bring his own ruin.

A new dramatic unit begins with the arrival of the Commendatore, Donna Anna's father. He demands a duel with the unknown intruder. Don Giovanni reluctantly accepts, and deals the Commendatore a mortal wound. Again, Leporello comments on the scene as it transpires before him, this time with an even greater sense of gloom. There follows a brief dialogue in secco recitative between Don Giovanni and Leporello, after which they exit. We then move directly into another dramatic unit, still with no real break in the music. Donna Anna returns, having summoned the aid of her kind-hearted but rather boring fiancé, Don Ottavio. During the accompanied recitative that follows they discover her father's body and she faints. Don Ottavio revives her so efficiently, however, that she is soon able to launch into her part of a powerfully dramatic duet (*Fuggi, crudele, fuggi*) at the end of which they swear together to avenge her father's death. The music, agitated and virtuosic, comes from the world of *opera seria*. Mozart fuses the reflective power of aria (Donna Anna's shock at the death of her father) with the interchange of duet (Don Ottavio's promise of consolation and revenge), all interrupted at unpredictable moments by powerful outbursts of accompanied recitative.

Clearly, Mozart wanted to create a sense of dramatic continuity for the entire opening sequence of events, for it is only now, at the end of this extended duet, that he gives the audience its first opportunity to applaud. The arias and ensembles are not, as is so often the case in *opera seria*, reflections on events that have already happened. On the contrary, they are part of the action, propelling it forward. The events of the drama, in other words, move through the music.

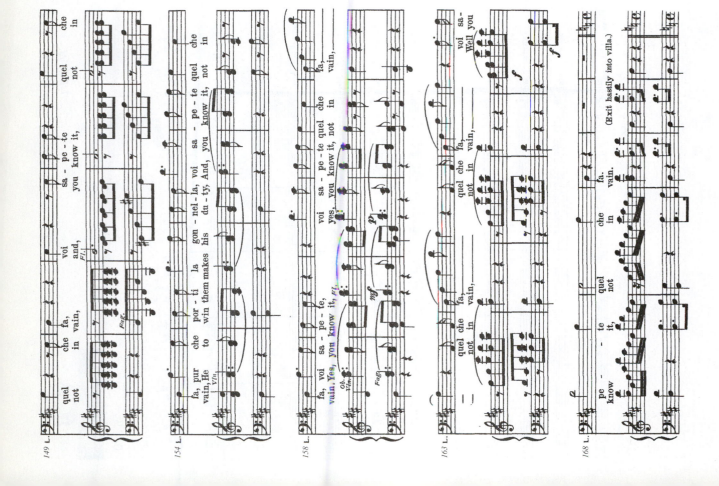

One of the devices Mozart uses to structure this extended series of units is tonality. The sequence begins and ends in D minor, and the choice of key in between is closely coordinated with the drama unfolding on stage. Each dramatic unit has its own distinctive key, different from yet related to the one before and the one after.

The integration of music and drama is evident as well in the two subsequent numbers. The first of these, *Ah, chi mi dice mai* ("Ah, who shall ever tell me"), begins like an aria. Donna Elvira, who had been seduced and abandoned by Don Giovanni long before the curtain has gone up, is asking herself if she will ever again find that "barbarian," promising to "cut out his heart" if she does. Her demanding vocal line, full of large leaps and covering a wide range, signals that she is a noblewoman, a character who would be at home in an *opera seria*. As she is singing, Don Giovanni and Leporello see her from a distance, and the aria becomes a trio. Don Giovanni does not at first recognize her (a curious reversal from the previous scene in which he escaped unrecognized), and so he is unaware that it is he she is raging about. With another seduction clearly in mind, he steps forward to console her. The moment they recognize each other, the ensemble ends. The music changes without a pause to secco recitative, and the drama presses on. Once again Mozart deprives the audience of an opportunity to applaud. Instead, we watch Donna Elvira's astonishment turn to rage as Don Giovanni slips away, leaving Leporello to deal with her. In his ensuing aria, *Madamina! il catalogo è questo* ("Madam! Here is the catalogue"), Leporello tries to assuage Donna Elvira with evidence that she is "neither the first nor the last" of Don Giovanni's conquests. He shows her a catalogue he has kept of all of Don Giovanni's lovers. In the first part of the aria Leporello enumerates his master's seductions by country; in the second part he describes them by type (old or young, fair-haired or dark-haired, large or small). The music reflects this shift of focus. The first part is allegro; the second part, with its own theme, moves at a more leisurely tempo (Andante con moto).

112 Requiem, K. 626, Introit (1791)

Mozart

P. 370

CD8 Track 28

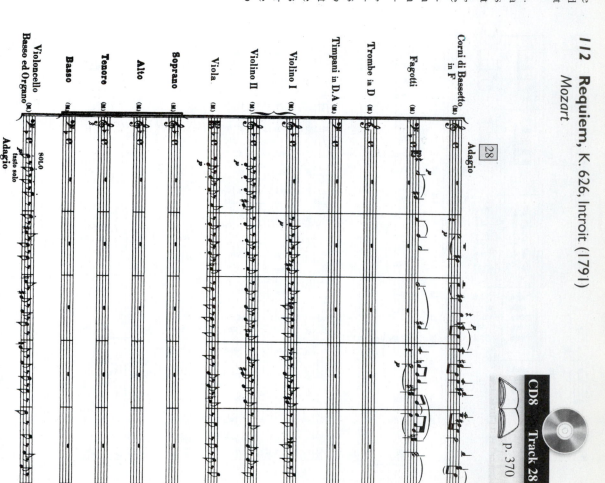

No. 112 Mozart: *Requiem*

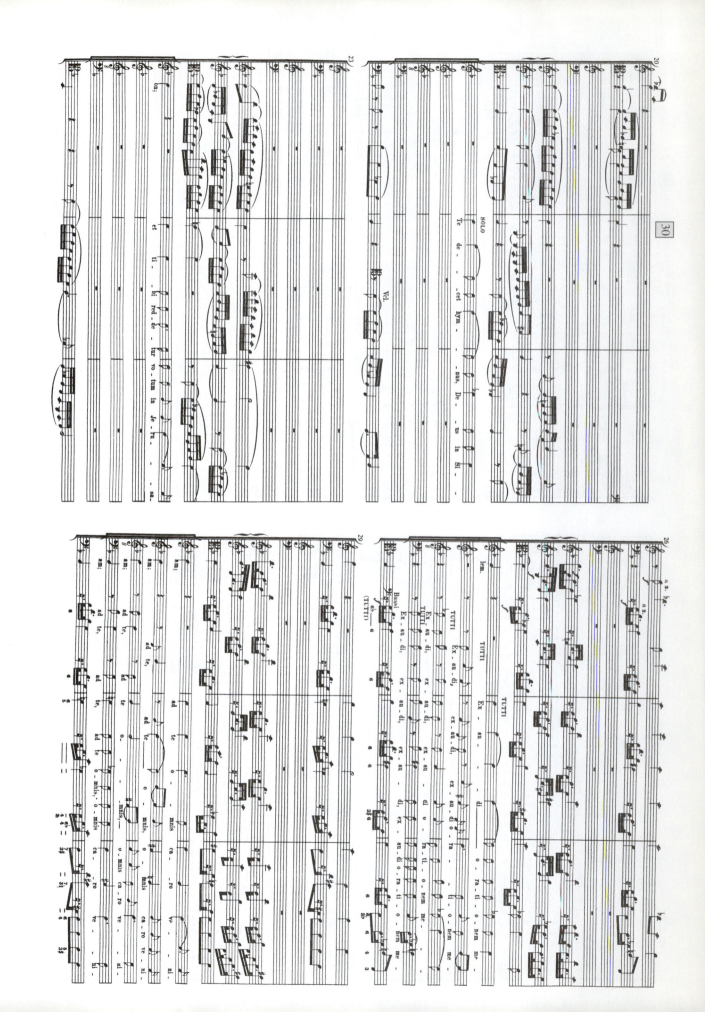

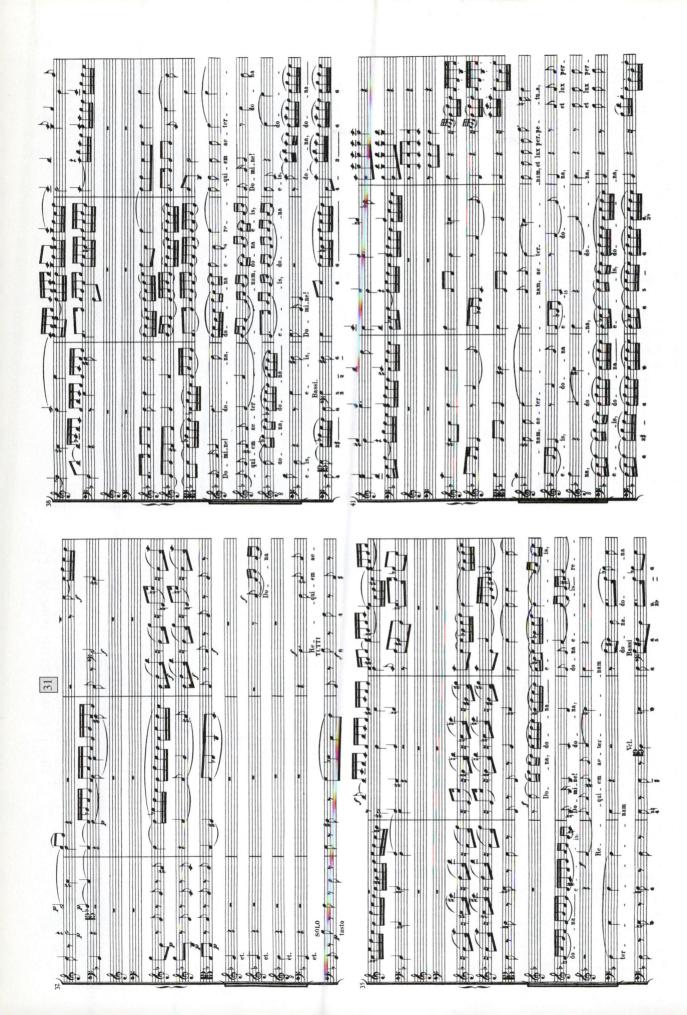

No. 112 Mozart: *Requiem*

The Introit of Mozart's unfinished *Requiem*, K. 626, offers a good example of the synthesis of older and newer styles often found in the sacred music of the Classical era. For this movement, Mozart drew on the opening chorus from Handel's *Funeral Anthem for Queen Caroline*, written in 1737. For the section beginning with the words *Te decet hymnus Deus in Sion* ("To thee, Lord in Zion, we sing a hymn"), Mozart brings in an even older source of sacred music, Gregorian chant. Here, in the soprano, he introduces the Ninth Psalm Tone (see Textbook, Chapter 1), also associated in German-speaking lands with the Magnificat, another hymn of praise to God. The concluding *Dona eis pacem* ("Grant them peace") section brings back the opening theme (*Requiem aeternam*), but now combines it with a new countersubject.

Mozart's *Requiem* has been surrounded in controversy since the time of its composition. It was known at the time that Mozart had died before he could complete the work, yet it was in his widow's interest to portray the efforts of the various collaborators who finished it—mostly students of her late husband—as inconsequential. Scholars have been trying to sort out Mozart's work from those of others since at least the 1820s. There is no dispute, however, about the authorship of the opening half of the work, including the Introit, because it has been preserved in manuscript in the composer's own hand.

Requiem aeternam dona eis, Domine.
Et lux perpetua luceat eis.
Te decet hymnus, Deus, in Sion,
Et tibi reddetur votum in Jerusalem
Exaudi orationem meam
Ad te omnis caro veniet.

Rest eternal grant unto them, O Lord.
And may light perpetual shine upon them.
A hymn, Lord, becometh thee in Zion,
And a vow shall be paid to thee in Jerusalem.
Hear my prayer,
To thee all flesh shall come.

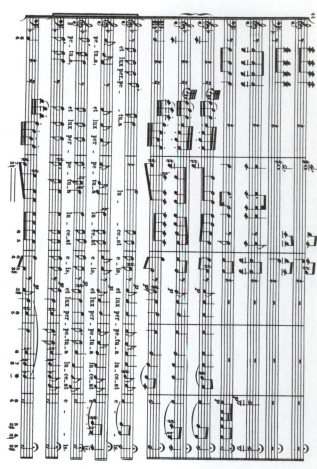

113 Kennst du das Land (1796)
Carl Friedrich Zelter (1758–1832)

CD8 Track 32 p. 373

No. 113 Zelter: *Kennst du das Land*

Kennst du das Land, wo die Zitronen blühn,
Im dunkeln Laub die Goldorangen glühn,
Ein sanfter Wind vom blauen Himmel weht,
Die Myrte still und hoch der Lorbeer steht,
Kennst du es wohl?
Dahin! dahin
Möcht' ich mit dir, o mein Geliebter, ziehn.

Kennst du das Haus? Auf Säulen ruht sein
Dach,
Es glänzt der Saal, es schimmert das Gemach,
Und Marmorbilder stehn und sehn mich an:
Was hat man dir, du armes Kind, getan?
Kennst du es wohl?
Dahin! dahin
Möcht' ich mit dir, o mein Beschützer, ziehn.

Kennst du den Berg und seinen Wolkensteg?
Das Maultier sucht im Nebel seinen Weg;
In Höhlen wohnt der Drachen alte Brut;
Es stürzt der Fels und über ihn die Flut.
Kennst du ihn wohl?
Dahin! dahin
Geht unser Weg! o Vater, lass uns ziehn!

Do you know the land where the lemon trees
blossom?
Among dark leaves the golden oranges glow.
A gentle breeze leaves from blue skies drifts.
The myrtle is still, and the laurel stands high.
Do you know it well?
There, there
would I go with you, my beloved,

Do you know the house? On pillars rests its
roof.
The great hall glistens, the room shines,
and the marble statues stand and look at me,
asking:
"What have they done to you, poor child?"
Do you know it well?
There, there
would I go with you, oh my protector,

Do you know the mountain and its path?
The muletier searches in the clouds for his way;
in the caves dwells the dragon of the old breed.
The cliff falls, and over it the flood.
Do you know it well?
There, there
leads our way; oh father, let us go!

Carl Friedrich Zelter's *Kennst du das Land?* ("Do You Know the Land?") exemplifies the strophic and largely syllabic approach to song writing that characterizes the genre during the Classical era. Both the vocal and piano parts are straightforward and technically undemanding; the range of the vocal line barely exceeds an octave. The text is from Goethe's widely read novel *Wilhelm Meisters Lehrjahre* ("Wilhelm Meister's Years of Apprenticeship"), the story of a young man's coming of age. Wilhelm is an aspiring actor who falls in with an odd assortment of characters, one of whom is a mysterious young girl named Mignon. She has no family, and Wilhelm becomes something of a father figure to her, but there is a powerful erotic tension beneath the surface of their relationship. From time to time throughout the novel, Mignon sings songs, of which Goethe gives only the words. Zelter (1758–1832) was one of the first composers to set these texts to music, and Goethe expressed his pleasure with Zelter's settings of his texts.

114 Wake Ev'ry Breath: A Canon of 6 in One with a Ground (1770)

William Billings (1746–1800)

CD8 Track 35 p. 374

[Billings's note on performance:] N.B. The Ground Bass to be continually sung by 3 or 4 deep voices with the 6 other parts

William Billings' "Wake Ev'ry Breath," the opening song of his *New-England Psalm Singer* (1770), illustrates what in its time was called a "social song"—that is, one intended to be sung by many voices at a social gathering like the one depicted on the frontispiece to his collection (see Textbook, p. 373). Social singing was a tradition brought to the American colonies from England, which had long cultivated imitative partsongs of various kinds. Catches tended to be humorous, while glees were generally more folk-like in nature; the texts of canons usually addressed moral or religious subjects. Billings (1746–1800), a native of Boston, was one of the first American-born composers to achieve international fame. He was largely self-taught, and his musical style, although indebted to English precedents, exhibits a certain roughness that gives it great energy. Billings's partsong *Chester* ("Let tyrants shake their iron rod / And slav'ry clank her galling Chains / we fear them not we trust in God / New England's God for ever reigns") became an unofficial anthem of the American Revolution.

Performance notes: This recording doubles each line with instruments. Although not indicated in the score, the practice of doubling vocal lines with instruments in hymns and hymn-like works was common in this era. The recording also captures something of the amateur quality of social gatherings in 18th-century New England. This music was not written for professional musicians.

No. 114 Billings: *Wake Ev'ry Breath: A Canon of 6 in One with a Ground*

115 Symphony No. 3 in E♭ Major ("Eroica"), Op. 55 (1803)
Ludwig van Beethoven (1770–1827)

115a First Movement

CD8 Track 36
P. 408

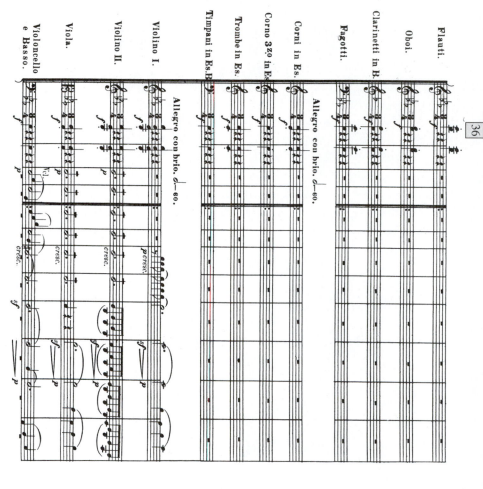

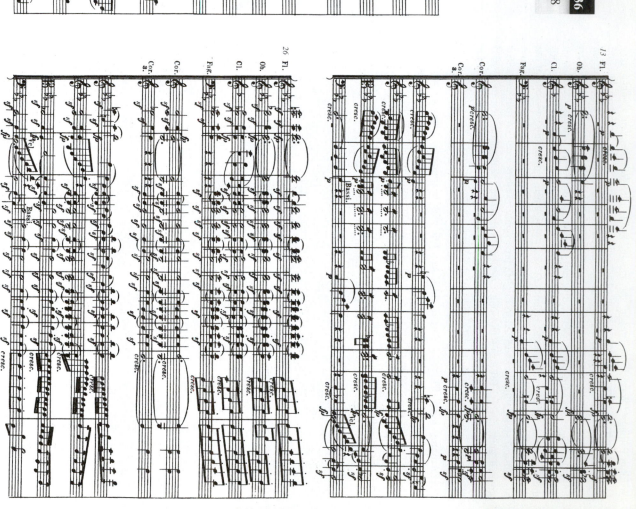

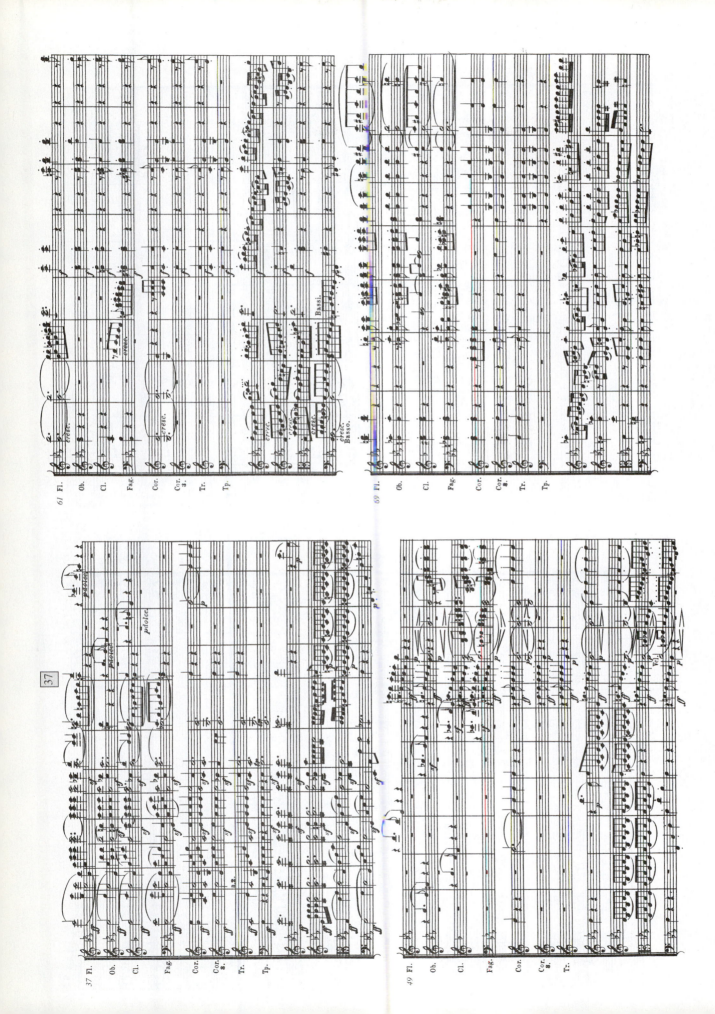

No. 115 Beethoven: Symphony No. 3 in E♭ Major

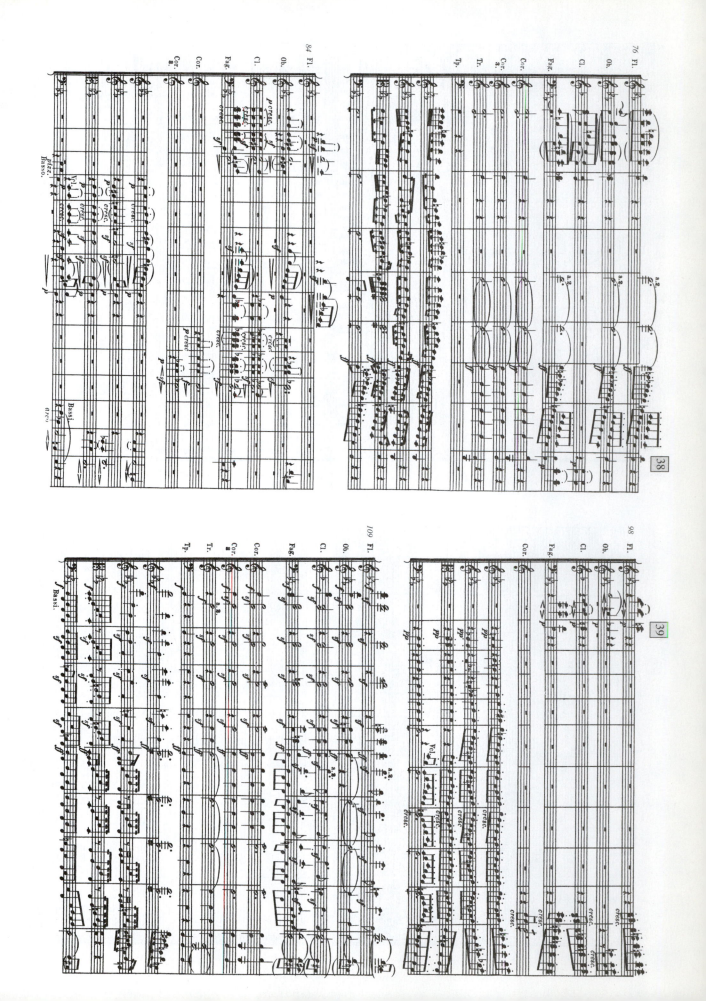

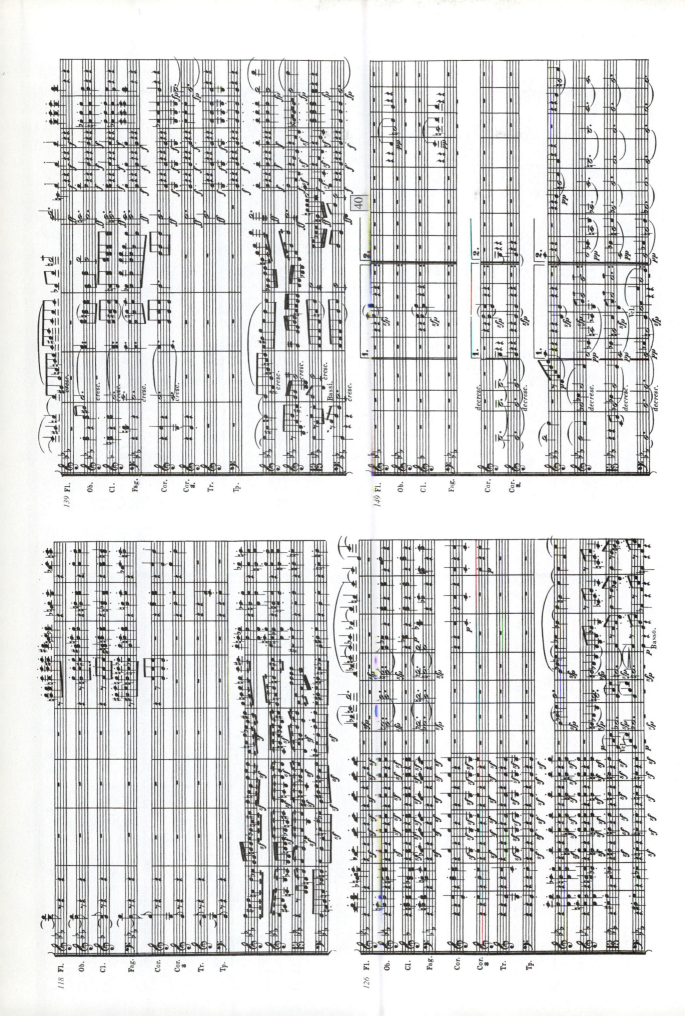

No. 115 Beethoven: Symphony No. 3 in E♭ Major

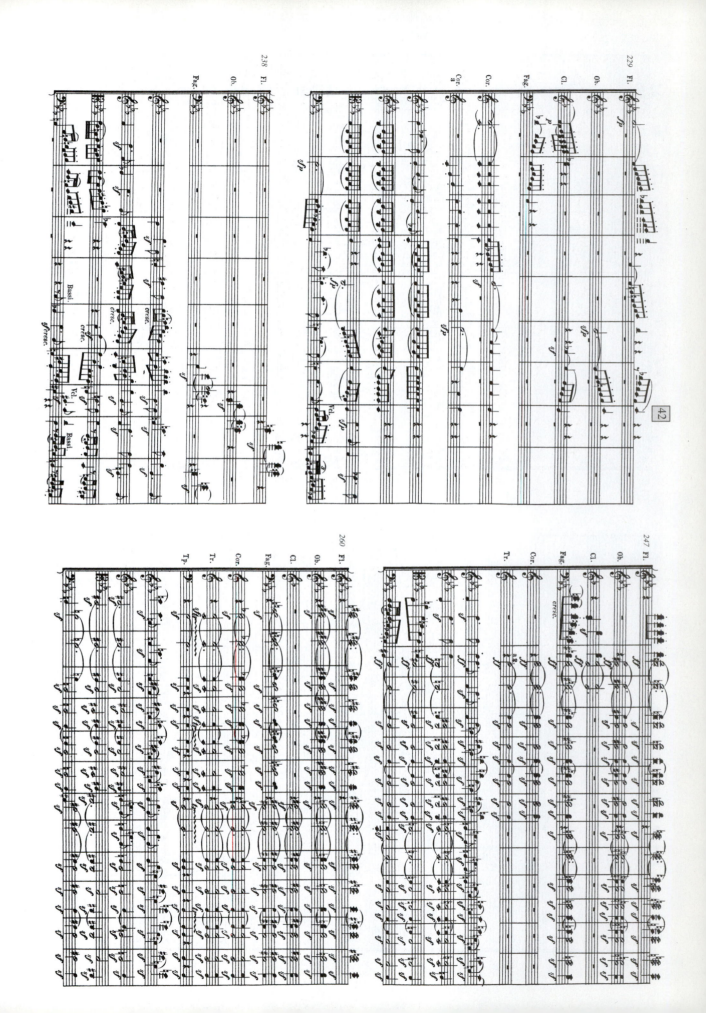

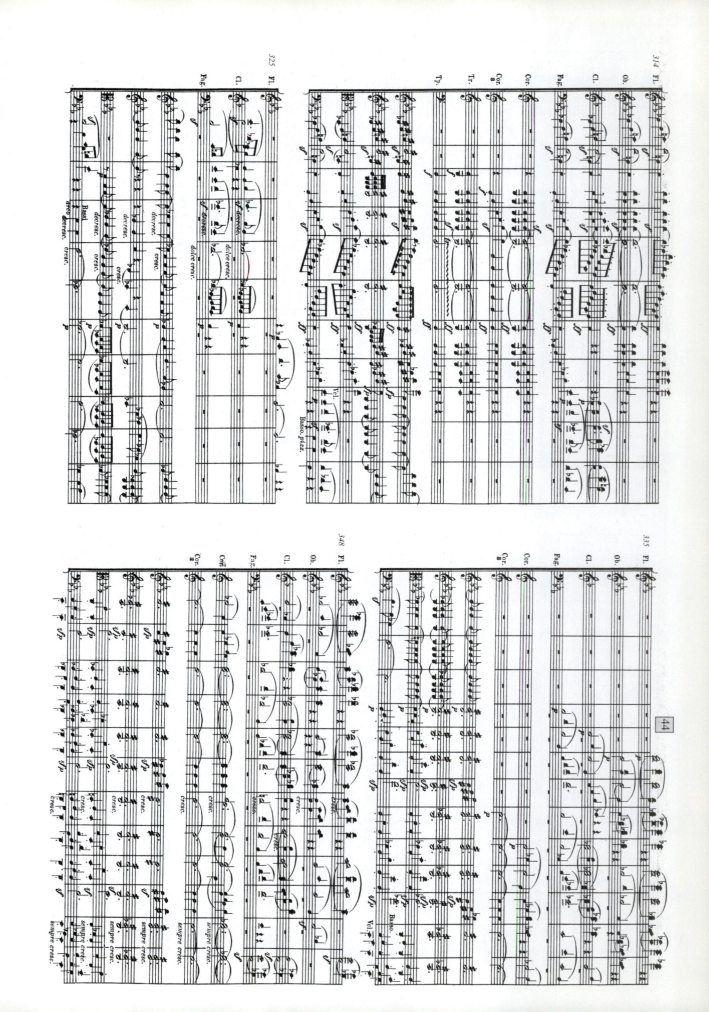

No. 115 Beethoven: Symphony No. 3 in E♭ Major

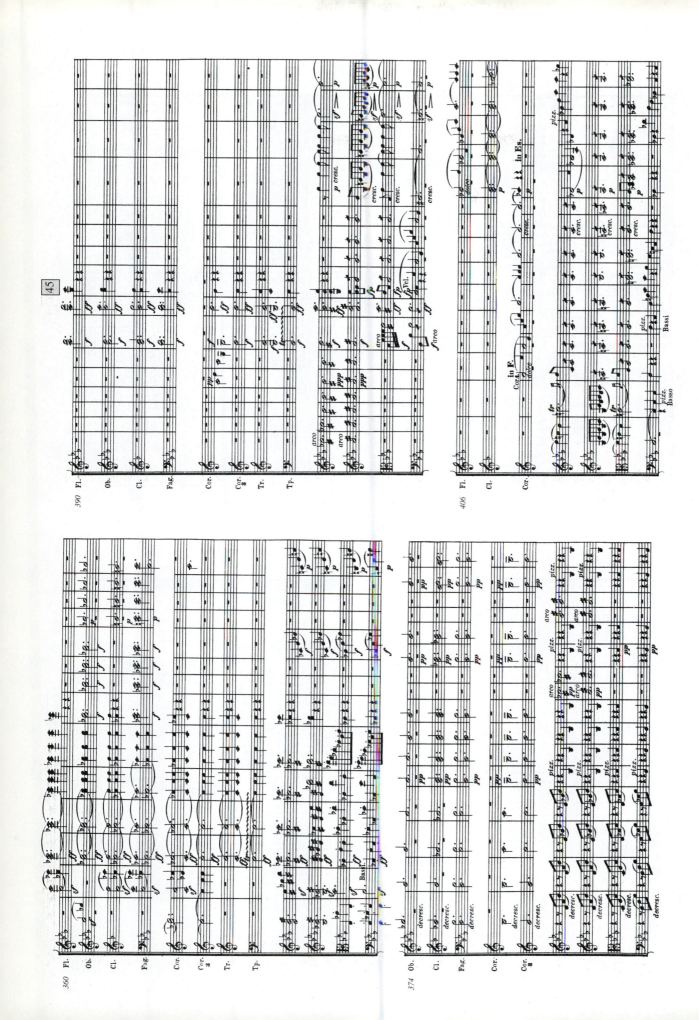

No. 115 Beethoven: Symphony No. 3 in E♭ Major

No. 115 Beethoven: Symphony No. 3 in E♭ Major

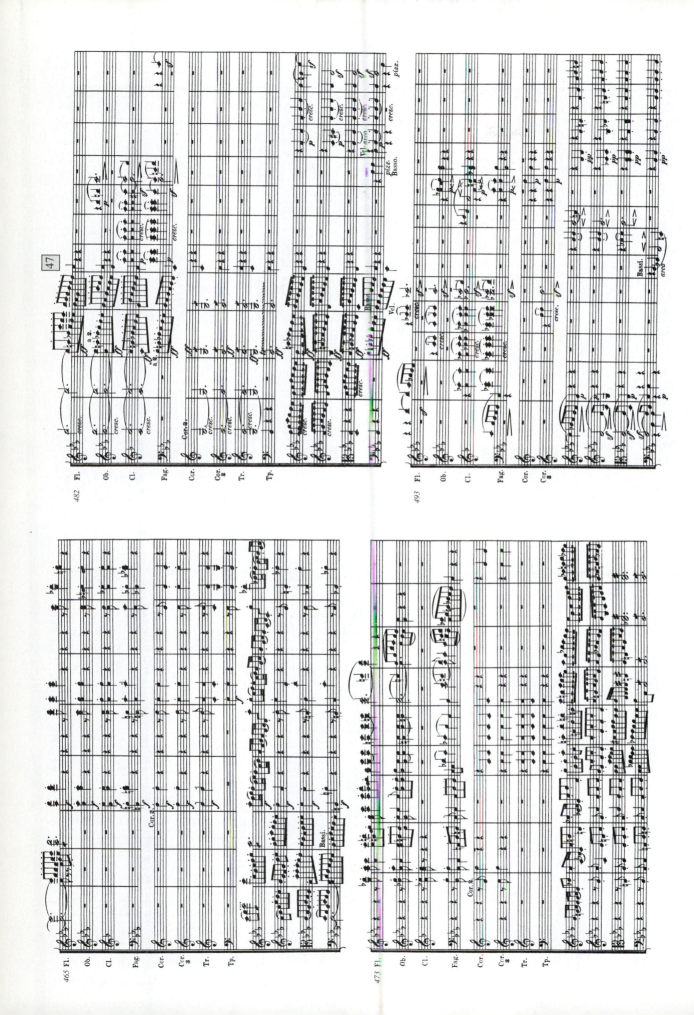

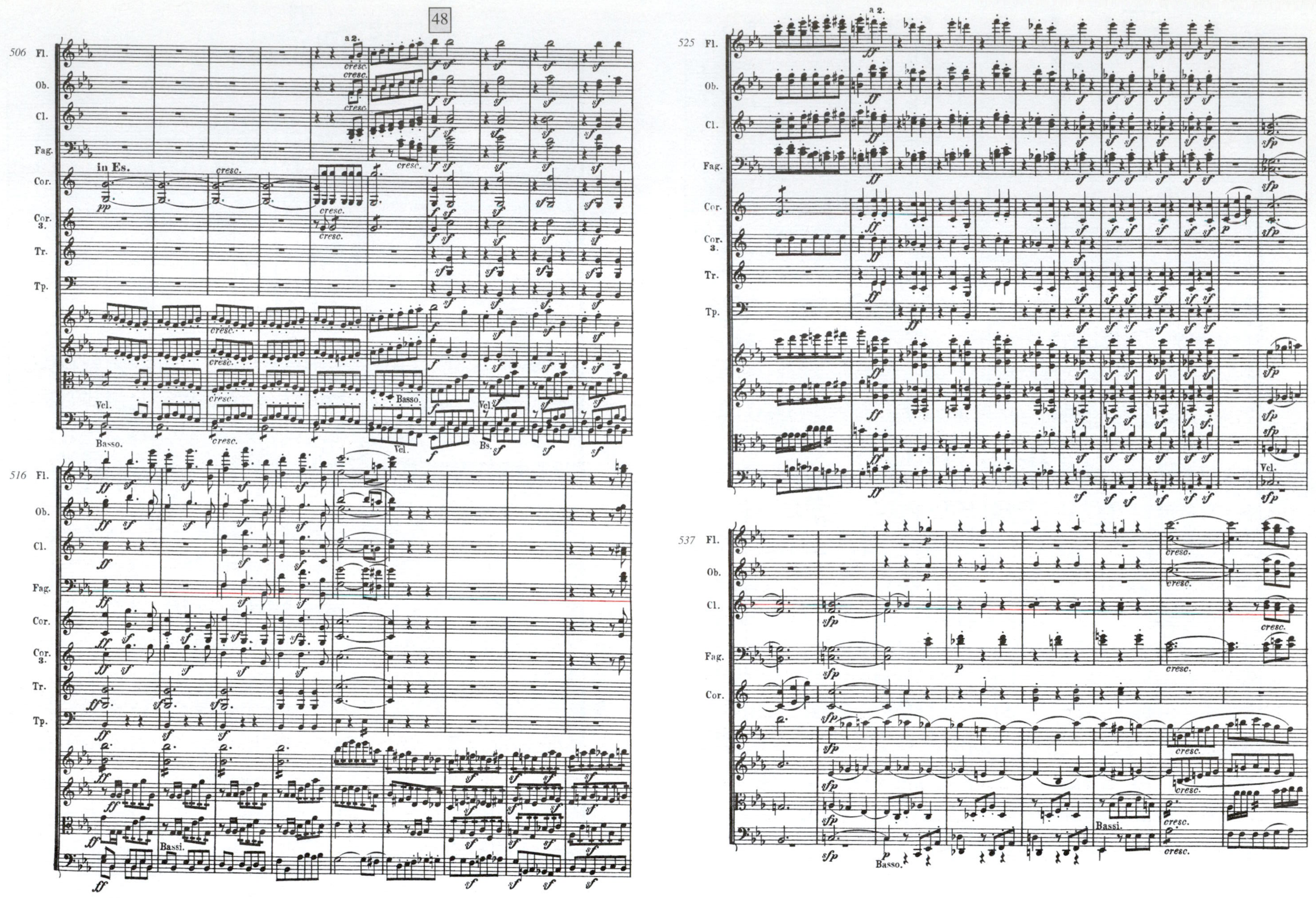
48
506 Fl.
Ob.
Cl.
Fag.
Cor.
Cor. 3.
Tr.
Tp.
in Es.
a 2.
cresc.
pp
Vel.
Basso.
Bs.
516 Fl.
Bassi.
525 Fl.
537 Fl.
Basso.

No. 115 Beethoven: Symphony No. 3 in E♭ Major

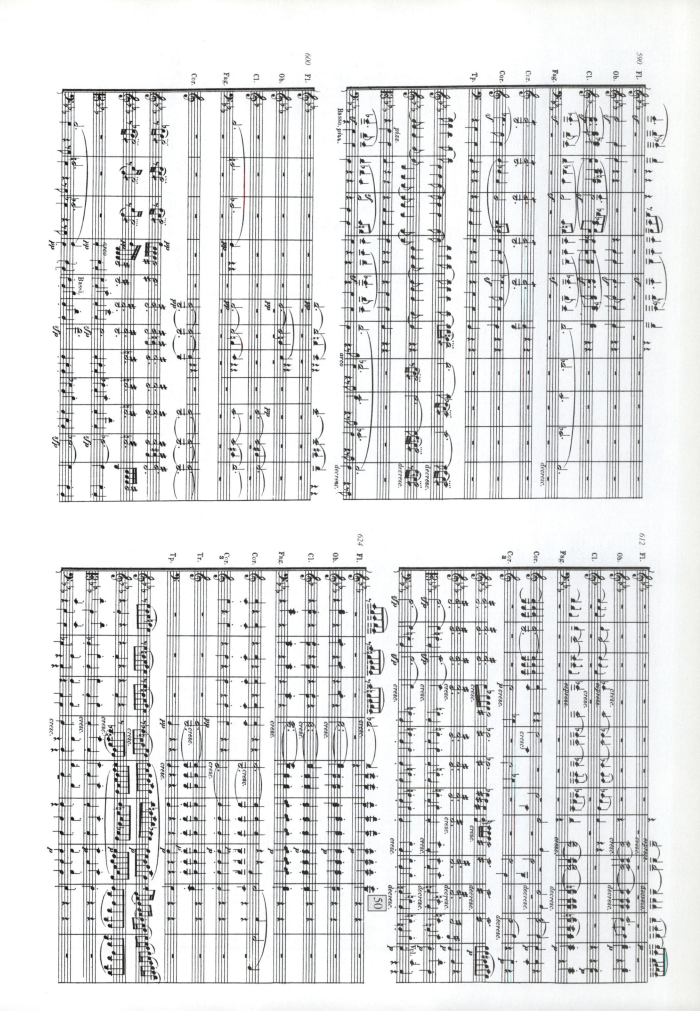

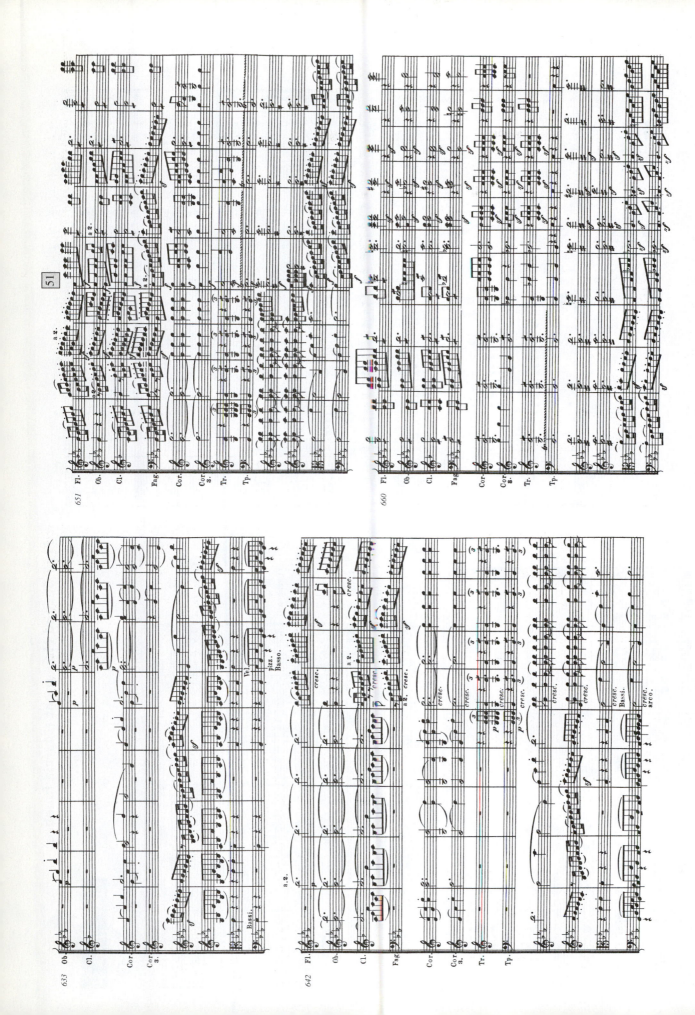

No. 115 Beethoven: Symphony No. 3 in E♭ Major

■ 121

No. 115 Beethoven: Symphony No. 3 in E♭ Major

670

679

115b Second Movement (Marcia funebre)

CD8 Track 52

P. 408

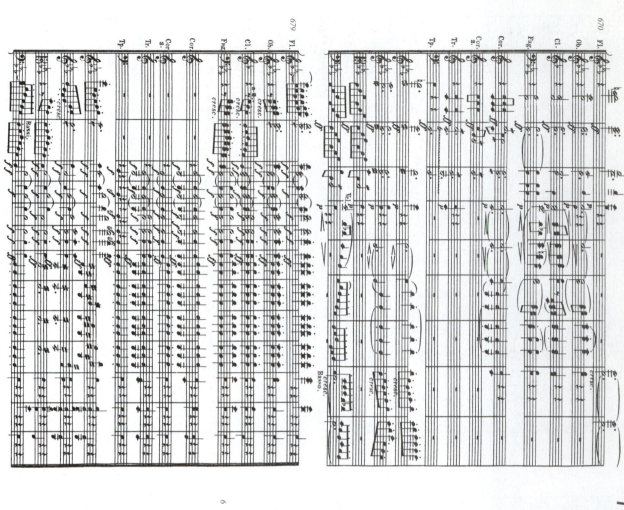

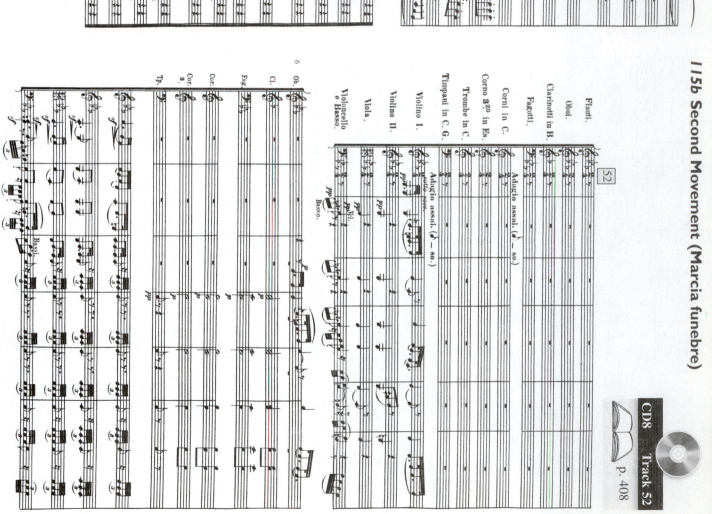

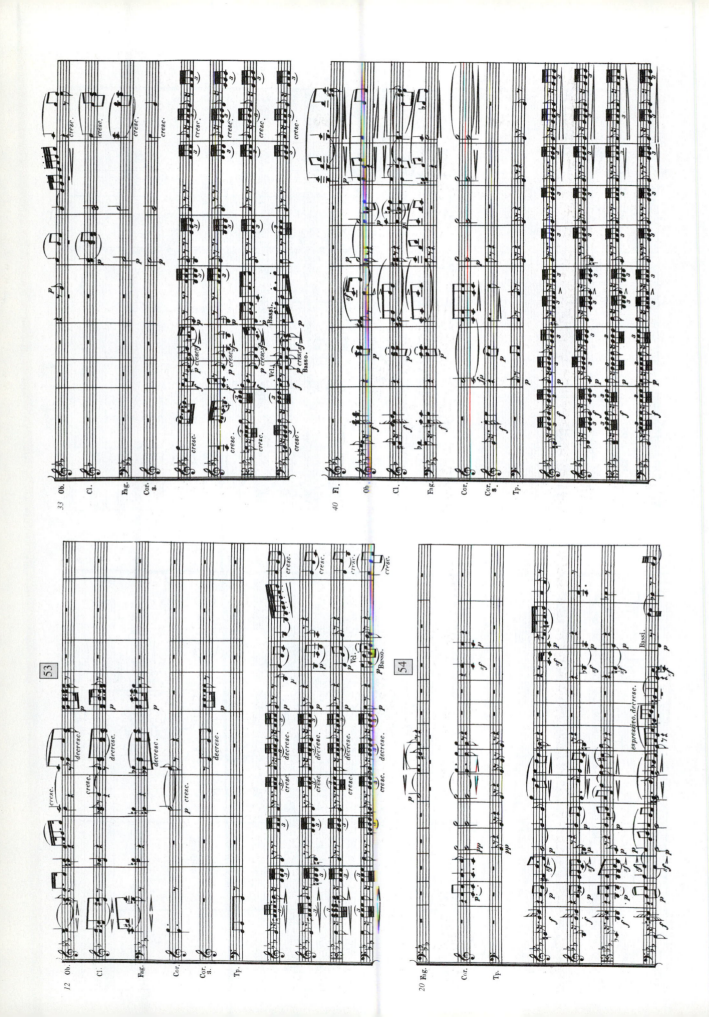

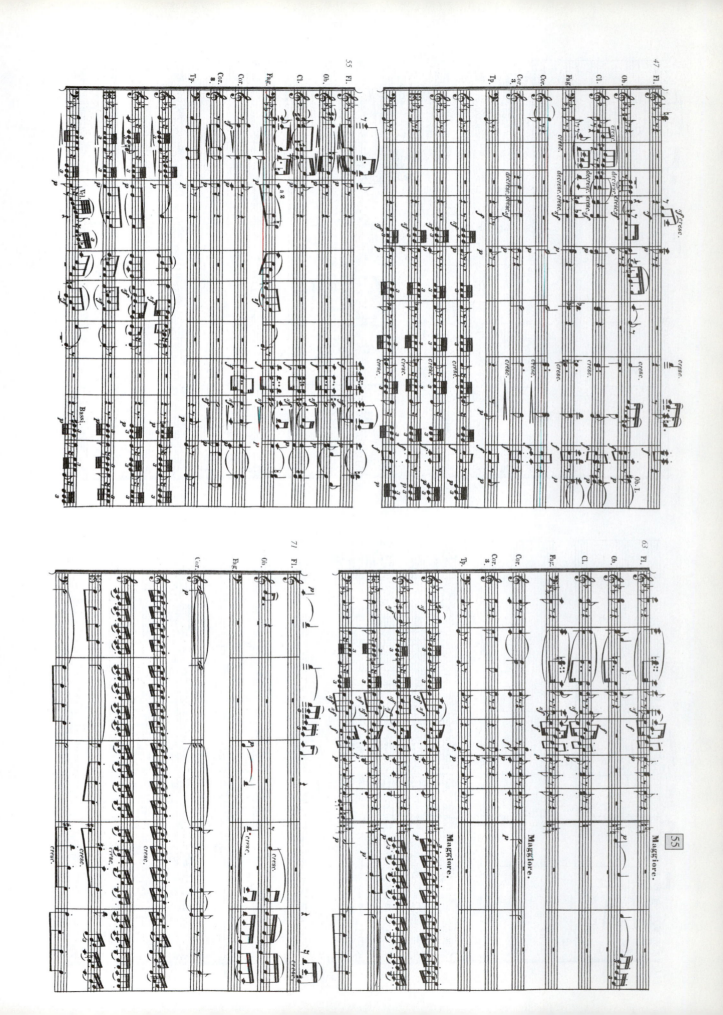

55

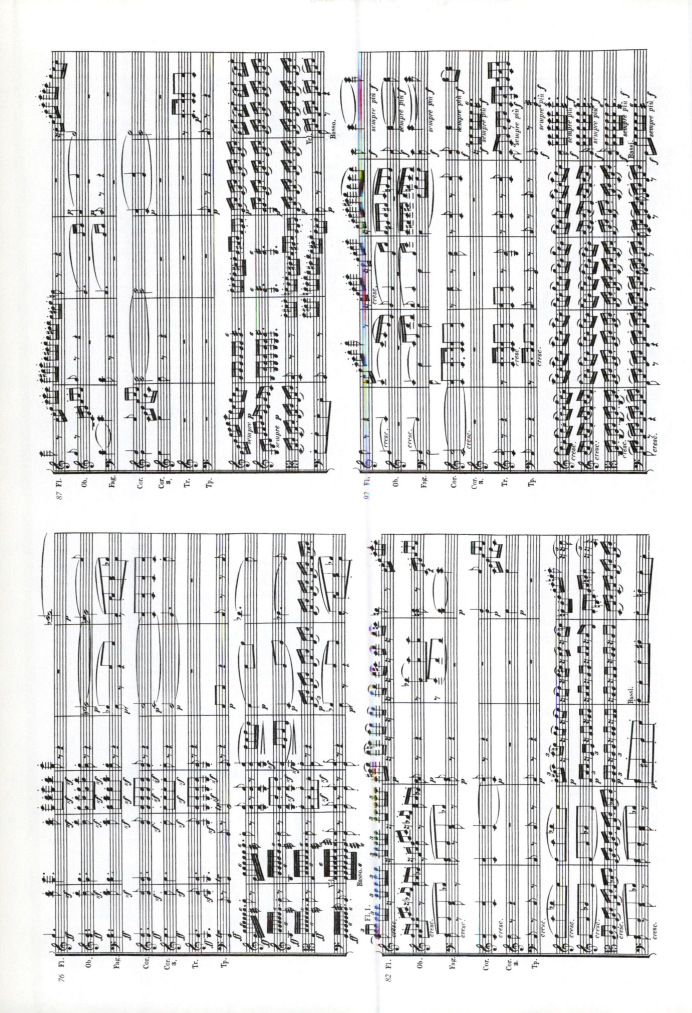

No. 115 Beethoven: Symphony No. 3 in E♭ Major

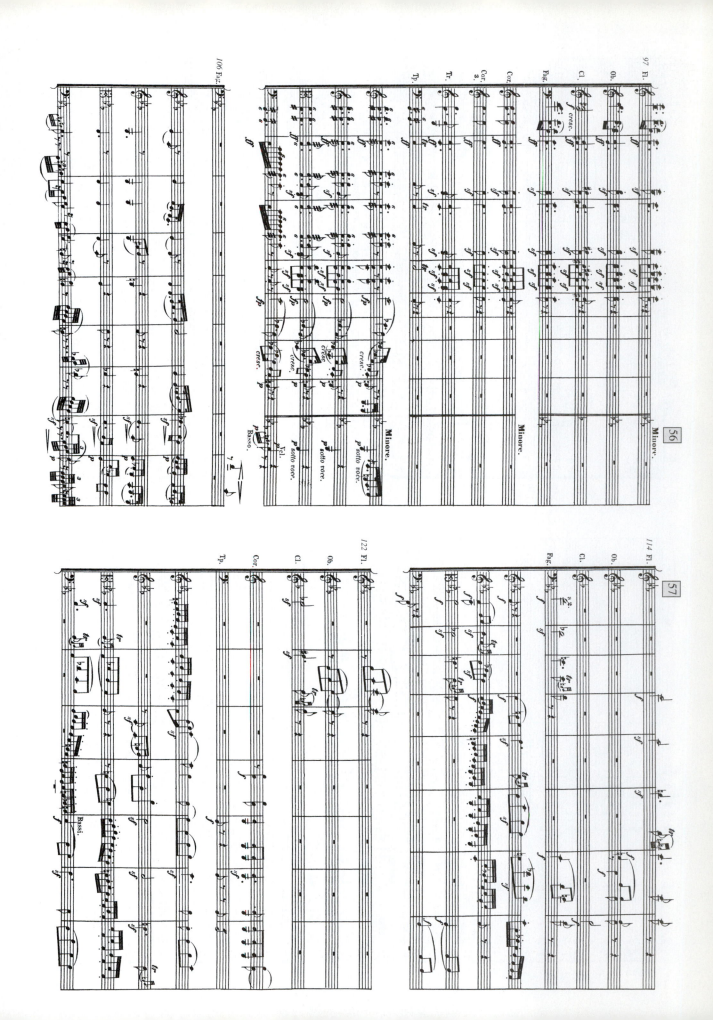

No. 115 Beethoven: Symphony No. 3 in E♭ Major

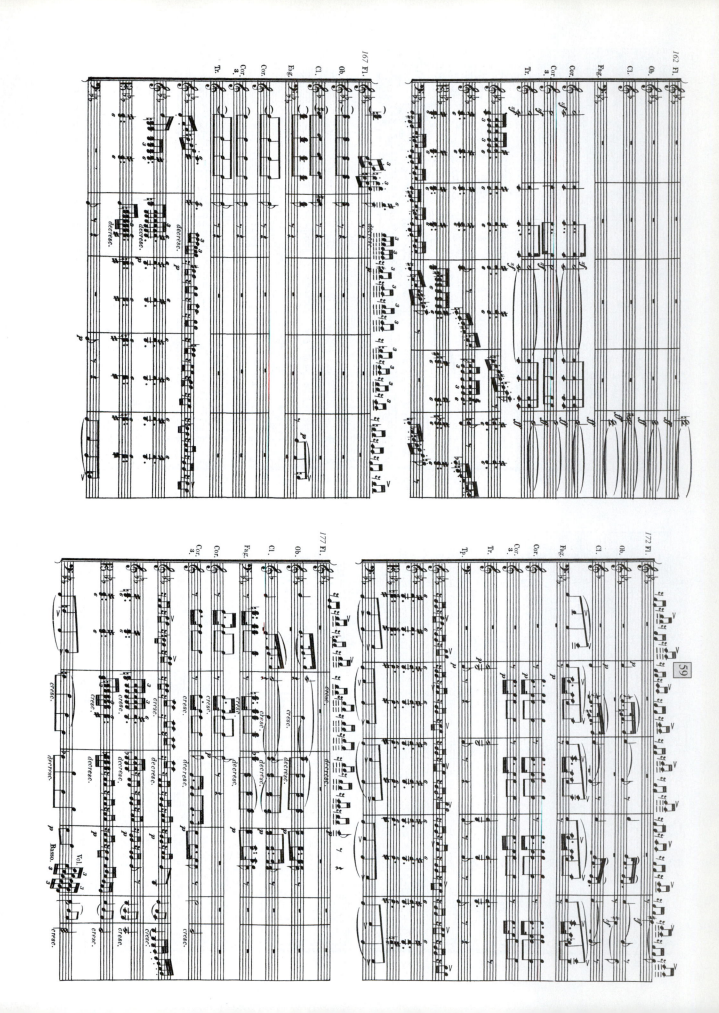

■ No. 115 Beethoven: Symphony No. 3 in E♭ Major

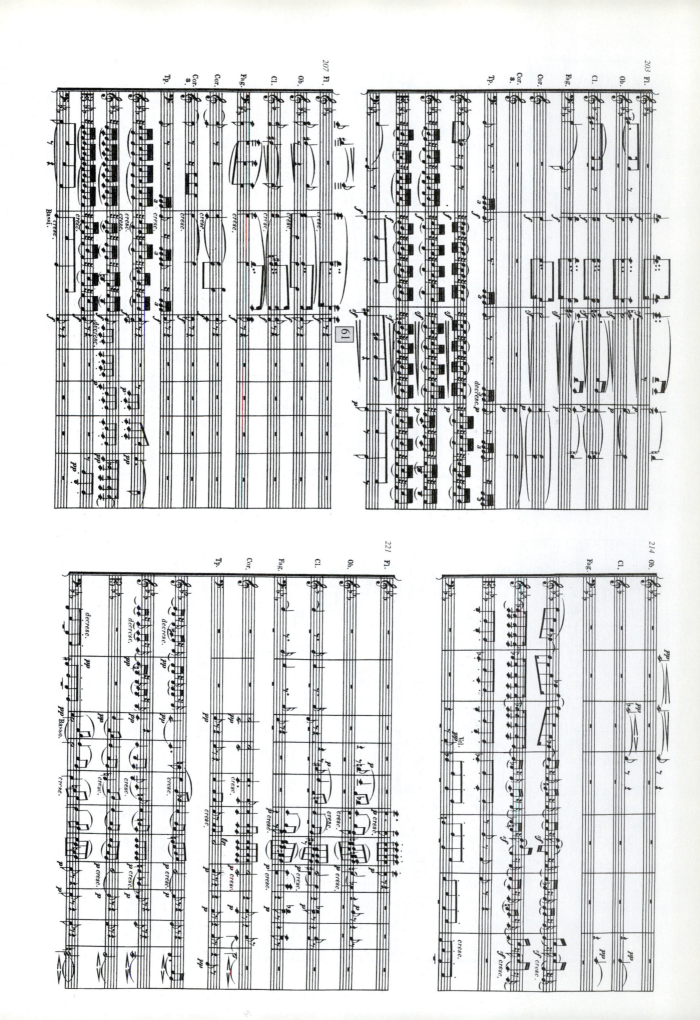

Beethoven's *Eroica* breaks new ground in many respects. The sonata-form first movement is of an unprecedented length; at 691 measures, it dwarfs any previous sonata-form first movement, and in the slow movement, Beethoven became the first composer to make symphonic use of the march.

First movement: The two loud tonic chords at the opening of the first movement (Allegro con brio) provide the briefest of introductions and serve a double function: to catch the audience's attention and to allow Beethoven to introduce the principal theme at a soft volume. The metrically regular, triadic opening of this theme (m. 3–6) contrasts with its syncopated, chromatic continuation (m. 7–10). The transition section (m. 45–83) is unusually long, occupying roughly 25 percent of the exposition. It contains three distinct thematic ideas, each of which will be developed later in the movement. The first idea in this secondary key area (the dominant, B♭ major), beginning in m. 83, offers a distinct but brief contrast to the turbulence of the opening and the transition. The sense of forward momentum soon returns, however, culminating in a series of syncopated chords (m. 123–131) just before the end of the exposition.

Within the development (m. 152–398), the fugato—a passage that begins like a fugue but does not sustain itself after a series of initial entries—that begins at m. 236 leads to a thematic standstill in a series of loud repeated chords (m. 248–283). Syncopation is emphasized at the expense of melody. The theme beginning in m. 284 that follows these chords is one we have not heard before. The introduction of an entirely new theme in the development of a sonata-form movement was not without precedent—Haydn did it in his *Farewell* Symphony of 1772. Beethoven, however, expands on this device in an innovative way by working his new theme into the remainder of the movement and restating it prominently in the tonic in the coda.

Beethoven has additional surprises in store before the recapitulation. The long passage on the dominant between m. 338 and 358 seems to signal the end of the development section and the beginning of the retransition to the tonic. But Beethoven avoids the tonic and extends the development still further. The true retransition begins at m. 382 with a thinning-out of the orchestral texture over an extended V⁹ harmony. Then, in a quiet yet deeply bizarre gesture, Beethoven has a solo horn enter with the opening theme in the tonic (m. 395) while the strings are still sounding a dominant harmony. In effect, Beethoven has deliberately written an apparent mistake into the score, making it seem to an unsuspecting listener that one of the hornists has come in too early.

The recapitulation itself, which begins at m. 398, is highly unstable at first, moving from the tonic to the supertonic (F major) after only eleven measures. The harmony finally settles firmly on the tonic with the full orchestral passage that begins in m. 430. From this point onward, the recapitulation is fairly stable. The coda, which begins in m. 557, is substantial. It amounts, in effect, to a second development section, during which the new theme introduced in m. 284 is finally restated in the tonic (beginning at m. 589).

Second movement: Beethoven's label at the head of the second movement—*Marcia funebre* ("Funeral March")—is in a sense superfluous, because the music itself bears all the characteristic features of a funeral march: minor mode, slow tempo (Adagio assai), the imitation of muffled drums in the double basses, dotted rhythms in the melody, and a subsequent alternation between minor- and major-mode themes. The movement is structured to feature the prominent return of the mournful opening figure (A) at key points (m. 1, 105, 173) between contrasting ideas.

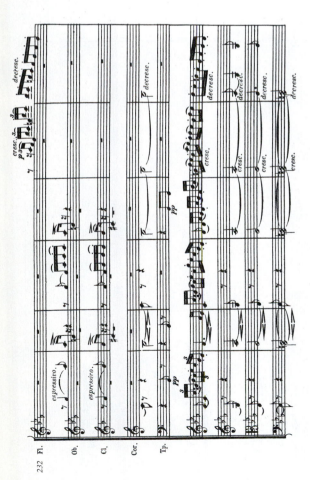

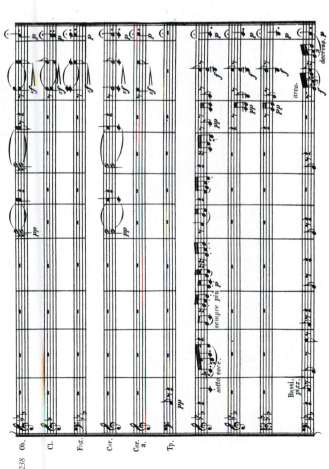

No. 116 Berlioz: *Symphonie fantastique*

62
16
mf
dim.
I.
sf > pp
con sordino III.
pppp
sf > pp
sf > pp
sf > pp
sf > pp
I.
sf > pp
f
pp
sf > p
div.
mf
62
2
Allegro. (♩. = 112.)
21
(lointain)
(entfernt)
(distant)
ppp
cresc. poco a poco
senza sord.
p cresc. poco a poco
cresc. poco a poco
senza sord.
Allegro assai. (𝅝 = 67.)
ff
a 2.
Allegro. (♩. = 112.)
Allegro assai. (𝅝 = 67.)

No. 116 Berlioz: *Symphonie fantastique*

55
Fl. I.
Fl. picc.
Ob.
Clar.
Cor.
Fag.
Viol.
(cresc.)
(mf cresc.)
(mf)
mf
a 2
64
Fl.
Fl. pic.
(cresc. sempre)
ff

67
Fl. I.
Fl. picc.
Ob.
Clar.
Cor.
Fag.
a 4.
a 2.
Tr.
Ctti
Tromb.
Tuba I.
Timp.
Viol.
ff

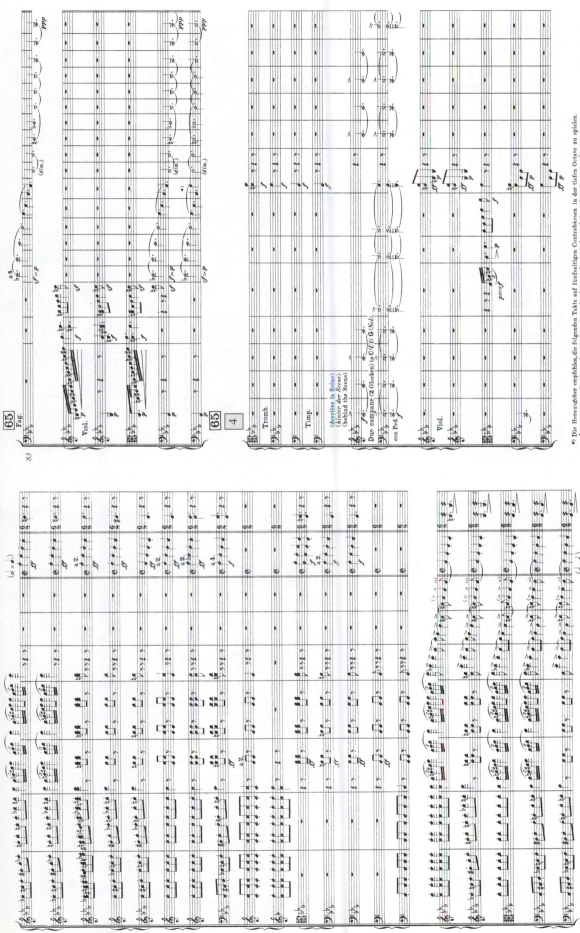

*) Die Herausgeber empfehlen, die folgenden Takte auf fünfsaitigen Contrabässen in der tiefen Octave zu spielen.
Les mesures suivantes se jouent une octave plus bas sur la contrebasse à 5 cordes. (Note des Éditeurs.)
The editor wishes the following bars to be played on a 5-stringed double-bass in the lower octave.

No. 116 Berlioz: *Symphonie fantastique*

115
Ob. I.
mf
a 2.
Cor.
Tr.
Tromb.
ff
Timp.
f
Camp.
p
pp
Viol.
mf
66
5
Dies iræ.
senza accel.
Fag. a 4.
Tube. a 2.
f
Camp.
Viol.
senza accel.
146
Fl. I.
Fl. picc.
Ob.
Clar.
Cor.
Fag.
Tr.
C^tti
Tromb.
Tube.
Gr. Tamb.
Camp.
Viol.
pizz.

No. 116 Berlioz: *Symphonie fantastique*

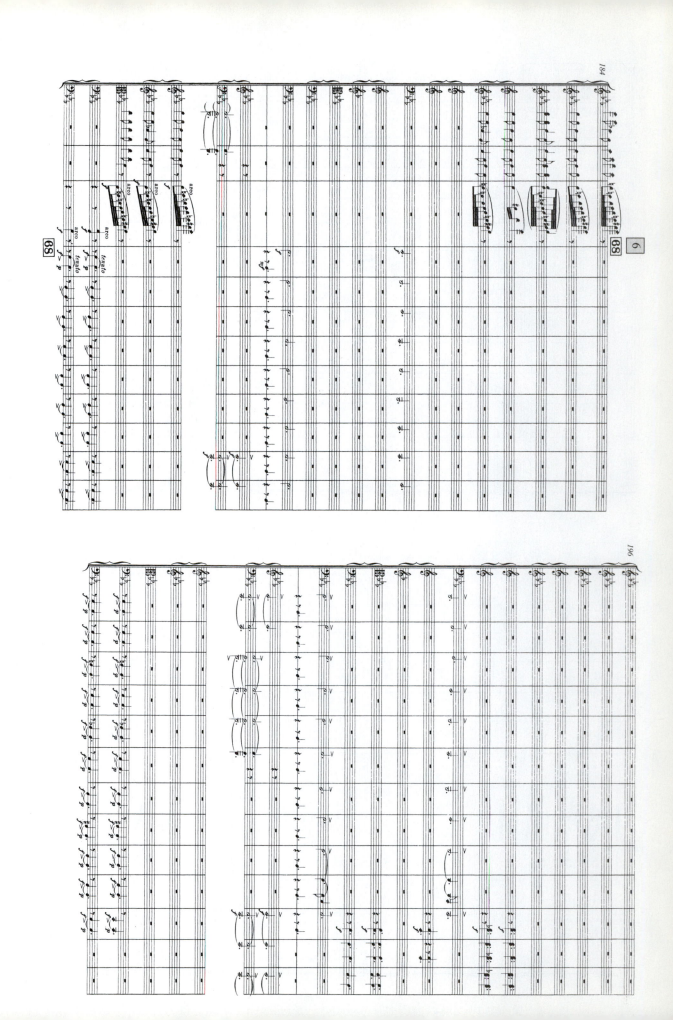

No. 116 Berlioz: Symphonie fantastique

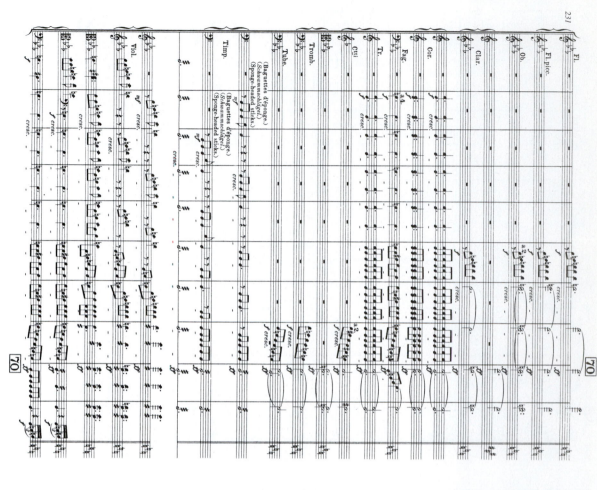

*) Le mouvement, qui a dû s'animer un peu, redevient ici comme au chiffre 63 Allegro (♩ = 104)
Das Zeitmaass, welches sich etwas belebt hat, wird hier wieder wie bei Ziffer 63 Allegro (♩ = 104)
The movement, which has animated itself, is here again as at number 63 Allegro (♩ = 104)

No. 116 Berlioz: *Symphonie fantastique*

No. 116 Berlioz: *Symphonie fantastique*

No. 116 Berlioz: Symphonie fantastique

No. 116 Berlioz: *Symphonie fantastique*

No. 116 Berlioz: *Symphonie fantastique*

No. 116 Berlioz: *Symphonie fantastique*

No. 116 Berlioz: *Symphonie fantastique*

79
371
con sord.
II.
poco sf > p
Les deux Timbalier réunis.
Beide Schläger zusammen.
Both drummers together.
p cresc. poco a poco
p
p
79
380
mf
I.
mf
senza sord.
senza sord.
a 4.
cresc. poco a poco
f cresc. sempre
cresc. sempre

No. 116 Berlioz: *Symphonie fantastique*

Dies irae et Ronde du Sabbat (ensemble).
Dies irae and witches' round dance (together).

No. 116 Berlioz: *Symphonie fantastique*

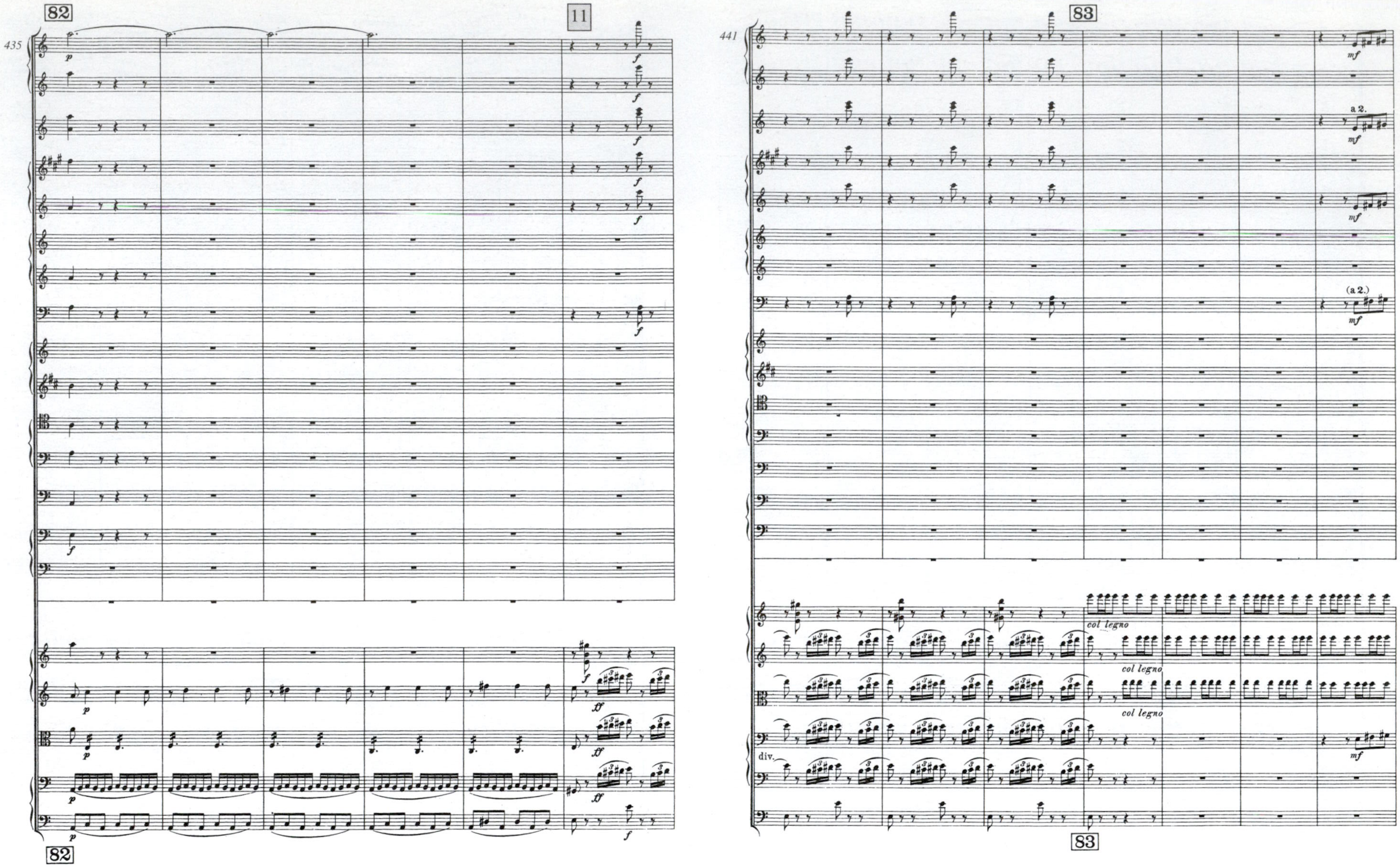
82
11
83
435
441
col legno
col legno
col legno
a 2.
(a 2.)
div.

No. 116 Berlioz: Symphonie fantastique

464
84
p leggiero
a 2.
p leggiero
ff (a 4.)
a 2.
I.
arco
pp cresc.
84

474
mf
cresc.
I.
a 2.
a 4.
I.

No. 116 Berlioz: *Symphonie fantastique*

No. 116 Berlioz: *Symphonie fantastique*

Berlioz's "Fantastic Symphony" is a deeply autobiographical work. Inspired by the composer's infatuation with an actress named Harriet Smithson, the symphony's prose program narrates the emotional turmoil of a young musician as he falls in love (the first movement), sees her at a ball (second movement), realizes that she may be spurning him (third movement), is executed for murdering her (fourth movement), and then finally sees her in hell, transformed into a witch (fifth movement, the "Dream of a Witches' Sabbath").

Berlioz's prose program for the finale, distributed at the work's premiere, reads as follows:

Dream of a Witches' Sabbath. He [the artist] sees himself at the Sabbath, in the middle of a frightening troupe of ghosts, sorcerers, monsters of every kind, all gathered for his funeral rites. Strange noises, groans, bursts of laughter, distant cries to which other cries seem to respond. The beloved melody reappears, but it has lost its noble and shy character. It is nothing more than the melody of a common dance, trivial and grotesque; it is she who comes to join the Sabbath . . . A roar of joy at her arrival . . . She throws herself into the diabolical orgy . . . Funeral knell, burlesque parody of the *Dies irae*. Witches' Round Dance. The dance and *Dies irae* combined.

The structure of this finale is appropriately unconventional. After an extended introduction (m. 1–39), we hear what Berlioz himself called a "trivial and grotesque" version of the original *idée fixe* on the Eb clarinet. In its original form in the first movement, this had been a lyrical, flowing melody played by violins and flutes:

Berlioz, *Symphonie fantastique*, first movement, m. 72–111: the initial appearance of the principal melody.

In the finale, this graceful idea becomes four-square and common. It is followed by a contrasting section based on the *Dies irae* (beginning at m. 127), followed in turn by the "Witches' Round Dance" (beginning at m. 241). In a brief but spectacular display of counterpoint, Berlioz then presents both the Witches' Round Dance and the *Dies irae* simultaneously (beginning at m. 414).

Berlioz's orchestration is particularly noteworthy in this work. In additon to the standard strings, winds, and percussion, he calls for an orchestra that includes piccolo, English horn, Eb clarinet, four horns, two cornets, three trombones, two ophicleides (a forerunner of the tuba), a bass drum, a snare drum, cymbals, bells, and two harps. Berlioz also draws sounds out of these instruments that are something less than beautiful. Listen, for example, to the downward flute glissandos at m. 8–9; it is almost as if the instruments (or their players) have lost all energy. The tapping of the strings with the wooden part of the bow (*col legno*, m. 444) is another sonority that strives to create a sensation lying out of the realm of the ordinary.

CD9 Track 13

p. 422

117 Overture to A Midsummer Night's Dream (1826)
Felix Mendelssohn (1809–1847)

Allegro di molto

[13]

2 Flauti
2 Oboi
2 Clarinetti in A
2 Fagotti
2 Corni in E
2 Trombe in E
Ophicleïde
Timpani in E-H
Violino I
Violino II
Viola
Violoncello e Contrabasso

Vl.
sempre stacc.
sempre stacc.
div.
20
unis.
div.
pizz.
Vla.
p
pp stacc.
stacc.
pp pizz.
pizz.
pp
30
unis.
arco
40
Fl.
Cl. (A)
Fg.
Cor. (E)
pp
arco
pizz.
50

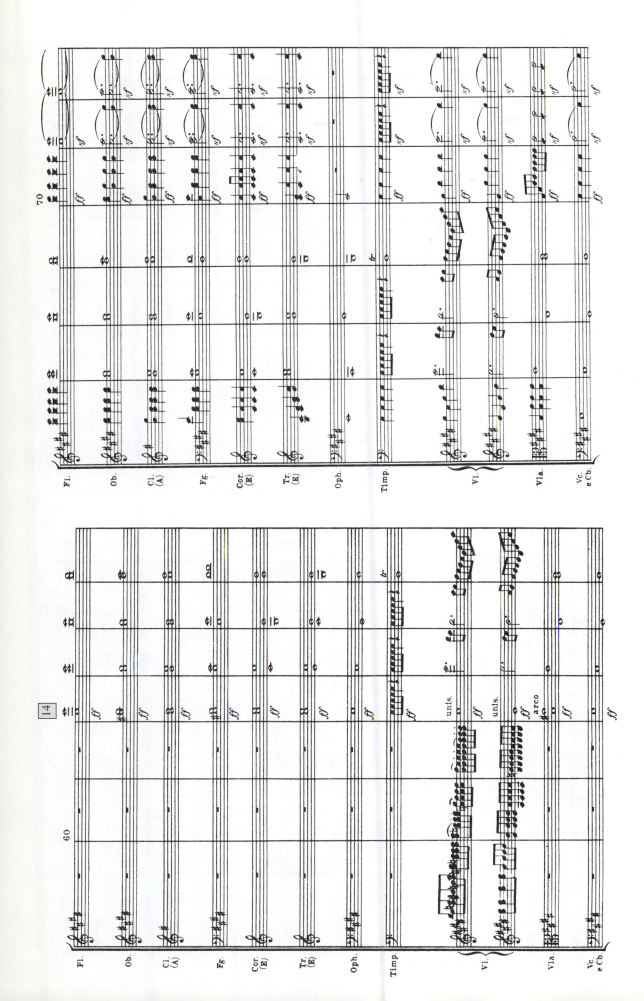

No. 117 Mendelssohn: Overture to A Midsummer Night's Dream

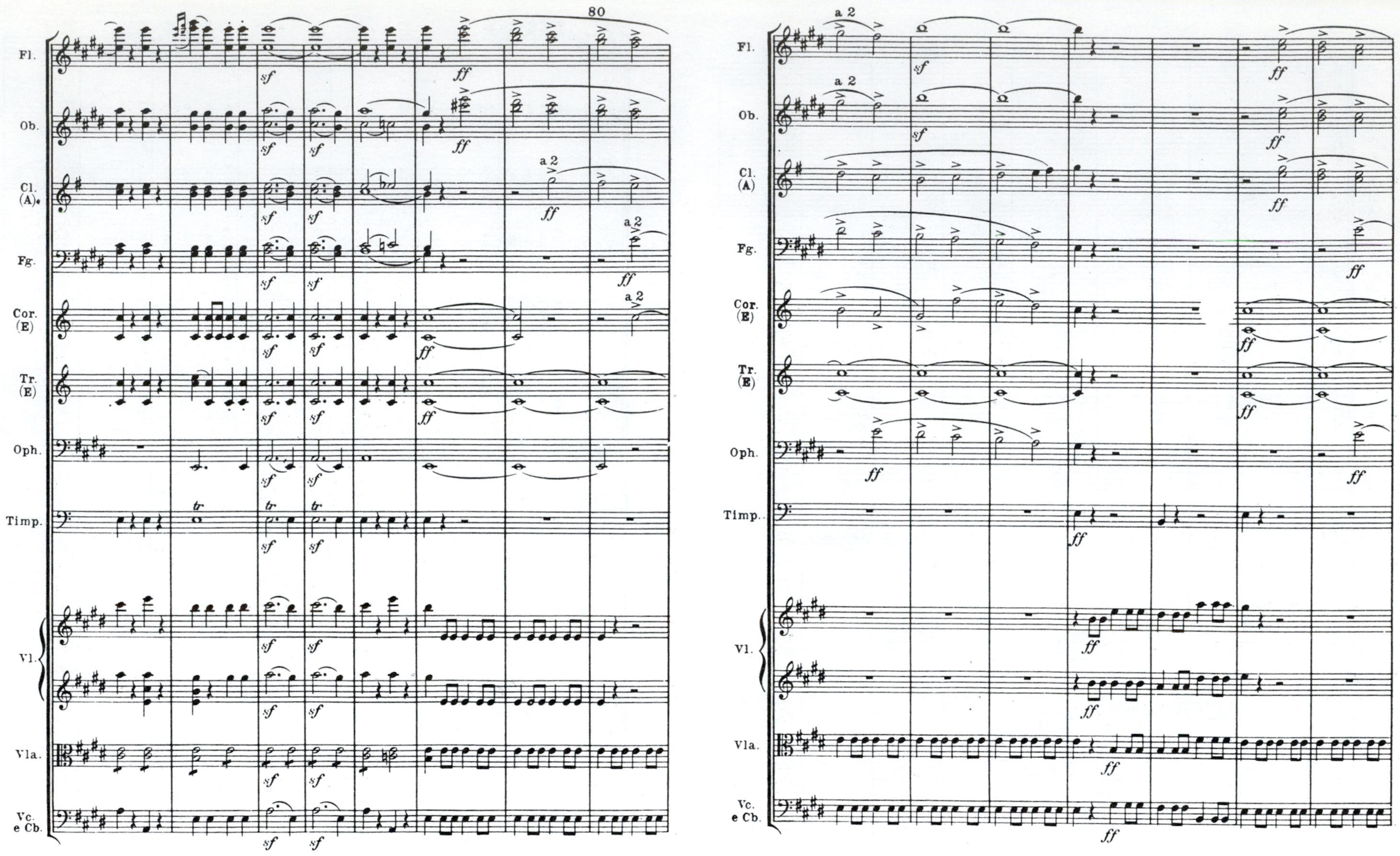
80
Fl.
Ob.
Cl. (A)
Fg.
Cor. (E)
Tr. (E)
Oph.
Timp.
Vl.
Vla.
Vc. e Cb.
a 2
sf
ff
tr

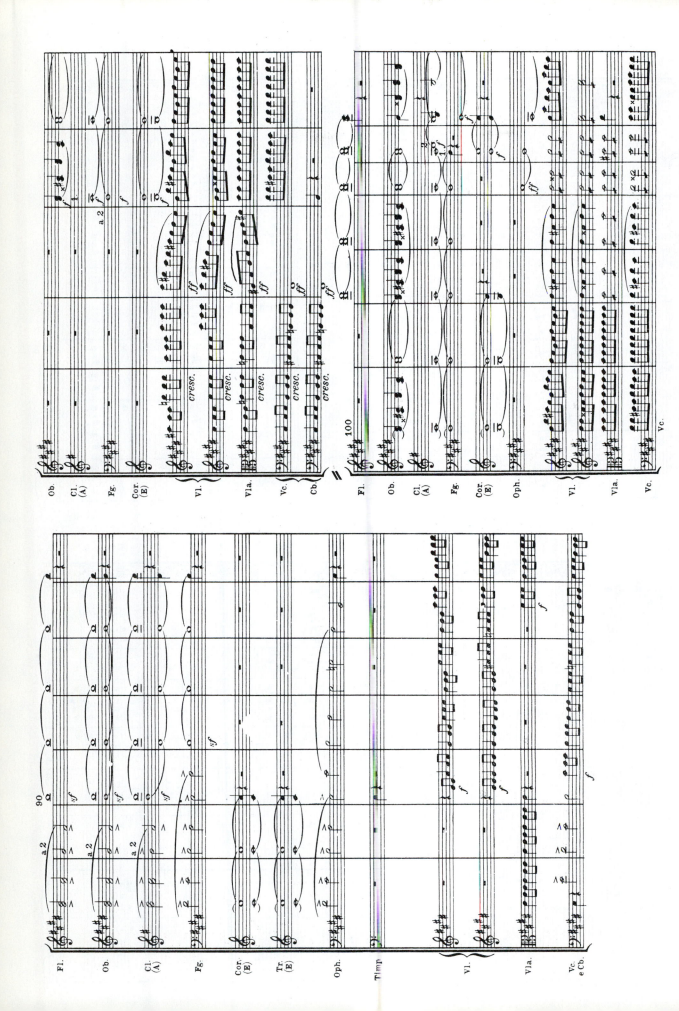

No. 117 Mendelssohn: *Overture to A Midsummer Night's Dream*

163

No. 117 Mendelssohn: Overture to A Midsummer Night's Dream

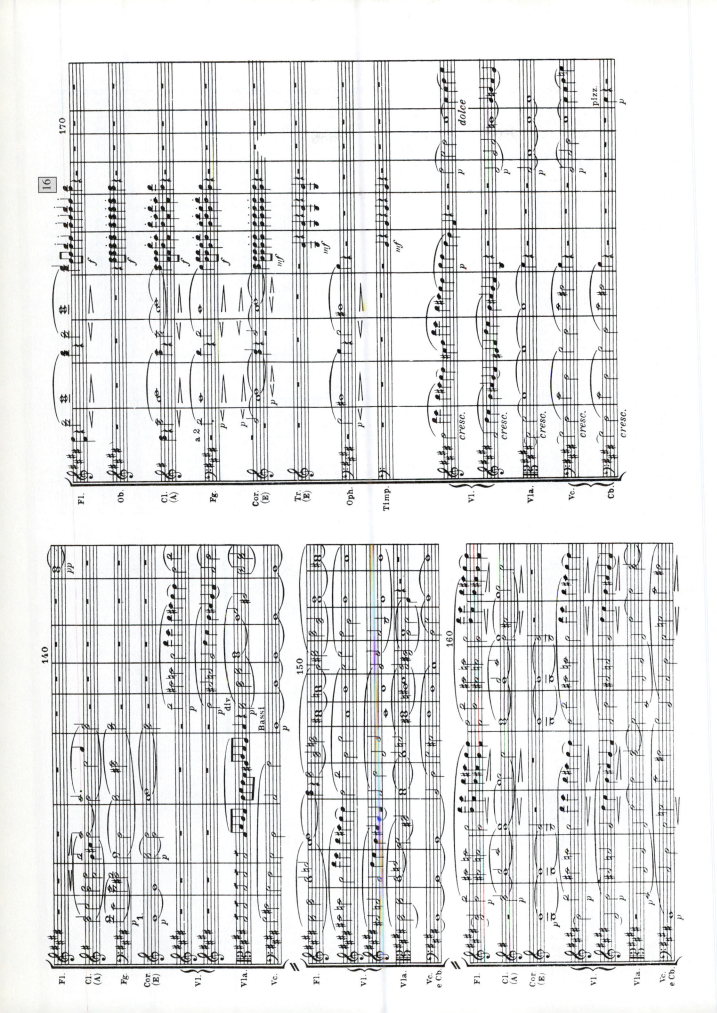

No. 117 Mendelssohn: Overture to A Midsummer Night's Dream

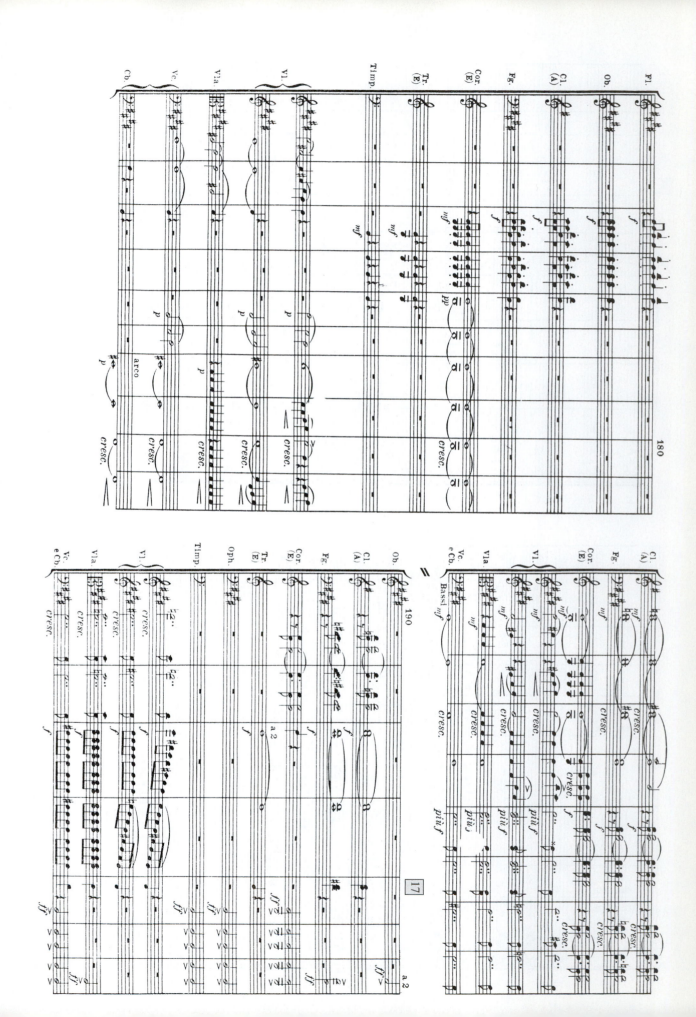

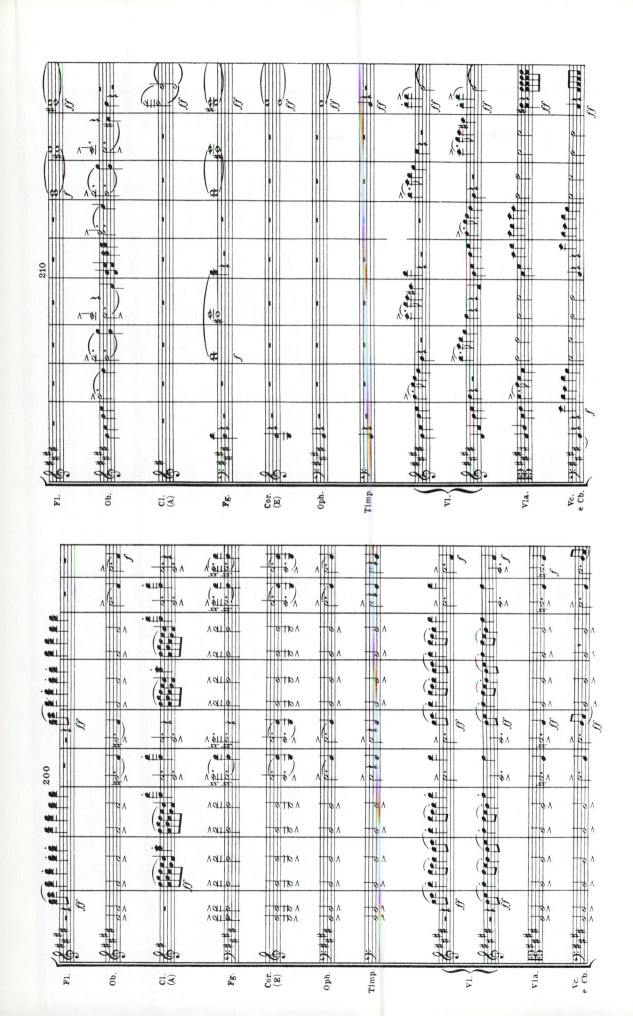

No. 117 Mendelssohn: Overture to *A Midsummer Night's Dream*

No. 117 Mendelssohn: Overture to A Midsummer Night's Dream

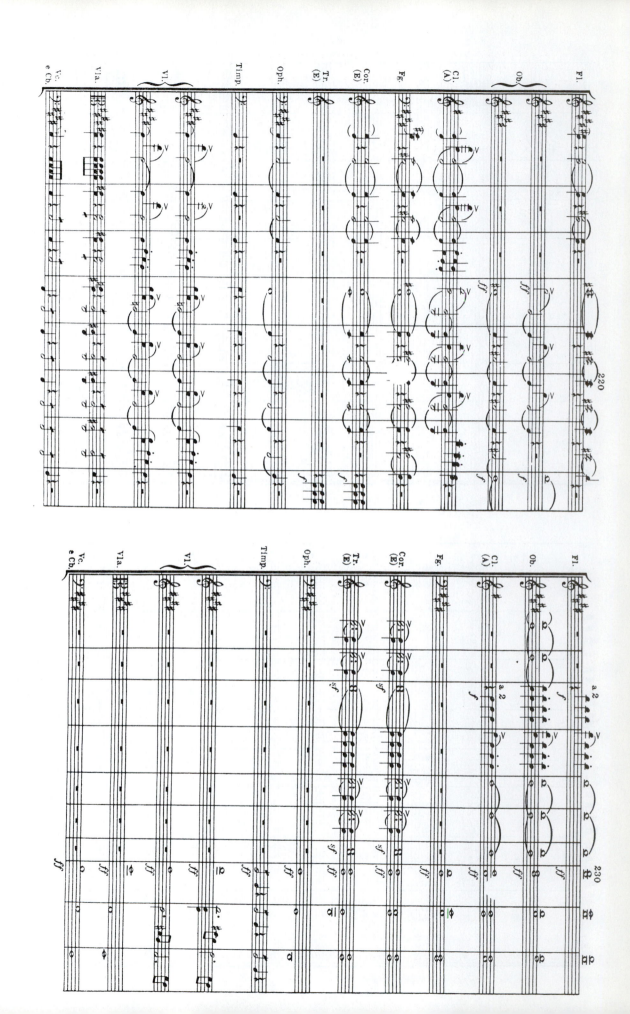

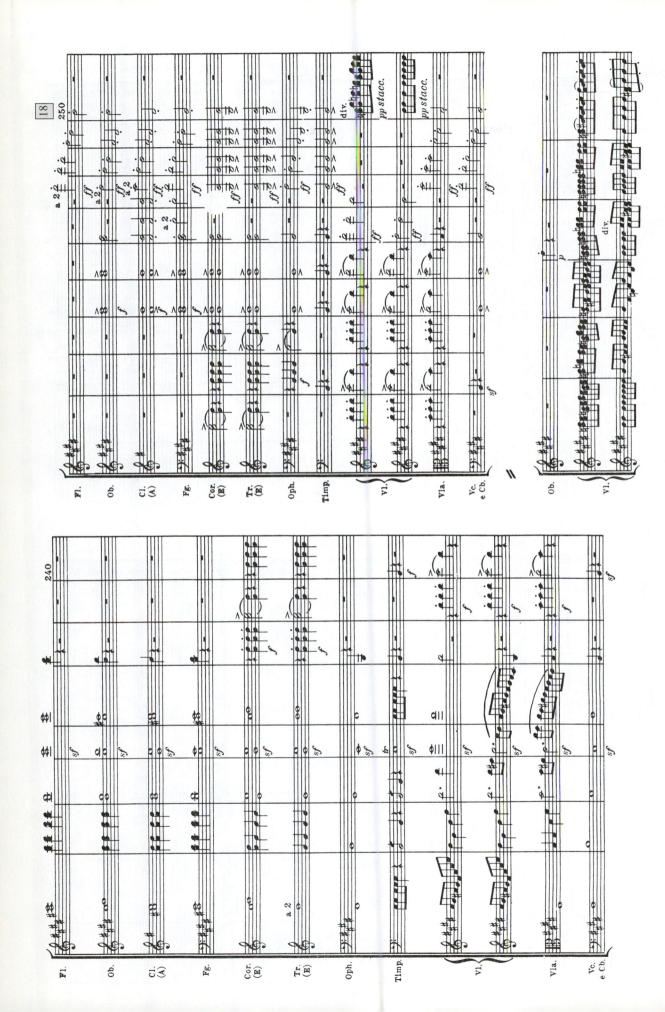

No. 117 Mendelssohn: Overture to A Midsummer Night's Dream

No. 117 Mendelssohn: Overture to A Midsummer Night's Dream

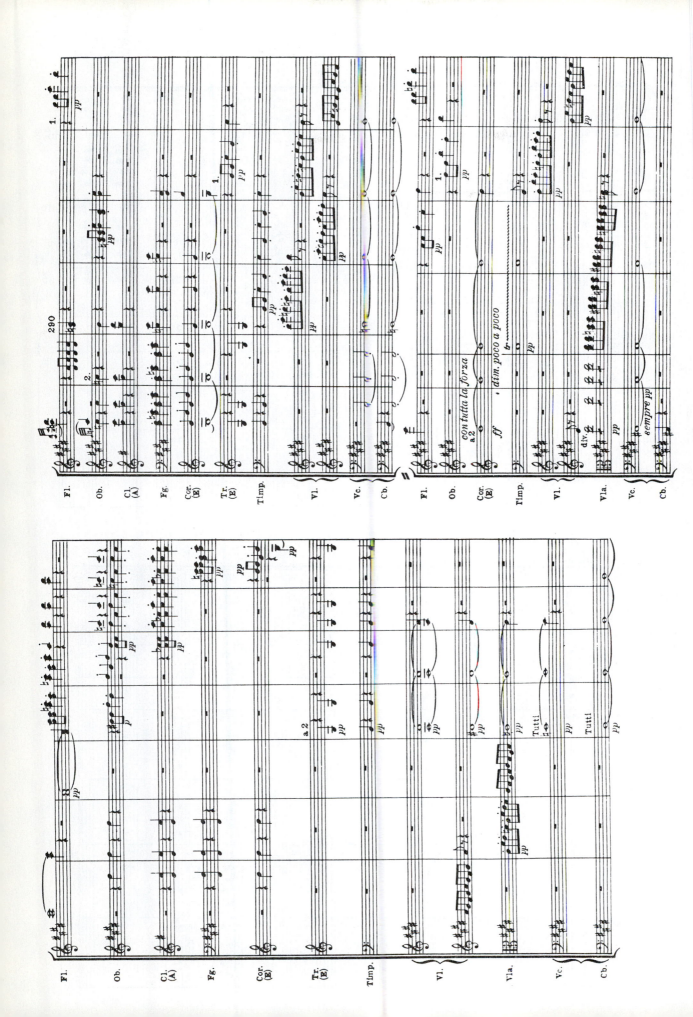

No. 117 Mendelssohn: Overture to A Midsummer Night's Dream

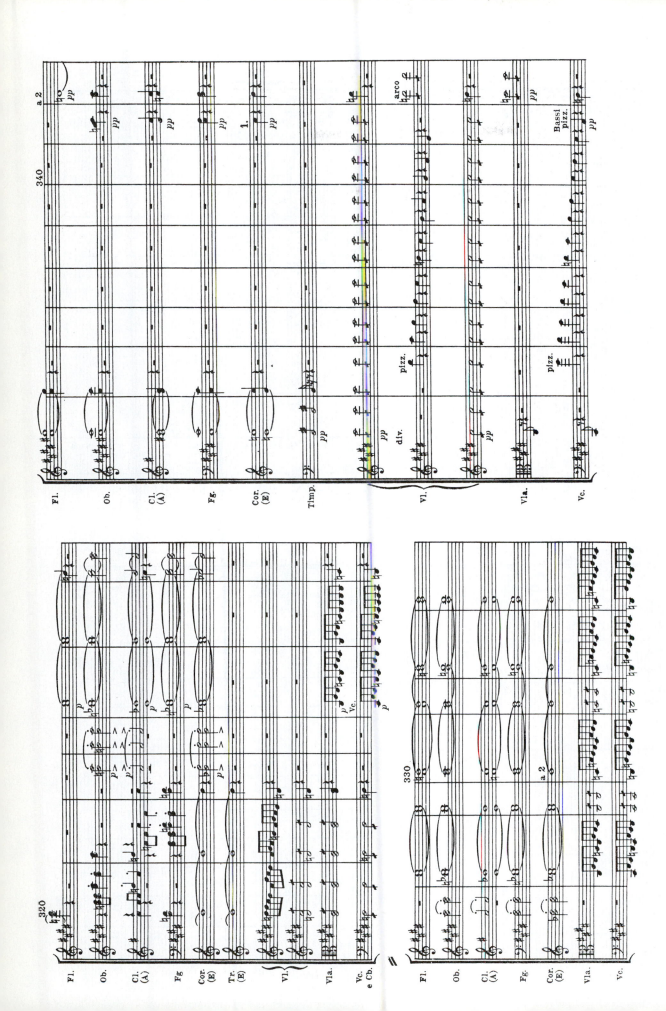

No. 117 Mendelssohn: Overture to A Midsummer Night's Dream

No. 117 Mendelssohn: Overture to A Midsummer Night's Dream

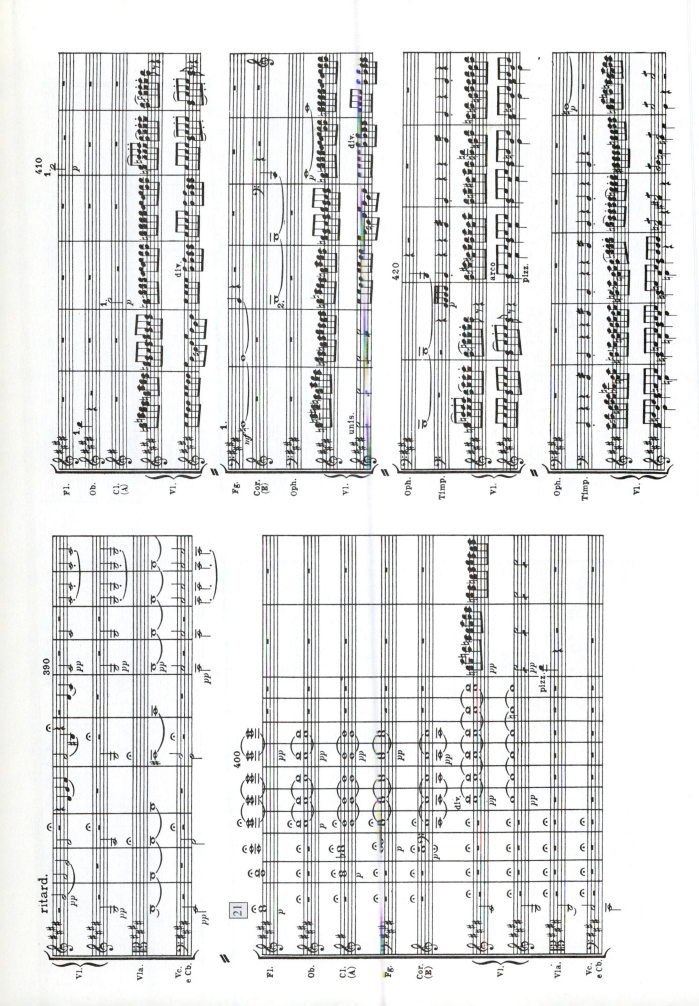

No. 117 Mendelssohn: Overture to A Midsummer Night's Dream

No. 117 Mendelssohn: Overture to A Midsummer Night's Dream

No. 117 Mendelssohn: Overture to *A Midsummer Night's Dream*

490
Fl.
Ob.
Cl. (A)
Fg.
Cor. (E)
Tr. (E)
Oph.
Timp.
Vl.
Vla.
Vc. e Cb.
Vc.
Bassi
500
510
23
cresc.
più f

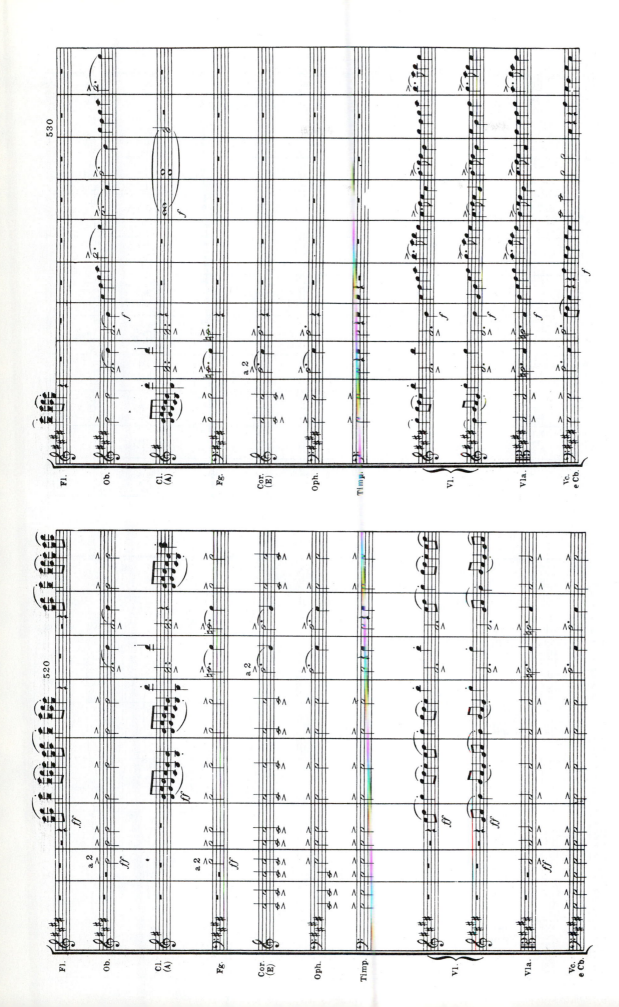

No. 117 Mendelssohn: Overture to A Midsummer Night's Dream

■ No. 117 Mendelssohn: Overture to *A Midsummer Night's Dream*

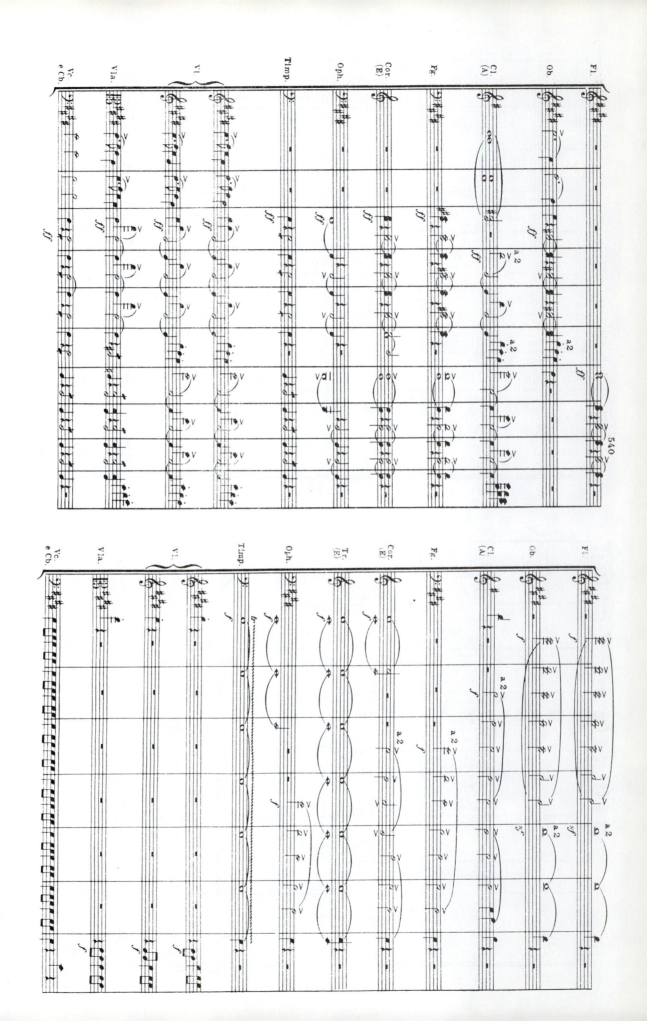

No. 117 Mendelssohn: *Overture to A Midsummer Night's Dream*

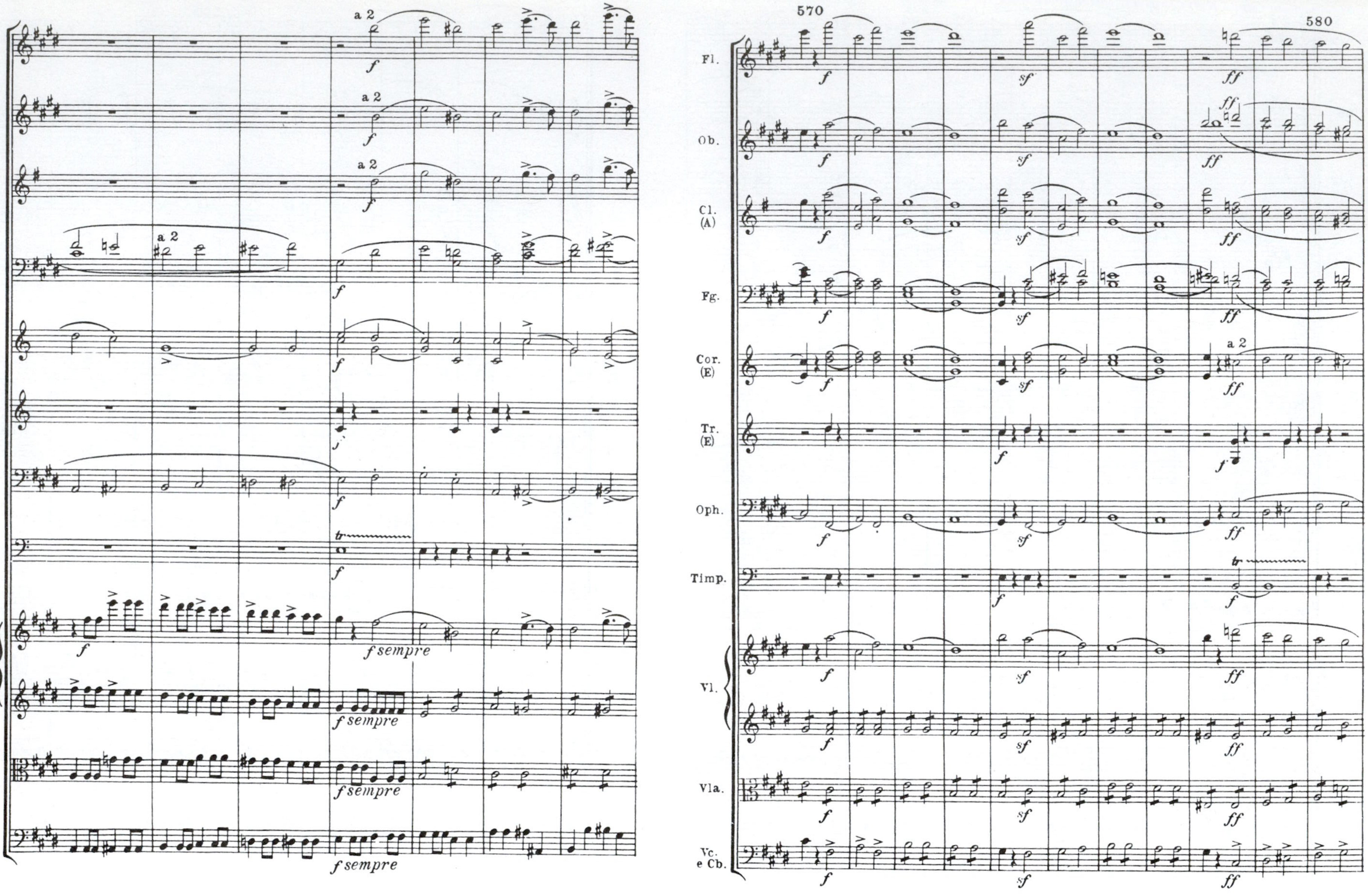
570
580
Fl.
Ob.
Cl. (A)
Fg.
Cor. (E)
Tr. (E)
Oph.
Timp.
Vl.
Vla.
Vc. e Cb.
a 2
f
f sempre
sf
ff

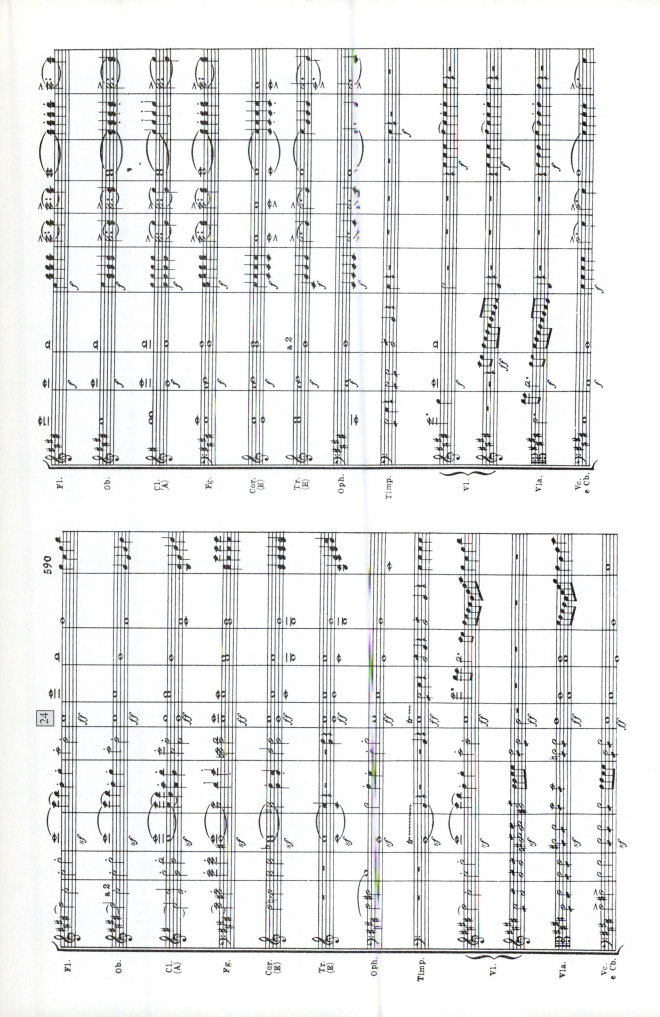

600
610
Fl.
Ob.
Cl. (A)
Fg.
Cor. (E)
Tr. (E)
a 2
Oph.
Timp.
Vl.
Vla.
Vc. e Cb.

25
620
Fl.
Ob.
Cl. (A)
Fg.
a 2
Cor. (E)
Tr. (E)
Oph.
Timp.
con tutta la forza
div.
Vl.
Vla.
Vc.
Cb.

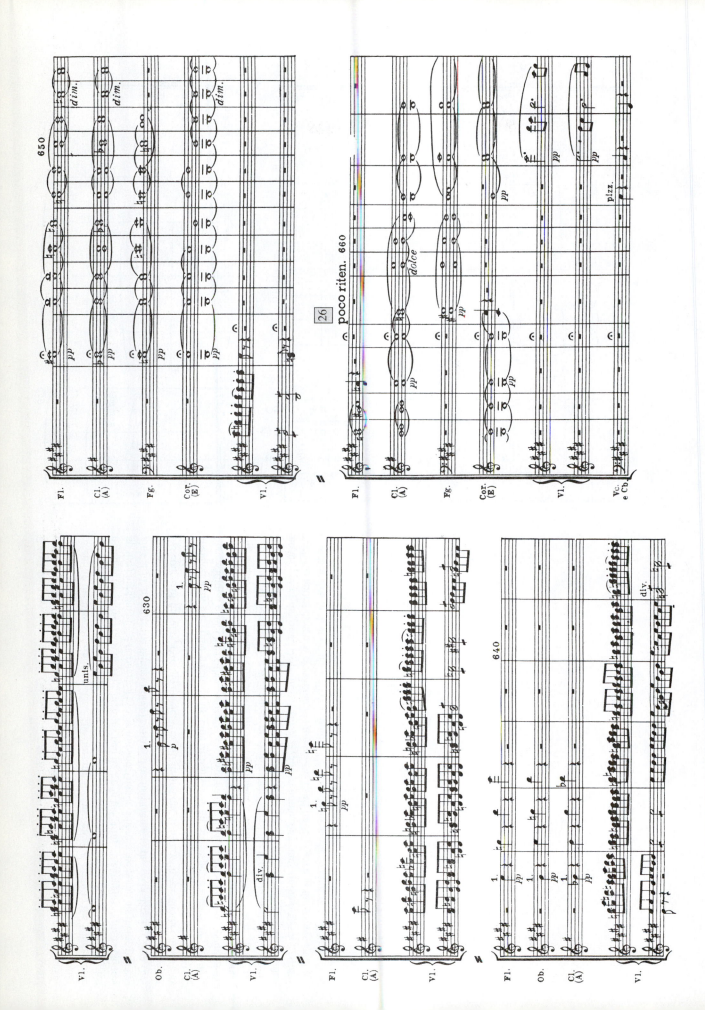

No. 117 Mendelssohn: Overture to A Midsummer Night's Dream

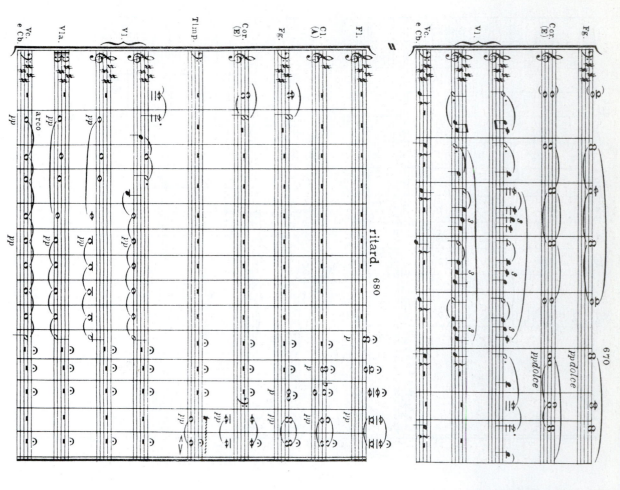

Felix Mendelssohn wrote his *Overture to A Midsummer Night's Dream* when he was 17 years old; only later did he compose additional movements called for within the course of Shakespeare's play. In this sonata-form overture, Mendelssohn presents a succession of themes representing the play's main characters. The opening five m., given entirely to the winds, serve as an introduction to the whole and draw us into the enchanted forest that is the setting for much of the play. The scurrying, high-pitched figure in the strings that begins in m. 5 conjures up the kingdom of the fairies, led by Oberon and Titania, whereas the pompous theme that begins at m. 62 corresponds to the human ruler, Theseus. The first theme in the secondary key area (beginning at m. 130) suits the young humans—two women and two men—who over the course of the play, through magic, will fall in and out of love with one another in various combinations. Finally, the exposition's closing theme (beginning at m. 195) can be readily associated with the "rude mechanicals," the artisans who in Shakespeare's comedy present a play-within-a-play. One of these artisans, a weaver named Bottom, appears at one point in the play with the head of an ass, a transformation reflected in the music by an unmistakable braying sound at m. 200 and elsewhere. In the development section (beginning at m. 250), the scurrying theme associated with fairies predominates. One of the ways Mendelssohn captures the sometimes chaotic magical spirit of the midsummer night's forest is through the simultaneous use of disparate dynamics. At m. 294, for example, he brings in the horns *fortissimo*, with the added direction of *con tutta la forza*—"with all force"—even as the strings and high winds maintain their elfin *pianissimo* figure. The dreamy coda (beginning at m. 260) leads us to wonder, as in Shakespeare's play, if all we have witnessed has been real or imagined.

118 Piano Concerto No. 4 in G Major, Op. 58, second movement (1806)
Beethoven

CD9 Track 27 p. 428

Andante con moto

Tutti

Pianoforte

Violino I

Violino II

Viola

Violoncello e Contrabasso

Solo

(p) molto cantabile

sempre stacc.

sempre stacc.

sempre stacc.

sempre stacc.

Tutti

Solo

molto espressivo

Solo

(Tutti)

Tutti

sempre f

sempre f

sempre f

sempre f

(Solo)

(Tutti)

Solo

Tutti

(Solo)

p dim.

sempre dim.

sempre dim.

sempre dim.

sempre dim.

pp

pp

pp

pp

p dim.

p dim.

p dim.

p dim.

pizz.

pizz.

pizz.

pizz.

*) Während des ganzen Andantes hat der Klavierspieler ununterbrochen die Verschiebung (una corda) anzuwenden, das Zeichen „℔" bezieht sich außerdem auf den zeitweisen Gebrauch des gewöhnlichen Pedalzuges.

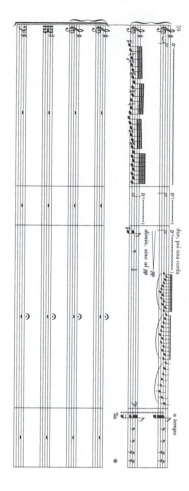

The second movement of Beethoven's Fourth Piano Concerto, Op. 58, illustrates the kind of dramatic contrast between soloist and orchestra that would become a staple of the 19th-century concerto repertory. The soloist and the orchestra—limited in this movement to the strings—engage in an extended dialogue that moves from confrontation to resolution. The strings open with a loud unison figure characterized by dotted rhythms and staccato articulation. The piano responds with an utterly different kind of statement, a lyrical, hymn-like theme that Beethoven marks *molto cantabile*. To underscore the timbral difference between soloist and orchestra, Beethoven calls on the pianist to play the entire movement *una corda* ("one string")—that is, using one of the pedals to shift the entire keyboard action so that the hammers strike only a single string. Orchestra and soloist alternately present their respective ideas. Neither gives ground at first, but the tutti eventually diminishes in volume. At m. 47, the soloist moves on to a new idea, a soaring melody that sounds very much like a singer's aria. This gives way to a dramatic series of simultaneous runs and trills in an extended (and written out) cadenza. Beethoven asks the soloist to increase the sound first to two strings, then to the full complement of three, before receding back to the original *una corda* sound.

At least some listeners have interpreted this movement as a musical reenactment of part of the myth of Orpheus and Euridice. According to this interpretation, m. 1–5 and 14–18 represent Orpheus descending into the underworld and confronting Charon; m. 38–48 represent him charming Charon with music; m. 47–54 represent him crossing the river Styx to the underworld to retrieve Euridice; m. 55–63 (the solo cadenza) represent his doubts about whether Euridice is still behind him as he ascends back to the world of the living; and finally, the empty-sounding final cadence reflects his despair at the second loss of his beloved. Although Beethoven himself left no direct evidence to support this interpretation, accounts by friends and acquaintances suggest that it is at least plausible.

Piano Sonata in C Major, Op. 53
("Waldstein"), first movement (1804)
Beethoven

47
p
cresc.
50
f
53
56
decresc.
cresc.
59
f
62
ff
65
sf
68
p
fp
decresc
71
pp
cresc.
74
fp
79
cresc.
p
84
cresc.
p
pp
1.
2.
88
cresc.
p
pp
32
93

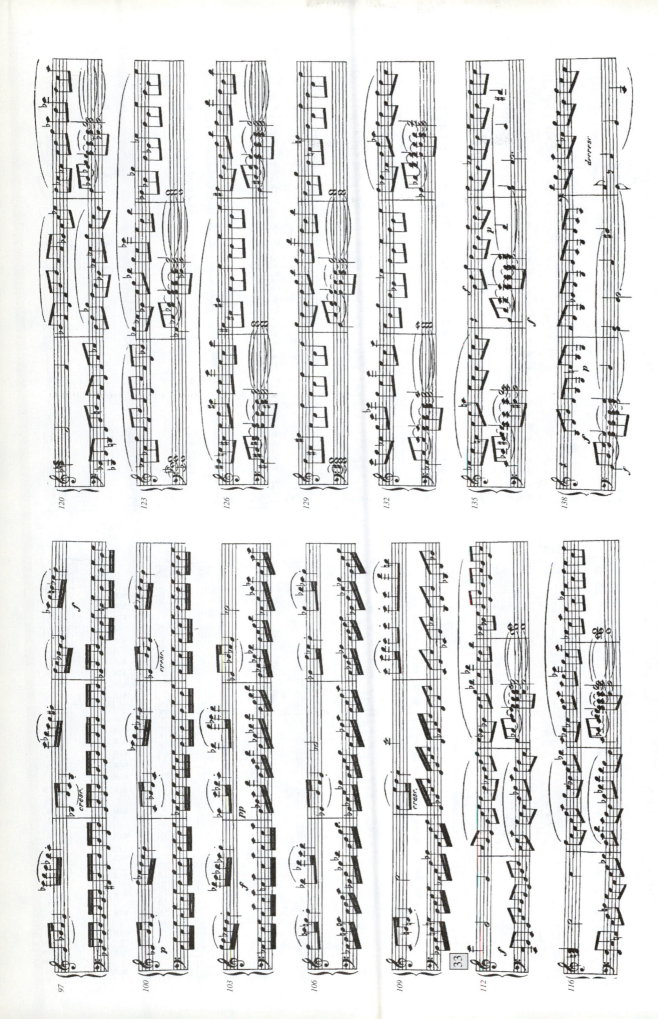

No. 119 Beethoven: Piano Sonata in C Major, Op. 53

No. 119 Beethoven: Piano Sonata in C Major, Op. 53

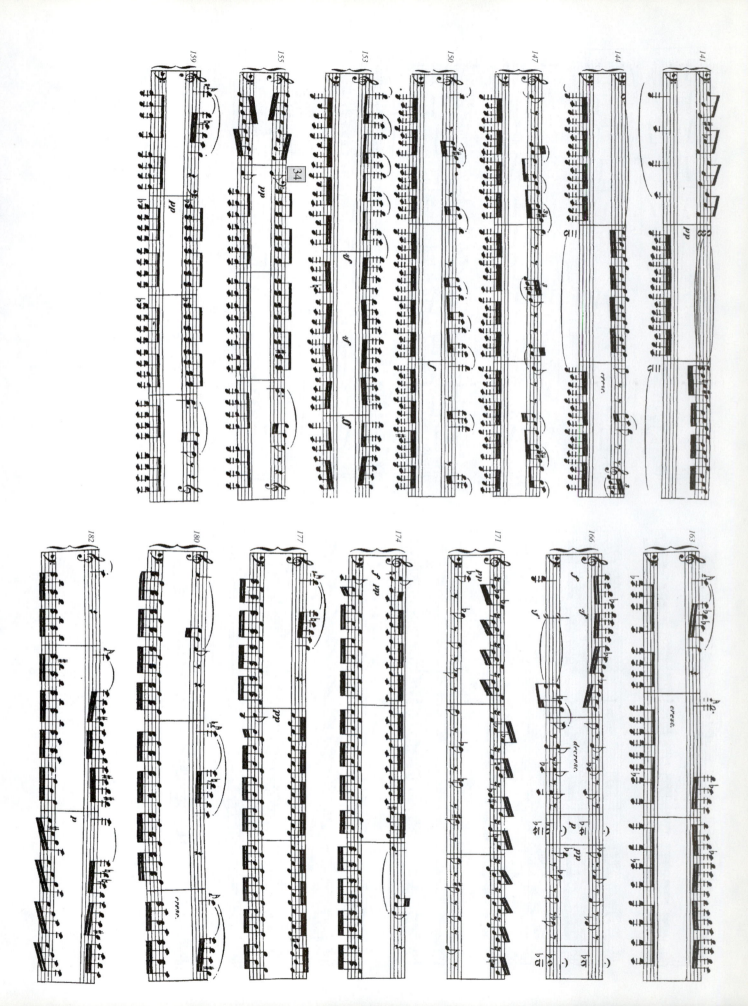

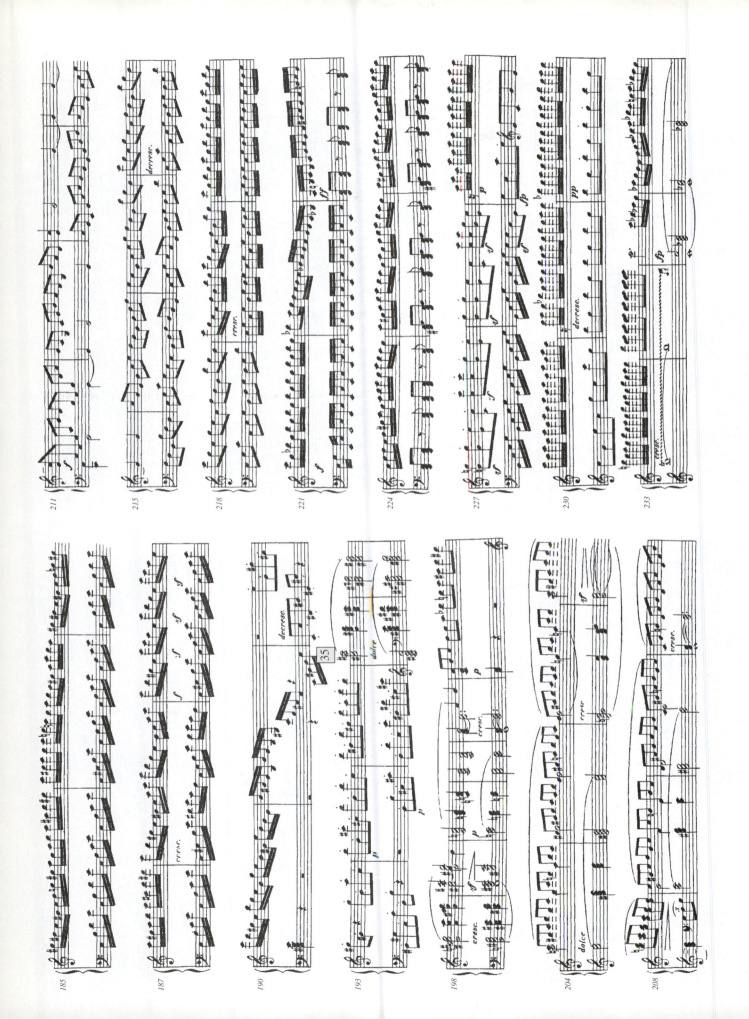

No. 119 Beethoven: Piano Sonata in C Major, Op. 53

No. 119 Beethoven: Piano Sonata in C Major, Op. 53

120 String Quartet in B♭ Major, Op. 130
(excerpts) (1826)
Beethoven

CD9   Track 37   p. 431

First movement

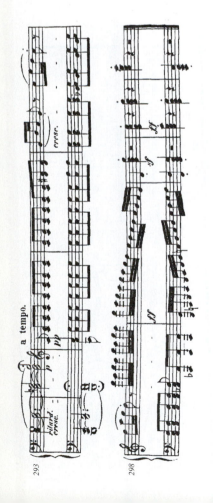

Original-Verleger: C. Haslinger qm Tobias in Wien.   Stich und Druck von Breitkopf & Härtel in Leipzig.

The gulf between music written for amateurs and professionals expanded greatly during the 19th century. Beethoven's piano sonatas, although widely admired, were repeatedly criticized during his lifetime for their technical difficulty. His Sonata in C Major, Op. 53, completed in 1804 and dedicated to Count Waldstein, an early patron from Bonn, may seem relatively undemanding compared to later works, but its rapid passagework and broken octave scales put it beyond the reach of most amateurs at the time it was written.

In a break with what had become standard practice in the Classical era, the exposition of the first movement modulates to the mediant (E major, which later becomes E minor) instead of the dominant (G major). This kind of modulation reflects the increasing chromaticism of 19th-century harmonic practice and the consequent erosion of the polarity between tonic and dominant that had characterized the formal structures of the mid- to late 18th century. Later composers working within the conventions of sonata form would often modulate to keys other than the dominant or relative major.

While looking forward in terms of its technical demands and harmonic structure, the "Waldstein" also looks back for thematic inspiration, illustrating Beethoven's ability to transform a predecessor's idea into an entirely new creation. The opening bears striking parallels to Haydn's String Quartet Op. 33, No. 3 (Anthology No. 105, discussed in Chapter 12). Like Haydn's quartet, Beethoven's sonata is in the key of C major, begins with a series of repeated notes, introduces its thematic idea in fragments, and repeats this idea on a series of unusual scale degrees before finally reestablishing the tonic (m. 14). We do not know if Beethoven was conscious of these underlying connections, but we do know that he studied the works of Haydn and Mozart carefully, even copying out entire quartets or quartet movements on occasion to better understand their craft of composition.

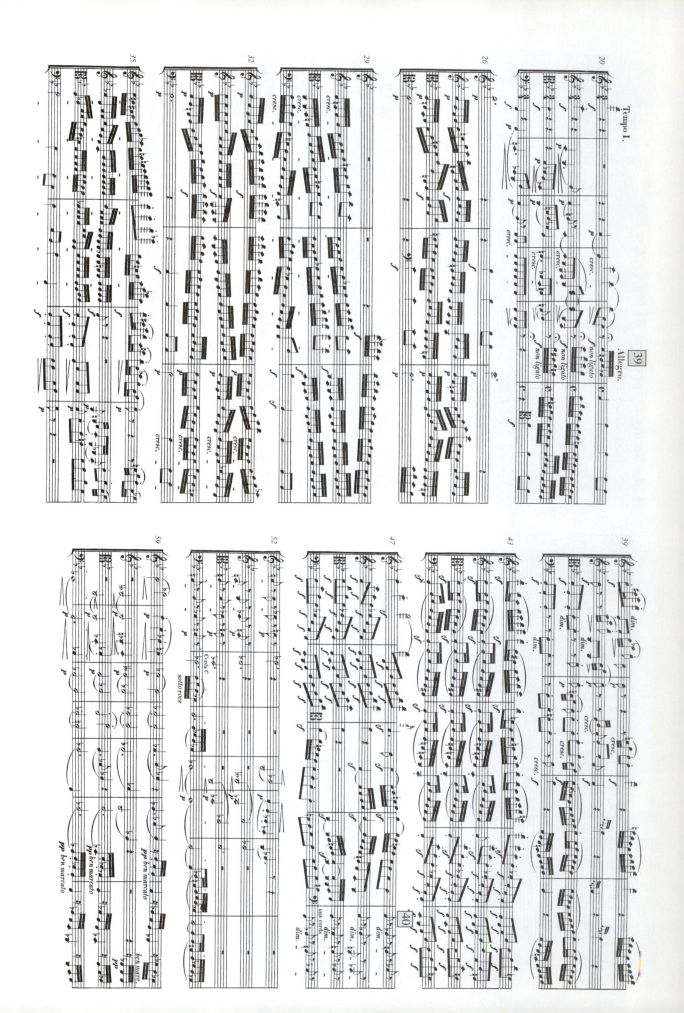

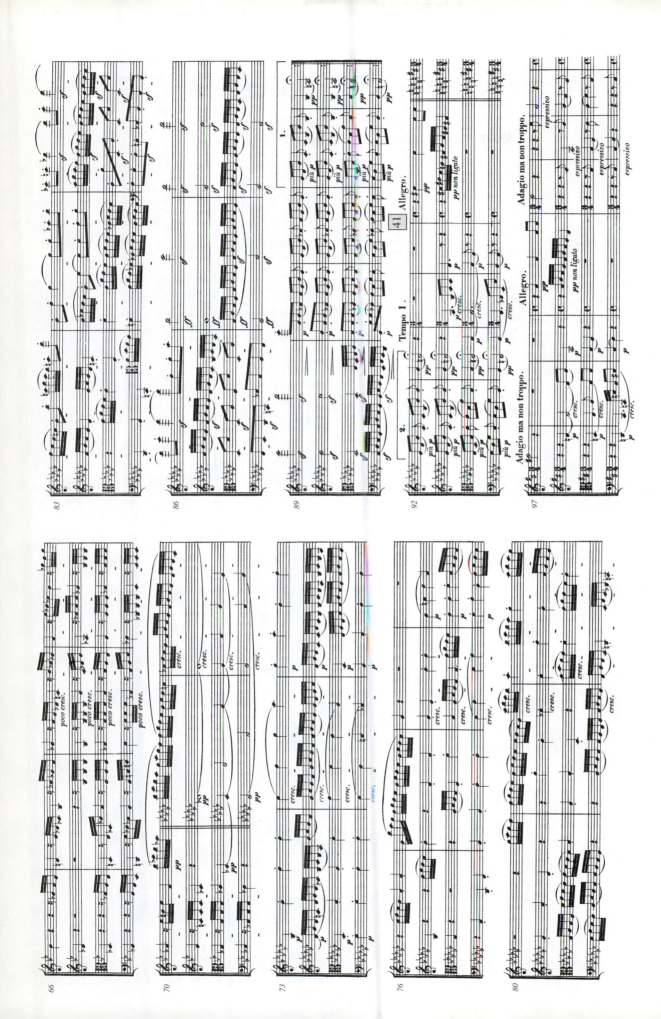

No. 120 Beethoven: String Quartet in B♭ Major, Op. 130

Allegro.
104
sempre p
non ligato
110
116
122
128
dim.
pp
cresc.
non ligato
42
f
133
p
f
cresc.
136
ten.
ben marcato
140
non ligato
143
146

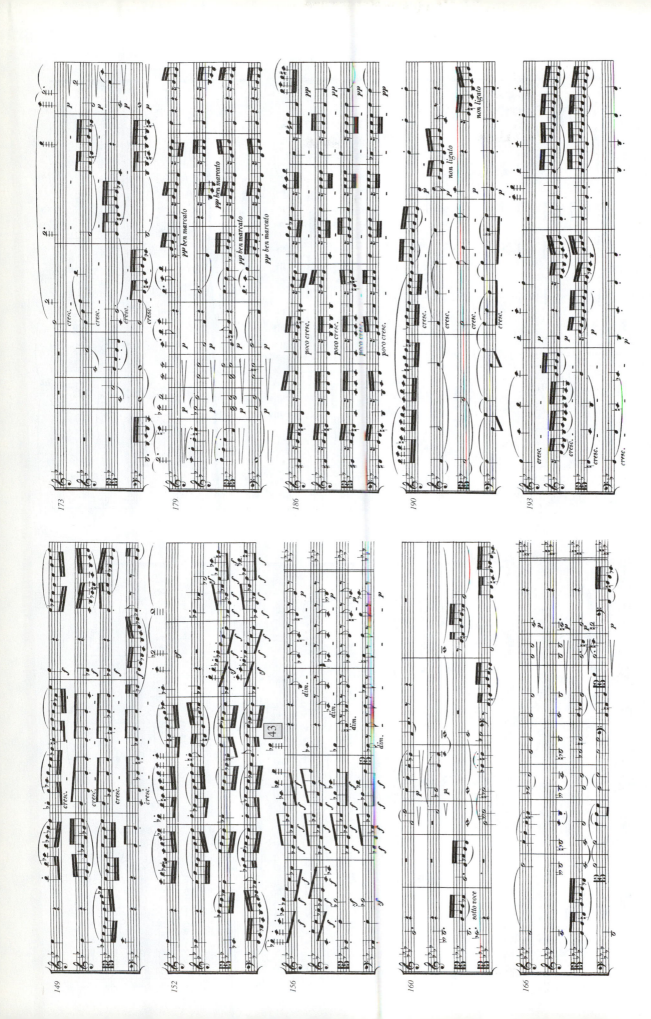

No. 120 Beethoven: String Quartet in B♭ Major, Op. 130

■ **199**

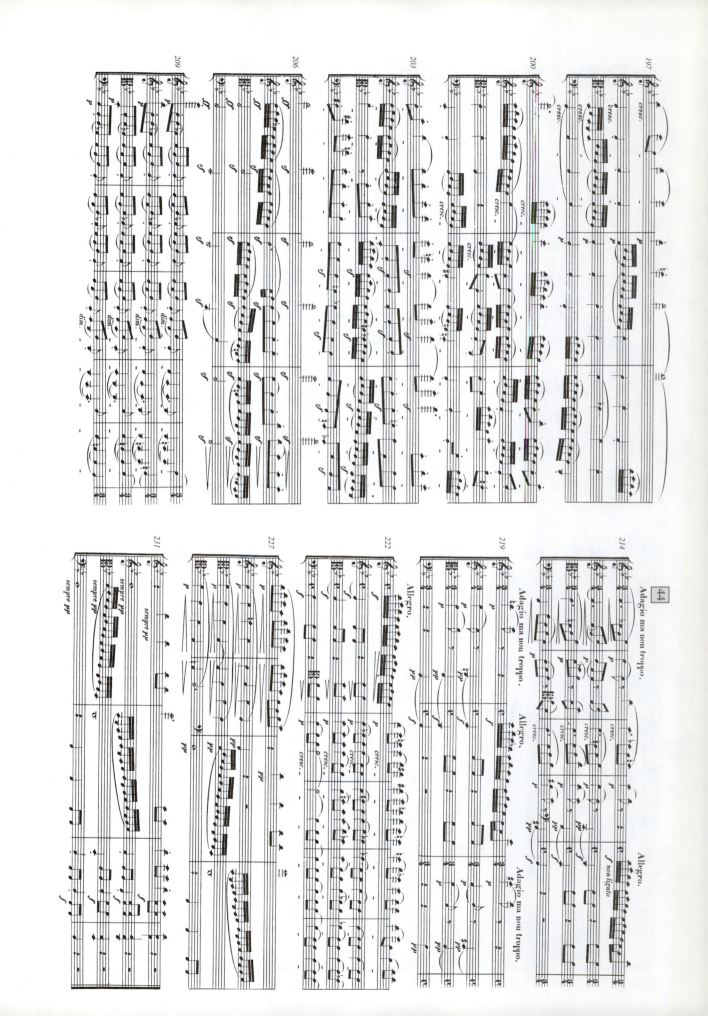

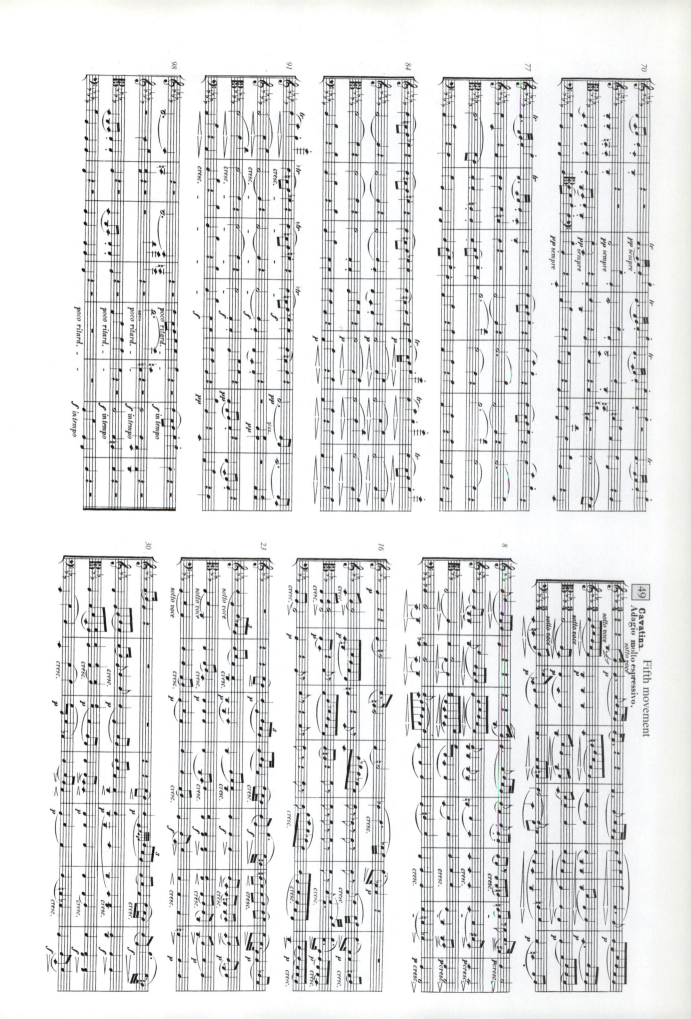

Like his piano sonatas, Beethoven's string quartets also reflect the trend toward increasing technical difficulty. Good amateurs could readily have performed the six quartets he published as Op. 18 in 1801, but not the three substantially longer quartets he published as Op. 59 in 1808. Beethoven's late quartets—Opuses 127, 130, 132, and 135, composed between 1824 and 1826—are among the most challenging works he wrote in any genre, for performers and listeners alike. Contemporary listeners had never heard anything quite like the opening of the Quartet in B♭ Major, Op. 130. The music is full of unexpected starts and stops. What appears at first to be a slow introduction, for example, turns out to be an integral part of the sonata-form exposition. And instead of modulating to the expected dominant (F) in the exposition, Beethoven dramatically overshoots it (m. 51) and lands instead in the unlikely key of G♭ (♭VI, m. 55).

Subsequent movements are similarly full of formal and technical surprises. The second movement scherzo, marked *Presto*, runs less than two minutes in many performances, even those that observe all of Beethoven's repeat signs. (The first movement, in contrast usually runs between 12 and 13 minutes.) The third movement, marked *Andante con moto, ma non troppo*, is a study in equal-voiced texture. In the opening measures, for example, melody and accompaniment are nearly indistinguishable. The fourth movement, a German dance (*Alla danza tedesca*) also features unusual textures, especially toward the end (m. 129–140). Here the melodic line bounces from instrument to instrument, each playing solo but completing together a continuous line of melody. Some later writers have compared this technique to pointillism, a painting technique developed in the late 19th century in which recognizable images are created from a pattern of tiny, discrete dots of color.

The fifth movement of this quartet, labeled "Cavatina," is of particular interest. In Italian opera, *cavatina* designated any introductory aria sung by a main character. In Germany, however, the term was reserved largely for simple arias of an introspective quality, free of virtuosic display, and it is clearly this kind of cavatina that Beethoven had in mind. It is in effect an aria without words, with the first violin clearly imitating a solo voice. Many composers had written aria-like string quartet movements before; what makes this one different is the interplay of the ensemble as a whole. The other three voices create a texture that is at once homophonic and contrapuntal. The soloist, moreover, "sings" in a voice that is almost sobbing, choking—as Beethoven marks it, *beklemmt* ("as if caught in a vise"). Violinists produce this effect by reducing pressure on the bow, letting it ride lightly across the string. The resulting tone is neither full nor beautiful, but nonetheless dramatically moving.

The original finale of Op. 130 was an enormous fugue that Beethoven later published as a separate work with its own opus number, the *Grosse Fuge* ("Great Fugue"), Op. 133. This work has justly been called Beethoven's equivalent to *The Art of Fugue*, Johann Sebastian Bach's compilation of fugues on a single theme. It is no coincidence that it should have originally been intended to provide the capstone to a work so thoroughly occupied with issues of texture. In its place, Beethoven wrote a shorter finale in which an apparently simple opening, based on a kind of folk-like dance, becomes increasingly complex, with a remarkable multiplicity of textures.

No. 120 Beethoven: String Quartet in B♭ Major, Op. 130

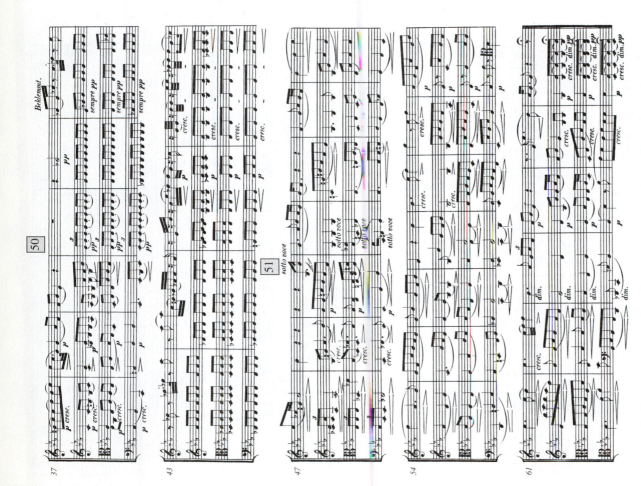

121 Three Lieder

Franz Schubert (1797–1828)

121a Erlkönig, D. 328 (1815)

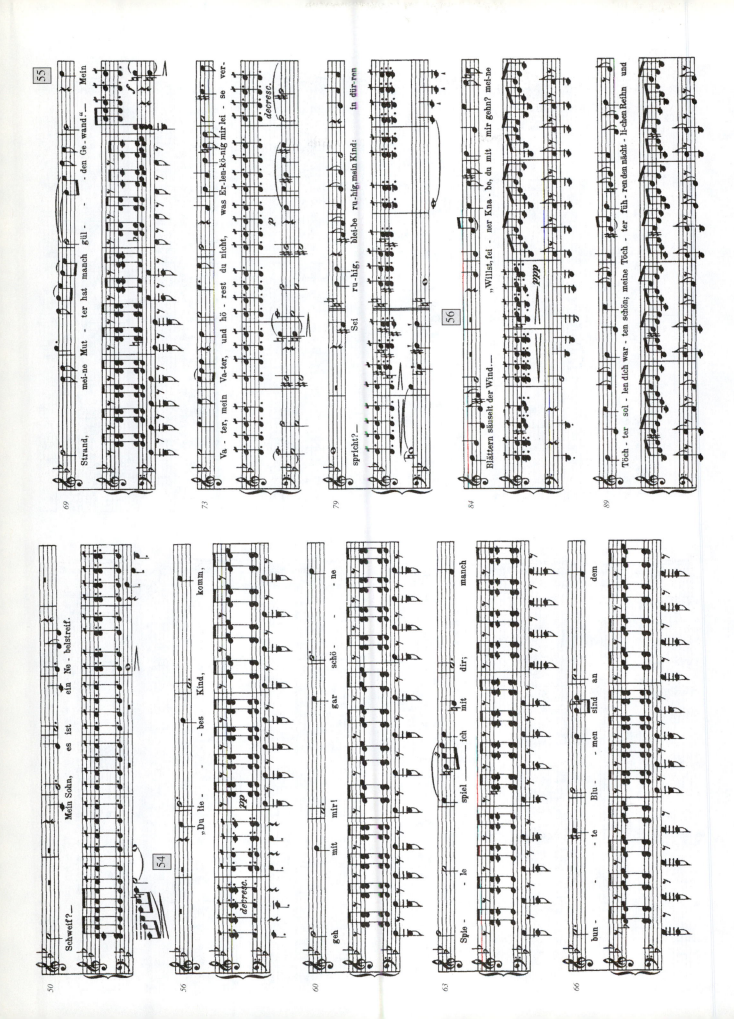

No. 121a Schubert: *Erlkönig*

No. 121a Schubert: Erlkönig

121b Prometheus, D. 674 (1819)

CD9 Track 60 p. 434

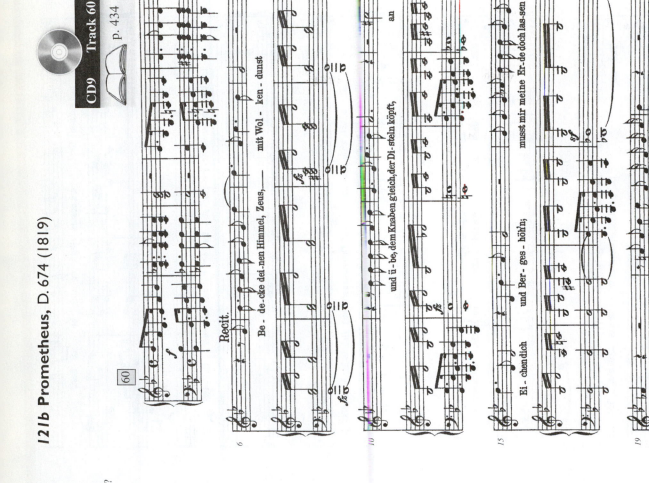

Who rides so late through night and wind?
It is the father with his child;
He holds the boy fast in his arms
He holds him tightly, he holds him warm.

My son, why do you hide your face so anxiously?
Do you not see, father, the elf-king?
The elf-king with crown and train?
My son, it is a streak of clouds.

"You dear child, come with me!
Such wonderful games I will play with you;
So many beautiful flowers are on the shore,
My mother has many a golden robe."

My father, my father, do you not yet hear,
What the elf-king softly promises me?
Be calm, stay calm, my child:
Through the dry leaves rustles the wind.

"Will you, dear child, come with me?
My daughters shall wait on you well;
my daughters dance at night
and will cradle and dance and sing to you."

My father, my father, do you not see there
Elf-king's daughters in the desolate place?
My son, my son, I see it clearly,
The old fields appear so gray.

"I love you, your lovely form charms me,
and if you're unwilling, I'll use force."
My father, my father, now he grabs me!
Elf-king has done me harm!

The father, filled with horror, rides fast,
He holds in his arms the groaning child,
Reaches the courtyard with toil and trouble,
In his arms the child was dead.

Wer reitet so spät durch Nacht und Wind?
Es ist der Vater mit seinem Kind;
er hat den Knaben wohl in dem Arm,
er fasst ihn sicher, er hält ihn warm.

Mein Sohn, was birgst du so bang dein Gesicht?
Siehst, Vater, du den Erlkönig nicht?
den Erlkönig mit Kron und Schweif?
Mein Sohn, es ist ein Nebelstreif.

"Du liebes Kind, komm, geh mit mir!
gar schöne Spiele spiel' ich mit dir;
manch bunte Blumen sind an dem Strand,
meine Mutter hat manch gülden Gewand."

Mein Vater, mein Vater, und hörest du nicht,
was Erlenkönig mir leise verspricht?
Sei ruhig, bleibe ruhig, mein Kind:
in dürren Blättern säuselt der Wind.

"Willst, feiner Knabe, du mit mir gehen?
meine Töchter sollen dich warten schön;
meine Töchter führen den nächtlichen Reihn
und wiegen und tanzen und singen dich ein."

Mein Vater, mein Vater, und siehst du nicht dort
Erlkönigs Töchter am düstren Ort?
Mein Sohn, mein Sohn, ich seh es genau,
es scheinen die alten Weiden so grau.

"Ich liebe dich, mir reizt deine schöne Gestalt,
und bist du nicht willig, so brauch ich Gewalt."
Mein Vater, mein Vater, jetzt fasst er mich an!
Erlkönig hat mir ein Leids getan!

Dem Vater grauset's, er reitet geschwind,
er hält in Armen das ächzende Kind,
erreicht den Hof mit Müh und Not;
in seinen Armen das Kind war tot.

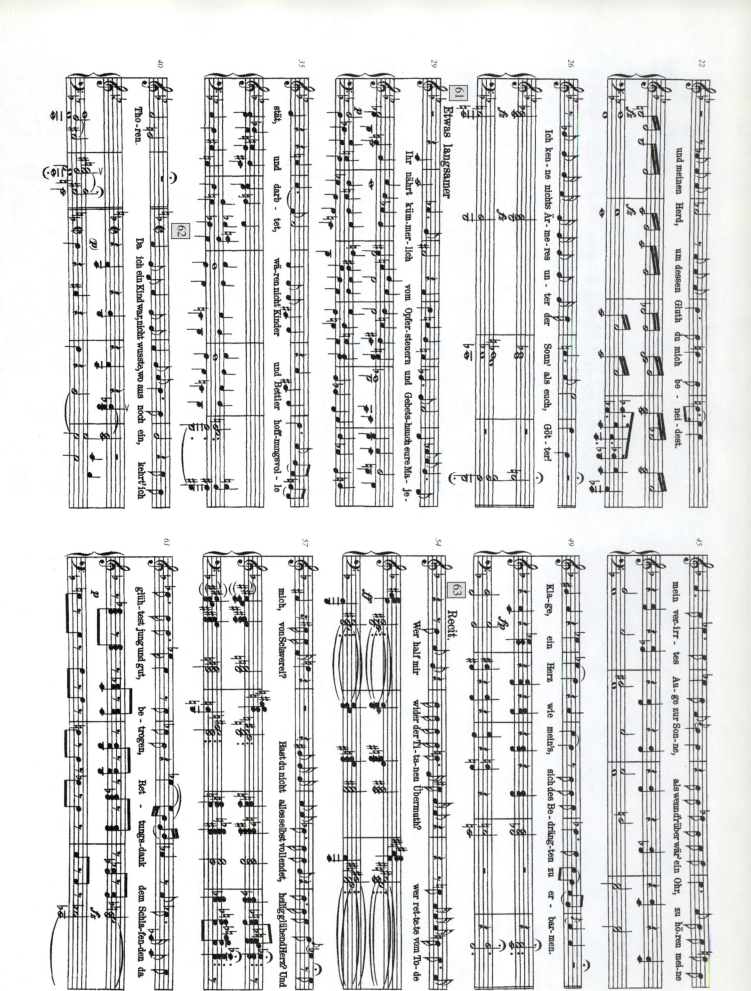

No. 121b Schubert: *Prometheus*

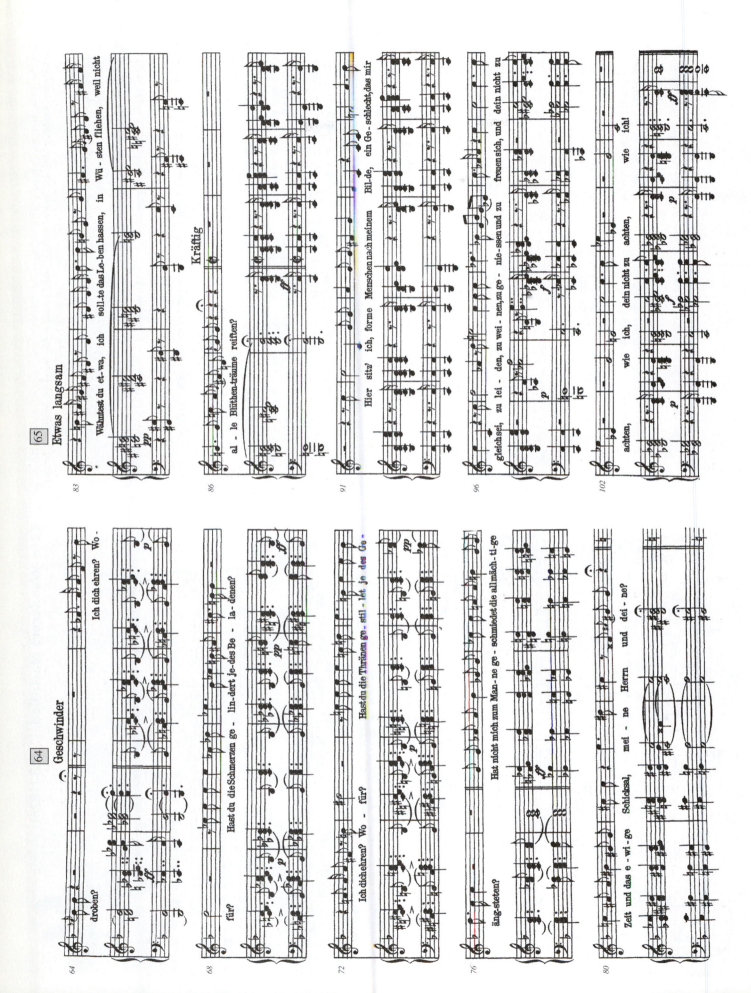

No. 121b Schubert: *Prometheus*

Bedecke deinen Himmel, Zeus, mit Wolkendunst,
und übe, dem Knaben gleich, der Disteln köpft,
an Eichen dich und Bergeshöh'n;
musst mir meine Erde doch lassen steh'n,
und meine Hütte, die du nicht gebaut,
und meinen Herd, um de Gluth du mich
beneidest.

Ich kenne nichts Ärmeres unter der Sonn',
als euch, Götter!
Ihr nähit kümmerlich
vom Opfersteuern und Gebetshauch eure
Majestät,
und darbtet,
wären nicht Kinder und Bettler hoffnungsvolle
Thoren.

Da ich ein Kind war, nicht wusste wo aus noch
ein,
kehr' ich mein verirrtes Auge zur Sonne,
als wenn d'rüber wär'ein Ohr, zu hören meine
Klage,
ein Herz, wie mein's,
sich des Bedrängten zu erbarmen.

Wer half mir wider der Titanen Übermuth?
Wer rettete vom Tode mich, von Sclaverei?
Hast du nicht alles selbst vollendet,
heilig glühend Herz?
Und glühtest jung und gut, betrogen,
Rettungsdank dem Schlafenden da droben?

Ich dich ehren? Wofür?
Hast du die Schmerzen gelindert je des
Beladenen?
Ich dich ehren? Wofür?
Hast du die Thränen gestillet je des
Geängsteten?

Hat mich nicht zum Manne geschmiedet die
allmächtige Zeit
und das ewige Schicksal, meine Herrn und
deine?

Wähntest du etwa, ich sollte das Leben hassen,
in Wüsten fliehen,
weil nicht alle Blüthenträume reiften?

Hier sitz' ich,
forme Menschen nach meinem Bilde,
ein Geschlecht, das mir gleich sei,
zu leiden, zu weinen, zu geniessen und zu
freuen sich,
und dein nicht zu achten, wie ich!

Cover your heaven, Zeus, with cloud-dust
and practice—like the youth who blows the tops
off dandelions—
on oak trees and mountaintops.
You must, however, let my earth be,
and my hut, which you did not build,
and my hearth, whose glow you envy.

I know nothing more pitiful under the sun
than you gods!
You nourish yourselves miserably
on sacrifice and the breath of prayers
and would wither away,
were not children and beggars hopeful fools.

When I was a child, not knowing anything,
I turned my mistaken eye to the sun,
as if up above there were an ear to hear my cry,
a heart, like mine,
that could comfort the oppressed.

Who helped me against the arrogance of Titans?
Who saved me from death, from slavery?
Have you not perfected everything yourself,
holy, glowing heart?
And glowed young and well, deceived,
Saying thanks for rescue to the sleeping one up
there?

I should honor you? For what?
Have you ameliorated the pain for the
downtrodden?
I should honor you? For what?
Have you ever stilled the tears of the anguished?

Has not the almighty time forged me into a man
and the eternal fate, the masters of both you and
me?

Did you perhaps think I should hate life,
flee to the deserts,
just because not all dreams of flowers grow ripe?

Here I sit,
formed human according to my image,
a race that resembles me,
to suffer, to weep, to enjoy and to rejoice,
and not to obey you but rather myself!

121c Wanderers Nachtlied, D.768 (1824)

CD9 Track 66 P. 435

CD10 Track 1 p. 435

Über allen Gipfeln ist Ruh,
in allen Wipfeln spürest du kaum einen Hauch;
die Vöglein schweigen,
schweigen im Walde.
Warte nur, balde ruhest du auch.

Over all summits is calm,
in every corner you feel barely a breath;
the birds are silent,
silent in the woods.
Wait yet, soon you, too, shall rest.

122 Three Settings of Goethe's Kennst du das Land

For translations of this text, see No. 113.

122a Kennst du das Land (Mignons Gesang), D. 321 (1815)
Schubert

From the perspective of form, songs generally fall into one of three categories: strophic, modified strophic, or through-composed. In strophic form, the simplest of the three, each verse (strophe) of a poem is set to the same music. In modified strophic form, as in a variation on a theme, the music varies from strophe to strophe—with melodic embellishment, for example, or alteration of texture or harmony—but remains otherwise recognizably the same. A through-composed song, in contrast, has no recognizable pattern of repetition, and often no repetition at all. *Erlkönig* is in modified strophic form; *Prometheus* and *Wanderers Nachtlied* are through-composed; for an example of a strophic song, see Schubert's *Kennst du das Land* (Anthology 2/#122a).

Song composers in the 19th century were judged according to the extent to which their music enhanced the words of the poems they set. The repetitive rhythmic insistence of Franz Schubert's *Erlkönig* ("Elf-king") reflects the content and iambic meter of Goethe's strophic poem. Schubert, however, goes beyond this rhythmic device to magnify the poem's emotional force in his modified-strophic setting. *Erlkönig* tells a chilling tale of a father riding home with his feverish son in his arms. The boy hears the Elf-king calling to him with seductive blandishments and cries out in fear as his father tries vainly to calm him. When they arrive, the boy is dead in his father's arms. The poem has four voices—a narrator, the Elf-king, the boy, and the father—and Schubert gives each of them a distinctive character through the strategic use of key, mode, texture, and register.

Free verse, as is found in a poem like Goethe's *Prometheus*, calls for a flexible musical structure. Schubert's through-composed setting emphasizes the declamatory tone and irregular rhythms of the poetry. The music and the text are equally dramatic. In Greek myth it was Prometheus who, against the will of Zeus, gave fire to humanity. As punishment for this transgression, Prometheus was chained to a rock, where every day an eagle came to eat out his liver, which grew back every night. In the poem the unrepentant Prometheus hurls scorn and defiance on Zeus. Schubert's setting conveys this defiance with the dotted rhythms of the piano introduction. The passages marked "Recit." (for recitative) are to be sung in the relatively free, declamatory style characteristic of operatic recitative.

Goethe's *Wanderers Nachtlied* ("Wanderer's Night Song"), a brief poem of a single strophe, elicited from Schubert an intense attention to detail. The limited melodic motion and straightforward rhythms of the opening capture the sense of calm that pervades the text ("Above all summits is calm…") and make the subsequent syncopation (m. 5–8) all the more pronounced. The repeated horn call-like figures in m. 9–13 take on added importance through repetition. In so brief a setting, every gesture carries added weight. Even the one-measure epilogue in the piano (m. 14) resonates with significance, given the remarkably small scale of this work.

No. 122a Schubert: Kennst du das Land

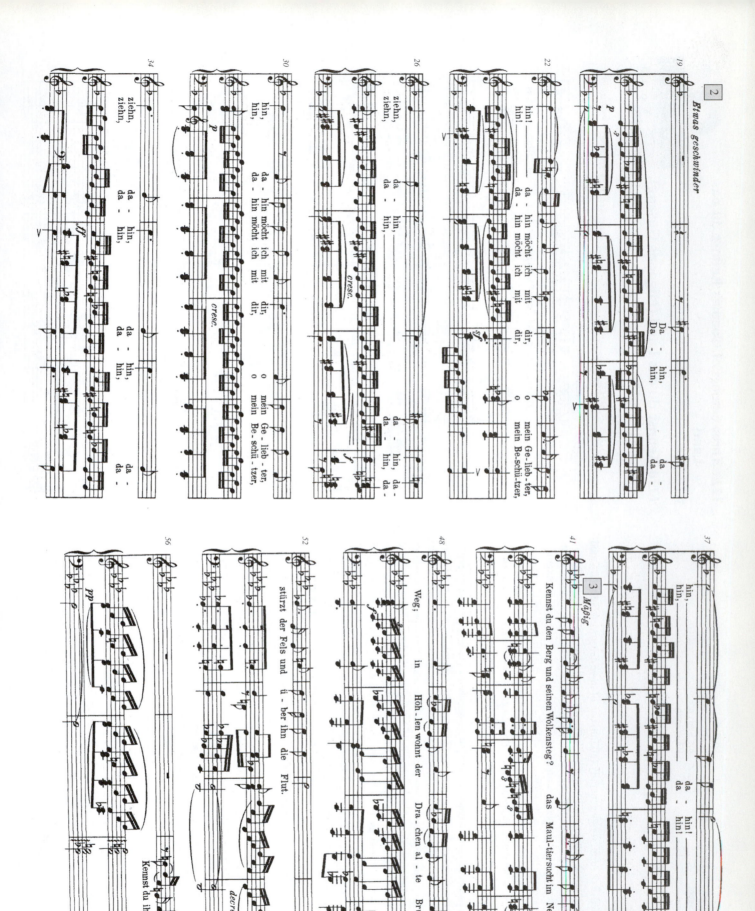

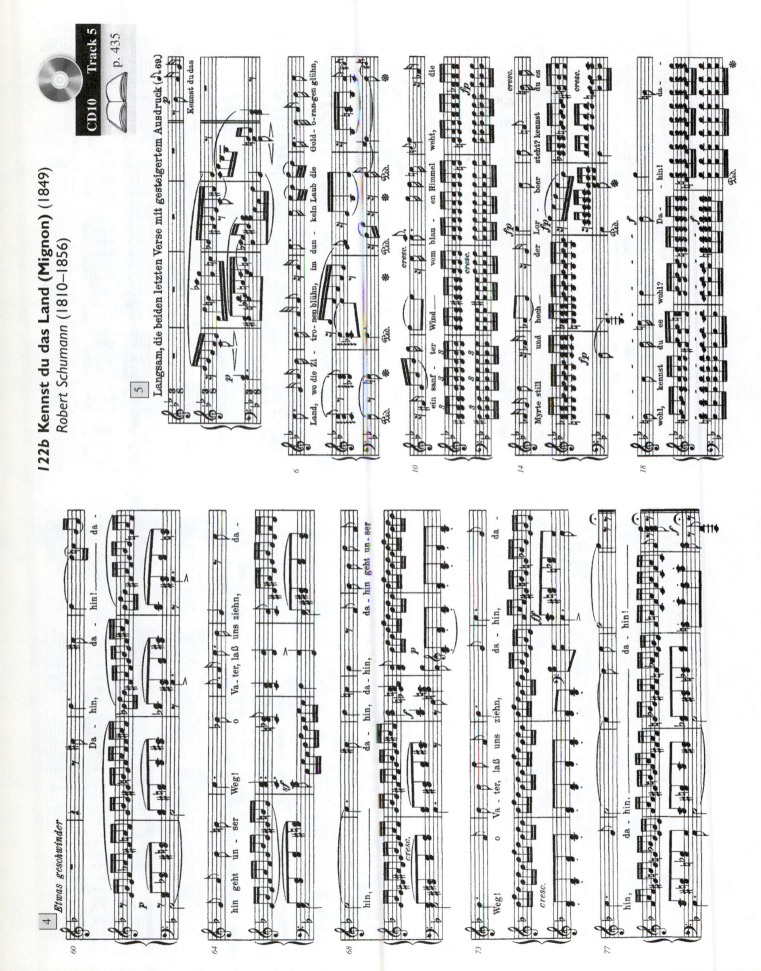

122b Kennst du das Land (Mignon) (1849)
Robert Schumann (1810–1856)

No. 122b Schumann: Kennst du das Land

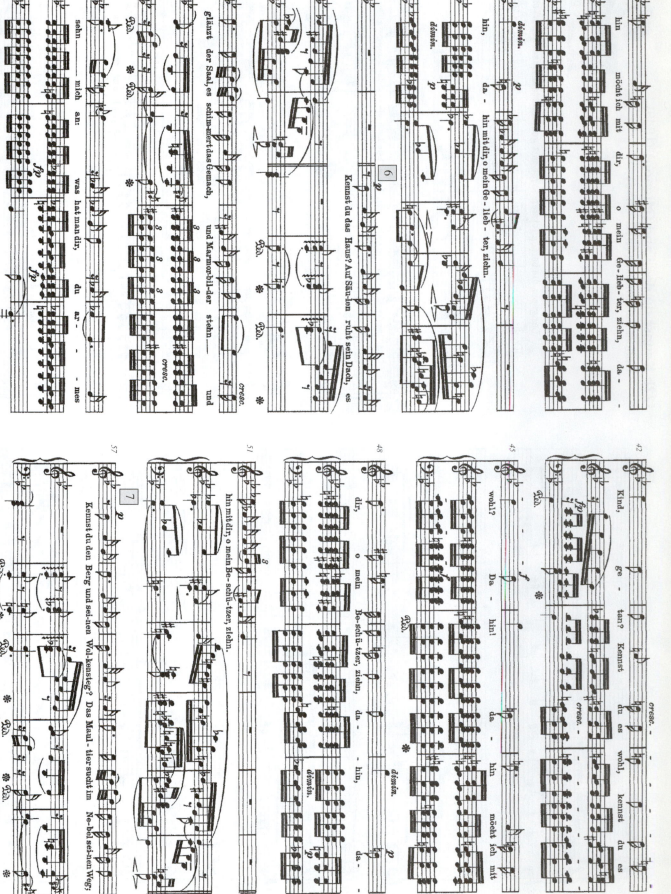

122c Mignon (1888)
Hugo Wolf (1860–1903)

CD10 Track 8 p. 435

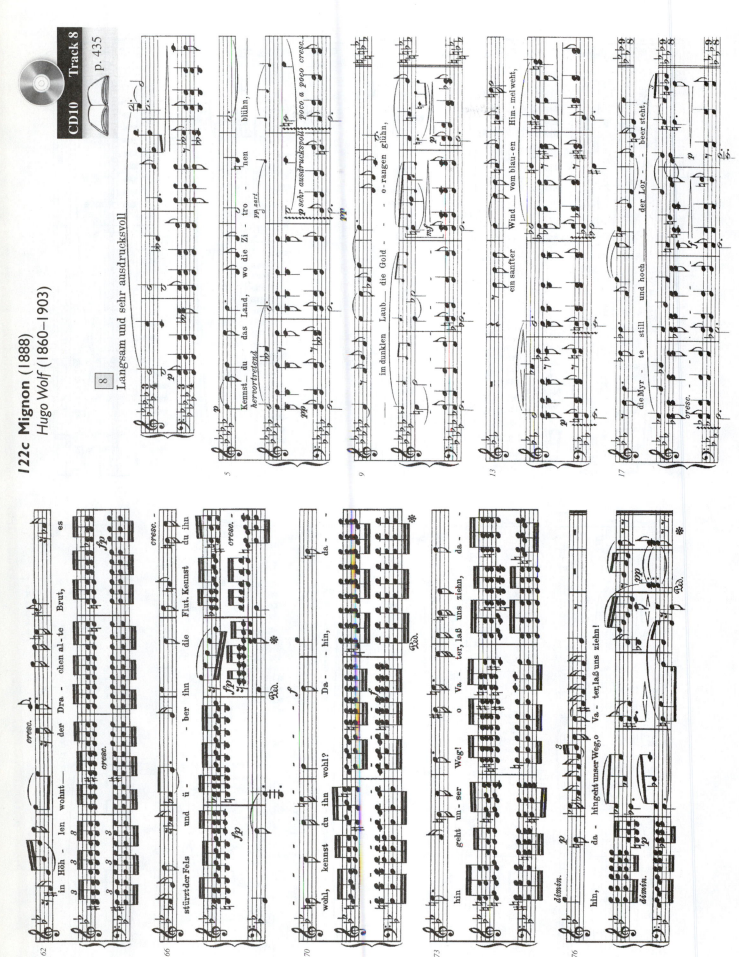

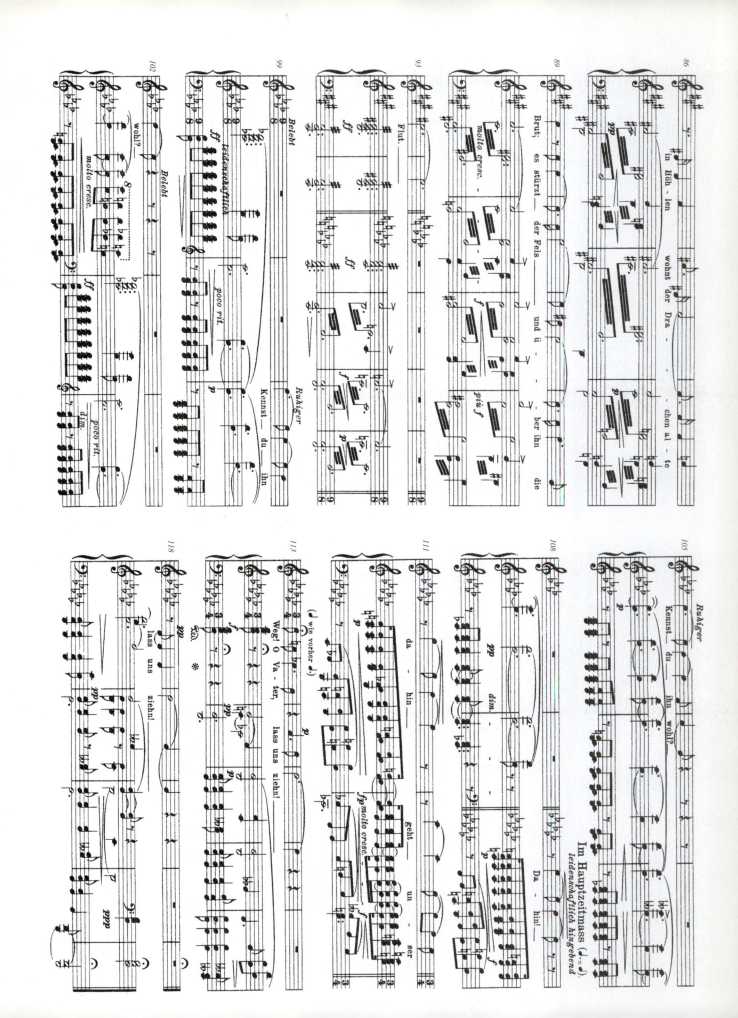

123 Liebst du um Schönheit (1841)
Clara Wieck Schumann (1819–1896)

CD10 Track 13

p. 435

Different composers were often drawn to the same text, bringing to it a variety of interpretations that reflect changing styles and expanding musical options. Carl Friedrich Zelter's late-18th-century setting of Goethe's poem *Kennst du das Land* ("Do You Know the Land?" Anthology No. 113), for example, is relatively straightforward, with a limited melodic range and restrained chromaticism. Later settings—like those by Schubert, Schumann, and Wolf—have more intricate vocal lines, richer textures, and increasingly chromatic harmonies that reflect the 19th century's ever-expanding harmonic vocabulary. Wolf's setting, in particular, illustrates the move away from the aesthetic of simplicity among composers of the latter part of the 19th century. His *Mignon*, composed in 1888, reflects none of the strophic elements of the original poetry but is instead wholly through-composed, with multiple changes of tempo and key.

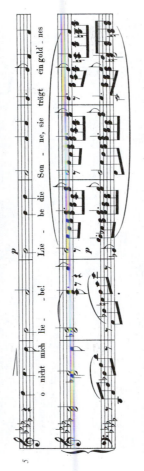

219

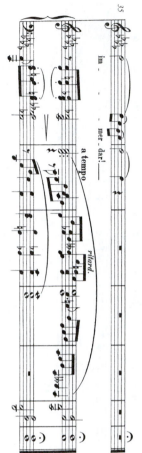

Liebst du um Schönheit,
O nicht mich liebe!
Liebe die Sonne,
Sie trägt ein gold'nes Haar!

Liebst du um Jugend,
O nicht mich liebe!
Liebe der Frühling,
Der jung ist jedes Jahr!

Liebst du um Schätze,
O nicht mich liebe.
Liebe die Meerfrau,
Sie hat viel Perlen klar.

Liebst du um Liebe,
O ja, mich liebe!
Liebe mich immer,
Dich lieb' ich immerdar.

If you love because of beauty,
Oh, do not love me!
Love the sun,
It has golden hair!

If you love because of youth,
Oh, do not love me!
Love the spring,
It is young every year!

If you love for treasures,
Oh, do not love me!
Love the mermaid,
She has many bright pearls!

If you love because of love,
Oh yes, love me!
Love me ever,
You I shall love evermore!

Clara Wieck Schumann's *Liebst du um Schönheit* ("If You Love for Beauty") is typical of the song at midcentury. It remains well within the technical grasp of amateur musicians and places its focus squarely on the voice. Its modified strophic form captures the trajectory that moves from a series of negatives ("... do not love me [for my beauty, for my youth, for treasures]") to the overwhelming positive at the end of the song ("... love [me] because of love"). The text, by Friedrich Rückert, speaks of the kind of idealized love that appealed to middle-class households.

124 Beautiful Dreamer (1862)
Stephen Foster (1826–1864)

CD10 Track 15 p. 438

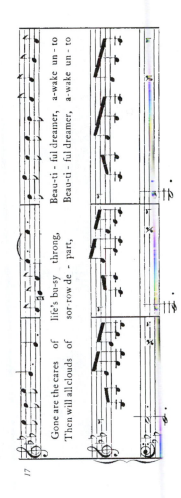

Published by permission of Wm. A. Pond & Co., owners of the copyright.

Beautiful Dreamer epitomizes the 19th-century American parlor song, so called because of its place of performance in the equivalent of today's living room—which is to say, at home, in a domestic setting. Its tone is sentimental and earnest, its strophic form straightforward, its technical demands extremely modest.

A note on the edition: The edition here reproduces a typical late-19th-century edition of the song. It is not particularly attractive but the movable type used here—note the many visible breaks between the individual pieces of type, particularly in the staff lines—made this kind of publication inexpensive to produce and thus affordable to a large base of consumers. Metal type could withstand far more pressure over a longer period of time than the more malleable (and more attractive but less durable) metal alloy plates commonly used for engraving.

125 V chetyrjokh stenakh ("In Four Walls"), from the song cycle **Bez solnca** ("Sunless") (1874)
Modeste Mussorgsky (1839–1881)

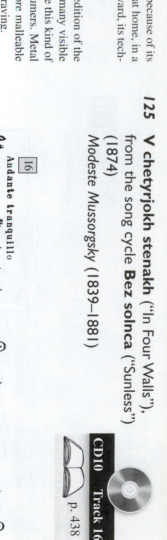

CD10 Track 16
p. 438

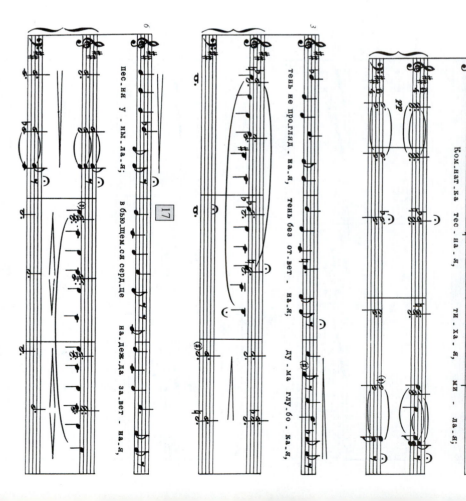

Komnatka tesnaja, tikhaja, milaja,
Ten' neprogljadnaja, ten' bezotvetnaja,
Duma glubokaja, pesnja unylaja,

V b'jushchemsja serdce nadezhda zavetnaja.

Bystryj polet za mgnoven'jem mgnovenija,
Vzor nepodvizhnyj na schast'je dalekoje,
Mnogo sommenija, mnogo terpenija,
Vot ona, noch' moja, noch' odinokaja.

I lie here in my room, sleeplessly,
Dark fathomless night all around me.
Gently a sigh is heard, one sad complaining
    word.

A faint hope remains in my aching heart.

Every moment rushes by so quickly,
Anxiously gazing on joy that is far away,
Ever doubting, ever suffering—
So the lonely night passes.

Mussorgsky's *V chetyrjokh stenakh* ("In Four Walls"), from the song cycle *Bez solnca* ("Sunless"), illustrates the ever-expanding presence of chromaticism in music from the later decades of the 19th century. Notice, for example, the series of triadic yet disjointed harmonies in the higher register in m. 9–12; these in turn clash with the persistent low D in the bass. And even though the work closes with a tonic D major triad, its ending fails to give a sense of resolution. Mussorgsky's naturalistic declamation—no melodic interval larger than a fifth, with relatively little rhythmic variety—fits well with this dark and brooding text.

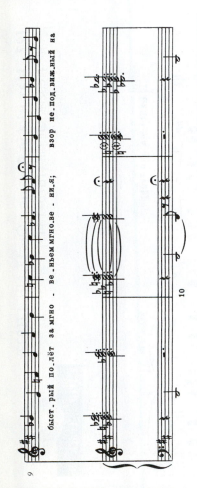

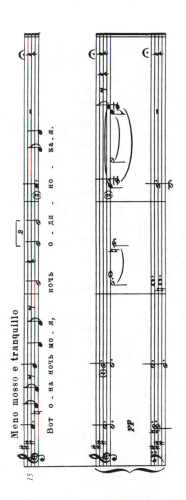

126 Lieder ohne Worte: Op. 30, No. 3 (1837)
Mendelssohn

CD10 Track 18 p. 439

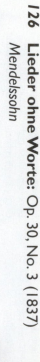

127 Mazurka in A minor, Op. 17, No. 4 (1833)
Frédéric Chopin (1810–1849)

CD10 Track 19 p. 441

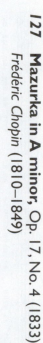

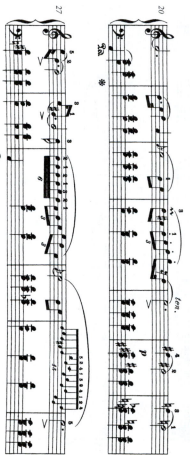

By its very nature, the character piece operates on the border between programmatic and absolute music. Mendelssohn's provocatively titled *Lieder ohne Worte* ("Songs Without Words") invites—indeed challenges—performers and listeners to imagine the nature of the words that the composer so pointedly omits. The song-like nature of this particular work is emphasized through the "instrumental" introduction and coda (m. 1–3, 25–27) and the lyrical "vocal" line m. 4–25. The simplicity of the melody, which avoids florid embellishment and stays within a well-defined vocal range, reinforces the conception of this instrumental work as a "song."

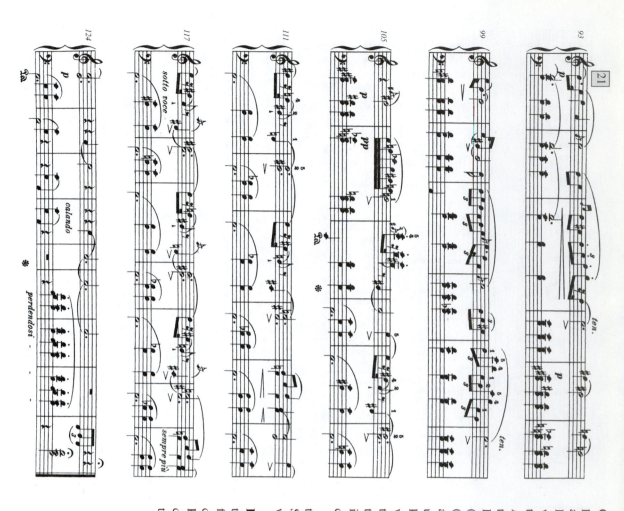

Chopin's Mazurka Op. 17, No. 4, is one of many 19th-century character pieces modeled on a particular dance—in this case, the mazurka, a Polish peasant dance in triple meter, often with an accent on the second or third beat. The work is harmonically ambiguous in several ways. It opens with three three-note chords that do not follow a harmonic progression in any conventional sense. The focus, instead, appears to be the motion of the middle note in each chord, the only one of the three to change. The progression B-C-D within the framework of the F and A in the outer voices prefigures a harmony that will prove repeatedly elusive. The cadence at the end of m. 4 can be read as an F major chord in first inversion (A-C-F), but the absence of Bb gives the work more a modal sound, either Lydian (a scale on F without the Bb) or Aeolian (a scale on A with no accidentals). The chromatic descent of linked thirds beginning in m. 9 (F♯–D♯ followed by F♮–D♮) further undermines the sense of a strong tonal center. Chopin creates the expectation of a strong cadence on A minor at the downbeat to m. 13, but delays it until m. 20. And even then, he gives us just enough stability in A minor to make us think we know where we are going, and that the piece has a tonal center. The middle section of this work, by contrast (m. 61–92) hammers away at A major triads so relentlessly that it seems to take all the energy it can muster to move to a dominant harmony even briefly. But with the return of the opening section at m. 93, we are thrust back into the realm of harmonic ambiguity. At the end of the piece, Chopin repeats the opening sequence of harmonically ambiguous chords followed by an A-C-F triad, giving us a conclusion but no harmonic closure.

A harmonically ambiguous opening had many distinguished precedents. One need think only of such works as Mozart's "Dissonant" Quartet, K. 465, or Haydn's "Drumroll" Symphony, No. 103 (Anthology No. 106). But a harmonically ambiguous close like this one was a phenomenon essentially new to the 19th century.

Performance notes: This recording by the great pianist Artur Rubinstein (1887–1982) reflects the state of recording technology in the late 1930s. Even though the quality of sound that falls far short of today's standards, recordings like this continue to be reissued commercially because they reflect outstanding interpretations that transcend the limitations of technology. Rubinstein himself recorded the complete Mazurkas of Chopin at three different points in his career (in 1938–1939, 1952–1953, 1965–1966), and all have found a ready audience among the pianist's admirers, for each reflects a different stage of the artist's long career.

Prelude in A Minor

128 Preludes, Op. 28, Nos. 1–4 (1839)

Chopin

Prelude in C Major

Prelude in G Major

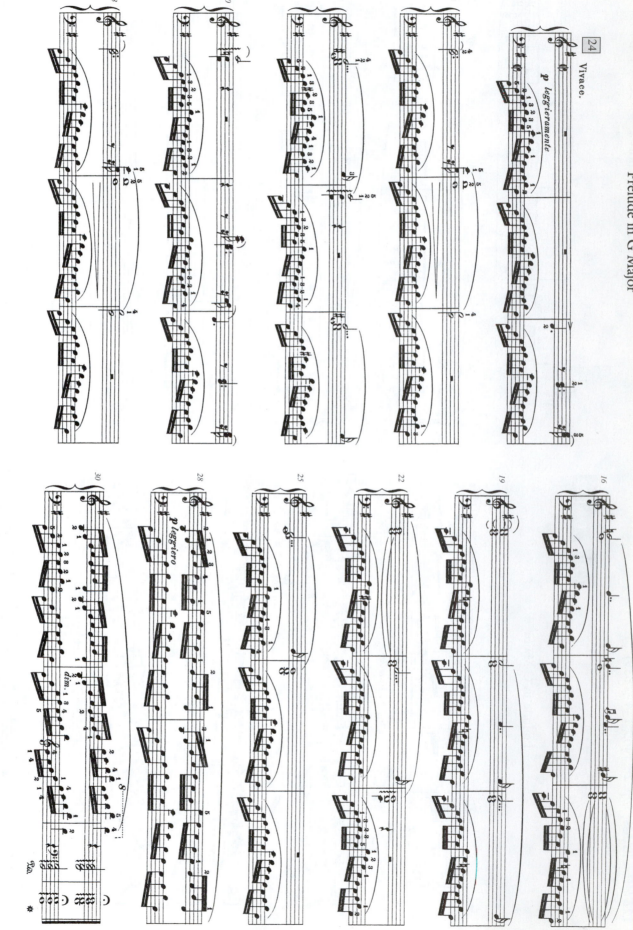

Chopin's *Preludes*, Op. 28, consist of 24 individual works presented in an order that follow the circle of fifths, moving systematically through all 24 major and minor keys of the twelve-note scale (from C major and A minor to G major and E minor, and so forth). The homage to J. S. Bach's *Well-Tempered Clavier* is unmistakable (Anthology No. 95). The first Prelude, in C major, imitates the broken chordal writing in the corresponding prelude of the first book of Bach's collection and uses harmonic progressions rather than a distinctive melodic line to create a sense of overall shape. And even though Chopin's preludes lack fugues, many of them explore unusual possibilities of voice leading. In the A minor Prelude, for example, a back-and-forth half-step motion in one voice is framed by another voice making leaps of a tenth. The Prelude in G Major is rather like an etude, emphasizing a single constant motion throughout in the rapid passagework in the left hand. And the Prelude in E minor recreates the mood of a lament, possibly from a tragic heroine in an opera; the steady chromatic descent in the lower voices echo the age-old connection of the falling chromatic line with suffering and pain.

Prelude in E Minor

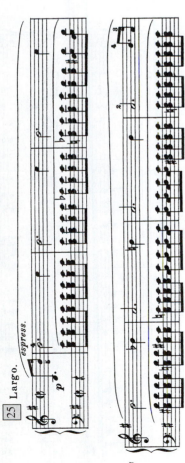

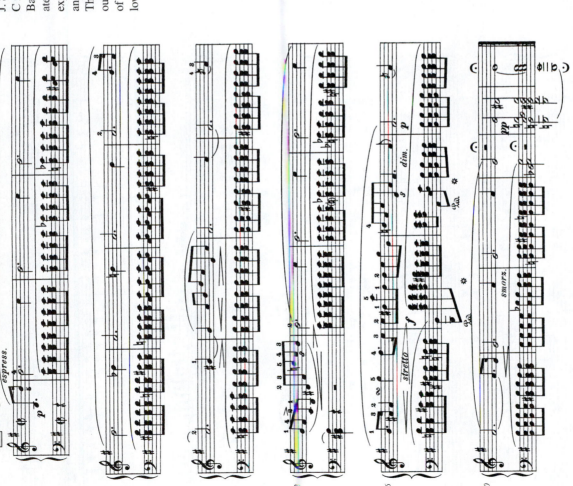

229

No. 128 Chopin: *Preludes*

129 Ballade No. 1 in G minor, Op. 23

(1835)

Chopin

*) The Princess M. Czartoryska, Frau F. Streicher, and Dr. F. von Hiller maintain the authenticity of this Eb in opposition to the D of earlier editions.

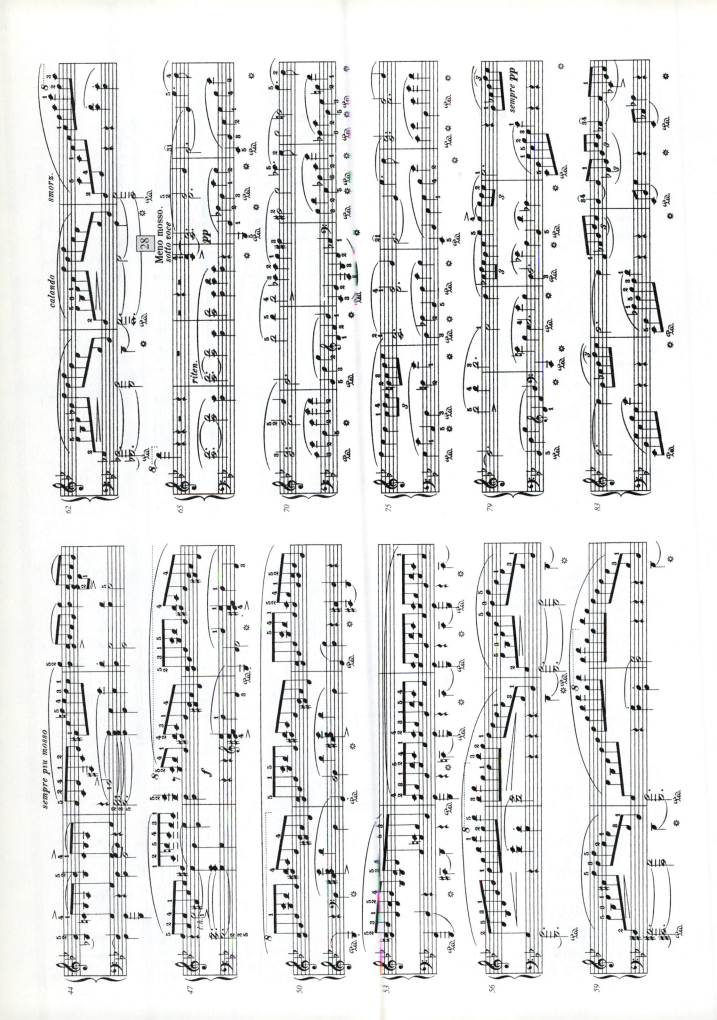

No. 129 Chopin: Ballade No. 1 in G minor

No. 129 Chopin: Ballade No. I in G minor

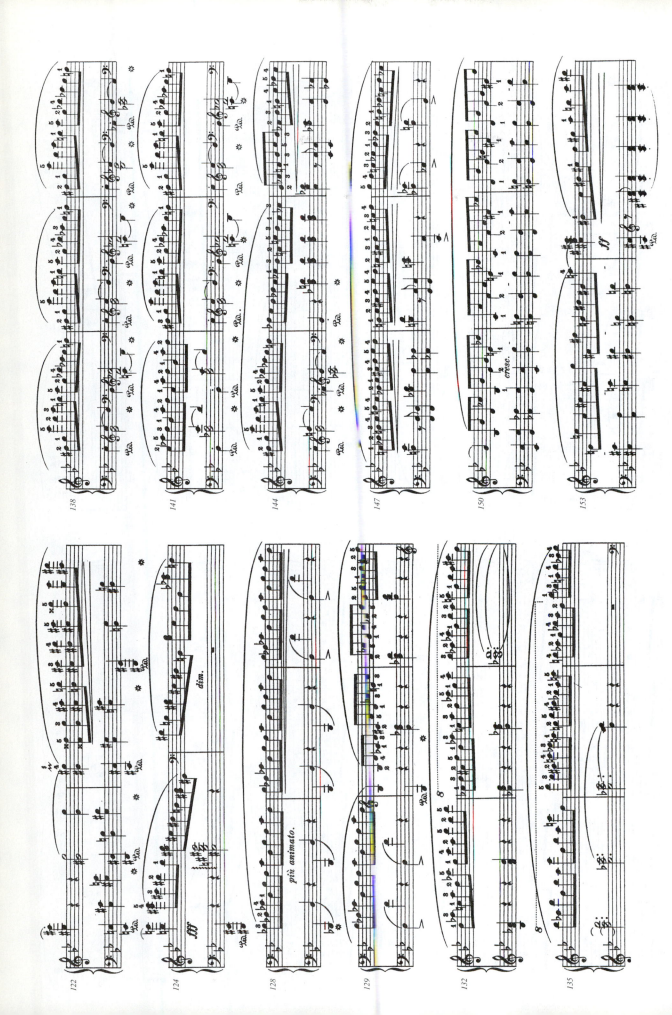

No. 129 Chopin: Ballade No. I in G minor

233

No. 129 Chopin: Ballade No. I in G minor

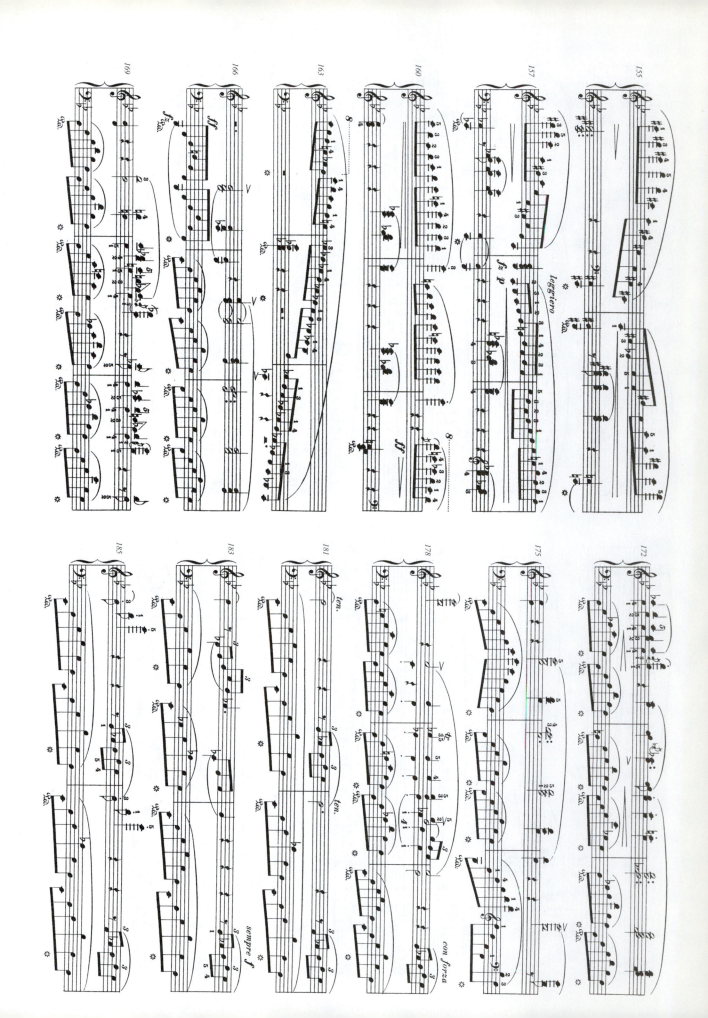

No. 129 Chopin: Ballade No. 1 in G minor

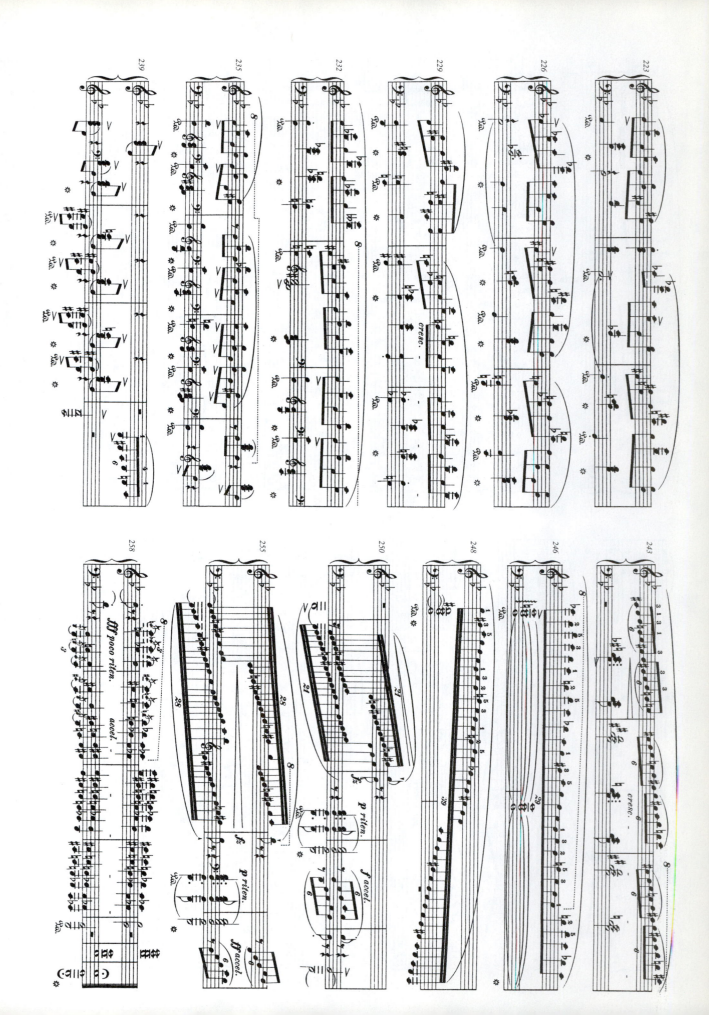

130 Galop de bal (ca. 1840)
Franz Liszt (1811–1886)

p. 445

CD10 Track 30

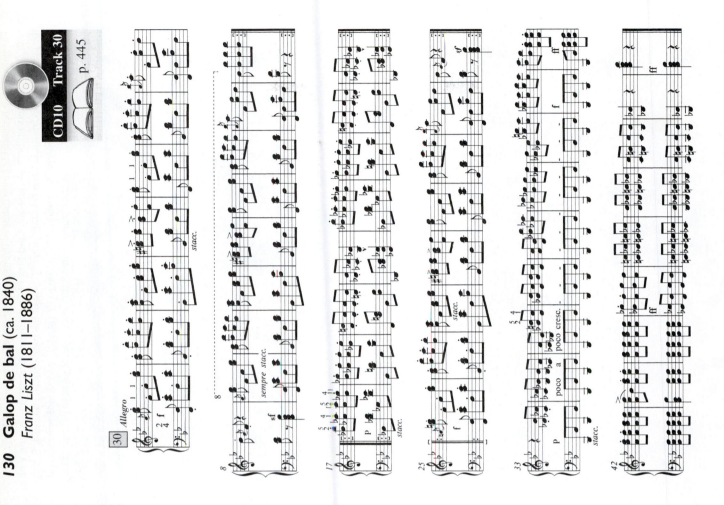

Although composers in the generations after Beethoven never abandoned the multimovement sonata entirely, it gradually gave way to larger-scale forms in a single movement such as the ballade, cultivated by Chopin, Liszt, Brahms, and Fauré, and the scherzo, cultivated by Chopin and Brahms. Chopin's Ballade in G minor, Op. 23, is an extended work with many elements of sonata form. After a brief introduction (m. 1–7), Chopin establishes two main key areas, G minor (m. 8–44) and E♭ major (m. 67–93), connected by a transition section (m. 44–67). Although the modulation here is from i to VI rather than the more typical i to III, the form of this opening corresponds to the conventions of a sonata-form exposition. Then, as in the development section of a sonata-form movement, Chopin takes the two main ideas through a variety of new key areas and manipulates them thematically before introducing a new idea (m. 138). The recapitulation deviates from the conventions of sonata form in that the theme originally presented in E♭ major returns in that same key (m. 166) rather than in the tonic. Only later does the first theme finally return to reestablish the tonic (m. 194). A coda (m. 208–264) introduces yet another new theme. Given so many deviations from the conventions of sonata form, it would be misleading to say that Chopin's G minor Ballade is "in sonata form." At the same time, it would be wrong to deny altogether that it reflects the influence of sonata form. Many 19th-century instrumental works share this kind of formal ambiguity, simultaneously operating within and pushing beyond the conventions of established forms.

It was long believed that Chopin based each of his four Ballades on one of the poetic ballads of the 19th-century Polish poet Adam Mickiewicz, but no evidence supports this belief. The G minor Ballade nevertheless projects a strong sense of narrative direction. The powerful unison opening is a call to attention, and the rhythmic regularity of the subsequent moderato (m. 8–32) conveys a sense of metered verse. Each section of the work embodies a particular affect, moving from the resigned (m. 8–32) to lyrical (m. 68–93), ecstatic (m. 106–124) to agitated (m. 124–137), waltz-like (m. 138–154) to furious (m. 208–242). The cataclysmic conclusion (m. 244–end), with its abrupt ending, brings to mind the abrupt and tragic end of Goethe's well-known poetic ballad Erlkönig (see Anthology No. 121a for Schubert's setting).

The galop was a fashionable group dance of the mid-19th century that moved at a lively pace, with steady accents on both the first and third beat of every duple measure. In keeping with the genre's origins in dance, Liszt constructs this "Galop of the Ball" around units of 4, 8, and 16 measures. But the unprepared harmonic deflection to ♭VI in m. 17 adds a nice twist against the rhythmic regularity, as does the chromatic instability over a pedal point tonic toward the end.

131 Carnaval, Op. 9 (excerpts) (1835)
Robert Schumann

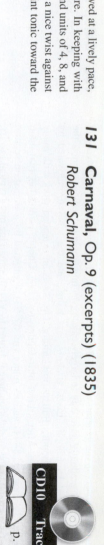

CD10 · Track 31 · p. 445

Papillons.

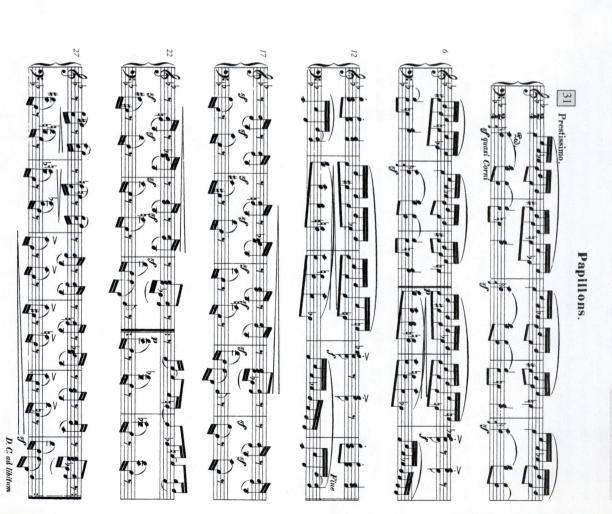

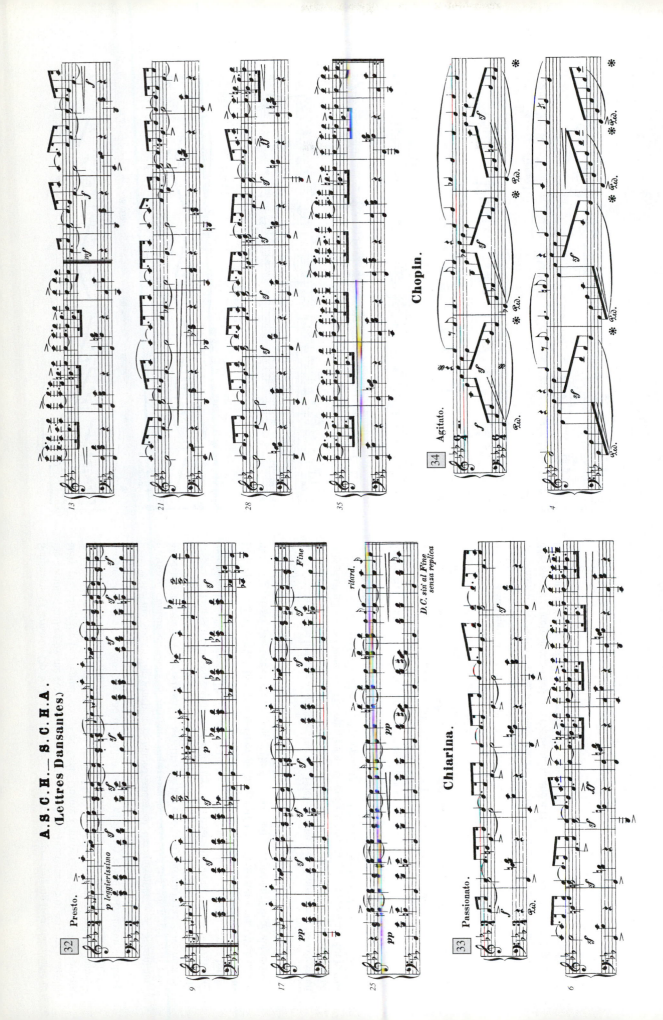

Chopin.

Chiarina.

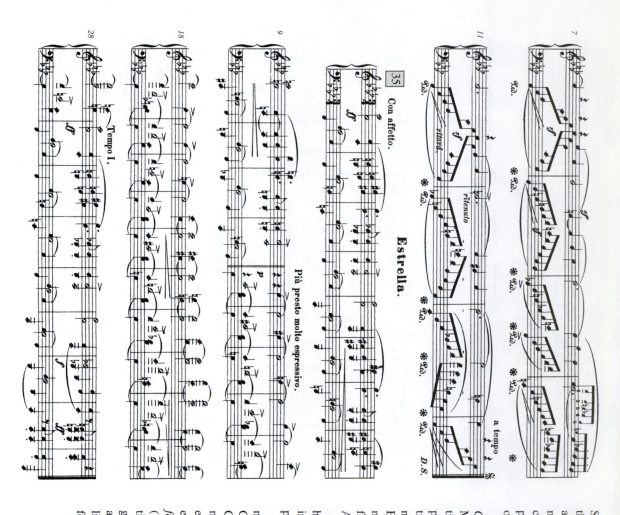

Schumann's *Carnaval*, Op. 9 (1835), is a cycle of character pieces ranging from the simple to the complex, linked by the common theme of Carnival, the brief season of revelry immediately preceding the penitential season of Lent. During Carnival—whose only high-profile manifestation in the United States today is the Mardi Gras celebration in New Orleans—conventional social standards are set aside. In Schumann's time it was perfectly acceptable for people to go about in costume and do behind masks what they could only dream of doing openly.

Like the season for which it is named, many of the movement's of Schumann's *Carnaval* contain elements of intrigue, impersonation, excess, and downright nonsense. Musically, the entire cycle is based on a riddle, the key to which is given in the movement entitled "Sphinxes." In Greek mythology, the sphinx was a creature who posed a riddle to passersby, killing those who couldn't solve it. Here, Schumann presents a series of brief motivic ideas in archaic breves. The key to the riddle is to be found in the German names for the notes of each motivic idea. Adding "s" to any note name in German designates it as flat. Thus Eb is "Es" and Ab is "As." In addition, Germans designate B♮ with the letter "H." With this in mind, we can see that one of the sequences (Eb-C-B-A) spells "Schumann" in an abbreviated form (Es=S,C,H,A) and the other two (Ab-C-B and A-Eb-C-B) spell "Asch" (As,C,H and A,S,C,H).

"Asch" is the hometown of Ernestine von Fricken, who was Schumann's fiancée when he wrote *Carnaval*. Schumann embeds the second and third sequences of notes throughout the individual pieces in *Carnaval*. The opening notes in the upper part of "Papillons," for example, are A, Eb, C, and Cb(= B♮ = H). The opening of "Chiarina" is Ab, C, B♮ (=H).

As the Sphinxes suggest, *Carnaval* is an autobiographical work: Schumann uses the mask of music to say things he would not otherwise have ventured to acknowledge openly. Consider, for example, the trio of movements labeled "Chiarina," "Chopin," and "Estrella." Chiarina was the nickname of the fifteen-year-old Clara Wieck, the daughter of his own former piano teacher. Schumann would later marry Clara, but when he wrote *Carnaval* he was engaged to Ernestine, whose nickname was Estrella. In a gesture clearly anticipating the inevitable end of his engagement to Ernestine, Schumann marks "Estrella" to be played *con affetto* ("with affection") and, in pointed contrast, marks "Chiarina" to be played *passionate* ("passionately"). The two women in question surely grasped the significance of these indications. The two movements are mediated by one named after Chopin, a composer Schumann greatly admired, who had paid personal visits to both Clara and Robert in September 1835. In an imitation of Chopin's style, the piece titled "Chopin" has a graceful and soaring melodic line, an elaborately arpeggiated accompaniment, and a clear homophonic texture. It also offers plenty of opportunity for *tempo rubato* in performance.

132 Nuages gris (1881)
Liszt

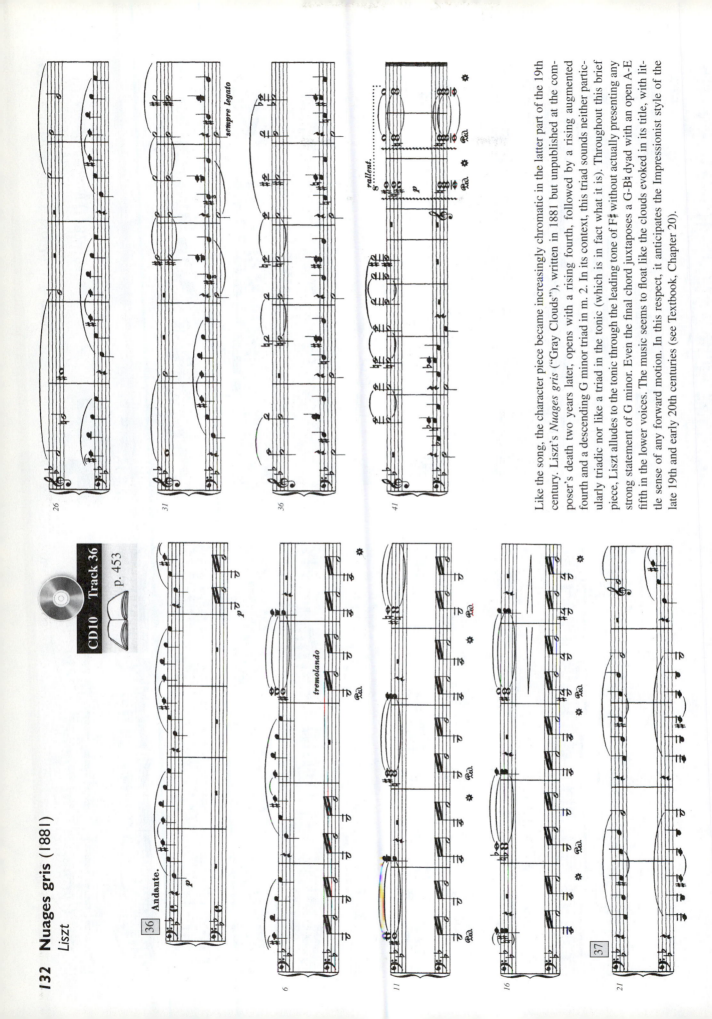

Like the song, the character piece became increasingly chromatic in the latter part of the 19th century. Liszt's *Nuages gris* ("Gray Clouds"), written in 1881 but unpublished at the composer's death two years later, opens with a rising fourth, followed by a rising augmented fourth and a descending G minor triad in m. 2. In its context, this triad sounds neither particularly triadic nor like a triad in the tonic (which is in fact what it is). Throughout this brief piece, Liszt alludes to the tonic through the leading tone of F♯ without actually presenting any strong statement of G minor. Even the final chord juxtaposes a G-B♭ dyad with an open A-E fifth in the lower voices. The music seems to float like the clouds evoked in its title, with little sense of any forward motion. In this respect, it anticipates the Impressionist style of the late 19th and early 20th centuries (see Textbook, Chapter 20).

241

133 Caprices, Op. 1, No. 24, in A minor

(ca. 1810)

Niccolò Paganini (1782–1840)

Companion CD
Track 15
p. 454

XXIV.

Tema.
Quasi Presto.

Var. 1.

Var. 2.

Var. 3.

D.C. al Fine.

Edition Peters.

63386

Var. 4.

Var. 5.

Var. 6.

Var. 7.

Var. 8.

Edition Peters.

63386

Paganini's *Caprices*, Op. 1 (published in 1820 but probably written at least a decade before), are 24 in number and pay homage to a set of 24 caprices published by Pietro Locatelli, an earlier violin virtuoso, in 1733. The last of Paganini's 24 caprices makes an unusually wide variety of technical demands on the violinist. Formally, it is a set of variations on a theme, with each variation highlighting a particular technique:

- Variation 1: Spiccato arpeggiation. This technique involves bouncing the bow lightly on the string.
- Variation 2: Bariolage. The rapid and repeated alternation between two adjacent strings, one open, the other fingered.
- Variation 3: Octaves. Because the violin does not feature fixed pitches, like a piano, octaves require absolutely perfect placement of two fingers in relation to each other.
- Variation 4: High chromatic passages. The higher the hand moves on the fingerboard, the smaller the physical space between the finger placements of the individual notes.
- Variation 5: String crossing. This variation requires the player to move quite rapidly between strings.
- Variation 6: Thirds and octaves. Again, both pitches must be perfectly fingered.
- Variation 7: Bowing. The player must pick up and replace the bow in a downstroke rapidly in succession while playing a triplet figure that moves through all registers of the instrument.
- Variation 8: Triple stopping. The performer rolls a series of chords on three different notes, each played on a different string.
- Variation 9: Harmonics. The small circle above the notes indicate that the finger is to be placed at the appropriate point on the string but not depressed; the resulting sound has a hollow timbre at a pitch two octaves higher than that of the pitch indicated.
- Variation 10: High position. The performer must execute rapid runs in a very high register.
- Variation 11: Successive double stops.
- Finale: Long runs and successive double stops.

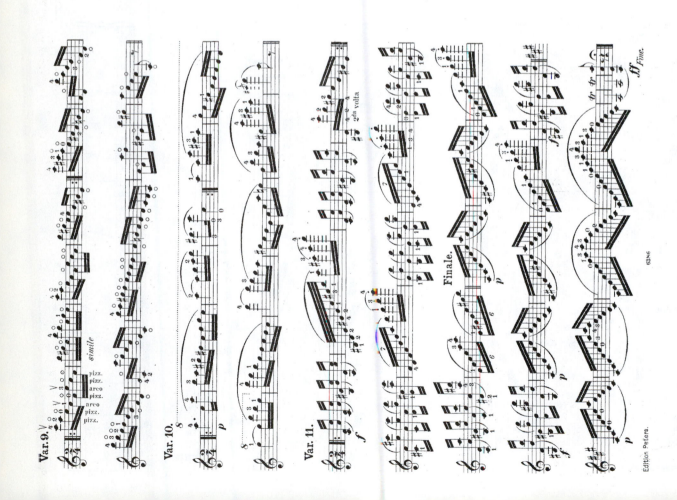

134 Etudes d'exécution transcendante, No. 1 in C Major (1838; revised 1851)

Franz Liszt (1811–1886)

Companion CD
Track 16
p. 455

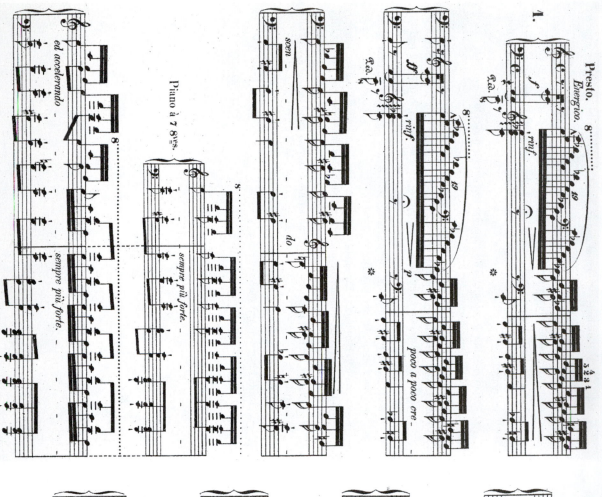

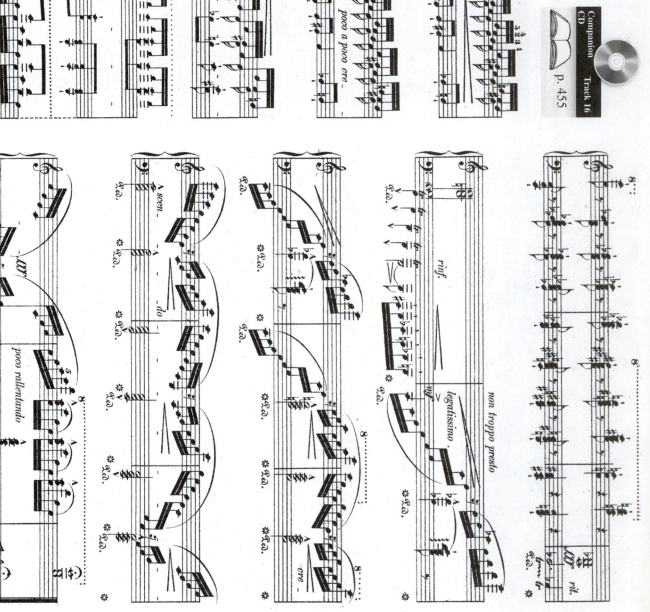

135 The Banjo (1855)
Louis Moreau Gottschalk (1829–1869)

Liszt's *Etudes d'exécution transcendante*, as their title suggests, require a technical facility that transcends the ordinary. The first of these etudes, in C major, clearly fits into the tradition of C major works that open large, systematically ordered sets: Bach's C Major Prelude in the *Well-Tempered Clavier* (Anthology No. 95), Chopin's C Major Prelude in his *Preludes*, Op. 24 (Anthology No. 128), as well as the opening C Major Etude in Chopin's *Etudes* for piano, Op. 10. (Liszt follows the same pattern in these etudes that Chopin had used in his preludes: a circle of descending fifths in the major keys, with each major-mode work followed by one in the relative minor.) But from the perspective of technical demands, Liszt's opening salvo in these "Transcendental" etudes leaves all earlier works in its wake. Robert Schumann, reviewing an earlier version of these etudes, called them "studies in storm and dread . . . fit for ten or twelve players in the world."

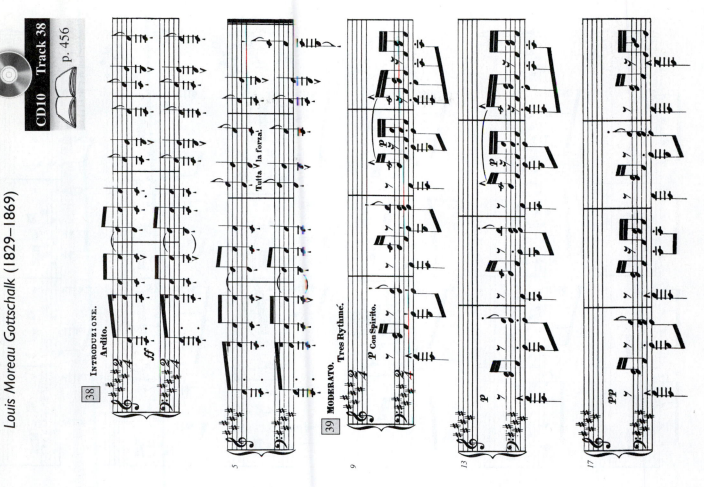

p. 456

245

No. 135 Gottschalk: The Banjo

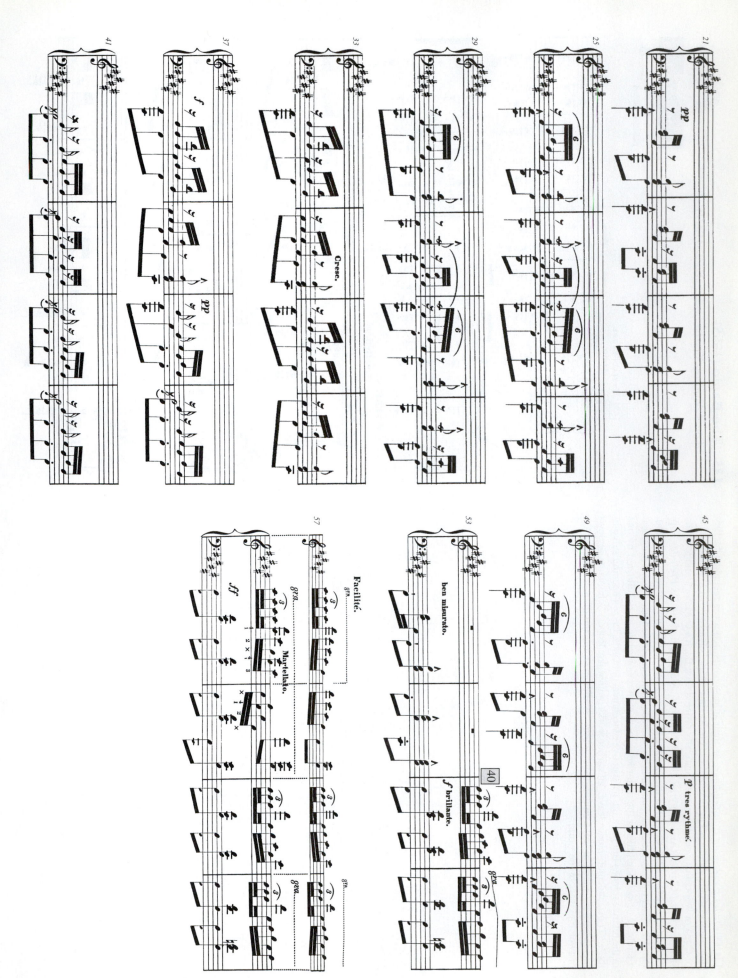

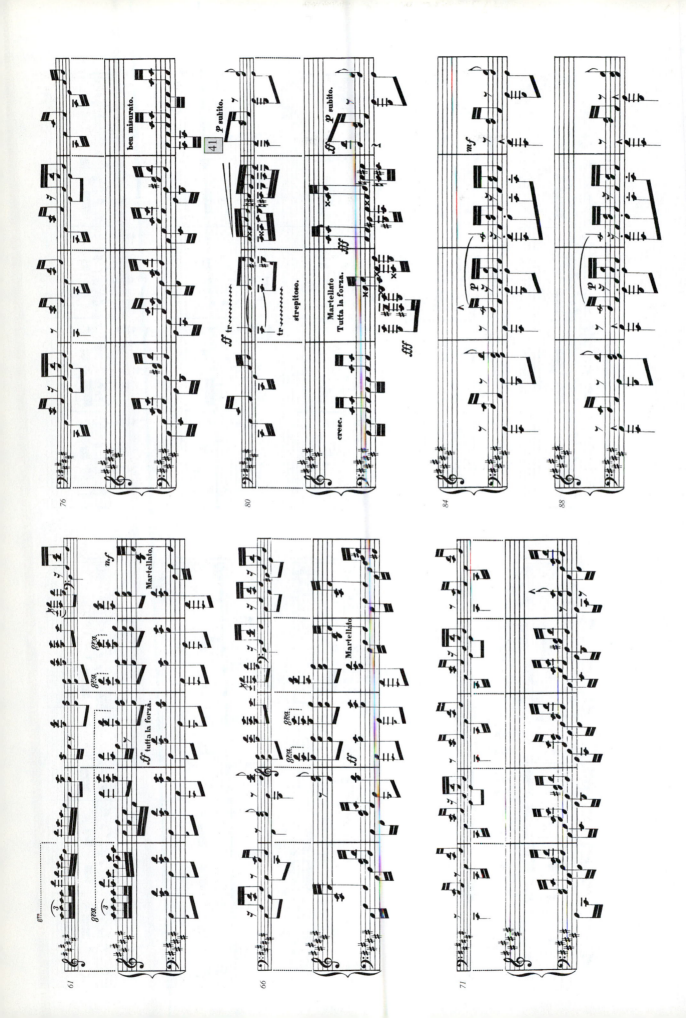

No. 135 Gottschalk: *The Banjo*

■ No. 135 Gottschalk: The Banjo

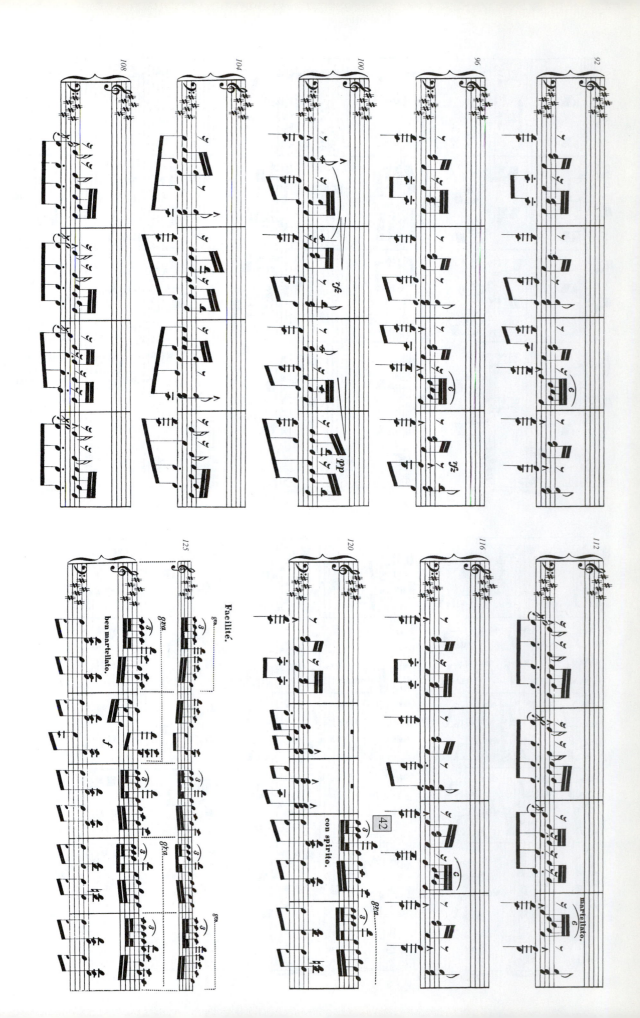

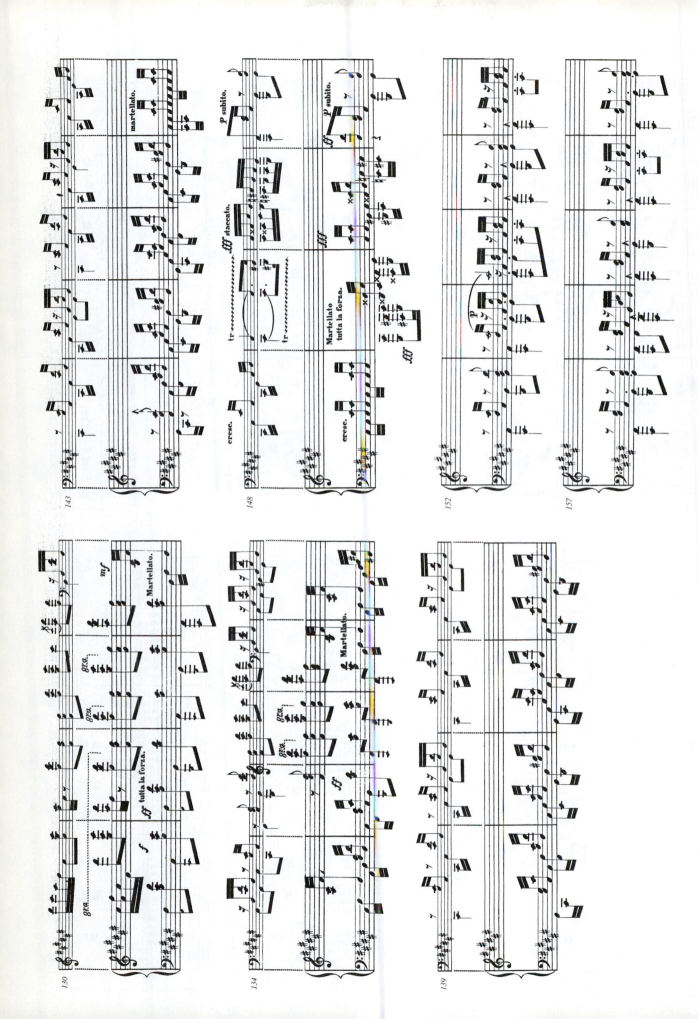

No. 135 Gottschalk: *The Banjo*

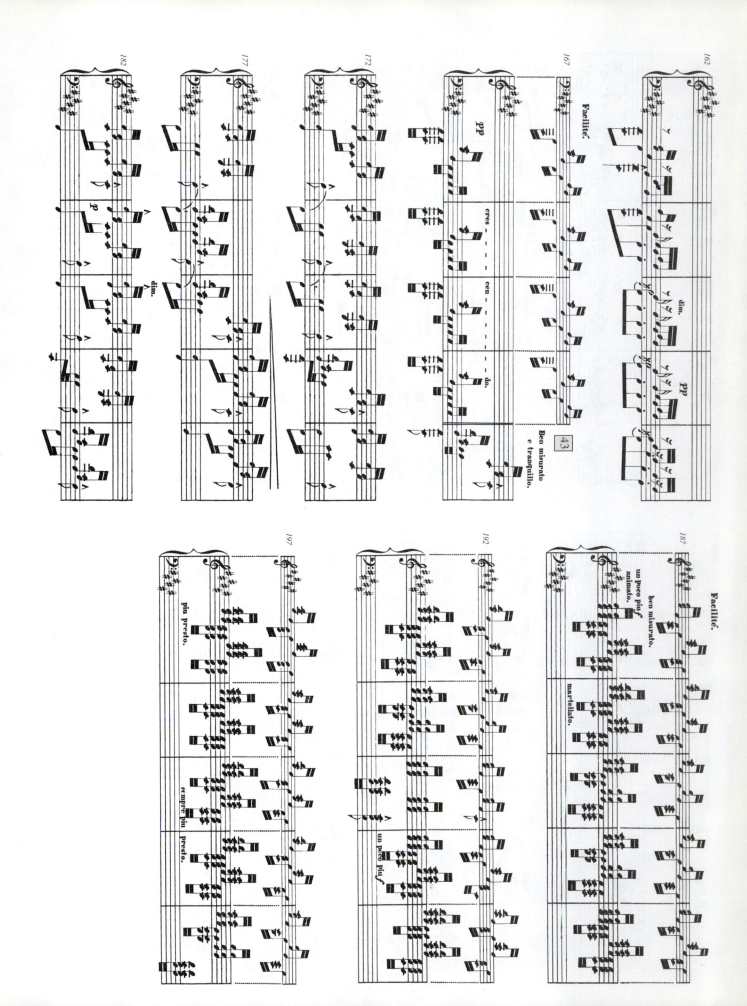

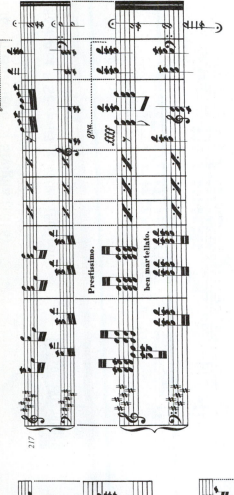

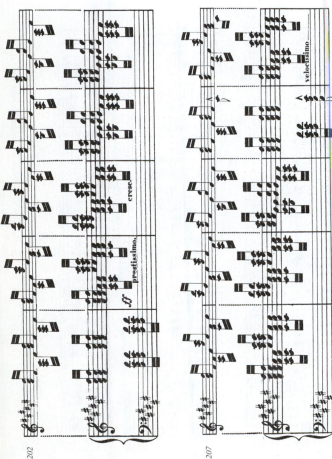

Gottschalk's *The Banjo* captures on the piano the idiomatic vitality of the banjo, that quintessentially American instrument. The music's constant strumming rhythms and jaunty syncopations anticipate the ragtime style that would become popular in the United States a few decades later (see Textbook, Chapter 20). Subtitled "An American Sketch," the work incorporates a clever reference to Stephen Foster's immensely popular song *The Camptown Races*, the theme of which begins to creep in around m. 178, blossoms shortly thereafter, and then is swallowed up in the volley of rapid-fire "strumming" that ends the work. In a concession to public sales, Gottschalk at various points offers alternative, slightly easier ways of performing some of the work's more difficult passages; these are marked "Facilité" in the score and notated above the standard line of music.

136 Il Barbiere di Siviglia (1816)

Gioacchino Rossini (1792–1868)

136a Act I, Scene 2, cavatina (Figaro):
"Largo al factotum"

CD10 Track 44 P. 459

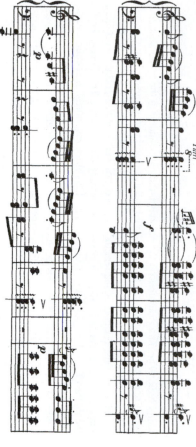

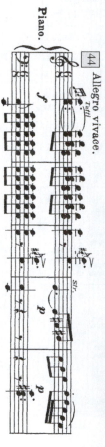

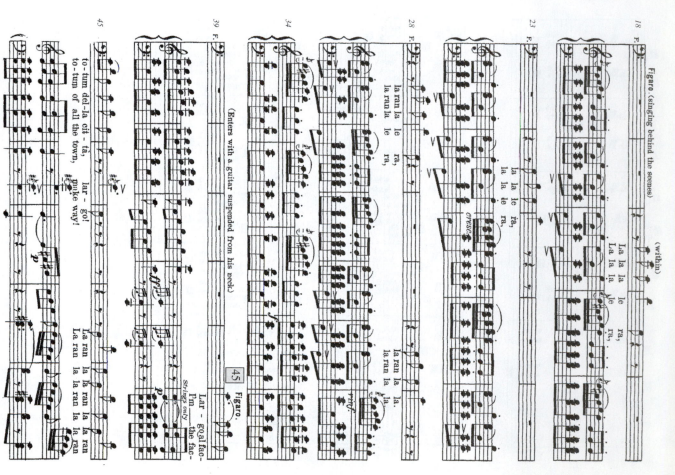

Note: This edition is a piano-vocal reduction of Rossini's original score for voices and orchestra.

No. 136 Rossini: *Il Barbiere di Siviglia*

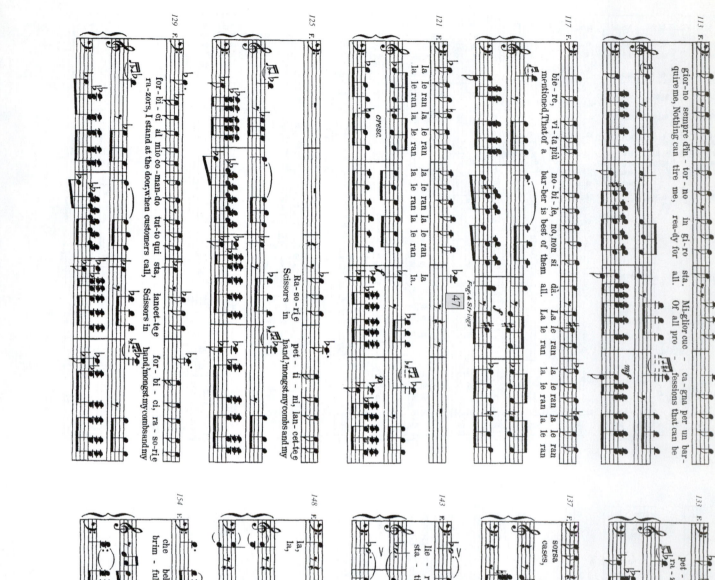

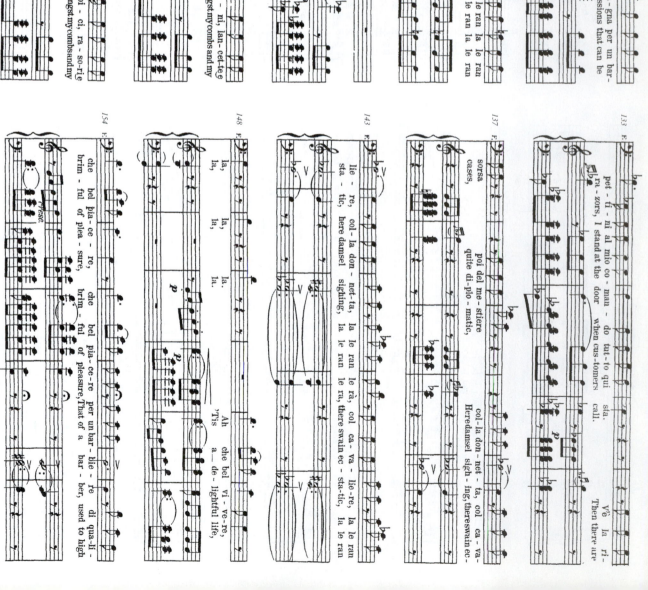

No. 136 Rossini: *Il Barbiere di Siviglia*

255

136b Act I, Scene 5, cavatina (Rosina): "Una voce poco fa"

A room in the house of Dr. Bartolo. The windows closed with Venetian blinds. Rosina has a letter in her hand.

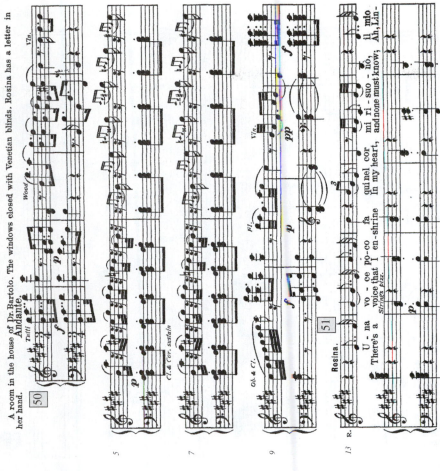

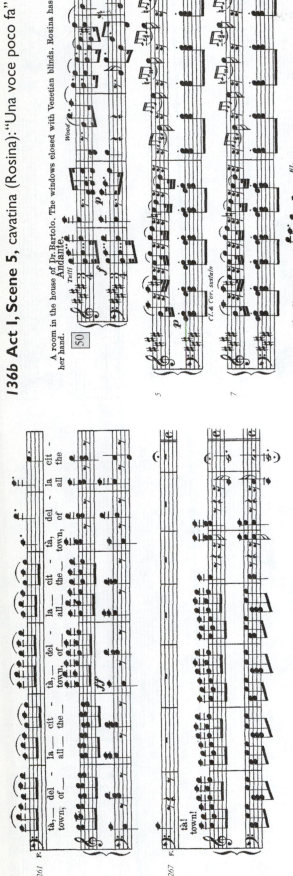

No. 136 Rossini: *Il Barbiere di Siviglia*

No. 136 Rossini: *Il Barbiere di Siviglia*

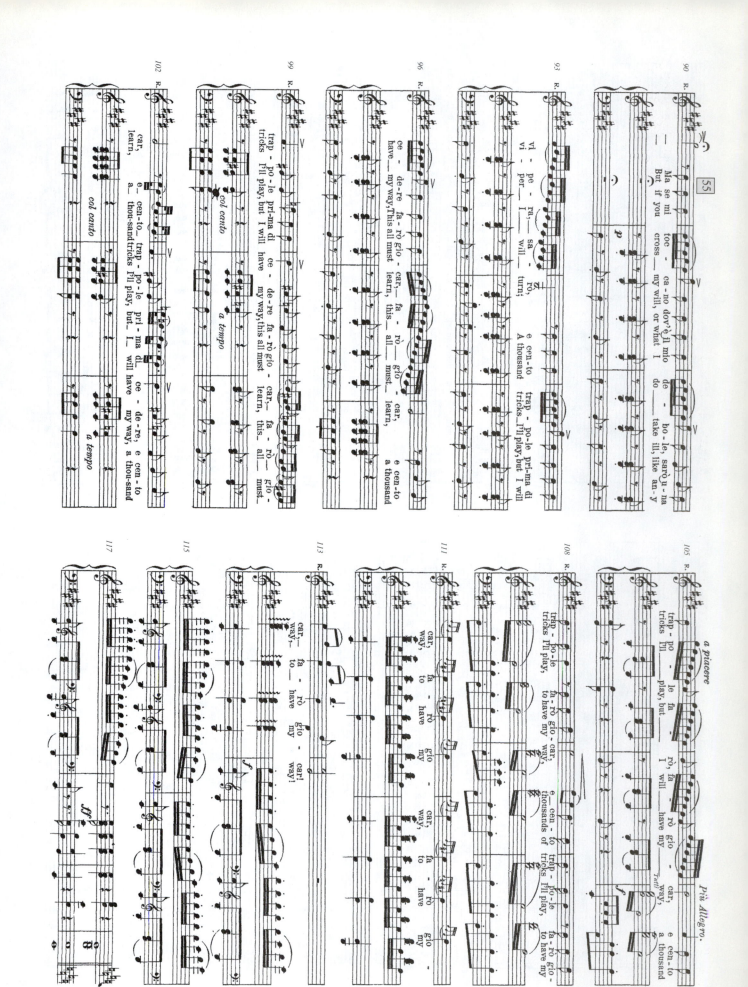

p. 459

CD11 · Track 1

Rossini's *Il Barbiere di Siviglia* ("The Barber of Seville") narrates a series of intrigues that entangle a nobleman (Count Almaviva) who, disguised as the poor student "Lindoro," seeks to win the affections of a beautiful young woman (Rosina), who stands under the watchful eye of her guardian, the prim and proper Doctor Bartolo. The town's barber, Figaro, acts as a go-between for the many complications of the plot.

Figaro's opening number, *Largo al factotum* ("Make way for the factotum"), does a marvelous job introducing the title character. He half complains, half boasts that his services are in such demand among people of quality that he is always busy. Constantly repeating the same lines of text, Figaro works himself into frenzy, imitating people calling him—"Figaro! Figaro!"—in that famous three note melody (m. 187–192) that has come to be indelibly associated with his character. "One at a time!" he half shouts to himself in response.

Rosina's *Una voce poco fa* ("A voice a short while ago") is very much in the *bel canto* tradition and draws an equally sharp characterization. Like many arias of this period, it consists of two sections, a slow opening and a lively conclusion, known as the *cabaletta*. Rosina sings while writing a letter to Lindoro—who is in fact Count Almaviva in disguise. After declaring Lindoro her chosen suitor, she professes to be "docile, respectful, and obedient." The music, however, gives the lie to this claim, changing from reserved to lively and spontaneous in the cabaletta, as she goes on to sing: "But if you push me the wrong way, I'll be a viper, and the last laugh will be on you." By the time she returns to her profession of docility, the feistiness of the music has infected the orchestra, leaving no doubt that the music, not the words, represents Rosina's true character.

The performance. Note the considerable liberties the singers take with the written notation, particularly in Rosina's aria (for example, at m. 32–42 and 89–98). This is part of the *bel canto* tradition, in which singers were expected to embellish their parts, often quite elaborately. At times, the music calls out for embellishment, as at the cadenza-like high G♯ with the fermata at m. 90. But even seemingly florid passages (such as m. 39–40) are fair game for alteration. This practice prevailed during Rossini's era and has continued down to the present day. Different recordings of the same aria readily demonstrate that virtually every singer uses Rossini's notation more as a point of departure than as something to be followed precisely.

137 Rigoletto (1851)
Giuseppe Verdi (1813–1901)
137a Act I (excerpts)

ATTO PRIMO. PRELUDIO ED INTRODUZIONE.

PRELUDIO.

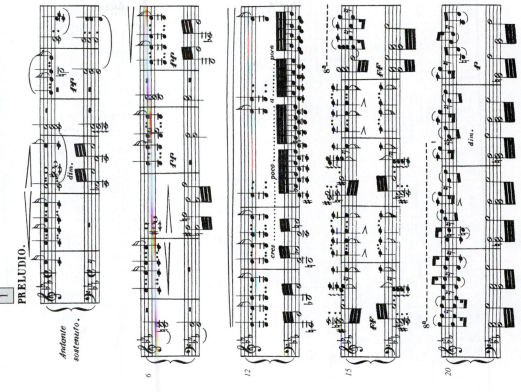

Note: This edition is a piano-vocal reduction of Verdi's original score for voices and orchestra.

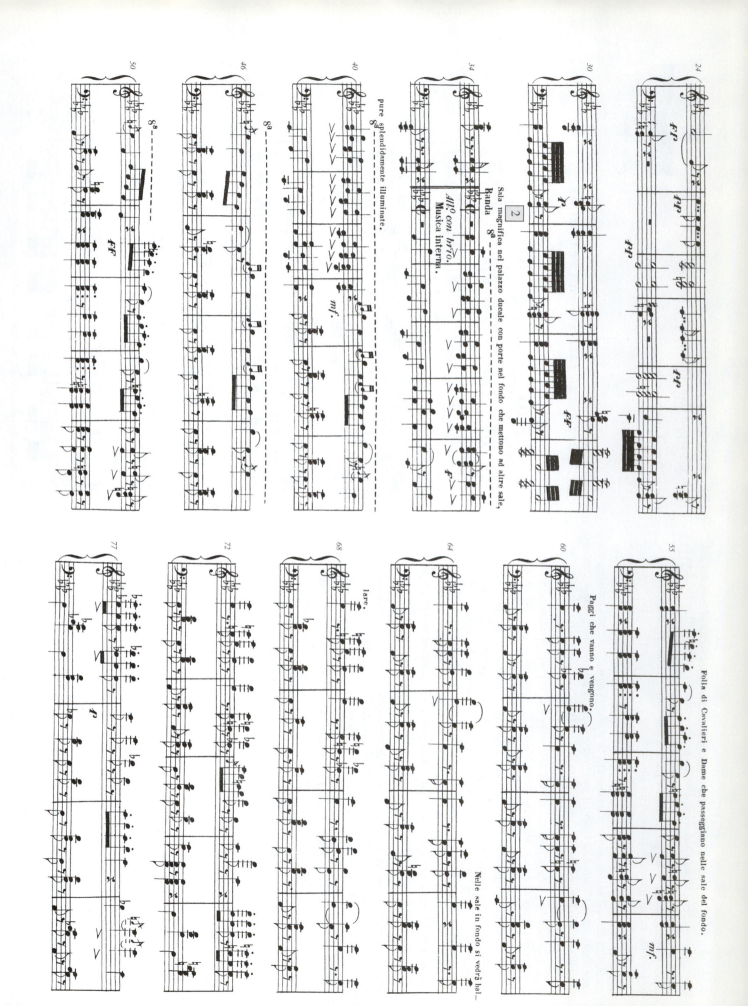

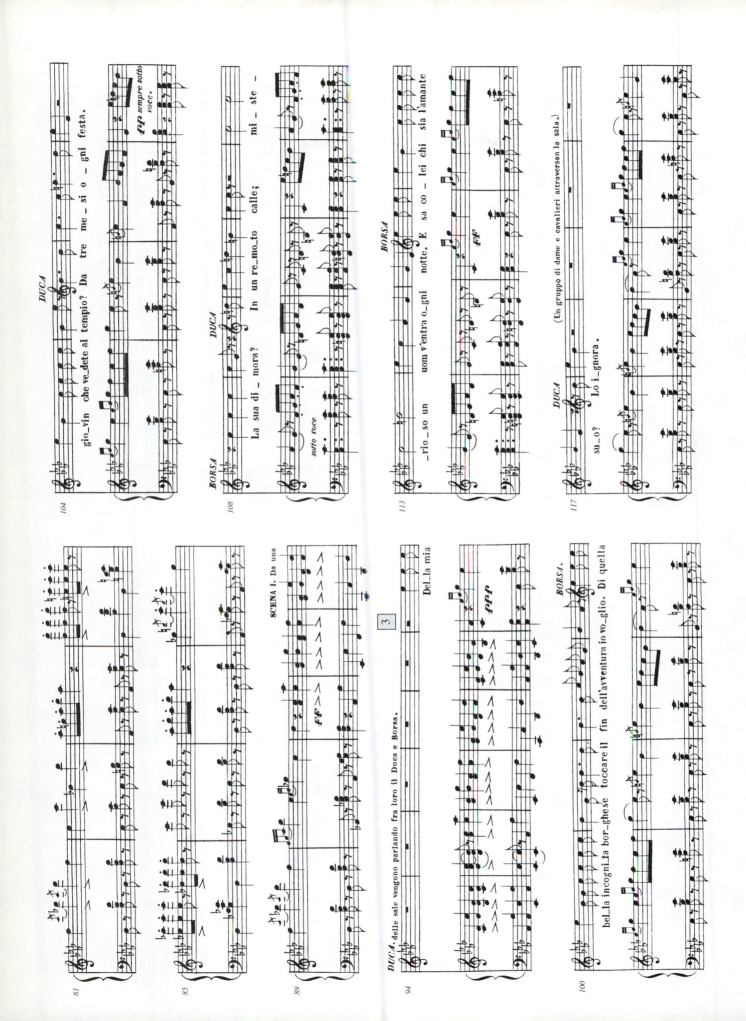

No. 137 Verdi: *Rigoletto*

BALLATA

ATTO I. SEGUITO della SCENA I.

4

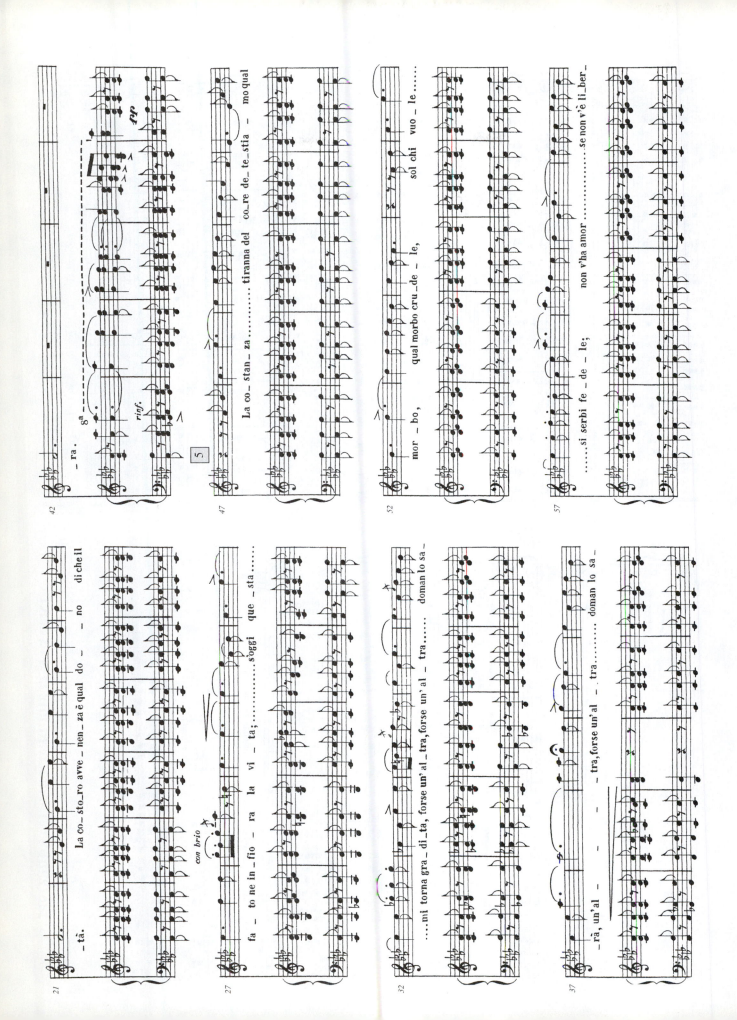

No. 137 Verdi: *Rigoletto*

No. 137 Verdi: Rigoletto

MINUETTO E PERIGODINO NELL'INTRODUZIONE.

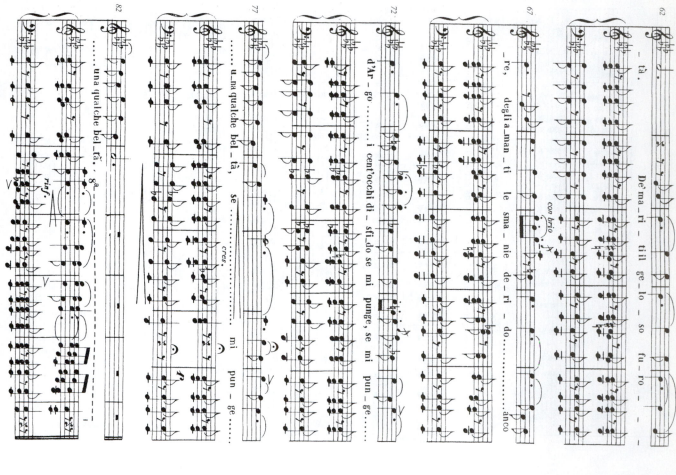

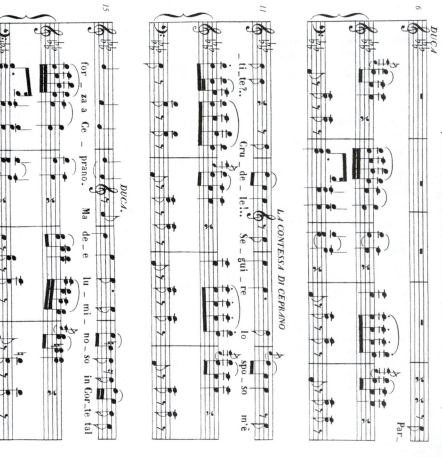

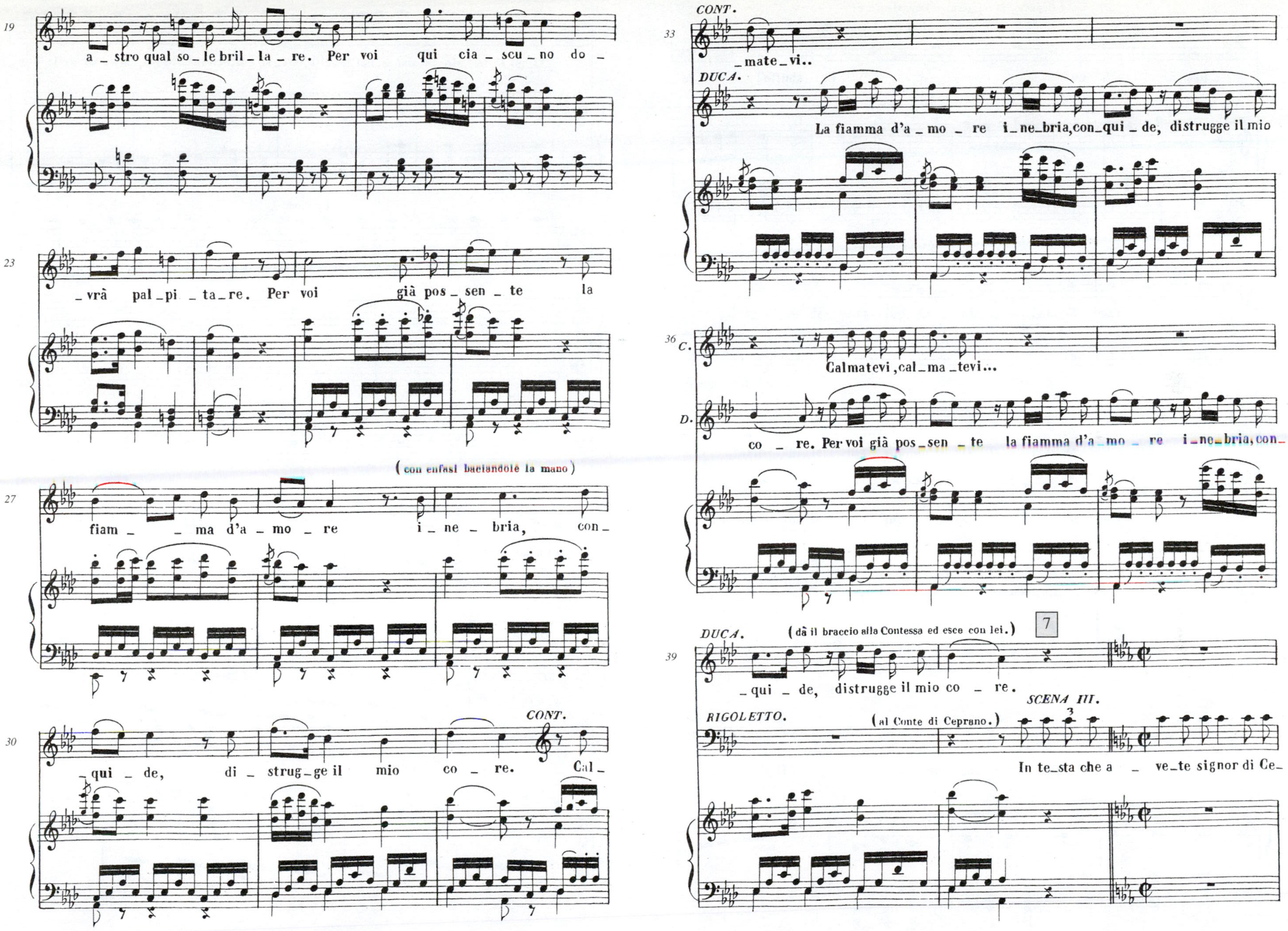
a _ stro qual so _ le bril _ la _ re. Per voi qui cia _ scu _ no do _
_ vrà pal _ pi _ ta _ re. Per voi già pos _ sen _ te la
(con enfasi baciandole la mano)
fiam _ _ ma d'a _ mo _ re i _ ne _ bria, con _
CONT.
_ qui _ de, di _ strug _ ge il mio co _ re. Cal _
_ mate _ vi..
DUCA.
La fiamma d'a _ mo _ re i_ne_bria,con_qui _ de, distrugge il mio
C.
Calmatevi, cal _ ma _ tevi...
D.
co _ re. Per voi già pos _ sen _ te la fiamma d'a _ mo _ re i _ ne _ bria, con _
(dà il braccio alla Contessa ed esce con lei.)
7
_ qui _ de, distrugge il mio co _ re.
SCENA III.
RIGOLETTO.
(al Conte di Ceprano.)
In te_sta che a _ ve_te signor di Ce_

No. 137 Verdi: Rigoletto

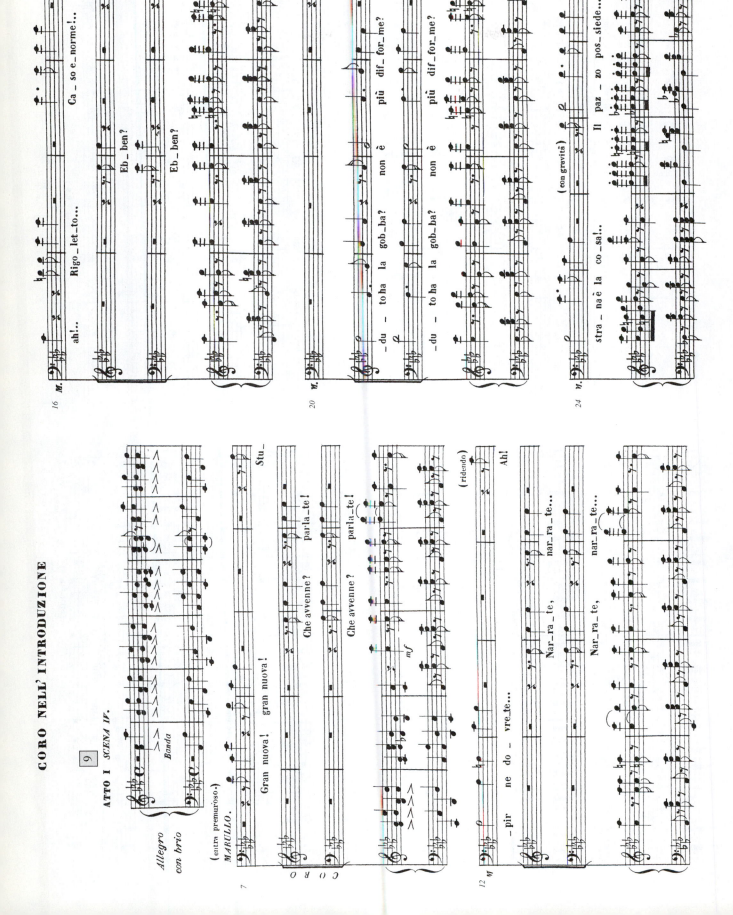

No. 137 Verdi: *Rigoletto*

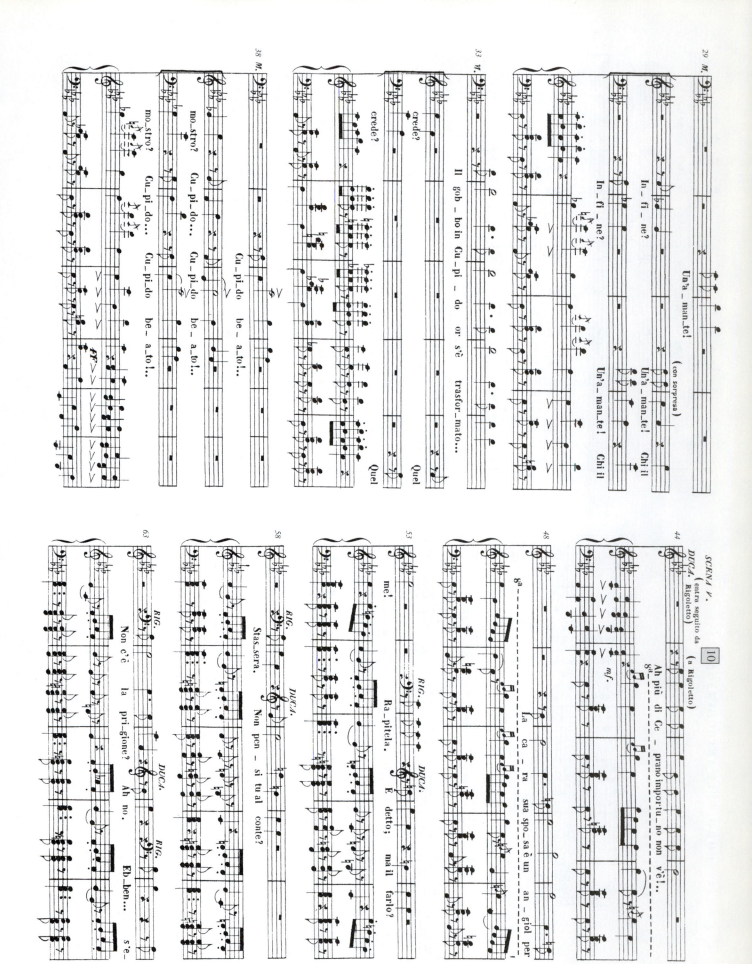

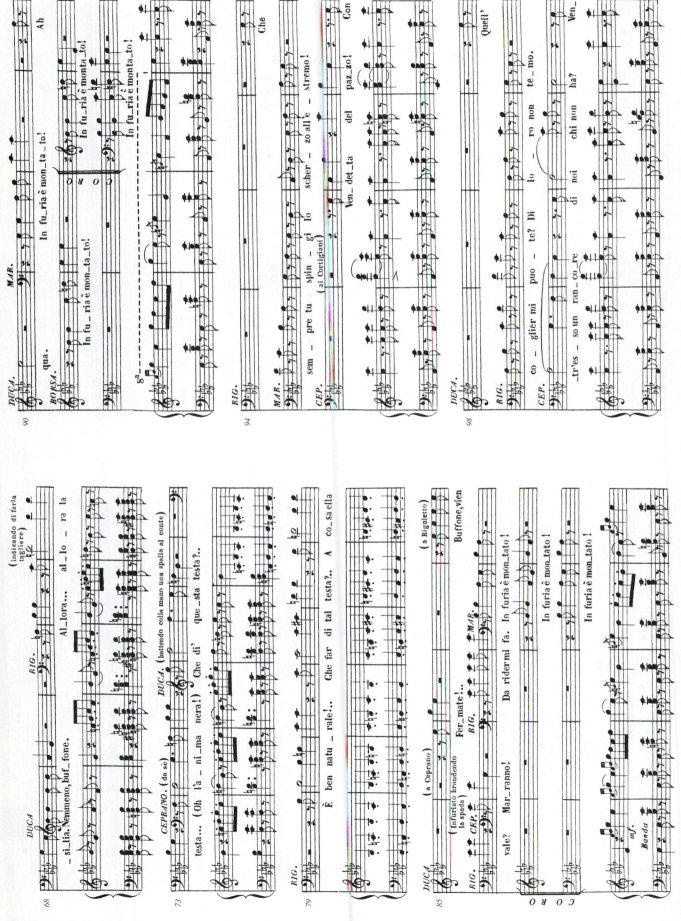

No. 137 Verdi: Rigoletto

No. 137 Verdi: *Rigoletto*

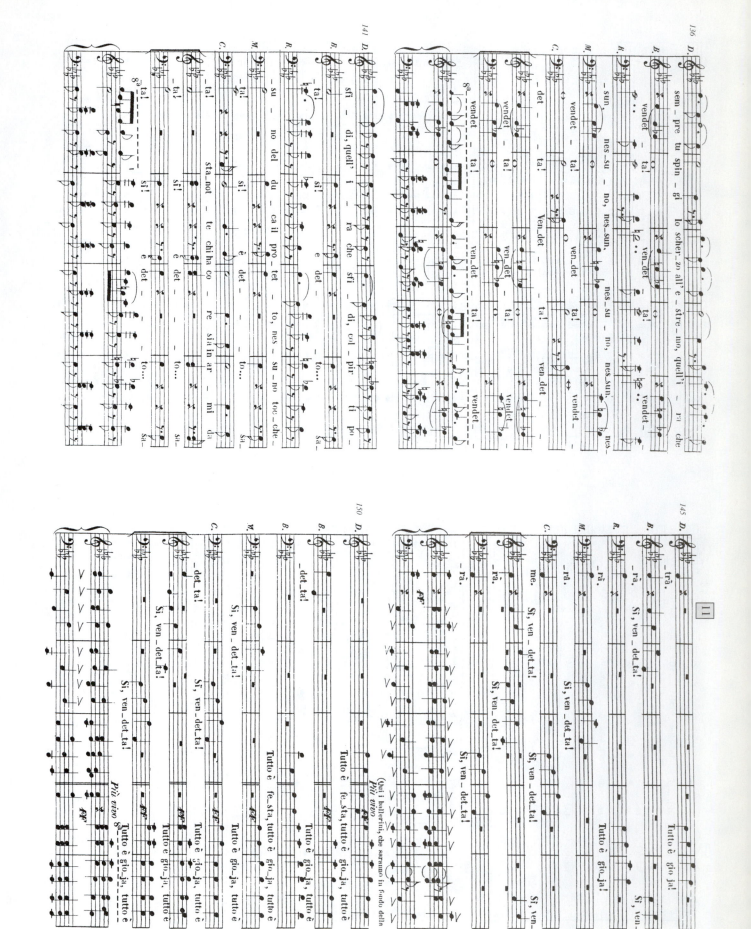

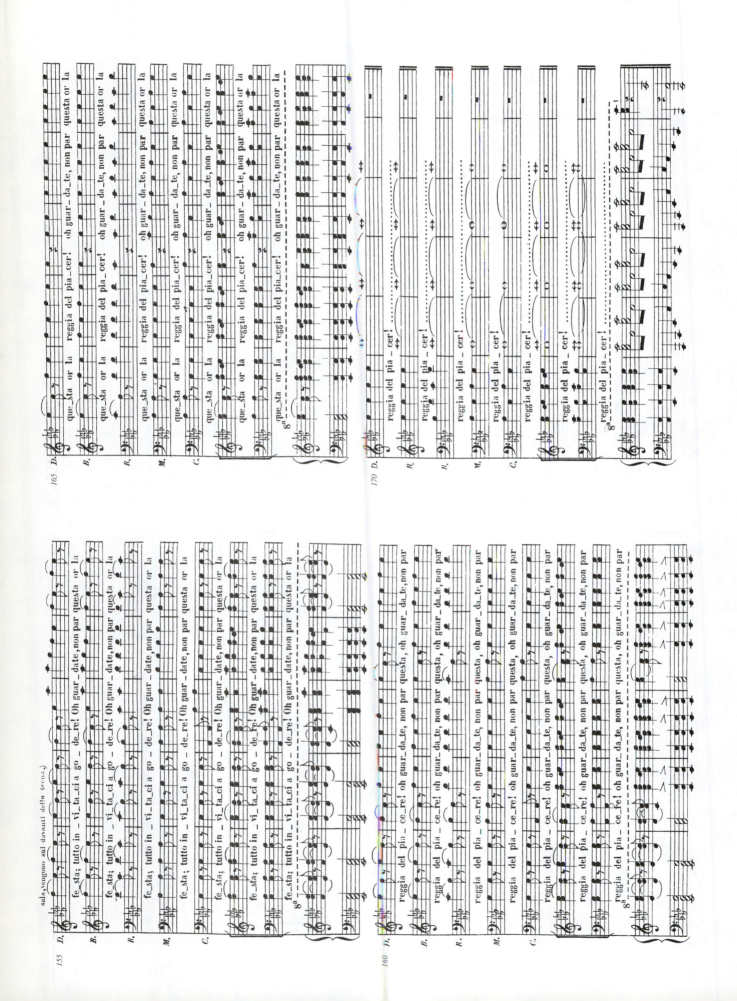

No. 137 Verdi: *Rigoletto*

SEGUITO E STRETTA DELL' INTRODUZIONE.

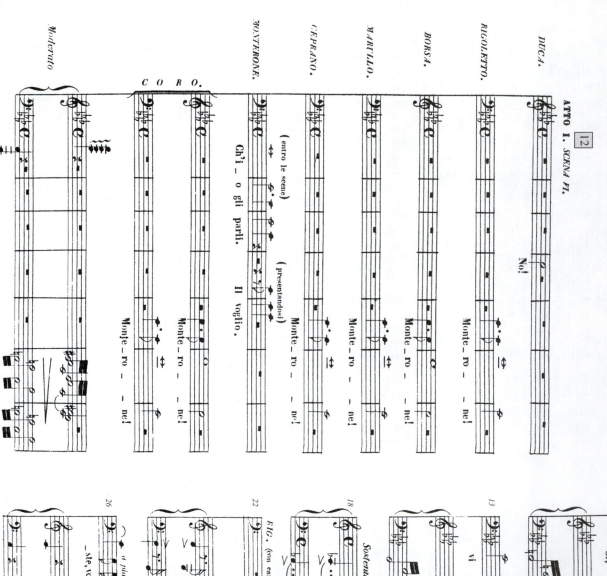

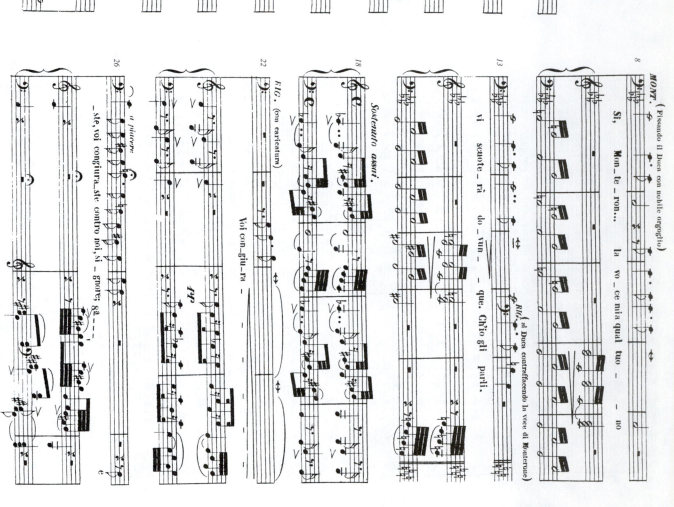

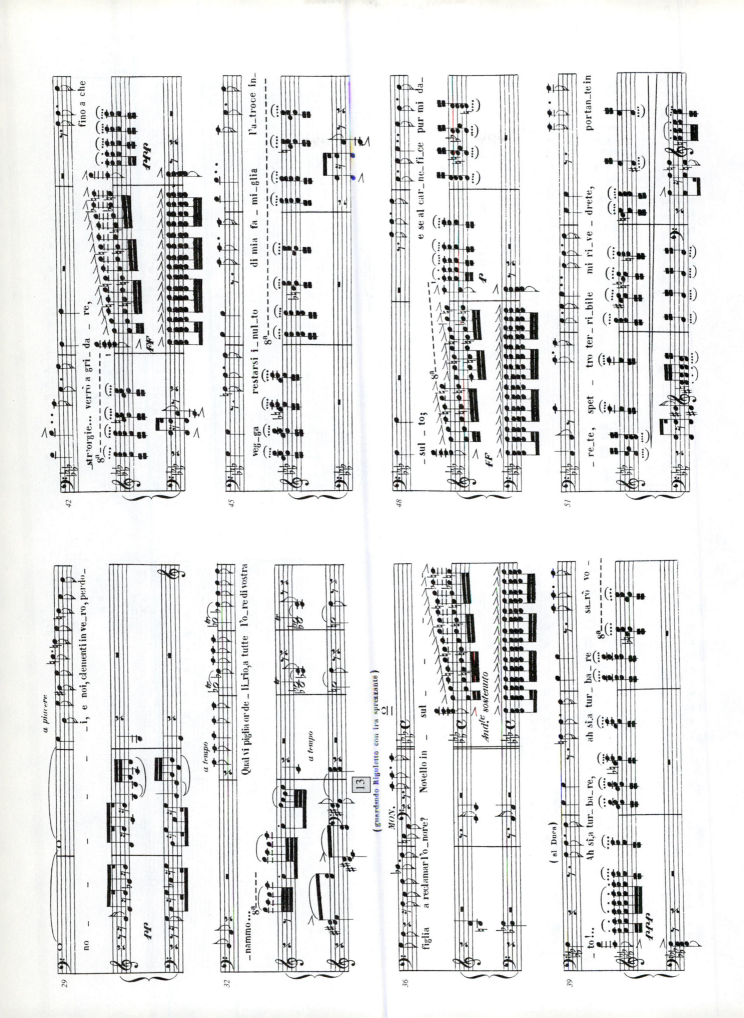

No. 137 Verdi: *Rigoletto*

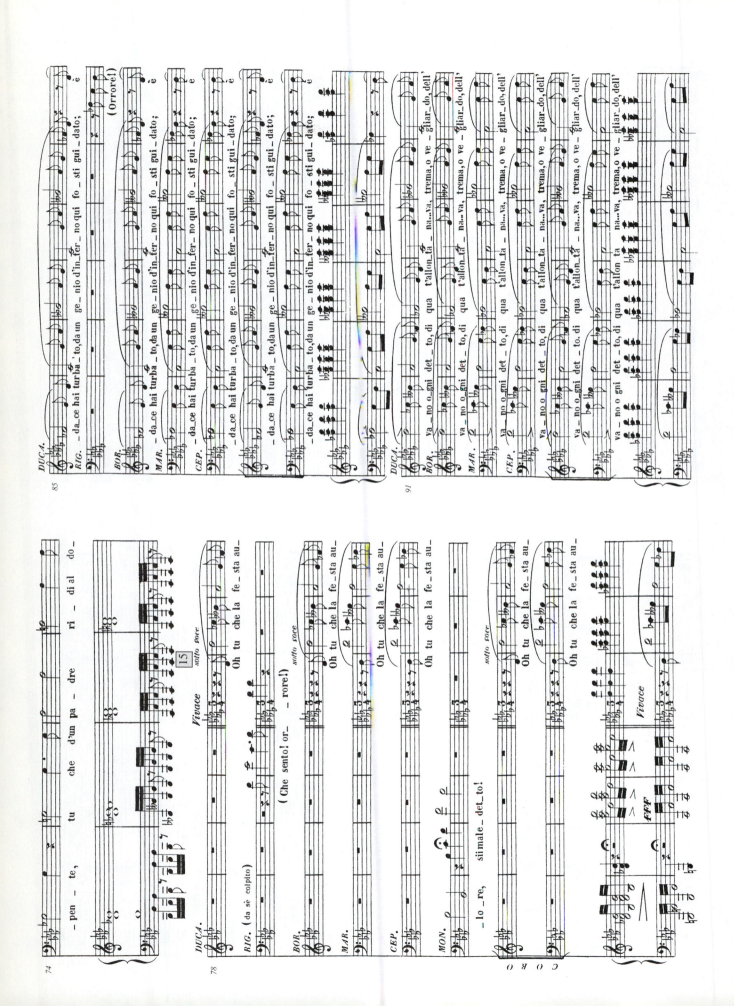

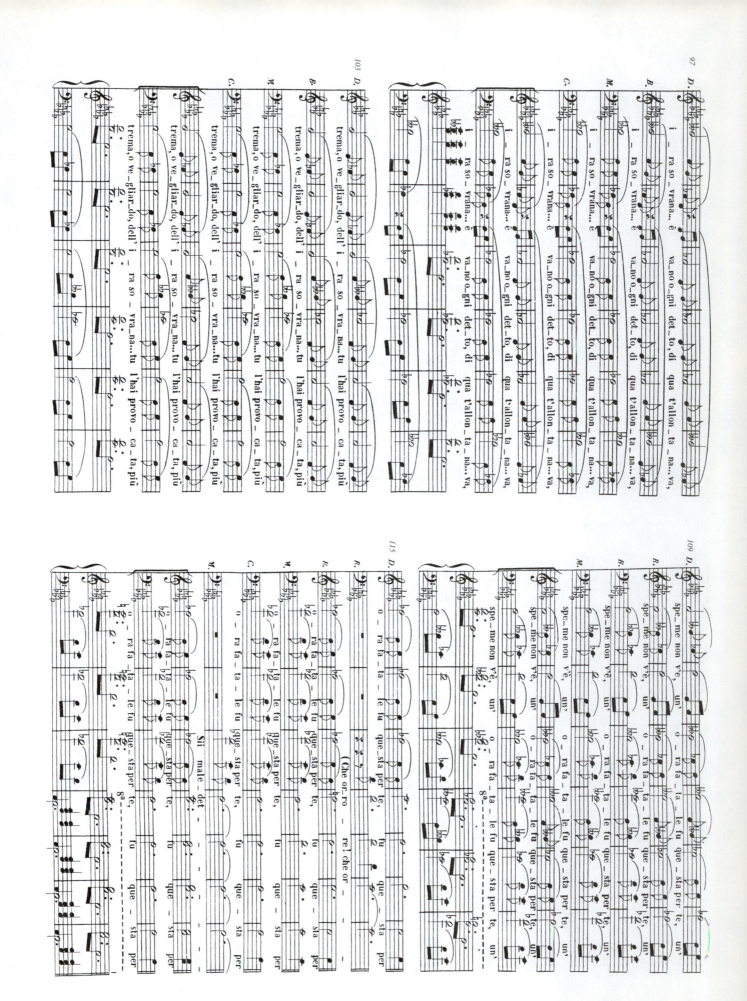

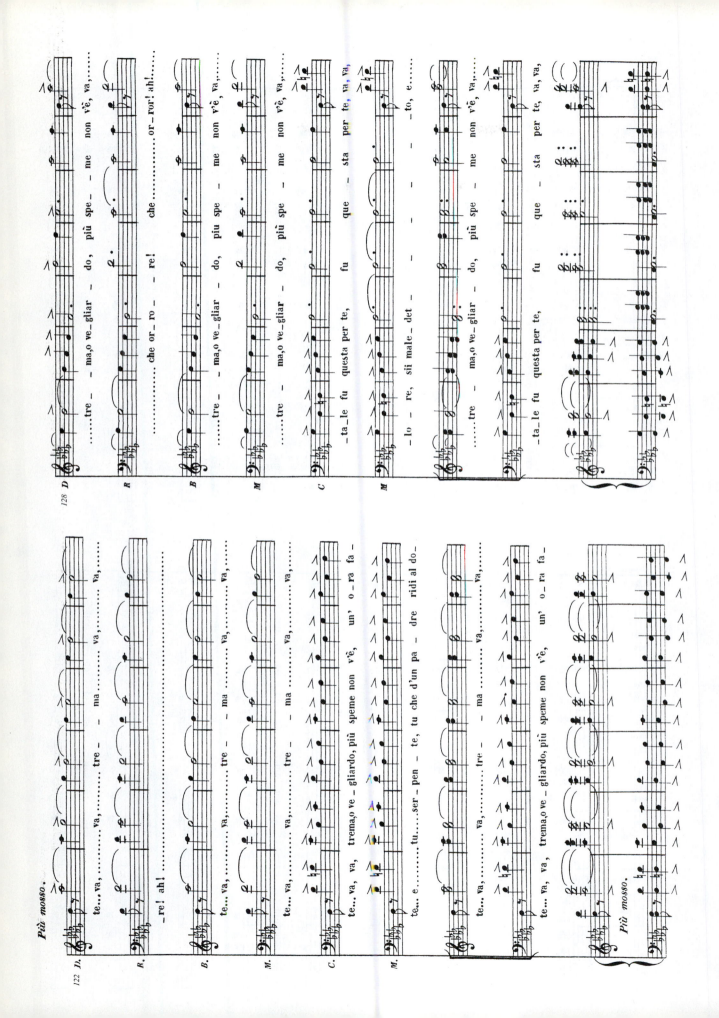

No. 137 Verdi: *Rigoletto*

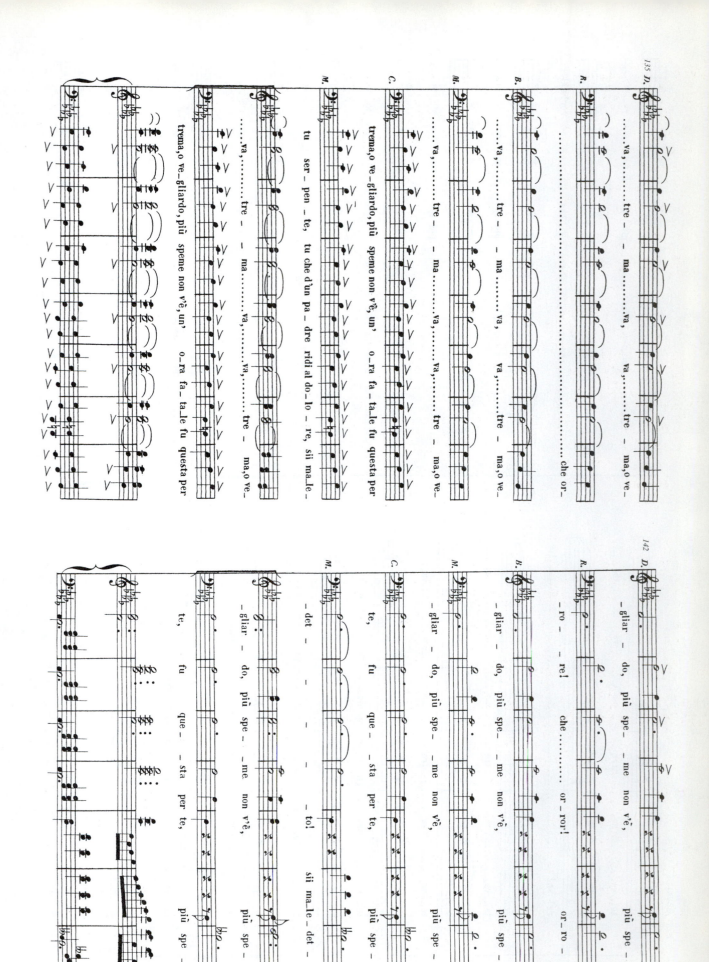

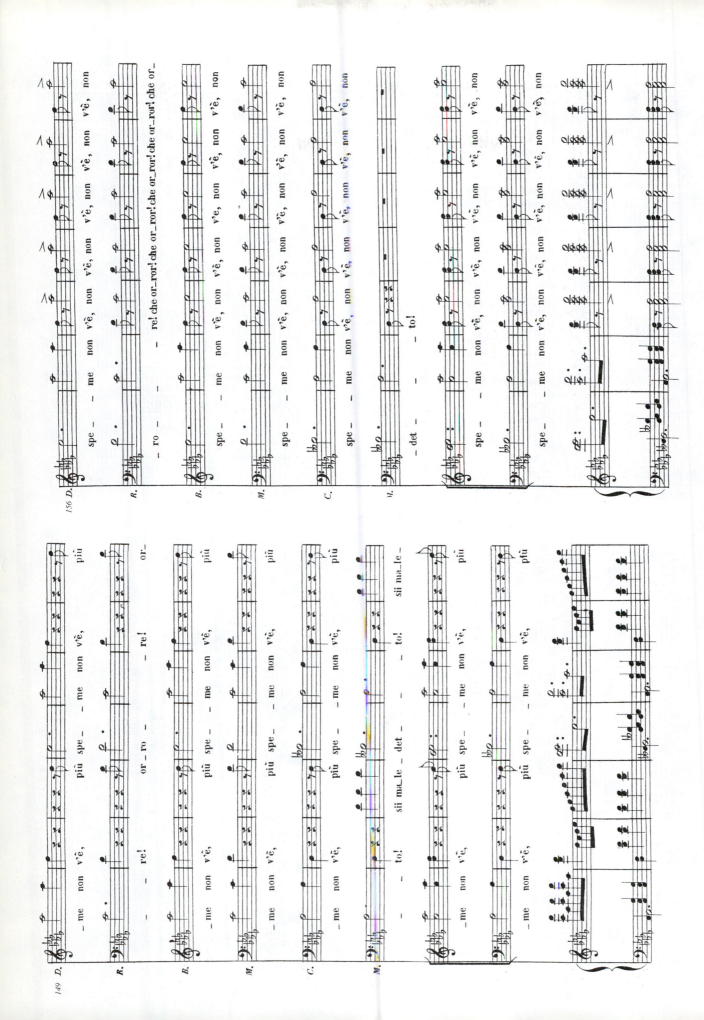

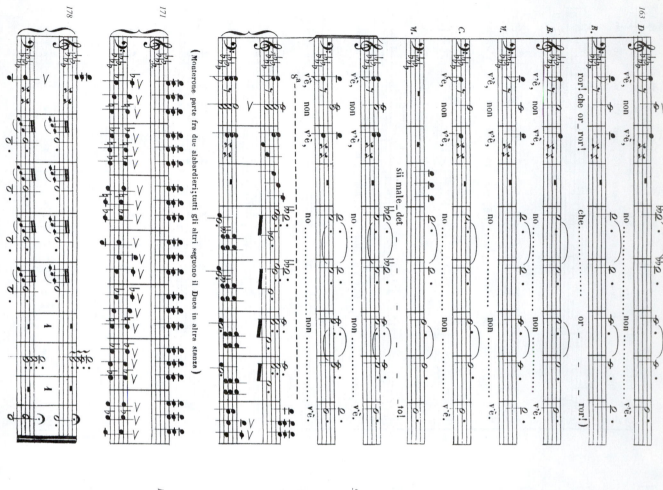

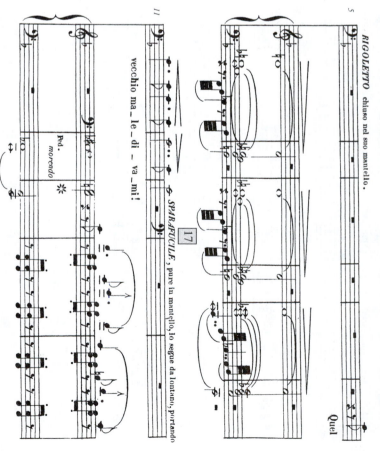

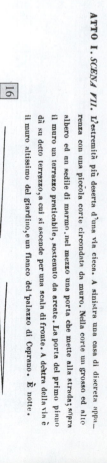

(Monterone parte fra due alabardieri; tutti gli altri seguono il Duca in altra stanza)

DUETTO

ATTO I. *SCENA VII.* L'estremità più deserta d'una via cieca. A sinistra una casa di discreta apparenza con una piccola corte circondata da muro. Nella corte un grosso ed alto albero ed un sedile di marmo; nel mezzo una porta che mette alla strada; sopra il muro un terrazzo praticabile, sostenuto da arcate. La porta del primo piano dà su detto terrazzo, a cui si ascende per una scala di fronte. A destra della via è il muro altissimo del giardino, e un fianco del palazzo di Ceprano. È notte.

Andte mosso.

RIGOLETTO chiuso nel suo mantello.

SPARAFUCILE, pure in mantello, lo segue da lontano, portando vecchio ma_le_di_va_mi!

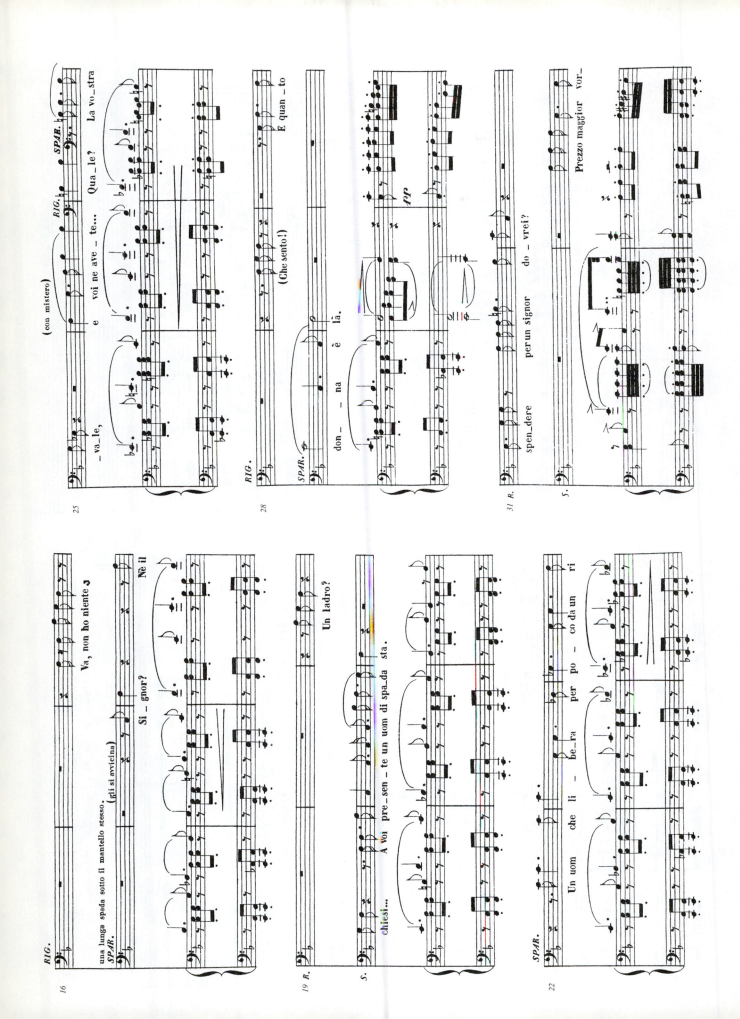

No. 137 Verdi: *Rigoletto*

285

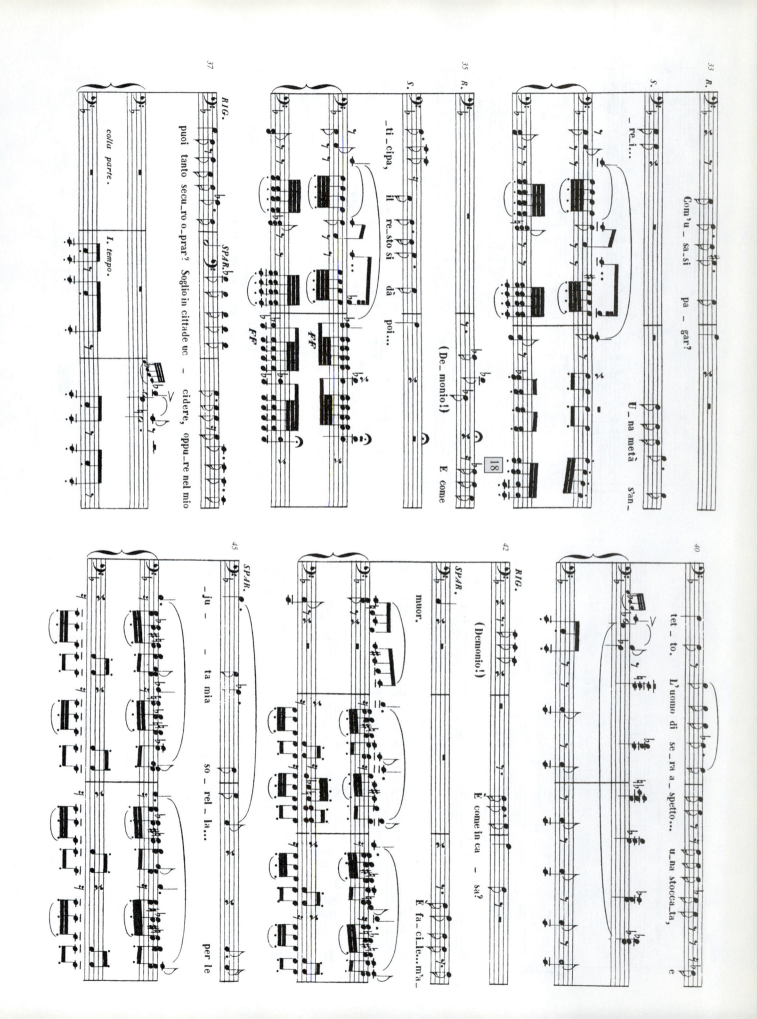

No. 137 Verdi: Rigoletto

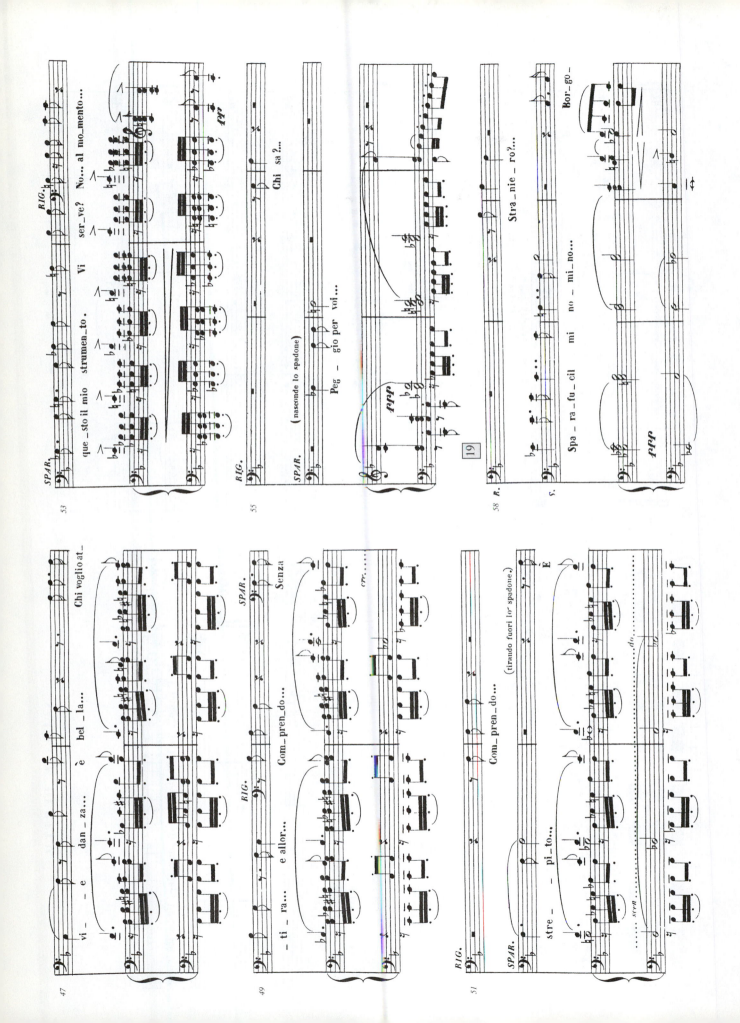

No. 137 Verdi: *Rigoletto*

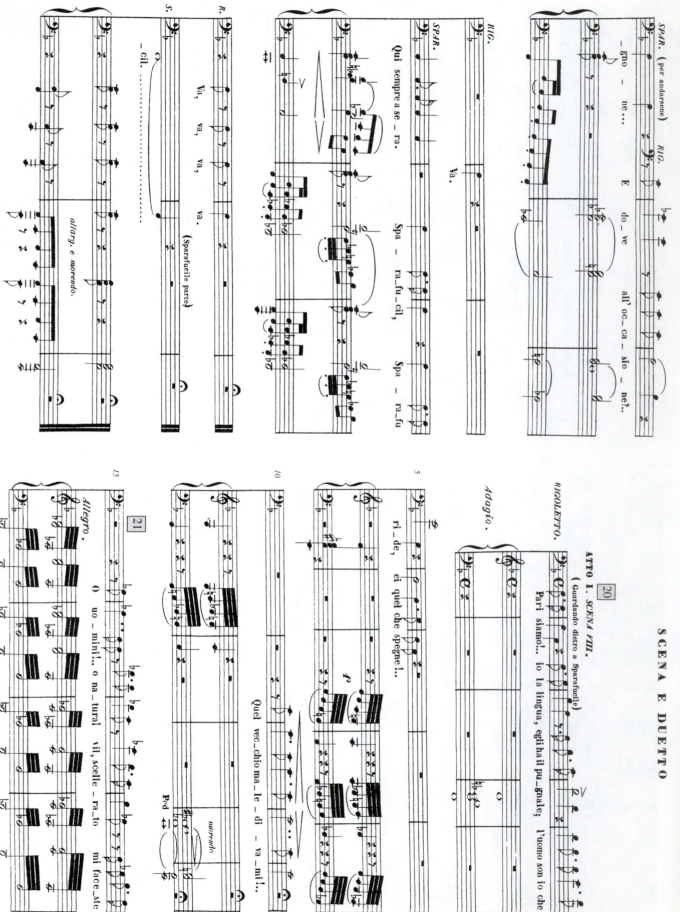

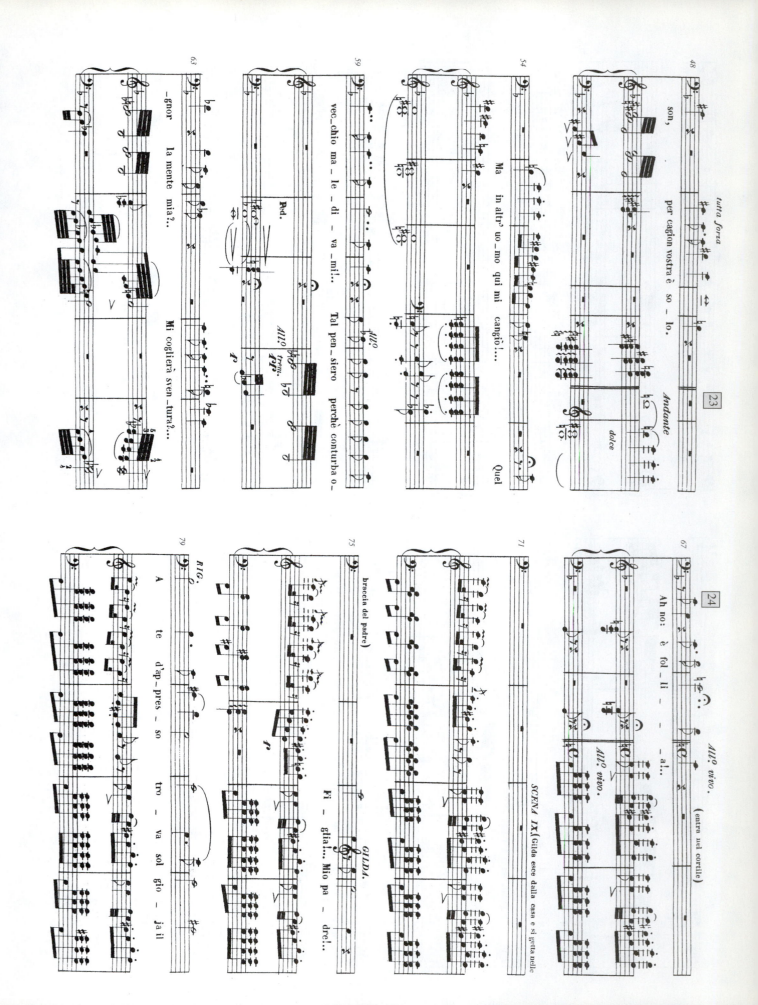

No. 137 Verdi: *Rigoletto*

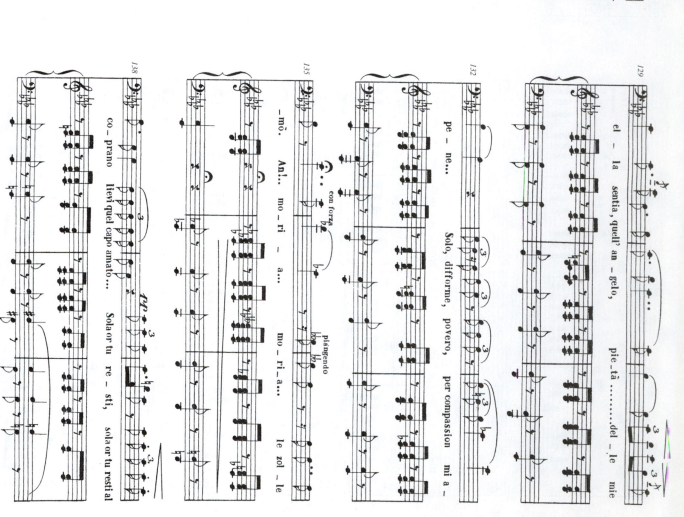

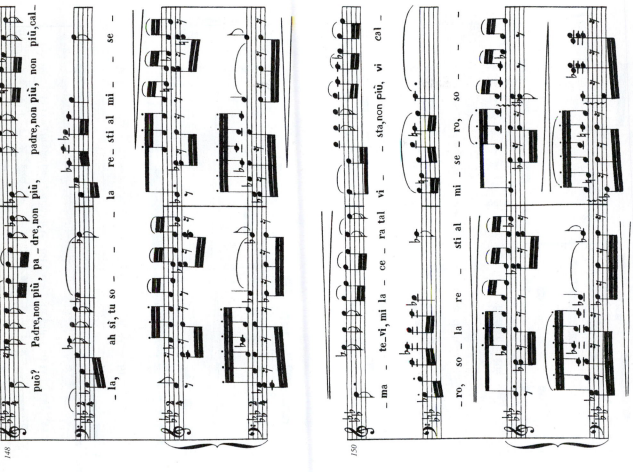

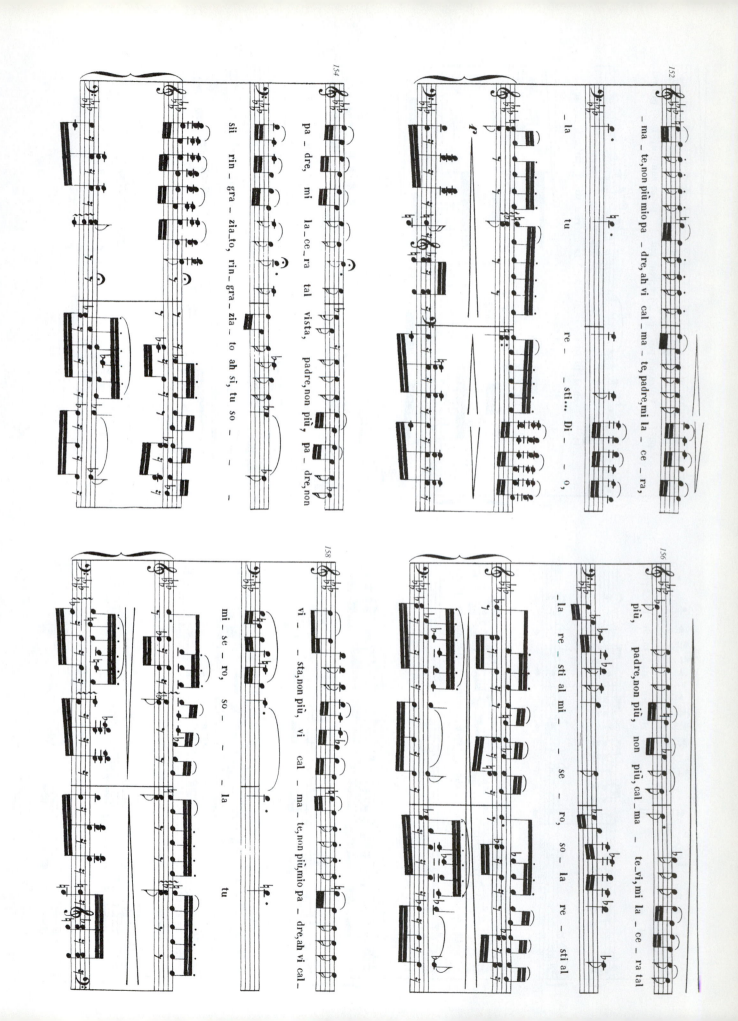

No. 137 Verdi: *Rigoletto*

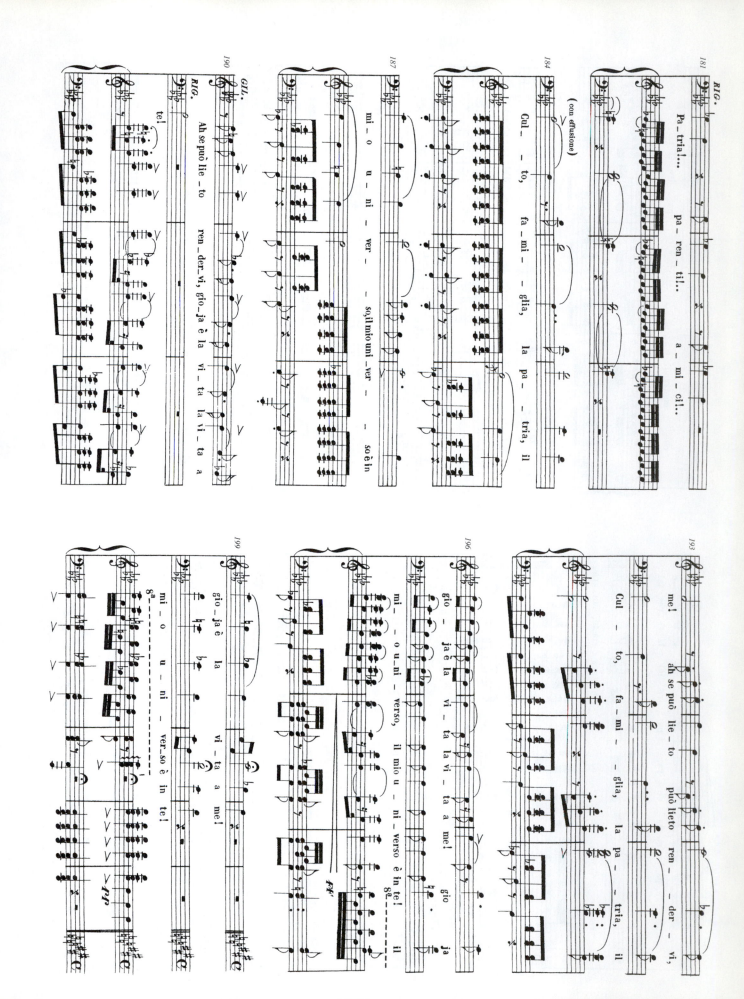

No. 137 Verdi: Rigoletto

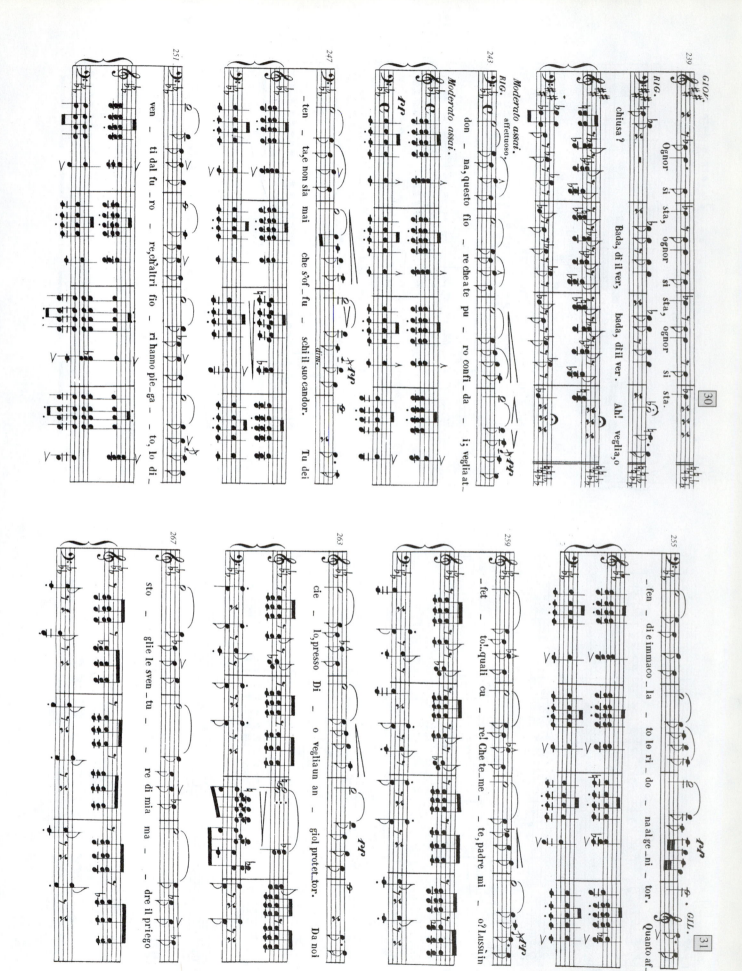

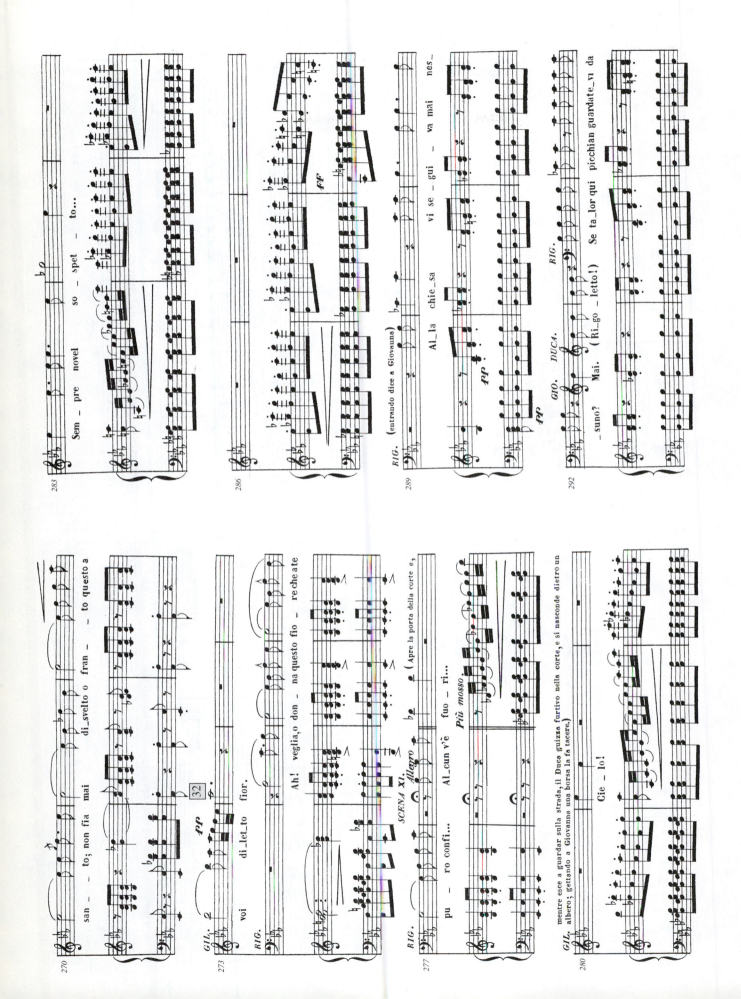

No. 137 Verdi: *Rigoletto*

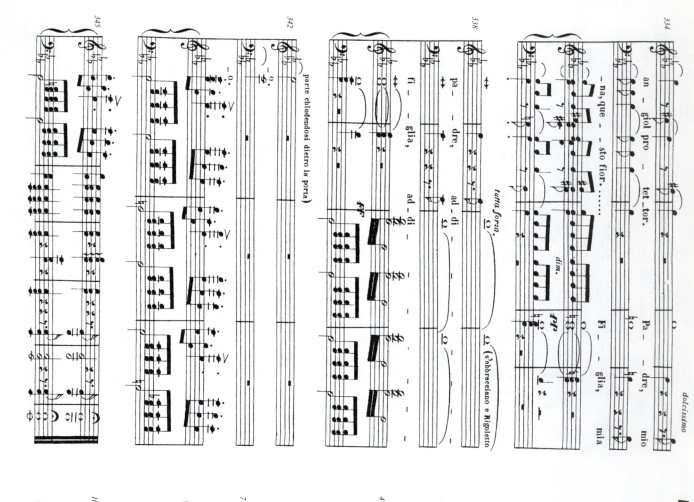

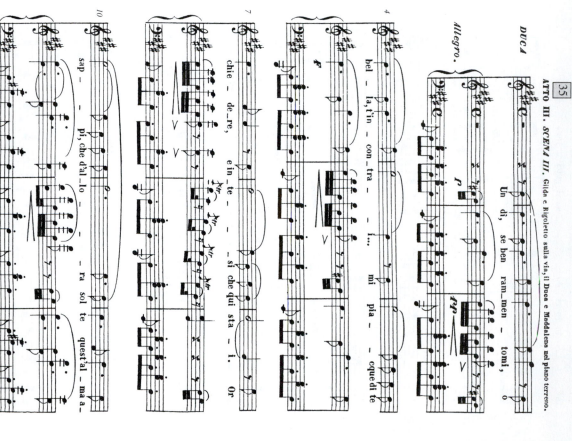

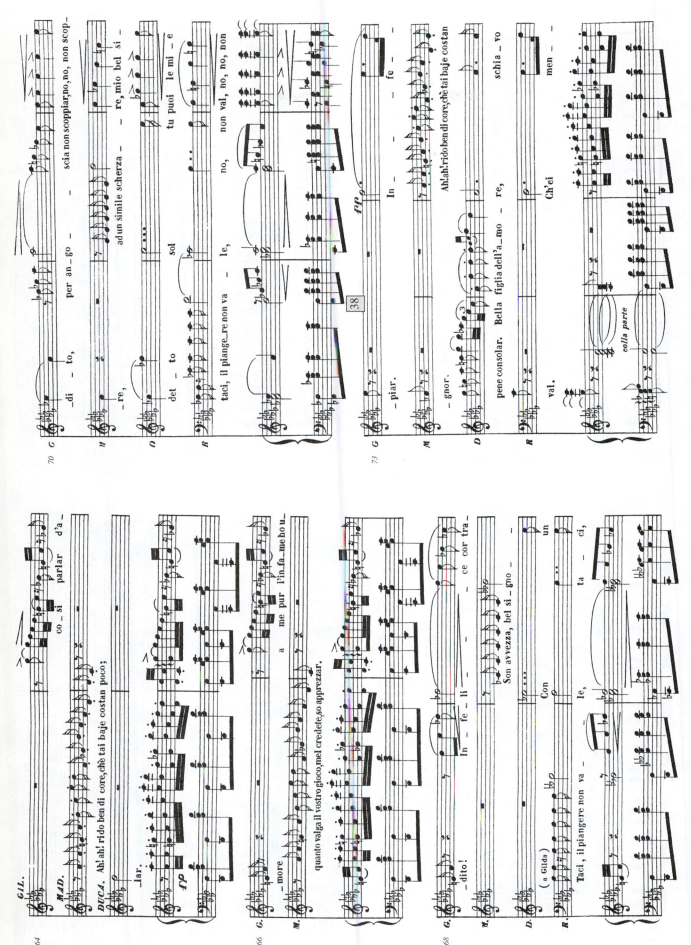

No. 137 Verdi: *Rigoletto*

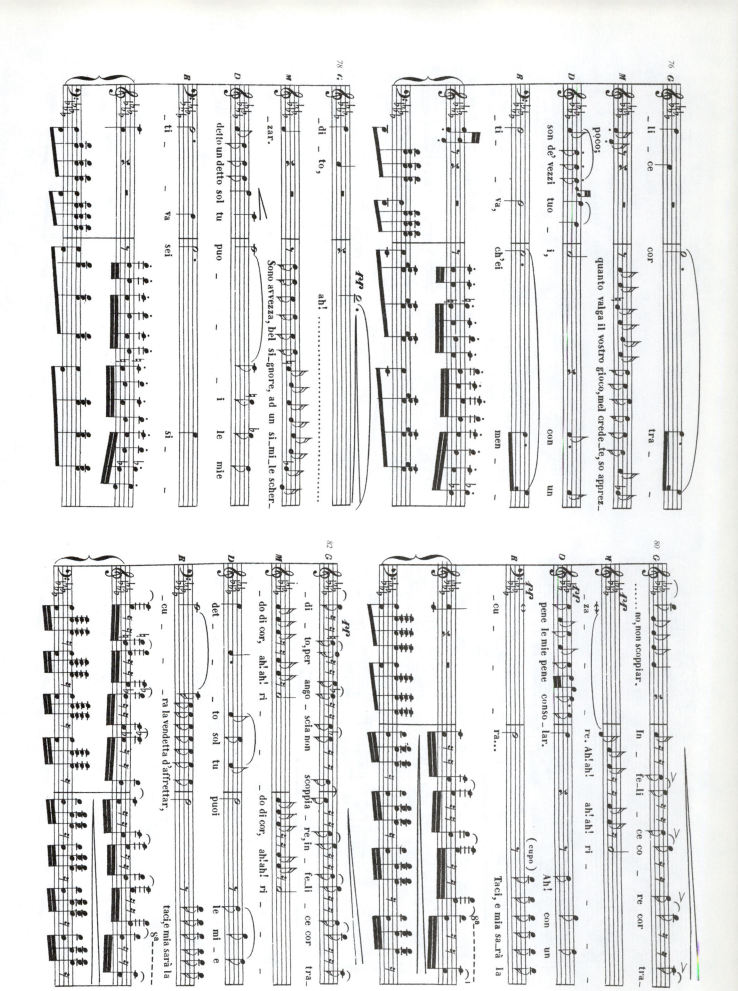

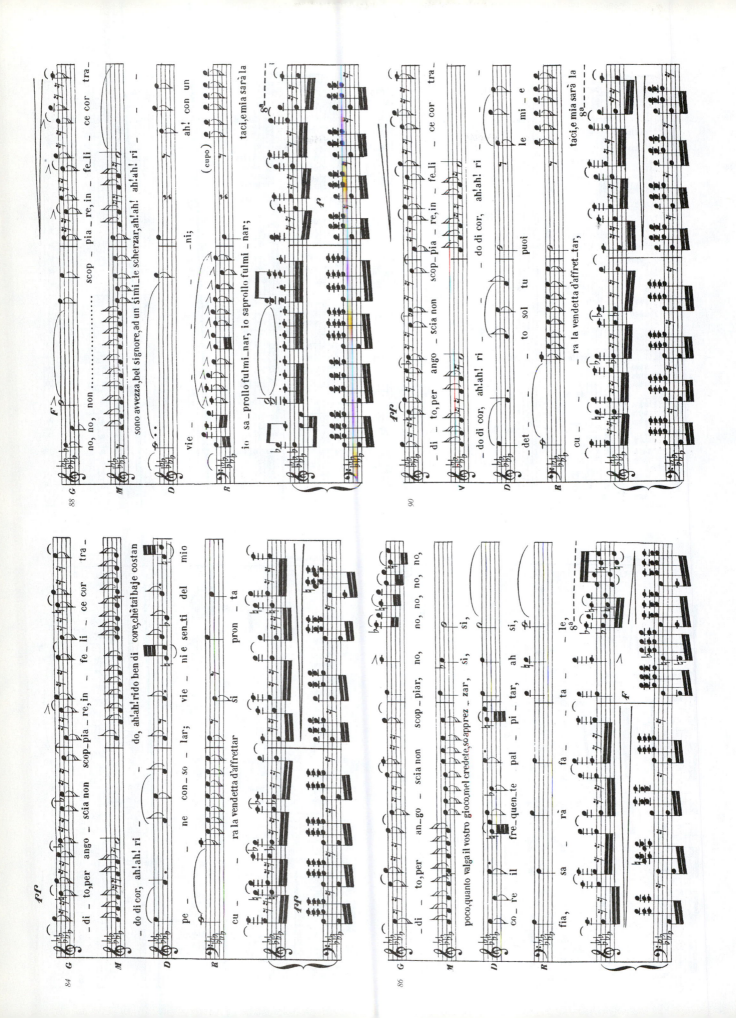

No. 137 Verdi: *Rigoletto*

No. 137 Verdi: Rigoletto

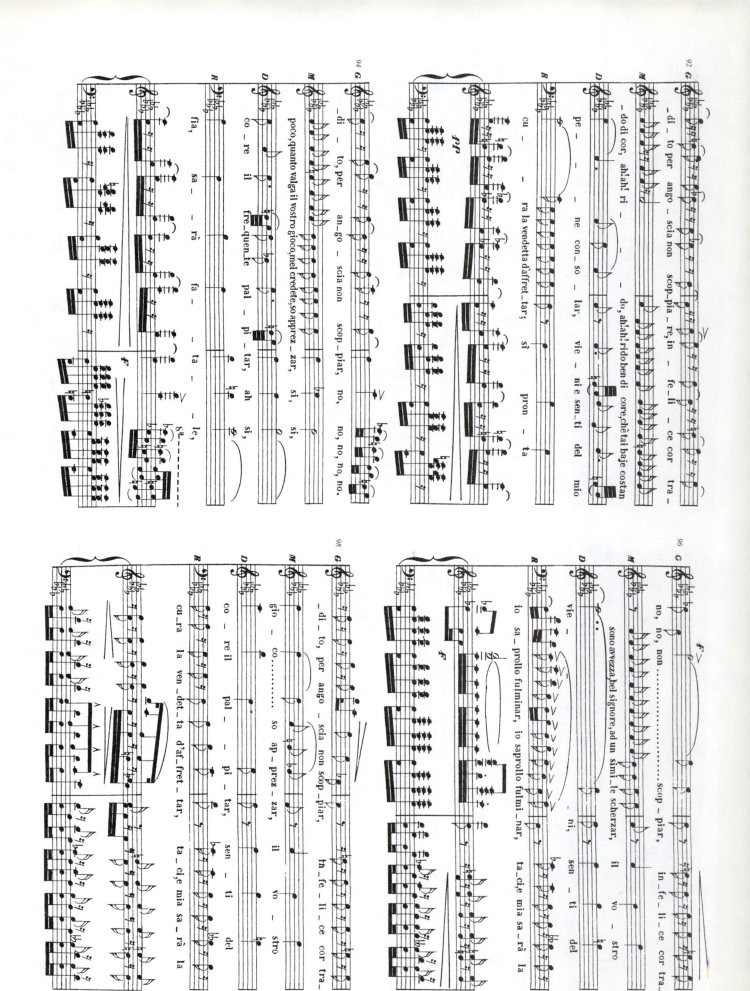

NO. 1 PRELUDE
SCENE I

A Ball-room in the Ducal Palace. Ladies and Gentlemen, Pages and Servants, cross the scene. Music is heard at a distance, and now and then bursts of laughter. Enter the Duke and Borsa.

DUKE: I am quite resolved to follow to the end My new adventure with this youthful lady.

BORSA: You mean the one you meet while going to church?

DUKE: Yes, in a lonely street, and every day she receives a visit from a dubious man.

BORSA: But does she know him?

DUKE: Yes, every Sunday for the last three months.

BORSA: Know you where she resides?

DUKE: No, I think not.

(A group of Ladies and Gentlemen cross the scene.)

BORSA: Behold those charming ladies.

DUKE: Yes, but Ceprano's wife outshines them all.

BORSA: Ah! but mind her husband, Duke.

DUKE: What matters?

BORSA: It might be spread about.

DUKE: What then—no great misfortune.

Amongst the beauties here around,
Over me none have control;
None can say: "I am preferred;"
Equal love I feel for all.
Yes, all women are to me
Like the flowers of the field.
Now to this, I am inclined,
Now to that by chance I yield.
As one flies from a great peril,
So from constancy I fly;
Those who will, may faithful be,
In freedom only does love lie.
I despise a jealous husband,
And I laugh at lover's sighs—
If a beauty strikes my fancy,
I defy one hundred eyes.

SCENA I

Sala magnifica nel Palazzo Ducale. Il Duca e Borsa che vengono da una porta del fondo.

DUCA: Della mia bella incognita borghese Toccare il fin del' avventura io voglio.

BORSA: Di quelli giovin che vedete al tempio?

DUCA: Da tre lune ogni festa.

BORSA: La sua dimora?

DUCA: In un remoto calle; Misterioso un uom v' entra ogni notte.

BORSA: E sa colei chi sia L'amante suo?

DUCA: Lo ignora.

(Un gruppo di Dame e Cavalieri attraversan la sala.)

BORSA: Quante beltà!—Mirate.

DUCA: Le vince tutte di Ceprano la sposa.

BORSA: Non v' oda il Conte, o Duca—
(Piano.)

DUCA: A me che importa?

BORSA: Dirlo ad altra ei potria—

DUCA: Nè sventura per me certo saria.

Questa o quella per me pari sono
A quant' altre d' intorno mi vedo,
Del mio core l'impero non cedo
Meglio ad una che ad altra beltà.
La costoro avvenenza è qual dono
Di che il fato ne infiora la vita;
S' oggi questa mi torna gradita,
Forse un' altra doman lo sarà.
La costanza tiranna del core
Detestiamo qual morbo crudele,
Sol chi vuole si serbi fedele;
Non v' ha amor, se non v' è libertà.
De' mariti il geloso furore,
Degli amanti le smanie derido,
Anco d' Argo i cent' occhi disfido
Se mi punge una qualche beltà.

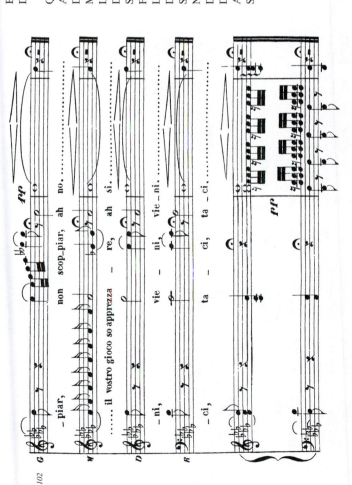

No. 137 Verdi: *Rigoletto*

SCENA II

Detti, il Conte di Ceprano, che segue da lungi la
sua sposa seguita da altro Cavaliere. Dame e
Signora entrano da varie parti.

DUCA: (Alla Signora di Cep., movendo ad
incontrarla con molta galanteria.) Partite?
Crudele!
CEP: Seguire le sposo
M'è forza a Ceprano.
DUCA: Ma dee luminoso
In Corte tal astro qual sole brillare.
Per voi qui possente la fiamma d' amore
Inebria, conquide, distrugge il mio core.
(Con enfasi, baciandole la mano.)
CEP: Calmatevi—
DUCA: No.
(Le da il braccio ed esce con lei.)

SCENA III

Detti e Rigoletto che s'incontra nel Signor di
Ceprano; poi Cortigiani.

RIG: In testa che avete,
Signor di Ceprano?
(Ceprano fa un gesto d'impazienza e segue il
Duca.)
RIG: (Ai Cortigiana.) Ei sbuffa, vedete
CORO: Che festa!
RIG: Oh sì—
BORSA: Il duca qui pur si diverte
RIG: Così non è sempre? Che nuove scopete.
Il giuoco ed il vino, le feste, la danza
Battaglie, conviti, ben tutto gli sta.
Or della Contessa l'assedio egl' avanza,
E intanto il marito fremendo ne va.
(Esce)

SCENA IV

Detti e Marullo premuroso

MAR: Gran nuova! gran nuova!
DUCA: Che avvenne? Parlate!
MAR: Stupir ne dovrete—
CORO: Narrate narrate
MAR: Ah! ah! Rigoletto—
CORO: Ebben?
MAR: Caso enorme!
CORO: Perduto ha la gobba? non è più difforme?

MAR: Più strana è la cosa! il pazzo possiede—
CHO: Infine?
MAR: Un amante—
CORO: Amante! Chi il crede?
MAR: Il gobbo in Cupido or s' è trasformato!
CORO: Quel mostro Cupido! Cupido beato!
Cupido!

SCENA V

Detti ed il Duca seguita da Rigoletto, indi
Ceprano.

DUCA: Ah, più di Ceprano, importuno non v' è!
La cara sua sposa è un angiol per me.

(A Rig.)
RIG: Rapitela.
DUCA: E detto! ma il farlo?
RIG: Stassera—
DUCA: Non pensi tu al Conte?
RIG: Non c' è la prigione?
DUCA: Ah, no.
RIG: Ebben—s' esilia.
DUCA: Nemmeno, buffone.
RIG: Allora la testa—
(Indicando di farla tagliare.)
CEP: (Oh l'anima nera!)
DUCA: Che di' questa testa?—
(Da se.)
(Battendo colla mano una spalla al Conte.)
RIG: Che far di tal testa?—A cosa ella vale?
CEP: Marrano!
(Infuriato battendo la spada.)
DUCA! Fermate—
(A Cep.)
RIG: Da rider mi fa.
CORO: In furia è montato!
(Tra loro.)
DUCA: Buffone, vien quà.
(A Rig.)
A sempre tu spingi lo scherzo all' estremo.
Quell' ira che sfidi colpir ti potrà.
RIG: Che coglier mi puote? Di lor non temo;
Del duca un protetto nessun toccherà.
CEP: Vendetta dal pazzo—
(Ai Cortigiani, a parte.)
CORO: Contr' esso un rancore
Pei tristi suoi modi, di noi chi non ha?

NO. 3 ACT 1
SCENE II

Enter Count Ceprano, watching at a distance the
Countess, who is followed by a Gentleman.
Ladies and Lords cross the scene.

DUKE: (To the Countess, with great politeness.)
You go already, cruel one?
COUN: I must obey my husband, I am obliged to
leave.
DUKE: But you must shine at Court,
As Venus amongst the stars—
Here all must sigh for you.
Already, behold here
A victim of your charms.
COUN: Ah! silence—
DUKE: No.
(The Duke kisses her hand.)

SCENE III

Enter Rigoletto, who meets Count Ceprano and
Courtiers.

RIG: What troubles you, dear Count?
You seem in deepest thought.
(The Count makes a sign of impatience, and
follows the Duke.)
RIG: (To the Courtiers.) The Count is furious!
See.
CHO: A fine ball!
RIG: Indeed.
BORSA: And even the Duke enjoys the feast.
RIG: Is it not always so? What news is this?
Wine and feasting—dancing and games—
Battles and banquets—for him all's the same.
Now against the Countess he tries to lay the
siege,
And cares not for the jealousy of her liege.
(Exit.)

NO. 4 ACT 1
SCENE IV

Enter Marullo, with great anxiety.

MAR: Great news! fine news!
DUKE: Quick, what has happened, say?
MAR: You will all be surprised.
CHO: Speak on, speak on.
MAR: Ah, ah! Rigoletto—
CHO: Well
MAR: Strange case.
CHO: What, has he lost his hump? Is he now
straight?

NO. 4 ACT 1 continued

MAR: More strange still, the foolish man
possesses—
CHO: What? say—
MAR: A lover.
CHO: A lover! who could ever have thought of
this?
MAR: The hump-back is transformed into a
Cupid.
CHO: Oh, what a monstrous Cupid! charming
Cupid!

SCENE V

Enter the Duke, followed by Rigoletto, afterwards
Ceprano.

DUKE: No man can be more vexing than
Ceprano,
His wife is a sweet angel.

(To Rig.)
RIG: Steal her away.
DUKE: 'Tis easier said than done.
RIG: This evening.
DUKE: You think not of the Count.
RIG: Have you no prisons?
DUKE: Ah! no.
RIG: Well, banish him.
DUKE: No, no, buffoon.
RIG: His head, then.
(Marking signs of having it cut off.)
CEP: (Villain!)
DUKE: What do you mean? this head?—
(Tapping the Count on the shoulder.)
RIG: Yes, what is it good for?
What can he do with it?
CEP: Miscreant!
(Unsheathing his sword.)
DUKE: Stop—stop.
(To the count.)
RIG: He makes me laugh.
CHO: He is frantic!
(Among themselves.)
DUKE: Now, buffoon, come here.
(To Rig.)
You carry your jokes too far,
His sword might reach your heart.
RIG: I fear him not. No one will dare to teach
The favorite of the Duke.
CEP: He must be punished.
(Aside to the Courtiers.)
CHO: And who has not some injuries
To avenge on him.

CEP: Vendetta!
CORO: Ma come?
CEP: Domani, chi ha core
Sia in armi da me.
TUTTI: Sì.
CEP: A notte.
TUTTI: Sarà.
(La folla de' danzatori invade la sala.)
Tutto è gioia, tutto è festa,
Tutto invitaci a goder!
Oh, guardate, non par questa
Or la reggia del piacer!

NO. 5 ACT I
SCENA VI
Detti ed il Conte di Monterone.
MON: Ch' io gli parli. (Dall' interno.)
DUCA: No.
MON: Il voglio.
(Entrando.)
TUTTI: Monterone!
MON: (fissando il Duca con nobile orgoglio.) Sì,
Monteron—la voce mia qual tuono
Vi scuoterà dovunque—
RIG: (al Duca, contraffacendo la voce di Mon.)
Ch' io gli parli.
(Si avanza con ridicola gravità.)
Voi congiuraste contro noi, signore,
E noi, clementi in ver, perdonammo—
Qual vi piglia or delirio—a tutte l'ore
Di vostra figlia reclamar l'onore?
MON: (guardando Rig. con ira sprezzante.)
Novello insulto!—Ah sì, a turbare (al Duca.)
Sarò vostr' orgie—verrò a gridare,
Fino a che vegga restarsi insulto
Di mia famiglia l'atroce insulto;
E se al carnefice pur mi darete
Spettro terribile mi rivedrete,
Portante in mano il teschio mio,
Vendetta chiedere al mondo e Dio.
DUCA: Non più, arrestatelo.
RIG: È matto!
CORO: Quai detti!
MON: Oh siate entrambi voi maledetti.
(Al Duca e Rig.)
Slanciare il cane al leon morente
È vile, o duca—e tu serpente, (a Rig.)
Tu che d'un padre ridi al dolore,
Sii maledetto!
RIG: Che sento? orrore!
(Da sè colpito.)

NO. 4 ACT 1 continued
CEP: Revenge, revenge!
CHO: But how?
CEP: If you fear not, tomorrow
Come with your swords to me.
ALL: We will.
CEP: At night.
ALL: Decreed.
(A crowd of dancers invades the scene.)
To dance, to feast, to pleasure,
Here everything invite,
Look around, does this not seem
The palace of delight.

NO. 5 ACT I
SCENE VI
Enter Count Monterone.
MON: (from without) I must see him.
DUKE: No, no.
MON: I will. (Entering.)
ALL: Monterone!
MON: (looking at the Duke, with pride.) Yes,
Monterone.—My voice
For ever I will raise against your crimes,
RIG: (to the Duke, counterfeiting Mon.'s voice.) I
must see him.
(He advances with ridiculous seriousness.)
You have conspired against our name, my lord.
And we have granted pardon—
What madness now is yours? In this glad hour
To come and claim the honor of your daughter!
MON: (looking at Rig. with contempt.)
A new insult! but your nefarious orgies
I will disturb. Here I will raise my voice
Until the honor of an injured family
Shall be restored.
And even if you were
To sign my death and send me to the block,
My shade will claim revenge!
DUKE: No more—arrest him.
RIG: He is mad!
CHO: He is mad!
MON: Be both for ever accursed.
(To Rig. and the Duke.)
To strike the dying lion,
'Tis base—but you, reptile,
Who dares to laugh at an old father's grief
Malediction fall on you!
RIG: What do I hear!
Oh, terror! (Aside)

NO. 5 ACT I continued
TUTTI: (meno Rig.) Oh tu che la festa andace hai
turbato,
Da un genio d'inferno qui fosti guidato;
È vano ogni detto, quà t'allontana—
Va, trema, o vegliardo, dell' ira sovrana—
Tu l' hai provocata, più speme non v' è.
Un' ora fatale fu questa per te.
(Mon. parte fra due alabardieri; tutti gli altra
seguono il Duca in altra, stanza.)

ATTO I
SCENA VII
L'estremita più deserta d'una via cieca, Casa di
Rigoletto e terazzo. Rigoletto chiuso nel suo man-
tello. Sparafucile lo segue portando sotto il man-
tello una lunga spada.
RIG: (Quel vecchio maledivami!)
SPA: Signor?—
RIG: Va, non ho niente.
SPA: Nè il chiesi—a voi presente
Un uom di spada sta.
RIG: Un ladro?
SPA: Un uom che libera
Per poco da un rivale,
E voi ne avete—
RIG: Quale?
SPA: La vostra donna è là.
RIG: (Che sento?) E quanto spendere
Per un signor dovrei?
SPA: Prezzo maggior vorrei—
RIG: Com' usasi pagar?
SPA: Una metà as' anticipa,
Il resto si da poi—
RIG: (Dimonio!) E come puo
Tanto securo oprar?
SPA: Soglio in cittade uccidere,
Oppure nel mio tetto.
L'uomo di sera aspetto—
Una stoccata, e muor.
RIG: E come in casa?
SPA: È facile—
M'aiuta mia sorella—
Per le vie danza—è bella—
Chi voglio attira—e allor—
RIG: Comprendo—
SPA: Senza strepito...
E' questo il mio stromento.
(Mostra la spada.)
Vi serve;

NO. 5 ACT I continued
ALL, EXCEPT RIG: Rash man, your evil spirit
Has brought you to disturb this feast,
Your words are vain. Away!
The Duke's revenge you raise:
No hope for you remains,
This is your fatal day.
(Mon. is led away by the soldiers, the others
follow the Duke.)

NO. 6 ACT I
SCENE VII
The end of a Street. House and Garden of
Rigoletto, with flight of stairs. Enter Rigoletto en-
veloped in his cloak, and followed by Sparafucile,
carrying a long sword.
RIG: (That man has cursed me.)
SPA: Sir?
RIG: Go: I need you not.
SPA: I have not spoken! Only I showed myself
There with my dagger, ready for your orders.
RIG: You are a thief.
SPA: A man,
That for a trifle will free you from enemies,
And you have one.
RIG: Who is he?
SPA: Is your mistress here?
RIG: (What do I hear?) How much have I to pay
To rid me of this man?
SPA: A little more.
RIG: And when must you be paid?
SPA: One half before the deed,
The other after.
RIG: (O wretch!) And how can you
Be sure of the success?
SPA: I kill them in the street,
Or even in my own house.
I await my man at night;
A single blow—he dies.
RIG: But how in your own house?
SPA: Nothing can be more easy,
My sister helps me.
She dances in the streets—she is handsome;
And she attracts the man I want—I then—
RIG: I understand!
SPA: Without the slightest noise,
This is my trusty weapon!
(Shows his sword.)
Can I serve you?

NO. 6 ACT I continued
RIG: No—al momento—
SPA: Peggio ver voi—
RIG: Chi sa?
SPA: Sparafucile mi nomino—
RIG: Straniero?
SPA: Borgognone— (Per andarsene.)
RIG: E dove all' occasione?
SPA: Qui sempre a sera.
RIG: Va. (Spa. parte.)

NO. 7 ACT I
SCENA VIII
RIG: (guardando dietro a Sparafucile)
Pari siamo!—io la lingua, egli ha il pugnale;
L'uomo son io che ride, ei quel che spegne!
Quel vecchio maledivami—
O uomini!—o natura!—
Vil scellerato mi faceste voi!—
Oh rabbia!—esser difforme!—un buffone!—
Non dover, non poter altro che ridere!—
Il retaggio d'ogni uom m' è tolto il pianto!—
Questo padrone mio,
Giovin, giocondo, sì possente, bello,
Sonnecchiando mi dice;
Fa ch' io rida, buffone.
Forzarmi deggio, e farlo!—Oh, dannazione!
Odio a voi, cortigiani schernitori!—
Quanta in mordervi ho gioia!
Se iniquo so, per cagion vostra solo—
Ma in altr' uom qui mi cangio!...
Quel vecchio maledivami!—Tal pensiero
Perchè conturba ognor la mente mia?—
Mi coglierà sventura? Ah no, è follia.
(Apre con chiave, ed entra nel cortile)
(Detto e Gilda ch' esce dalla casa e si getta nelle sue braccia.)

SCENA IX
RIG: Figlia—
GILDA: Mio padre!
RIG: A te d'appresso
Trova sol gioia il core oppresso.
GILDA: Oh quanto amore!
RIG: Mia vita sei!
Senza te in terra qual bene avrei?
(Sospira)
GILDA: Voi sospirate!—che v' ange tanto?
Lo dite a questa povera figlia—
Se v' ha mistero—per lei sia franto—

NO. 6 ACT I continued
RIG: No, not now.
SPA: The worse for you.
RIG: Perhaps another day.
SPA: Sparafucile I am called.
RIG: A foreigner?
SPA: From Burgundy. (In the act of going away.)
RIG: But where could I meet you?
SPA: At this spot, always at night.
RIG: Well, go. (Spa. exit.)

NO. 7 ACT I
SCENE VIII
RIG: (looking after Sparafucile)
My weapon is my tongue—and his the dagger;
I make the people laugh, he makes them mourn!
We are alike!—That man has cursed me!
Men and nature,
'Tis you that made me wicked;
O rage! to be deformed—and a buffoon!
To be condemned to laugh against my will:
To ask in vain the common gift—of tears!
Alas! my master, young,
And full of mirth,
At every moment says,
Now make me laugh, buffoon.
I must do it. Oh! rage.
I hate you all, vile courtiers!
On you, therefore, my tongue delights to dwell;
For you I am depraved—
But here I am not the same;
That man has cursed me! But why does this thought
Haunt my mind?
What can I have to fear? No, it's madness.
(He opens and enters.)
(Enter Gilda from house and throws herself in his arms.)

SCENE IX
RIG: My daughter!
GILDA: Father.
RIG: Near to you, alone,
My poor dejected heart returns to joy.
GILDA: Ah, so much love!
RIG: You are my only hope,
What else have I on earth except my Gilda?
(Sighing.)
GILDA: You sigh! What is the cause of your affliction?
Tell it to your poor daughter

NO. 7 ACT I
SCENE VIII
RIG: Deh non parlare al misero
Del suo perduto bene—
Ella sentia quell' angelo,
Pietà delle mie pene—
Solo, difforme, povero
Per compassion mi amò.
Moria—le zolle coprano
Lievi quel capo amato—
Sola or tu resti al misero—
O Dio, sii ringraziato!—
(Singhiozzande.)
GILDA: Quanto dolor!—che spremere
Sì amaro pianto può?
Padre, non più, calmatevi—
Mi lacerà tal vista—
Il nome vostro ditemi,
Il duol che si v' attrista—
RIG: A che nomarmi?—è inutile!—
Padre, ti sono, e basti—
Me forse al mondo temono,
D'alcuno ho forse gli asti—
Altri mi maledicono—
GILDA: Patria, parenti, amici,
Voi dunque non avete!
RIG: Patria!—parenti!—dici?—
Culto, famiglia, patria,
Il mio universo è in te!
(Con effusione.)
GILDA: Ah, se può lieto rendervi,
Gioia è la vita a me!
Già da tre lune son qui venuta,
Nè la cittade ho ancor veduta;
Se il concedete, farlo or potrei—
RIG: Mai!—mai!—uscita, dimmi, unqua sei!
GILDA: No.

NO. 7 ACT I
SCENE VIII
RIG: Ah, do not awake. I pray,
A memory so sad;
Of my dejected state
She alone had compassion,
Despised, deformed, and poor,
Through pity, she loved me,
She died—ah, may the earth
Lay lightly on her head—
You are my only treasure—
O God! Are you her aid?
(Sighing.)
GILDA: Alas, what grief! ah, never
Saw I such bitter tears!
Ah, father, be calm.
Or you will break my heart.
To me reveal your name;
To me your grief impart.
RIG: Why this?—I am your father,
This is enough for you.
I might perhaps be hated,
Or be by others feared.
Alas! I have been cursed!
GILDA: No country, no relations,
No friends, you then possess?
RIG: What do you say, my love?
You are my god, my country,
You are the world to me!
GILDA: If I could see you glad,
I would be happy too.
It has been three months now, since we here arrived,
And nothing I have seen yet of the city.
I wish to see it now, if you will grant it.
RIG: Have you never left this house?
GILDA: Never!

NO. 7 ACT I continued
Ch' ella conosca la sua famiglia.
RIG: Tu non ne hai—
GILDA: Qual nome avete;
RIG: A te che importa?
GILDA: Se non volete
Di voi parlarmi—
RIG: Non uscir mai, (Interrompendola her.)
GILDA: Non vo che al tempio.
RIG: Or ben tu fai.
GILDA: Se non di voi, almen chi sia
Fate ch' io sappia la madre mia.

NO. 7 ACT I continued
Entrust me with your secrets,
And let me know my family
RIG: Ah! You have none!
GILDA: Your name
RIG: What does it matter to you?
GILDA: If you object to speak
Of our relations—
RIG: Do you ever leave this house? (Interrupting her.)
GILDA: I only go to church.
RIG: That's right, my child.
GILDA: If you will not reveal your name or rank,
Ah, let me know, at least, who my mother is.

RIG: Guai!
GILDA: (Che dissi?)
RIG: Ben te ne guarda!
(Potrian seguirla, rapirla ancora!
Qui d'un buffone si disonora
La figlia, e se ne ride—Orror!) Olà?
(Verso la casa.)

SCENA X
Detti e Giovanna della casa.
GIO: Signor?
RIG: Venendo mi vede alcuno?
Bada, di il vero.
GIO: Ah no, nessuno.
RIG: Sta ben—la porta che dà al bastione
È sempre chiusa?
GIO: Lo fu e sarà.
RIG: Veglia, o donna, questo fiore (A Gio.)
Che a te puro confidai;
Veglia attenta, e non sia mai
Che s' offuschi il suo candor.
Tu dei venti dal furore,
Ch' altri iori hanno piegato,
Lo difendi, e immacolato
Lo ridona al genitor.

GILDA: Quanto affetto!—quali cure!
Che temete, padre mio?
Lassù in cielo, presso Dio
Veglia un angiol protettor.
Da noi stoglie le sventure
Di mia madre il priego santo;
Non fia mai disvelto o franto
Questo a voi diletto fiore.

SCENA XI
Detti ed il Duca in costume borghese dalla strada.
RIG: Alcuno v'è fuori—
(Apre la porta della Corte, e mentre esce a sulla strada il Duca guizza-furtivo nella corte e si nasconde dietro l'albero; gettando a Giovanna una borsa la fa tacer)
GIL: Cielo!
Sempre novel sospetto—
RIG: (a Gil. tornando.)
Vi seguiva alla chiesa mai nessuno!
GIO: Mai.
DUCA: (Rigoletto.)
RIG: Se talor qui picchiano
Guardatevi da aprir—
GIO: Nemmeno al duca?—
RIG: Meno che a tutti a lui—Mia figlia, addio.

NO: 7 ACT I continued
RIG: Mind!
GILDA: (What do I say?)
RIG: Nor must you ever leave it.
(She might be followed, she might be stolen,
And they would laugh at the dishonor
Of a buffoon. Oh shame!) Ho! there!
(Towards the house.)

SCENE X
Enter Giovanna from the house.
GIO: Sir?
RIG: Has no one seen me while coming here?
Mind, speak the truth.
GIO: No one.
RIG: That's well! The door that leads to the
Ramparts, is it always closed?
GIO: Yes, it has always been so, and always shall.
RIG: Oh, woman, watch over this flower,
Which I trust unto your care;
Be mindful, it may never
Fall the victim of dark snare.
O, save this fragile stem
From the hail and from rain:
As it was to you confided,
May I receive it back again.

GILDA: O, be cheerful, my dear father.
Chase your starting tears away;
There, in heaven, is an angel
Who protects us night and day.
There the prayers of my mother
From all danger keeps us free;
Never, never, from your side,
Never distant will I be.

SCENE XI
The Duke in disguise arrives in the street.
RIG: Some one outside—(Rigoletto opens the
street gate, and whilst he goes out, the Duke
slides in, hiding himself behind a tree, and
throwing a purse to Giovanna.)
GILDA: Oh, heavens!
He is always suspicious.
RIG: (To Gilda, returning.)
Has any one ever followed you to church?
DUKE: No, never. (Aside.)
RIG: (It is Rigoletto.)
If any one knocks here
You must not open.
GIO: Not even to the Duke?
RIG: Still less to him than others—Child, adieu.

DUCA: Sua figlia!
GIO: Addio, mia padre. (S'abbraciano, e Rigoletto parte chiudendosi dietro la porta.)

* * *

NO. 16 ACT III
SCENA III
Gilda e Rigoletto sulla via, il Duca e Maddalena nel piano terreno.
DUCA: Un dì, se ben rammentomi,
O bella, t'incontrai—
Mi piacque di te chiedere,
E intesi che qui stai.
Or sappi, che d'allora
Sol te quest' alma adora.
MAG: Ah, ah!—e vent' altre appresso
Le scorda forse adesso?—
Ha un' aria il signorino
Da vero libertino—
DUCA: Sì?—un mostro son—(Por abbracciarla.)
MAG: Lasciatemi, stordito.
DUCA: Ih, che fracasso!
MAG: Stia saggio.
DUCA: E tu sii docile,
Non farmi tanto chiasso.
Ogni saggezza chiudesi
Nel gaudio e nell' amore—
La bella mano candida!—
(Le prende la mano.)
MAG: Scherzate, voi signore.
DUCA: No, no.
MAG: Son brutta.
DUCA: Abbracciami.
MAG: Ebro—
DUCA: D'amore ardente. (Ridendo)
MAG: Signor l'indifferente,
Vi piace canzonar?—
DUCA: No, no, ti vo' sposar.
MAG: Ne voglio la parola—
DUCA: Amabile figliuola! (Ironico.)
RIG: Ebben?—ti basta ancor?—(A Gilda che avra tutto osservato ed inteso)
GIL: Iniquo traditor!
DUCA: Bella figlia dell'amore,
Schiavo son de' vezzi tuoi;
Con un detto sol tu puoi
Le mie pene consolar.
Vieni, e senti del mio core
Il frequente palpitar.

NO: 7 ACT I continued
DUKE: His child!
GILDA: Adieu my father. (They embrace; and Rigoletto going out, shuts the door after him.)

* * *

SCENE III
Gilda and Rigoletto on the road. Magdalen and the Duke in the Inn.
DUKE: If I remember well, my pretty girl,
I have seen your face before.
I tried to find your house,
At length I see you here.
Believe that from that time
I loved you to despair.
MAG: And others, score by score,
Do you forget them now?
To tell the truth, good sir,
You are a gay deceiver.
DUKE: Yes, yes, just so.
MAG: Leave me, rude man.
DUKE: Eh! eh! what noise!
MAG: Be quiet.
DUKE: And you be kind,
And do not scream so loud,
For wisdom ever lies
In pleasure and in love.
What pretty hands! how white!
(He takes her by the hand.)
MAG: You like to laugh at me.
DUKE: No, no.
MAG: I know I am not pretty.
DUKE: Kiss me.
MAG: Sir, you are drunk—
DUKE: Yes, drunk of love for you.
MAG: And can you be so unkind,
As thus to laugh at me.
DUKE: I do not joke—I wish to marry you.
MAG: If so, give me your word of honor.
DUKE: You are a charming girl! (Ironically.)
RIG: Well then, is this not yet enough?
GIL: The cruel traitor!
DUKE: Lovely woman, of your charms
At your feet the victim see,
But one word, and changed to joy
All my sorrows soon will be.
Yes, be assured, my lady sweet,
This fond heart for you does beat.

No. 137   Verdi: Rigoletto

NO. 16 ACT III continued

MAD: Ah! ah! rido ben di core,
Che tai baie costan poco;
Quanto valga il vostro giuoco,
Mel credete, so apprezzar.
Sono avezza, bel signore,
Ad un simile scherzar.

GIL.: Ah, così parlar d'amore!
A me pur l'infame ho udito
Infelice cor tradito,
Per angoscia non scoppiar.

RIG: Taci, il piangere non vale; (A Gil.)
Ch'ei, mentiva or sei secura—
Taci, e mia sarà la cura
La vendetta d'affretar.
Pronta fia, sarà fatale;
Io saprollo fulminar.

MAG: Do you take me for a fool,
To think your words are true;
Full well I know what they mean,
I give them their right value,
Jokes like these I often hear,
But I laugh at them, dear sir.

GIL.: Thus my heart he did deceive,
Thus the traitor spoke to me.
All my joys, my hopes are gone,
Now my wretched doom I see.

RIG: Hush! your sorrows are all vain,
That he deceived you is now sure—
Hush! it now belongs to me
Dreadful vengeance to procure.
It shall be done quickly, it shall be fatal;
I know how to shoot.

Throughout *Rigoletto*, Verdi incorporates traditional elements of Italian opera (accompanied recitatives, arias, duets, choruses) into an extended whole.

Track 1: Preludio: This brief "Prelude" takes the place of a more extended overture. Its somber tone conveys at once that the work to follow will be a tragedy. The "curse" motif figures prominently throughout.

Track 2: The curtain rises to reveal a scene of dancing, drinking, and revelry in the ballroom of the Duke's palace. This extended opening unit of music consists of eight discrete yet interconnected subsections, in each of which the music underscores the dramatic action:

2 The opening dance, played by an onstage band, has the kind of frenzied beat associated with the *galop*.

3 When the Duke and one his courtiers enter, the music shifts to a dance that has a lighter texture with emphasis only on beats one and three of a four-beat measure. This change allows the recitative-like patter of the voices to be heard clearly over the orchestra.

4 The Duke's first aria (*Questo o quella*) is also the first moment in the opera in which the voice carries the melody completely. The texture here is pointedly homophonic, with the orchestra providing a demure accompaniment. The Duke sings two musically identical strophes (the second begins at m. 48), ending with a vocal cadenza that matches perfectly the boastful nature of his words.

6 With the entrance of the Countess of Ceprano, the music changes to a minuet played by an onstage string ensemble. This decidedly old-fashioned dance fits perfectly with the Countess's traditional character. When the Duke leaves with the reluctant countess, Rigoletto and the courtiers ridicule her husband (m. 40). One of the festive dance melodies from the opening returns briefly here. Rigoletto exits and the on-stage ensemble strikes up a *perigordino* (m. 62), a frenzied dance in 6/8 meter.

8 The opening galop-like dance resumes briefly with the entrance of Marullo, a courtier who brings "great news.". Rigoletto, he reports, has a secret lover.

9 The Duke, Rigoletto, and Count Ceprano return, and with them the opening galop-like theme. The Duke rebukes Rigoletto for his excessive jesting about the Count. The chorus of courtiers joins in and in a general frenzy all agree to get their revenge on Rigoletto.

12 The music now shifts ominously to accompanied recitative with the entrance of Monterone, whose daughter has earlier been abducted by the Duke. Monterone, in response, lays a curse on the entire court, particularly on Rigoletto, who has taunted him.

Track 16 Act I, Scene 7: Duet. A duet between Rigoletto and the assassin Sparafucile. Note in particular the unusually dark orchestration, using low strings (no violins and only four violas, plus cellos and double basses), a solo double bass and solo cello playing the same melodic line at the interval of an octave, clarinets and bassoons playing in their lowest range, and a bass drum.

Track 20 Act 1, Scene 8: Scene and Duet. The "scene" is a monologue in which Rigoletto muses on his deformity, his malicious wit, and his contempt for the Duke and courtiers. In the duet with Gilda, Rigoletto reveals another, more compassionate side to his character. For a detailed diagram of this unit, see Textbook, p. 466.

The final duet within the Duet (m. 243–343) has its own internal structure, a series of variations on a single theme. It follows the traditional pattern of love duets: he sings, she sings, and then they both sing; and in this respect, Verdi adheres to convention. But he also slips in important plot developments within the duet. At m. 279, Rigoletto hears a prowler—the Duke, it turns out—and interrupts himself to launch into an agitated inquisition of Gilda's nursemaid, Giovanna. Thus we have a dramatic dialogue in the middle of the duet (Rigoletto: "No one has followed her from church?" Giovanna (lying): "Never!" and so on). Meanwhile, the Duke himself has been listening in on all this and realizes that the woman he has been pursuing (Gilda) is the daughter of his court jester (Rigoletto), and he interjects a few asides to express his astonishment at this revelation. With his fears calmed, Rigoletto resumes his duet with Gilda, who sings a glorious descant to his original melody (m. 303). The protracted farewell provides the traditional cabaletta, an extended concluding section that accelerates as it nears the end of this very long unit of music.

138 Tristan und Isolde (1859)
Richard Wagner (1813–1883)

138a Prelude

CD11 Track 39
p. 474

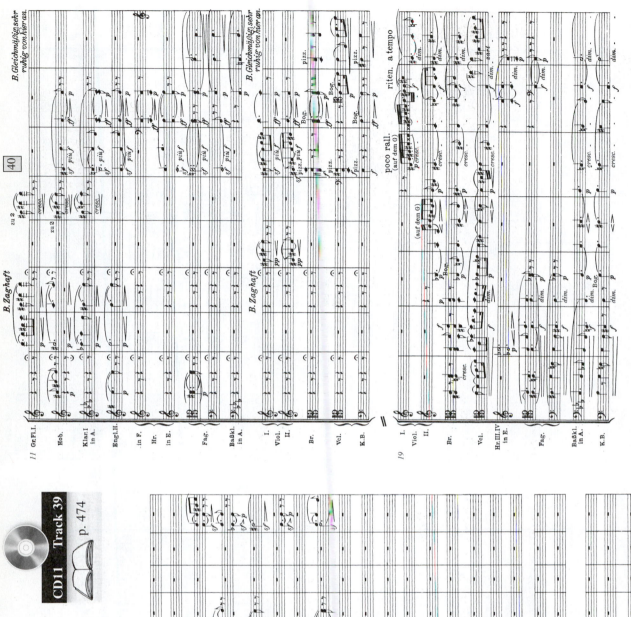

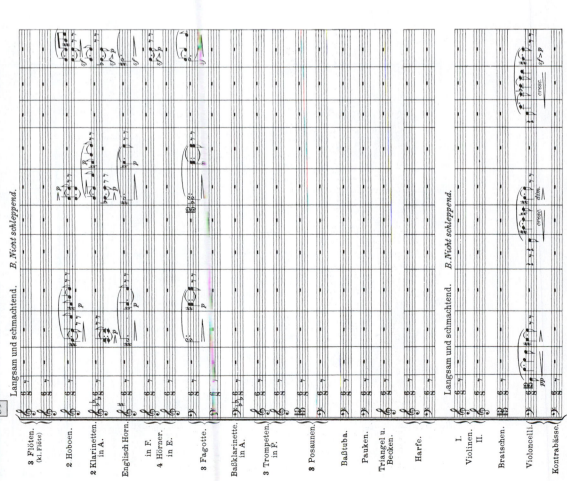

26
Hob.I.
Klar. in A.
Engl.H.
in F. Hr. in E.
Fag.
Baßkl. in A.
I. Viol. II.
Br.
Vcl.
K.B.
B. Nicht eilen!
zu 2
ten.
cresc.
dim.
più p
33
belebt
zart
(get.)
pp
40 Gr.Fl.I.
41
Belebend.
rallent.
a tempo
molto cresc.
(zus.)
(G)

No. 138 Wagner: *Tristan und Isolde*

No. 138 Wagner: *Tristan und Isolde*

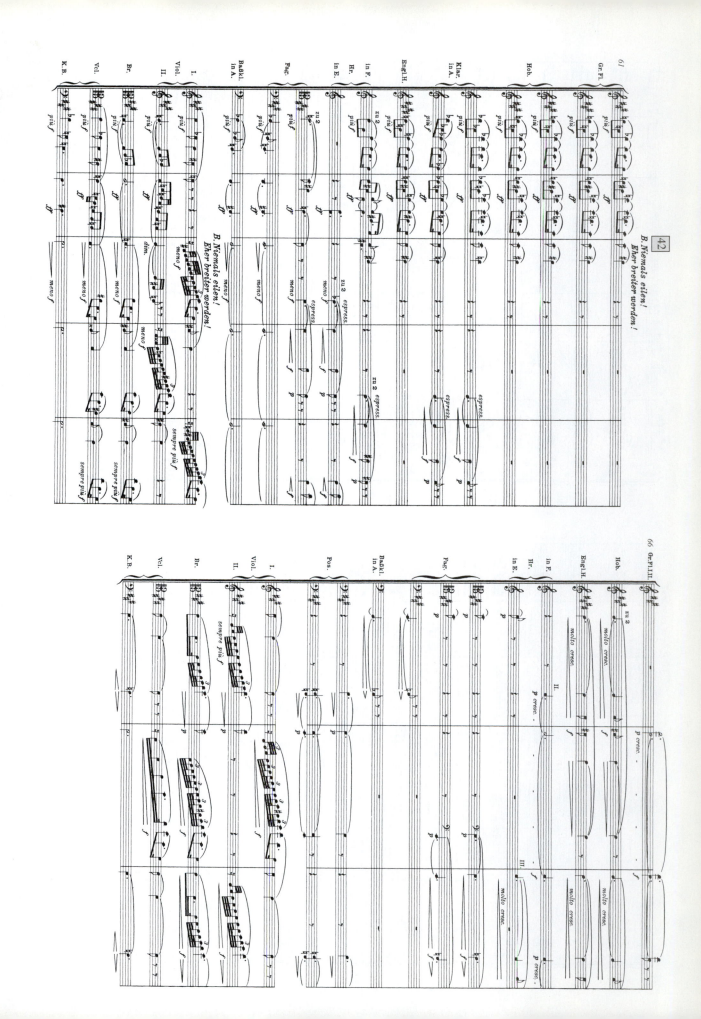

No. 138 Wagner: *Tristan und Isolde*

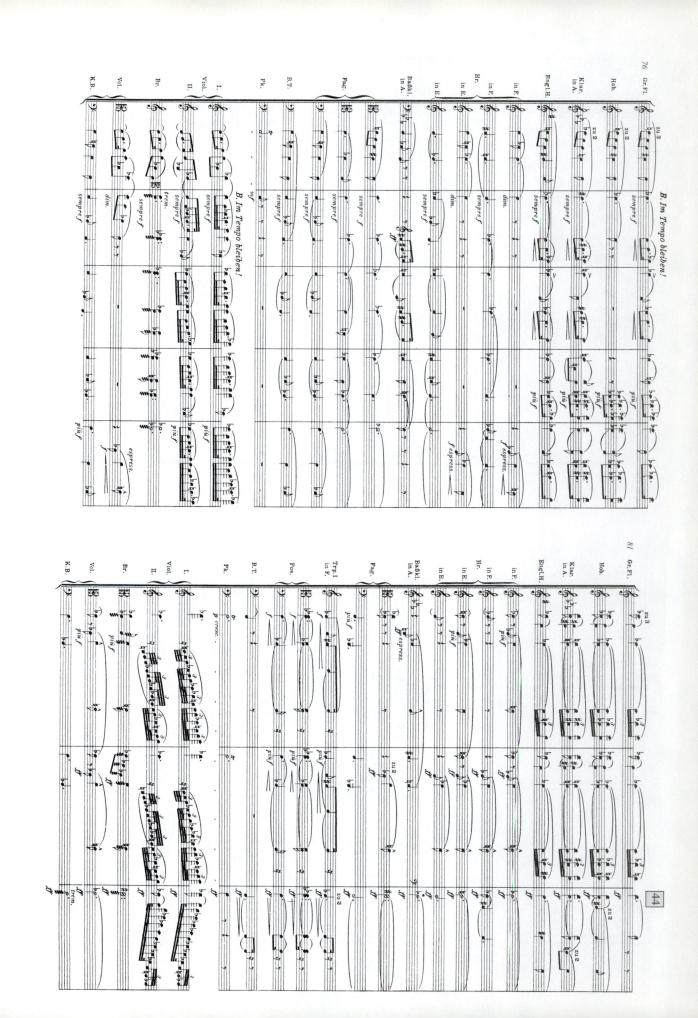

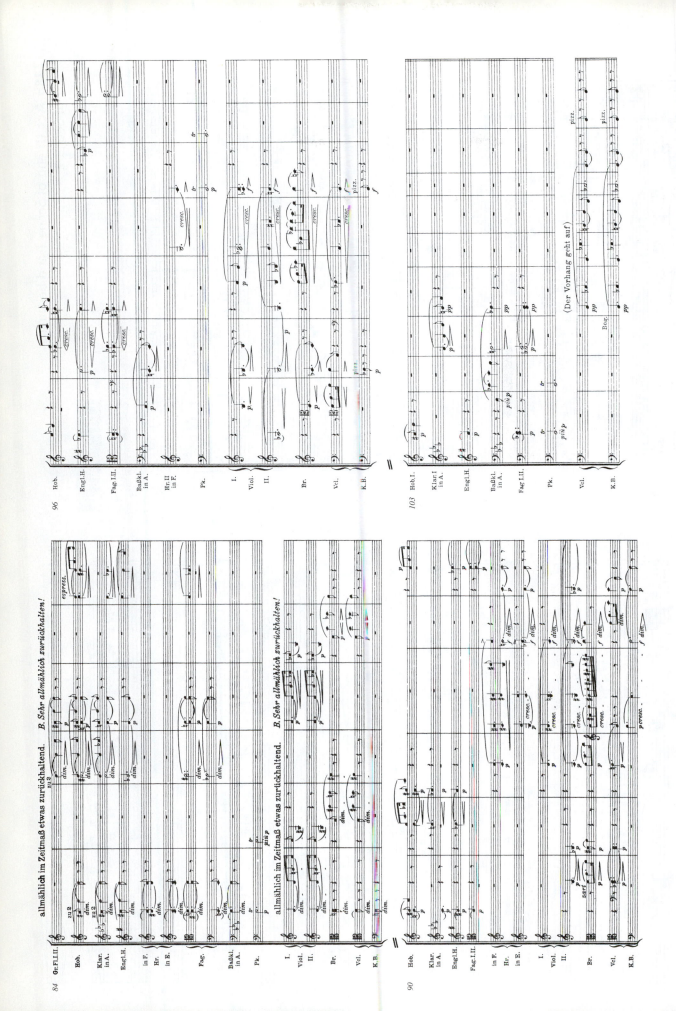

No. 138 Wagner: *Tristan und Isolde*

138b Act II: end of Scene I and beginning
of Scene 2

p. 474

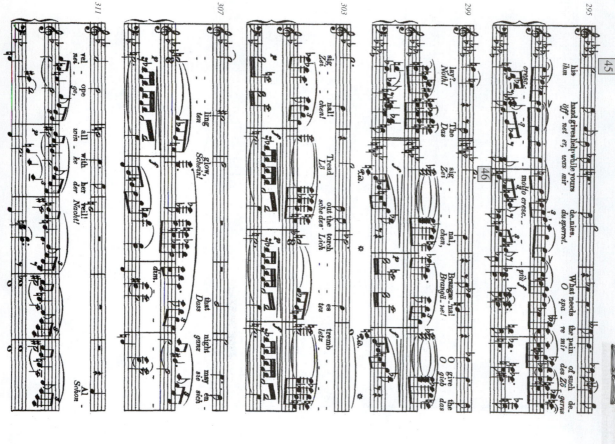

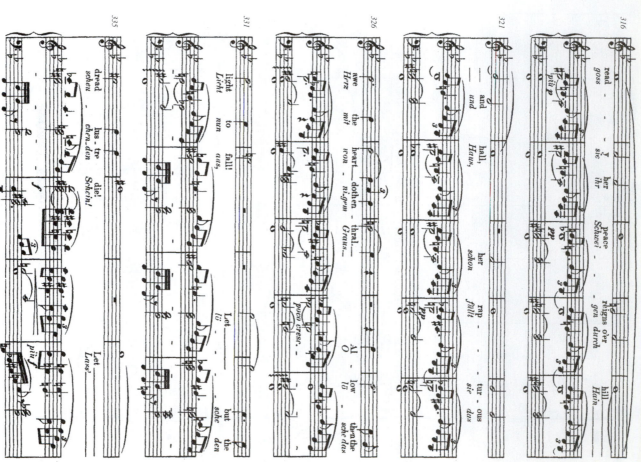

Note: This edition is a piano-vocal reduction of Wagner's original score for voices and orchestra.

No. 138 Wagner: *Tristan und Isolde*

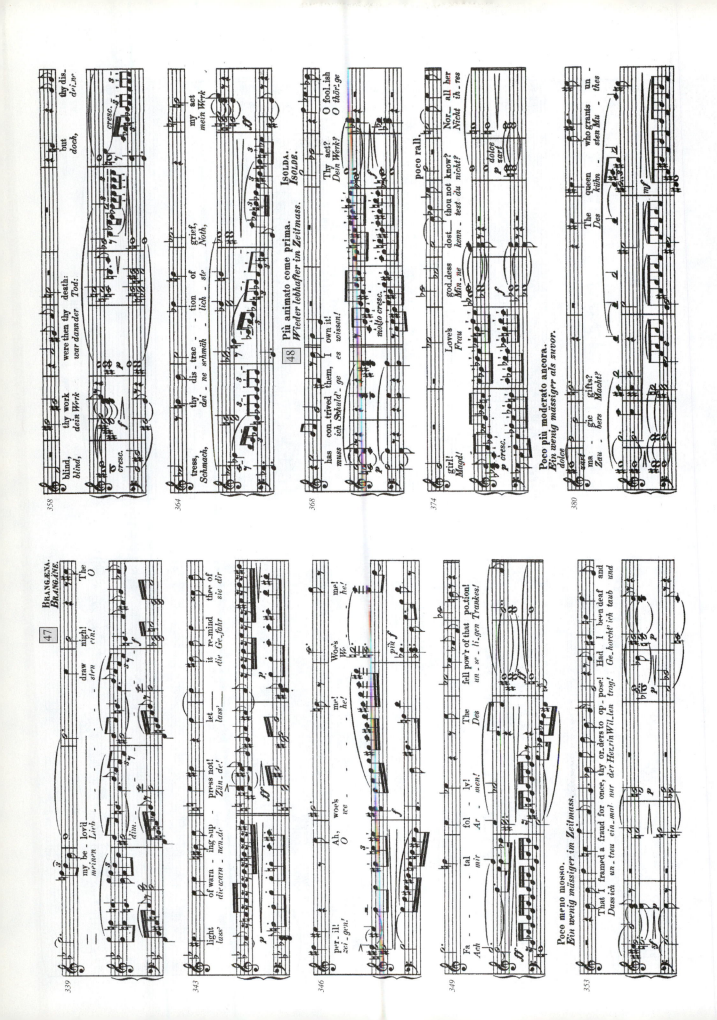

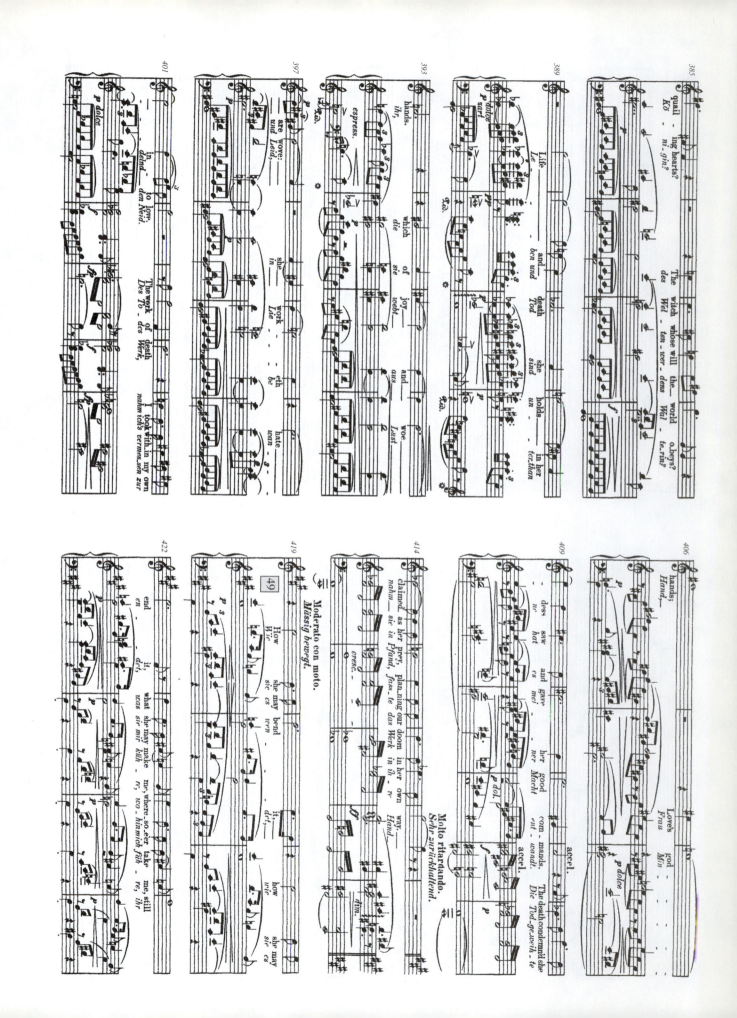

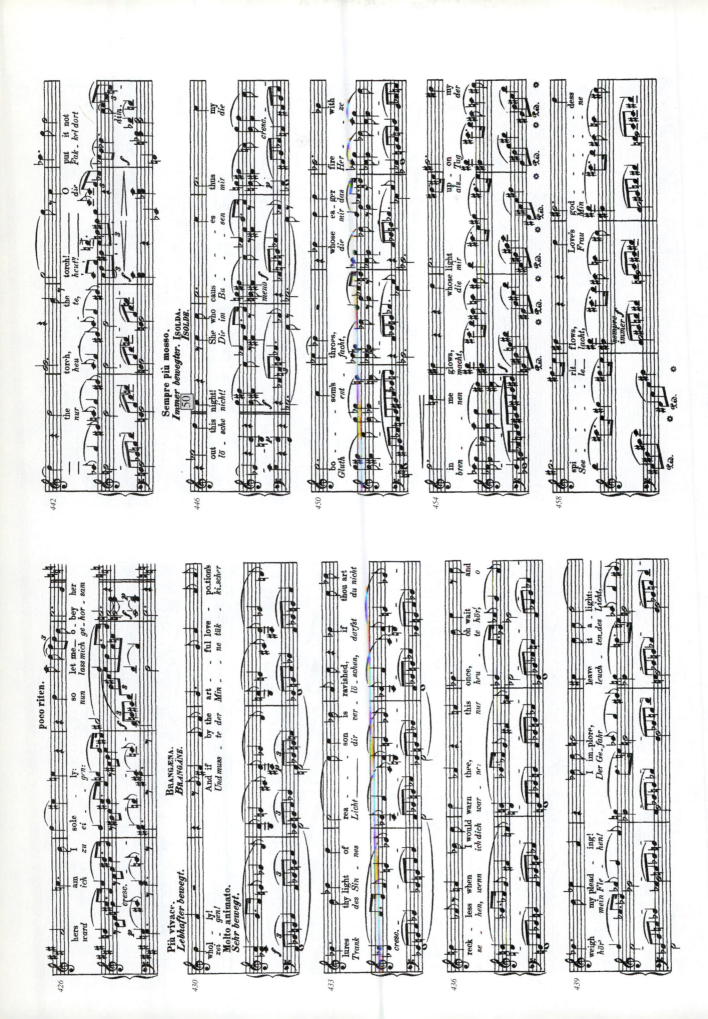

No. 138 Wagner: *Tristan und Isolde*

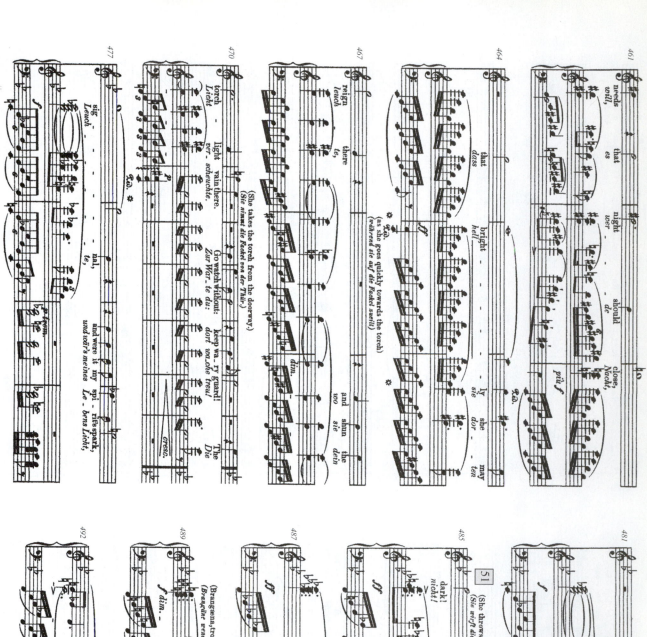

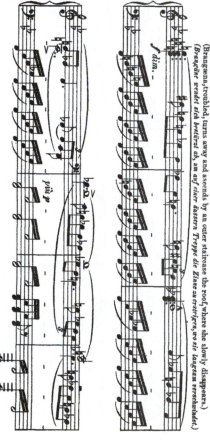

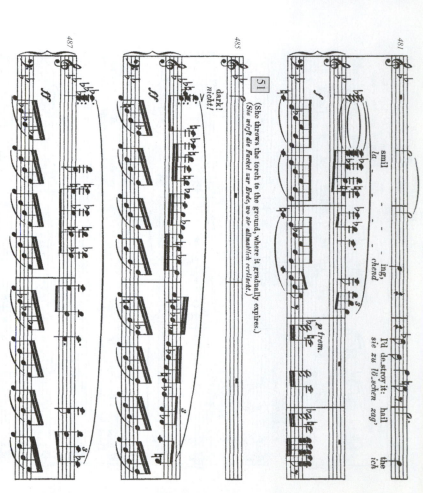

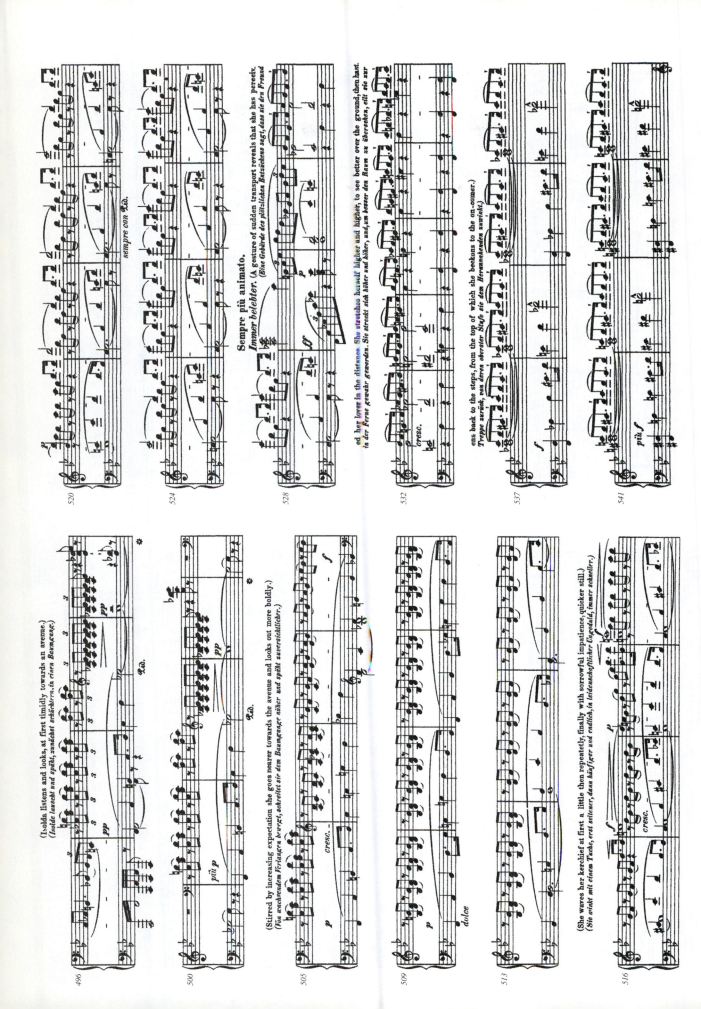

No. 138 Wagner: *Tristan und Isolde*

Scene II.— Zweite Scene.

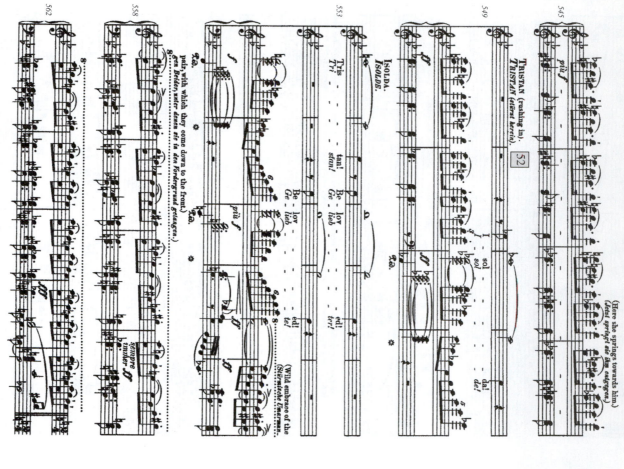

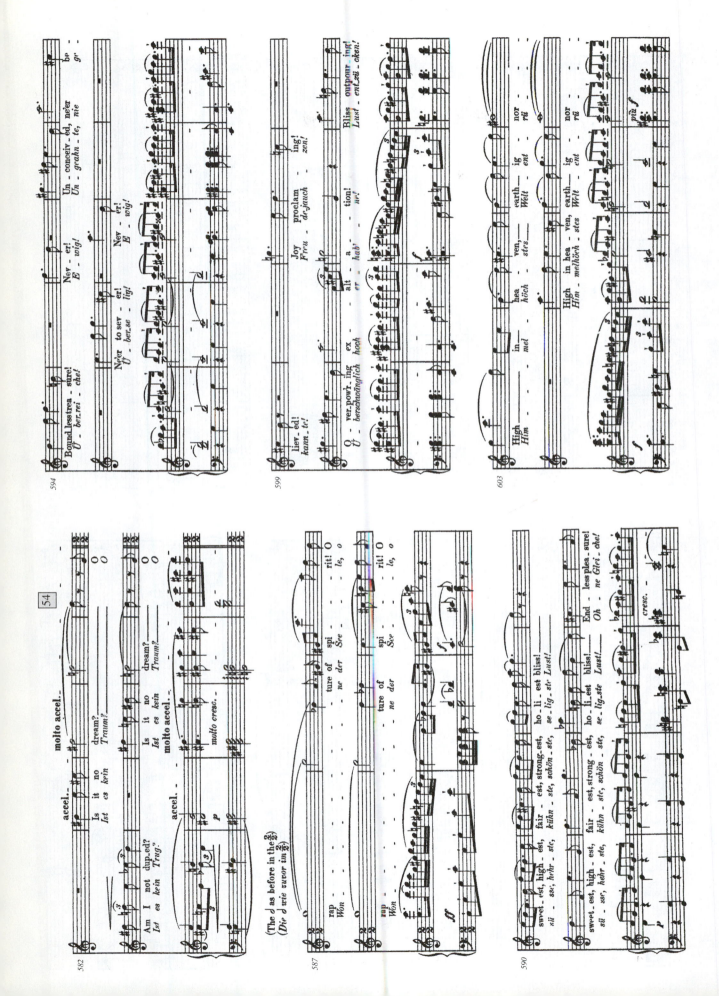

No. 138 Wagner: *Tristan und Isolde*

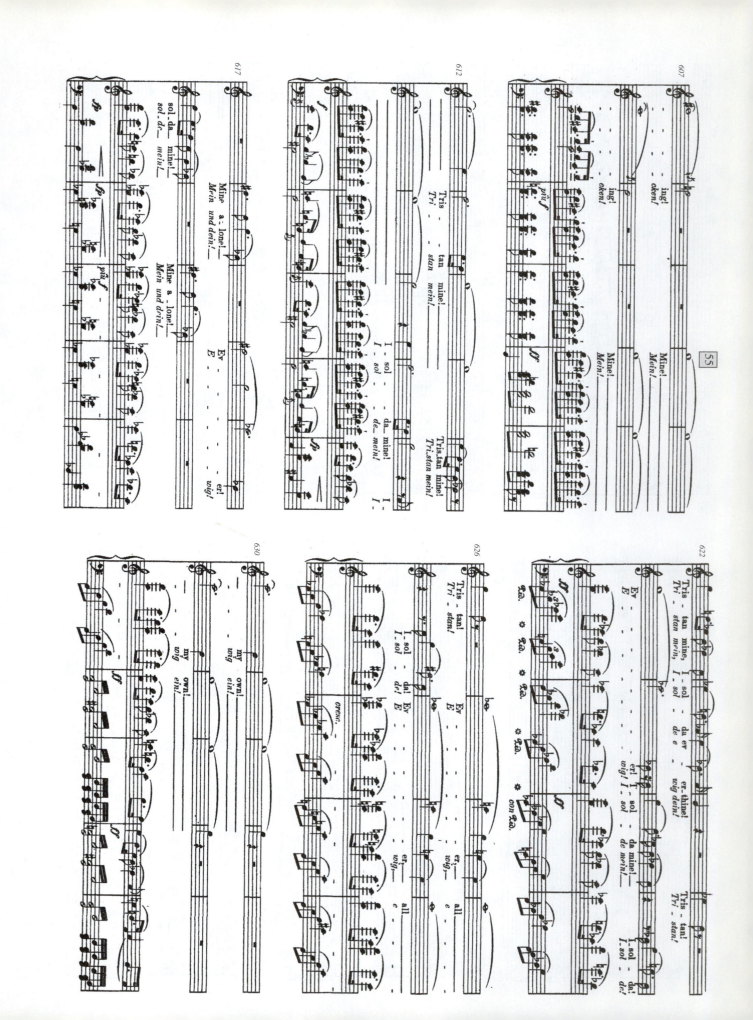

No. 138 Wagner: *Tristan und Isolde*

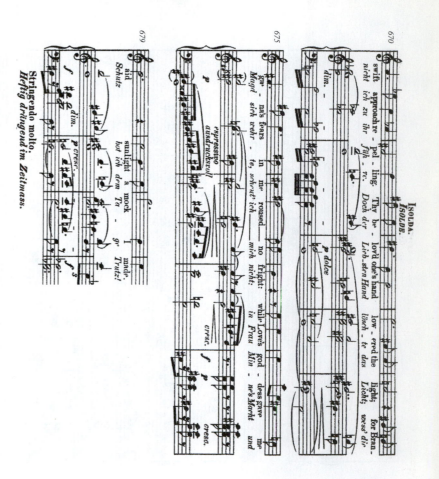

ISOLDA.
ISOLDE.

Stringendo molto.
Heftig drängend im Zeitmass.

The Prelude (overture) begins with what will prove to be the most important musical idea over the course of the drama, one associated with the love potion Tristan and Isolde will drink in Act I (see Example 2).

The extended dissonance on the so-called "Tristan chord" (on the downbeat of m. 2) and its upward chromatic "resolution" (m. 3) convey the sense of painful yearning that dominates love's longing. The formal structure of the prelude as a whole does not follow sonata form or any other conventional pattern. Instead, Wagner goes on to fragment, extend, transpose, invert, and otherwise manipulate the opening idea in a variety of ways. The rising minor chromatic third first heard in m. 2–3 assumes special importance. Wagner manipulates a fragment of this theme (Example 3a, first measure; Example 3b) by using repetition, harmonic variation, melodic variation, and silence to enrich each successive statement. The Prelude as a whole follows no established convention of large-scale form. Instead, the music seems to propel itself forward through a series of constant transformations. For example, the rising three-note figure that first appears in the cellos in m. 17 (see Example 3, m. 2) represents a metamorphosis of the rising minor chromatic third from m. 2–3. This new idea, in turn is further fragmented and manipulated in m. 36–37. The orchestra, all the while, builds gradually in size and volume, reaching a high point of sorts with the fortissimo statement of yet another

version of the cello's theme at m. 74. But a crashing dissonance (m. 83) turns out to be the true climax, however, for it ushers in a return to the quiet tension of the opening (m. 85). There is no sense of resolution here: the music closes pianissimo and leads without a pause into the opening scene of Act I.

Example 2 The "love potion" motif, with the "Tristan chord" highlighted

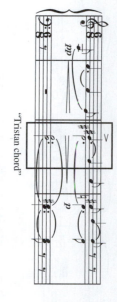

"Tristan chord"

In the excerpt from Act II, Isolde and her maidservant Brangaene await the onset of night; Tristan has left with King Mark's hunting party, but at a signal from Isolde—the moment she extinguishes the torch on the castle's ramparts—Tristan will return. The musical transformations of the love potion motif continue throughout, as for example when Brangaene laments having substituted a love potion for what was supposed to be a death potion (m. 351–353), and then again more tellingly shortly afterward (m. 380–382), when Isolde explains that it was the power of love that caused the potion to transform itself. Here, underneath Isolde's declamation (beginning at m. 385), the orchestra spins out a series of thematic variants based on the characteristic rising chromatic third we first heard in the work's opening measures. Isolde now views the love potion quite differently, and the orchestra reflects this by presenting the motif within the guise of a softer, more lyrical tone. In Wagnerian terms, Isolde gives voice to what the orchestra is already expressing through music alone.

The motif known as "love's longing" (Example 4) represents yet another manipulation of the rising chromatic third. Here, the melodic trajectory is reversed: the chromatic line moves downward and is supported by a clearly outlined triadic base. The feeling here is more confident, more directional, as befits the dramatic situation. This motif dominates the tension that builds toward Tristan's return. Still another metamorphosis of this motif (Example 5) emerges when Tristan finally arrives: the theme becomes ecstatic, rising in its opening to a high note before descending; rather than descending from the very start. Such changes, subtle but effective, have led more than one commentator to accord this idea a separate identity, associating it with the idea of "bliss"—which is of course the desired consequence of longing. The musical and dramatic parallels function in tandem.

Another prominent *Leitmotiv* in *Tristan and Isolde* is associated with death (*Tod* in the German text). Like the "love potion" motif, the "death" motif (Example 6) is chromatic and harmonically unusual. (Wagner often used chromatic themes or unusual harmonic progressions to evoke conditions of pain, such as love and death.) Although the "death" motif manifests itself in many different ways, its characteristic harmonic feature is the juxtaposition of two otherwise distant chords (such as Ab major and A major, as in Example 6, combined with a distinctive dotted rhythm.

Having established these and other motifs in the listener's mind (conscious or unconscious), Wagner is free to use it in any number of ways, some of them obvious, some of them

Example 6 "Death"

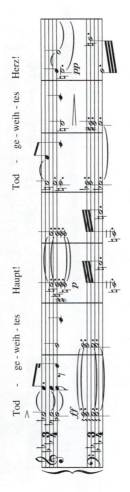

Tod - ge - weih - tes   Haupt!   Tod - ge - weih - tes   Herz!

Death-destined head! Death-destined heart!

Example 3 Subsequent transformations of the "love potion" motif

(a)

(b)

Example 4 "Love's longing"

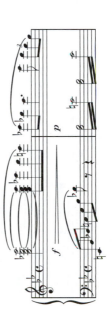

Example 5 "Bliss"

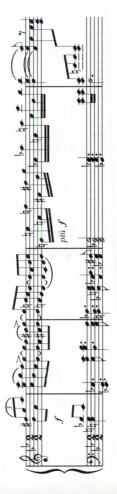

not. Near the end of Act II Scene 1, for example, at the moment when Isolde extinguishes her torch, thereby giving Tristan the signal to leave the hunting party and return to the castle, Wagner embeds the "death" motif in the orchestra (beginning at m. 485). (The texture is so thick at this point that the motif is not evident in the piano reduction of the score in the Anthology.) What is the connection between this moment and death? Once Tristan returns, the lovers will consummate their passion, which in turn will lead to their deaths. By linking the extinguishing of the torch to the "death" motif, Wagner is telling us, in musical terms, that the act carries ultimately fatal consequences.

The labels we have been using to identify these Leitmotivs, although useful for analyzing Wagner's music, can lead us to think of them (incorrectly) as fixed entities, both musically and in terms of their dramatic associations. Probably for this reason, Wagner himself almost never explicitly identified any of these themes. It would be tedious, pointless, and ultimately impossible to ascribe an individual name to every different manifestation of every motif, in any event. More important is to recognize how Wagner works his Leitmotivs into an ever-evolving web of complementary and contrasting musical and dramatic relationships that can sustain a work lasting many hours in performance.

The performance: Improvisation and embellishment have never played an important role in Wagner's. The demands on the singers' voices are nevertheless considerable. In *Tristan und Isolde*, the two main characters remain on stage for very long stretches at a time: vocal endurance is a prerequiste of great Wagnerian voices. They must also be able to project through the sound of a large orchestra that is itself richly textured. Beyond all this, singers must negotiate a dauntingly wide register. This is particularly true of sopranos (see, for example, Isolde's high C two octaves above middle C in m. 589). The recording here, made during a live performance in 1972, features Birgit Nilsson (b. 1918), the greatest Wagnerian soprano of her generation.

No. 138 *Wagner: Tristan und Isolde*

139 The Pirates of Penzance (1879)
William S. Gilbert (1836–1911) and
Arthur Sullivan (1842–1900)

Mabel, Samuel, Major-General, Girls, and Pirates

CD11 Track 57

p. 484

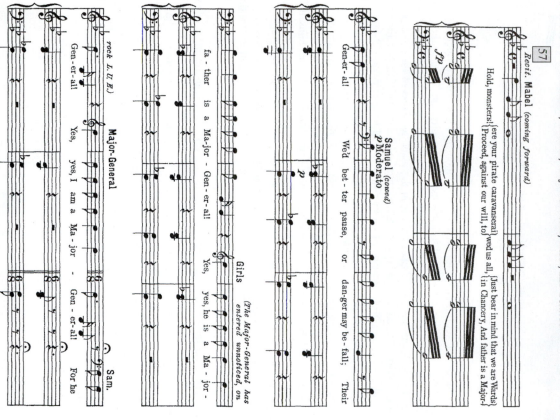

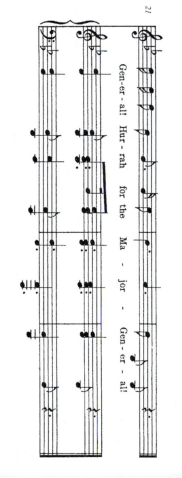

58 Allegro vivace

ff

2

Major-General

1. I am the ver-y mod-el of a mod-ern Ma-jor-Gen-er-al; I've
2. I know our myth-ic his-to-ry, King Ar-thur's and Sir Car-a-doc's; I

pp

in - for - ma - tion veg - e - ta - ble, an - i - mal, and min - er - al: I
an - swer hard a - cros - tics; I've a pret - ty taste for par - a - dox; I

know the kings of Eng-land, and I quote the fights his-tor - i - cal, From
quote, in el - e - gi - acs, all the crimes of He - lio - gab - a - lus; In

Mar - a - thon to Wa - ter - loo, in or - der cat - e - gor - i - cal; I'm
con - ics I can floor pe - cu - li - ar - i - ties pa - rab - o - lous; I can

ver - y well ac-quaint-ed, too, with mat - ters math - e - mat - i - cal, I
tell un - doubt-ed Ra - pha - els from Ger - ard Dows and Zof - fa - nies I

un - der-stand e - qua-tions,both the sim - ple and quad-rat - i - cal, A -
know the croak-ing cho - rus from the *Frogs* of Ar - is - toph - a - nes! Then

bout bi - no - mial the - o - rem I'm teem - ing with a lot o' news,
I can hum a fugue of which I've heard the mu - sic's din a - fore,

17

19

21

23

25

No. I39 Gilbert and Sullivan: *The Pirates of Penzance*

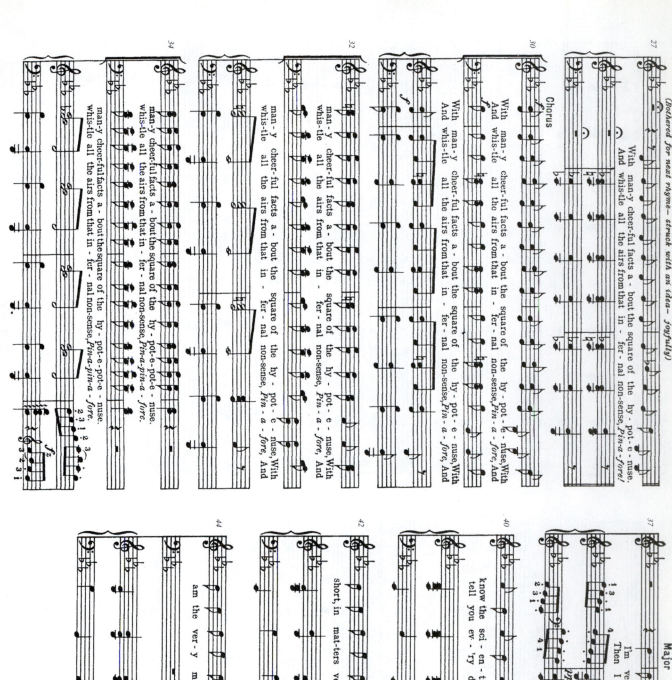
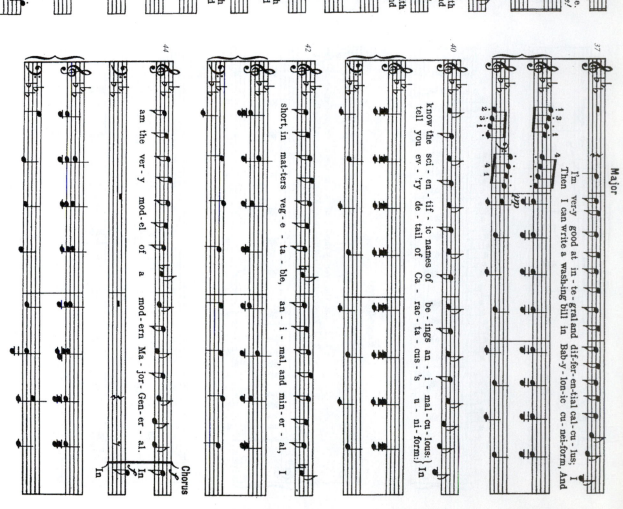

No. 139 Gilbert and Sullivan: *The Pirates of Penzance*

46
short, in mat-ters veg-e-ta-ble, an-i-mal, and min-er-al, He
short, in mat-ters veg-e-ta-ble, an-i-mal, and min-er-al, He
f
48
is the ver-y mod-el of a mod-ern Ma-jor-Gen-er-al.
is the ver-y mod-el of a mod-ern Ma-jor-Gen-er-al.
59
Slower
50
3. In fact, when I know what is meant by
pp
53
"mam-e-lon" and "rav-e-lin", When I can tell at sight a Mau-ser
55
ri-fle from a jav-e-lin, When such af-fairs as sor-ties and sur-
57
pris-es I'm more wa-ry at, And when I know pre-cise-ly what is
59
meant by "com-mis-sa-ri-at", When I have learnt what prog-ress has been
61
made in mod-ern gun-ner-y, When I know more of tac-tics than a
63
nov-ice in a nun-ner-y— In short, when I've a smat-ter-ing of

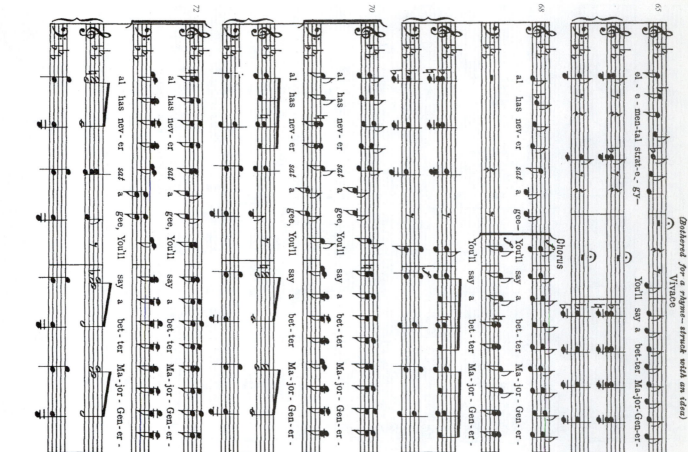

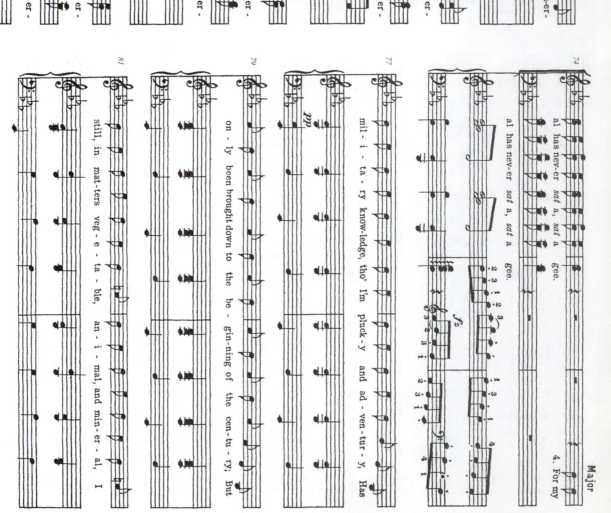

Gilbert and Sullivan's operettas—plays with significant quantities of sung music—draw heavily on the principal forms of opera, with numbers that are easily recognizable as arias, duets, ensembles, and even accompanied recitatives. At the same time, their works manage to poke fun these very same conventions. The sustained tremolo in the opening recitative of this scene from *The Pirates of Penzance*, for example, suggests a matter of grave importance, and the pirates are indeed cowed when Mabel informs them that her father is major general. The ensuing aria ("I am the Very Model of a Modern Major General") parodies the kind of rapid-fire declamation so popular in Italian opera (see, for example, Figaro's aria, Anthology No. 136). This "patter song" is all the more amusing coming from a major general rather than a servant.

Performance notes: The performance here is from the D'Oyly Carte Opera Company production recorded in 1949. Established by Richard D'Oyly Carte in 1875 and still in operation today, this troupe gave the premiere performances of many of Gilbert and Sullivan's most celebrated operettas. Every generation of this company has interpreted these works in its own way, but the degree of historical continuity in a single institution remains remarkable.

No. 139 Gilbert and Sullivan: *The Pirates of Penzance*

140 Virga Jesse floruit (1885)

Anton Bruckner (1824–1896)

CD11 Track 60

p. 485

Alla breve, feierlich langsam.

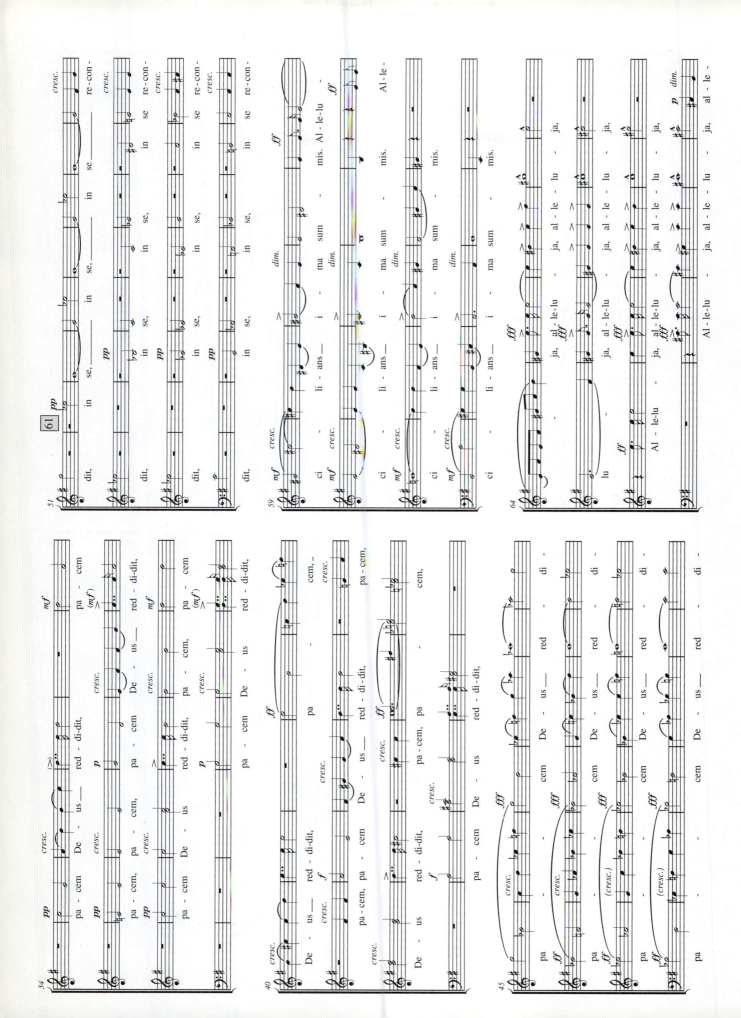

No. 140 Bruckner: *Virga Jesse floruit*

No. 140 Bruckner: *Virga Jesse floruit*

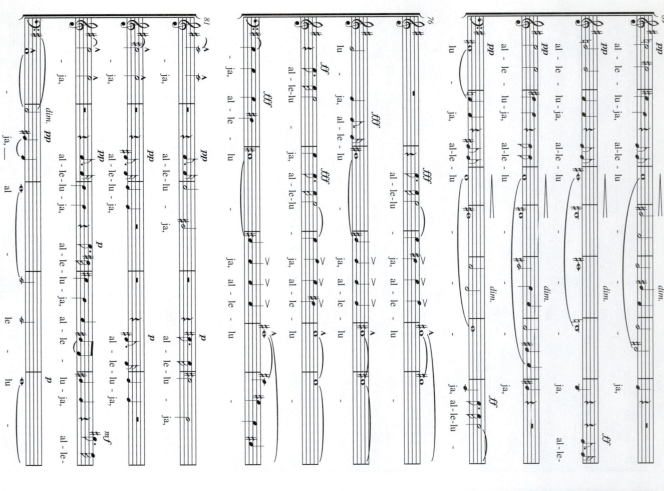

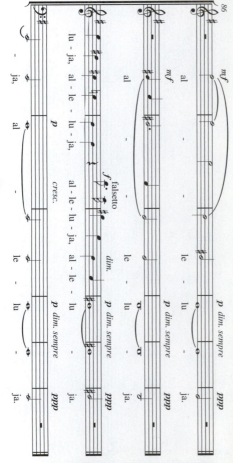

Virga Jesse floruit:
Virgo Deum et hominem genuit:
pacem Deus reddidit,
in se reconcilians ima summis.
Alleluja.

The rod of Jesse blossomed:
A virgin brought forth [both] God and man:
God restored peace,
in Himself reconciling the lowest [and] highest.
Alleluia.

The text of this motet is the Alleluia of any Mass for the Feast of the Blessed Virgin Mary during Paschal time. It refers to Isaiah's Old Testament prophecy that an offshoot of Jesse (the father of King David) would blossom and give birth to the Messiah. The strict four-part counterpoint and a cappella setting suggest at first a motet in the style of the late Renaissance. But the unusual harmonic turn and crescendo on the first *floruit* ("flourished") in m. 7–9 reveal this to be a work of the Caecilian movement, an attempt by various composers of the 19th century to recreate—without imitating precisely—the style of Renaissance polyphony. The linear chromaticism, the sudden harmonic turns, and the wide melodic leaps in the individual voice parts are all typical of the late 19th century.

141 An der schönen blauen Donau,
Op. 314 (On the Beautiful Blue Danube)
(Original orchestral version reduced for piano) (1867)
Johann Strauss, Jr. (1825–1899)

No. 141 Strauss: An der schönen blauen Donau

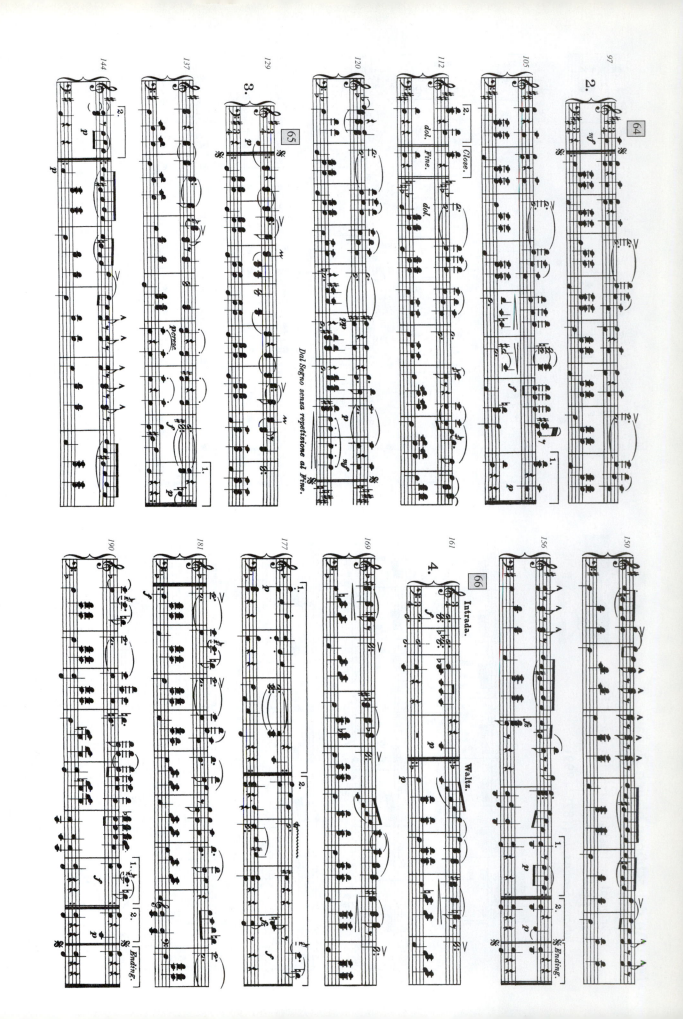

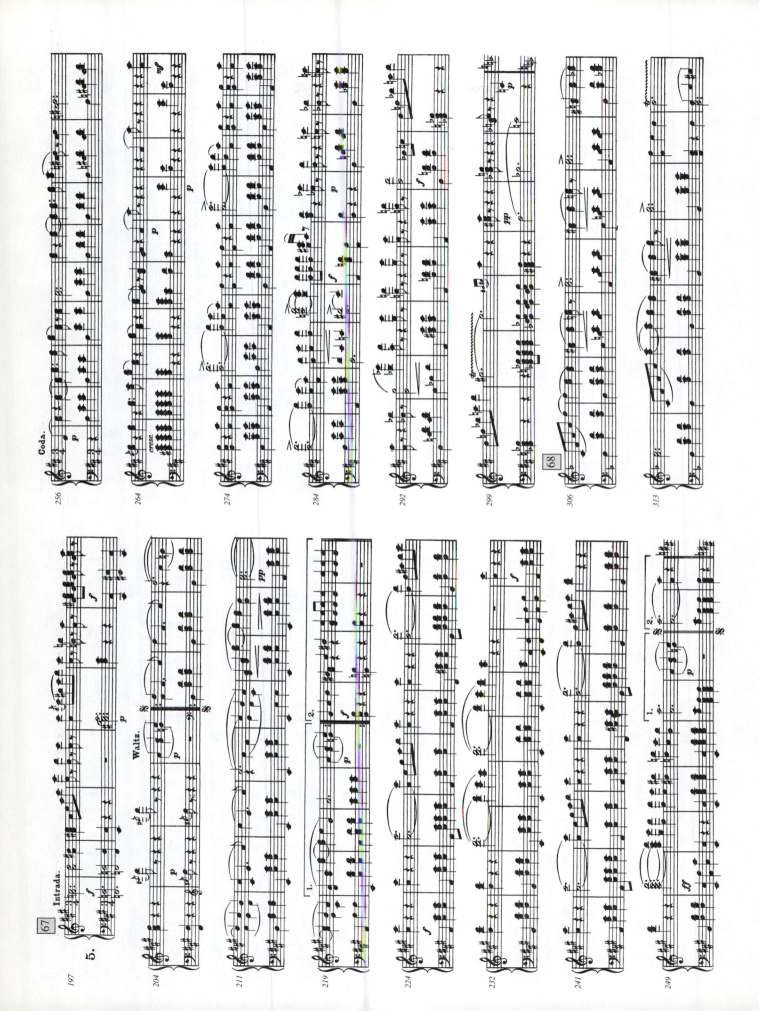

No. 141 Strauss: *An der schönen blauen Donau*

No. 141 Strauss: *An der schönen blauen Donau*

The form of Strauss's "On the Beautiful Blue Danube" is typical of many dances from the late 19th century. It consists of an extended introduction followed by a series of individual waltzes (numbered 1, 2, 3, etc.), most in binary form, each with its own thematic idea, and some with their own introductions (marked "Intrada" in the score). This modular structure allowed ensembles to repeat any individual waltz as often as needed. At the same time, Strauss was careful to integrate the sequence of dances into a coherent whole. The introduction (notated in A major but heard as the dominant of D) establishes the tonic key of D major for most of the waltzes. The fourth waltz modulates to F major for the sake of harmonic variety, and an extended coda brings the work to a close in the tonic and reprises the theme of the opening waltz. Typically for dance music, each of the individual waltzes within *An der schönen blauen Donau* is built on units of four or eight measures, which join to create larger units of 16 or 32 measures. This kind of rhythmic and structural predictability was essential for the function of social dance and would become the basis for many forms of dance or dance-related genres in the 20th century, including ragtime, the blues, and even rock-and-roll.

142 King Cotton (Original band version
reduced for piano) (1895)
John Philip Sousa (1854–1932)

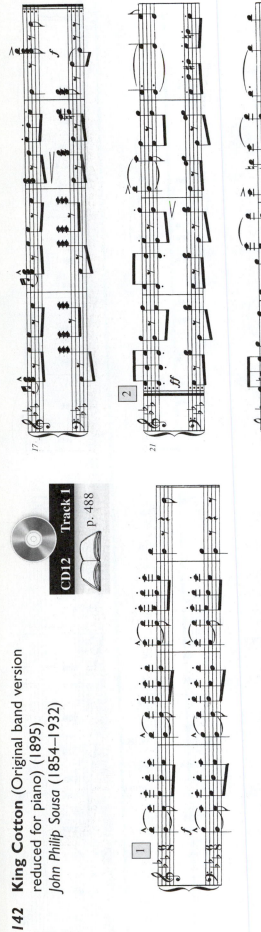

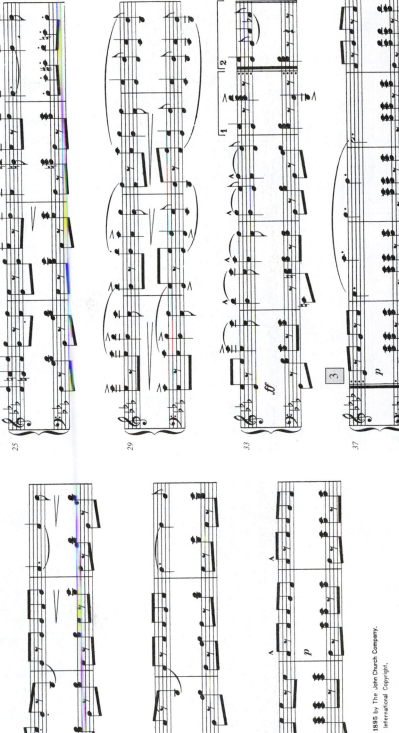

No. 142 Sousa: *King Cotton*

The march, like dance music, was written to coordinate physical movement—in this case, of soldiers. Like Strauss's waltzes, Sousa's marches are invariably modular in structure, built on units of 4, 8, 16, and 32 measures, and in performance, each unit can be repeated as often as desired. In *King Cotton*, every unit marked by a repeat sign consists of 16 measures, with an extended closing section of 32 (16+16 measures). For each of these, Sousa wrote out altered orchestrations and added new contrapuntal lines to be played the second time around; note, for example, the added trombone line that stands out prominently (but is not conveyed in the piano reduction) in the repetition of the last half of the march's last unit. Tonal closure is not an issue of great concern in the march repertory: Sousa's marches often begin in one key and end in another. *King Cotton*, starts in the key of E♭, and ends in A♭ major.

143 The Nutcracker (excerpts) (1892)
Peter Ilyich Tchaikovsky (1840–1893)

CD12   Track 5   p. 490

Le café (Danse Arabe)

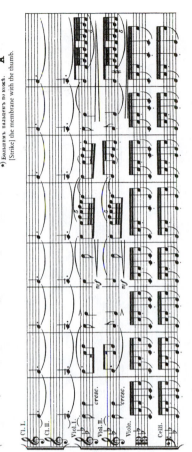

*) Большимъ пальцемъ по кожѣ.
[Strike] the membrane with the thumb.

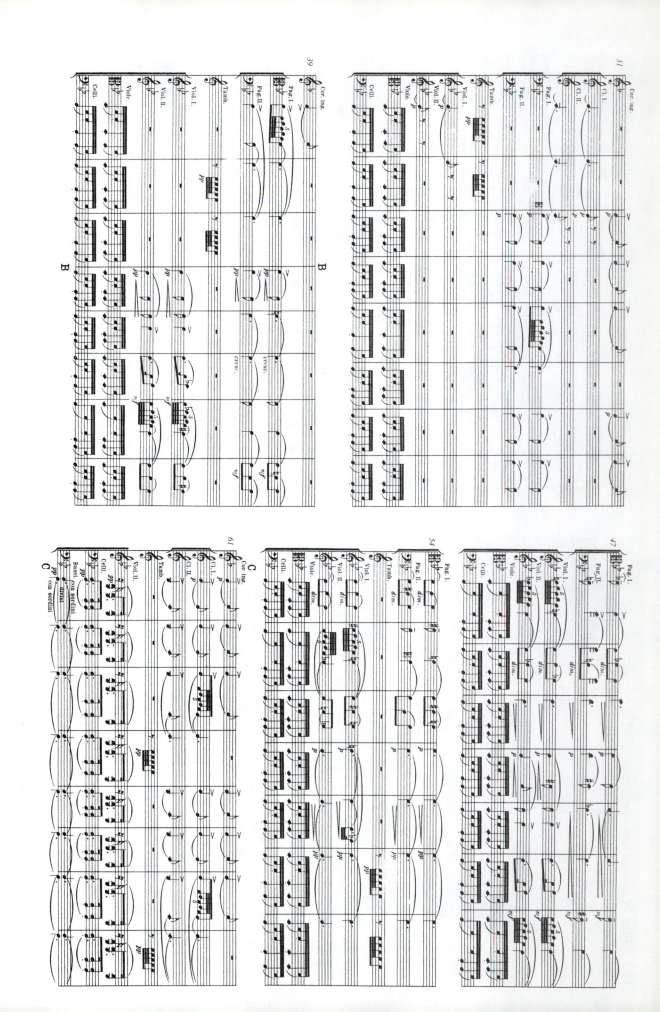

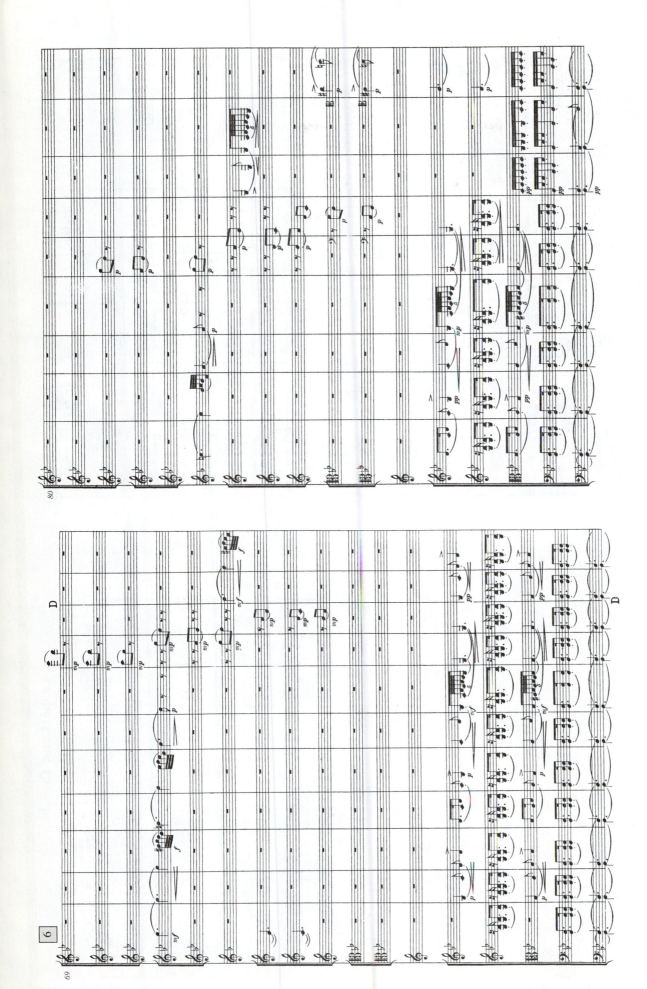

No. 143 Tchaikovsky: The Nutcracker

■ No. 143 Tchaikovsky: The Nutcracker

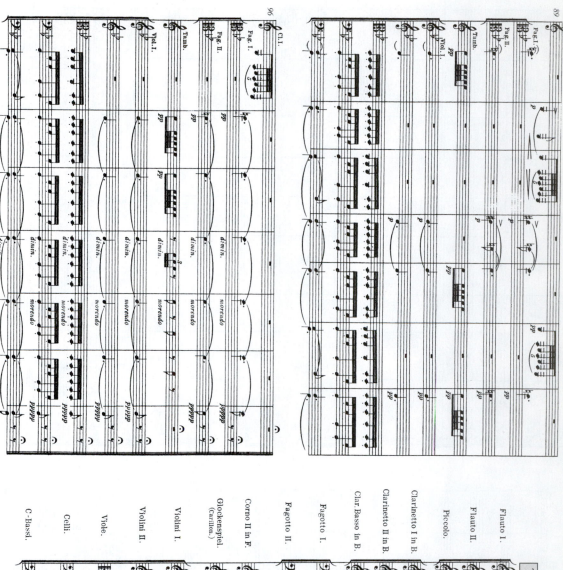

Le thé (Danse Chinoise)

No. 143 Tchaikovsky: *The Nutcracker*

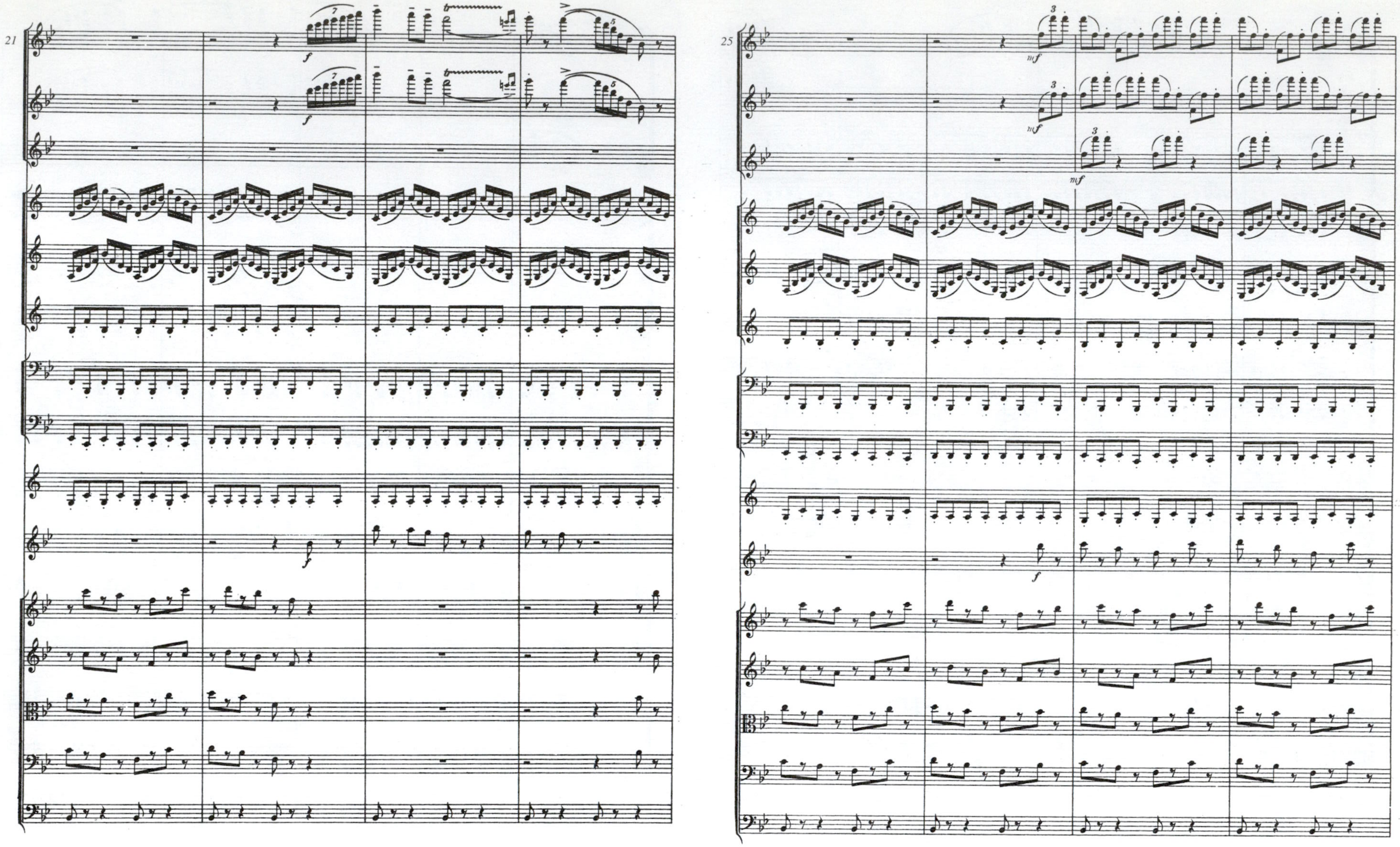
21
f
f
f
25
mf
mf
mf
f

Trépak (Danse Russe)

Tempo di trepak, molto vivace.

Tempo di trepak, molto vivace.

No. 143 Tchaikovsky: *The Nutcracker*

No. 143 Tchaikovsky: *The Nutcracker*

No. 143 Tchaikovsky: *The Nutcracker*

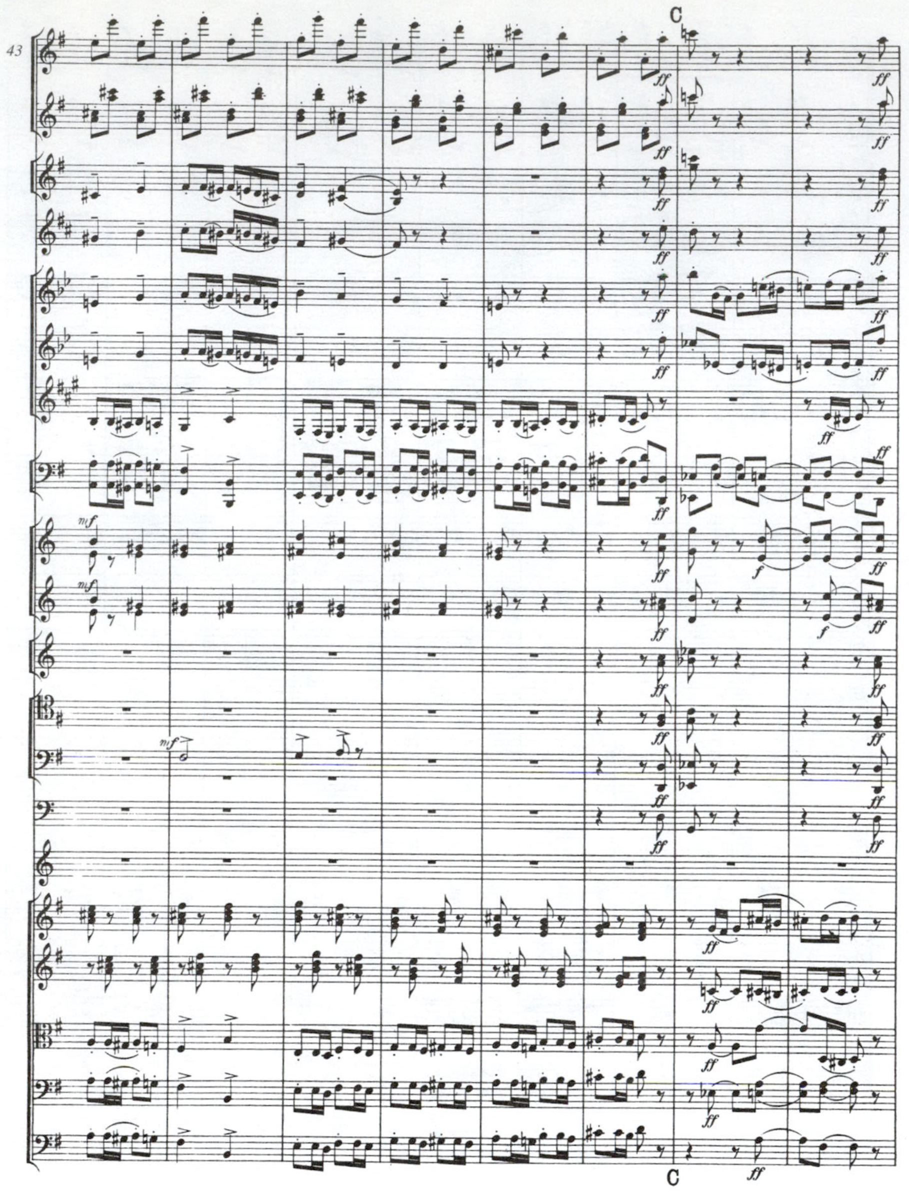
43
C
C

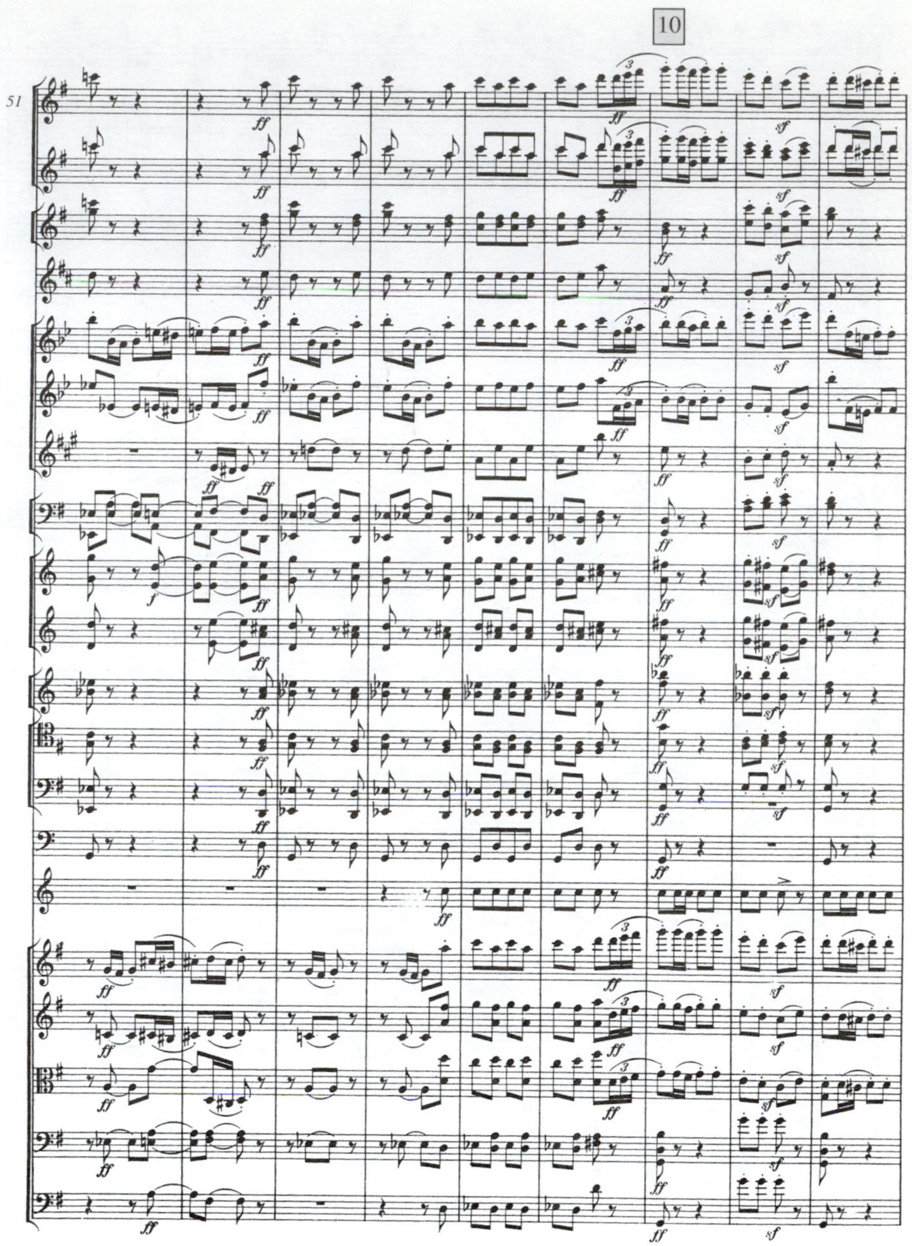
10
51

No. 143 Tchaikovsky: *The Nutcracker*

77

Prestissimo.

In the last third of the century, Tchaikovsky emerged as the preeminent composer of ballet music. His lyrical melodies and rich orchestrations combined to make his *Swan Lake* (1876), *Sleeping Beauty* (1889), and *The Nutcracker* (1892) among the most enduringly popular works of their kind. *The Nutcracker*, based on the well-known story by E. T. A. Hoffmann, combines a real-life plot with fairy-tale fantasy. In Act I, a mysterious inventor named Drosselmeyer gives a young girl, Clara, a magical nutcracker as a present. At night the nut-cracker comes to life and leads an army of toy soldiers into battle with an army of mice. When Clara saves the Nutcracker's life, he transforms into a handsome young man. In Act II, the transformed Nutcracker takes Clara on a magical journey that ends in the Land of Flowers, where they meet the Sugar Plum Fairy. The *divertissements* of Act II allow Tchaikovsky to construct a series of loosely connected vignettes, each of which presents the characteristic sound (or what at least was believed at the time to be the characteristic sound) of a variety of exotic lands. In "Le café" ("Coffee"), Tchaikovsky uses a drone-like bass beneath a trio of single-reed instruments (English horn and two clarinets), muted strings, and tambourine to evoke images of Arabia. "Le thé" ("Tea") takes us to China, for which Tchaikovsky creates a very different kind of sound based on the contrast of flutes and piccolo against pizzicato strings, all inflected melodies based on a pentatonic or quasi-pentatonic scale, traditionally as-sociated (at least in the Western mind) with the music of China. The initial statement of the pizzicato figure in the strings, for example, is constructed solely on the pitches F-A-B♭-C-D. The ensuing "Trépak" takes up the rhythms of this characteristically Russian dance. The mu-sical exoticism of all these dances held particular appeal for audiences of the late 19th cen-tury at a time when the European world was claiming dominion over vast portions of the earth.

Symphony No. 9 in E minor, Op. 95
("From the New World"), Largo (1893)
Antonín Dvořák (1841–1904)

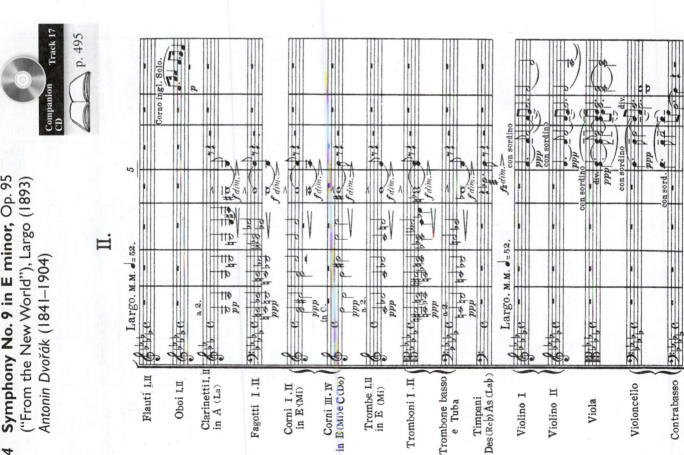

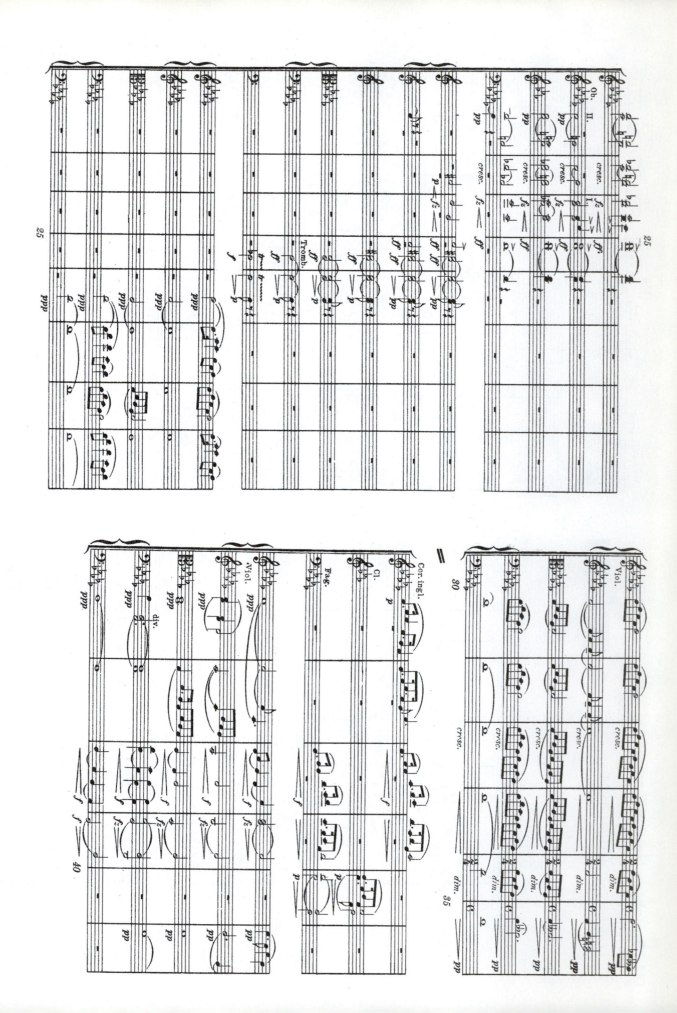

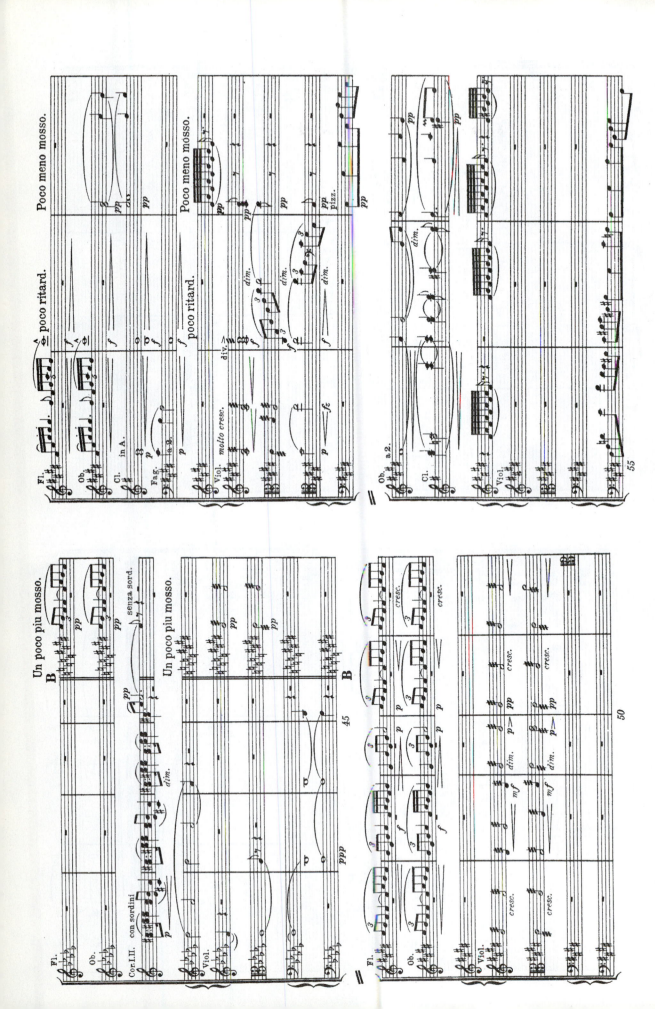

No. 144 Dvořák: Symphony No. 9 in E minor

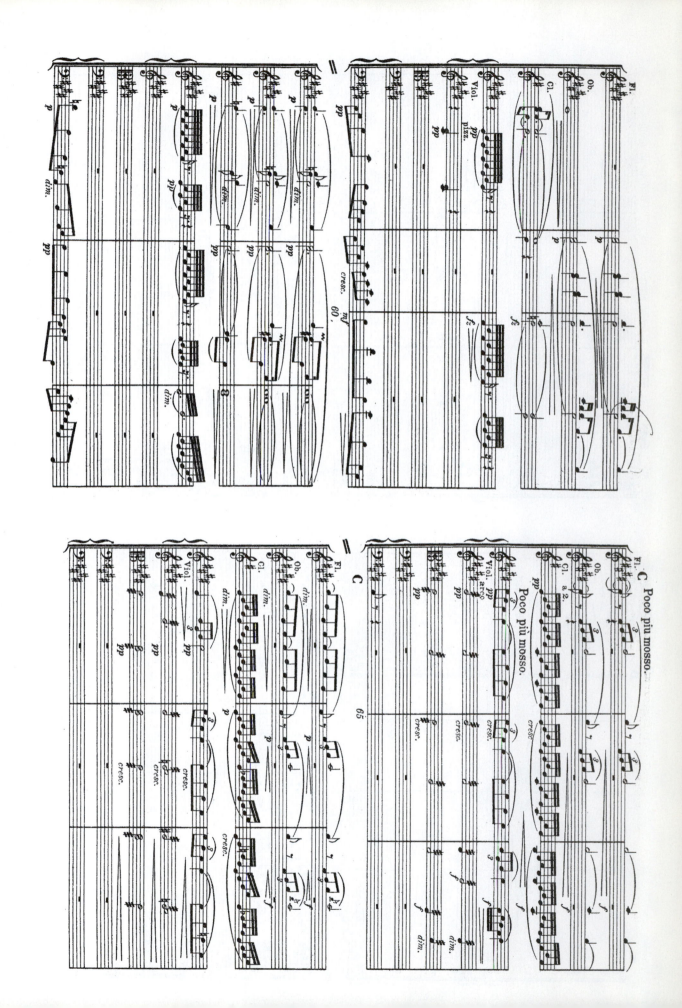

No. 144 Dvořák: Symphony No. 9 in E minor

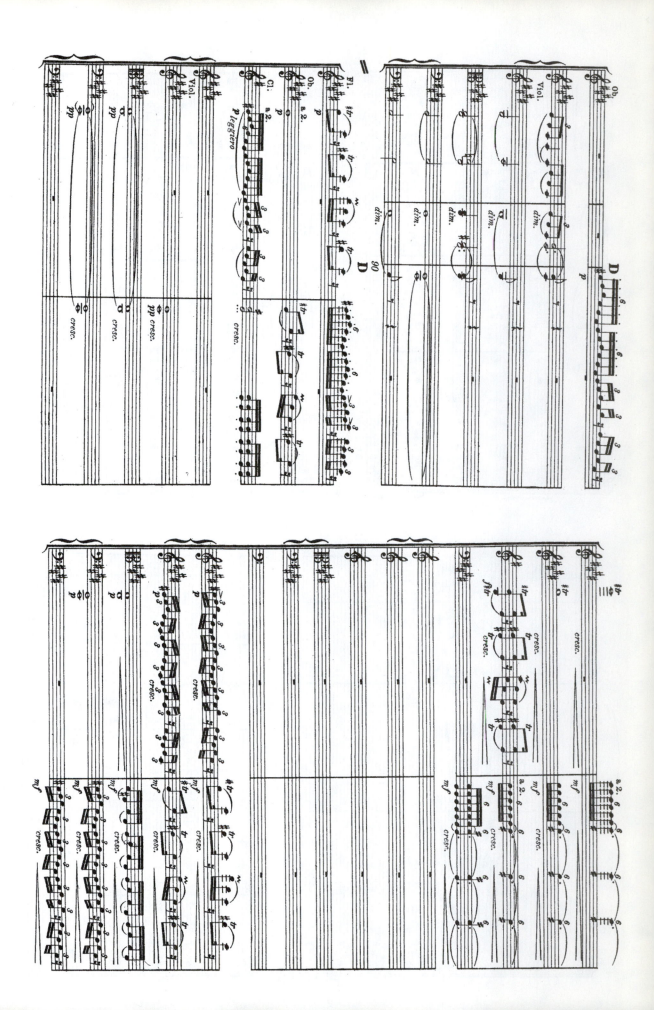

No. 144 Dvořák: *Symphony No. 9 in E minor*

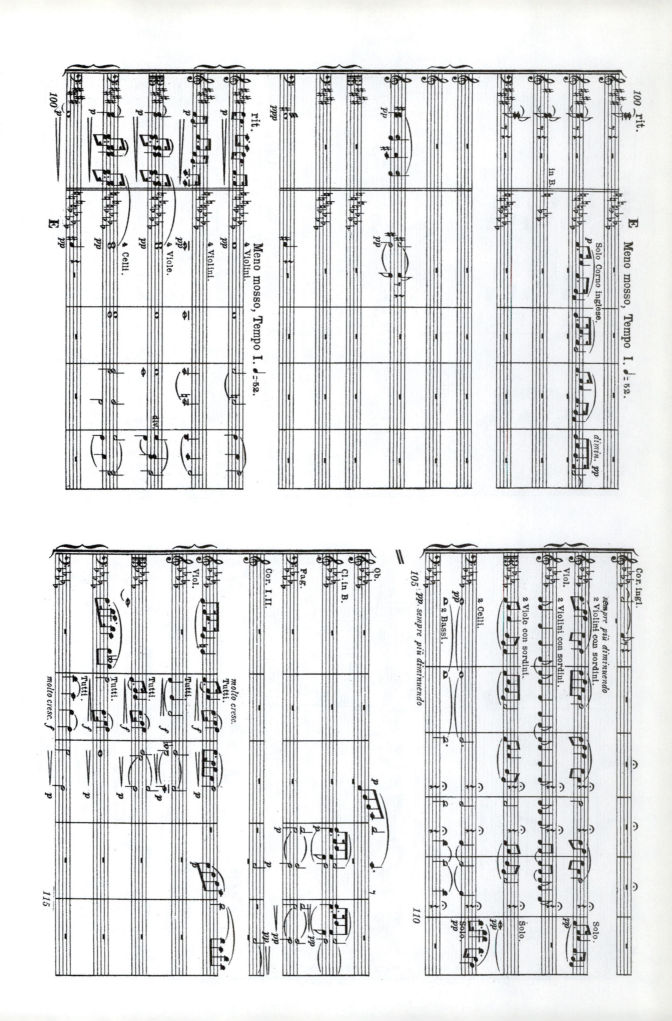

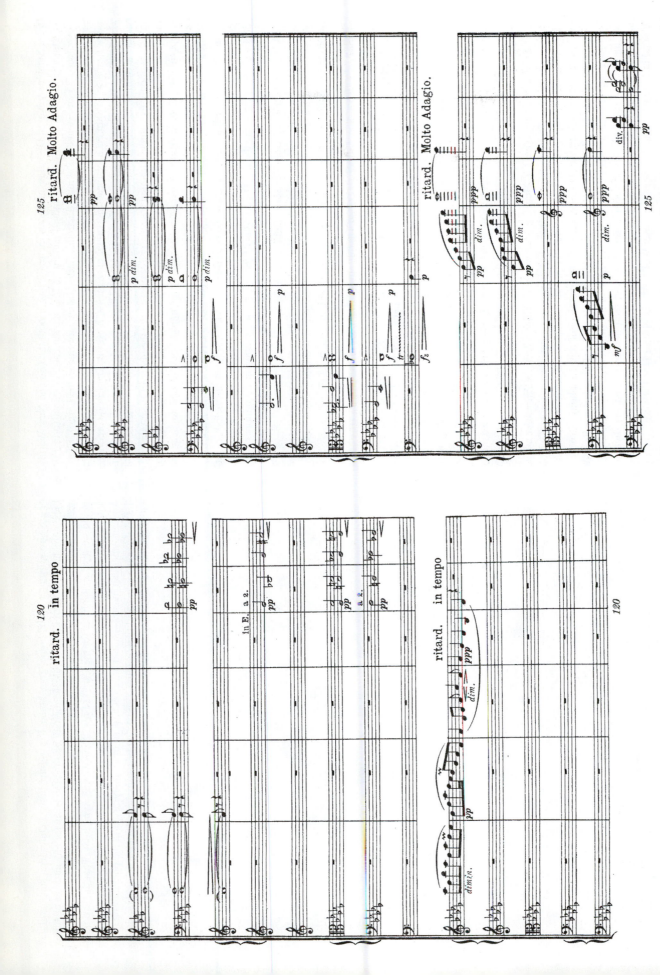

No. 144 Dvořák: Symphony No. 9 in E minor

In his Symphony No. 9, Dvořák synthesizes the traditions of both the Old and New Worlds. Structurally, the work follows the standard pattern of four movements: a sonata-form first movement with an extended slow introduction; a pastoral slow movement (the Largo); a fast, dance-like third movement in triple meter; and a rousing finale that breaks through from minor to major. Within each of these individual movements, however, Dvořák incorporates what he considered to be characteristic elements of indigenous American music. The principal theme of the Largo, for example (beginning at m. 7), is largely pentatonic—that is, based on a scale of only five notes. Although frequently associated with the music of East Asia, pentatonic scales figure large in many traditional ("folk") idioms of the West as well, and when Europeans like Dvořák heard Native Americans making music, they tended to hear the melodies as characteristically pentatonic. The opening phrase on the English horn (which sounds a fifth lower than notated) uses primarily the pitches Db, Eb, F, Ab, and Bb. The Cb that first appears in m. 11 functions as a leading tone to the tonic, but the scale of the melody pointedly avoids the fourth scale degree in the key of Db (that is, Gb), thereby lending a strongly pentatonic coloring to the theme. The melody of the contrasting section in C# minor (beginning at m. 46), played on flutes and oboes, is also constructed on a pentatonic scale (C#–D#–E–G#–B), again omitting the fourth scale degree (F#).

The orchestration and harmonization of both these melodies contribute to the pastoral tone of the movement. The English horn and oboe are both reed instruments and thus connected, at least indirectly, to the shepherd's reed pipe; the flute, too, is an instrument associated with the idealized serenity of the countryside. The drone bass underneath both melodies, reminiscent of a bagpipe, further contributes to this air of calm. But pastoral scenes are almost inevitably disrupted at some point, and Dvořák's Largo holds true to form: the C# minor section introduces a dark and at times threatening tone to the whole. The extended section over a "walking bass" (beginning at m. 54) includes still more pentatonically inflected melodies. The idea in the flute incorporates the so-called Scotch snap, a short note on the accented beat followed by a longer note. In m. 60, for example, the sixteenth note in the flute is followed by a dotted quarter tied to a half, emphasizing rhythmically the melodic absence of the fourth scale degree in the melodic fragment (E–F#–G#–B–C#). Yet another important interruption, a lively major-mode section (beginning at m. 90) leads to a portentous reference back to the main theme of the first movement (m. 96)—Dvořák carefully integrates all four movements of the symphony—before the original mood of calm is restored with the return of the English horn theme in the tonic (m. 101).

Dvořák himself pointed to Henry Wadsworth Longfellow's *Song of Hiawatha* as the source of inspiration for this movement, though it is not altogether clear whether Dvořák meant a particular passage in this long poem or the mood of the poem as a whole. For many listeners, however, including even those attending the premiere of this symphony, Dvořák's work was primarily based on what they called "Negro melodies." "The composer has not taken the external forms of plantation music," one critic of the time noted, "but has used his own themes suggested by the southern music. Now and then the motifs and the rhythms strongly suggest the origin of the symphony."[1] These connections were reinforced in the public mind in 1922 when the American composer William Arms Fischer (1861–1948), who had studied with Dvořák, set the Largo's English horn theme to a text he had written in the style

of a Negro spiritual ("Goin' home, goin' home, I'm a-goin' home / Quiet like, some still day, I jes' goin' home"). With these words, the melody became the basis for any number of subsequent arrangements, and to this day many concert-goers believe that Dvořák had in fact used an old spiritual as the basis for the Largo of his "New World" Symphony. That the two traditions of American music Dvořák considered so potentially fruitful—Native American and African-American music—should have become so thoroughly fused in the public mind testifies to the composer's ability to capture a spirit that was somehow "American" without being either specific or immediately identifiable.

[1]James Creelman, "Dvořák's Negro Symphony," *Pall Mall Budget*, 21 June 1894, reproduced in *Dvořák and His World*, ed. Michael Beckerman (Princeton, NJ: Princeton University Press, 1993), p. 179.

145 Symphony No. 4 in E minor, Op. 98, fourth movement (finale) (1885)
Johannes Brahms (1833–1897)

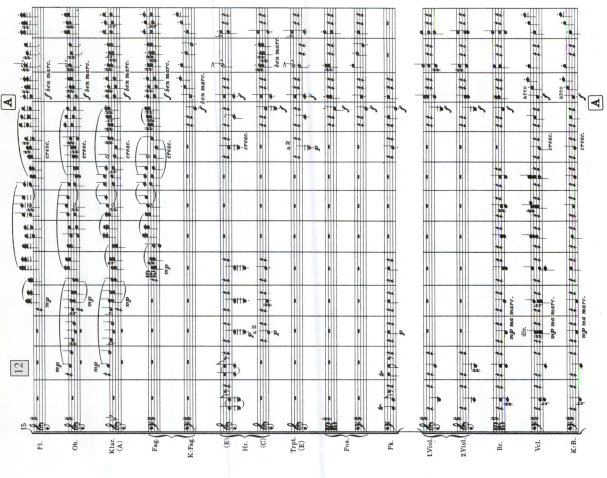

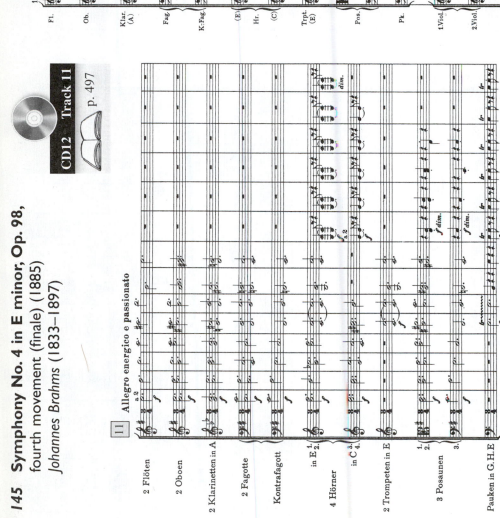

CD12 Track 11 p. 497

28
13
a 2
Fl.
Ob.
Klar. (A)
Fag.
K.-Fag.
(E) Hr. (C)
Trpt. (E)
Pos.
Pk.
1.Viol.
2.Viol.
Br.
Vcl.
K.-B.
arco
f ben marc. largamente
38
B
1.
2.
poco f
sim.
cresc. sempre più
pizz.
47
14
cresc.
espress. cresc.
K. B.

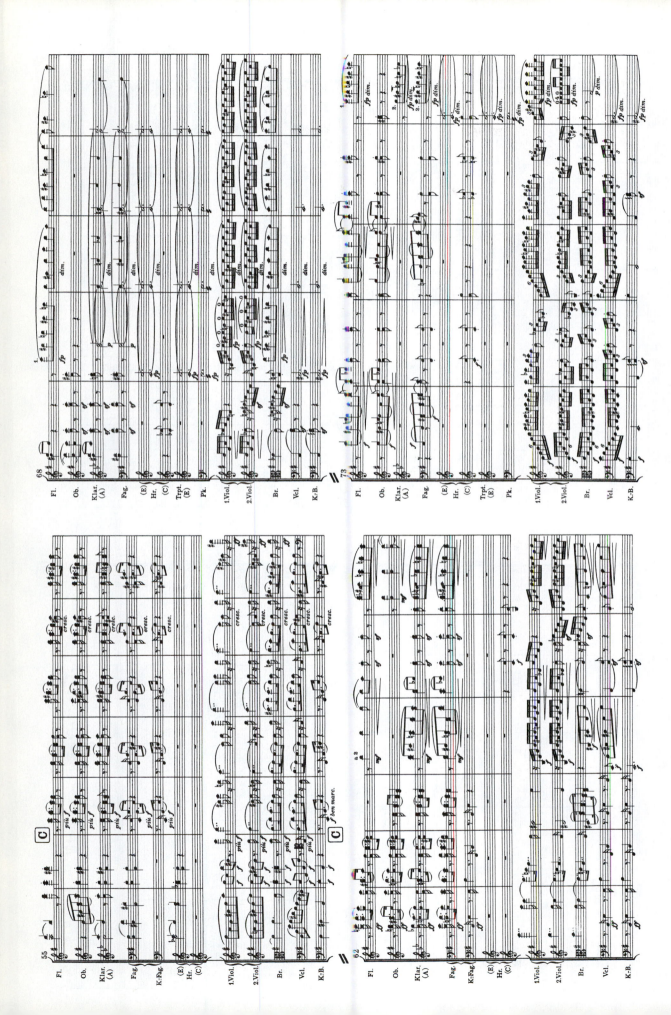

373 ■ No. 145 Brahms: Symphony No. 4 in E minor

15
16
D
78
89
97
102
Fl.
Ob.
Klar. (A)
Fag.
(E) Hr. (C)
Trpt. (E)
Pk.
1.Viol.
2.Viol.
Br.
Vcl.
K.-B.
espressivo
poco cresc.
p dolce
p molto dolce
dim.
espress.
dolce
arco
pp dolce
pizz.

No. 145 Brahms: *Symphony No. 4 in E minor*

No. 145 Brahms: *Symphony No. 4 in E minor*

No. 145 Brahms: Symphony No. 4 in E minor

163
Fl.
Ob.
Klar. (A)
Fag.
K.-Fag.
(E) Hr. (C)
Trpt. (E)
Pos.
Pk.
1.Viol.
2.Viol.
Br.
Vcl.
K.-B.
20
G
169
a 2

No. 145 Brahms: Symphony No. 4 in E minor

■ No. 145 Brahms: *Symphony No. 4 in E minor*

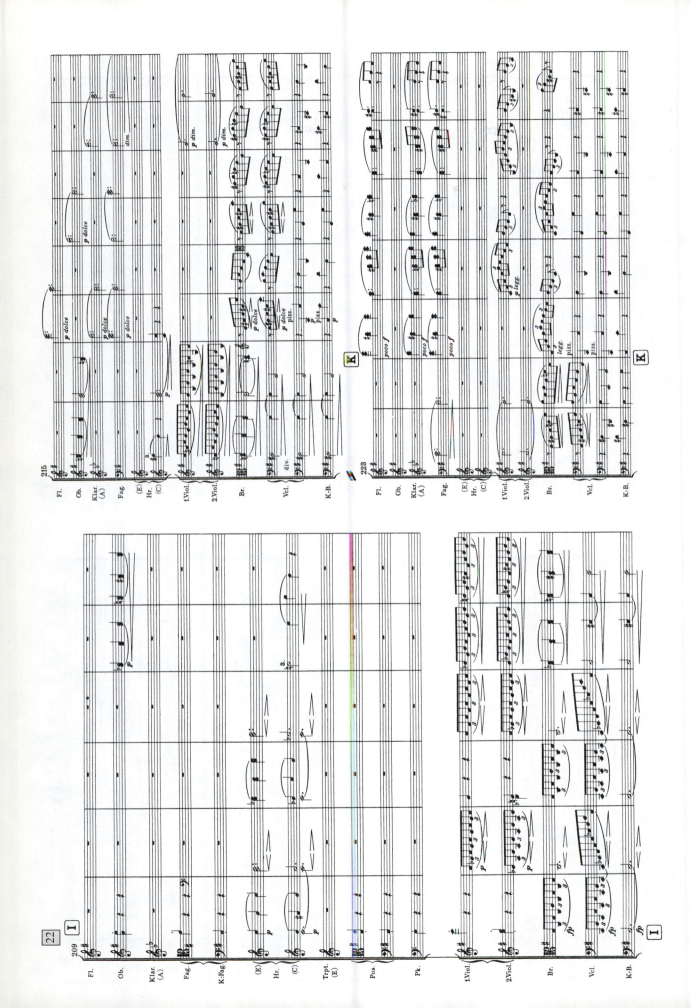

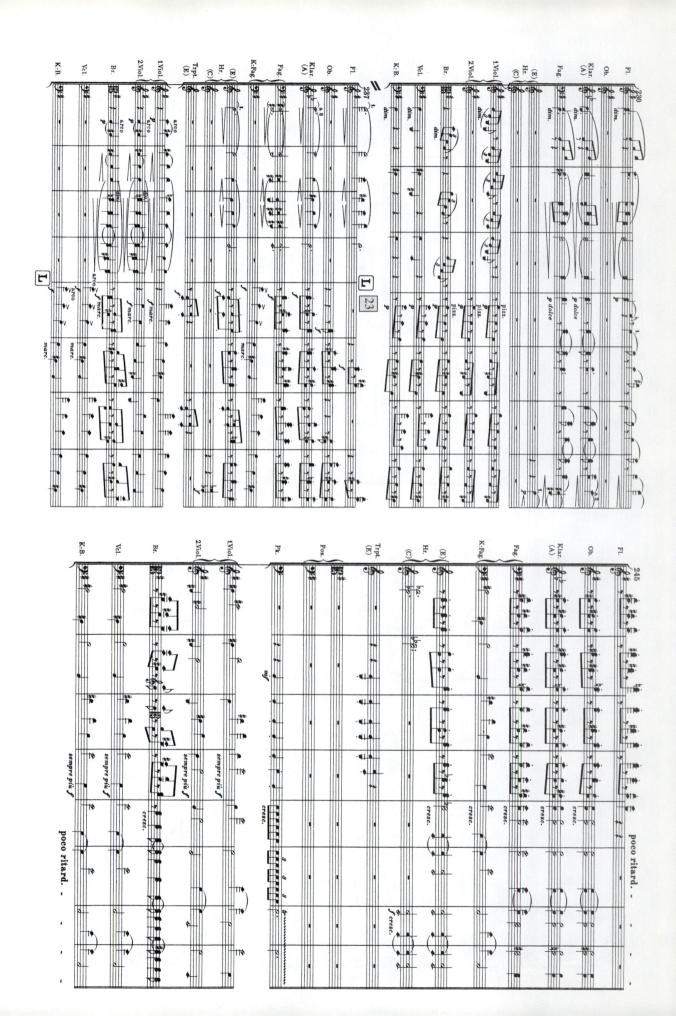

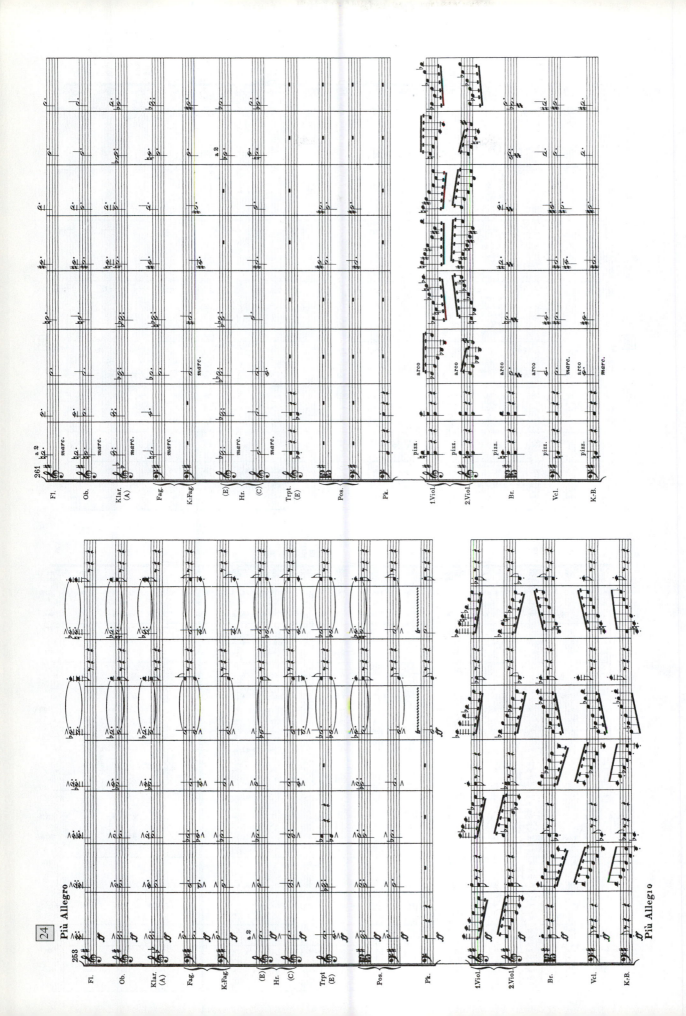

No. 145 Brahms: *Symphony No. 4 in E minor*

269
M
Fl.
Ob.
Klar. (A)
Fag.
K-Fag.
Hr. (E) (C)
Trpt. (E)
Pos.
Pk.
1.Viol.
2.Viol.
Br.
Vcl.
K-B.
a 2
cresc.
marc.

277
Fl.
Ob.
Klar. (A)
Fag.
K-Fag.
Hr. (E) (C)
Trpt. (E)
Pos.
Pk.
1.Viol.
2.Viol.
Br.
Vcl.
K-B.
p cresc.
p
cresc.
div.

No. 145 Brahms: Symphony No. 4 in E minor

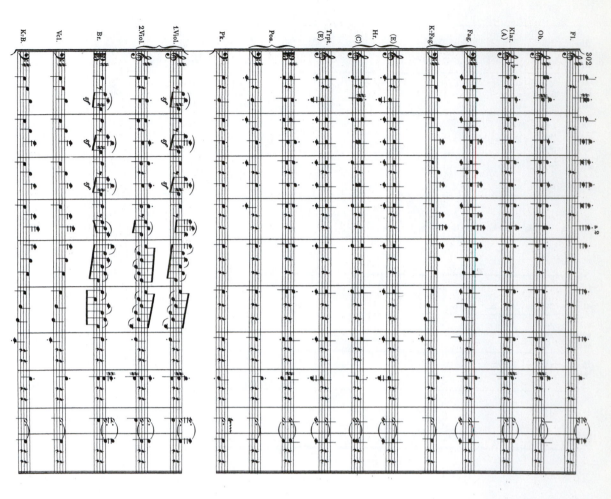

The finale of Brahms's last symphony is an enormous set of variations on a theme. On one level, the structure of this movement is quite simple: it is a series of 30 variations, each eight measures long and based on the same eight-measure theme (see examples below). Within this relatively simple—one might be tempted to say restrictive—framework, Brahms introduces a stunning variety of thematic ideas, textures, harmonies, and colors. The theme is derived from the ostinato finale of Bach's Cantata No. 150, a work that Brahms knew well.

Example 7 Ostinato theme of Bach, Cantata no. 150, finale (transposed)

Example 8 Brahms's ostinato bass for the finale of his Symphony no. 4

Allegro energico e passionato

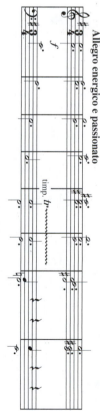

Bach's ostinato theme is not particularly distinctive: it fills in the interval of a fifth and ends with an octave leap on the dominant, which in turn sets up the repetition of the theme. Brahms extends the theme to eight measures (one note per measure), moves the melodic idea to the uppermost voice, and adds a striking dissonance by sharpening the second iteration of the fourth scale degree (A♯). He further deviates from Bach's theme by ending on the first scale degree. The resulting harmonic closure increases the challenge of composing a continuous movement from a string of such sequences, but it is a challenge Brahms confronts with zeal. By the time we reach the middle of this movement, we have to remind ourselves that it is in fact a set of variations on a theme. The division between variations 6 and 7 (m. 49–56 and 57–64), is almost imperceptible even when we listen for it. The movement nevertheless holds consistently to the repeating eight-measure structure all the way through Variation 30. Only the coda, beginning in m. 253 after a few introductory measures, is freely composed.

Within this self-imposed structure of variations on a theme, Brahms integrates another formal principle, that of sonata form. In a strict sense, the movement is not in sonata form because it lacks the essential modulation to a secondary key. Still, there is an unmistakable sense of transition in variations 10 and 11 (m. 81–88, 89–96) and a clear change of mood with variation 12 (m. 97–104); the meter changes, the music is marked *dolce* for the first time, and the timbre of the solo flute dominates the substantially thinned texture. The impression of change is reinforced in variation 13 (m. 105–112) with a shift to E major. Variation 16 marks the onset of what corresponds to the development, and variation 24 sounds very much like the beginning of a recapitulation. The material after variation 30, as noted above, constitutes a freely composed coda.

With this finale of his last symphony, Brahms seems to be reminding the musical world that old forms are capable of rejuvenation, that it is possible to search for the new without abandoning tradition entirely. With its ostensibly simple construction, this movement is firmly rooted in tradition, but in its harmony, orchestration, and sense of flow, it is distinctly progressive.

146 Symphony No. 1 in D Major,
third movement (1888)
Gustav Mahler (1860–1911)

CD12 · Track 25 p. 502

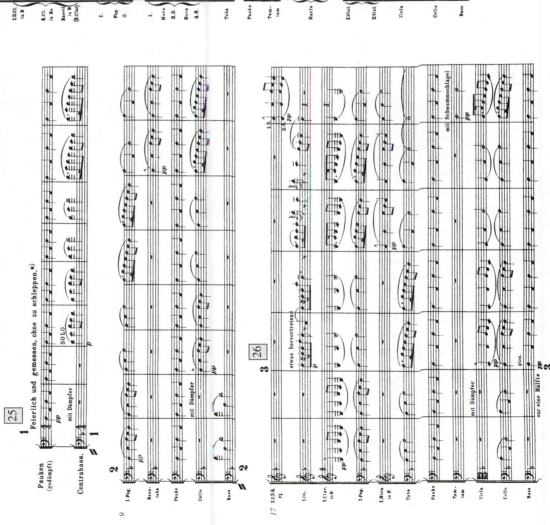

Anmerkung: Sämmtliche Stimmen vom Einsatz bis zu „Langsam" in gleichmässigem pp ohne crescendo

Feierlich und gemessen, ohne zu schleppen.)

27
Zurückhaltend
Rit.
pp aber ausdrucksvoll (rit.)
nehmen C-Clar.
dim.
Dämpfer ab
pizz. nicht sordinirt
Doppelgriff
geth.
Zurückhaltend.
5 a tempo. Ziemlich langsam.
p subito
Dämpfer ab
ausdrucksvoll
6 Mit Parodie.
Nicht schleppen
gut hervortretend
Die Becken sind an dieser Stelle an der grossen Trommel anzuhängen und Becken- und Trommelstimme sind von einem und demselben Musiker zu schlagen.
col legno
immer pizz.
poco rit.
sehr zarte Betonungen
7 a tempo

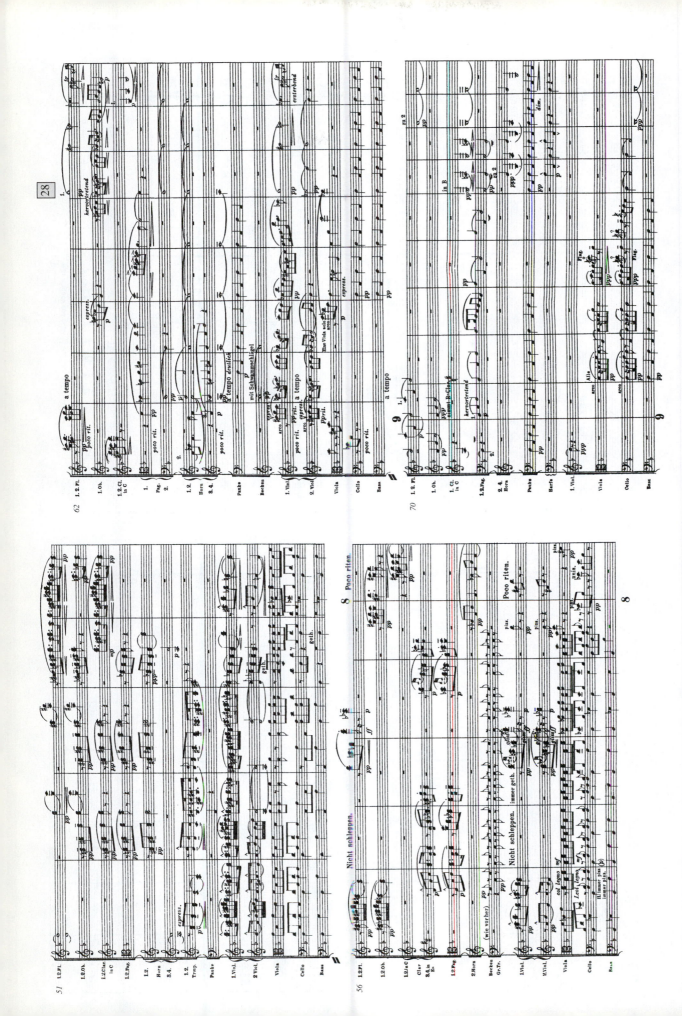

No. 146 Mahler: Symphony No. I in D Major

■ No. 146 Mahler: Symphony No. 1 in D Major

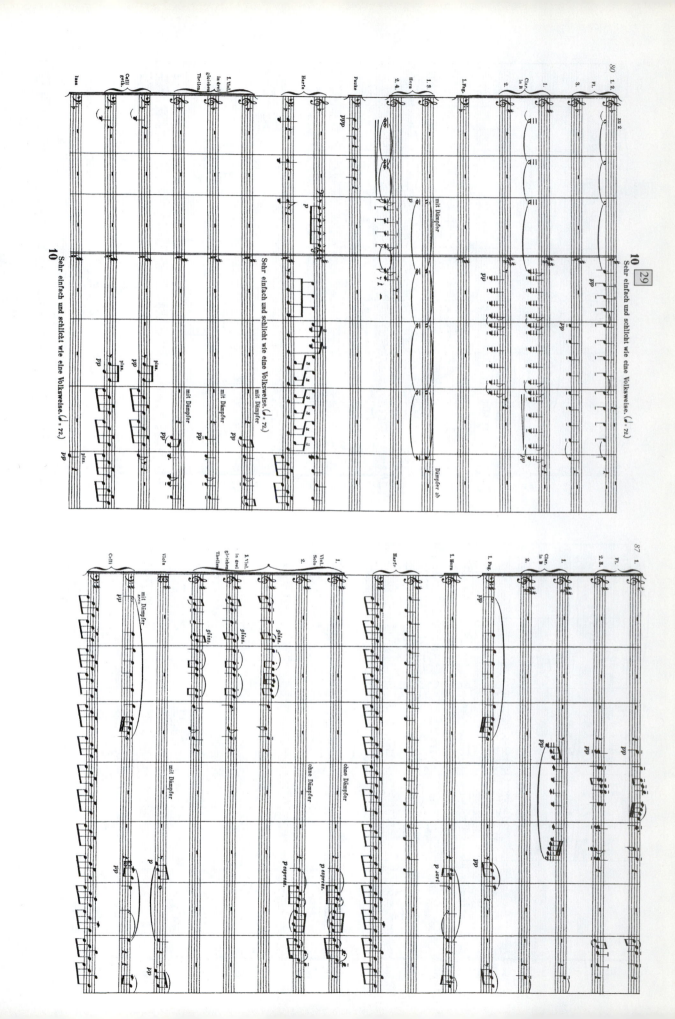

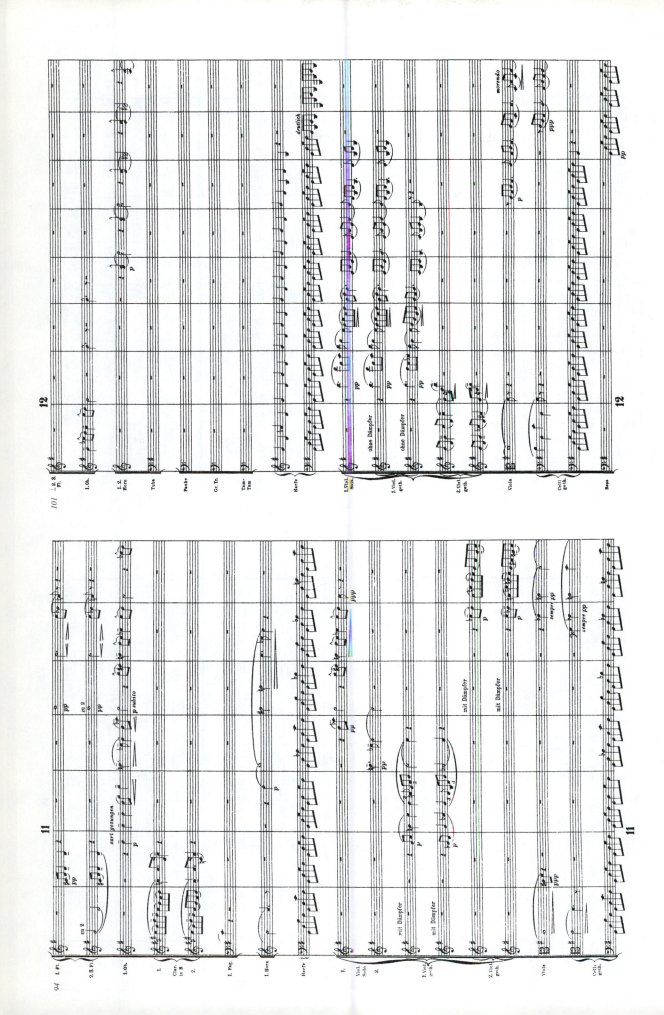

No. 146 Mahler: *Symphony No. 1 in D Major*

No. 146 Mahler: Symphony No. 1 in D Major

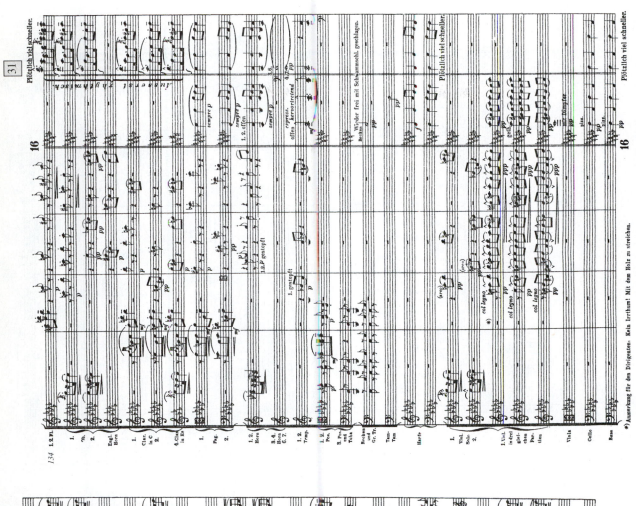

No. 146 Mahler: *Symphony No. 1 in D Major*

*) Anmerkung für den Dirigenten. Kein Irrthum! Mit dem Holz zu streichen.

■ No. 146 Mahler: Symphony No. 1 in D Major

The third movement of Mahler's First Symphony careens wildly from the beautiful to the grotesque, the sincere to the ironic. Mahler himself once suggested that the entire movement was inspired by a well-known illustration (see p. 499 of the Textbook) showing wild animals bearing a hunter to his grave. By writing a funeral march into this symphony, Mahler is of course directly linking it to the funeral march in the second movement of Beethoven's "Eroica." But the ironic tone of this music, inspired by a grotesque ceremony in which the hunted bury the hunter, mocks the somberness of the movement, combined with its slow tempo, low register, and minor mode all combine to announce that this will be a funeral march befitting the slow movement of a symphony. The instrument playing the melody is a solo double bass, and it is playing in a torturously high range for that instrument. The tone is not deep and resonant, but pinched and forced. Odder still, the melody turns out be a minor-mode variant of the children's tune "Frère Jacques" (or "Bruder Martin," as it is known in German-speaking lands). A children's play song in minor in the slow movement of a symphony? We can begin to understand why so many contemporary critics found Mahler's music perplexing and at times exasperating.

Still other critics (many of them motivated by anti-Semitism) criticized the passage immediately following for its "Jewish" or "eastern" qualities. The sound world evoked here (beginning in m. 39) is that of the *Klezmorin*, the professional Jewish musicians of eastern Europe—what we refer to today as Klezmer music, characterized by a steady "oompah" sound in the bass (here, in low strings, bass drum, and cymbals) and rhythmically free winds above. Chromatic passages in thirds, exaggerated accents, repeated half-steps back and forth, and the prominence of the shrill-sounding E♭ clarinet all contribute to what many critics dismissed as the music of peasants, not suited to the lofty realm of the symphony. After a brief return of the "Bruder Martin" theme (m. 71), the mood shifts yet again, introducing a passage of lyrical beauty accompanied now by the harp (beginning in m. 83). Mahler uses here a melody from a song he himself had written several years before entitled "The Two Blue Eyes of My Beloved," and the tone is decidedly sincere: the composer indicates that this section is to be played "very simply and unadorned, like a folk melody," in contrast to the Klezmer-like passages, which he directs at one point to be played "like a parody" (m. 45).

All these contrasts are intentionally jarring, and Mahler uses them to drive home his belief that a symphony can and should encompass the banal and mundane as well as the beautiful. The contrast between the funeral marches of Beethoven's Third Symphony and Mahler's First Symphony manifests the enormous changes music had experienced in less than a century. Beethoven's music is earnest, sincere, unselfconscious; Mahler's by contrast, combines hauntingly beautiful melodies with passages that fairly drip with irony. Mahler's subsequent symphonies manifest similar contrasts of tone, at times deadly serious, at times light-hearted and remote. All of his symphonies are large-scale works: unlike Mendelssohn, Schumann, and Brahms, he built on the monumental aspect of the genre as embodied above all in Beethoven's Ninth Symphony, but also in Schubert's "Great" C Major Symphony, D. 944, and the symphonies of Bruckner.

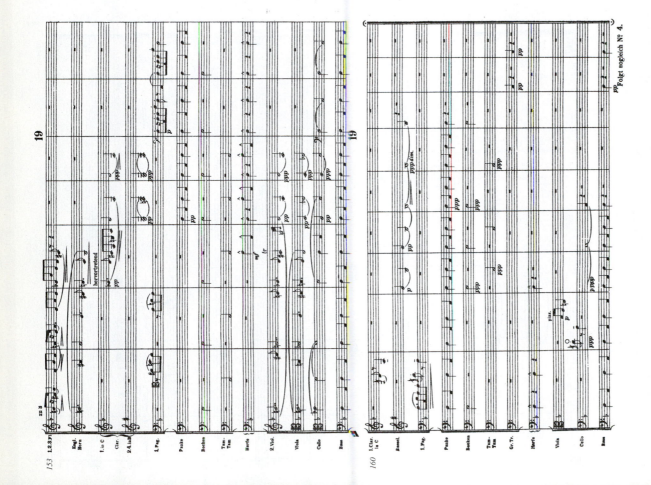

No. 146 Mahler: *Symphony No. 1 in D Major*

147 Prélude à l'Après-midi d'un faune
(1894)
Claude Debussy (1862–1918)

CD12 Track 32

p. 544

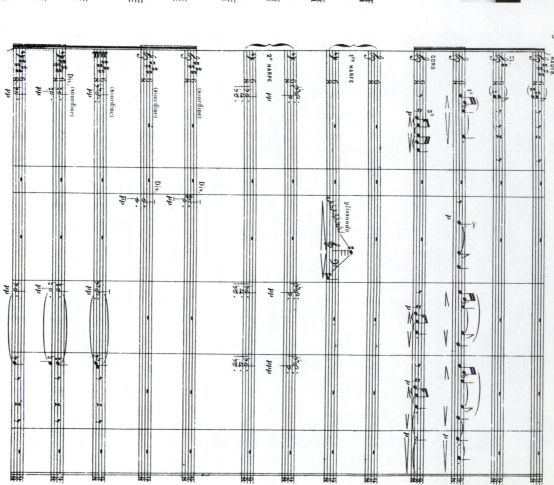

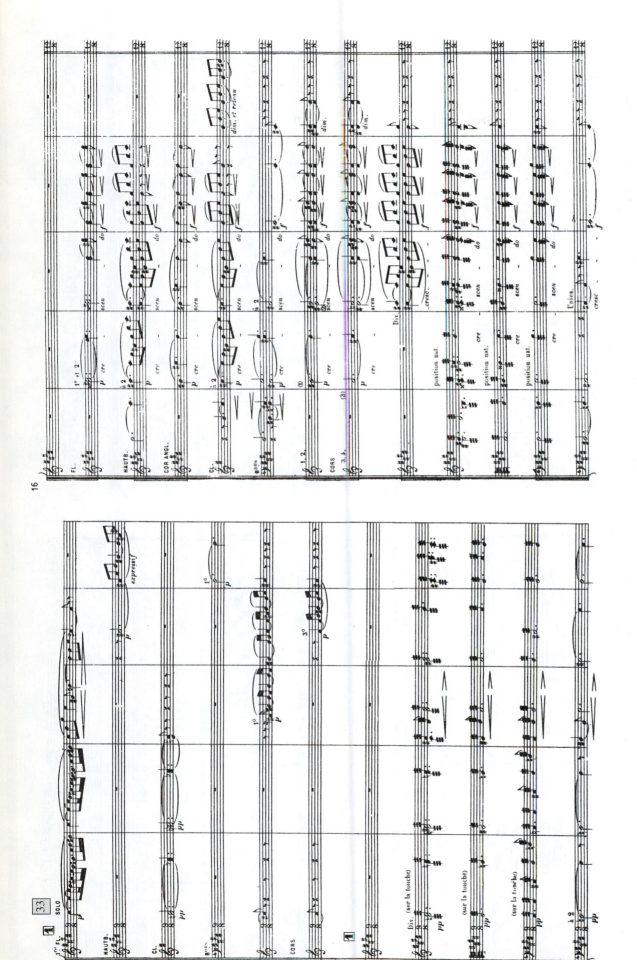

No. 147 Debussy: *Prélude à l'Après-midi d'un faune*

No. 147 Debussy: *Prélude à l'Après-midi d'un faune*

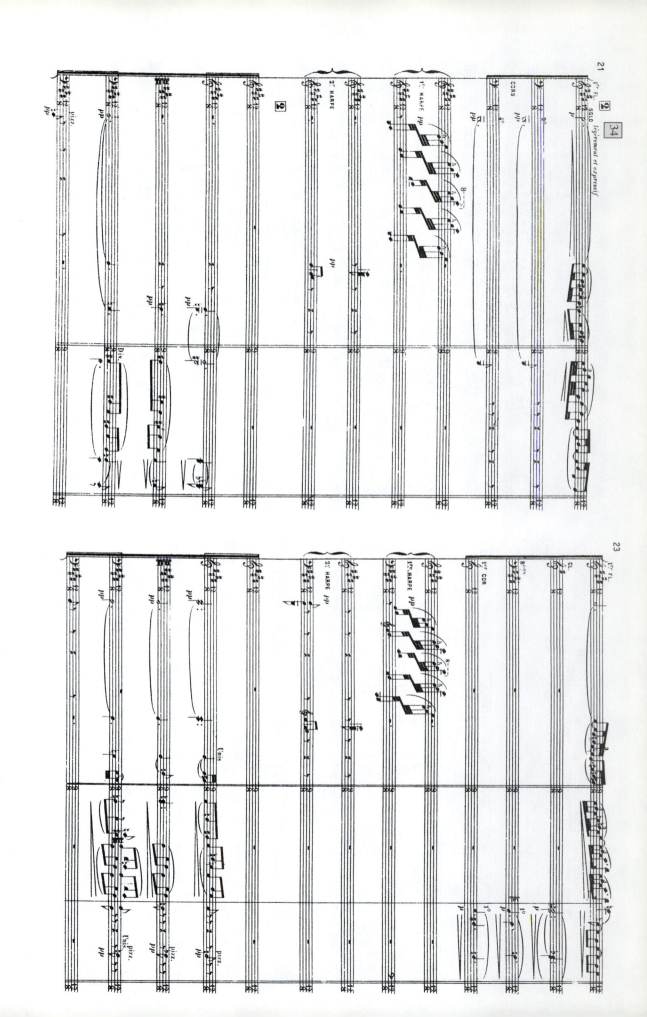

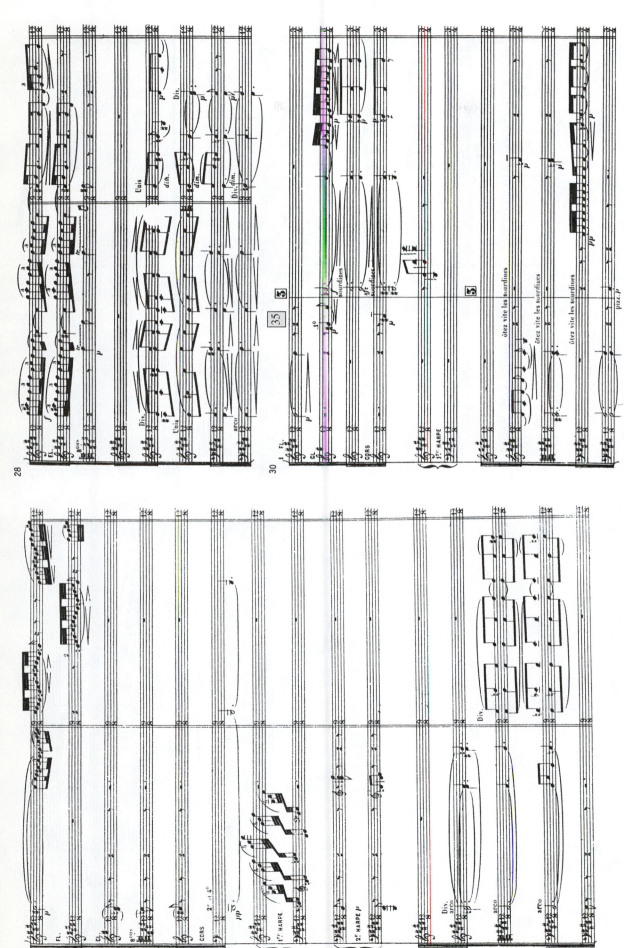

No. 147 Debussy: *Prélude à l'Après-midi d'un faune*

No. 147 Debussy: *Prélude à l'Après-midi d'un faune*

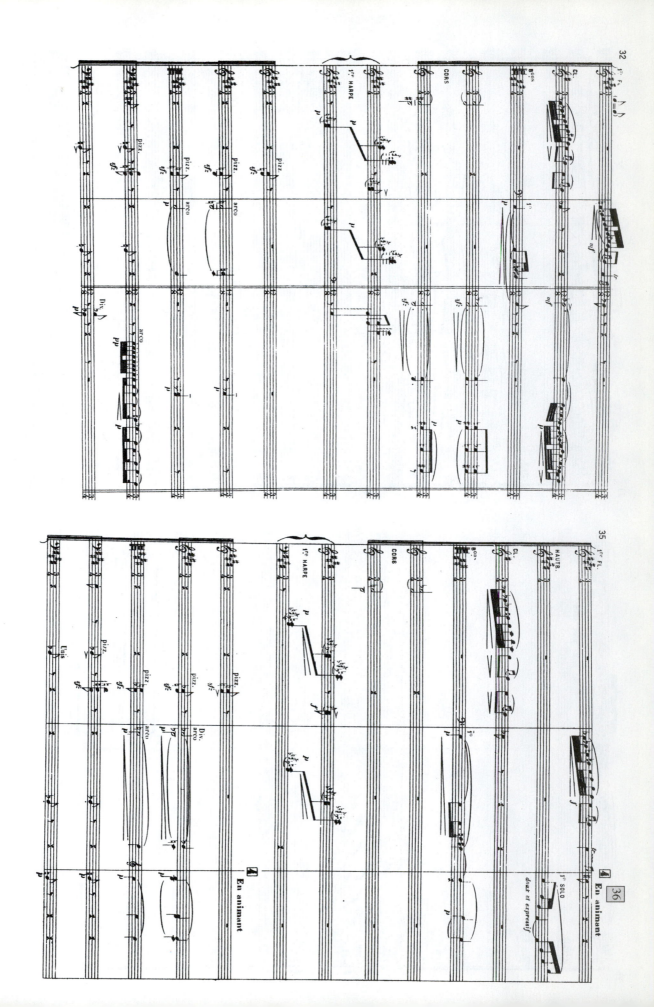

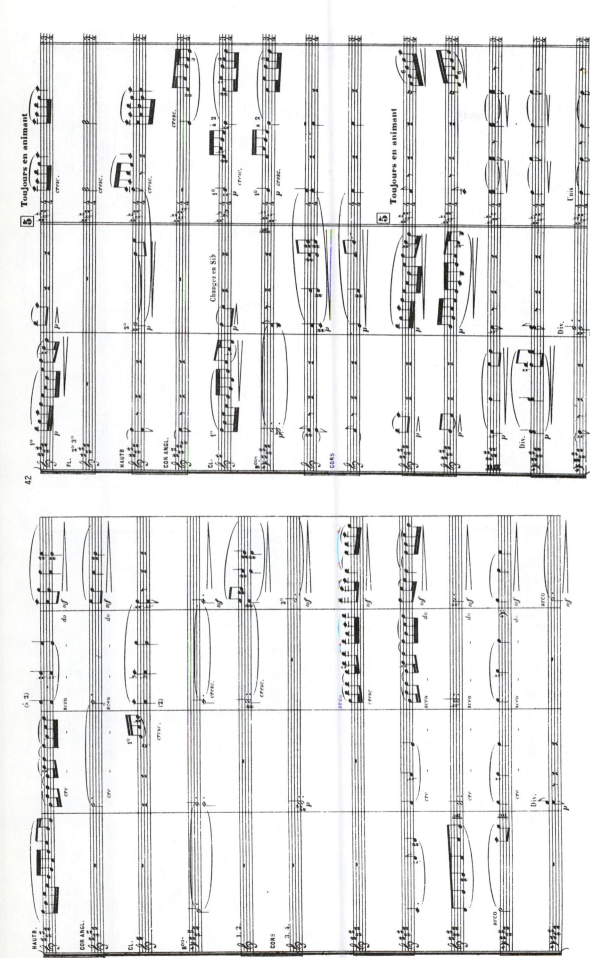

No. 147 Debussy: *Prélude à l'Après-midi d'un faune*

No. 147 Debussy: Prélude à l'Après-midi d'un faune

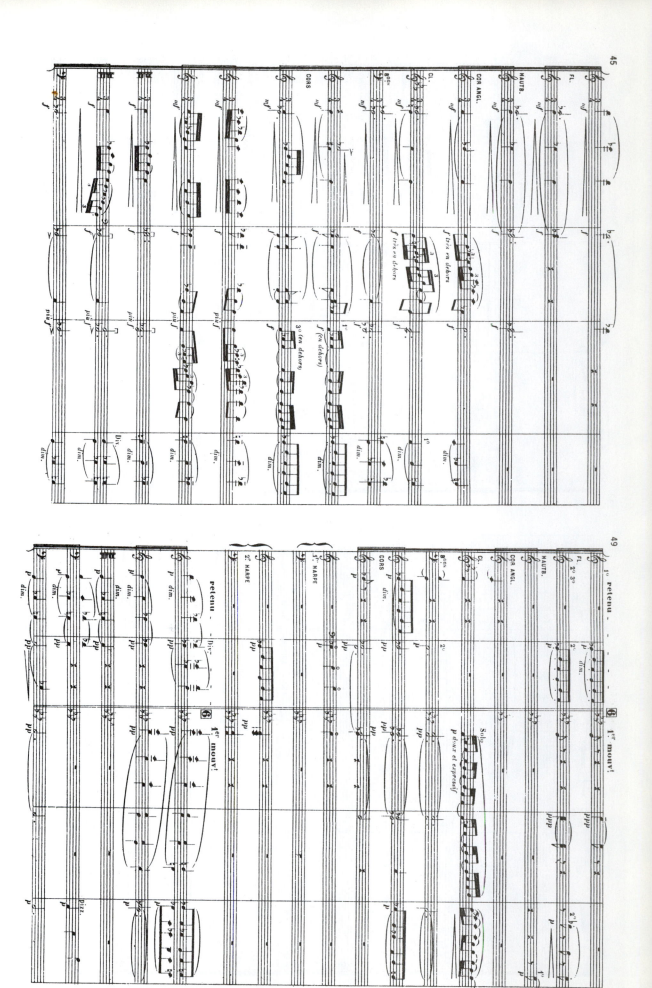

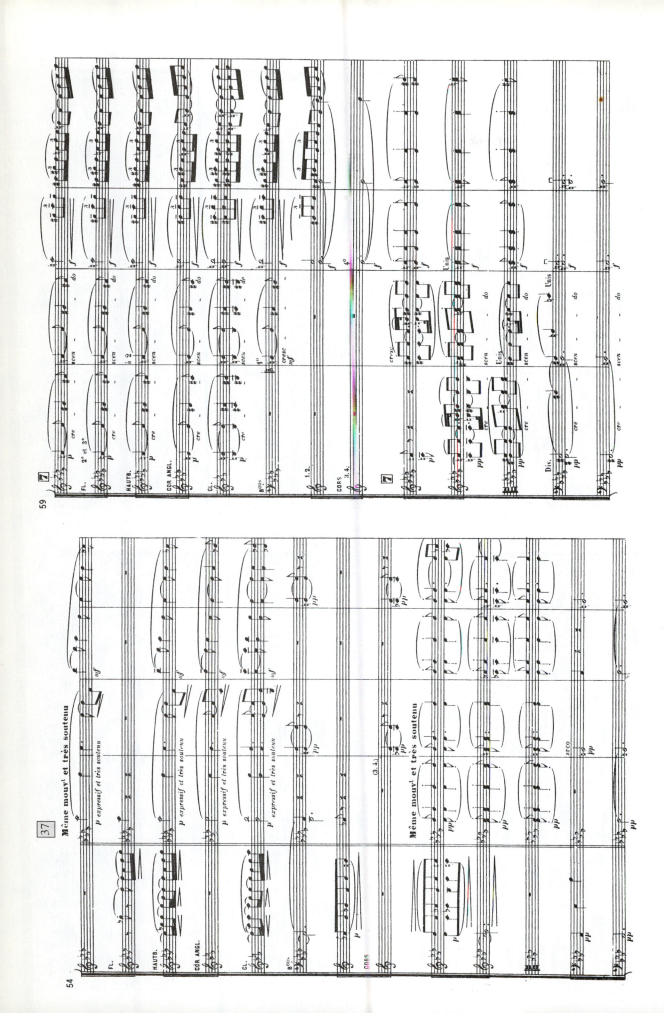

No. 147 Debussy: *Prélude à l'Après-midi d'un faune*

■ No. 147 Debussy: *Prélude à l'Après-midi d'un faune*

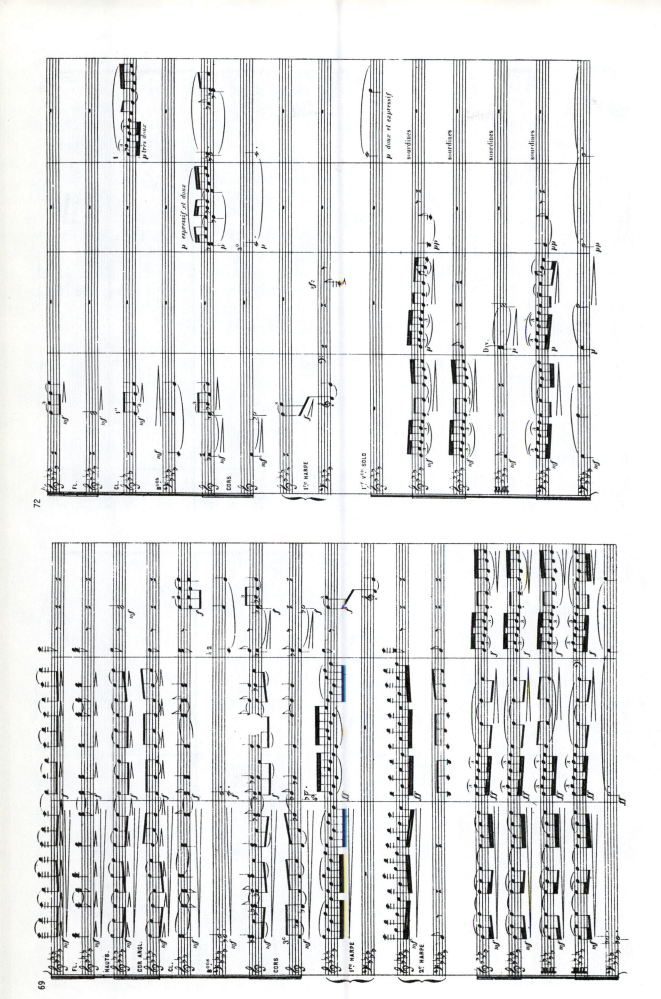

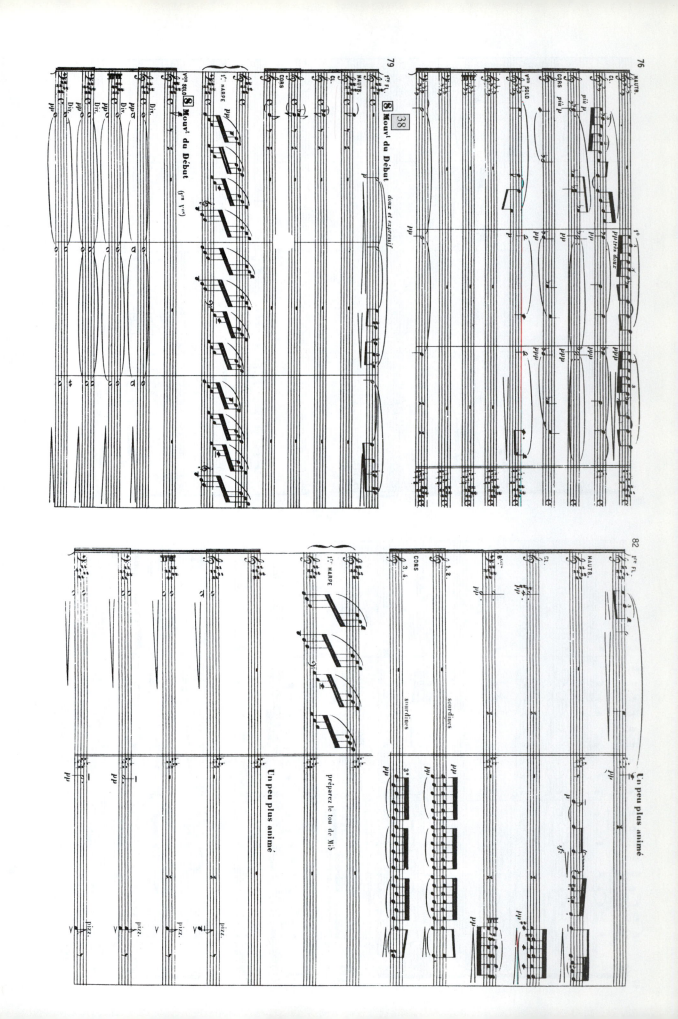

No. 147 Debussy: *Prélude à l'Après-midi d'un faune*

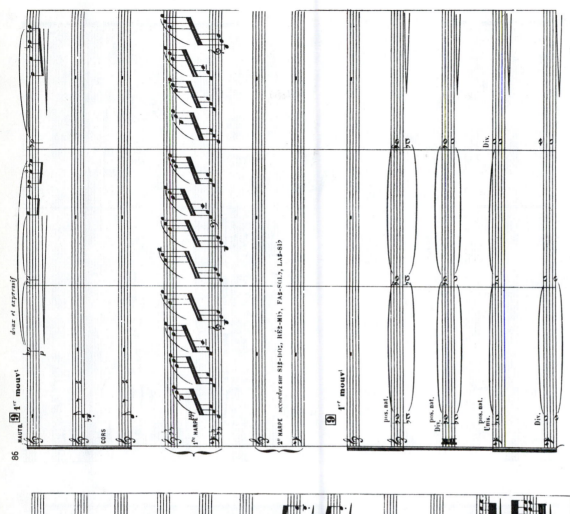

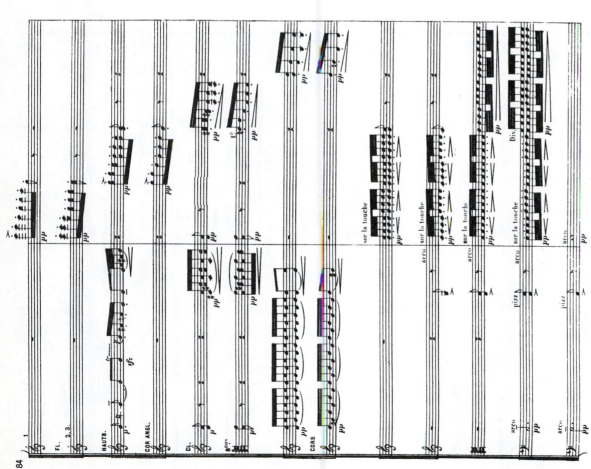

No. 147 Debussy: *Prélude à l'Après-midi d'un faune*

No. 147 Debussy: Prélude à l'Après-midi d'un faune

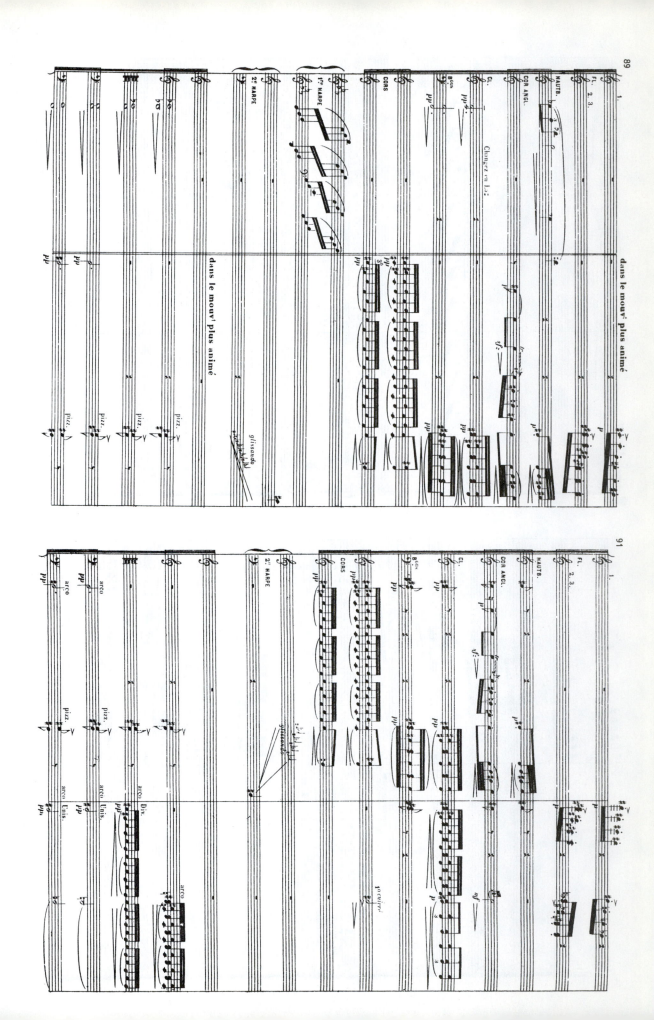

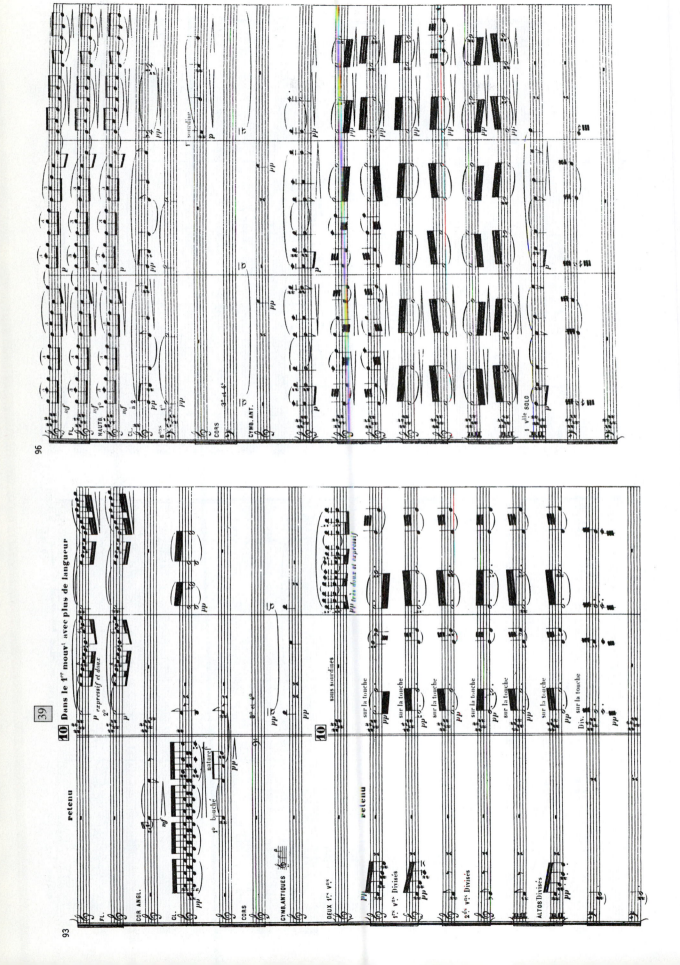

No. 147 Debussy: *Prélude à l'Après-midi d'un faune*

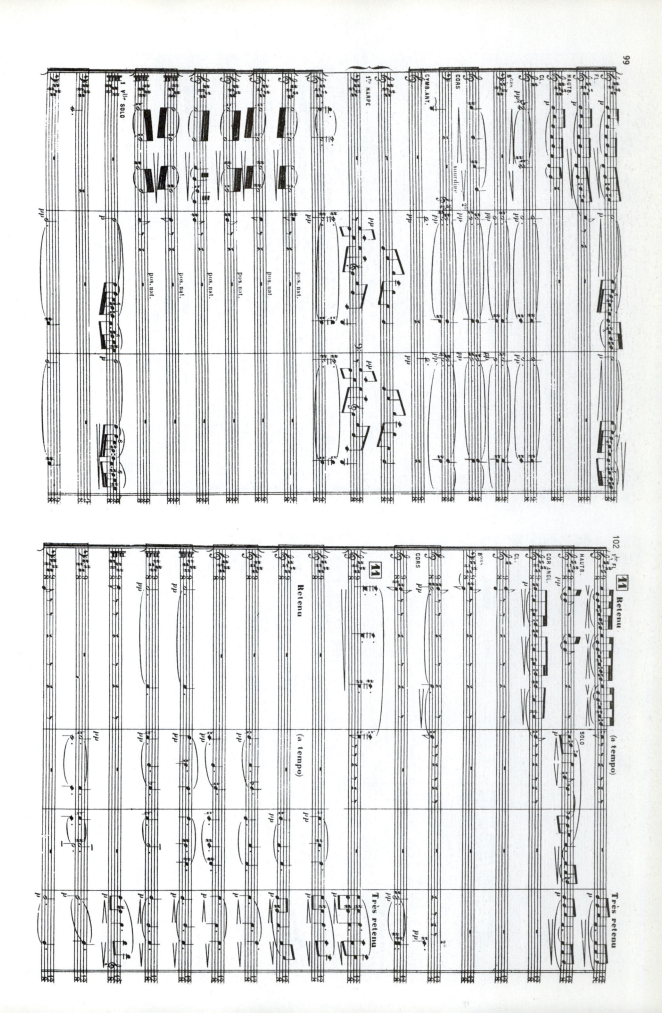

Debussy's "Prelude to an Afternoon of a Faun" was inspired by a symbolist poem, Stéphane Mallarmé's *L'Après-midi d'un faune* ("Afternoon of a Faun," 1876). Evocative and at times obscure, Mallarmé's poem captures the ruminations of a mythological faun, a half-man, half-goat who remembers—or did he only dream about?—his erotically charged encounter with a pair of wood nymphs. The opening line reads: "Those nymphs, I want to make them permanent," and the rest of the poem floats between dream and consciousness. Illusion and reality are indistinguishable.

Critics have drawn many indirect and a few direct connections between Mallarmé's poetry and Debussy's music. The faun's instrument is traditionally the flute, and it is this instrument that opens Debussy's work. The languorous chromatic line falls and rises like the faun's own fantasy. Debussy himself was evasive about further particulars, however, stating merely that his piece conveyed "a general impression of the poem, because if music were to follow more closely it would run out of breath, like a dray horse competing for the Grand Prize with a thoroughbred . . ." Yet the consistent opposition between flute and strings and the points of structural articulation (m. 30–31, 37, 55, 80, 94) resonates subtly with both the design and content of Mallarmé's poem.

It is also unclear why Debussy called this the "Prelude" to the faun's afternoon. At one point he had announced a forthcoming work entitled *Prélude, interludes et paraphrase finale pour: l'Après-midi d'un faune*, and it would seem that the first of these, the prelude, was the only movement the composer actually completed. In a way, though, the title fits the poetry, which holds many mysteries that cannot be rationally explained.

For traditionally minded listeners of the late 19th century, Debussy's *Prélude à l'Après-midi d'un faune* was an enigma. They found the lack of clearly defined themes, the successions of seventh chords (m. 48–49), and the parallel fifths (m. 102) primitive in the worst sense of the word. Almost thirty years after the work's premiere, Camille Saint-Saëns (1835–1921), one of the leading French composers of his generation, wrote privately to a friend that he could make little sense of the work, accusing it of cultivating an "absence of style." But others found in this "absence of style" an inspiration, a new approach to music that opened the door to writing in a manner that was decidedly modern. While no single work can be said to represent birth of modernism, Debussy's *Prélude à l'Après-midi d'un faune* epitomizes the assault on traditional elements and attitudes that characterizes a great deal of music written at the end of the 19th century and at the beginning of the 20th.

No. 147 Debussy: *Prélude à l'Après-midi d'un faune*

148 Préludes, Book I: "Voiles" (1910)

Debussy

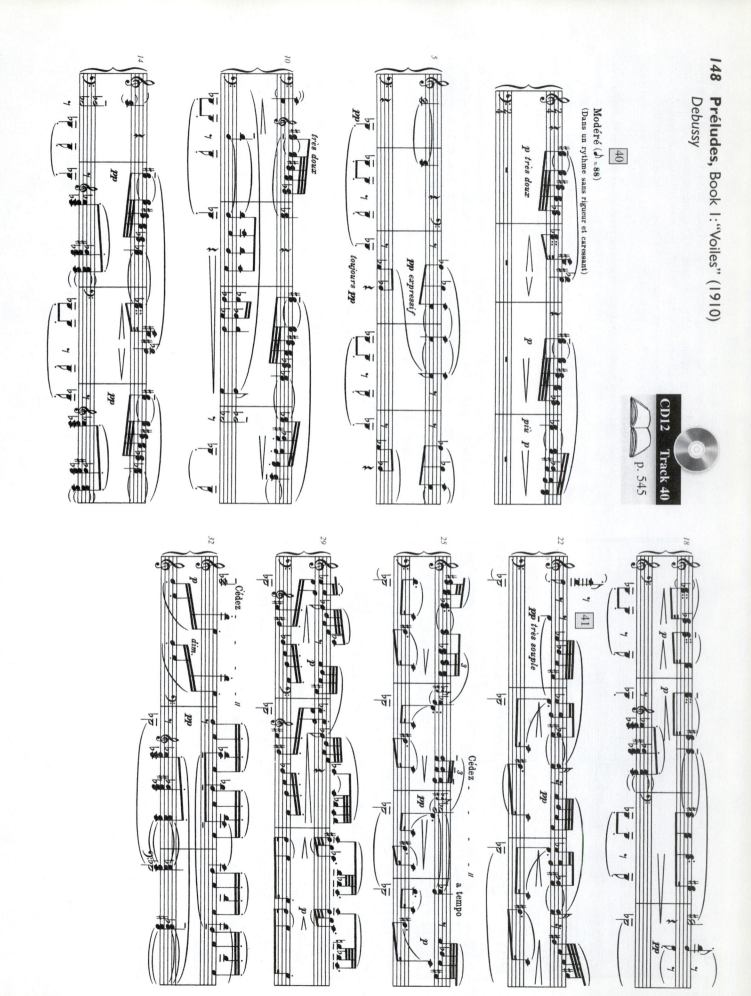

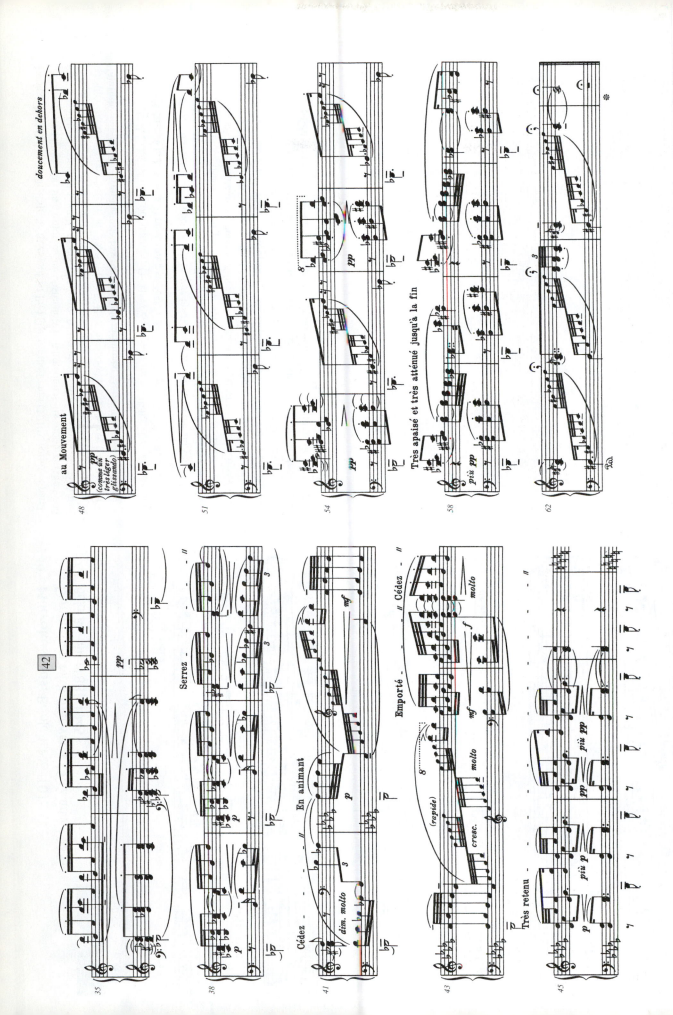

Debussy's *Voiles*, published in the first book of Preludes for the Piano (1910), is full of parallel octaves and fifths, and its harmonies are obstinately nondirectional. Its supple rhythms add to a sensation of constant fluidity, as does its form. Although the work follows an ABA pattern in its broadest outlines, with the A section returning at m. 58, critics disagree as to whether the B section starts at m. 23, 37, or 55. Here as elsewhere, Debussy's music is delightfully ambiguous. Even the title has two possible meanings: "sails" or "veils."

More important, *Voiles* also illustrates the increasing use of nontraditional scale forms in the early decades of the 20th century. Debussy constructs the melodic ideas of this work primarily from whole-tone and pentatonic scales:

- Based on six notes, each a whole tone apart, the whole-tone scale subverts some of the most basic elements of diatonic harmony: it cannot be used to construct major and minor triads, and it permits a few seventh chords. In *Voiles*, Debussy uses a whole tone scale in the outer sections. Here again, the effect is one of a freely floating tonality with no clear center—very much in keeping with the work's evocative title ("Sails" or "Veils"). The opening figure is based on the scale built on C, but with no half-steps.

- Although frequently associated with East Asian music, pentatonic scales—scales based on five notes—are found in many traditional ("folk") idioms of the West as well. Debussy uses one such scale in the inner section of *Voiles*, beginning at m. 42.

149 Mikrokosmos, Book 4, No. 101: Diminished Fifth (between 1932 and 1939)
Béla Bartók (1881–1945)

CD12 Track 43 · p. 548

Con moto ♩ = 110

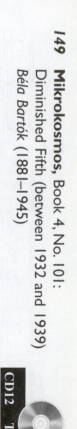

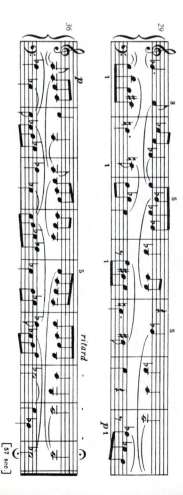

Bartók's *Mikrokosmos* is a set of 153 etude-like works issued in six volumes between 1926 and 1937. The short piece entitled "Diminished Fifth," which explores various compositional possibilities of this interval, is based on the octatonic scale, a scale that alternates between half and whole steps and contains within itself all possible intervals, from the minor second to the major seventh. "Diminished Fifth" repeatedly juxtaposes two tetrachords (four-note units) that together make up the octatonic scale outlined here:

Example 9 Octatonic scale used in m. 1–5 of Béla Bartók, *Diminished Fifth*

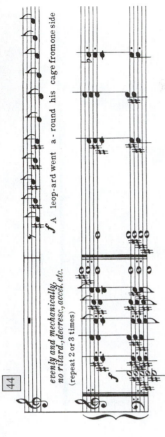

whole   half   whole   whole   half   whole   whole

Because of its symmetrical construction and strict alternation between half and whole steps, an octatonic scale tends to subvert the idea of a tonal center.

p. 548

150 The Cage (1906)
Charles Ives (1874–1954)

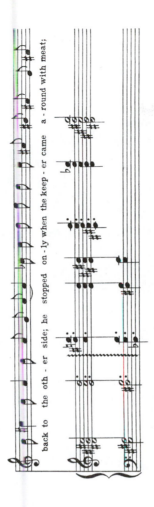

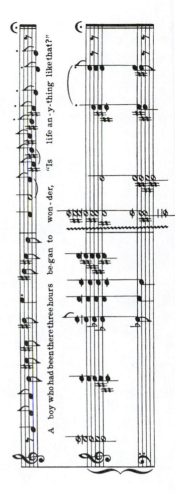

NOTE.- All notes not marked with sharp or flat are natural.

415

Ives's *The Cage* is an early attempt to write using quartal harmonies, that is, chords built on the interval of a fourth rather than a third. The unsettling text, about a leopard pacing in his cage, receives an appropriately repetitive and unsettling melody whose relentless up-and-down progression creates a kind of "cage" in its own right. The accompaniment provides little sense of direction, at least not within the expected conventions of triadic harmony. This brief song, in effect, is in no key at all. Notice, too, the absence of any meter or bar lines.

151 The Things Our Fathers Loved (1917)

Ives

CD12 Track 45 p. 549

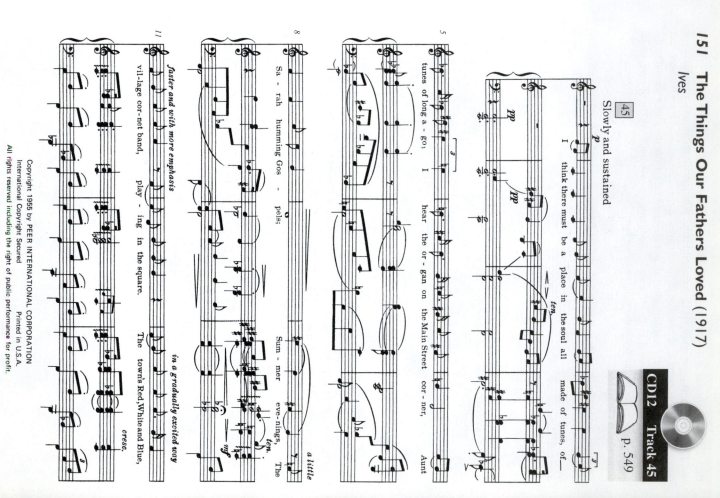

Slowly and sustained

I think there must be a place in the soul all made of tunes, of

tunes of long a - go; I hear the or - gan on the Main Street cor - ner, Aunt

Sa - rah humming Gos - pels; Sum - mer eve-nings, The

Faster and with more emphasis vil-lage cor - net band, play - ing in the square. The town's Red, White and Blue,

in a gradually excited way

a little

This song, written to a text by the composer himself, plays with traditional harmony by string-ing together a series of tunes from popular songs but joining and harmonizing them in an ex-tremely unusual manner, often in the "wrong" key. *Dixie*, at the very beginning, merges im-perceptibly into *My Old Kentucky Home*, followed by *On the Banks of the Wabash* (at the words "I hear the organ on the Main Street corner"), then the hymn tune *Nettleton* ("Aunt Sarah humming Gospels"), and *The Battle Cry of Freedom* ("The village cornet band, playing in the square. The town's Red, White, and Blue"), and finally *In the Sweet Bye and Bye* ("Now! Hear the songs!"). The harmonizations of these tunes—all of them familiar to Ives's contemporaries—create a strange sense of distance. The familiar becomes unfamiliar, and the way in which one melodic fragment flows into the next, always to words from a different source, seems very much in keeping with the literary technique of the stream of conscious-ness developed by the modernist author James Joyce. The net result is a song that insists on its modernity even while celebrating (and quoting from) songs of the past.

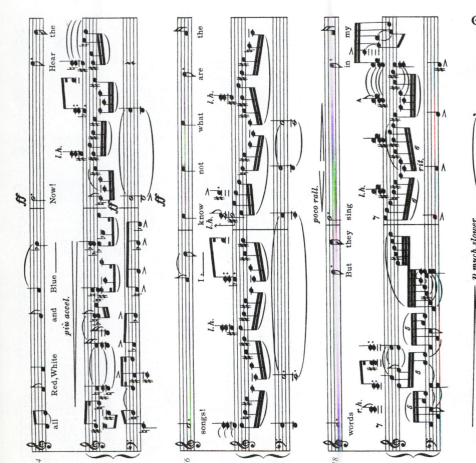

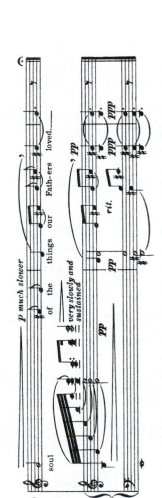

No. 151 Ives: *The Things Our Fathers Loved*

Charles E. Ives
(ca. 1930-35)
Edited by Paul C. Echols and Noel Zahler

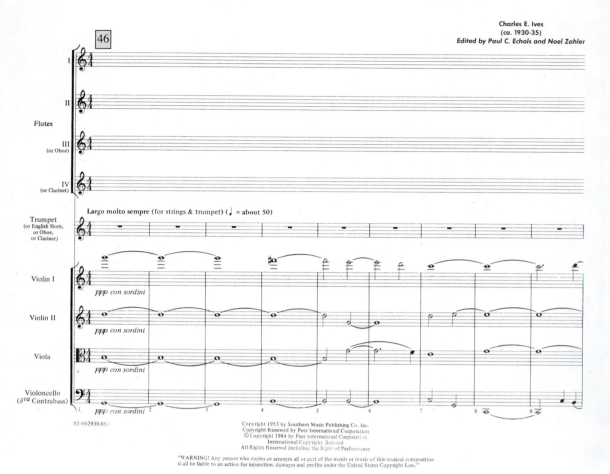

CD12 Track 46 p. 549

NOTE: The publisher of this music refused permission to reproduce more than two pages of the score here. We regret the subsequent omission of the remaining three pages of the score. The work is recorded in its entirety on the anthology of recordings accompanying this textbook.

Ives's *The Unanswered Question* directly juxtaposes traditional and nontraditional harmonies. The solo trumpet and the small ensemble of flutes seem to occupy an entirely different musical sphere from the strings. The strings speak in slow, measured, chorale-like tones, using the tonal language of conventional triads. Dissonance in the strings is carefully controlled and resolved: the entire string part, in fact, looks and sounds almost like a student essay in species counterpoint. The solo trumpet, by contrast, repeatedly poses a five-note figure that implies no harmonic center at all (Bb–C#–E–Eb–C), or, in some instances, ending with a Bɦ instead of a C). The flutes, in turn, are even more tonally diffuse and grow rhythmically more independent. The work ends with a serene, perfect authentic G-major triad, yet the sensation it creates is not one of resolution.

In his foreword to the score of *The Unanswered Question*, Ives gave some hint as to the symbolism behind these contrasting elements:

The strings play *ppp* throughout with no change in tempo. They are to represent "The Silence of the Druids—Who Know, See and Hear Nothing." The trumpet intones "The Perennial Question of Existence," and states it in the same tone of voice each time. But the hunt for "The Invisible Answer" undertaken by the flutes and other human beings, becomes gradually more active, faster and louder through an *animando* [animatedly] to a *con fuoco* [with fire]. This part need not be played in the exact time position indicated. It is played in somewhat of an impromptu way; if there be no conductor, one of the flute players may direct their playing. "The Fighting Answerers," as the time goes on, and after a "secret conference," seem to realize a futility, and begin to mock "The Question" —the strife is over for the moment. After they disappear, "The Question" is asked for the last time, and "The Silences" are heard beyond in "Undisturbed Solitude."

153 Le Sacre du printemps, excerpt (1913)
Igor Stravinsky (1882–1971)

CD12 Track 49   p. 552

PREMIÈRE PARTIE.
L'ADORATION DE LA TERRE.

Introduction.

ЧАСТЬ ПЕРВАЯ.
ПОЦЪЛУЙ ЗЕМЛИ.

Вступление.

Igor Strawinsky.

Droit d'exécution réservé
Edited by F. H. Schneider.

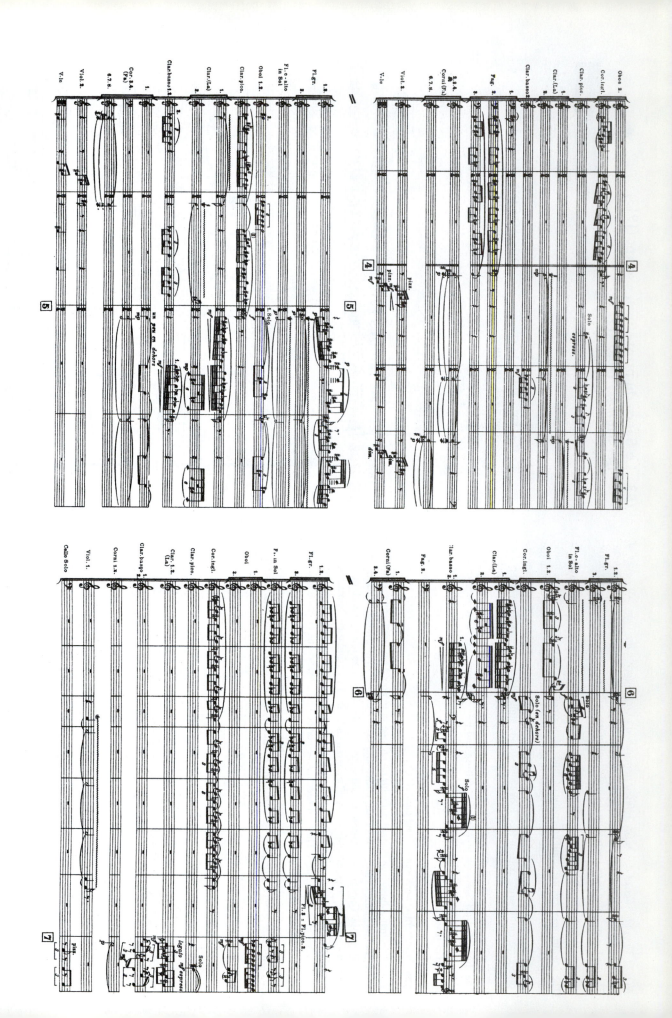

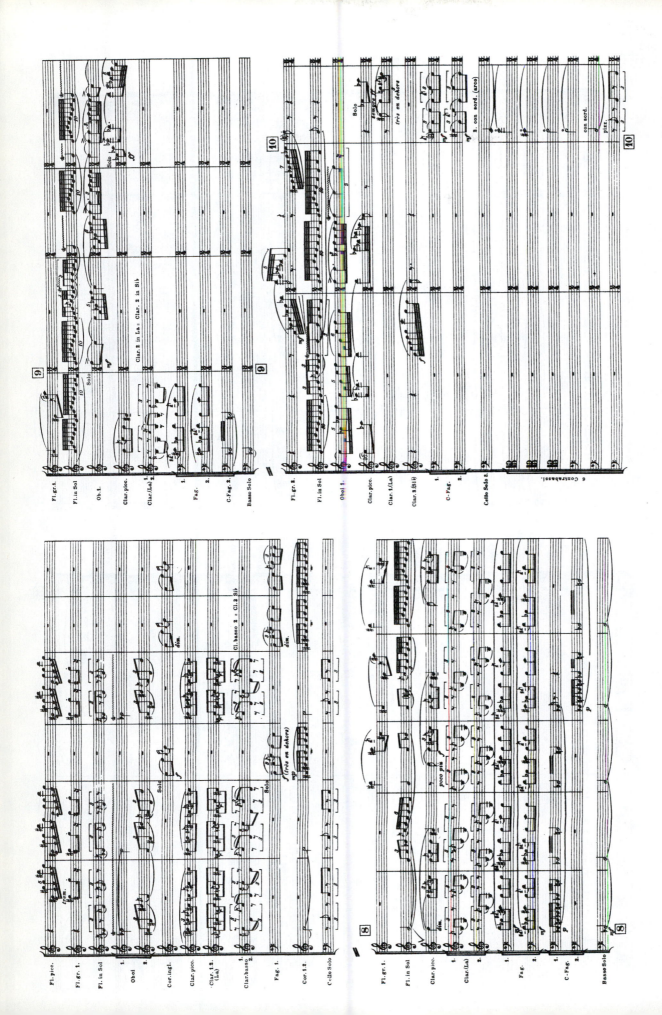

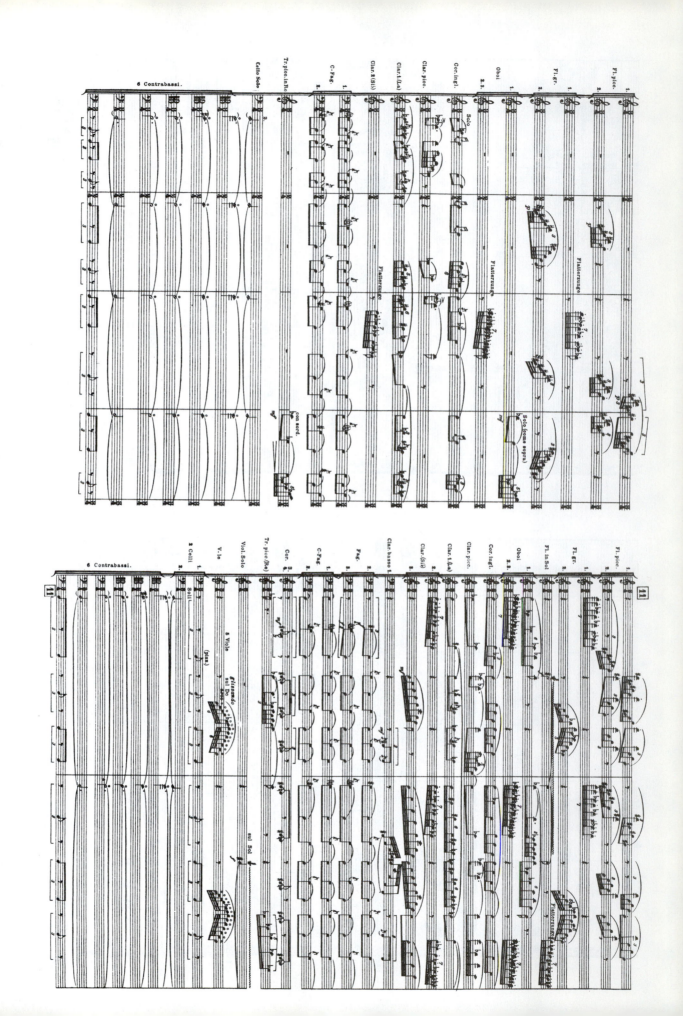

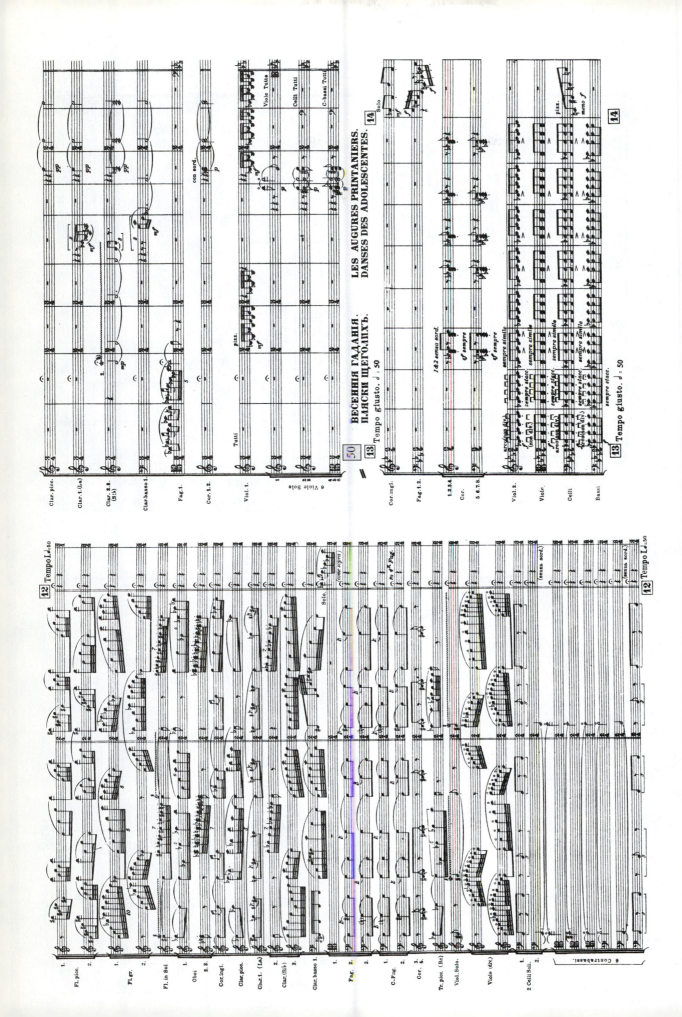

■ No. 153 Stravinsky: *Le Sacre du printemps*

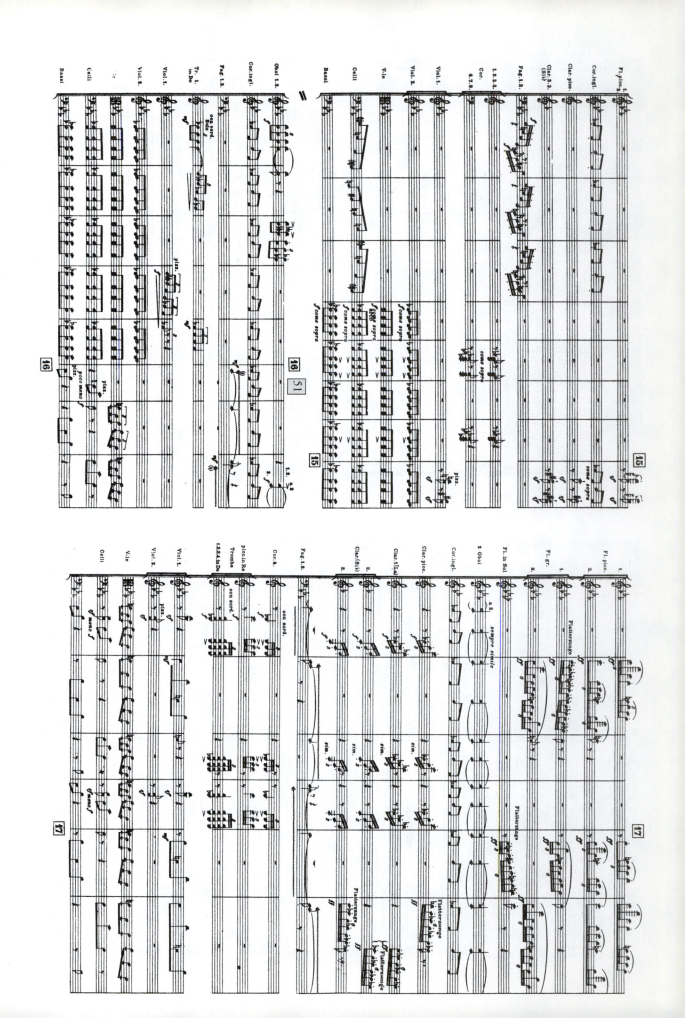

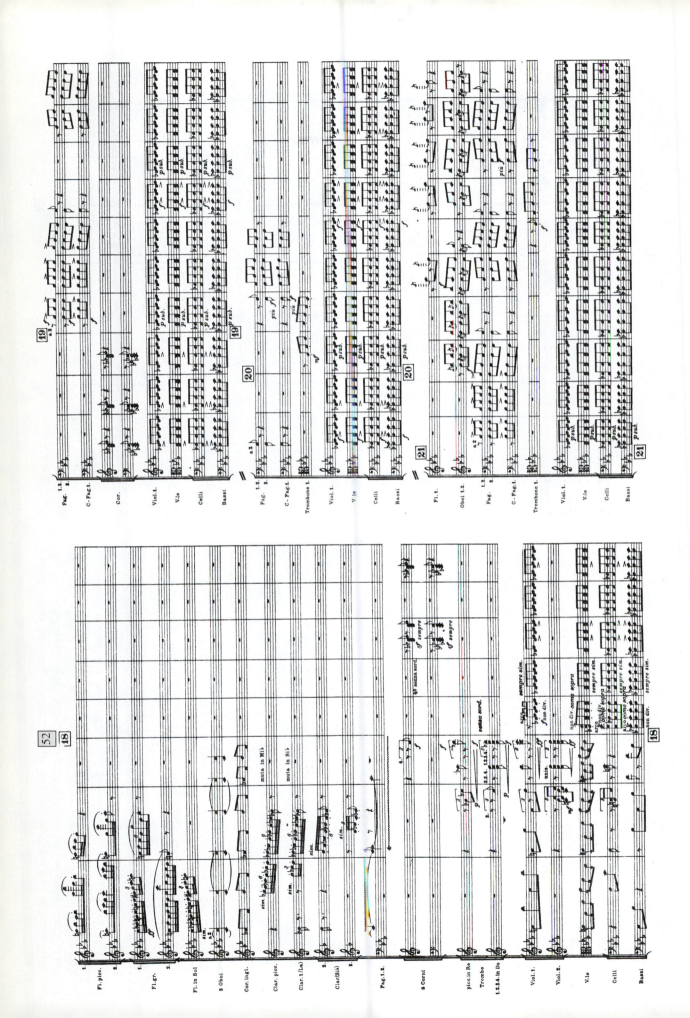

No. 153 Stravinsky: *Le Sacre du printemps*

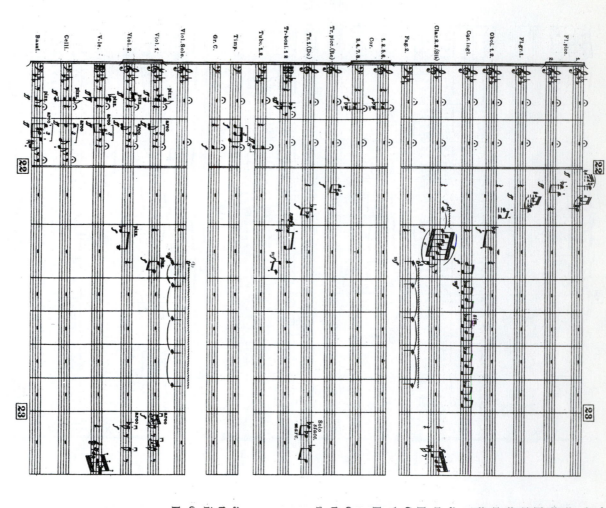

The scenario of Stravinsky's ballet *Le Sacre du printemps* ("The Rite of Spring," subtitled "Pictures from Pagan Russia") centers on a pre-Christian ritual that welcomes the coming of spring and offers in thanks to the gods a human sacrifice—primitive and uncivilized to be sure, but consequently all the more elemental and powerful. By rejecting traditional harmonic progressions, timbres, and above all rhythms, Stravinsky was able to create a score that reflected the same kind of raw, elemental relationship between man and nature that is represented on stage through the story of the dance. Stravinsky elevates the role of rhythm—the most basic of all musical elements—in a number of ways, sometimes through complexity, sometimes through simplicity.

The passage beginning at figure 13 (m. 76) is unpredictable, even though it is based on a series of repeating eighth-note chords. Stravinsky strips the music of all harmonic and melodic variety. The orchestra, in effect, functions as a kind of giant, polychordal drum, repeating the same chord 32 times in succession (see Textbook, Example 20-6). By marking each iteration with a down bow, Stravinsky eliminates the slight alternation of strong and weak that is often perceptible from standard back-and-forth (down-and-up) bowing, and by placing accents at irregular intervals, he eradicates any sense of a rhythmic pattern.

The polytonal harmony of this same passage posed further challenges to early listeners. Contrasting triads are juxtaposed simultaneously, with each of two instrumental groups—two sets of horns, high strings, low strings—playing its own chord in such a way that an E major chord sounds simultaneously with an $E\flat^7$ chord.

Violins, violas, horns 1–4: $E\flat^7$ chord ($E\flat$-G-$B\flat$-$D\flat$)

Cellos, basses, horns 5–8: E major chord ($F\flat$-$A\flat$-$C\flat$ = E-G#-B)

At figure 14, Stravinsky juxtaposes arpeggiated chords in an even more jarring fashion: an implied $B\flat^7$ arpeggio in the English horn, against C major in the bassoons, against an alternation of E major and E minor in the cellos (see Example 20-7 in the Textbook). Each chord is perfectly tonal within itself, but the simultaneous sounding of these chords rubbed many ears the wrong way, at least on first hearing in 1913. Within a decade, however, the elemental power of the score had won over a large following of critics and listeners alike.

154 Maple Leaf Rag (1899)

Scott Joplin (1868–1917)

CD12 Track 53

p. 558

53

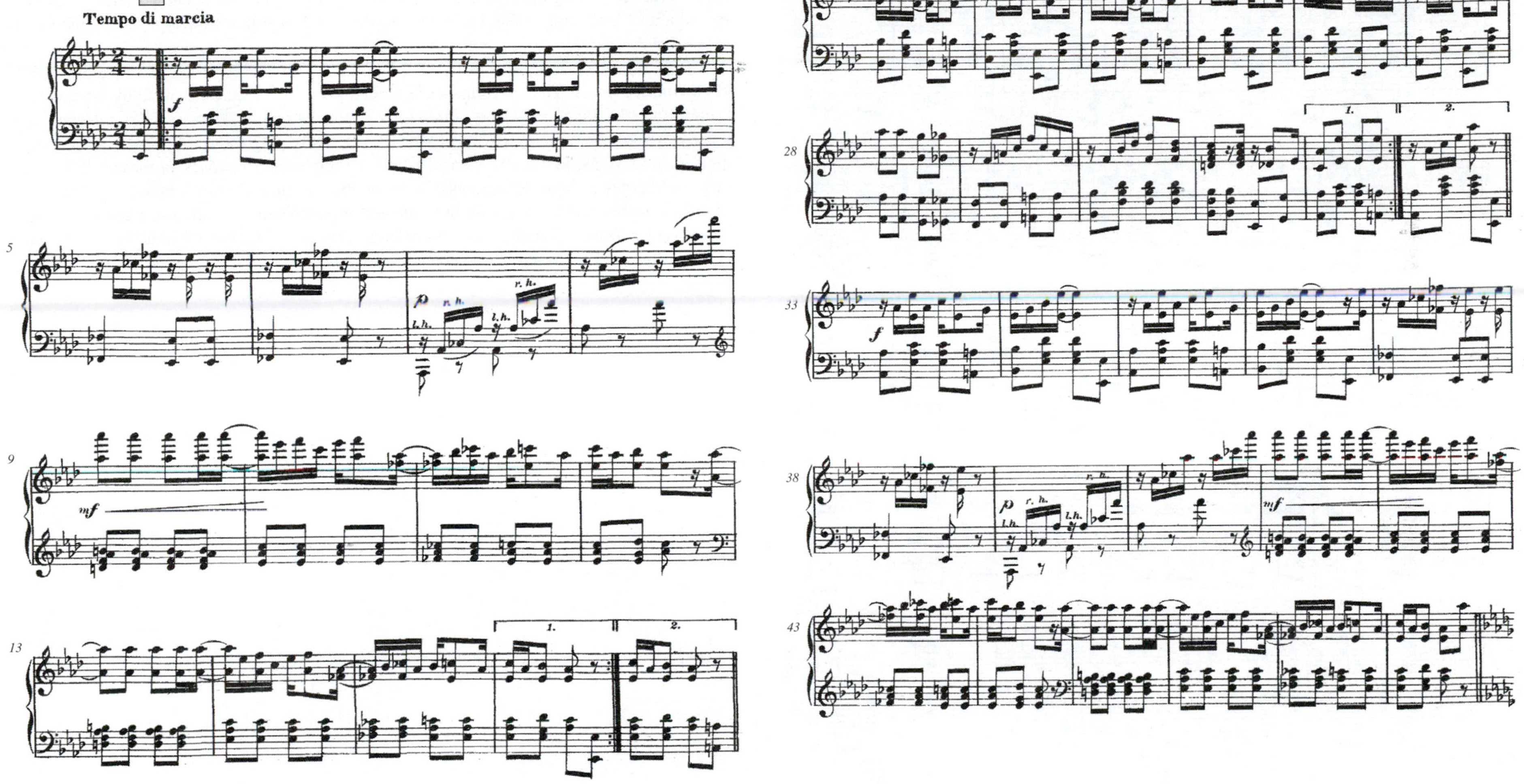
Tempo di marcia
f
p
r. h.
l. h.
mf
1.
2.
f stacc.

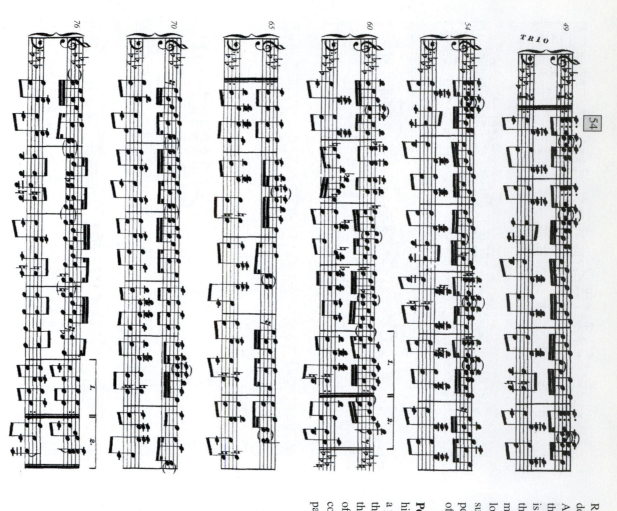

■ No. 154 Joplin: *Maple Leaf Rag*

Ragtime first flourished in the United States at the end of the 19th century and in the early decades of the 20th. It grew out of the confluence of the largely unwritten tradition of African-American dance, minstrel dance (particularly the cakewalk), and such ballroom dances as the two-step and polka. Joplin's enormously popular *Maple Leaf Rag* exemplifies the style: it is in duple meter and based on units of eight or sixteen measures. Syncopation is prevalent throughout, thrown into relief by the steadiness of the bass line typically heard in the banjo music of minstrel shows (see Chapter 16). The *Maple Leaf Rag* is also typical in that it follows the basic form of a march: three or four different themes, each running to sixteen measures, with connecting material between sections. In ragtime, the opening theme is often repeated after the second theme. Formally, *Maple Leaf Rag* follows the typical ragtime pattern of AA BB A CC DD.

Performance notes: This performance is from a piano roll recording made by the composer himself in 1916. Piano rolls were coiled rolls of punched paper, each punch corresponding to a particular key on a piano specially made or adapted to play these rolls. Piano rolls enjoyed their greatest vogue in the 1910s and 1920s. One important drawback of these rolls was that they could not reproduce gradations of volume; thus Joplin's recording here conveys no sense of difference between loud or soft. Still, the performance helps capture some sense of how the composer performed his own music. Embellishments and slight variations abound throughout, particularly when a given section is being repeated.

155 Children's Corner Suite: "Golliwog's Cakewalk" (1908)
Debussy

CD12 | Track 55
p. 559

No. 155 Debussy: *Children's Corner Suite*

156 St. Louis Blues (1914)
W. C. Handy (1873–1958)

Words and Music by
W. C. HANDY

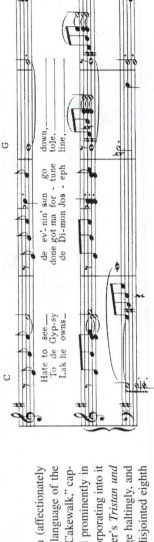

Debussy wrote his *Children's Corner Suite* (1908) for his daughter Emma (affectionately known as "Chou Chou"). The English title and movement titles reflect the language of the child's governess, a Miss Gibbs. The last movement of the suite, "Golliwog's Cakewalk," captures the syncopated rhythms of the cakewalk, a strutting dance that figured prominently in minstrel shows of the day. Debussy adds a touch of irony to his work by incorporating into it (m. 61–63) an oblique reference to the celebrated "Tristan chord" of Wagner's *Tristan und Isolde* (see Anthology 2/#138). He instructs the performer to play this passage haltingly, and "with great emotion," only to answer the quotation with a series of jaunty, disjointed eighth notes.

■ No. 156 Handy: St. Louis Blues

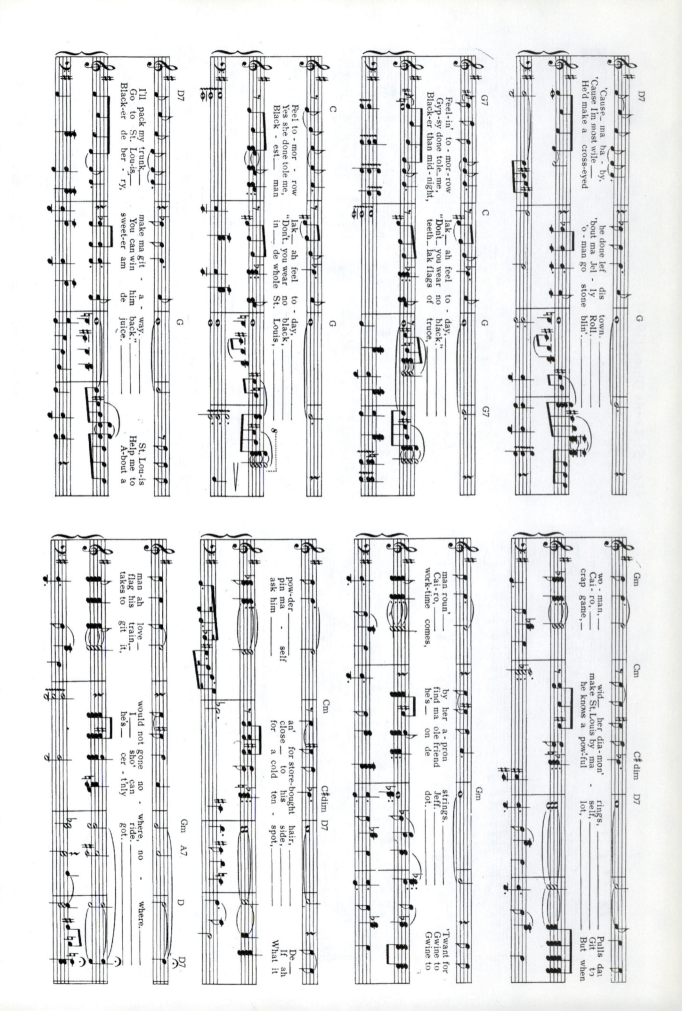

St. Louis Blues is constructed on a standard pattern known as the 12-bar blues form. This consists of a series of variations on a repeated harmonic pattern of 12 measures in 4/4 time. Each of these 12-measure units is known generically as a chorus and is in turn divided into three groups of four measures each. The harmonic progression in *St. Louis Blues* follows a harmonic pattern typical for the blues:

Measure number	1	2	3	4	5	6	7	8	9	10	11	12
Harmony	I				IV		I		V		I	

Like a great many blues numbers, *St. Louis Blues* opens with a vamp, a short progression of chords (and in this particular case, a melody as well) whose function is to introduce the basic harmonies, tempo, and mood of the whole. The vamp in *St. Louis Blues* is unusual in that it contrasts markedly with the chorus that follows. Handy explained this unusual feature in his autobiography:

When *St. Louis Blues* was written the tango was in vogue. I tricked the dancers by arranging a tango introduction, breaking abruptly then into a low-down blues. My eyes swept the floor anxiously, then suddenly I saw lightning strike. The dancers seemed electrified. Something within them came suddenly to life. An instinct that wanted so much to live, to fling its arms and to spread joy, took them by the heels. By this I was convinced that my new song was accepted.[1]

But the notated score gives only the barest of outlines for what the blues actually sound like in performance. As with *basse danse* forms of the Renaissance (see Chapters 5 and 6), the basic structure leaves room for enormous variation. Harmonies can be altered, enriched, or made to move at a faster speed, and melodies can easily be changed to accommodate the text. In performance, a blues song is fluid in spite of its underlying form. As heard in the contrasting performances of *St. Louis Blues* by Bessie Smith and Louis Armstrong (see the Textbook, Performance Perspectives, p. 563), the same work can be realized in strikingly different ways.

[1]W. C. Handy, *Father of the Blues: An Autobiography*, ed. Arna Bontemps (New York: Macmillan, 1941), p. 122.

No. 156 Handy: *St. Louis Blues*

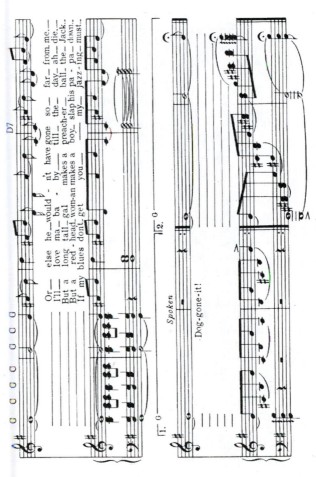

157 It Don't Mean a Thing (If It Ain't Got that Swing) (1930)

Duke Ellington (1899–1974)

CD12 Track 58 p. 562

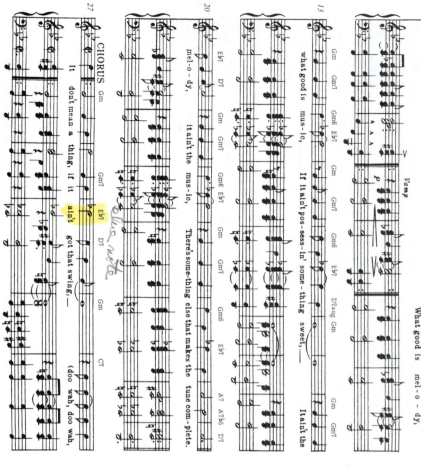

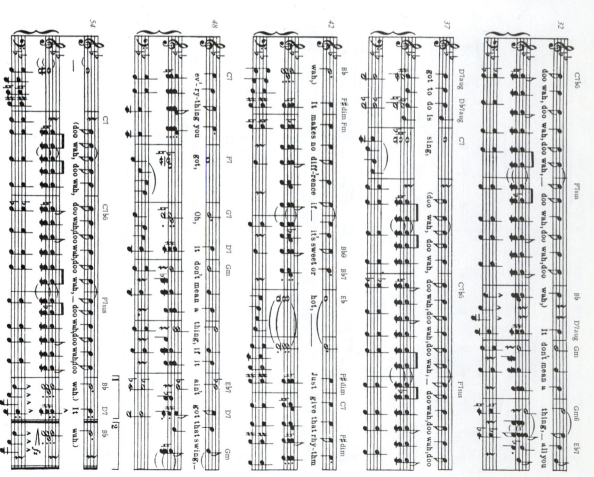

158 Mikrokosmos, Book 6, No. 148: Six Dances in Bulgarian Rhythm, No. 1 (between 1932 and 1939)
Bartók

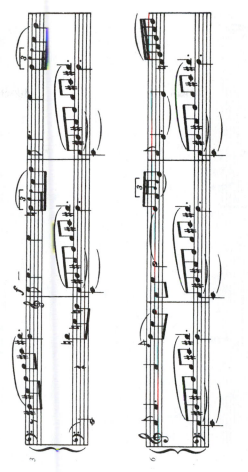

Duke Ellington's *It Don't Mean a Thing (If It Ain't Got that Swing)* represents jazz in the "Swing" era of the 1930s and 1940s. Swing rhythm features a hard meter but a subtle avoidance of cadences and downbeats, with the soloist placing notes either just ahead or just behind the beat in a way that heightened the music's rhythmic suppleness. Formally, the original song version of Ellington's *It Don't Mean a Thing* consists of an eight-measure instrumental introduction, followed by a two-measure vamp, a short progression of chords that can be repeated indefinitely before the entrance of the voice. The verse ("What good is melody...") consists of 16 measures (2 × 8) that end on a half cadence leading to the song's chorus or principal melody. The chorus itself consists of 16 measures, the thematic content of each following the pattern AABA. This pattern is so common in 20th-century song that it has come to be known as *song form*. The contrasting B section (here, from the words "It makes no diff'rence" through "ev'rything you got") is often known as the *bridge* because it connects statements of the A theme.

Performance notes: When Ellington recorded this number with his band in 1932, he substantially reworked the form of the piece. The recorded version omits the introduction and begins with ten measures of the vamp, in which the singer (Ivie Anderson) uses her voice as an instrument, singing syncopated nonsense syllables against the steady beat of the bass in a technique known as *scat* singing. The 32-measure verse, expanded from the song's 16-measure version, is allotted to a solo muted trombone. The voice, in turn, presents the chorus in its full 32-measure form. At this point, the instruments take over with a series of quasi-improvised solos. In rehearsal, Ellington and his group would have planned who would play these solos and in what order, but, beyond this, each instrumentalist was free to improvise at will, knowing in advance the basic chord progressions with which the band would support him. In this particular performance, we hear only one extended solo, given to the saxophonist (Johnny Hodges), who varies thematic elements of both verse and chorus. The full band then plays the opening of the chorus; the vocalist returns with the bridge passage, and the work concludes with the syncopated "doo-wah" fragmented on the muted brass. Other performances of this same work by Ellington vary the number and sequence of the soloists, the order in which verse and chorus are first presented, the final cadence, and countless other features large and small. Jazz performances by their very nature represent a fusion of composed and improvised elements.

No. 158 Bartók: *Mikrokosmos*

In his own compositions, Bartók often incorporated the kind of irregular meters that characterize a good deal of the folk music of eastern Europe. The first of his *Six Dances in Bulgarian Rhythm* from his *Mikrokosmos*, Book 6, is built on a metrical pattern notated as:

$$\frac{4+2+3}{8}$$

This kind of meter is sometimes referred to as complex meter, and although it ostensibly had its origins in folk music, it found its way into much modernist music as well. The simultaneous contrast of tonal centers is also notable here. In m. 4–12, for example, Bartók contrasts a rising seven-note motif outlining an E major scale in the left hand with a downward melodic idea that corresponds to a Phrygian scale (in keyboard terms, a downward scale from E on the white notes, without an F#).

No. 158 Bartók: *Mikrokosmos*

159 Saudades do Brasil (1921)

Darius Milhaud (1892–1974)

159a No. 5, "Ipanema"

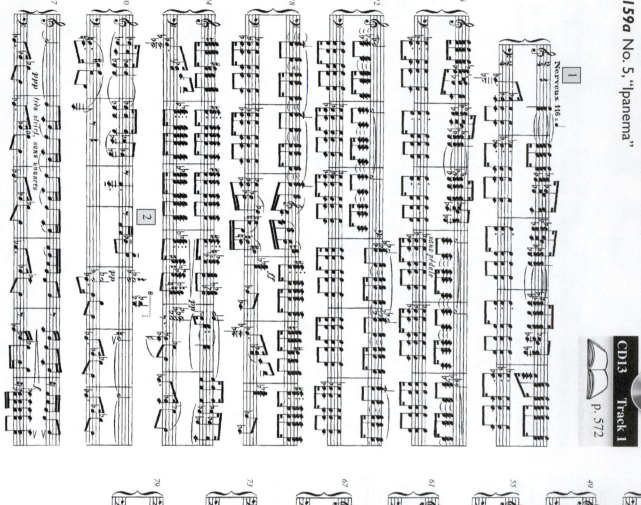

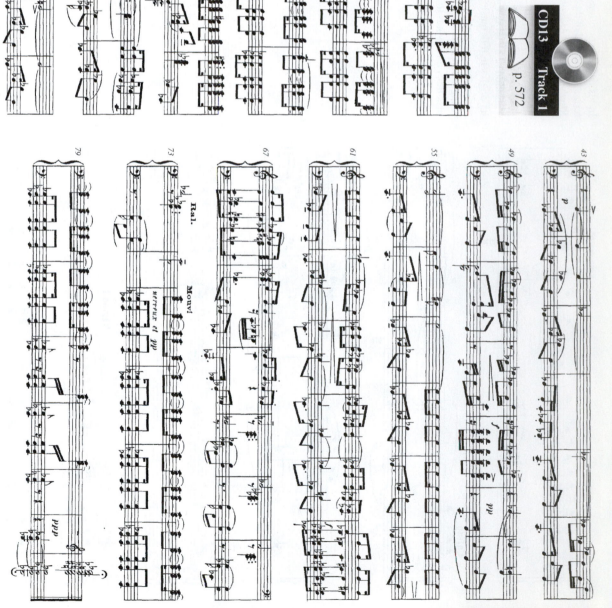

159b No. 6, "Gavea"

No. 159 Milhaud: *Saudades do Brasil*

Composers can and often do adapt the music of cultures not their own. The French composer Darius Milhaud (1892–1974) drew on Latin American tunes and dance rhythms in his *Saudades do Brasil* ("Nostalgia for Brazil"). These dances integrate popular dance rhythms into a harmonic idiom that is delightfully unpredictable. Milhaud's ample use of polytonality distinguishes his music from the sounds one would have actually heard in the streets of, say, Rio de Janeiro; yet the rhythms are true-to-life enough to provide the music with a decidedly Brazilian flavor.

CD13 Track 4 p. 572

"The Banshee" is played on the open strings of the piano, the player standing at the crook. Another person must sit at the keyboard and hold down the damper pedal throughout the composition. The whole work should be played an octave lower than written.

R. H. stands for "right hand." L. H. stands for "left hand." Different ways of playing the strings are indicated by a letter over each tone, as follows:

Explanation of Symbols

(A) indicates a sweep with the flesh of the finger from the lowest string up to the note given.

(B) sweep lengthwise along the string of the note given with flesh of finger.

(C) sweep up and back from lowest A to highest B-flat given in this composition.

(D) pluck string with flesh of finger, where written, instead of octave lower.

(E) sweep along three notes together, in the same manner as (B).

(F) sweep in the manner of (B) but with the back of finger-nail instead of flesh.

(G) when the finger is half way along the string in the manner of (F), start a sweep along the same string with the flesh of the other finger, thus partly damping the sound.

(H) sweep back and forth in the manner of (C), but start at the same time from both above and below, crossing the sweep in the middle.

(I) sweep along five notes, in the manner of (C).

(J) same as (I) but with back of finger-nails instead of flesh of finger.

(K) sweep along, in manner of (J) with nails of both hands together, taking in all notes between the two outer limits given.

(L) sweep in manner of (C) with flat of hand instead of single finger.

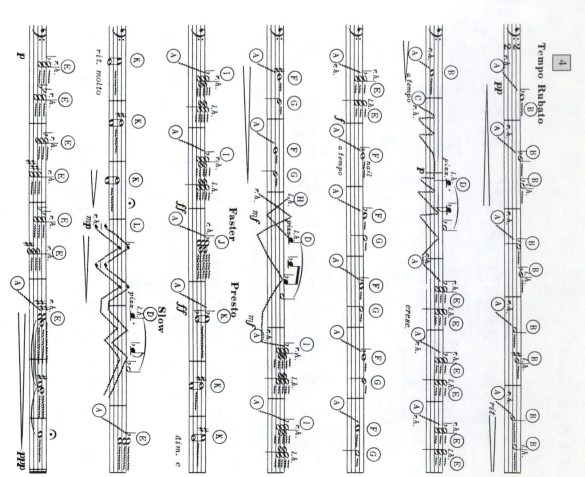

161 Pierrot lunaire (1912)
Arnold Schoenberg (1874–1951)

161a No. 7, "Der kranke Mond" ("The Sick Moon")

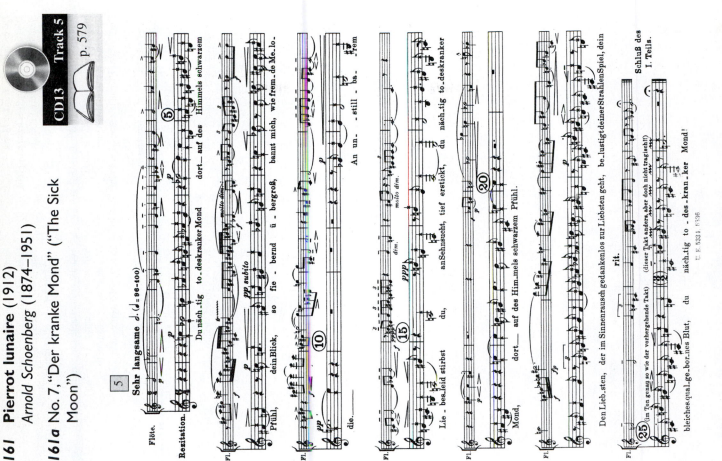

Although the 20th century brought relatively few technical changes to the piano itself, composers developed many novel ways of using the existing instrument. In *The Banshee*, the Californian composer Henry Cowell calls on the performer to manipulate directly by hand the strings inside the instrument. *The Banshee* actually requires two performers, although the only responsibility of the one at the keyboard is to keep the damper pedal down throughout the entire work. The other player stands in the crook of the instrument and touches the strings with his or her fingers. Cowell's explanation of the special performance symbols for the work takes up almost as much space as the score itself. The opening of the piece calls for the standing player to "sweep with the flesh of the finger from the lowest string up to the note given," ending with another lengthwise sweep of the finger on the string of that highest note. Different sounds are gradually introduced: the sweep concludes with a pluck of strings, then with a sweep along the strings of three notes together, then sweeping with the back of the fingernails instead of the fleshy part of the finger, and so on.

At the time of composition in 1925, the unearthly effect was unlike anything anyone had heard before that time. The eerie quality of the sound fits with the work's title. In Cowell's own words, a banshee is "a woman of the Inner World . . . who is charged with the duty of taking your soul into the Inner World when you die . . . She has to come to the outer plane for this purpose, and she finds the outer plane very uncomfortable and unpleasant, so you will hear her wailing at the time of a death in your family."

Performance note: The voice announcing the title of this work is Cowell's own, and he performs the more difficult part of the work's two parts in this recording made in 1963, only two years before his death.

p. 579

No. 161 Schoenberg: *Pierrot lunaire*

Du nächtig todeskranker Mond
Dort auf des Himmels schwarzem Pfühl,
Dein Blick, so fiebernd übergroß,
Bannt mich wie fremde Melodie.

An unstillbarem Liebesleid
Stirbst du, an Sehnsucht, tief erstickt,
Du nächtig todeskranker Mond
Dort auf des Himmels schwarzem Pfühl.

Den Liebsten, der im Sinnenrausch
Gedankenlos zur Liebsten schleicht,
Belustigt deiner Strahlen Spiel—
Dein bleiches, qualgebornes Blut,

Du nächtig todeskranker Mond.

You dark moon, deathly ill,
Laid over heaven's sable pillow,
Your fever-swollen gaze
Enchants me like alien melody.

You die of insatiable pangs of love,
Suffocated in longing,
You dark moon, deathly ill,
Laid over heaven's sable pillow.

The hotblooded lover
Slinking heedless to the tryst
You hearten with your play of light,
Your pale blood wrung from torment,

You dark moon, deathly ill.

161b No. 14, "Die Kreuze" ("The Crosses")

CD13 Track 6 P. 579

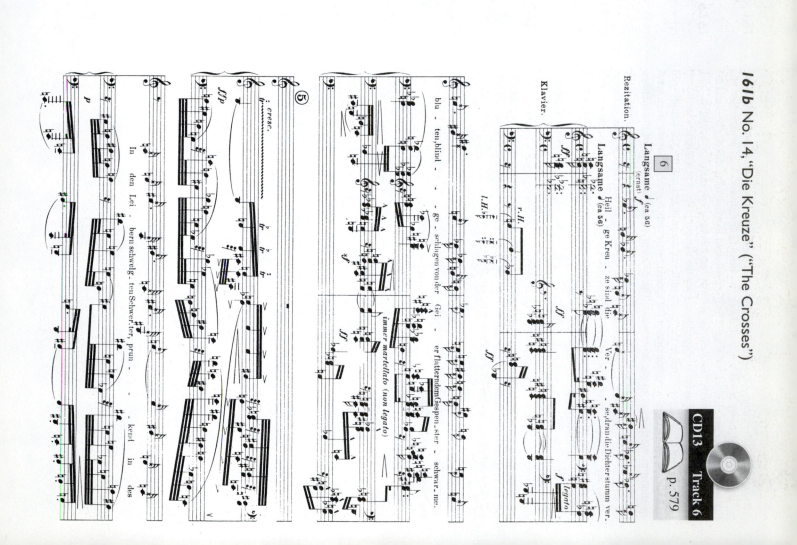

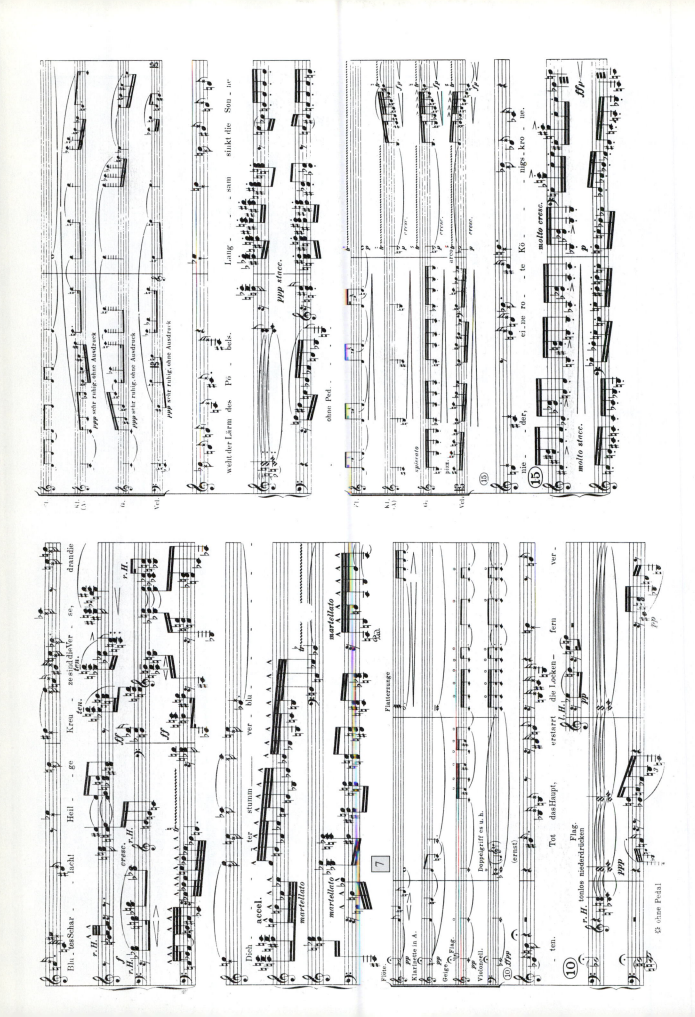

No. 161 Schoenberg: *Pierrot lunaire*

443

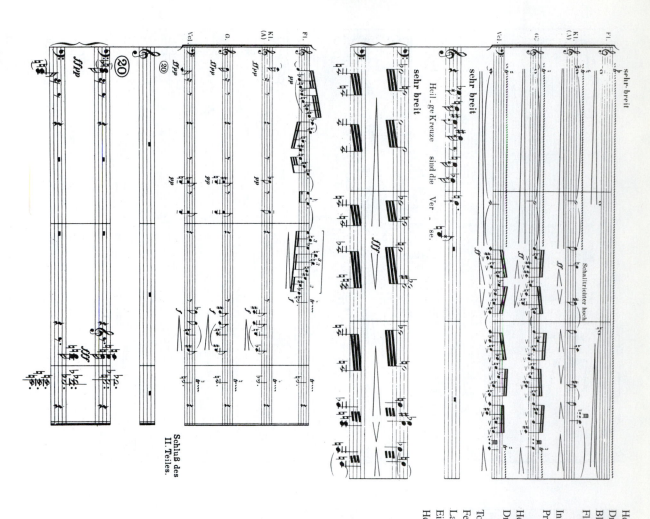

Heilge Kreuze sind die Verse,
Dran die Dichter stumm verbluten,
Blindgeschlagen von der Geier
Flatterndem Gespensterschwarme!

In den Leibern schwelgten Schwerter,
Prunkend in des Blutes Scharlach!
Heilge Kreuze sind die Verse,
Dran die Dichter stumm verbluten.

Tot das Haupt—erstarrt die Locken—
Fern, verweht der Lärm des Pöbels.
Langsam sinkt die Sonne nieder,
Eine rote Königskrone.—
Heilge Kreuze sind die Verse!

Poems are poets' holy crosses
On which they bleed in silence,
Struck blind by phantom swarms
Of fluttering vultures.

Swords have feasted on their bodies,
Reveling in the scarlet blood!
Poems are poets' holy crosses
On which they bleed in silence.

Dead the head, the tresses stiffened,
Far away the noisy rabble.
Slowly the sun sinks,
A red royal crown.—
Poems are poets' holy crosses.

161c No. 21, "O alter Duft" ("O redolence of Old")

No. 161 Schoenberg: *Pierrot lunaire*

445

O alter Duft aus Märchenzeit,
Berauschest wieder meine Sinne;
Ein närrisch Heer von Schelmerein
Durchschwirrt die leichte Luft.

Ein glückhaft Wünschen macht mich froh
Nach Freuden, die ich lang verachtet:
O alter Duft aus Märchenzeit,
Berauschest wieder mich!

All meinen Unmut gab ich preis;
Aus meinem sonnumrahmten Fenster
Beschau ich frei die liebe Welt

Und träum hinaus in selge Weiten . . .
O alter Duft—aus Märchenzeit!

O redolence from fairytale times,
Bewitch again my senses!
A knavish swarm of silly pranks
Buzzes down the gentle breeze.

A happy impulse calls me back
To joys I have long neglected:
O redolence from fairytale times,
Bewitch me again!

All my ill humors I've renounced;
From my sun-framed window
I behold untrammeled the beloved world

And dream me out to blissful vistas . . .
O redolence from fairytale times.

Pierrot is one of the stock masked characters from the Italian *commedia dell'arte*, a melancholy, moon-struck clown who lives in a state of constant longing. The poetic cycle *Pierre lunaire* by the Belgian poet Albert Giraud (1860–1929) draws on the mask as a metaphor for the human manners that conceal deeper emotions, and Schoenberg was deeply attracted to this imagery. The atonality of No. 7 ("The Sick Moon") makes the moon seem far more ill than any tonal idiom could. Schoenberg projects the violence of the text in No. 14 ("The Cross") by having the voice make leaps of ninths, diminished and augmented octaves, and other nontriadic intervals, thereby undermining any sense of a tonal center. The final work in Schoenberg's setting of 21 songs from this cycle is particularly haunting for the way in which it conjures up the specter of tonality. The text speaks of a longing for the old "fairy tale times," yet the poetic persona is fully aware that such times will never return, if indeed they existed at all. Schoenberg's music fits the text perfectly: in the opening piano passage, the "walking" bass and the triads in the upper voices sound almost like a chorale by J. S. Bach, but the harmonic distortions are more than enough to create a distorted, grotesque image of the musical past. The voice ends in a barely audible whisper in a barely audible range.

Sprechstimme, the style of singing called for throughout *Pierrot lunaire*, reinforces the surreal quality of the text and music. *Sprechstimme* (literally, "speech-voice," with "voice" understood here in the sense of "singing") is neither speech nor song, but a means of declamation somewhere between the two. Unlike speech, in *Sprechstimme* the vocalist must articulate specified pitches and rhythms. Instead of sustaining a pitch as in the conventional method of singing, however, the performer allows the pitch to drop rather in the same way one's voice drops with the enunciation of a spoken word. *Sprechstimme* is indicated by means of standard notes with a small *x* through the stem. The effect is unique: as song, it falls short of lyricism, and intentionally so, while as speech, it constitutes a purposefully exaggerated, overblown kind of delivery. It occupies a kind of twilight zone between speech and song that calls attention to the essentially artificial distinction between the two.

Anton Webern's *Five Pieces for String Quartet,* Op. 5 (1908) is a series of miniatures that concentrates its resources into a remarkably intense form of expression. Like most atonal works, the fourth of these five pieces uses a limited number of building blocks—in this case, groups of four or five notes—sometimes fewer, sometimes more, but rarely very many more. These units tend to avoid triads, both in their linear (melodic) and vertical (harmonic) alignments. Webern, like Schoenberg and Berg, saw himself as a traditionalist who continued in the tradition of Beethoven and Brahms by manipulating motivic ideas in a process that Schoenberg called "developing variation." The extreme brevity of the movements in Webern's Op. 5, the absence of a tonal center, and the consistent avoidance of strong cadences and any long-range sense of meter all make it difficult to hear this process of development, at least on first listening.

Fortunately, set theory, which was developed in the third quarter of the 20th century by the American scholar Allen Forte, among others, provides us with a framework for identifying the constituent elements that go into most atonal music. Forte proposed a system for identifying and clarifying the relationship of the relatively small units ("cells" or "sets") that together provide the building blocks for a typical atonal composition. These sets can consist of anywhere between two and ten *pitch-classes*. A pitch-class is any manifestation of a particular pitch, regardless of register; thus the pitch-class A-F can be used for units that go either down a major third or up a minor sixth—or down a tenth, and so on. There is a finite number of set types—220 to be exact—that can be created out of all the various combinations of pitch-classes (see Textbook, Focus, p. 584).

In analysis, these combinations of differing size are identified by a series of numbers reflecting the prime form of the set, beginning with 0 (the lowest note of the set) and moving upward by half-step. Thus the tetrachord set C-D♯-F-G would be called 0-3-5-7 because D♯ is three half-steps above C, F is 5 half-steps above C, and G is seven half-steps above C. Sets can be presented either simultaneously (as a "chord") or successively (as a "melody").

Looking at the score of Webern's Op. 5, No. 4, we can see that two sets play an important role in the opening measures. Set A (0-1-5-6 = B-C-E-F) is presented in the two upper voices in m. 1; set B (0-1-6-7 = B-C-F-F♯) at the beginning of m. 2. The pitches of set A recur on the final half-beat of m. 2; set B appears as a melodic line in the first violin in m. 3–4, then again in the second violin (m. 4) transposed down a fifth. Identifying pitch-class sets can be a hit-or-miss process at times: some sets occur only once or twice in a piece and cannot really be considered to have structural importance. The identification of sets can nevertheless be extremely helpful for making audibly coherent a work of music that might otherwise seem shapeless.

162 Five Pieces for String Quartet, Op. 5, No. 4 (1908)
Anton Webern (1883–1945)

CD13   Track 10   p. 581

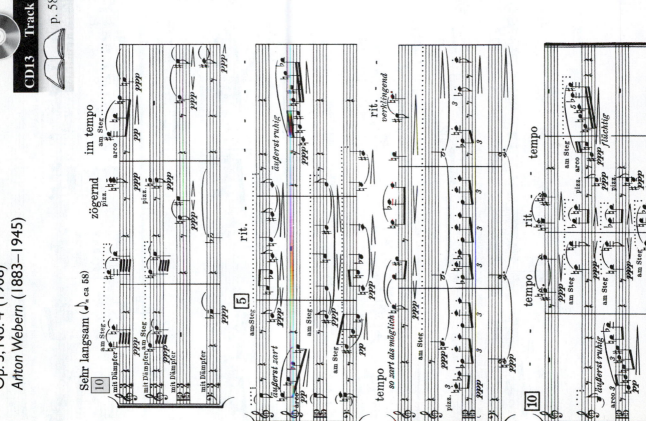

163 Wozzeck, Act I, Scene I (1925)
Alban Berg (1885–1935)

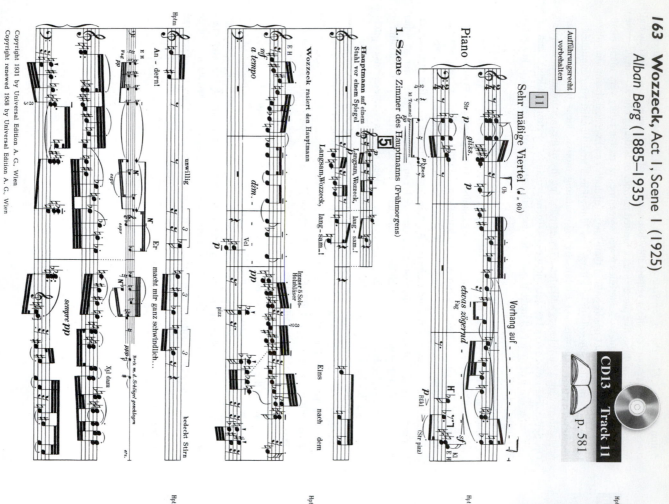

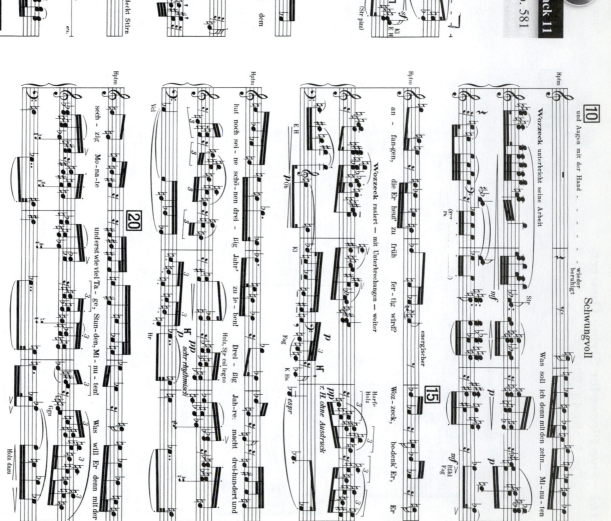

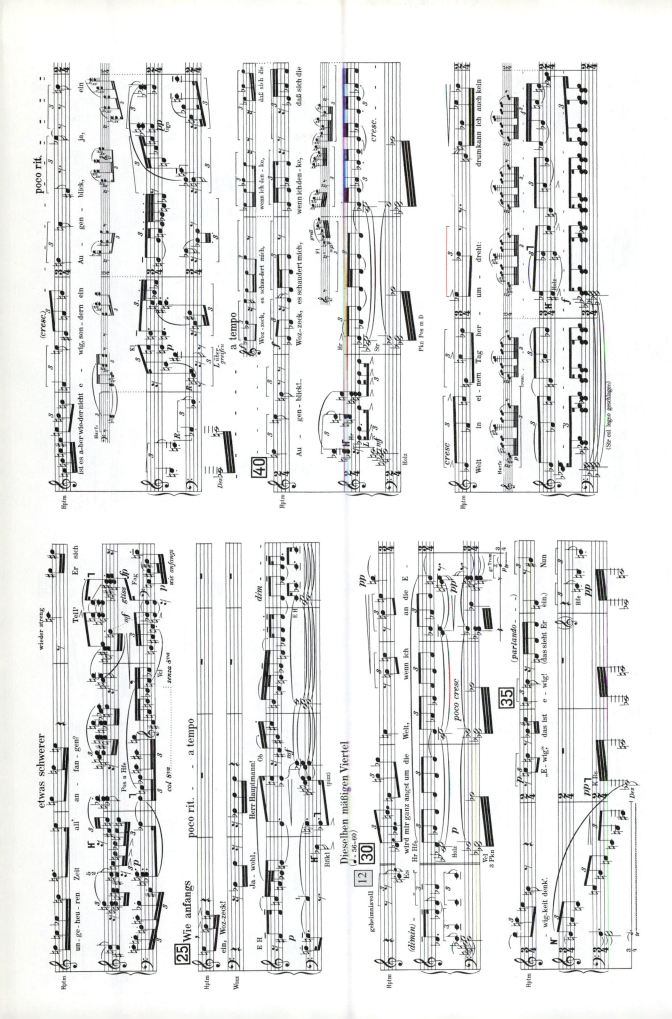

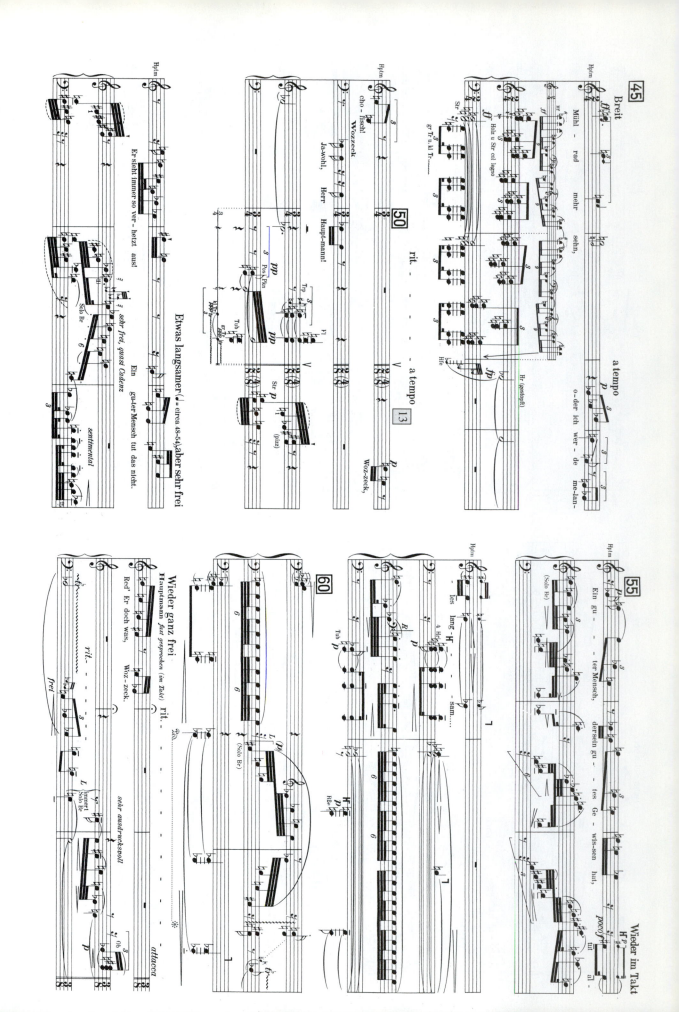

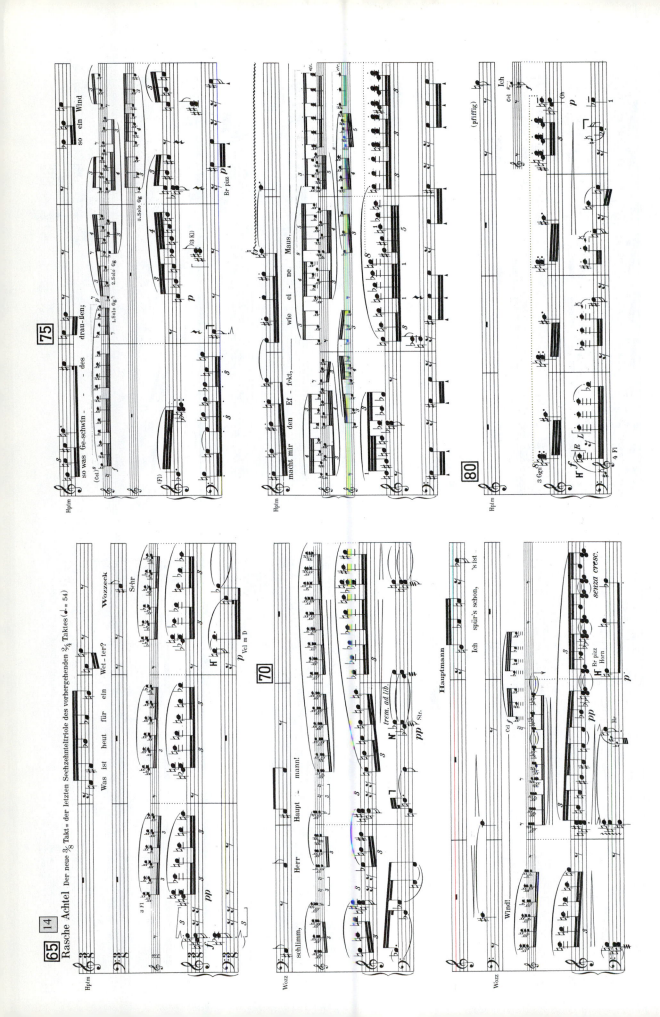

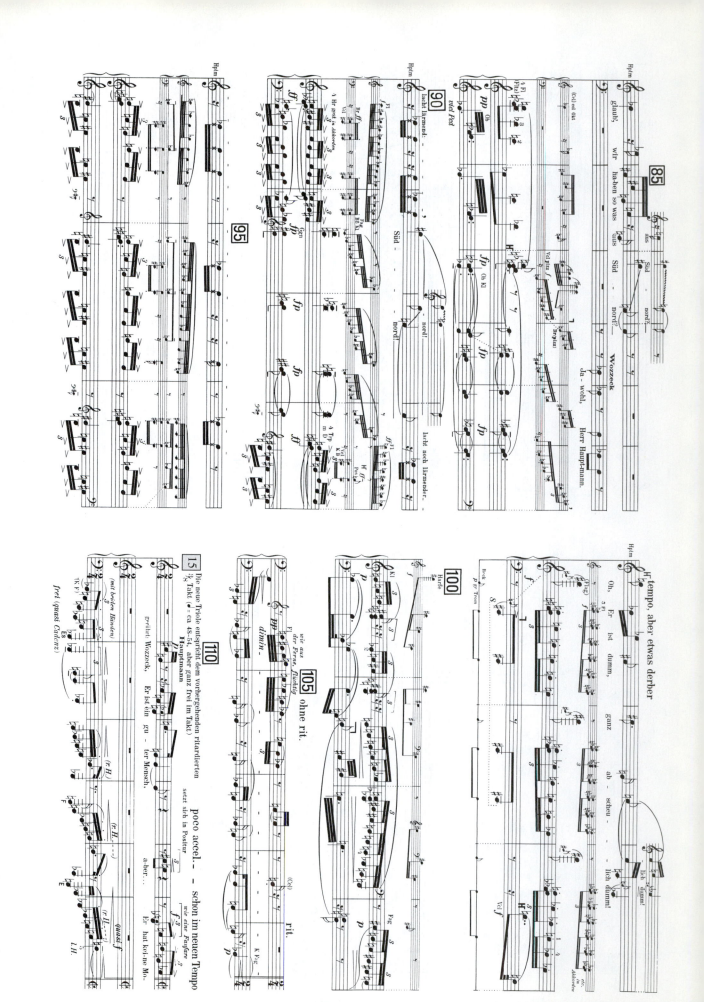

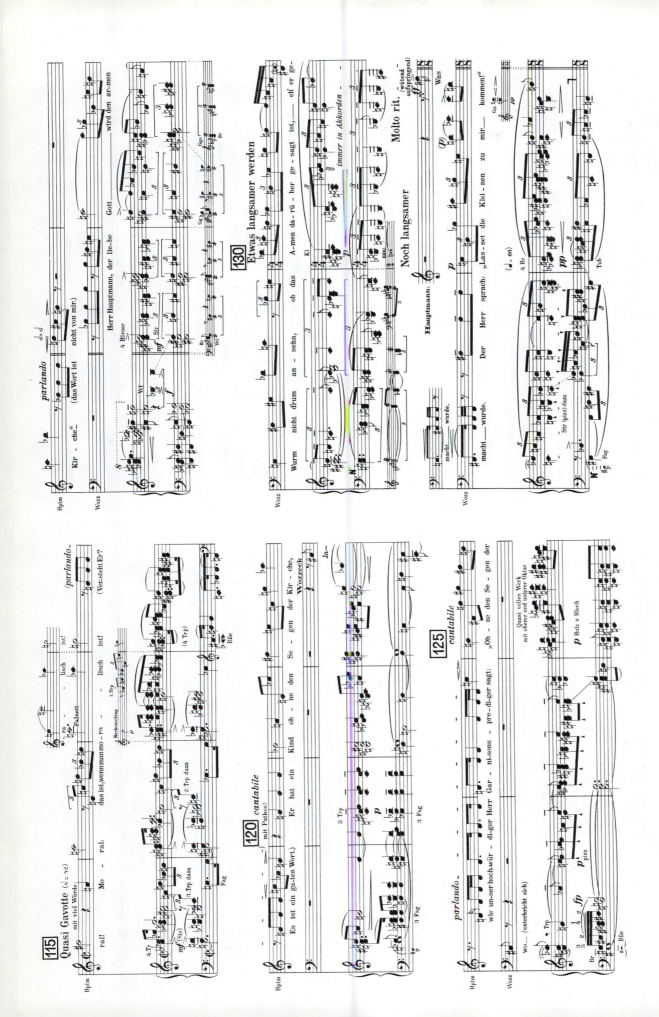

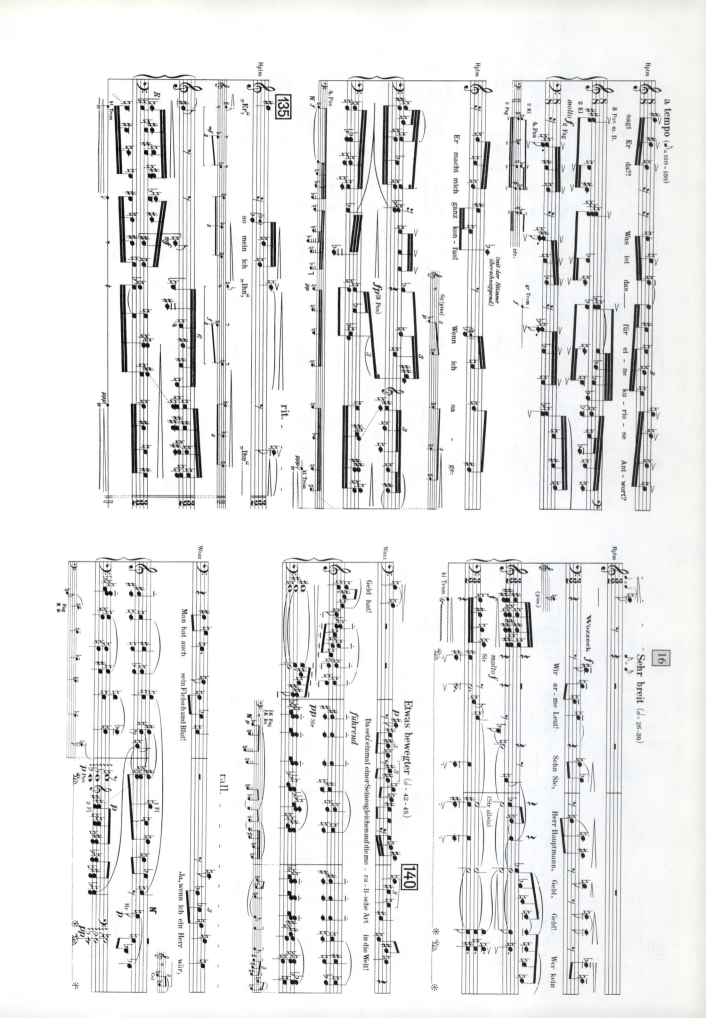

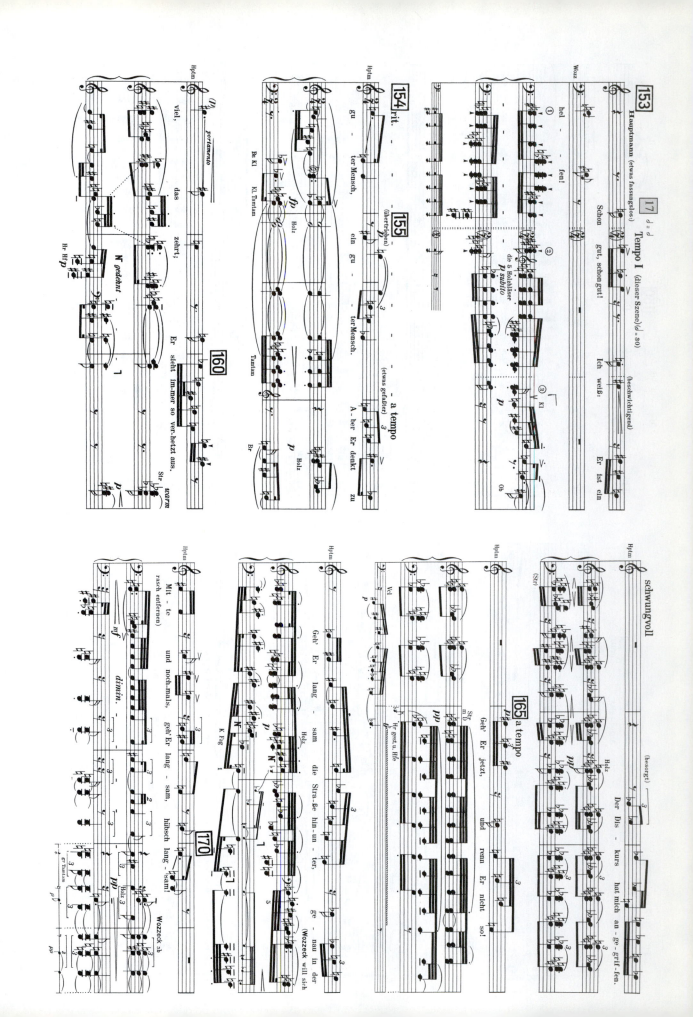

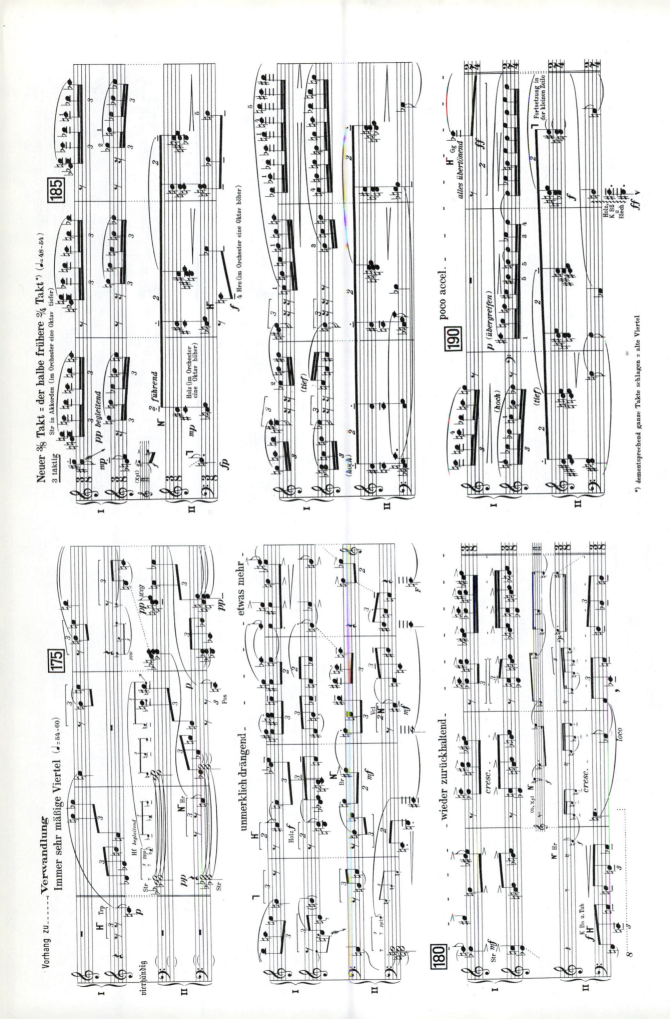

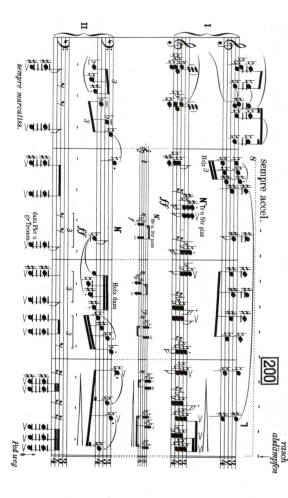
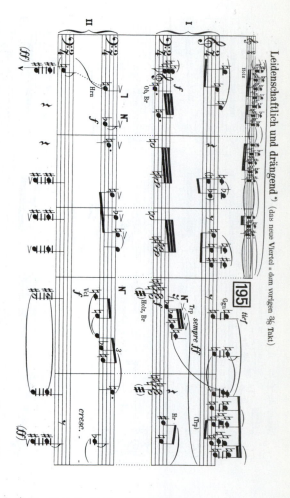

Leidenschaftlich und drängend*) (das neue Viertel = dem vorigen ⅜ Takt)

*) ♩=30 bis ♩=42-48 (entspricht dann dem Viertel des folgenden ¾ Takts 201)

sempre marcatiss.

1. AKT
1. SZENE

Zimmer des Hauptmanns (Frühmorgens). Hauptmann auf einem Stuhl vor einem Spiegel. Wozzeck rasiert den Hauptmann.

HAUPTMANN: Langsam, Wozzeck, langsam! Eins nach dem Andern! (unwillig) Er macht mir ganz schwindlich... (bedeckt Stirn und Augen mit der Hand—wieder beruhigt. Wozzeck unterbricht seine Arbeit)

HAUPTMANN: Was soll ich denn mit den zehn Minuten anfangen, die Er heut' zu früh fertig wird? (energischer) Wozzeck, bedenk' Er, Er hat noch seine schönen dreißig Jahr' zu leben! Dreißig Jahre: macht dreihundert und sechzig Monate und erst wie viel Tage, Stunden, Minuten! Was will Er denn mit der ungeheuren Zeit all' anfangen? (wieder streng) Teil' Er sich ein, Wozzeck!

WOZZECK: Jawohl, Herr Hauptmann!

HAUPTMANN: (geheimnisvoll) Es wird mir ganz angst um die Welt, wenn ich an die Ewigkeit denk'. "Ewig," das ist ewig! (das sieht Er ein.) Nun ist es aber wieder nicht ewig, sondern ein Augenblick, ja, ein Augenblick! Wozzeck, es schaudert mich, wenn ich denke, daß sich die Welt in einem Tag herumdreht: drum kann ich auch kein Mühlrad mehr sehn, oder ich werde melancholisch!

WOZZECK: Jawohl, Herr Hauptmann!

HAUPTMANN: Wozzeck, Er sieht immer so verhetzt aus! Ein guter Mensch tut das nicht. Ein guter Mensch, der sein gutes Gewissen hat, tut alles langsam... Red' Er doch was, Wozzeck. Was ist heut für ein Wetter?

WOZZECK: Sehr schlimm, Herr Hauptmann! Wind!

HAUPTMANN: Ich spür's schon, 's ist so was Geschwindes draußen; so ein Wind macht mir den Effekt, wie eine Maus. (pfiffig) Ich glaub; wir haben so was aus Südnord?

ACT ONE
SCENE ONE

(The Captain's room. Early morning. The Captain is sitting on a chair in front of a mirror, while Wozzeck is shaving him.)

CAPTAIN: Easy, Wozzeck, easy! Do take your time, man! (anxiously) You make me quite giddy. (Covers his forehead and eyes with his hand. Wozzeck stops what he is doing. The Captain steadies himself)

CAPTAIN: What shall I do with the time you save in ten minutes, if you finish early today? (more vigorously) Wozzeck, consider, you surely still have almost thirty years to live yet... Thirty years... that's three hundred and sixty months to go... and how many days and hours and minutes!... What will you do with the great expanse of time before you now? (serious again) Make up your mind, Wozzeck!

WOZZECK: Yes sir, I will sir.

CAPTAIN: (mysteriously) It makes me afraid for the world to think of eternity. Always—that's "eternal"... (you understand). But then again, it cannot be always... but a mere moment, yes, a moment. Wozzeck, I'm terrified when I'm thinking that the whole world in one short day revolves. And if I see a mill-wheel that turns, it always gives me melancholia.

WOZZECK: Yes sir, I see sir.

CAPTAIN: Wozzeck, your face always looks so harassed. A worthy man takes his time, a worthy man with a conscience that's undefiled does all things slowly. Do say something. Wozzeck. Come tell me, how's the weather?

WOZZECK: Not good. Not good, sir. Wind...

CAPTAIN: I feel it... there's something so swift outside there. Such a wind always seems to me just like a mouse. (artfully) I think there's something blowing from South-North...

Alban Berg's opera *Wozzeck* was by far the most successful atonal work of the early 20th century, both critically and commercially. The libretto, drawn from selected scenes of the drama *Woyzeck* by the Austrian playwright Georg Büchner (1813–1837), traces the mental and physical deterioration of a simple army soldier, who is treated abysmally by everyone: his captain, his doctor, and the woman by whom he has fathered a child. In the end, he goes mad and murders Marie, the mother of his young son.

Berg used a series of traditional instrumental forms to structure his opera. The opening scene (Act I, Scene 1) is a suite, a series of dance-types, very much in the tradition of the opening scene of Verdi's *Rigoletto*. Each change in the turn of conversation in the dance-type. The curtain goes up on a scene that is at once both mundane and chilling. We see Wozzeck shaving the Captain. With a flick of the wrist Wozzeck could kill him, and indeed the thought occurs to him as, in the process of trying to engage the laconic soldier in conversation, the Captain crosses the line by reminding Wozzeck of his illegitimate child. The scene is constructed as a suite, a series of dances (or rather, dance rhythms) that relate precisely to the nature of the conversation.

- Prelude (m. 1): The Captain, who, as we later realize, is obsessed with the passage of time, reminds Wozzeck to proceed slowly, "one step at a time." In the course of urging calm, the Captain himself becomes quite agitated.
- Pavane (m. 30): The Captain broods on eternity and mortality. This section ends with a cadenza for the viola.
- Gigue (m. 65): The Captain has not been able to engage Wozzeck in a conversation on morality, so he turns instead to the weather ("I believe the wind is from South-North"), but even these absurdities fail to capture Wozzeck's attention. The music ends with a cadenza for bassoon.
- Gavotte (m. 115): The captain returns to the idea of morality and scores a hit when he declares that Wozzeck's child was born out of wedlock, "without the blessings of the church."
- Double I (m. 127): Wozzeck finally responds and quotes Christ's words "Let the little children come unto me." At Double II (m. 133), the Captain's erratic rhythm takes over when he insists that he had not been talking about Wozzeck at all. Suddenly it is the Captain who does not want to talk.
- Air (m. 136): Wozzeck erupts in a passion of genuine emotion, a lyrical outburst: "We poor people," he sings, and the music to these words will return often in the course of the opera. Morality, he proclaims, is a function of affluence.
- Prelude (reprise) (m. 154): The Captain, quite shaken, tries to resume his original air of calm. The music of the opening returns, and he resumes his verbal harassment of Wozzeck as if nothing had happened in the meantime.

In addition to introducing the opera's central character, this opening scene also introduces one of the work's principal ideas: the consequences of emotional repression. At first, Wozzeck assumes the guise of an automaton, answering each of the Captain's provocative questions with a monotonous and unthinking "Yes, sir." Only when the Captain touches on the question of Wozzeck's child do we begin to see the soldier's true feelings emerge, but because they are so raw and powerful, the captain quickly seeks to put them back in place, insisting (quite absurdly) that he had not even been talking to Wozzeck at all during this time.

WOZZECK: Yes sir, quite so sir.

CAPTAIN: *(laughs loudly)* South-North! *(laughs still more loudly)* Oh, you are dense! Quite absurdly dense! *(sympathetically)* Wozzeck, you are a worthy man . . . *(striking an attitude)* and yet . . . you have no moral sense. Moral sense . . . *(very dignified)* . . . that is, acting quite morally. Is that clear? . . . it is a splendid word . . . *(very grand)* You have a child which is not blessed by the clergy . . .

WOZZECK: Well, yes . . . *(stops)*

CAPTAIN: . . . as our regimental chaplain says to us, preaching in church: ". . . which is not blessed by the clergy" (the words are not my own) . . .

WOZZECK: And yet sir, the good Lord God will not spurn the poor little fellow, all because the 'amen' was not spoken before a child was thought of. The Lord spake: "Suffer the children to come to Me" . . .

CAPTAIN: *(jumping up in a rage)* What do you mean? And what sort of curious answer is that? You make me quite confused. When I'm saying "you," then I mean *you, you . . .*

WOZZECK: Poor folk like us . . . see now . . . need money . . . look, sir . . . always money. Let one of us try to bring his own kind into the world in a good moral way . . . We're all made of flesh and blood. If I were a lord, sir, and wore a silk hat and had a watch and an eyeglass too, and could talk genteelly, then I would be virtuous too. It must be fine indeed to be virtuous, indeed, sir . . . and yet . . . I am a simple soul. Folk like us always are unfortunate . . . in this world and in any other world. I think that if we should go to heaven, then we shall be thunder-makers.

CAPTAIN: *(somewhat nonplussed)* All right, all right. *(pacifying)* I know that you're a worthy man *(exaggerating)* a worthy man . . . *(firmer, more controlled)* . . . but you do *think* too much; that hurts. Your face always looks so harrassed. *(anxiously)* This discussion has quite unnerved me. Run away, and yet do not run. Go quite slowly the length of the highway, and keep to the middle; and once more, do so slowly, quite slowly . . .

WOZZECK: Jawohl, Herr Hauptmann.

HAUPTMANN: *(lacht lärmend.)* Südnord! *(lacht noch lärmender)* Oh, Er ist dumm, ganz abscheulich dumm! *(gerührt)* Wozzeck, Er ist ein guter Mensch. *(setzt sich in Positur)* aber . . . Er hat keine Moral! *(mit viel Würde)* Moral: das ist, wenn man moralisch ist! *(Versteht Er?* Es ist ein gutes Wort.) *(mit Pathos)* Er hat ein Kind ohne den Segen der Kirche,

WOZZECK: Jawo . . . *(unterbricht sich)*

HAUPTMANN: wie unser hochwürdiger Herr Garnisonsprediger sagt: "Ohne den Segen der Kirche" (das Wort ist nicht von mir.)

WOZZECK: Herr Hauptmann, der liebe Gott wird den armen Wurm nicht d'rum ansehn, ob das Amen darüber gesagt ist, eh' er gemacht wurde. Der Herr sprach: "Lasset die Kleinen zu mir kommen!" *(wütend aufspringend)*

HAUPTMANN: Was sagt Er da?! Was ist das für eine kuriose Antwort? Er macht mich ganz konfus! Wenn ich sage: "Er," so mein ich "Ihn," . . .

WOZZECK: Wir arme Leut! Sehn Sie, Herr Hauptmann, Geld, Geld! Wer kein Geld hat! Da setz' einmal einer Seinesgleichen auf die moralische Art in die Welt! Man hat auch sein Fleisch und Blut! Ja, wenn ich ein Herr wär, und hätt' einen Hut und eine Uhr und ein Augenglas und könnt' vornehm reden, ich wollte schon tugendhaft sein! Es muß was Schönes sein um die Tugend, Herr Hauptmann. Aber ich bin ein armer Kerl! Unsereins ist doch einmal unselig in dieser und der andern Welt! Ich glaub', wenn wir in den Himmel kämen, so müßten wir donnern helfen!

HAUPTMANN: *(etwas fassungslos:)* Schon gut, schon gut! Ich weiß: *(beschwichtigend)* Er ist ein guter Mensch, *(übertrieben)* ein guter Mensch. *(etwas gefaßter)* Aber Er denkt zu viel, das zehrt; Er sieht immer so verhetzt aus. *(besorgt)* Der Diskurs hat mich angegriffen. Geh' Er jetzt, und renn Er nicht so! Geh' Er langsam die Straße hinunter, genau in der Mitte und nochmals, geh' Erlangsam, hübsch langsam!

459

No. 163 Berg: *Wozzeck*

164 Piano Suite, Op. 25 (1923)

Schoenberg

164a Praeludium

Rasch (♩.= 80)

CD13 Track 18 p. 590

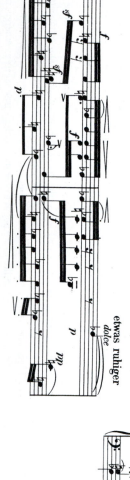
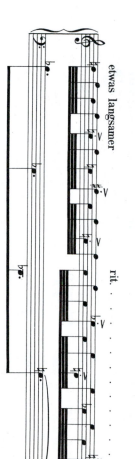

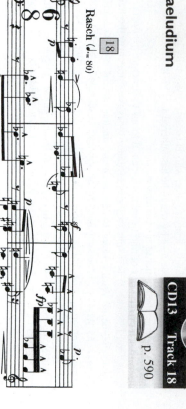

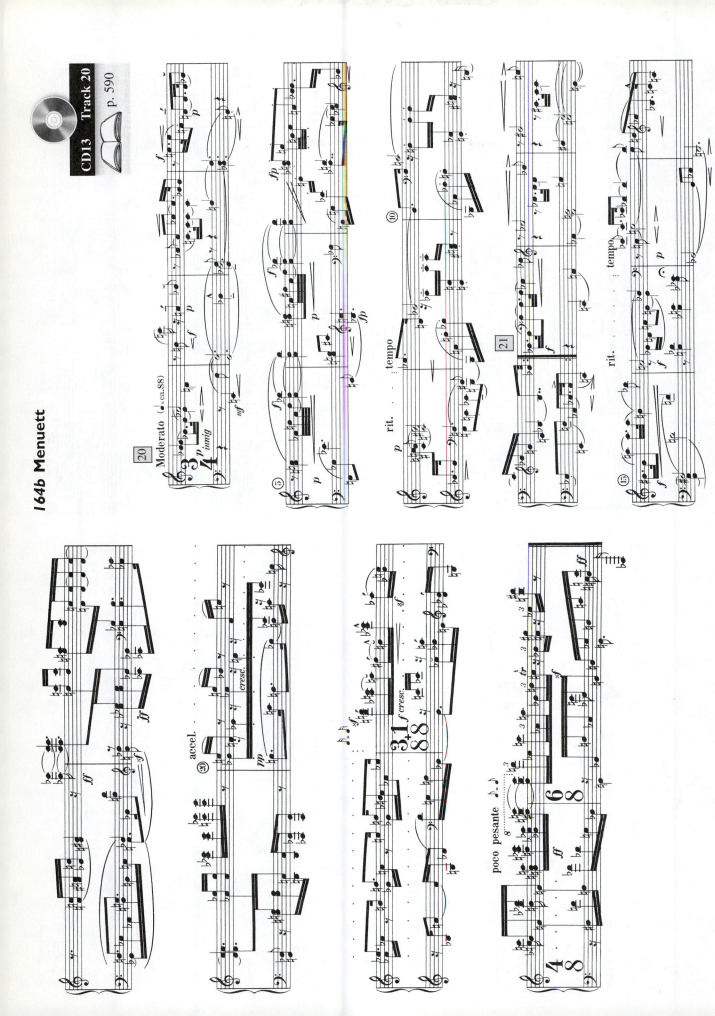

164b Menuett

Moderato (♩=ca.88)

No. 164 Schoenberg: *Piano Suite*

■ No. 164 Schoenberg: *Piano Suite*

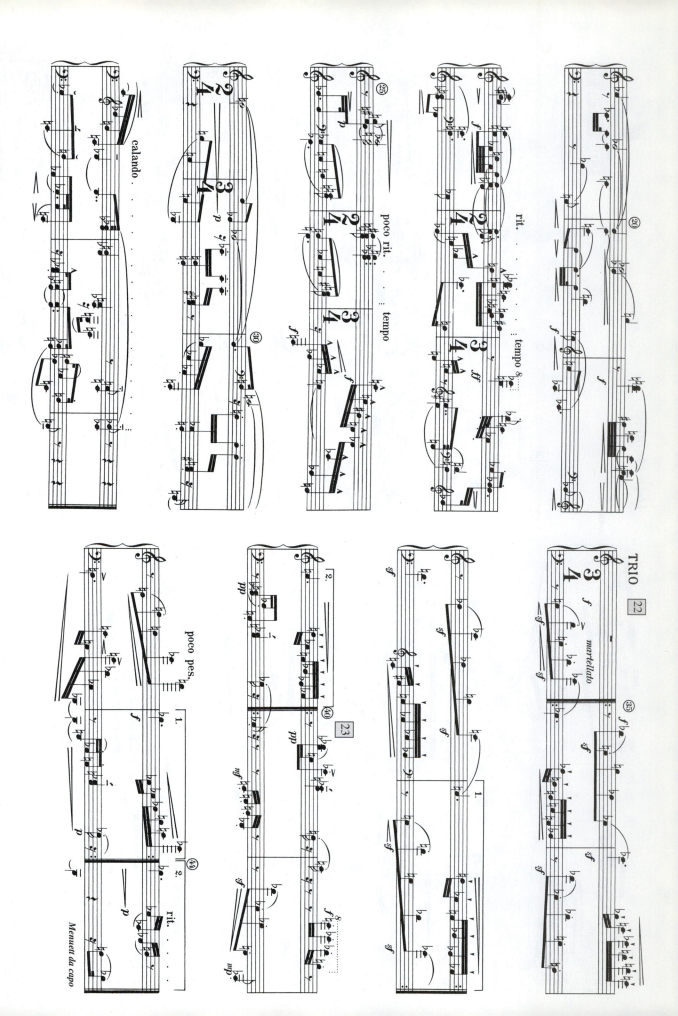

165 Lyric Suite, for String Quartet, third movement (1926)
Berg

Allegro misterioso
♩ = 150

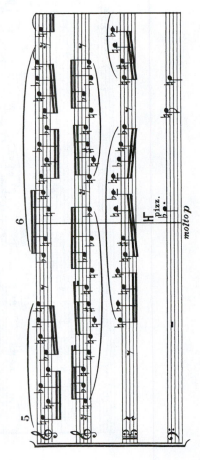

Schoenberg's *Piano Suite*, Op. 25, is one of the composer's earliest serial works, begun in 1921 and completed in 1923. The prime form of the row consists of the pitches E-F-G-C#-F#-D#-G#-D-B-C-A-Bb. A matrix (see Textbook, p. 590) shows at a glance all the 48 possibilities of this row in the transposed versions of Prime (P), Inverted (I), Retrograde (R), and Retrograde Inverted (RI). In practice, Schoenberg uses only eight different versions of the row:

Example 10 Forms of the row actually used in Schoenberg's *Piano Suite*, Op. 25

P-0

R-0

P-6

R-6

I-0

RI-0

I-6

RI-6

In the Prelude, the prime form of the row (P-0) is presented in the upper voice (right hand) of the first three measures. But what is going on in the left hand? Careful scrutiny of the first four pitches there (Bb-Cb, Db, G) reveals that they are the first four notes of the same series transposed up a tritone (P-6) to begin on the note Bb (=A#). The relationship of the pitches is identical to that of the upper voice: up a half step (Bb-Cb = A#-B), then up a whole step (Cb-Db = B-C#) the disposition of register is of no importance in identifying rows), then a tritone leap (Db-G = C#-G). The relationship is not audible on the surface (at least not to most people), yet the structure is every bit as present as the harmony of a I-IV-V progression in tonal work.

Matters become slightly more complicated in m. 2–3 in the left hand, where we see multiple pitches sounded simultaneously within the same row. Here, Schoenberg in effect divides the row in two: the "middle voice" (the upper line in the left hand) proceeds along the row with pitches 2-11-4-10 of P-6, while the left hand at the same time is playing pitches 7-8-5-6 of the same P-6 version of the row. The repetition of the Bb in m. 3 is "permitted" because no other pitches have sounded in that particular voice. Once that voice leaves Bb, that pitch does not return until all other eleven have sounded in that particular voice. ("Permitted" is in quotation marks here because composers can of course do whatever they like, including bending or breaking their own self-imposed limitations.)

The distribution of material between right and left hands in opening of the Minuet is fairly complicated, but if we pay close attention to the leading voice, we can see how consistently Schoenberg applies the serial process (see Textbook, Example 21-5, p. 593).

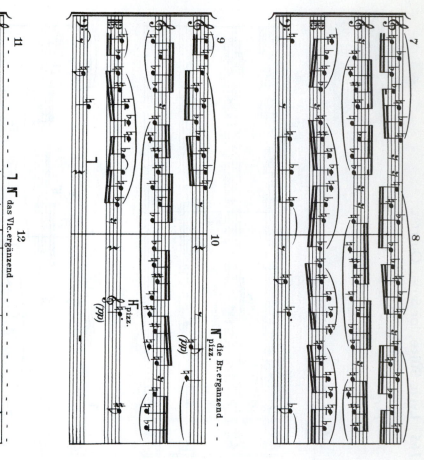

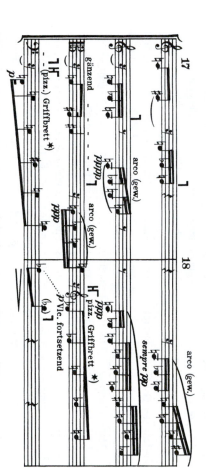

*) pizz. am Griffbrett d. h. nahe an den Fingern der linken Hand.

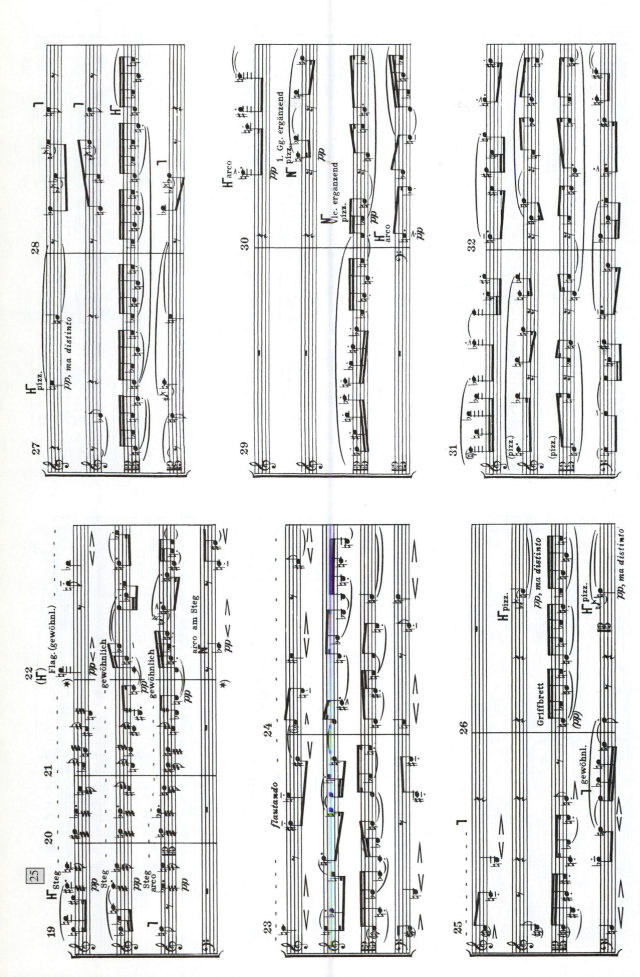

*) Alle > und << immer nur innerhalb des *pp*!

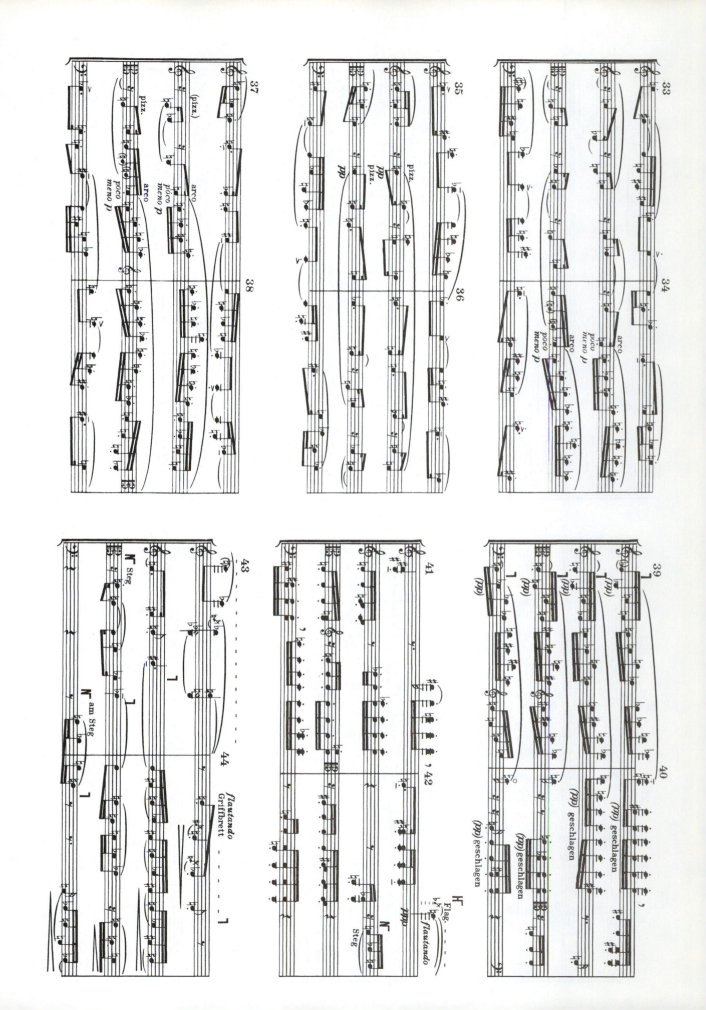

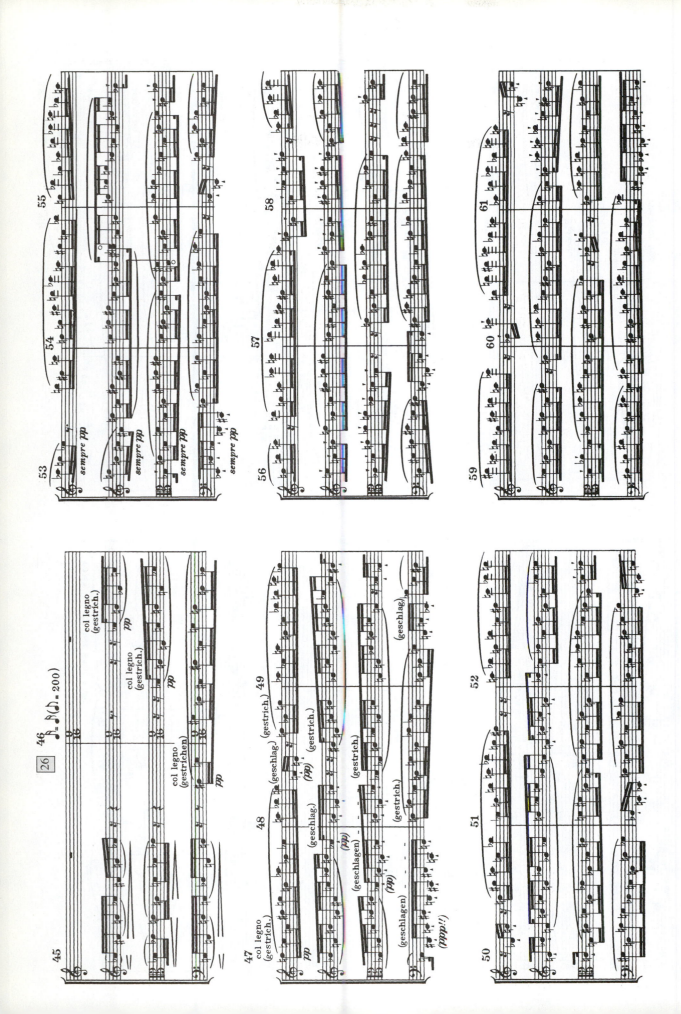

No. 165 Berg: Lyric Suite

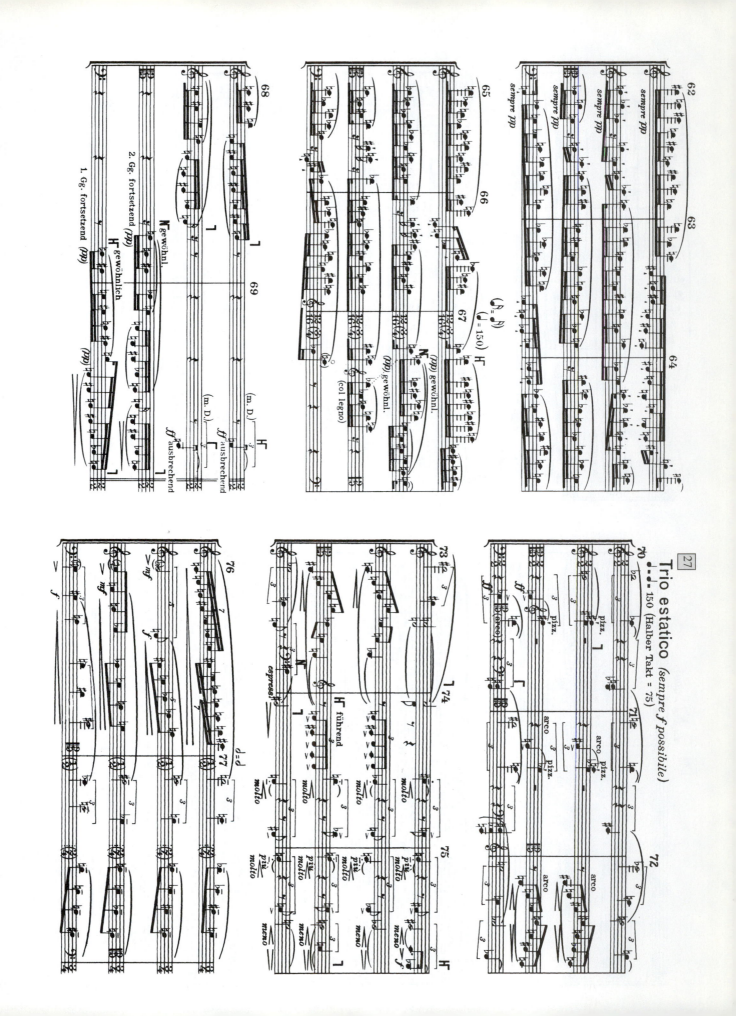

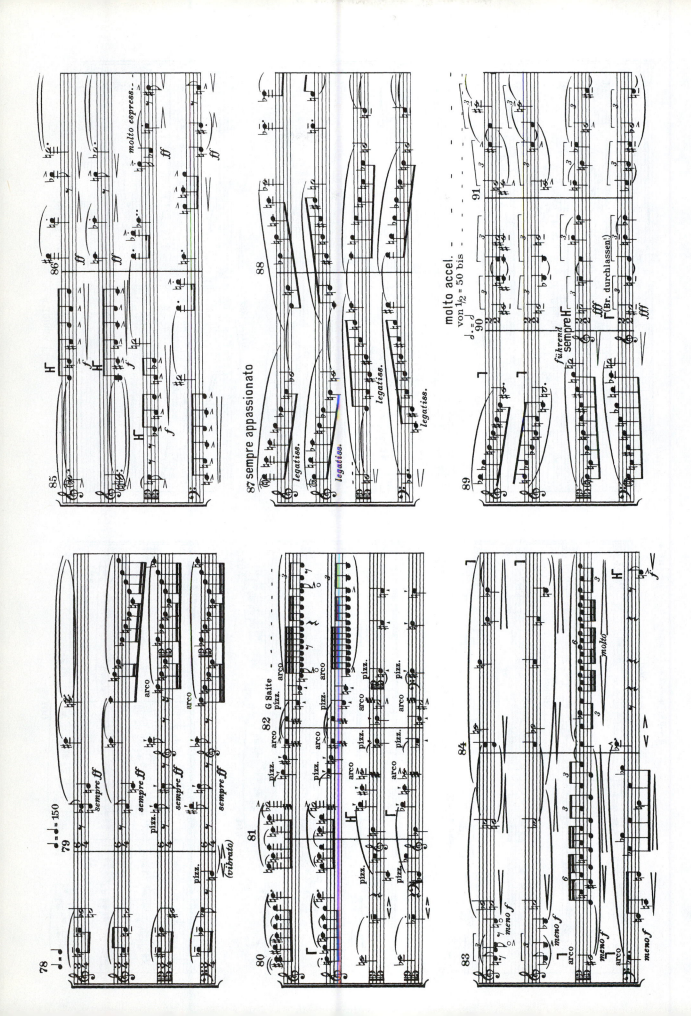

No. 165 Berg: *Lyric Suite*

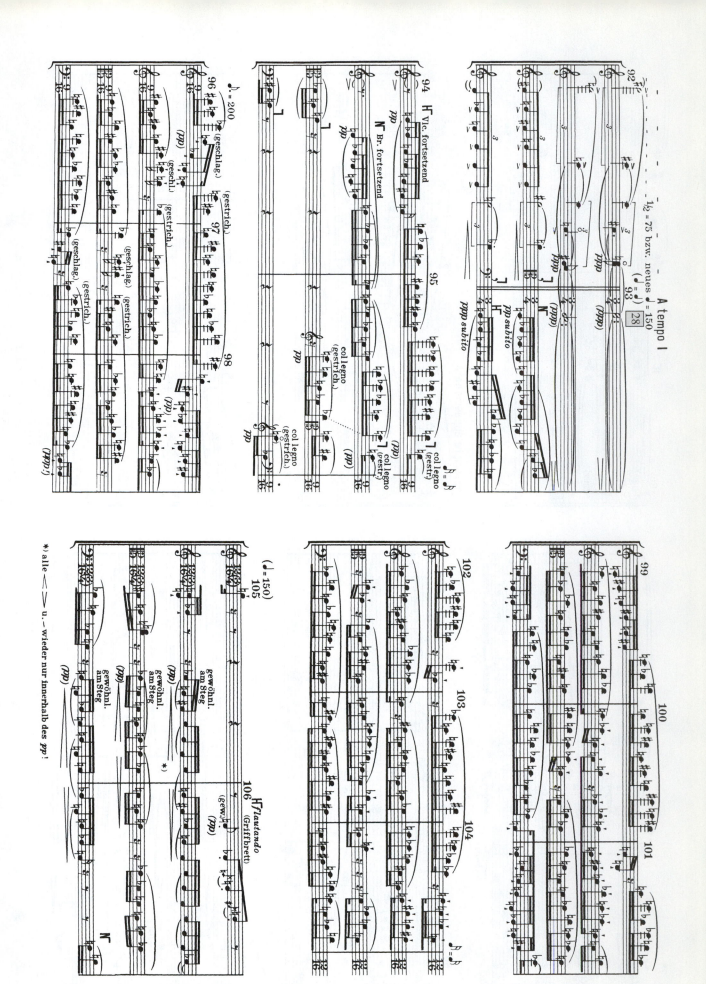

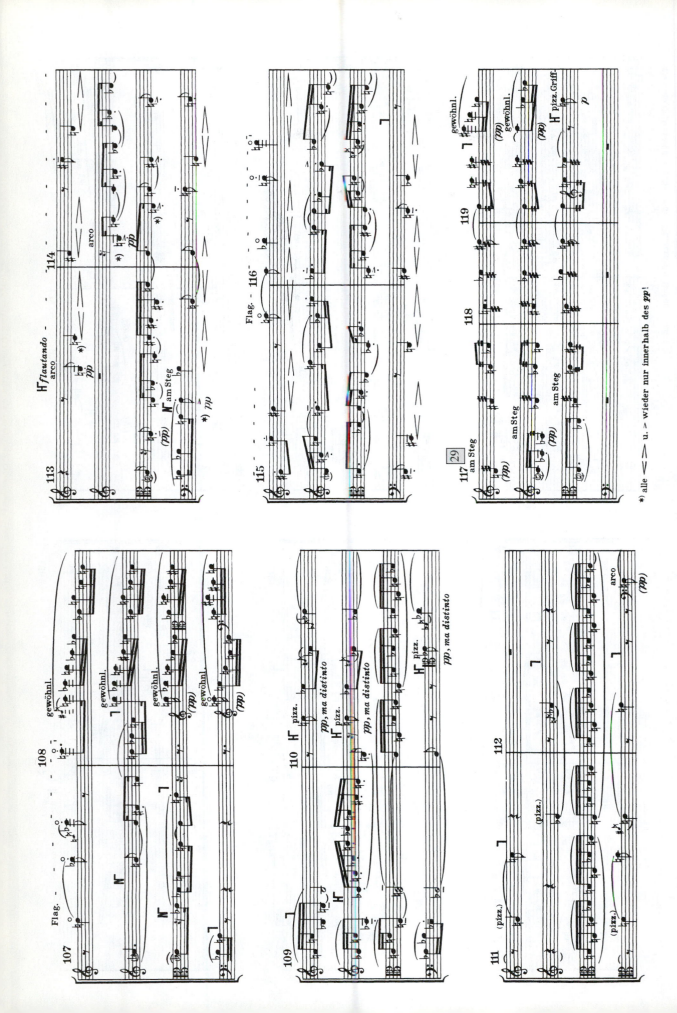

No. 165 Berg: Lyric Suite

*) alle <=> u. > wieder nur innerhalb des *pp*!

No. 165 Berg: *Lyric Suite*

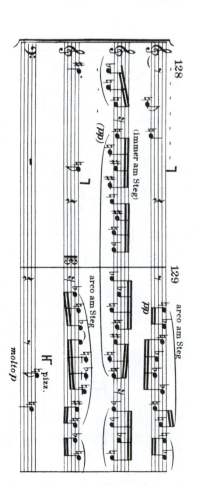

*) pizz. am Griffbrett d.h. nahe an den Fingern der linken Hand.

Berg tended to take a more liberal approach to serial composition than either Schoenberg or Webern. The first movement of his *Lyric Suite* for string quartet uses three different (yet related) rows, and not all of its six movements are serial: only the outer movements are entirely dodecaphonic. The third movement is serial in its outer sections but not in its trio, and only the trios of the fifth movement are written in the twelve-tone method. Berg manipulates the basic row of the work (See Textbook, Example 21-6a) in ingenious ways. By rotating one derivation of the row—that is, by beginning it on a pitch other than 0, Berg is able to create a derivative row with the succession of pitches A-Bb-B-F. These pitches hold a symbolic meaning for Berg: keeping in mind that in German, "B," is called "H" and "Bb" is called simply "B," these pitches represent the composer's own initials (A-B) and those of his secret lover, Hanna Fuchs (H-F). Berg calls special attention to this tetrachord—this group of four notes—at the beginning of the movement, where every voice plays some version of this grouping:

- First violin: P-0 (beginning on 0). The first full statement of P-0 occurs in m. 2–3.
- Second violin: P-7 (rotated, beginning on 9). The first full statement of P-7 occurs in m. 3–4.
- Viola: P-10 (rotated, beginning on 3). The first full statement of P-10 occurs in m. 3.

These three forms of the row, along with I-5, are the only ones Berg uses in this section. The *trio estatico* ("ecstatic trio") is freely composed, while the return of the opening section at m. 93 presents the opening section in a large-scale retrograde. The inverse relationship of opening and closing becomes especially clear when we compare the first and last few measures of the movement.

No. 165 Berg: *Lyric Suite*

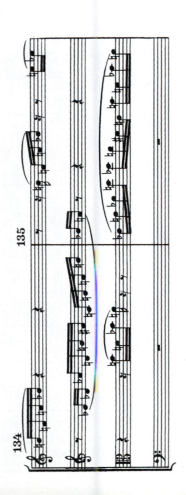

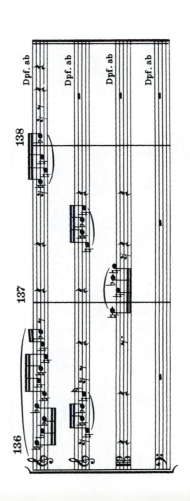

166 Classical Symphony, Op. 25, third movement (1917)

Sergei Prokofiev (1891–1953)

III

Gavotta

CD13 Track 30

p. 599

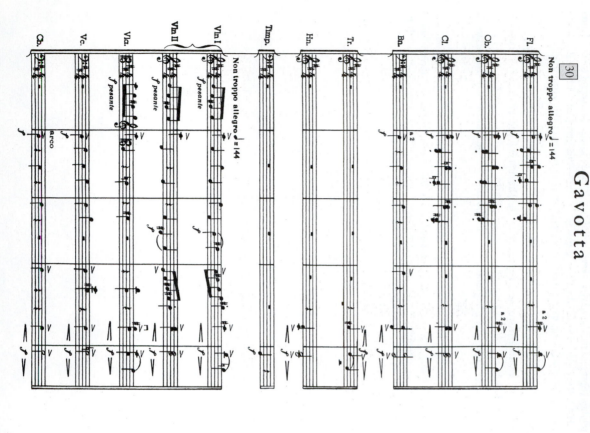

No. 166 Prokofiev: *Classical Symphony*

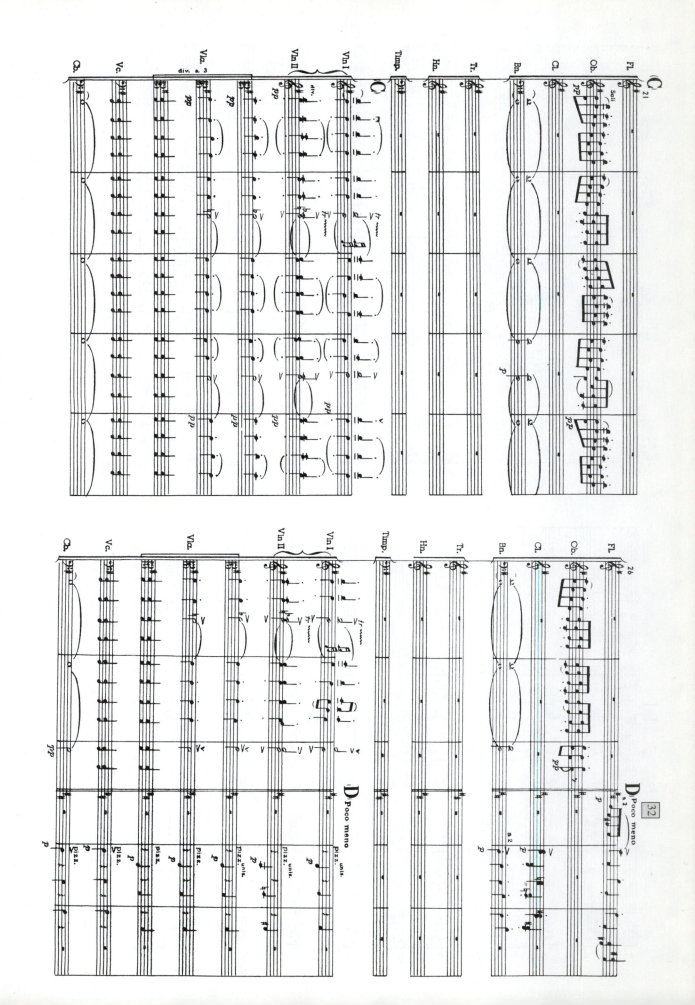

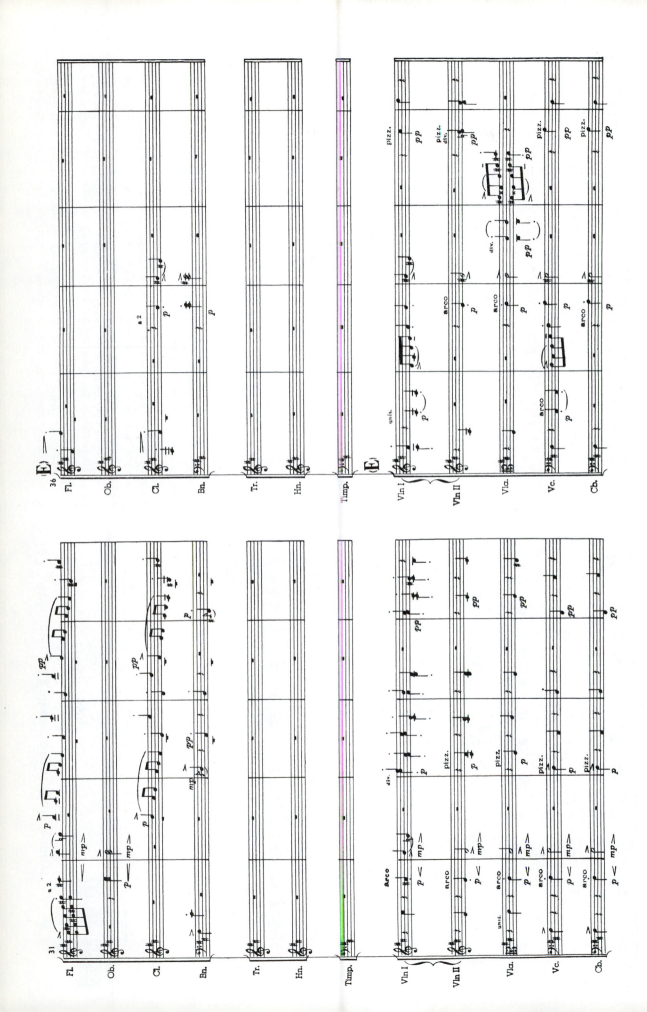

No. 166 Prokofiev: *Classical Symphony*

The "Gavotta" from Prokofiev's *Classical Symphony* represents the artistic movement known as neoclassicism. Prokofiev preserves the characteristic form and rhythms of the gavotte but transforms the melody and harmony in ways that are distinctively 20th-century. The movement is essentially in D major, yet the harmony consistently avoids any strong cadence in this key. When a cadence in the tonic finally arrives at the end of the second reprise, there is a strong sense of rhythmic arrival, but the harmony has been so skewed as to make the tonic sound unexpected at this point. The section that follows provides the thematic and textural contrast one would expect in the trio of such a dance: the droning open fifths evoke the sound of a bagpipe, hurdy-gurdy, or other similar folk instrument. And when the opening reprise returns in m. 29, it is now reorchestrated, with the winds taking the lead. The piece ends not with a bang but a whimper: pianissimo, understated, tongue in cheek. Neoclassical composers prided themselves on avoiding emotional extremes, bombast, and monumentality.

167 Aufstieg und Fall der Stadt Mahagonny:
"Alabama Song" (1927)
Kurt Weill (1900–1950)

CD13 Track 33

p. 601

Aus der geschlossenen Gardine treten mit einem großen Koffer Jenny und die 6 Mädchen, setzen sich auf den Koffer und singen den Alabama-Song.

Moderato assai (♩ = 69)

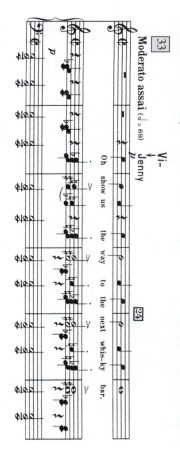

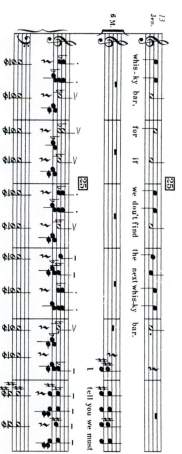

Note: This edition is a piano-vocal reduction of Weill's original score for voices and orchestra.

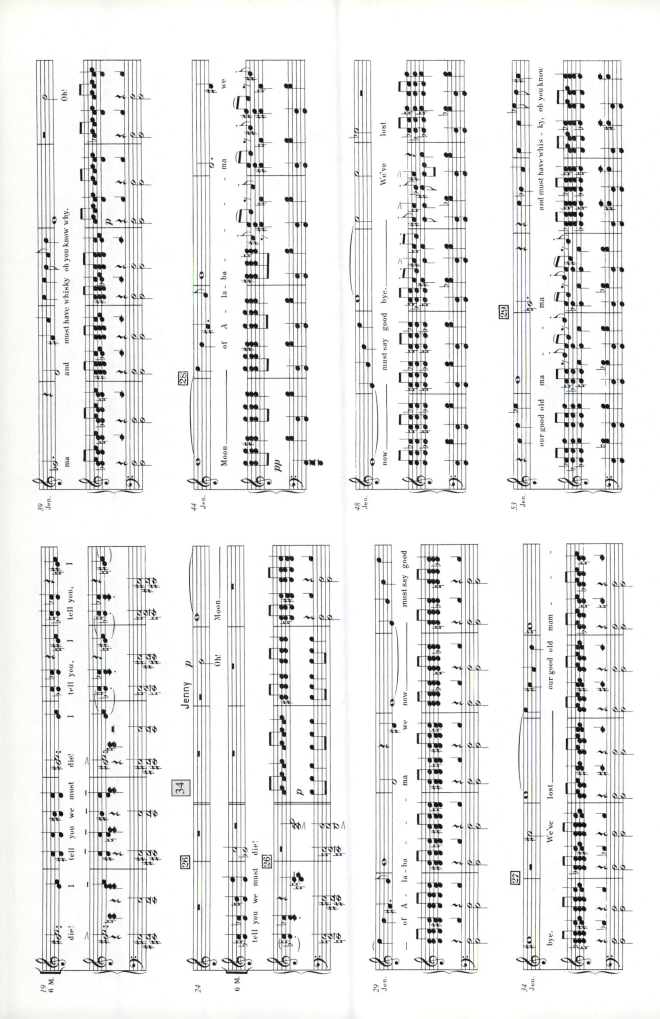

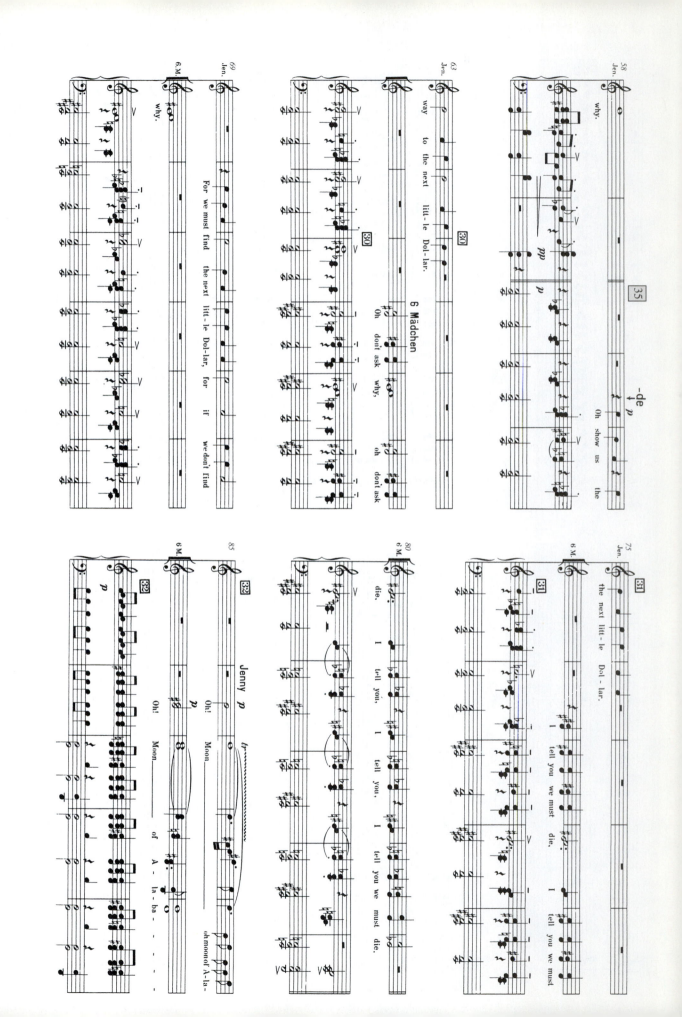

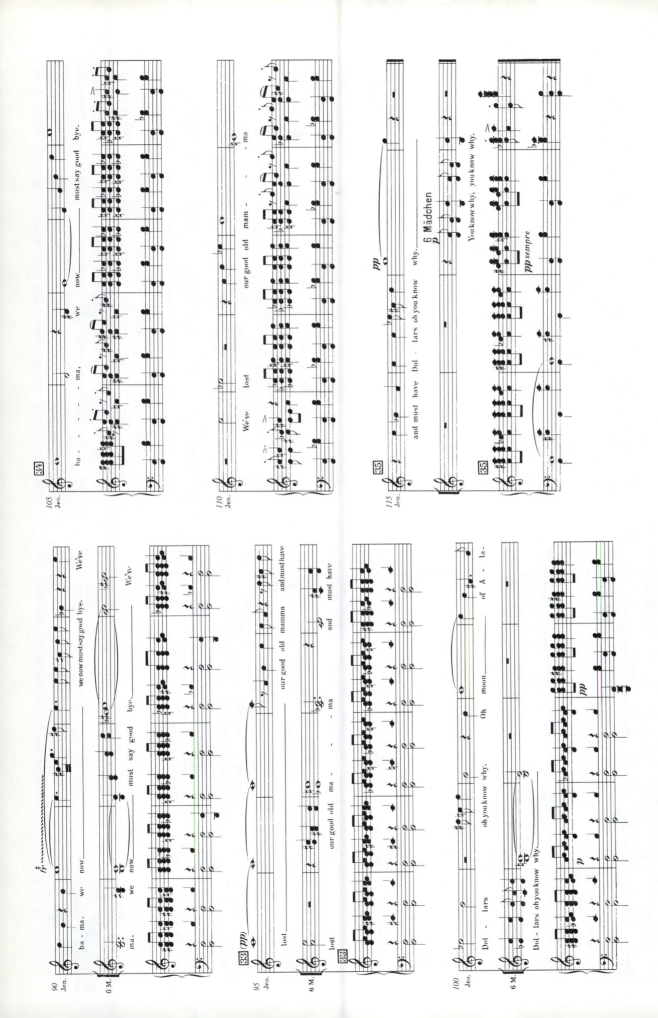

No. 167 Weill: *Aufstieg und Fall der Stadt Mahagonny*

Kurt Weill and the poet Bertolt Brecht (1898–1956) collaborated on a series of stage productions in the 1920s and 1930s that emphasized a sense of aesthetic distance between the artist and his work and the audience and the work. Speaking in the third person (a verbal technique of distancing), the composer announced that "Brecht and Weill have investigated the question of music's role in the theater. They have concluded that music cannot further the action of a play or create its background. Instead, it achieves its proper value when it interrupts the action at the right moments."

Weill's first collaboration with Brecht was *Aufstieg und Fall der Stadt Mahagonny* ("Rise and Fall of the City of Mahagonny," 1927), a satire on capitalism that takes place in a fictional city (Mahagonny) in which the only crime is poverty. Everything is legal as long as it can be paid for. The "Alabama Song," sung by Jenny (a prostitute) and her six cohorts, assumes the outward form of a traditional aria, with a declamatory introduction and a soaring conclusion, but the words are surreal ("Oh! Moon of Alabama we now must say goodbye, / We've lost our good old mama and must have whisky oh you know why") and, oddly enough for an opera otherwise in German, the text of this number is in English. All this creates a sense of distance—objectivity—that is magnified by the discordant sound of the honky-tonk-style accompaniment.

Performance note: The soloist heard in this recording, Lotte Lenya (1898–1981) was married to the composer Kurt Weill. She sang leading roles in the original productions of several of her husband's works, including *Die Dreigroschenoper* ("The Threepenny Opera"). The studio recording here was made in New York City in the 1950s. Lenya also appeared in several films late in her life, including the James Bond film *From Russia With Love* (1963), in which she played the evil Rosa Klebb.

168 Music for Strings, Percussion, and Celesta, third movement (1936)
Bartók

CD13 Track 36 p. 602

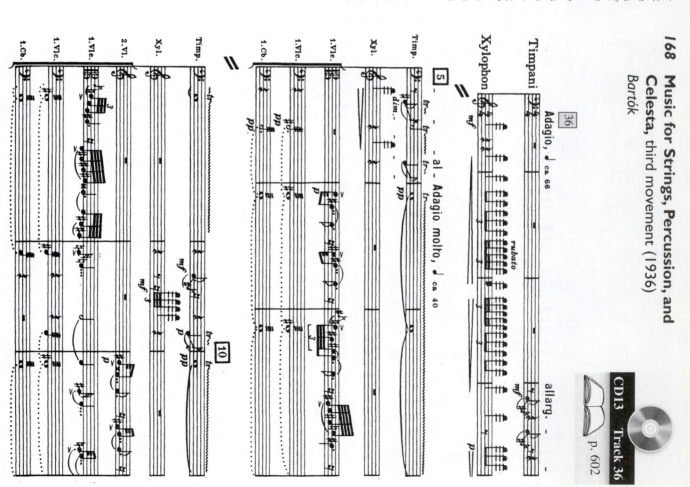

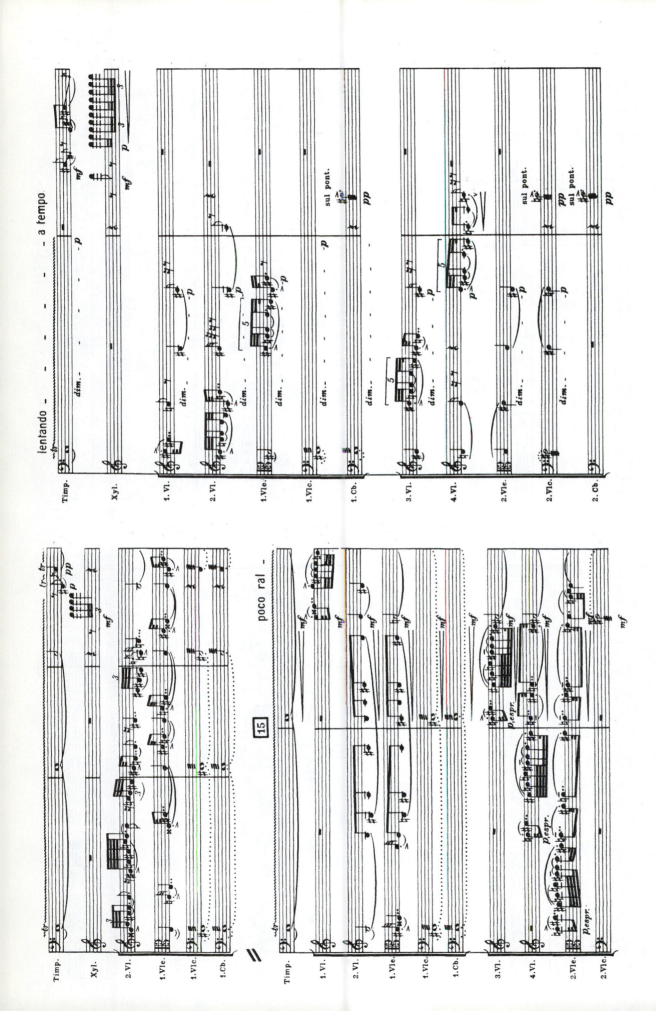

No. 168 Bartók: *Music for Strings, Percussion, and Celesta*

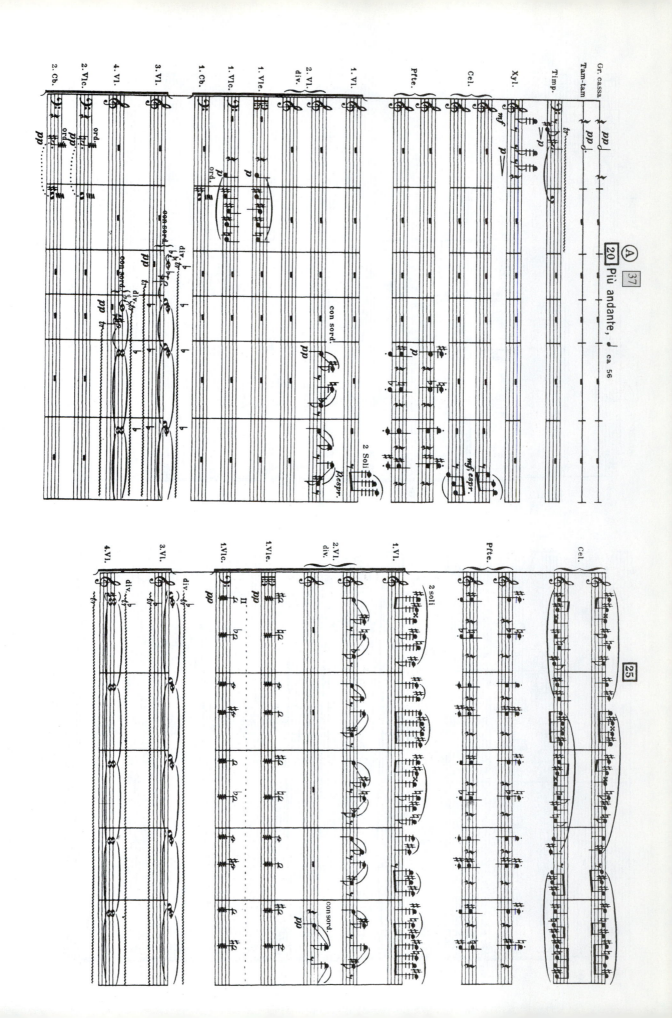

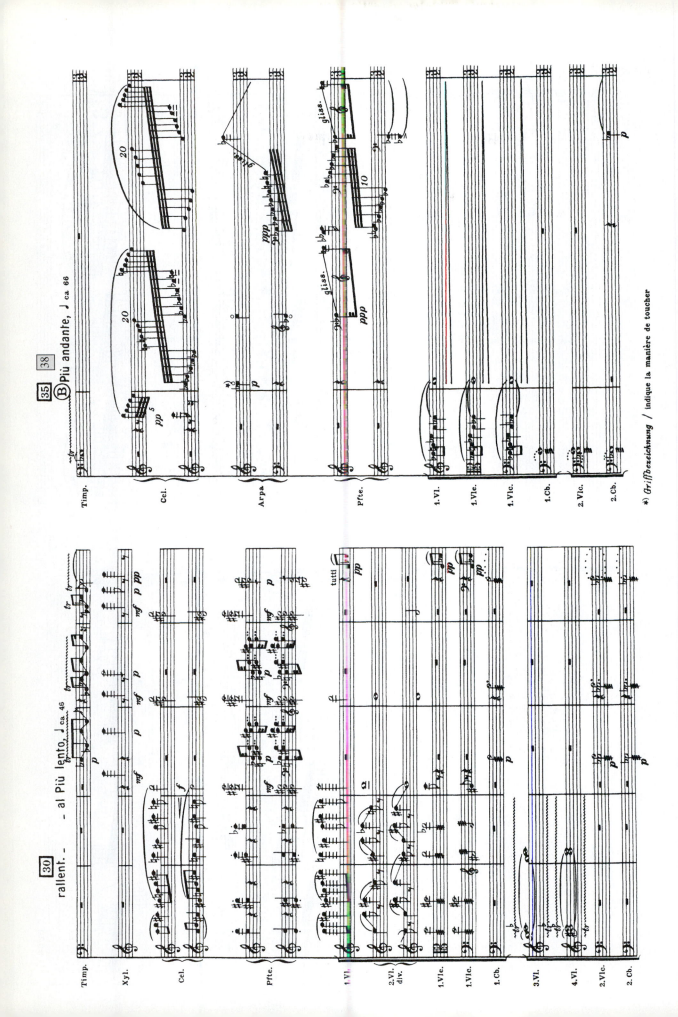

No. 168 Bartók: *Music for Strings, Percussion, and Celesta*

485

■ No. 168 Bartók: *Music for Strings, Percussion, and Celesta*

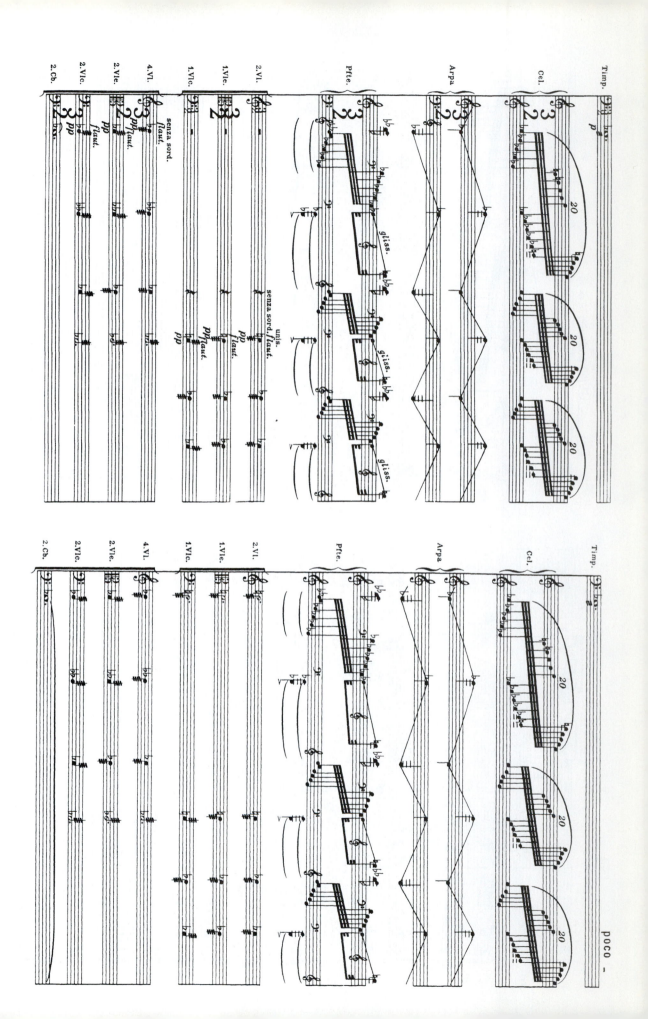

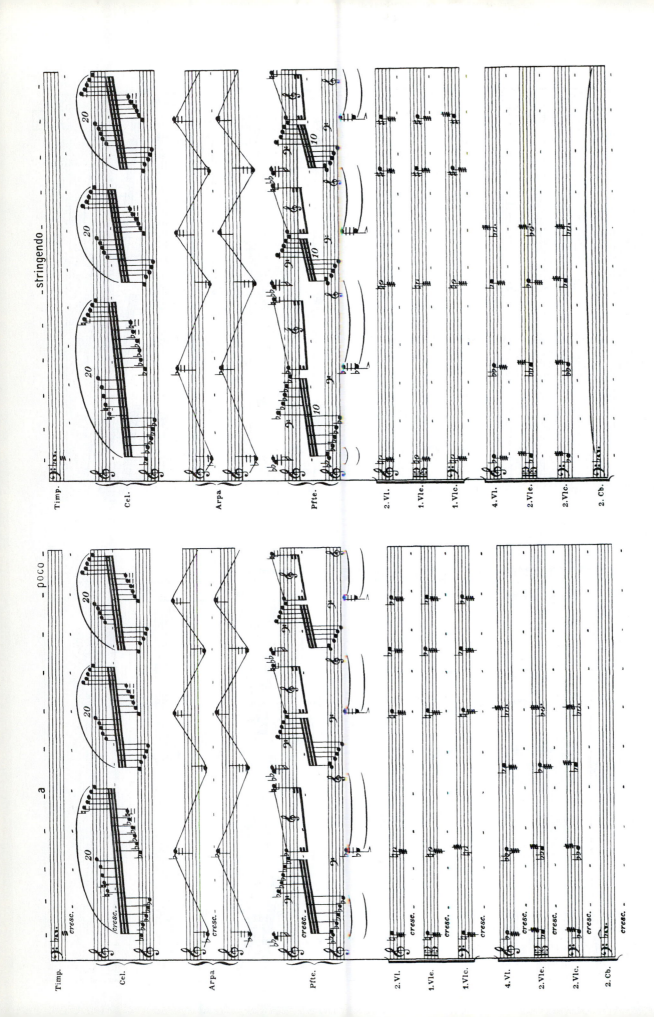

No. 168 Bartók: *Music for Strings, Percussion, and Celesta*

■ No. 168 Bartók: *Music for Strings, Percussion, and Celesta*

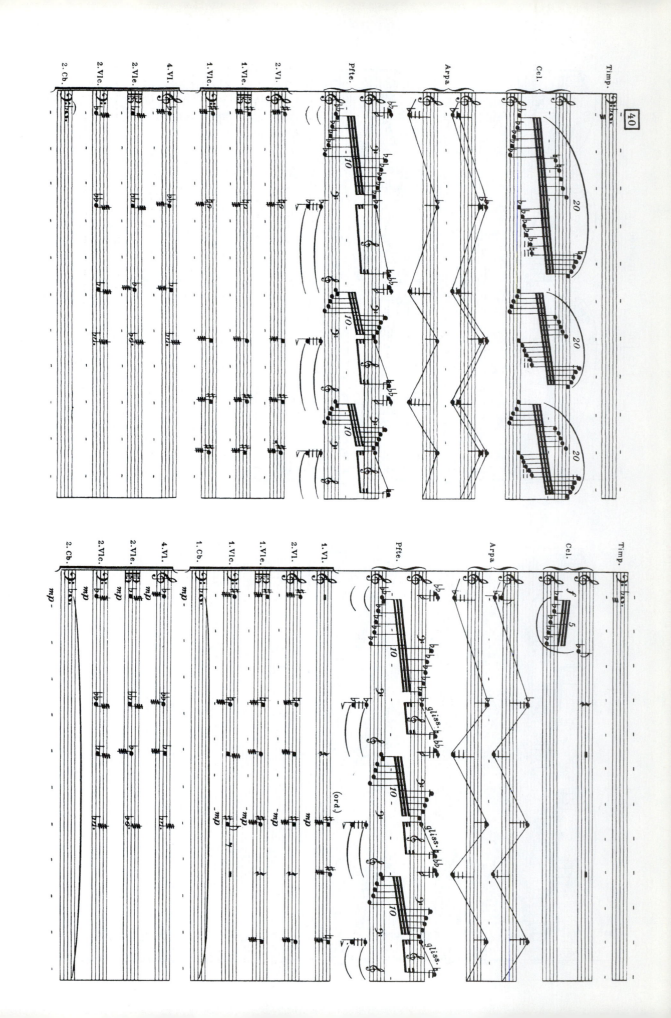

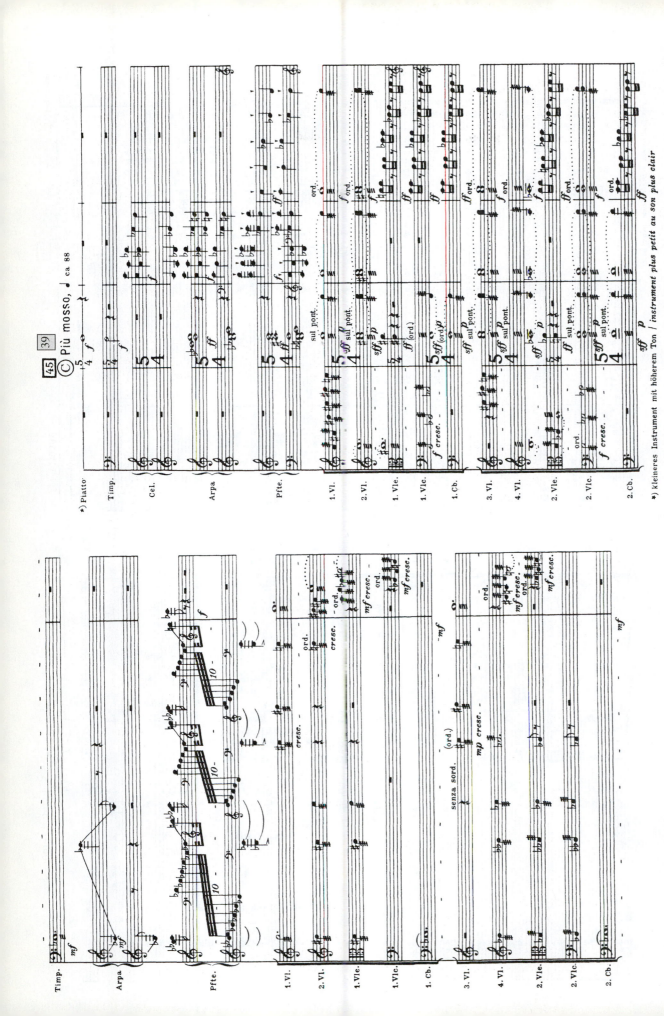

No. 168 Bartók: *Music for Strings, Percussion, and Celesta*

*) kleineres Instrument mit höherem Ton / instrument plus petit au son plus clair

No. 168 Bartók: *Music for Strings, Percussion, and Celesta*

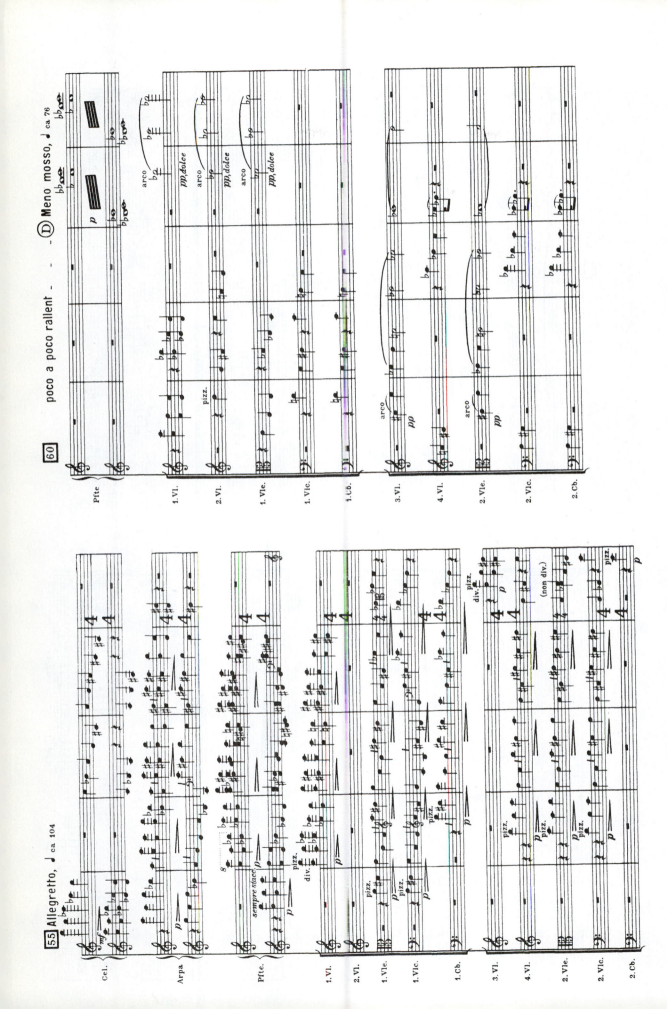

No. 168 Bartók: *Music for Strings, Percussion, and Celesta*

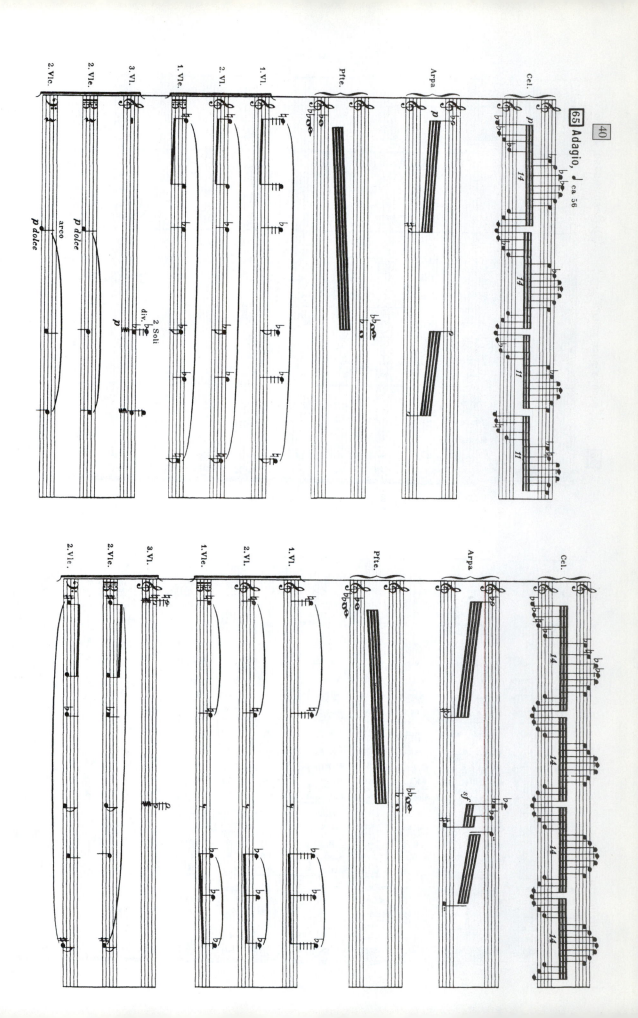

No. 168 Bartók: *Music for Strings, Percussion, and Celesta*

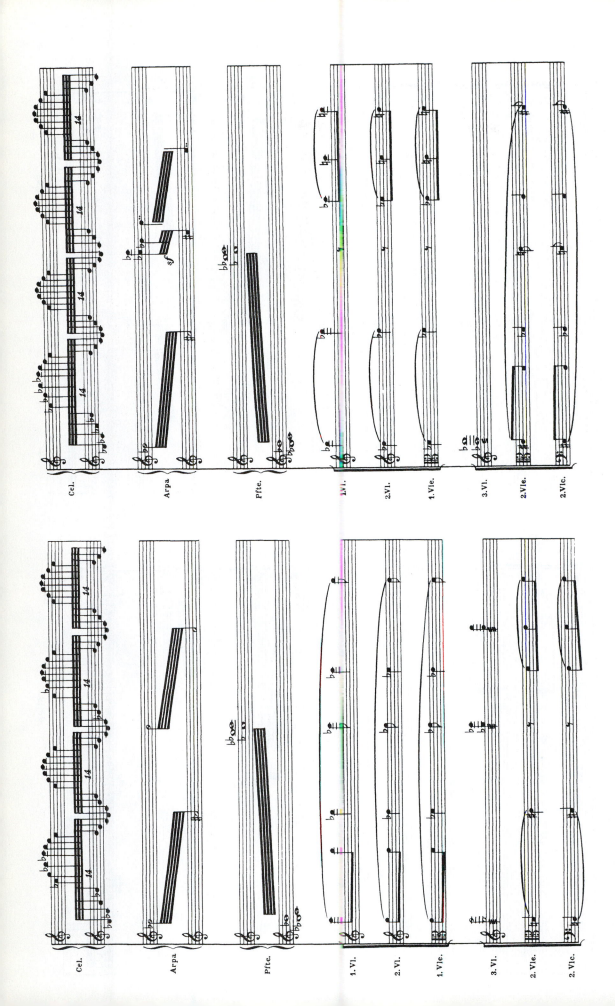

No. 168 Bartók: *Music for Strings, Percussion, and Celesta*

■ No. 168 Bartók: *Music for Strings, Percussion, and Celesta*

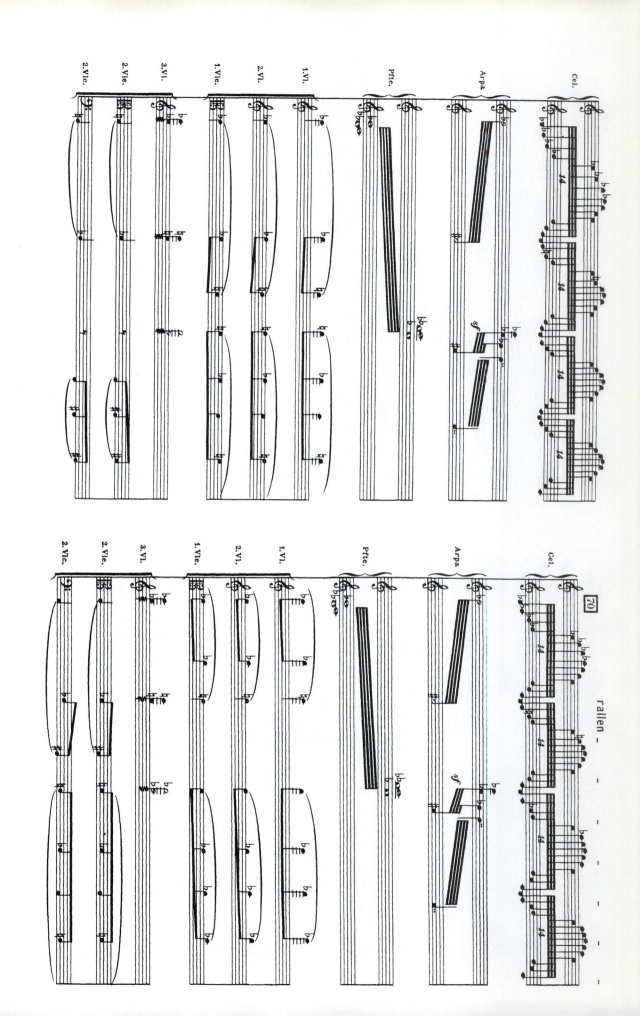

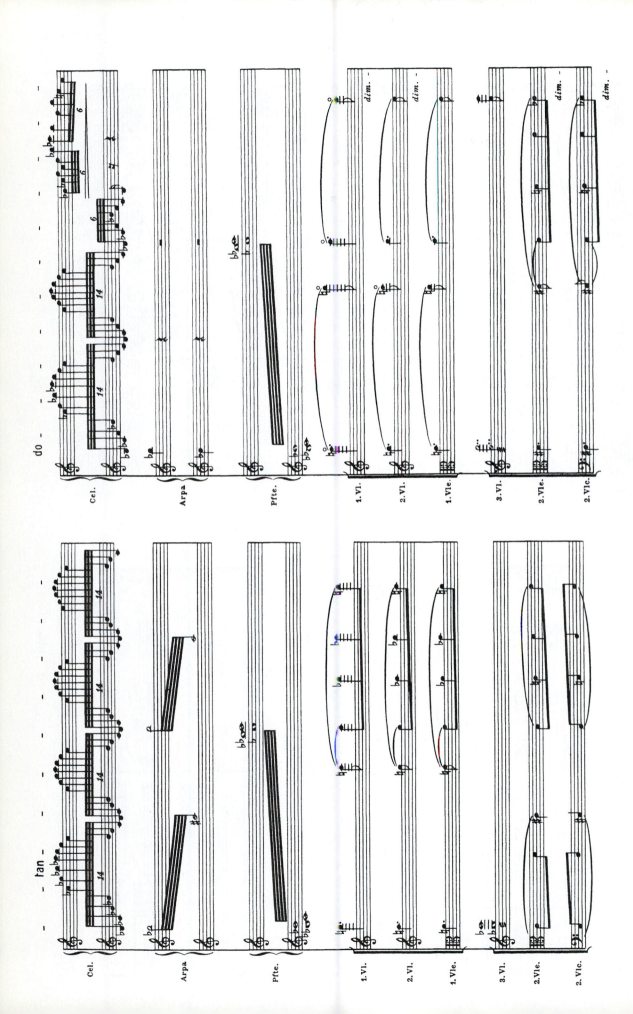

No. 168 Bartók: *Music for Strings, Percussion, and Celesta*

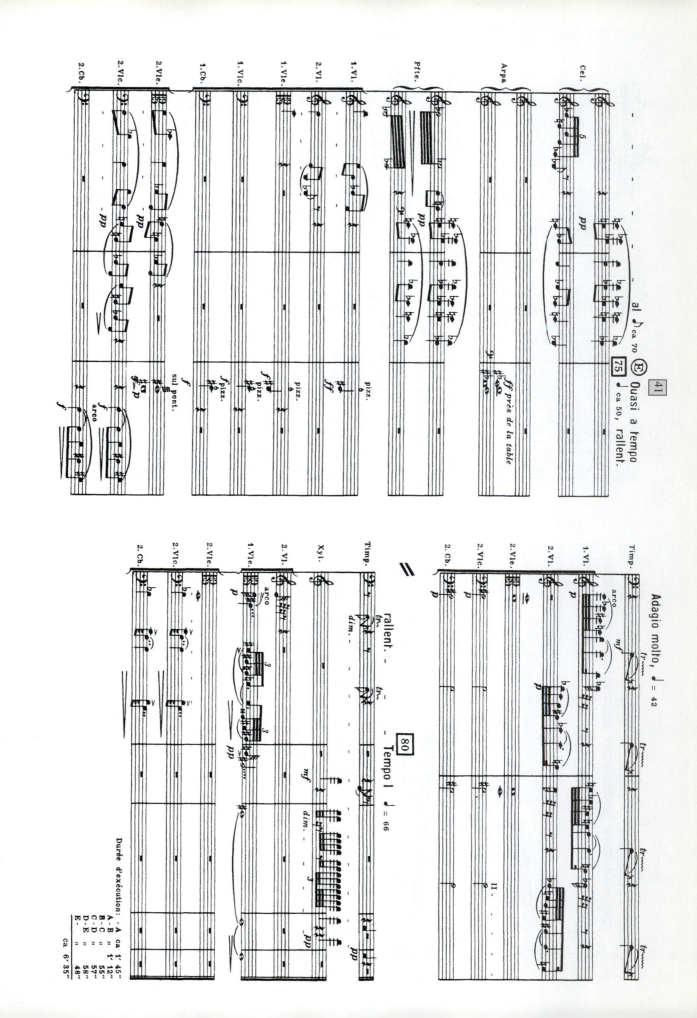

CD13 Track 42 p. 604

169 Alexander Nevsky, Op. 78, No. 4: "Vstavaite, ludi russkie" ("Arise, People of Russia") (1938)
Prokofiev

Béla Bartók's *Music for Strings, Percussion, and Celesta* (1936) is written for an unusual combination of instruments: a double string orchestra (including harp), celesta (a keyboard instrument that mimics the sound of small bells), and a battery of percussion instruments (timpani, piano, xylophone, bass drum, side drum, cymbals, tam-tam). The work is tightly integrated, with all four movements deriving their principal thematic ideas from the fugue subject of the opening movement.

The third movement of *Music for Strings, Percussion, and Celesta* is full of unusual sonorities. It opens with an extended solo on a single note in the upper reaches of the xylophone—a note so high, in fact, that its pitch (F) can scarcely be perceived as a pitch at all. The xylophone is soon joined by a timpani playing glissandos. The movement as a whole is structured around the principle of a symmetrical or arch form, by which the music progresses toward a mid-point and then more or less retraces its steps. This particular movement centers on m. 49–50, which present an essentially retrograde form of m. 47–48. The music "turns" upon this moment. On the whole, the movement can be broken down as follows:

Measure	A	B	C	D	E	D	C	B	A
	1	6	20	35	45	65	74	77	80

The proportions are not strict—Bartók was seldom pedantic about such matters—but the overall impression is one of growth, development, climax, and return to an original state. A glance at the opening and closing measures shows the gradual addition of instruments: xylophone, then timpani and cello. The movement ends with instruments dropping out, first the violas, then the xylophone, ending with the timpani. The idea of symmetry operates at various points throughout this movement on a smaller scale as well. The opening rhythm of the xylophone gesture, for example, is symmetrical in its own right, with its midpoint at the downbeat of m. 3.

42 Вставайте, люди русские   4.   Arise, Ye Russian People

Allegro risoluto ♩ = 72

2 Fl.
2 Cl.
Cl.b.
Sax.
C-fag.
4 Cor.
3 Tr-ni e Tuba
P-tti
C-na
T-tam
S.
A.
T.
B.
V-ni I
V-ni II
V-le
V-c.
C-b.
a 2
ff
div.
arco
unis.
рус-ски - е, на славный бой, на смертный бой, вста - вай-те, лю-ди воль-ны - е, за
Rus-sian folk, in bat-tle just, in fight to death. A - rise Ye Peo-ple, free, and brave, de -
25
T-ro
Arpa
Do♭ magg.
sol
f
на - шу зем-лю чест - ну - ю.
fend our fair, our na - tive land.
Жи - вым бой-цам по чёт и честь, а мерт-вым сла-ва
To liv-ing war-riors high es - teem, im - mor-tal fame to
unis.
pizz.

No. 169 Prokofiev: Alexander Nevsky

43
27 a tempo
poco rit.
Picc.
2 Fl.
2 Ob.
C.ingl.
2 Cl.
Cl.b.
Sax.
2 Fag.
C-fag.
Tr-be I.II
4 Cor.
3 Tr-ni e Tuba
P-tti
C-na
T-tam
Arpa
S.
A.
T.
Cl.b
Tuba
Alti
V-ni I
V-ni II
V-le
V-c.
C-b.
вай-те, лю-ди воль-ны-е, за на-шу зем-лю чест-ну-ю.
rise Ye Peo-ple, free and brave, defend our fair, our na-tive land.
На Ру-си род-ной, на Ру-си боль-шой не бы-вать вра-гу.
In our Rus-sia great, in our na-tive Rus-sia no foe shall live.
Под-ни-май-ся, встань,
Rise to arms, a-rise,
arco
div.
unis.
mp espress.
mf espress.
cresc.
p cresc.

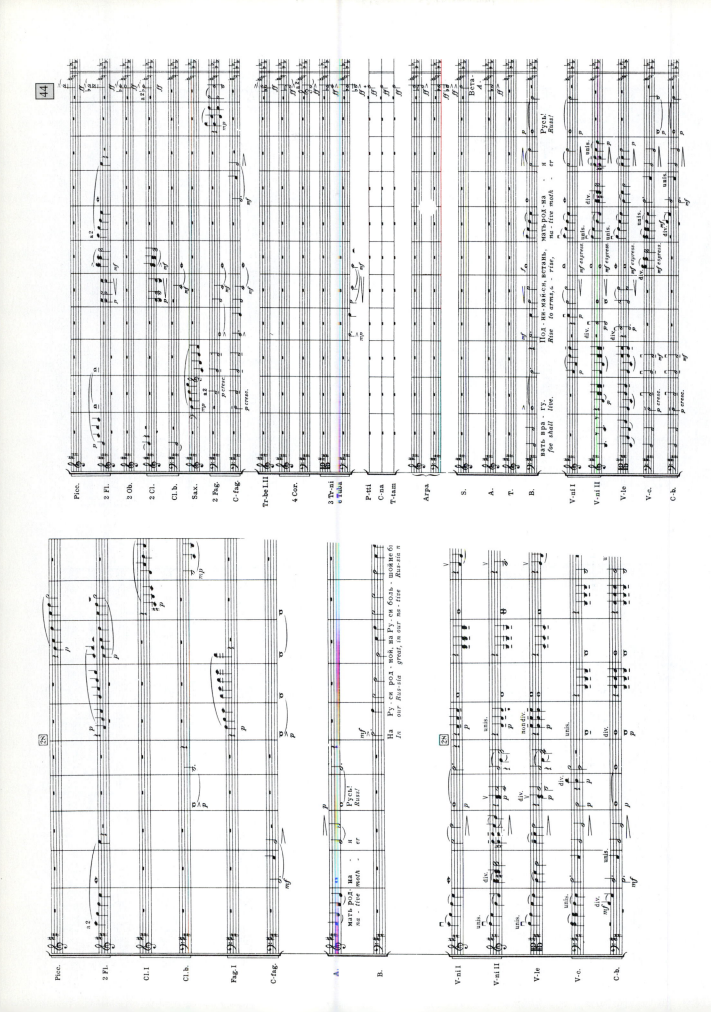

29
Picc.
2 Fl.
2 Ob.
2 Cl.
C-fag.
Tr-be I.II
4 Cor.
3 Tr-ni e Tuba
P-tti
C-na
T-tam
Arpa
S.
A.
T.
B.
вай-те, лю-ди
rise to arms, Ye
рус-ски-е.
Rus-sian folk.
Вста- вай-те, лю-ди
A - rise Ye Peo-ple,
На славный бой, на
In bat-tle just, in
смертный бой.
fight to death.
V-ni I
V-ni II
V-le
V-c.
C-b.
pizz.
div.
arco
unis.
30
2 Fl.
2 Cl.
Cl.b.
Sax.
2 Fag.
C-fag.
4 Cor.
3 Tr-ni e Tuba
P-tti
C-na
Cassa
T-tam
Sil.
solo
Arpa
S.
A.
T.
B.
воль-ны-е.
free and brave.
Вра-гам на Русь не ха - жи-вать, пол -
No foe shall march' cross Rus - sian land, no
За на-шу зем-лю чест-ну-ю.
De - fend our fair, our na - tive land.
V-ni I
V-ni II
V-le
V-c.
C-b.
arco
div.

No. 169 Prokofiev: Alexander Nevsky

The film *Alexander Nevsky*, directed by Sergei Eisenstein, is based on the true story of Grand Duke Alexander of Novgorod, who defeated the Swedes on the River Neva (hence "Nevsky" in his popular name) in the year 1240 and went on to repel an army of Teutonic knights in 1242 in a battle that took place on the frozen surface of Lake Chudskoye. In the film's climactic scene, the ice breaks and swallows the invaders. In 1939, Prokofiev turned his brilliant score for this movie into a cantata for mezzo-soprano, chorus, and large orchestra. The rousing fourth movement of this work ("Arise, People of Russia") like much of the rest of the score, integrates folksong-like melodies (of Prokofiev's own invention) with a harmonic idiom that is essentially triadic. The occasional modal and chromatic inflections are extremely limited, for this was music written to appeal to mass audiences and their spirit of patriotism. This kind of writing was actively promoted by Soviet authorities under the banner of what they called socialist realism, a readily accessible style that evokes the music of the people in an overwhelmingly optimistic tone (see Textbook, Primary Evidence: Socialist Realism).

The Soviet government was quick to recognize the potential of film and film music to galvanize patriotic fervor. The state itself financed Eisenstein's *Alexander Nevsky* in the late 1930s at a time when German invasion appeared imminent: the film's plot is deeply nationalistic and transparently anti-German. Soldiers of the Red Army were actually used as extras in the movie. But after signing the Non-Aggression Pact with Hitler in 1939 (the same agreement whose secret annex also spelled out the later dismemberment of Poland by both Germany and the Soviet Union), Stalin had the film removed from circulation, only to have it rushed back into theaters after Germany's surprise invasion of the Soviet Union in June of 1941. The film's powerful images were made all the more evocative by Prokofiev's stirring score.

170 **Appalachian Spring: Suite** (excerpt)
(1945)
Aaron Copland (1900–1990)

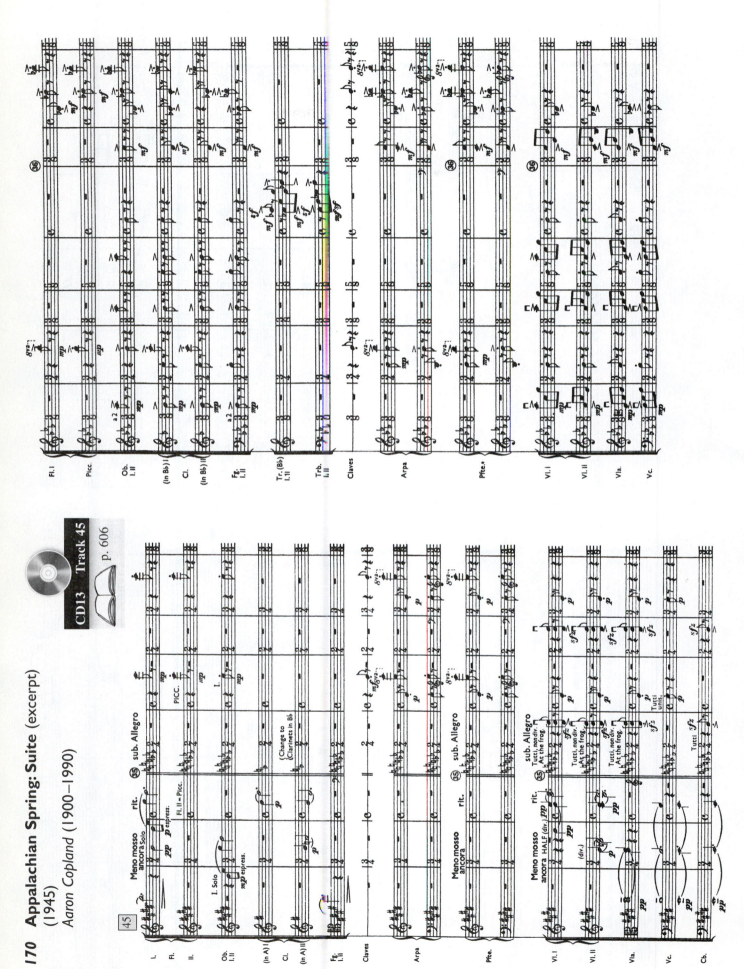

p. 606

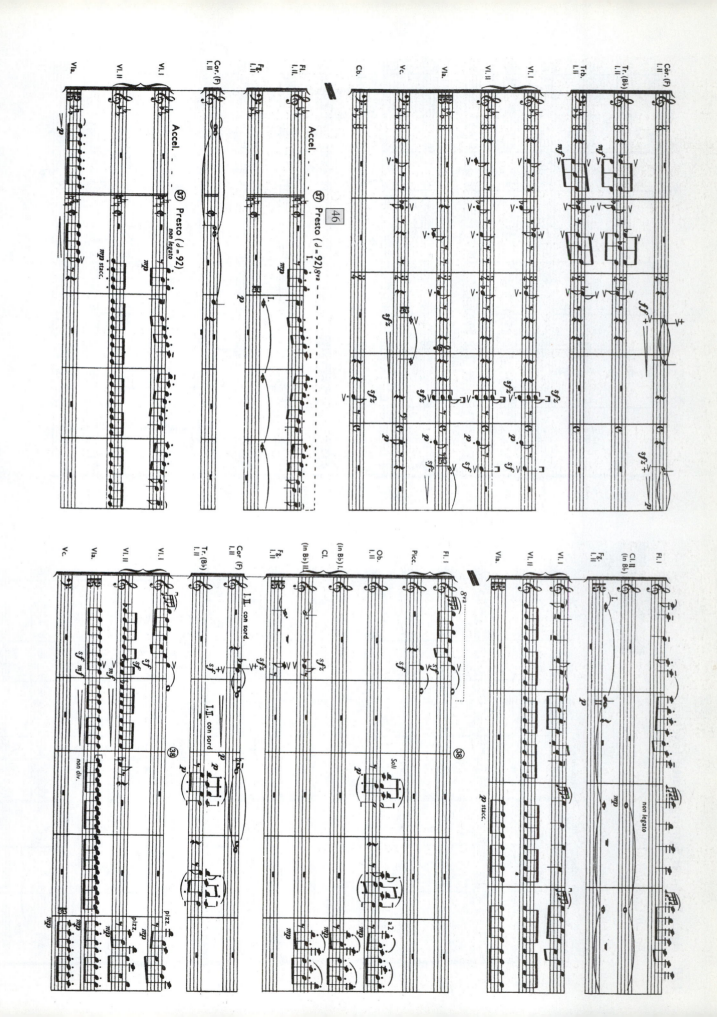

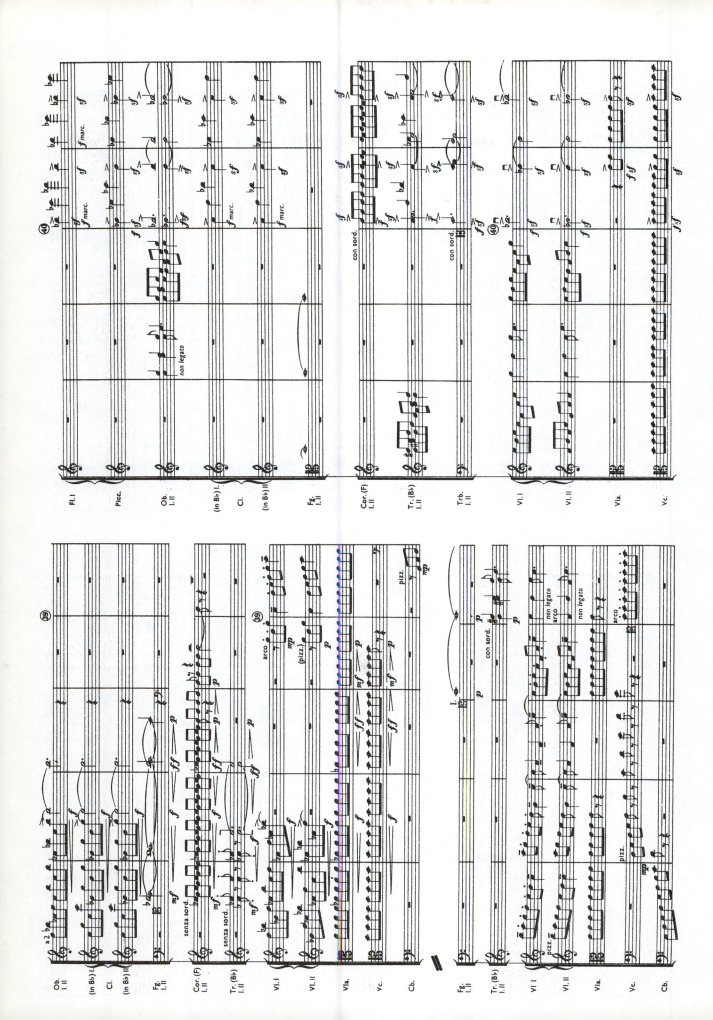

No. 170 Copland: Appalachian Spring

Fl. I.
Picc.
Ob. I. II
(in B♭) I.
Cl.
(in B♭) II
Cor. (F) I. II
Tr. (B♭) I. II
Trb. I. II
Timp.
Bass Dr.
Pfte.
Vl. I
Vl. II
Vla.
Vc.
Cb
41
8va
a2
f stacc.
div. marc.
marc.
arco
unis.
B. Dr.

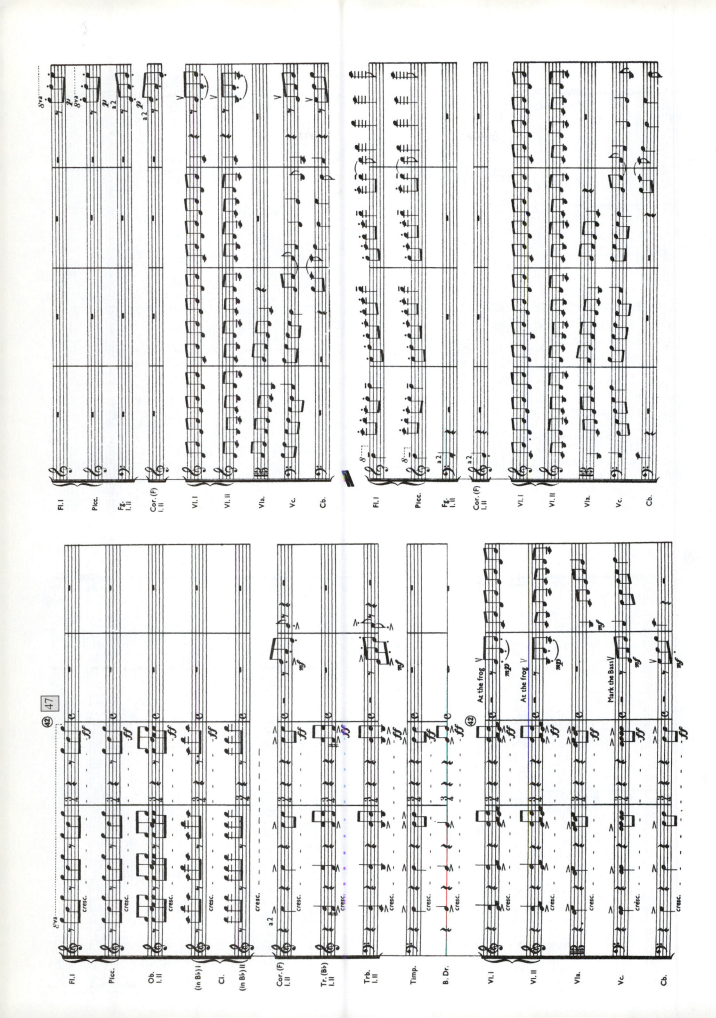

No. 170 Copland: *Appalachian Spring*

No. 170 Copland: *Appalachian Spring*

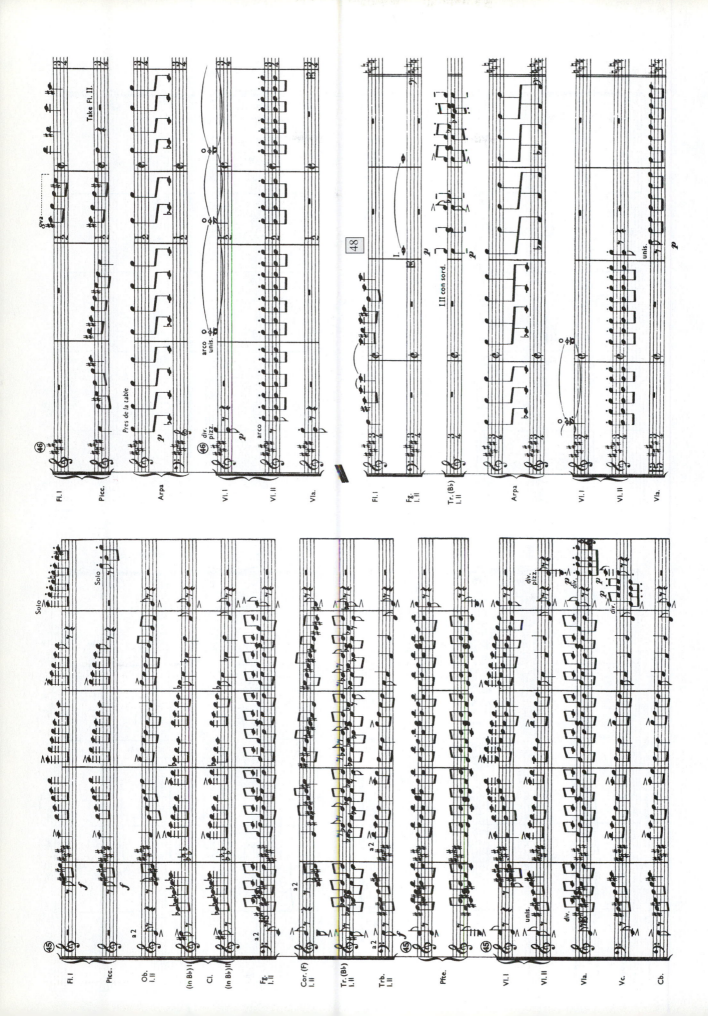

No. 170 Copland: *Appalachian Spring*

47
Fl. I. II.
Ob. I. II
a 2
Cl. (in B♭) I (in B♭) II
Fg. I. II
Tr. (B♭) I. II
Vl. I
Vl. II
unis.
Vla.
Vc.
Cb.
Cor. (F) I. II
II. (senza sord.)
I. senza sord.
div. pizz.
pizz.
sf-mf sf sf-p mf f ff p mp

No. 170 Copland: Appalachian Spring

49
I.
Fl.
II.
Ob. I. II
(in B♭) I
Cl.
(in B♭) II
Fg. I. II
Cor. (F) I. II
Tr. (B♭) I. II
Trb. I. II
Timp.
Xylo.
Pfte.
Vl. I
Vl. II
Vla.
Vc.
Cb.
Claves
Arpa
Pfte
a 2
II.
8va
div.
uns.
unis.
marc.
sf
ff

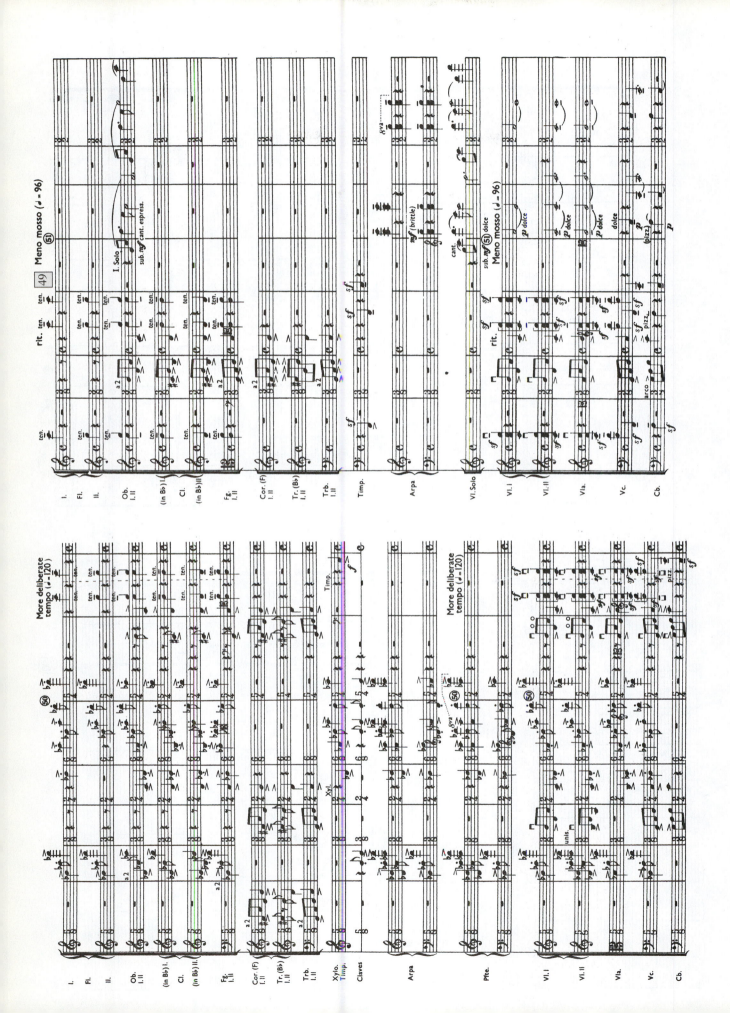

■

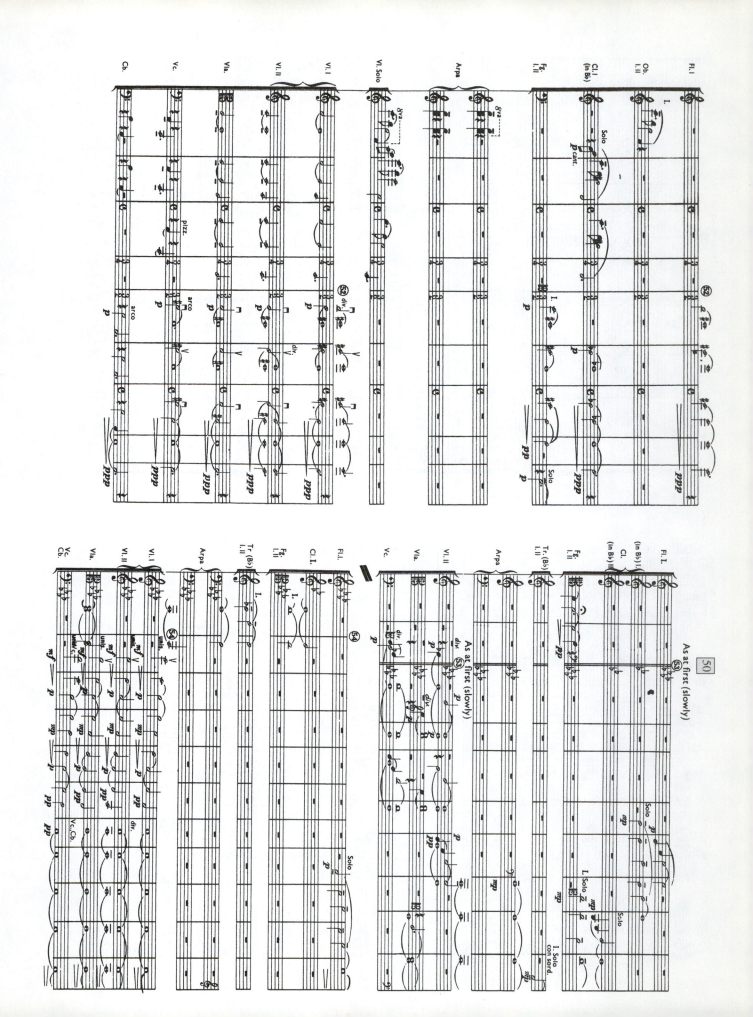

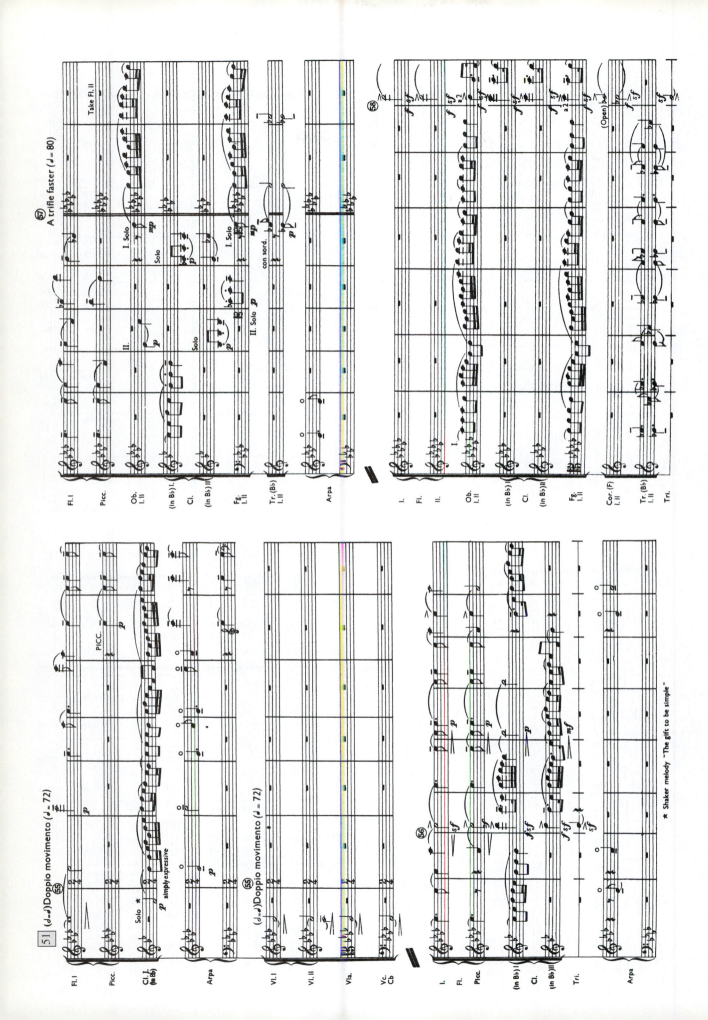

* Shaker melody "The gift to be simple"

No. 170 Copland: Appalachian Spring

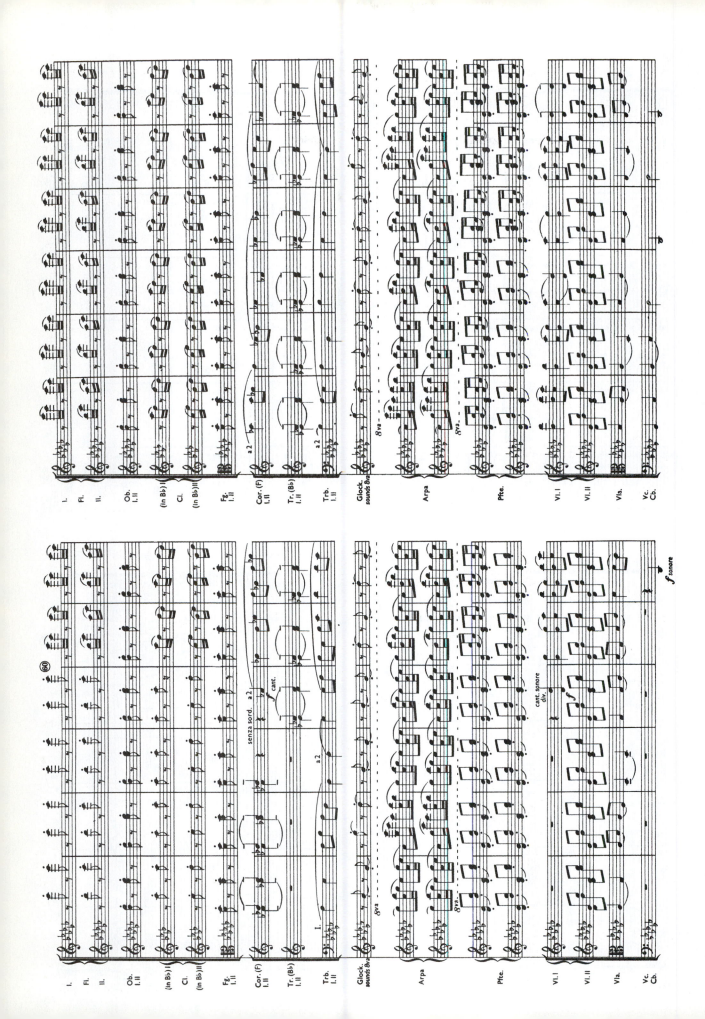

No. 170 Copland: *Appalachian Spring*

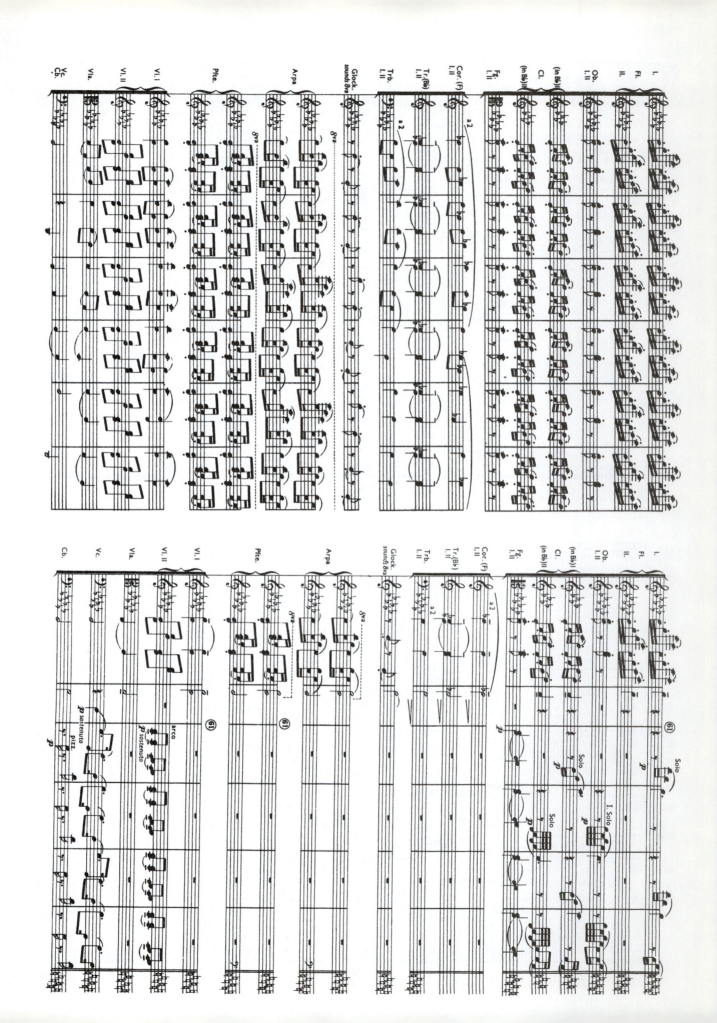

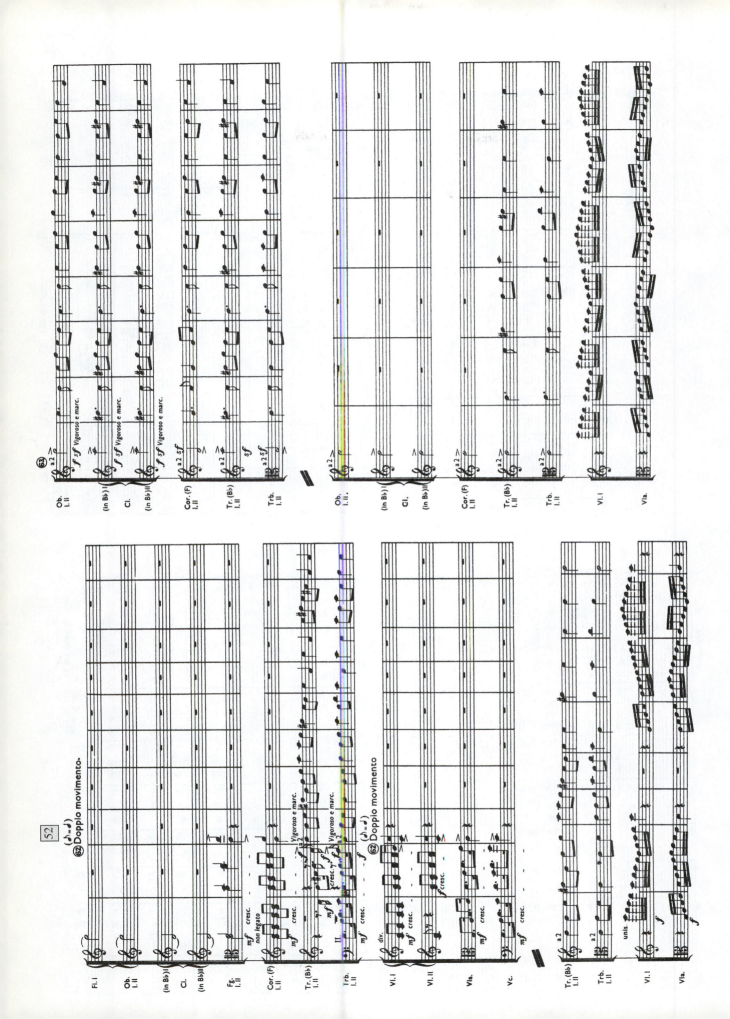

No. 170 Copland: Appalachian Spring

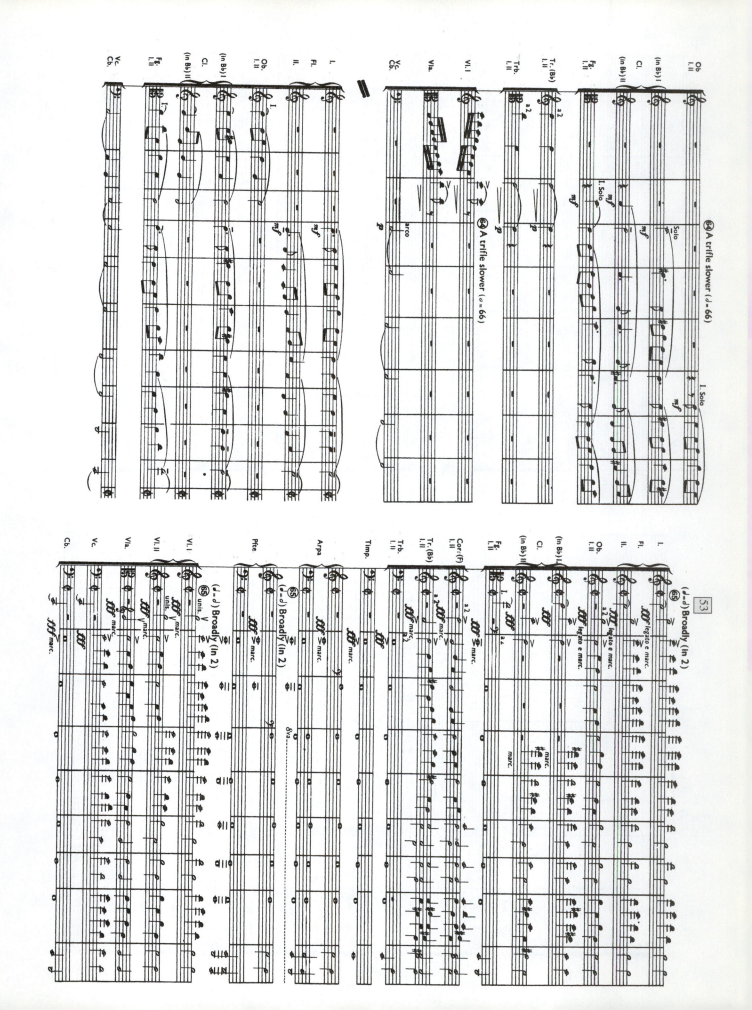

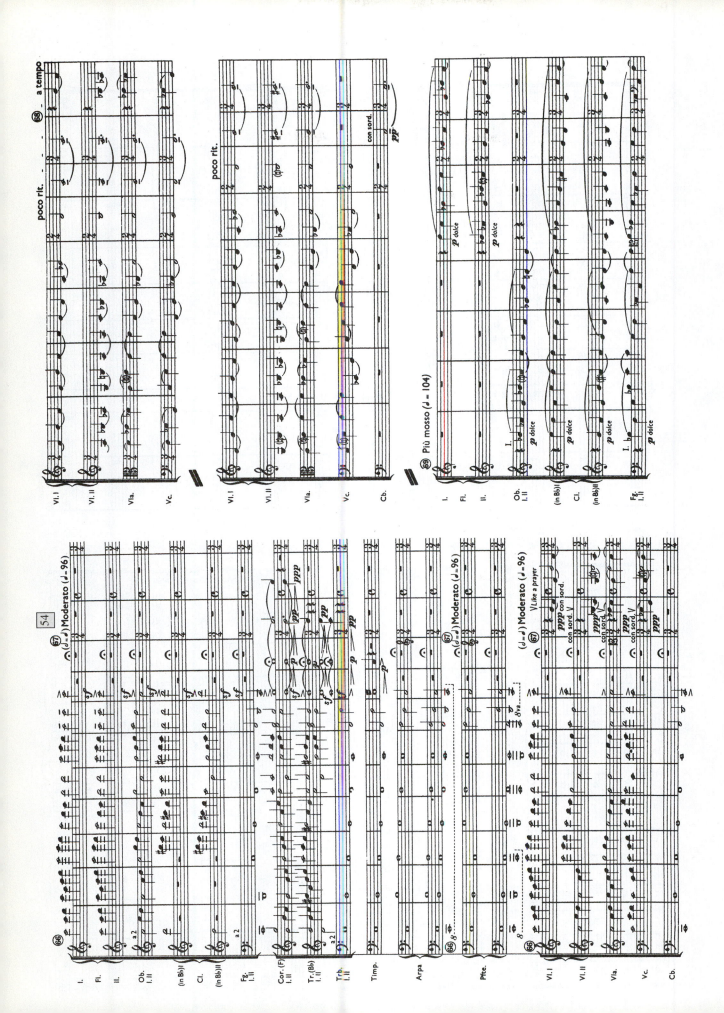

No. 170 Copland: *Appalachian Spring*

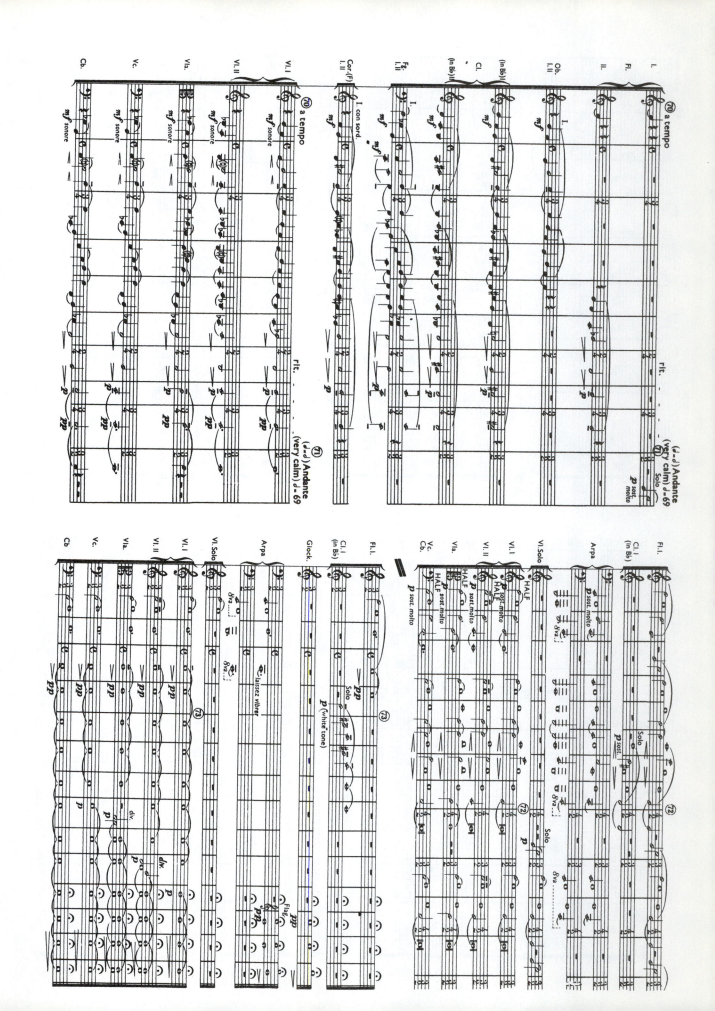

171 Quatuor pour la fin du temps, first movement: "Liturgie de cristal" (1940)
Olivier Messiaen (1908–1992)

(*) *Glissando brefs; id. aux passages similaires.*

Tous droits d'exécution réservés.
Copyright by DURAND & Cⁱᵉ 1942

Copland's *Appalachian Spring* is in many respects the American counterpart to Stravinsky's *Sacre du printemps*: both works involve springtime rituals in rural societies, and both draw on folk idioms for their musical materials. The scenario of the ballet, developed by the choreographer Martha Graham largely after Copland had written the music, revolves around a bride-to-be and her fiancee in a newly built farmhouse in the Pennsylvania countryside in the early 19th century. The couple, according to the note published in the score, "enact the emotions, joyful and apprehensive, their new domestic partnership invites. An older neighbor suggests now and then the rocky confidence of experience. A revivalist and his followers remind the new householders of the strange and terrible aspects of human fate. At the end the couple are left quiet and strong in their new house." Copland originally scored the ballet for an ensemble of thirteen musicians, but the music is best known from the suite the composer created in 1945, arranged for a small orchestra.

The influence of Stravinsky is clear: folk-derived melodies, polytonal harmonies, orchestration, shifting meters, propulsive rhythms—at times irregular, at times ostinato—all owe much to the work of the Russian master. Yet Copland's work is no mere imitation. Particularly in the variations on the Shaker hymn "Simple Gifts" (Example 11), the work projects what many listeners perceive to be a distinctly American sound. The widely spaced voices resonate with the open spaces of the American frontier, and the simplicity of the tune and its text capture the optimism and hope that were so basic to the pioneer mentality.

Example 11 Shaker hymn *Simple Gifts*

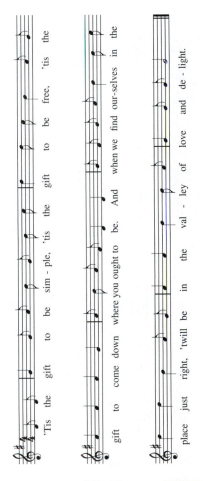

'Tis the gift to be sim - ple, 'tis the gift to be free, 'tis the gift to come down where you ought to be. And when we find our-selves in the place just right, 'twill be in the val - ley of love and de - light.

525

7 von
Clar.
velle
B
gliss.
10 von
Clar.
velle
gliss.
13 von
Clar.
velle
C
gliss.
16 von
Clar.
velle
glissando
gliss.
18 von
Clar.
velle
D
gliss.
21 von
Clar.
velle
gliss.

No. 171 Messiaen: *Quatuor pour la fin du temps*

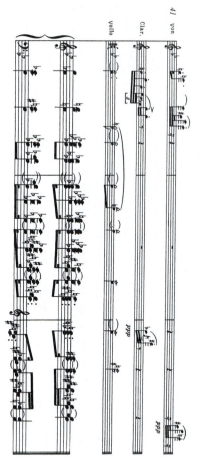

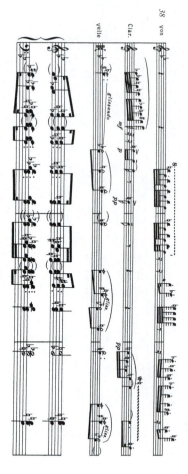

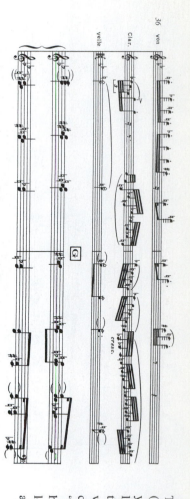

The French composer Olivier Messiaen (1908–1992) wrote his *Quatuor pour la fin du temps* ("Quartet for the End of Time") while interred in a German prisoner-of-war camp in the early years of World War II. The only instruments at his disposal at the time were a clarinet, a violin, a cello, and a rickety piano. Although many inmates interpreted its title as an allusion to the end of their time in prison, the composer himself insisted that the true inspiration for the work came from Chapter 10 of the New Testament book of Revelation, in which an angel causes time to cease at the end of the world. Messiaen compared the opening movement, "Liturgy of Crystal" to "the harmonious silence of the firmament." The harmonics in the cello help create a particularly light, ethereal timbre: by touching the string lightly wherever a lozenge-shaped note is indicated, the cellist creates a pitch—a harmonic overtone—that actually sounds two octaves higher than the notated pitch.

But the "End of the Time" in the work's title is most directly evident in its organization of rhythm. The four voices operate on entirely different rhythmic levels: the violin and clarinet—which by the composer's own account reflect the songs of a nightingale and blackbird, respectively—are free, random, unpredictable. The cello and piano, in contrast, adhere to strict rhythmic and melodic patterns. The cello presents a fifteen-note melody eight and one-half times over the course of the movement (see Example 22-3 in Textbook).

The rhythmic pattern of the melody is palindromic—the same forward as backward—or as Messiaen himself called it, nonretrogradable. This is not obvious at first because the note values begin in the middle of the rhythmic sequence: time, after all, has been going on before the piece begins.

The piano's rhythm of seventeen note values, although not palindromic, is also repeated many times. As in the case of the cello, the rhythmic pattern begins and ends in the middle of two different measures and thus shifts constantly in relation to the bar line. Thematically, the piano repeats a sequence of 29 chords throughout, but the thematic and rhythmic patterns do not coincide. This structure resembles that of the medieval isorhythm (see Chapter 3), in which a melodic pattern (*color*) is played against an independent rhythmic pattern (*talea*). Although Messiaen himself was well aware of the technique of isorhythm, he maintained that his more immediate sources were the rhythmic structures of certain Hindu modes.

This movement also reminds us just how remote a work can be removed from the framework of triadic harmony. Although many of the piano's 29 chords (see Example 22-4 in Textbook) incorporate triadic harmonies, they also have multiple additional nonharmonic tones. The inner voices of chords 9 through 12, for example, present a series of first-inversion harmonies on G♭ major, G major, A♭ major, and A major, but the nonharmonic notes of the outer voices mask the sound of these triads. At the same time, the insistent F in the bass, which has been present since the very first chord, grounds the music around a semblance of a tonal center. Messiaen himself described the opening sonority as a "chord on the dominant"—in this case, of B♭ major, the tonality implied by the key signature—even though it does not function as such in the traditional sense.

172 String Quartet No. 8, third movement
(1960)
Dmitri Shostakovich (1906–1975)

No. 172 Shostakovich: String Quartet No. 8

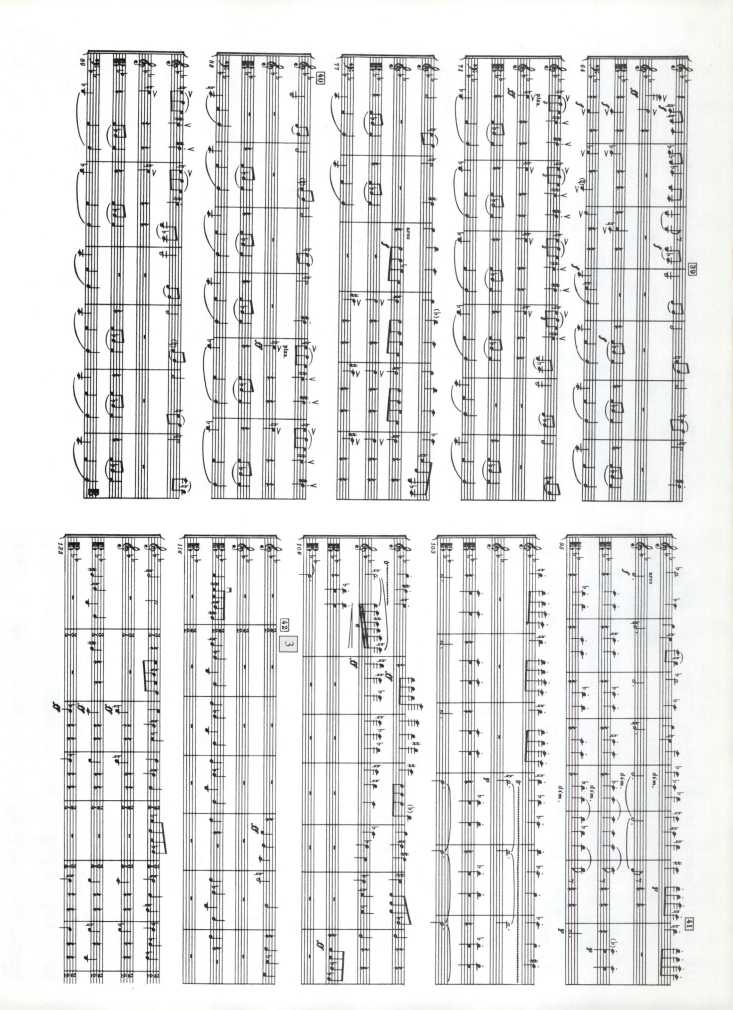

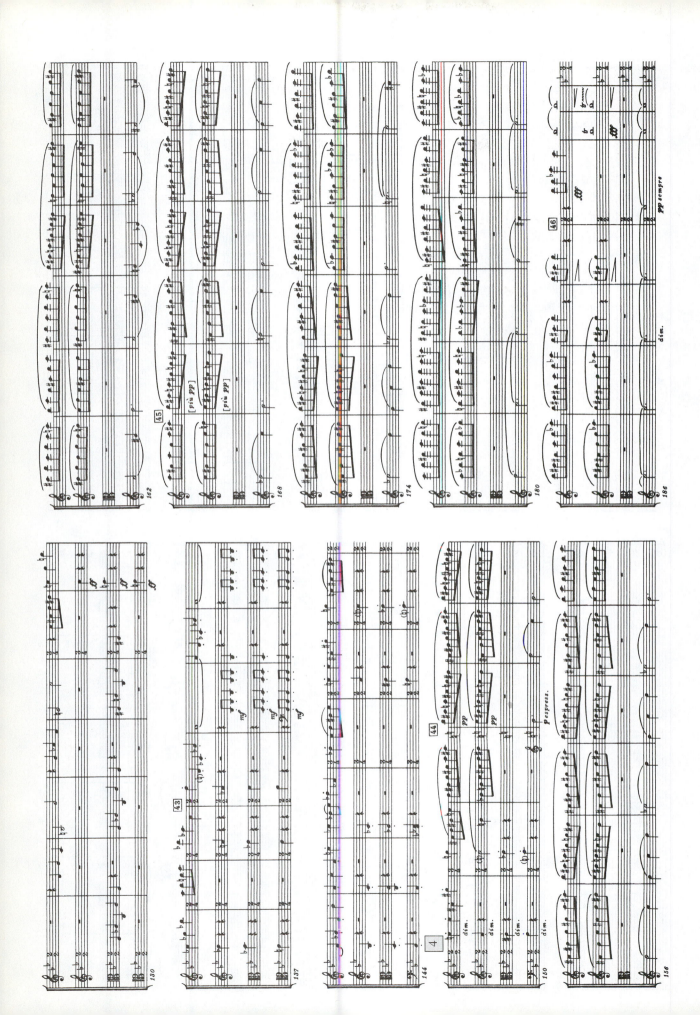

No. 172 Shostakovich: String Quartet No. 8

531 ■

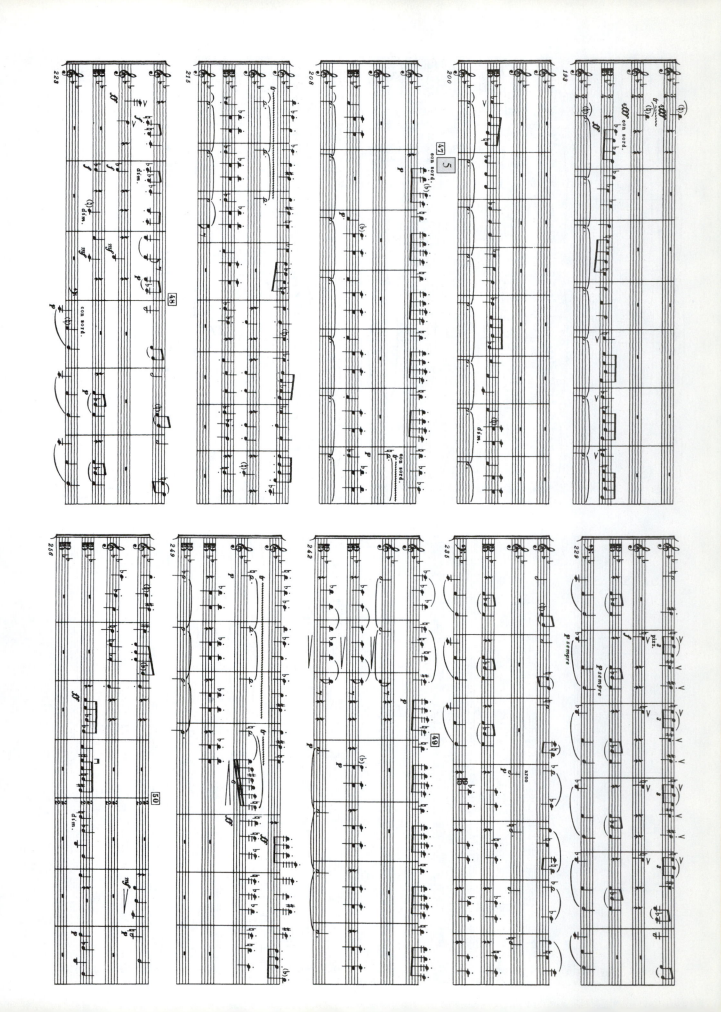

The String Quartet No. 8 of the Russian composer Dmitri Shostakovich is heavily autobiographical. "When I die," Shostakovich wrote to a friend, "it's hardly likely that someone will write a quartet dedicated to my memory. So I decided to write it myself." The work is saturated with a musical motif which the composer himself identified as his musical monogram: the notes D-E♭-C-B, which in the German system of notation (see Chapter 16) spell D-S (=Es =E♭)-C-H (=B♮), are shorthand for **Dmitri Schostakovich**, the German transliteration of the composer's name. The piece as a whole is full of quotations from Shostakovich's operas, symphonies, and chamber works; it also includes snippets from Siegfried's funeral music in Wagner's *Götterdämmerung* and the first movement of Tchaikovsky's Sixth Symphony. The latter two are directly associated with the idea of death, as is the recurring *Dies irae* plainchant melody, the same tune used by Berlioz in the finale of his *Symphonie fantastique* (see Chapter 14).

Shostakovich dedicated his Eighth Quartet "to the memory of the victims of fascism and war"—that is, to the victims of the struggle against Nazi Germany in World War II—a sentiment wholly acceptable to Soviet authorities. But several of the composer's friends have since asserted that the work was Shostakovich's "suicide note," that the composer planned to swallow an overdose of sleeping pills after finishing this work, so depressed was he at having been forced to join the Communist Party. As is so often the case with Shostakovich, truth and fiction are difficult to separate. Eyewitness accounts of events in his life are not always reliable, many of them never having been committed to paper until after the composer's death. The music itself, however, clearly connects the images of Shostakovich (through the many quotations of his own music and of his musical monogram) and death (through the quotation of death-related music by other composers). In the final movement, the DSCH motif appears as a counterpoint to a quotation from the last scene of Shostakovich's opera *Lady Macbeth of the Mtsensk District* (1934), banned by the Soviet government, in which prisoners are being transported to Siberia. This could easily have been Shostakovich's own fate had he not agreed to join the Communist Party. Shostakovich used the ambiguity of the music as a shield for his own self-expression.

The third movement functions as a scherzo and assumes the form of a waltz, but it is a macabre kind of dance. The introduction begins with the DSCH theme in the first violin (D-E♭-C-H[B♮]), which soon (m. 20) reenters as the main motive, now jarringly discordant with the simple G minor accompaniment. Formally, the movement follows the standard scherzo-trio-scherzo pattern. It leads without a break into the finale.

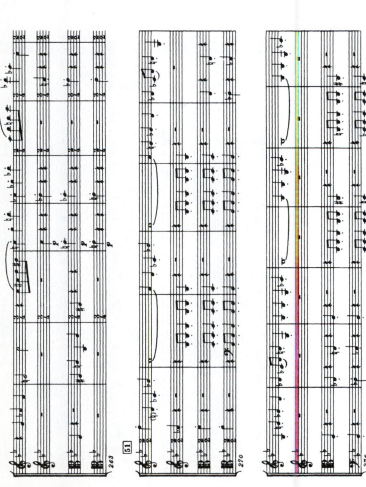
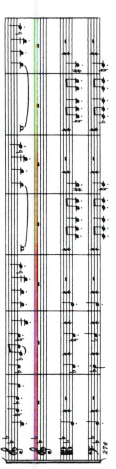
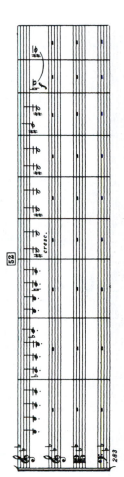
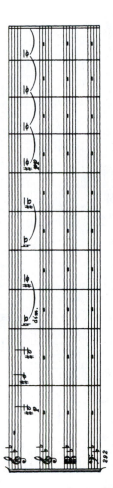

173 Night and Day (1932)

Cole Porter (1891–1964)

CD14 Track 6
p. 614

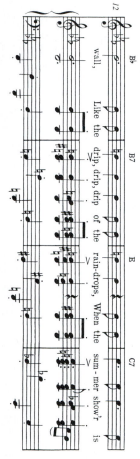

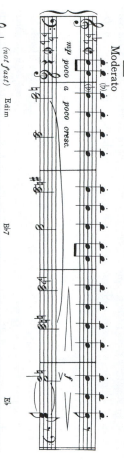

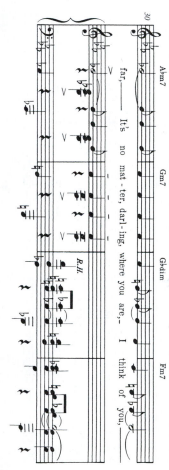

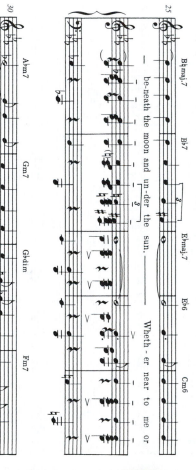

Songs like Porter's *Night and Day* and Ellington's *Sophisticated Lady* reflect the traditions of the 19th-century *Lied* in remarkable ways. The harmonic vocabularies of these works, although essentially tonal, are richly chromatic and far from straightforward. The poetry is elegant and witty, the melodies unforgettable, and the union of the two represents the genre at its best. In Porter's *Night and Day*, the juxtaposition of the wandering chromatic line in the bass against the repeated B♭ of the voice establishes the underlying tension between longing and insistency. Finally, after 35 iterations of B♭, the vocal line itself begins to rise and fall chromatically, gradually, languorously: the longing has become infectious. We do not feel a strong sense of tonic until the word "one" in the clinching phrase "…you are the one" (m. 23). In m. 52, the music moves to a remote key (G♭=♭III), the repeated notes grow into a back-and-forth a whole step (m. 57), and the tonic finally returns after a circuitous passage through a series of chromatic harmonies. Unlike Wagner in Act II of *Tristan und Isolde* (Anthology No. 138), or Leonard Bernstein in "Tonight" from *West Side Story* (Anthology No. 175), Porter erases the differences between night and day: the lover here is indifferent to the setting and rising of the sun.

Like many songs of this era, *Night and Day* has been subjected to countless arrangements, vocal and instrumental. It was first recorded by Fred Astaire for the movie *The Gay Divorcee* (1934), a comedy that revolves around mistaken identity and provides a platform for much singing and dancing. Within three months of the film's premiere, more than 30 artists had recorded the song. Within 25 years, the number had surpassed a hundred. And no two recordings are alike: the performance tradition of a song like *Night and Day* allows—and in fact encourages—performers to take considerable liberties with its rhythm, text, orchestration, harmonies, words, and even its melody. Frank Sinatra's version sounds very different from Ella Fitzgerald's, which in turn sounds very different from Fred Astaire's. Nor can any of these renditions really be said to represent the composer's original intentions, because Cole Porter did not really conceive of the song as a fixed entity. The notion of an "authentic" version of this song is in fact vaguely ridiculous. Is it Cole Porter's original manuscript? The first edition? The first recording? As in jazz, improvisatory freedom plays such a basic role in this kind of music that the idea of an authentic text loses all relevance.

174 Sophisticated Lady (1933)

Ellington

CD14 Track 8 p. 615

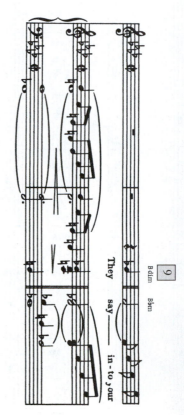

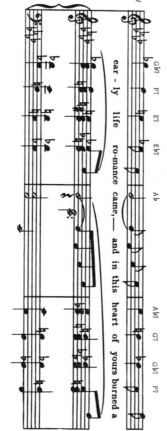

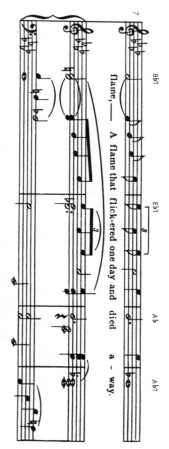

No. 174 Ellington: *Sophisticated Lady*

Ellington's *Sophisticated Lady* uses advanced melodic and harmonic chromaticism to project the idea of a woman who has assumed a worldly attitude toward life and love. Melodic chromaticism and rhythmic irregularity emphasize the woman's exterior life of glamor and uncaring attitude ("Smoking, drinking, never thinking of tomorrow, nonchalant . . ."). Only with the final word of the text—"cry"—does the music arrive at its long-avoided resolution on the tonic. The chromaticism, in the end, is revealed as a mask covering the woman's true feelings.

175 West Side Story: "Tonight" (1957)
Leonard Bernstein (1918–1990)

CD14 Track 11 p. 616

Ensemble
Maria, Tony, Anita, Riff, Bernardo*
Sharks and Jets

Fast and rhythmic ♩ = 132

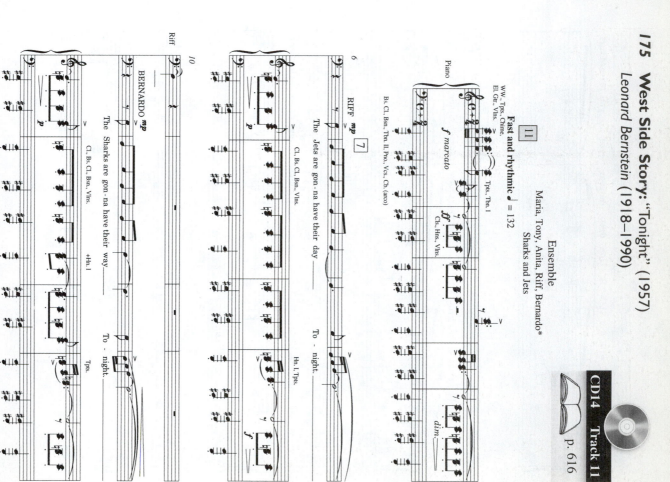

* If the scene is staged with more than the designated five people, the members of the gangs may sing with their respective leaders (except in bars 103 - 125).

No. 175 Bernstein: West Side Story

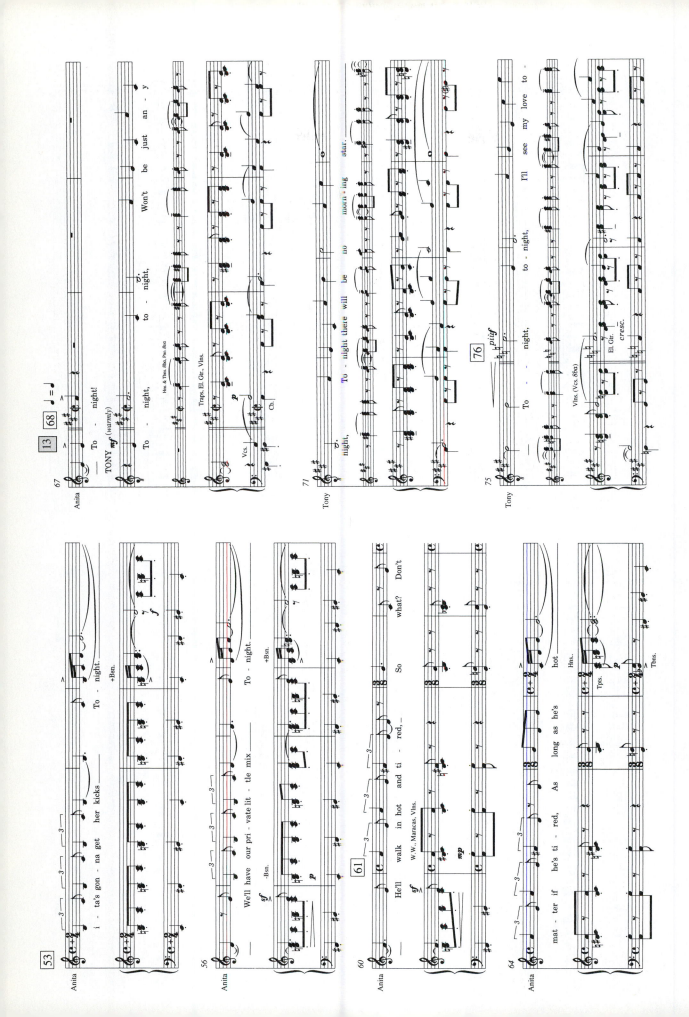

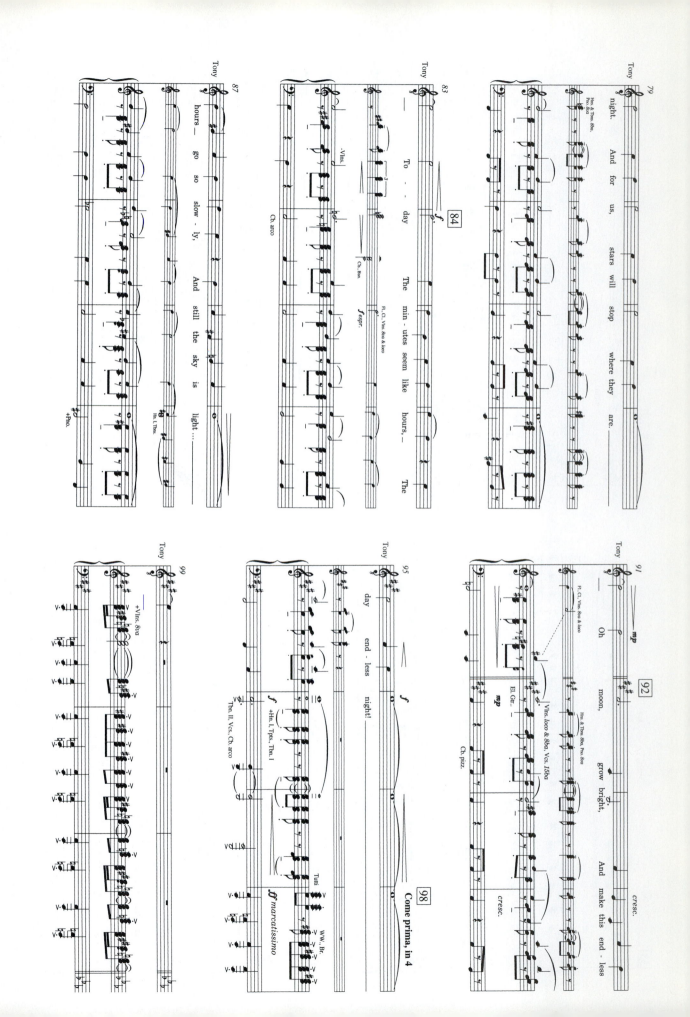

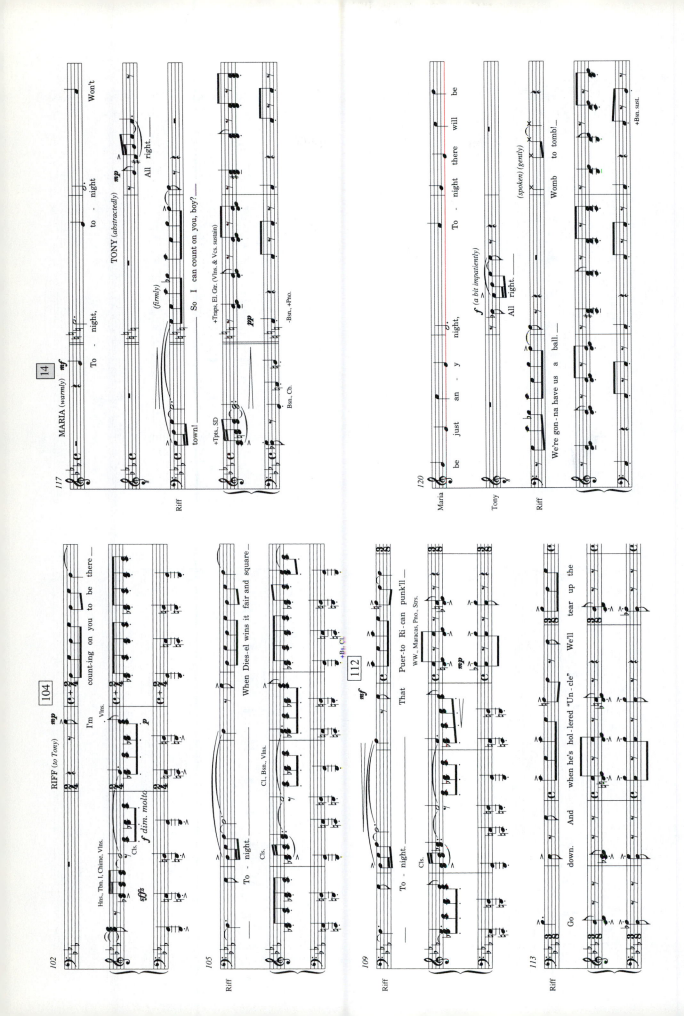

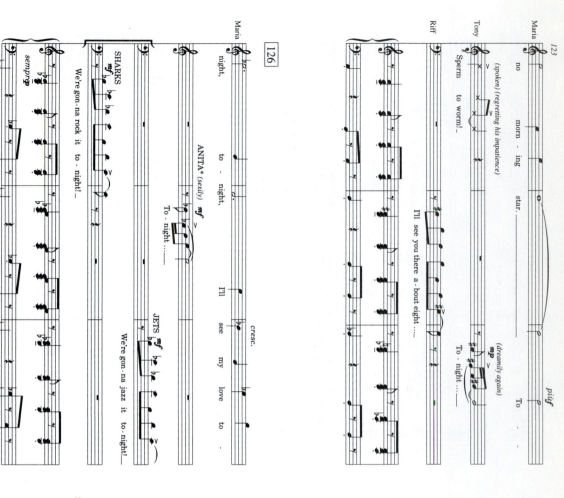

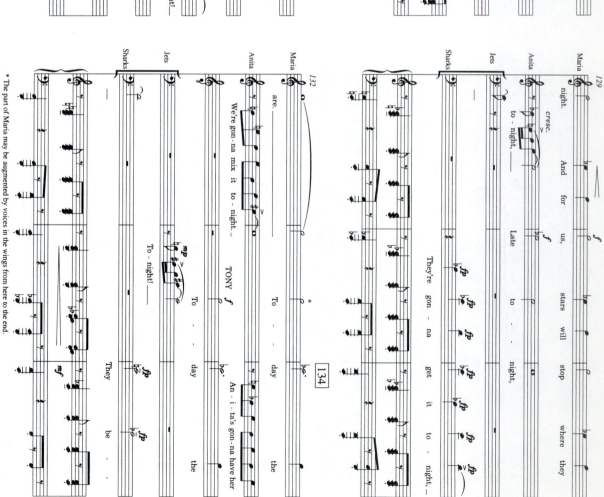

* The part of Anita may be augmented by voices in the wings from here to the end.

* The part of Maria may be augmented by voices in the wings from here to the end.

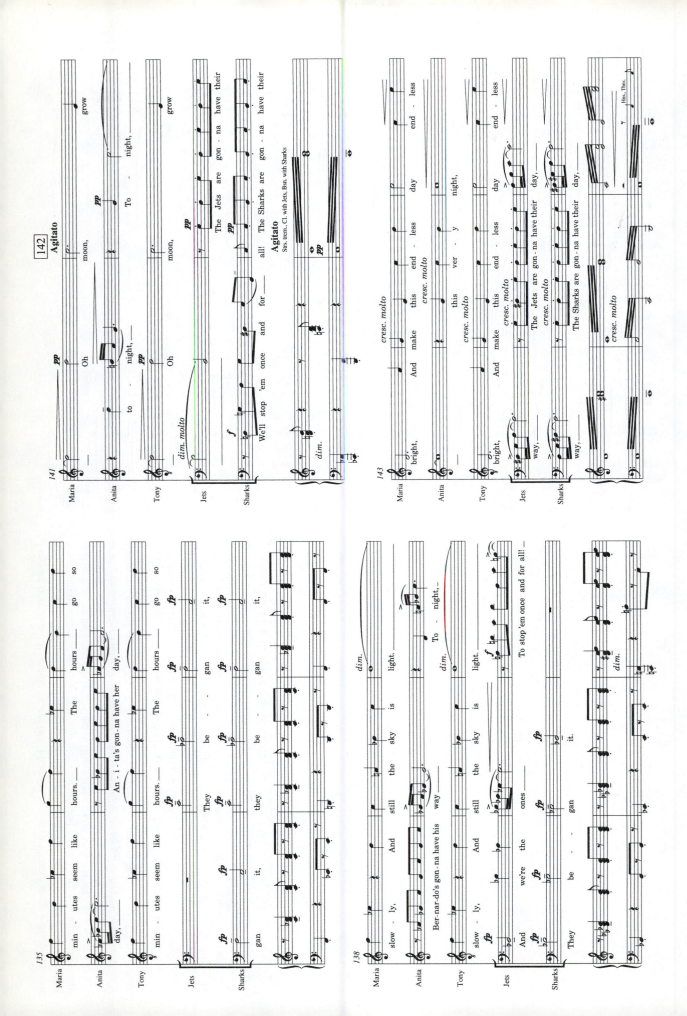

No. 175   Bernstein: West Side Story

[Piano reduction of the original orchestral version]

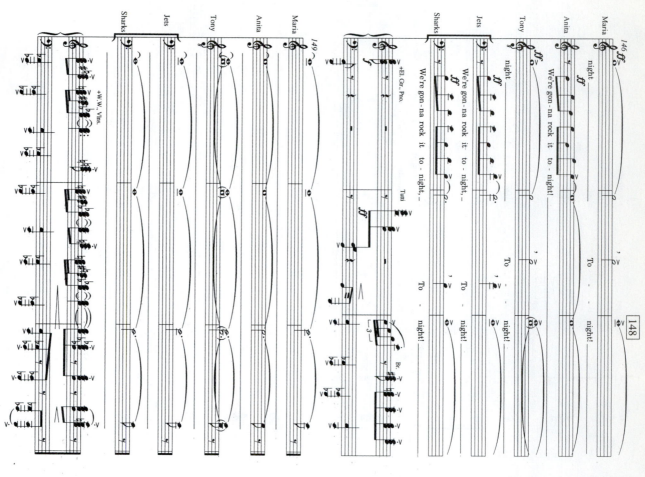

Leonard Bernstein's *West Side Story* (1957) focuses on the problem of gang warfare between Puerto Ricans (The Sharks) and whites (The Jets) in New York City. The libretto, by Stephen Sondheim (who would go on to compose many hit musicals of his own), was unusually gritty and realistic by the standards of its time. It draws liberally on Shakespeare's *Romeo and Juliet*, featuring a pair of lovers from rival groups and ending in the death of one of them.

"Tonight" is a quartet very much in the tradition of *Bella figlia del l'amore* from Verdi's *Rigoletto* (Anthology 2#137). Dramatically, both revolve around the feeling of anticipation: the Sharks and Jets await their climactic conflict; the sultry Anita knows that she will get "her kicks" that night ("He'll walk in hot and tired. So what? Don't matter if he's tired, as long as he's hot"); and the two lovers, Tony and Maria, await their meeting ("Tonight, tonight won't be just any night"). The number builds gradually and becomes increasingly contrapuntal as it progresses, with a lyrical love duet between Tony and Maria that unfolds above the animosity of the rival choruses. Bernstein uses a jazz-like orchestration, a rapid alternation of duple and triple meters, and even *Sprechstimme* at one point to give the music a decidedly modern sound. But the overall shape of the movement—contrasting emotions expressed simultaneously—owes much to the traditions of 19th-century opera.

176 Threnody for the Victims of Hiroshima (1960)
Krzysztof Penderecki (b. 1933)

CD14 Track 15 — p. 619

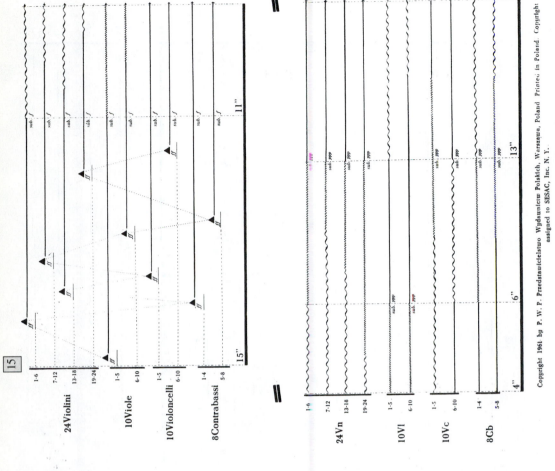

SKRÓTY I SYMBOLE	ABBREVIATIONS AND SYMBOLS	SIGNES D'ABREVIATION ET SYMBOLES	ABKÜRZUNGEN UND SYMBOLE
ordinario — ord. sul ponticello — s. p. sul tasto — s. t. col legno — c. l. legno battuto — l. batt.			
podwyższenie o ¼ tonu	raised by ¼ tone	hausse la note d'un quart de ton	Erhöhung um ¼ Ton
podwyższenie o ¾ tonu	raised by ¾ tone	hausse la note de trois quarts de ton	Erhöhung um ¾ Ton
obniżenie o ¼ tonu	lowered by ¼ tone	abaisse la note d'un quart de ton	Erniedrigung um ¼ Ton
obniżenie o ¾ tonu	lowered by ¾ tone	abaisse la note de trois quarts de ton	Erniedrigung um ¾ Ton
najwyższy dźwięk instrumentu (wysokość nieokreślona)	highest note of the instrument (indefinite pitch)	le son le plus aigu de l'instrument (hauteur indéterminée)	höchster Ton des Instrumentes (unbestimmte Tonhöhe)
grać miedzy podstawkiem i strunnikiem	play between bridge and tailpiece	jouer entre le chevalet et le cordier	zwischen Steg und Saitenhalter spielen
arpeggio na 4 strunach za podstawkiem	arpeggio on 4 strings behind the bridge	arpège sur 4 cordes entre le chevalet et le cordier	Arpeggio zwischen Steg und Saitenhalter (4 Saiten)
grać na strunniku (arco)	play on tailpiece (arco)	jouer sur le cordier (arco)	auf dem Saitenhalter spielen (arco)
grać na podstawku	play on bridge	jouer sur le chevalet	auf dem Steg spielen
efekt perkusyjny: uderzać w górną płytę skrzypiec żabką lub czubkami palców	percussion effect: strike the upper sounding board of the violin with the nut or the finger-tips	effet de percussion: frapper la table de dessus du violon avec le talon de l'archet ou avec les bouts des doigt	Schlagzeugeffekt: mit dem Frosch oder mit Fingerspitze die Decke schlagen
kilka nieregularnych zmian smyczka	several irregular changes of bow	plusieurs changements d'archet irréguliers	mehrere unregelmäßige Bogenwechsel
molto vibrato	molto vibrato	molto vibrato	molto vibrato
bardzo wolne vibrato w obrębie ćwierćtonu, uzyskane przez przesuwanie palca	very slow vibrato with a ¼ tone frequency difference produced by sliding the finger	vibrato très lent à intervalle d'un quart de ton par le déplacement du doigt	sehr langsames Vibrato mit ¼ - Ton-Frequenzdifferenz durch Fingerverschiebung
bardzo szybkie i nierytmizowane tremolo	very rapid not rhythmicized tremolo	trémolo très rapide, mais sans rythme précis	sehr schnelles, nicht rhythmisiertes Tremolo

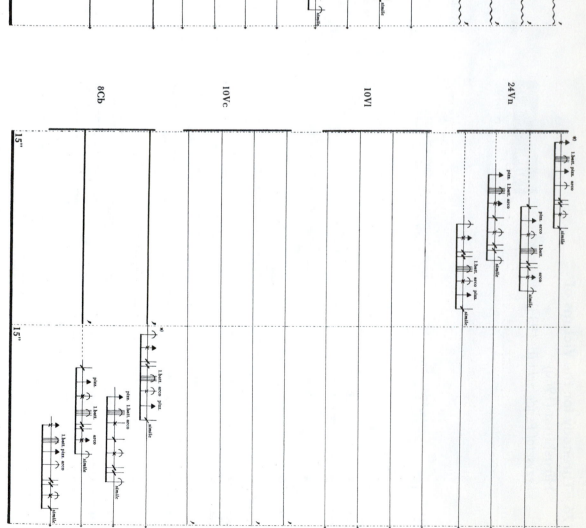

*)Każdy instrumentalista wybiera sobie jedno z 4 podanych ugrupowań i realizuje je (w wyznaczonym odcinku czasu) tak szybko, jak tylko można..
Jeder Instrumentalist wählt eine der angegebenen 4 Gruppierungen und spielt sie (im bestimmten Zeitabschnitt) so schnell wie möglich.
Each instrumentalist chooses one of the 4 given groups and executes it (within a fixed space of time) as rapidly as possible.
te exécutant choisi; un des 4 groupements donnés et l'exécute (dans le segment de temps indiqué) aussi vite que possible.

*) patrz uwaga na s.6 / vgl. Anmerkung auf Seite 6 / cf. note on page 6 / voir note à la page 6

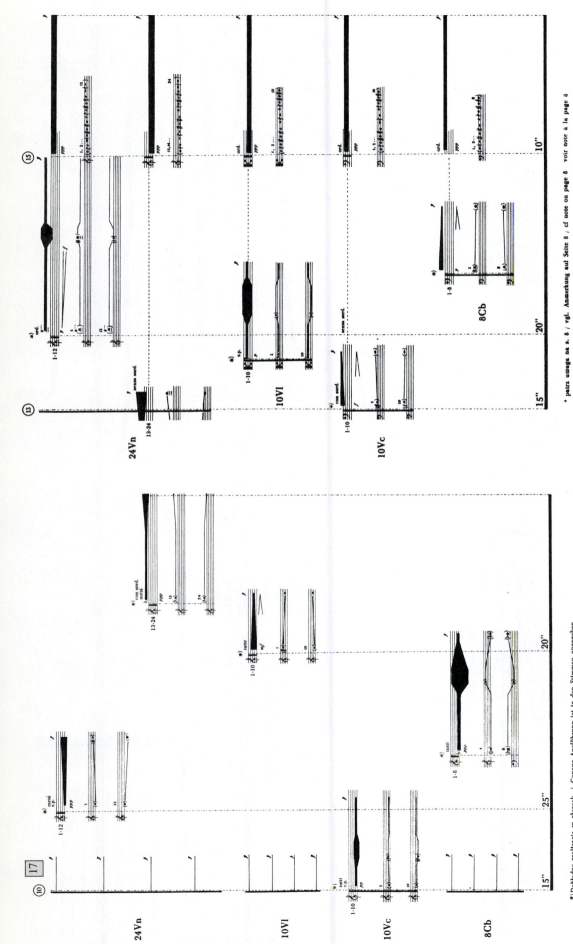

*) Dokładna realizacja w głosach. / Genaue Ausführung ist in den Stimmen angegeben.

Exact notation is given in the parts. / L'exécution précise est indiquée dans les parties.

* patrz uwaga na s. 8 / vgl. Anmerkung auf Seite 8 / cf note on page 8   voir note à la page 8

No. 176 Penderecki: *Threnody for the Victims of Hiroshima*

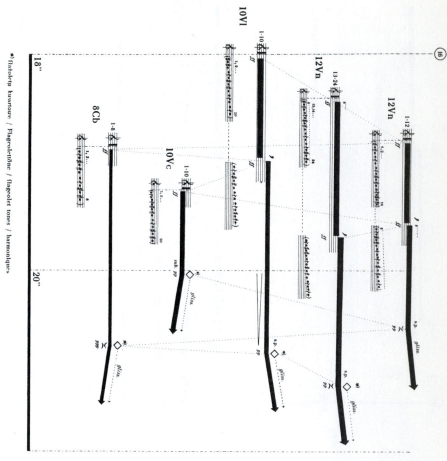

*) flażolety kwartowe / Flageolettöne / flageolet tones / harmoniques

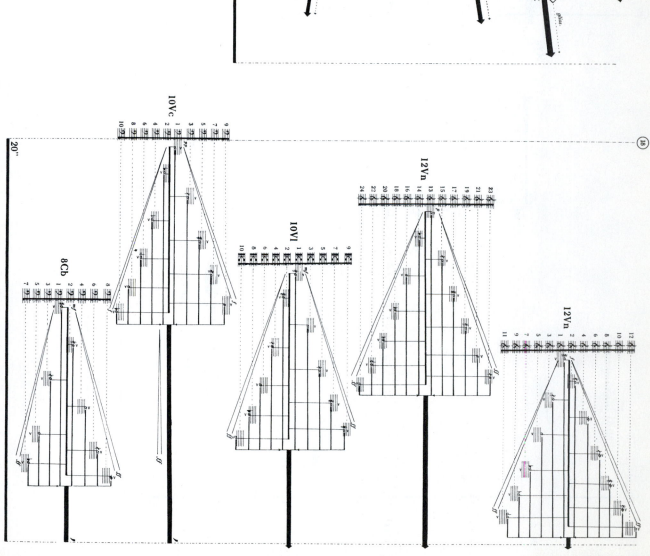

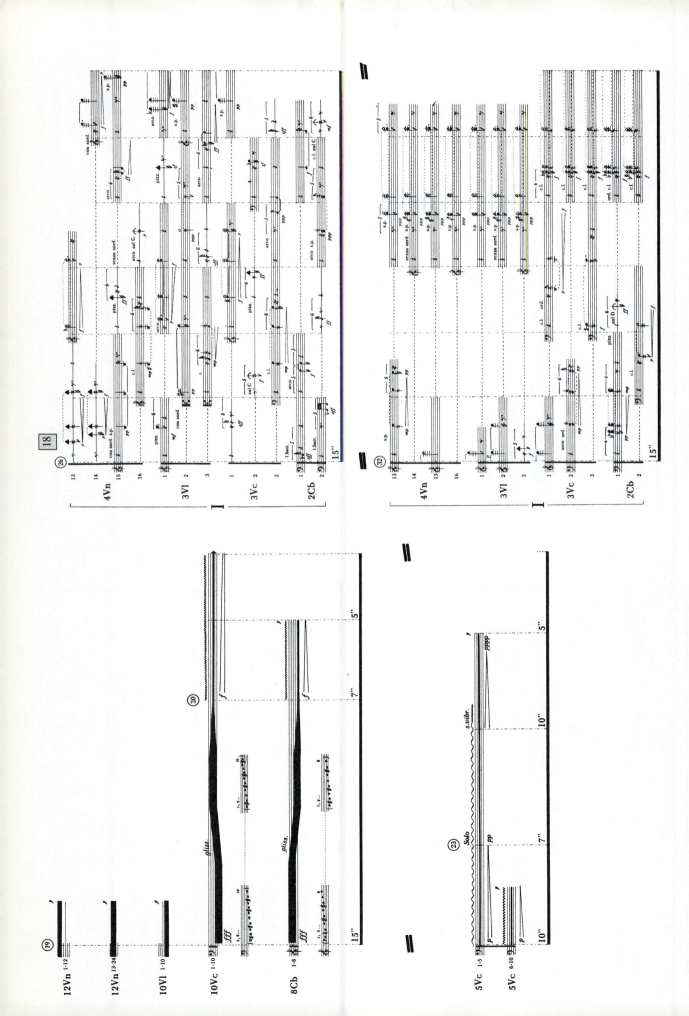

No. 176 Penderecki: *Threnody for the Victims of Hiroshima*

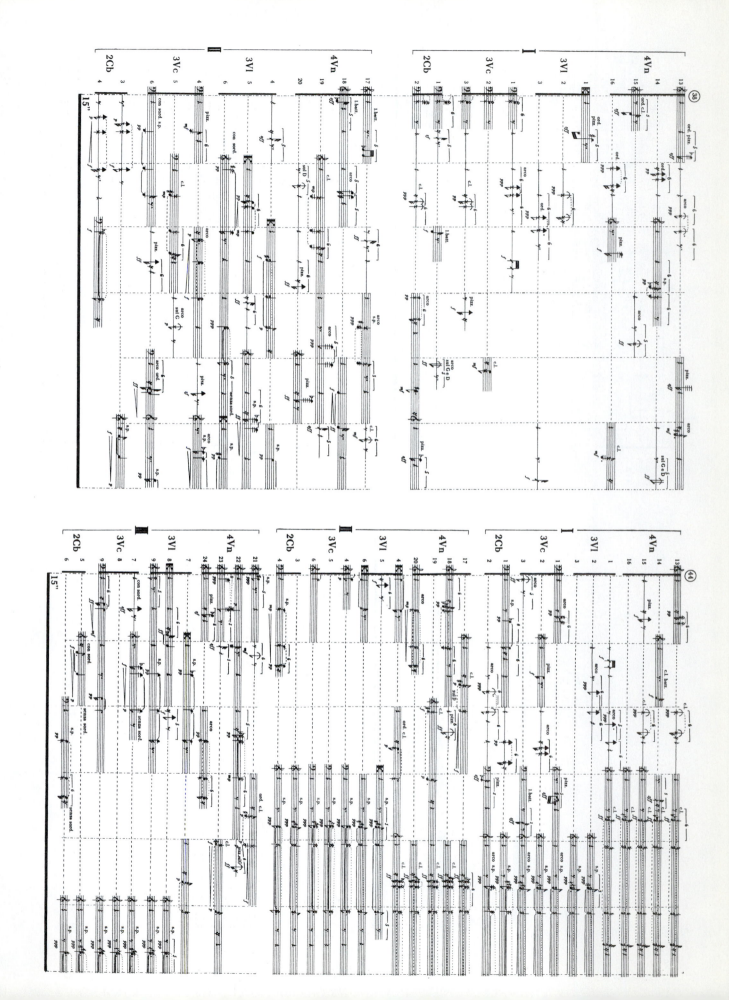

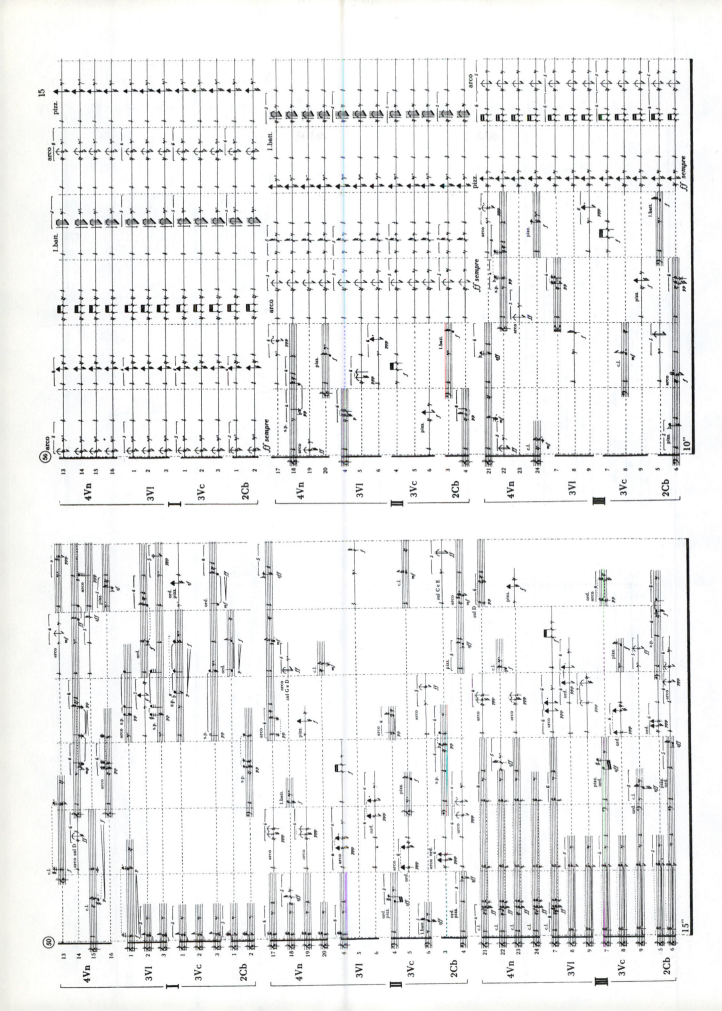

No. 176 Penderecki: *Threnody for the Victims of Hiroshima*

■ No.176 Penderecki: Threnody for the Victims of Hiroshima

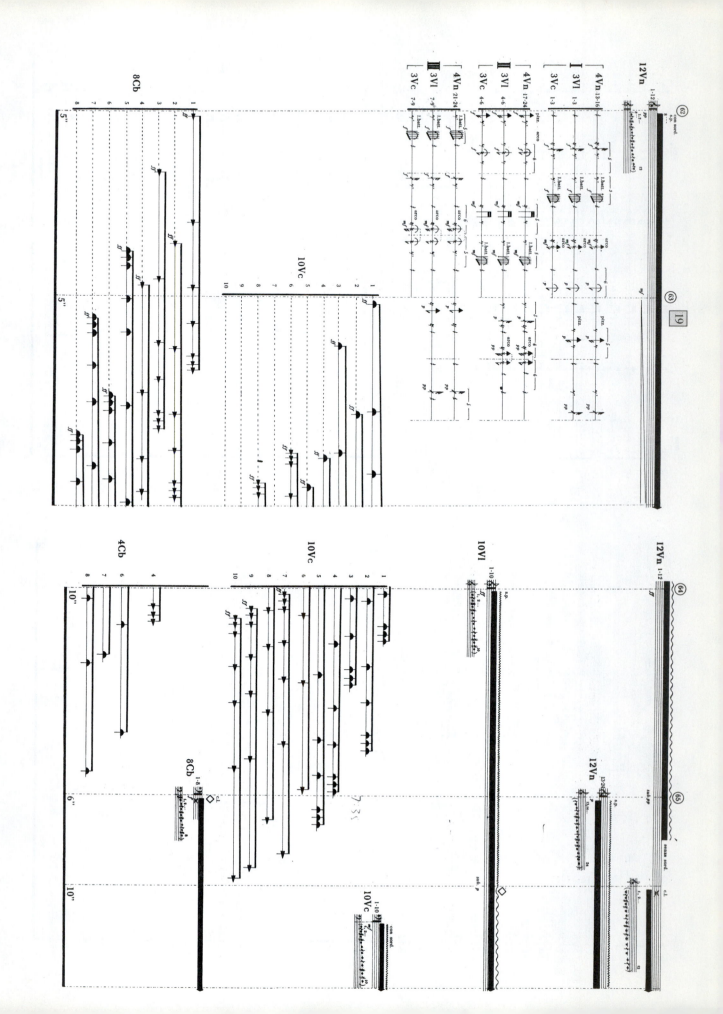

Moved by the devastation of Hiroshima, the Polish composer Krzysztof Penderecki (b. 1933) sought to express the grim reality of nuclear war in his *Threnody for the Victims of Hiroshima* (1960). Finding conventional sonorities and textures inadequate to capture the event and its aftermath, he calls in his score for unique combinations of sounds from an orchestra consisting of 52 stringed instruments (24 violins, 10 violas, 10 cellos, 8 double basses). At times the string players are asked to create sharp, percussive sounds by snapping strings against the fingerboard. At other times they must produce a different kind of percussive sound by striking the body of the instrument with the fingertips. Penderecki's score grants considerable freedom to the performers at many points. He asks individual players at several points to play simply "the highest note possible." At other points, he directs different groups of instruments to play with vibrato at different rates of speed, indicated only generally by the size of the wavy line in the score; the precise speed is left up to individual players. On still other occasions, individual performers are free to choose from a group of four different notational sequences and to perform the chosen group "as rapidly as possible." The work features no meter and no bar lines: durations are indicated by timings that run underneath the bottom of each system of the score.

Other elements of the score, however, are extremely precise. Penderecki uses microtones —intervals smaller than a half-step in the diatonic scale—at many points in the score. Western musicians had long been aware of microtones, but principally as a theoretical idea. It was not until the 20th century that composers like Ives, Bartók, Berg, Copland, and Ligeti began to use microtones in their works. Penderecki's *Threnody* explores these possibilities to an unprecedented degree, concluding with a massive quarter-tone cluster of tones and microtones spanning two octaves and played by all 52 instruments.

The form of Penderecki's *Threnody* offers a comparable mixture of precision and imprecision. It is structured around sonorities, dynamics, and textures rather than themes or key areas. Although it resists any ready-made formal category, its ever-changing surface suggests a division into five large sections:

1. m. 1–5   High register, varying vibrato
2. m. 6–9   Pizzicato and bowed passages played on the tailpiece
3. m. 10–25   Expanding and contracting tone clusters
4. m. 26–62   Percussive, pointillistic sounds, with much tremolo
5. m. 63–end Gradual return of tone clusters

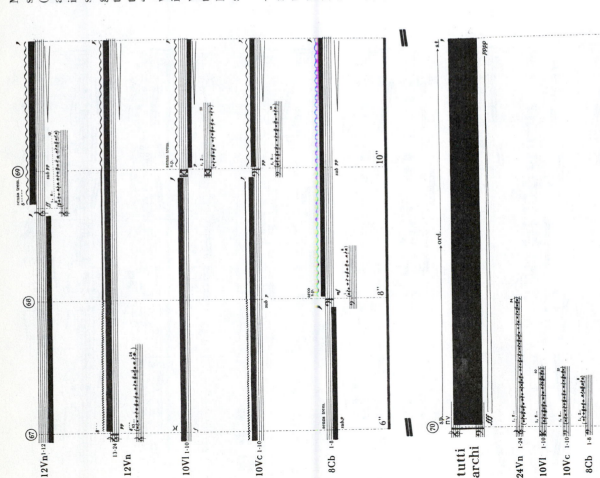

No. 176 Penderecki: *Threnody for the Victims of Hiroshima*

177 Three Compositions for Piano,
No. I (1947)
Milton Babbitt (b. 1916)

CD14 Track 20 p. 620

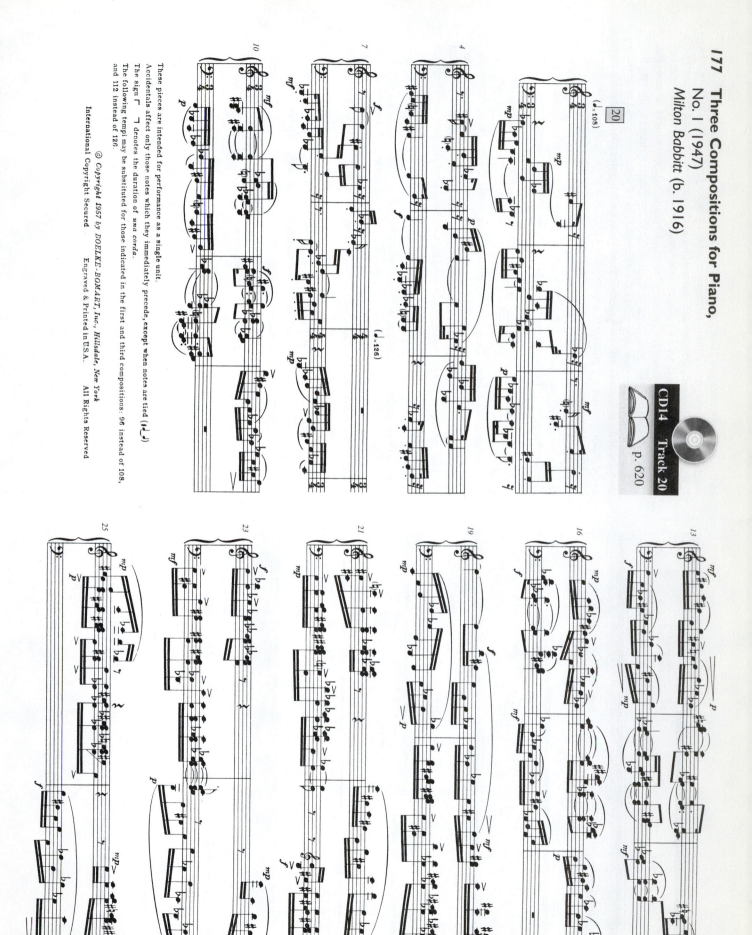

These pieces are intended for performance as a single unit.
Accidentals affect only those notes which they immediately precede, except when notes are tied (♩♩).
The sign ⌐ ⌐ denotes the duration of *una corda*.
The following tempi may be substituted for those indicated in the first and third compositions: 96 instead of 108, and 112 instead of 126.

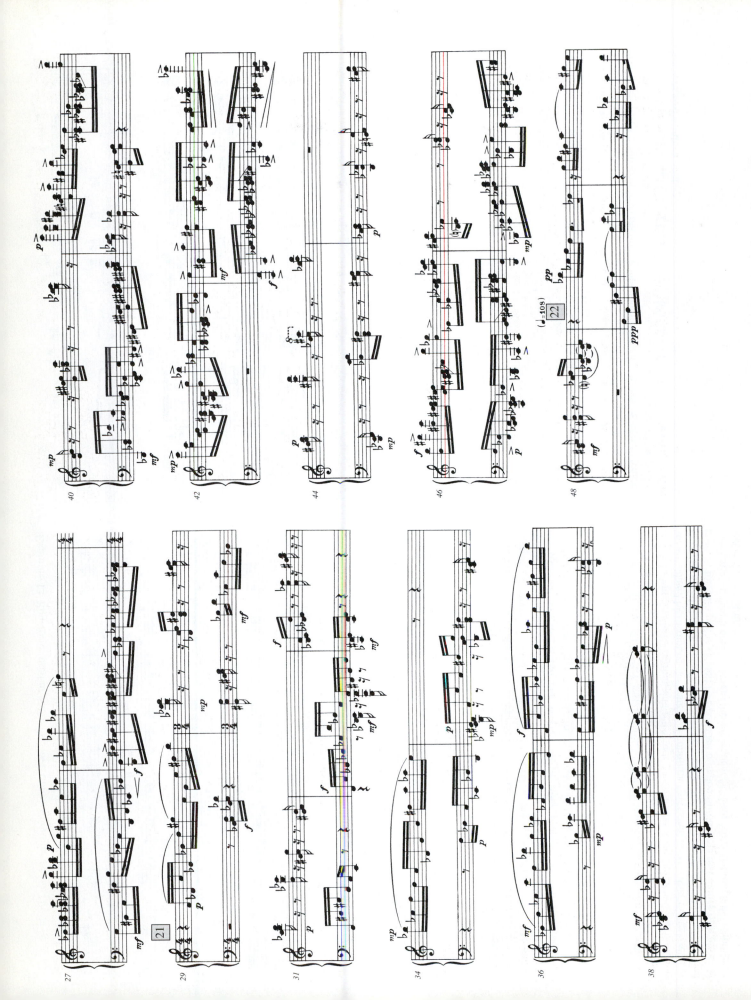

No. 177 Babbitt: *Three Compositions for Piano*

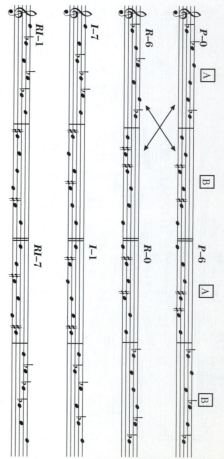

Example 12 Row forms used in Babbitt's *Three Compositions for Piano*, No. 1

The row for the first of Milton Babbitt's *Three Compositions for Piano* (1947) is combinatorial: its two hexachords (that is, its first six and six notes) can be combined with one of the hexachords of an inverted, retrograde, or retrograde inverted form of the same row without producing any duplication of pitches. Here, P-0 is combinatorial with R-6. In other words, hexachord A of P-0 combines with hexachord B of R-6 to produce all twelve pitches. The order of the pitches is different from that in P-0, but combinatoriality is concerned only with the content of the individual (and combined) hexachords, not the actual sequence of the pitches. The complementary hexachords of the two forms (hexachord B of P-0 and hexachord A of R-6) are also combinatorial.

Combinatoriality allowed composers to align different set-forms to sound at the same time without risking simultaneous or nearly simultaneous iterations of the same pitch-class. By exploiting the combinatorial properties of this row, Babbitt and others were able to create multiple statements of the twelve-tone row not only horizontally (in individual voices) but also vertically through the alignment of two different forms of the row sounding simultaneously. In the opening measures of the *Three Compositions for Piano*, No. 1, for example, we find the basic row both horizontally and vertically:

- Horizontally: the left hand in m. 1–2 presents P-0 in its entirety; the right hand presents P-6 in its entirety.

- Vertically: taking both voices together, all twelve pitches appear in m. 1; all twelve appear again in m. 2; in m. 3, and so on.

This same work also represents one of the earliest manifestations of integral serialism. In addition to manipulating the combinatorial properties of the row, Babbitt serializes the elements of rhythm, dynamics, and register as well. Using the sixteenth note as the unit of measure, he establishes a basic pattern of 5, 1, 4, 2 (that is, five sixteenth notes, followed by one sixteenth note, and so on) and "inverts" the rhythmic structure by subtracting these values from 6. Thus the rhythmic "matrix" of the work looks like this:

P = 5, 1, 4, 2   I = 1, 5, 2, 4
R = 2, 4, 1, 5   RI = 4, 2, 5, 1

Prime forms of the pitch row, regardless of the transposition, are always presented in the P rhythm (5, 1, 4, 2), inverted forms of the pitch row in the I rhythm (1, 5, 2, 4), retrograde inverted forms in the RI rhythm, and retrograde forms in the R rhythm. Rhythmic durations are articulated by disrupting the pattern of continuous sixteenth notes, either through rests or through slurred notes that create rhythms of longer duration. The grouping of 5 in the left hand in m. 1, for example, is created by the added duration on the note that comes fifth after the four initial sixteenth notes, whereas the subsequent "1" is articulated through the eighth-note rest at the end of m. 1.

4'33" (1952)
John Cage (1912–1992)

CD n/a   p. 623

I

TACET

II

TACET

III

TACET

The most celebrated of all aleatoric ("chance") compositions is *4'33"*, first performed on August 29, 1952, at the appropriately named Maverick Concert Hall in Woodstock, New York (near the site of the celebrated rock festival that would take place there 27 summers later). The work, which consists of three entirely silent movements, was inspired in part by the "white paintings" by one of Cage's friends, the artist Robert Rauschenberg. These "blank" canvases are by their very nature never truly blank, of course. Every canvas has its own unique color and textures, and each canvas is constantly changing because of the way it reflects the light of its surroundings. In much the same way, Cage's *4'33"* challenges the notion that there is such a thing as silence—the musical equivalent of a "blank" canvas—and by extension, the very idea of music itself. By listening to a "silent" work, we become acutely aware of the sounds around us: breathing, coughing, a room's ventilation system, a dog barking in the distance. We are listening to a work that is not silent at all, and that changes constantly and differs from performance to performance. These kinds of sounds, moreover, are always a part of the listening experience: if we choose to shut them out, it is because we have been conditioned to do so.

Many interpreted Cage's work as the epitome of the modernist composer's contempt for the audience. Other listeners reveled in the work's profoundly provocative absurdity. The piece is in some respects even more absurd than most people realize, for its score (and it does have a score) directs that the work "may be performed and last any length of time by any instrumentalist or combination of instrumentalists." Thus the most famous aspect of the piece—its meticulously precise duration—is optional.

NOTE: The title of this work is the total length in minutes and seconds of its performance. At Woodstock, N.Y., August 29, 1952, the title was 4' 33" and the three parts were 33", 2' 40", and 1! 20". It was performed by David Tudor, pianist, who indicated the beginnings of parts by closing, the endings by opening, the keyboard lid. However, the work may be performed by any instrumentalist or combination of instrumentalists and last any length of time.

FOR IRWIN KREMEN

JOHN CAGE

179 Roll Over, Beethoven (1956)
Chuck Berry (b. 1926)

Chuck Berry's *Roll Over, Beethoven* is typical of many early rock-and-roll songs of the 1950s and early 1960s. Its melodic range is limited, its formal structure and rhythms repetitive, its essential harmonies confined to the tonic and subdominant—and for all these reasons, the work is mesmerizing. The lyrics themselves—urging the most revered of all classical composers to turn over in his grave—evoke a cultural war between "high" and "low" art, contemplation and activity, old and young. The song spoke directly to a generation of teenagers, and it retains its elemental force today. Formally, *Roll Over, Beethoven* follows the 12-bar blues form. The published lead sheet provides only the barest outline of the melody, harmonies, and words; a great many aspects of the music are left to the discretion of the performer or performers.

180 Traditional, **Tom Dooley**
Arranged by *Charles Seeger (1886–1979)*
and *Ruth Crawford Seeger (1901–1953)*

CD14 Track 24

p. 634

CHORUS:
Hang down your head, Tom Dooley,
Hang down your head and cry,
Hang down your head, Tom Dooley,
Poor boy, you're bound to die.

1. I met her on the mountain
   And there I tuck her life;
   I met her on the mountain
   And stobbed her with my knife.

   CHORUS:
   Hang down your head, Tom Dooley,
   Hang down your head and cry,
   Hang down your head, Tom Dooley,
   Poor boy, you're bound to die.

2. This time tomorrer,
   Reckon where I'll be?–
   If it hadn'-a been for Grayson
   I'd-a been in Tennessee.

   CHORUS:
   Hang down your head, Tom Dooley,
   Hang down your head and cry,
   Hang down your head, Tom Dooley,
   Poor boy, you're bound to die.

3. This time tomorrer,
   Reckon where I'll be?—
   In some lonesome valley
   A-hangin' on a white oak tree.

   CHORUS:
   Hang down your head, Tom Dooley,
   Hang down your head and cry,
   Hang down your head, Tom Dooley,
   Poor boy, you're bound to die.

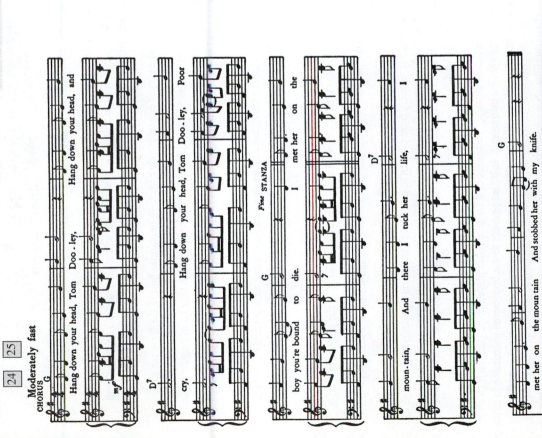

The song *Tom Dooley* illustrates the complexity of the ways in which music from the unwritten and unrecorded traditions was transmitted to a wider audience. The ballad "Tom Dooley" was a true folk ballad, a way of telling the news—in this case about the murder of one Laura Foster in 1865 in western North Carolina, allegedly at the hands of her lover, Tom Dooley. In 1938, the folklorist Frank Warner was traveling in that part of the state and took down the song as performed in unaccompanied form by a local resident named Frank Proffitt. Proffitt had learned the song from his father, who in turn had learned it from his mother, who had actually witnessed the hanging of Tom Dooley. Warner passed his transcription of the song on to his colleague Alan Lomax, who in 1947 published it in a collection called *Folk Song U.S.A.*, crediting Warner as the collector. Lomax carefully preserved the regional pronunciations ("stobbed" for "stabbed," "tuck" for "took") and commissioned Charles Seeger and his wife, Ruth Crawford Seeger (a significant composer in her own right) to add piano accompaniment. The first published version of the work thus represents a curious mixture of old (melody and text) with new (harmonizations and piano accompaniment).

Eleven years later, The Kingston Trio picked up the song from Lomax's anthology, made their own arrangement, recorded it, and scored their first hit. Warner and Lomax, realizing the immense popularity of the song, contacted Proffitt, and the three filed suit against the Kingston Trio. They began to receive small royalties on the Kingston Trio's recording after 1962—by which time the group had already sold four million copies of the song. Because of technology, what had been passed on from generation to generation orally and in a remote locale for almost 80 years had become a readily available commodity when it was first published in 1947—and an extremely valuable commodity, worth millions of dollars, when it was recorded by The Kingston Trio in 1958.

181 In C (1964)
Terry Riley (b. 1935)

CD14 Track 26 p. 637

IN C
Performing Directions

All performers play from the same page of 53 melodic patterns played in sequence.

Any number of any kind of instruments can play. A group of about 35 is desired if possible but smaller or larger groups will work. If vocalist(s) join in they can use any vowel and consonant sounds they like.

Patterns are to be played consecutively with each performer having the freedom to determine how many times he or she will repeat each pattern before moving on to the next. There is no fixed rule as to the number of repetitions a pattern may have, however, since performances normally average between 45 minutes and an hour and a half, it can be assumed that one would repeat each pattern from somewhere between 45 seconds and a minute and a half or longer.

It is very important that performers listen very carefully to one another and this means occasionally to drop out and listen. As an ensemble, it is very desireable to play very softly as well as very loudly and to try to diminuendo and crescendo together.

Each pattern can be played in unison or canonically in any alignment with itself or with its neighboring patterns. One of the joys of IN C is the interaction of the players in polyrhythmic combinations that spontaneously arise between patterns. Some quite fantastic shapes will arise and disintegrate as the group moves through the piece when it is properly played.

It is important not to hurry from pattern to pattern but to stay on a pattern long enough to interlock with other patterns being played. As the performance progresses, performers should stay within 2 or 3 patterns of each other. It is important not to race too far ahead or to lag too far behind.

The ensemble can be aided by the means of a 1/8 note pulse played played on the high c's of the piano or on a mallet instrument. It is also possible to use improvised percussion in strict rhythm (drum set, cymbals bells etc.), if it is carefully done and doesn't overpower the ensemble. All performers must play strictly in rhythm and it is essential that every one play each pattern carefully. It is advised to rehearse patterns in unison before attempting to play the piece to determine that everyone is playing correctly.

(continued on p. 564)

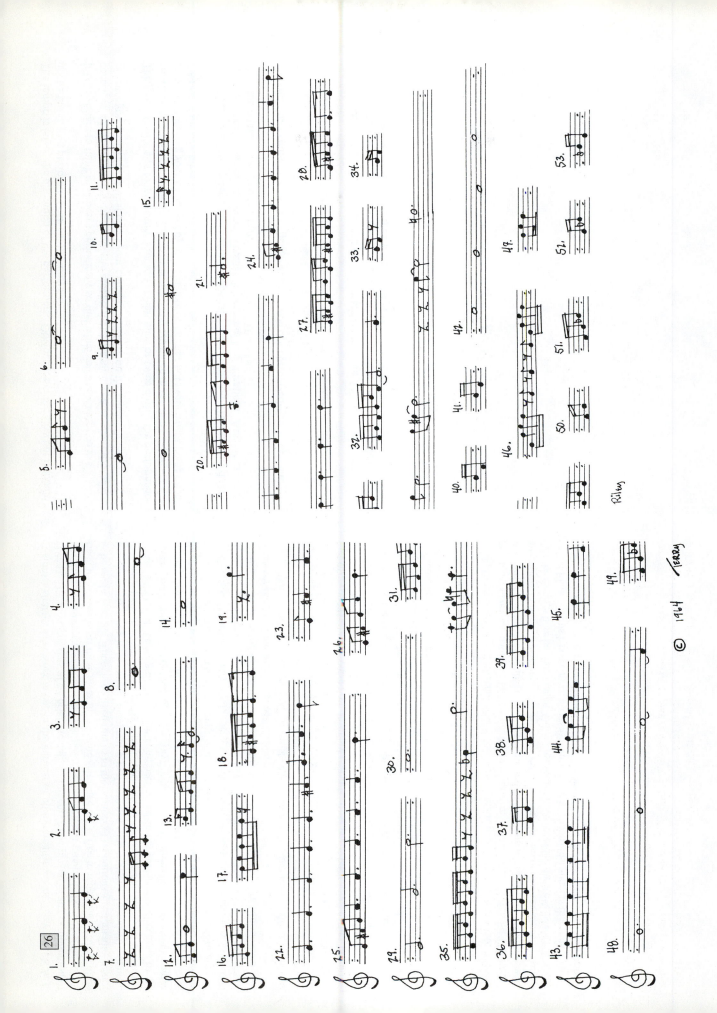

No. 181 Riley: *In C*

563

The tempo is left to the discretion of the performers. Obviously, not too slow but it should not be faster than performers can comfortably play.

It is important to think of patterns periodically so that when you are resting you are conscious of the larger periodic composite accents that are sounding and when you re-enter you are aware of what effect your entrance will have on the musics flow.

The group should aim to merge into a unison at least once or twice during the performance. At the same time if the players seem to be consistently too much in the same alignment of a pattern try shifting your alignment by an 1/8th note or quarter note with what's going on in the rest of the ensemble.

It is OK to transpose patterns by an octave, especially to transpose up. Transposing down by octaves works best on the patterns containing notes of long durations. Augmentation of rhythmic values can also be effective.

If a performer comes to a pattern that for some reason can't be played--just omit it and go on.

Instruments can be amplified if desired. Electronic keyboards are welcome also.

In C is ended in this way: When each performer arrives at figure #53 he or she stays on it until the entire ensemble has arrived there. The group then makes a large crescendo and diminuendo a few times and then each player drops out as he or she wishes.

Terry Riley

A similar strategy is at work in one of the earliest of all minimalist works, Terry Riley's *In C* (1964). The score consists of 53 brief thematic fragments to be played in any combination of any kind of instruments, though the composer recommends a group of about 35 if possible. Each player performs these ideas in the same sequence but is free to repeat each unit as often as he or she sees fit. "There is no fixed rule as to the number of repetitions a pattern may have," the composer notes in the score, though if a performance runs between 45 and 90 minutes, then each performer would ordinarily repeat each pattern for somewhere between 40 and 90 seconds. "One of the joys of *In C*," the composer noted in his performing directions to the score, "is the interaction of the players in polyrhythmic combinations that spontaneously arise between patterns. Some quite fantastic shapes will arise and disintegrate as the group moves through the piece when it is properly played." The one constant element of the piece is an ostinato C octave played on the high range of a piano or mallet instrument. If a performance of *In C* runs to 90 minutes, this would mean repeating this particular figure as many as 15,000 times in succession. While this might sound like a recipe for monotony, the process of unfolding is such that the work remains constantly in motion and gradually transforms itself into whatever the performers decide it will become.

What kind of a work is *In C*? It resists classification. It bears many hallmarks of jazz (individual "riffs," enormous latitude for improvisation), yet it is essentially a canon at the unison. Riley notes that "all performers must play strictly in rhythm," and he even recommends that musicians "rehearse patterns in unison before attempting to play the piece to determine that everyone is playing correctly." In many respects, *In C* harks back to an earlier period of time—its open-ended instrumentation and the tremendous latitude given to performers seem in some respects more typical of the Renaissance or Baroque eras than the 20th century. "At the time I wrote *In C*, I was almost ready to drop out of music," the composer once explained. "Classical music was very mental; the mind governed the musical activity. I think the shift in what this music [*In C*] was doing was letting the heart back into the game. I wanted to make the score so minimal that it wasn't important anymore."

Performance notes: Terry Riley has recorded *In C* on several occasions. The best known are those made in 1968 with Members of the New Music Center at the State University of New York, Buffalo, and the "25th Anniversary Recording" made in San Francisco in 1990. Not surprisingly, given the nature of this music, the two performances are quite different. The earlier was performed by an ensemble of 11 musicians and runs 43 minutes. The later recording, with an ensemble of 31 musicians, runs 76 minutes. It is from the second of these performances that the excerpt here has been taken. Other ensembles have recorded the work as well. A group called Piano Circus has recorded a version entirely on keyboard instruments that runs 20 minutes; and a 2002 electronic realization by the European Music Project is affectionately known as the "disco version" of *In C*.

182 Orfeo II (excerpt) (1976)
Thea Musgrave (b. 1928)

CD14 Track 28

p. 643

NOTES ON PERFORMANCE

Orfeo II is projected as a ballet for solo male dancer, although it can equally well be performed in concert form. The dancer takes the part of Orfeo, as does the solo flute. All other elements are represented by the orchestra — they are invisible: their presence is indicated by lighting effects, or laser beam projections etc. Orfeo's journey to the Underworld exists only in his imagination.

The flautist should also be on-stage (he is to some extent Orfeo's *alter ego*) and there should be close interaction between him and the dancer (though, of course, he is 'invisible' to the dancer). The principal 1st violin represents Euridice (that is, heard not seen) and so, in concert version, the player should sit at the back, hidden by the other players.

The solo flute should play with considerable rubato independently of the conductor. Where there are arrows synchronization must be exact, otherwise there can be some flexibility. Adjust tempo so that synchronization is *approximately* as written.

Accidentals in *unmeasured* bars apply only to the note they precede, except where one note or a pair of notes is immediately repeated.

↓ represents downbeat to an unmeasured bar: here, the music should continue in the same tempo (unless otherwise marked), though with rubato.

This work also exists in another version — *Orfeo I* for flute and pre-recorded tape. Like *Orfeo II*, this is projected as a ballet, but is equally suited to concert performance.

SCENARIO

1 Orfeo laments.

Orfeo stands alone on the banks of the river Styx and grieves for Euridice. He hears a distant echo of her voice and he listens. Then it disappears. Orfeo in despair pleads with Charon to ferry him across the river so that he may search for her.

2 Orfeo crosses the river Styx.

Charon consents to listen to his plea. The waves of the river begin to ripple and then surge up and part, and Orfeo can cross to the other side.

3 Orfeo calms the Furies.

Orfeo is confronted by the Furies, and eloquently he pleads with them. They gradually quieten as they listen. He is allowed to proceed, but on one condition . . . that he must not look at Euridice till he has returned to the other side of the river.

4 Orfeo searches amongst the Shades.

Orfeo searches for Euridice amongst the Shades. He hears her approaching . . . he steps towards her, then turns away and shields his eyes.

5 Orfeo hears Euridice's pleas.

Orfeo hears Euridice pleading with him to turn and look at her . . . he cannot resist and he turns. Euridice vanishes for ever.

6 Orfeo is attacked by the Bacchantes.

Orfeo is at once attacked violently by the Bacchantes. He makes a last desperate plea, but he finds himself back on the banks of the river Styx, alone and desolate.

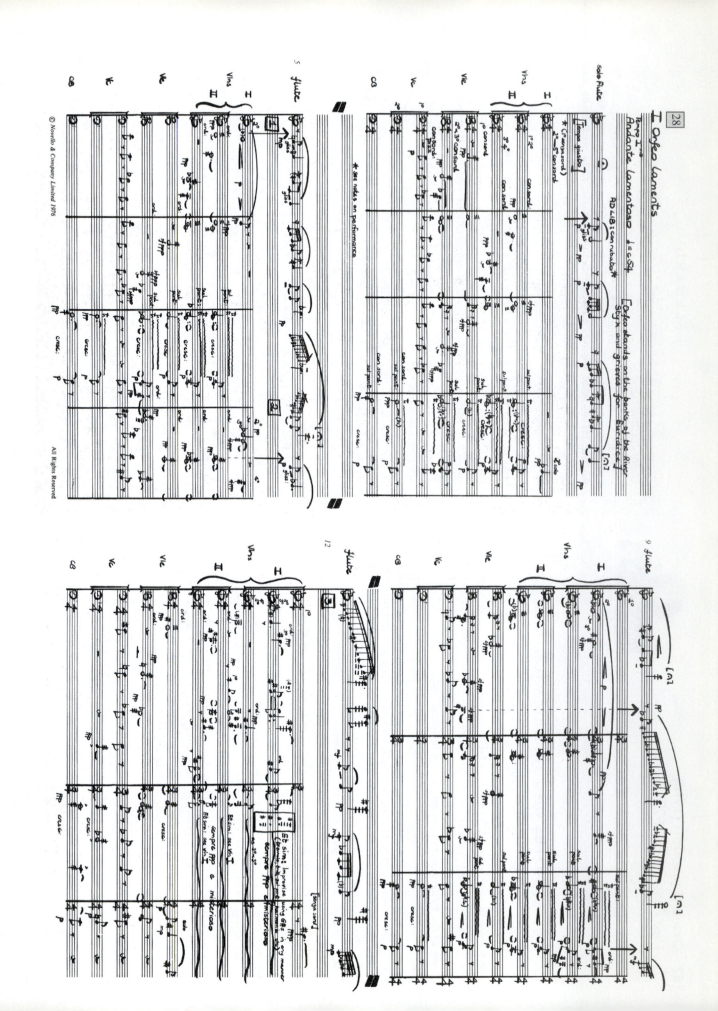

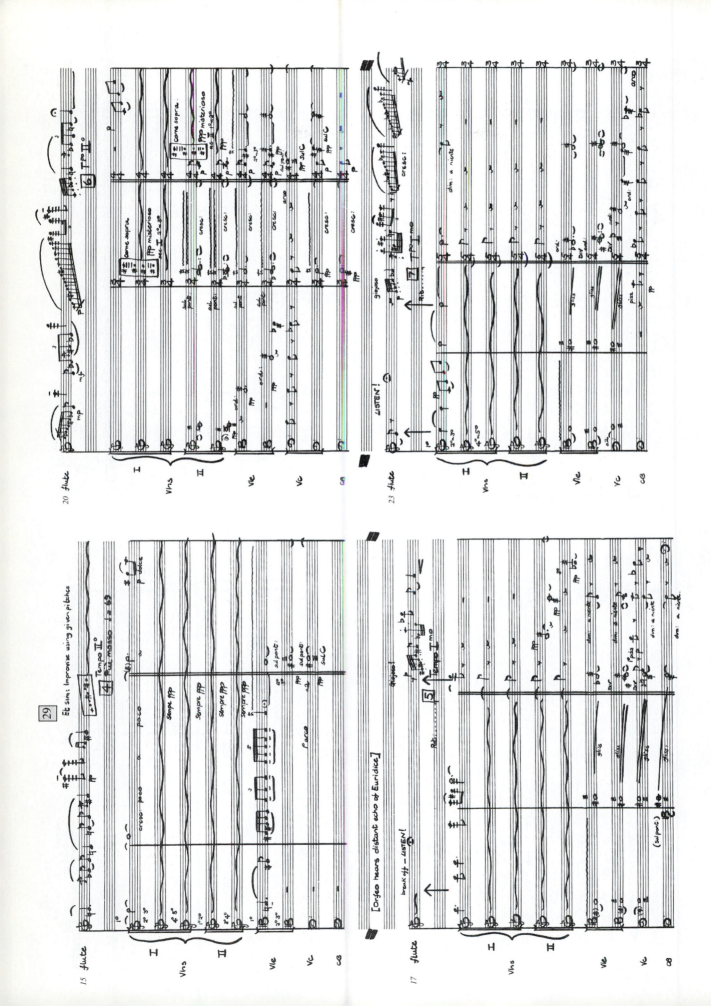

No. 182 Musgrave: Orfeo II

No. 182 Musgrave: *Orfeo II*

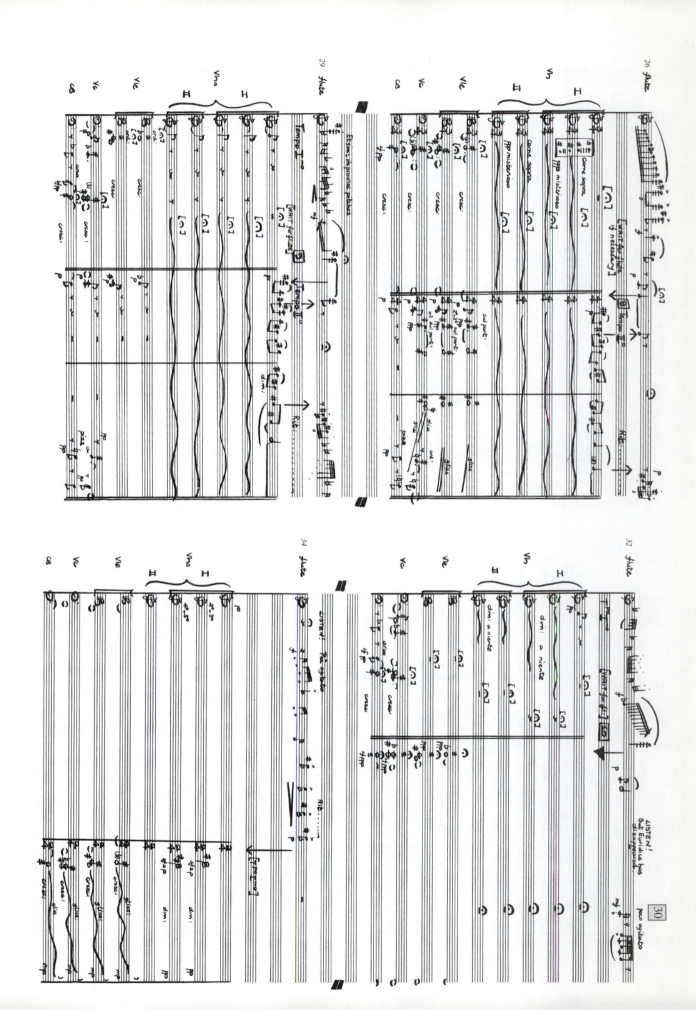

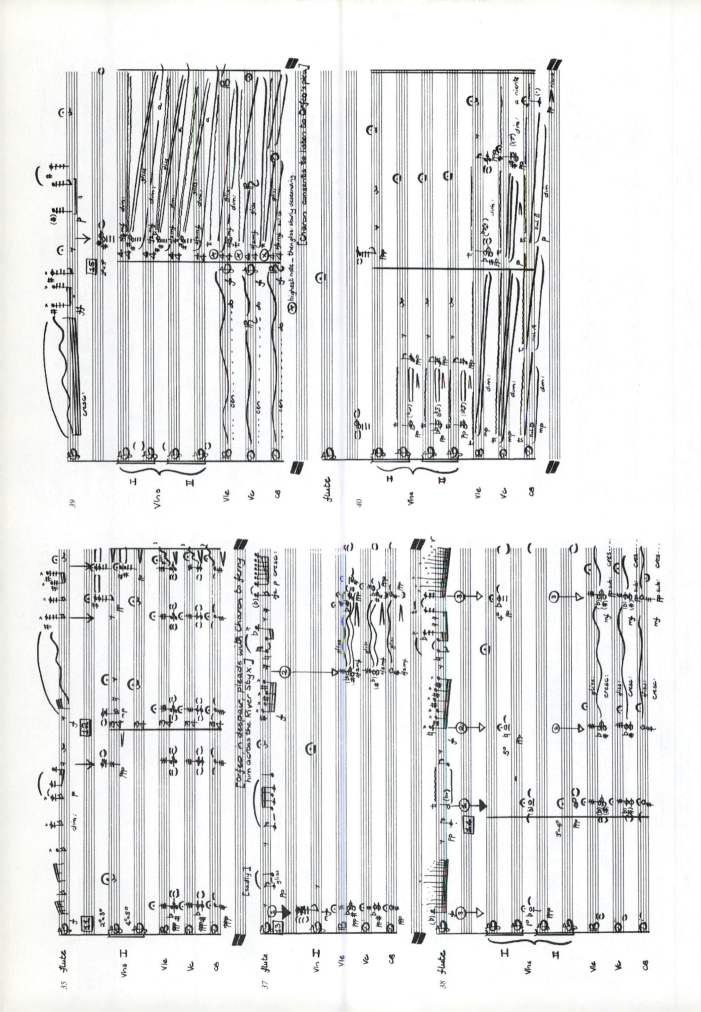

No. 182 Musgrave: *Orfeo II*

Thea Musgrave's *Orfeo II*, scored for solo flute and 15 strings, moves freely between tonal and atonal idioms. Long passages of its opening section ("Orfeo Laments") are centered on G and D. It would be misleading to say the music is "in" either of these keys, but it has a strong sense of a tonal center. The tonality is reinforced rhythmically by the steady, repeated pattern of eighth notes in the lower voices, almost in the fashion of a Baroque ground bass.

At figure 4, the first violin intones the opening phrase of the most famous aria from Christoph Willibald Gluck's opera *Orfeo* of 1762, *Che farò senza Euridice?* ("What shall I do without Euridice?"). Orpheus's moving lament at the loss of his beloved wife (Example 23-2). This reminiscence from another musical world—the middle of the 18th century—has an eerie effect within the context of Musgrave's *Orfeo II*. When it appears in the first violin at figure 4, it sounds like (and is) a fleeting memory. The flute soloist, representing Orpheus, listens to the fragments of this melody and tries to imitate them (just after figure 10 through figure 14) but cannot sustain the line. Orpheus's inability to recover the tonal melody parallels his inability to recover the dead Eurydice.

Example 13 Gluck, *Orfeo ed Euridice, Che farò senza Euridice?*

What shall I do without Euridice? Where shall I go without my beloved?

As in Ives's *Unanswered Question* (Anthology 2#152) and Schoenberg's "O alter Duff" from *Pierrot lunaire* (Anthology 2#161), Musgrave juxtaposes tonal and nontonal harmonies to create a sense of tonality that nevertheless sounds strangely discordant.

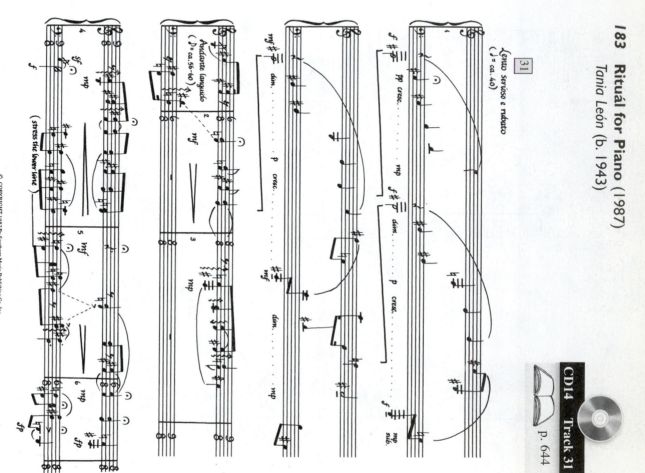

183 Ritual for Piano (1987)
Tania León (b. 1943)

CD14 Track 31   P. 644

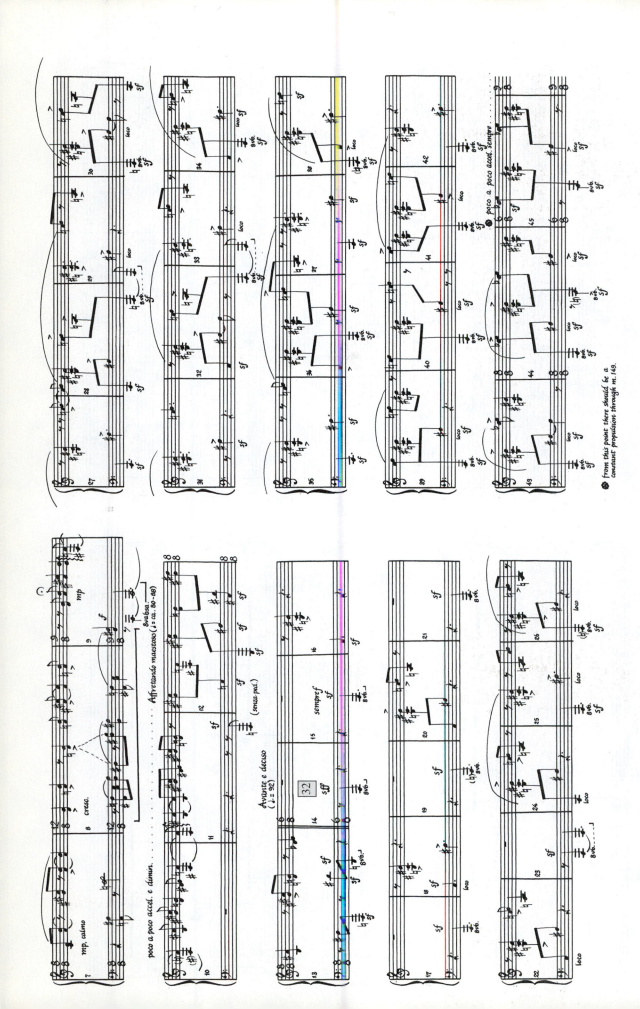

No. 183 León: *Ritmál for Piano*

No. 183 León: *Ritual for Piano*

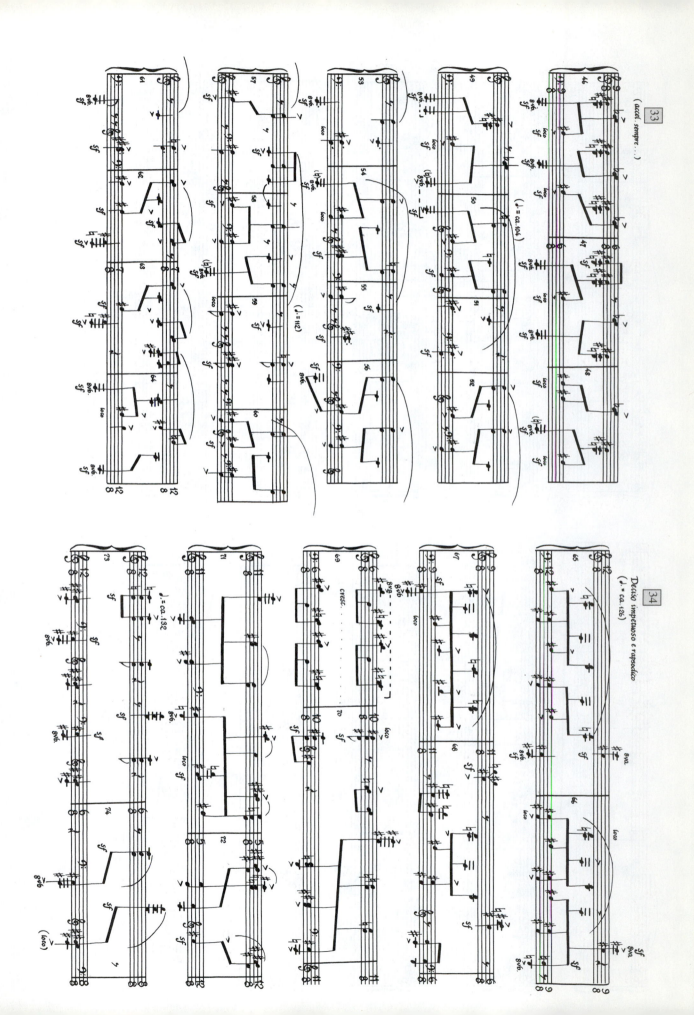

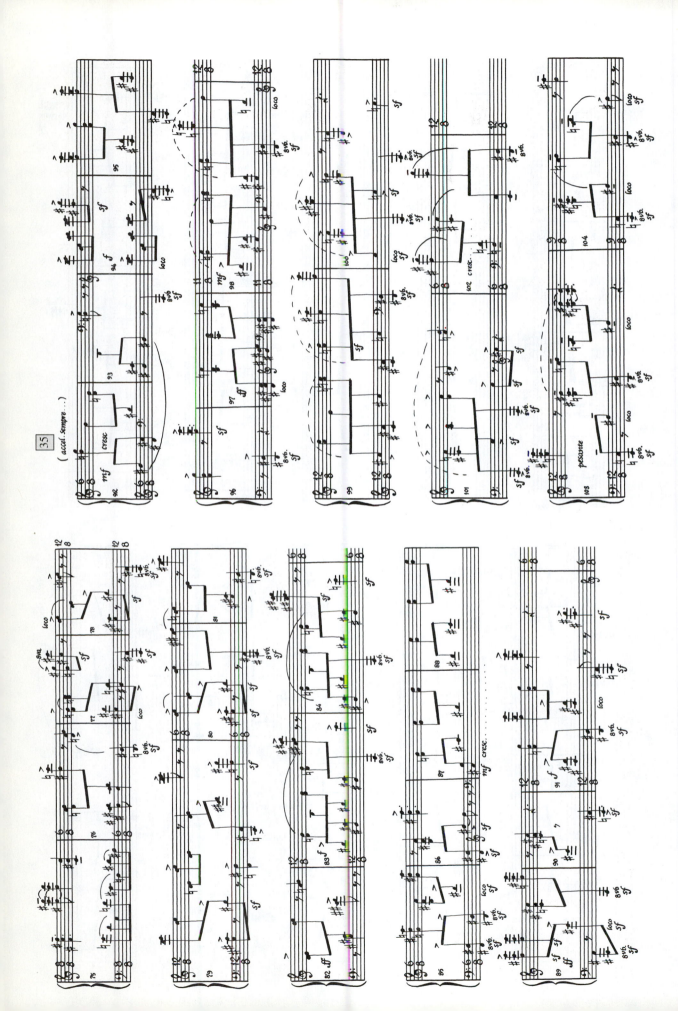

No. 183 León: *Ritual for Piano*

No. 183 León: *Ritual for Piano*

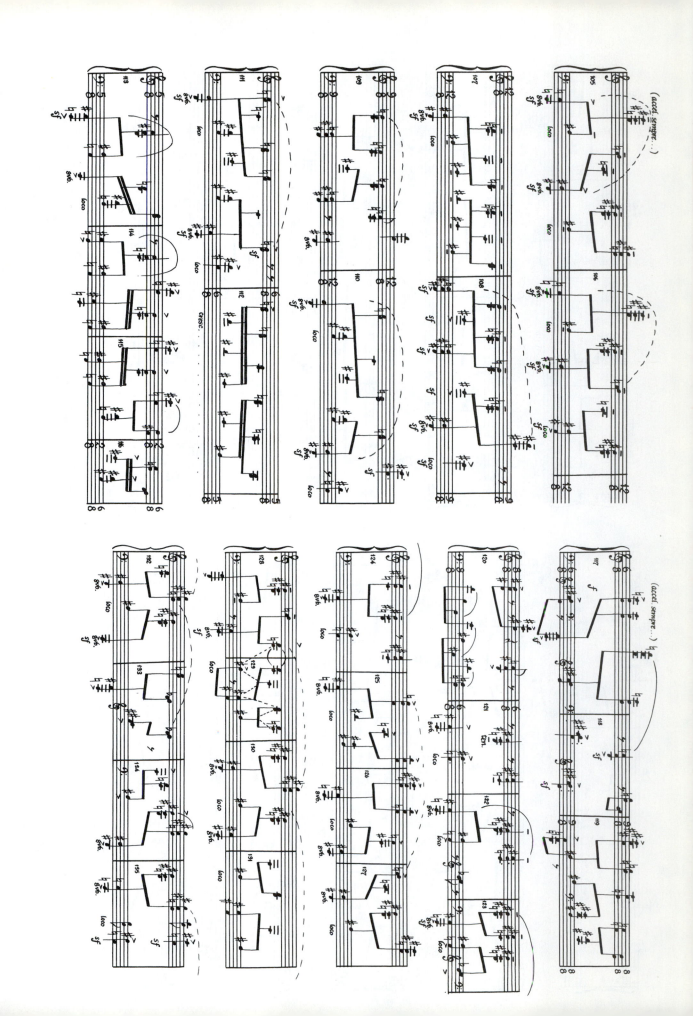

Tania León's *Rituál for Piano* (1987) synthesizes a variety of traditions even while establishing its own unique identity. It opens with an introductory series of slow, unmeasured arpeggios similar in their improvisatory mood to those found in the beginning of C. P. E. Bach's Fantasia in C minor (Anthology No. 103). After a brief section marked "Andante languido" (m. 1–13), the music hits its stride with the powerful rhythms of the "Avante e deciso" (beginning at m. 14). The harmonic idiom is tonal but not triadic: the emphasis on a series of repeated notes in the bass anchors the work tonally without situating it in any particular key. The driving rhythms owe as much to Afro-Cuban jazz elements and the artistry of jazz pianist Art Tatum as to the traditions of Stravinsky and Copland. Like the composer herself, *Rituál for Piano* resists easy classification. It represents instead the increasing tendency of music in the late 20th century toward a synthesis of diverse styles and traditions.

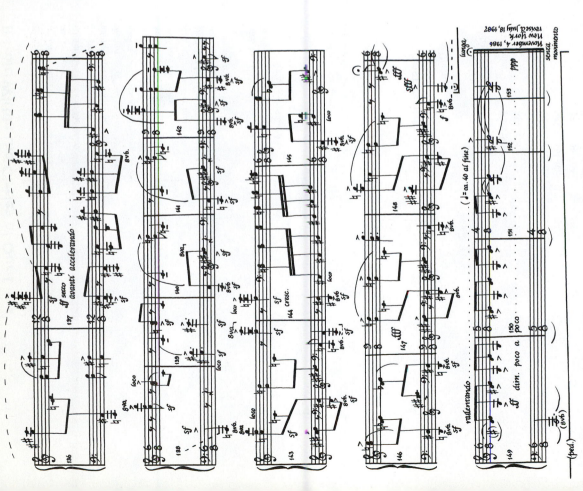

New York
November 4, 1986
revised July 18, 1987

No. 183 León: *Rituál for Piano*

184 Missa Gaia: Mass for the Earth, first movement (Introit—"Within the Circles of Our Lives") (1992)
Libby Larsen (b. 1950)

CD14 Track 36 p. 646

Program Notes

Missa Gaia: Mass for the Earth
SATB and SSA Choirs, oboe, percussion, string quartet, four-hand piano

The *Missa Gaia: Mass for the Earth* is a mass for our times which adopts the form and spirit of the traditional Mass and replaces the texts with words addressing human beings' relationship to the Earth. *Missa Gaia* is a celebration of those of us who live on this land, a land which can be terribly beautiful and gentle, a land which can be harsh—but which is always giving and always renewing. The texts are drawn from the Bible, from Native American poets Joy Harjo and Maurice Kenny, from medieval mystic Meister Eckhart, from the Chinook Psalter and from poets Wendell Berry and Gerard Manley Hopkins.

The theme of circles permeates the entire work from the texts to the music, which uses the circle of fifths both as a melodic theme and as an instrumental motive. Although I have not asked to oboe to do so in this work, the oboist is one of the few instrumentalists who can breathe circularly. The string quartet traditionally sits in a semi-circle.

The United States of America is not an old country. Most of us are really still pioneers. And we are still learning what it is to live on this land and what it is for the land to let us live here. Amidst the natural abundance of our country, I live with the blizzards and tornadoes of the Midwest. And I see the earthquakes of the West Coast, the hurricanes of the South and East coast, and the arid lands of the Southwest. I am reminded again and again that the Earth lets us live on it.

It seems to me that if we perform traditional Western rituals with new reverence, spirit and meaning, than perhaps we can help effect change. It is, at least, one of the efforts we who make music can give to assist Mother Earth and repay her in some small way for all she has given us.

Introit—Within the Circles of Our Lives—premiered by the Paul Hill Washington Singers at the Kennedy Center, May 13, 1992

Gloria—Pied Beauty—premiered by the combined choirs the University Lutheran Church of Hope, University Baptist Church, and First Congregational Church, Minneapolis, Minnesota, April 26, 1992

Credo—Speak to the Earth and It Shall Teach Thee—premiered by Waldorf College Choir and the Saint Paul Chamber Orchestra, November 4, 1991, Forest City, Iowa, Peter Bay, conductor

The entire Missa Gaia: Mass for the Earth, premiered by Schola Cantorum, Gregory Wait, director, Palo Alto, California, May 30, 1992.

Introit: Within the Circles of Our Lives

Within the circles of our lives
we dance the circles of the years,
the circles of the seasons
within the circles of the years,
the cycles of the moon
within the circles of the seasons,
the circles of our reasons
within the cycles of the moon.

Again, again we come and go,
changed, changing. Hands
join, unjoin in love and fear,
grief and joy. The circles turn,
each giving into each, into all.
Only music keeps us here,

each by all the others held.
In the hold of hands and eyes
we turn in pairs, that joining
joining each to all again.

And then we turn, alone,
out of the sunlight gone
into the darker circles of return.

Wendell Berry

Orchestration

String Quartet

Oboe

4-Hand Piano

Percussion: Bass drum—high and low
                  Maracas
                  Marimba
                  Orchestra bells
                  Suspended cymbal
                  Temple blocks
                  Triangle—medium
                  Tubular bells
                  Vibraphone
                  Woodblock—medium

Duration: approximately 35 minutes

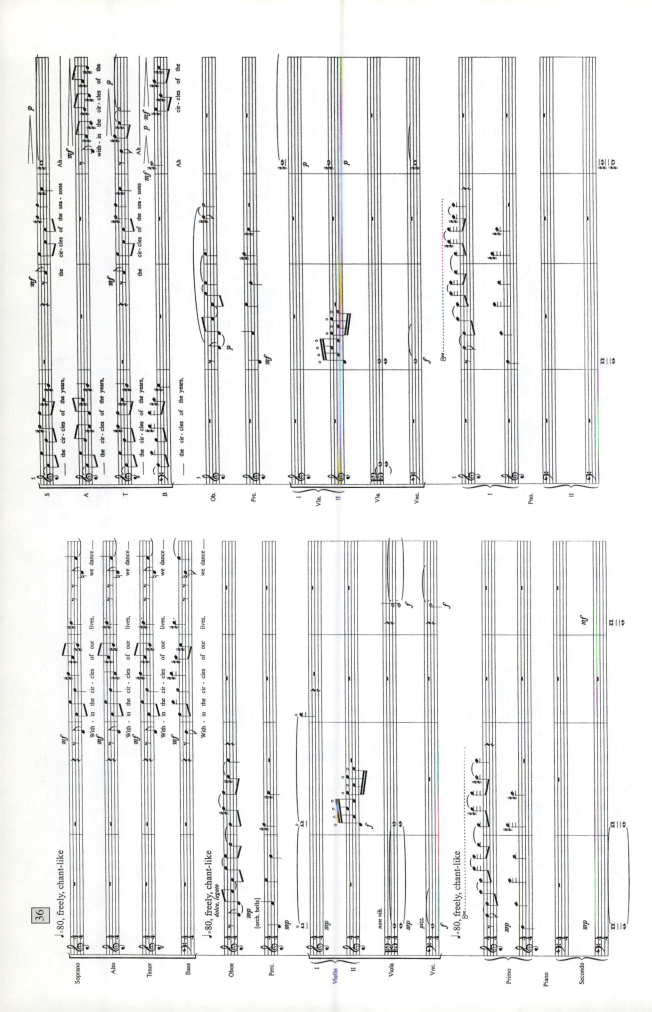

No. 184 Larsen: *Missa Gaia: Mass for the Earth*

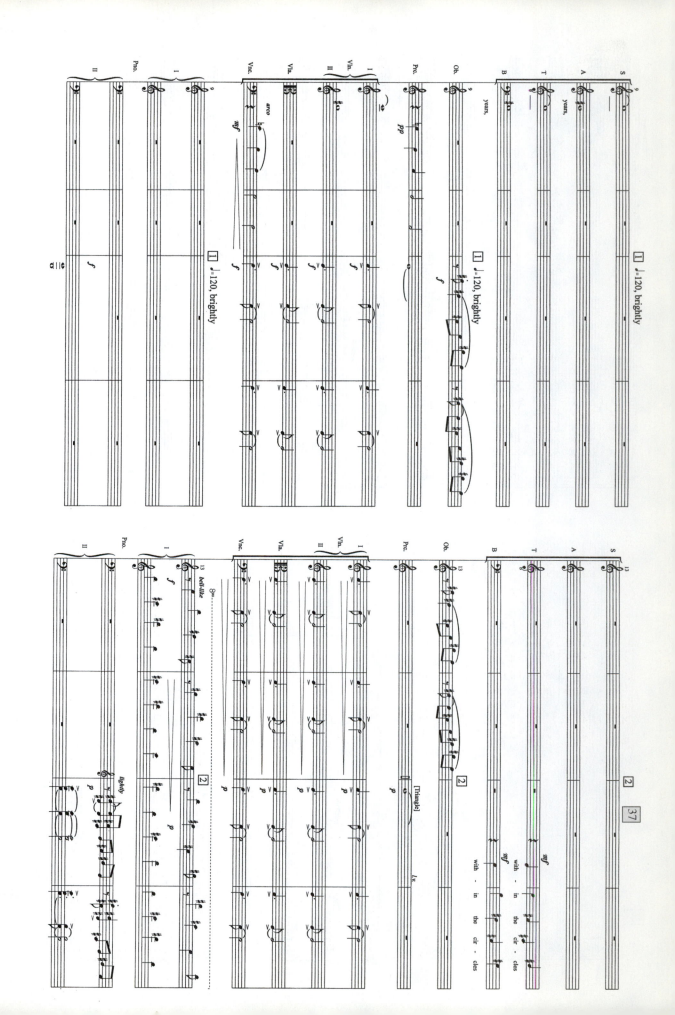

No. 184 Larsen: *Missa Gaia: Mass for the Earth*

No. 184 Larsen: *Missa Gaia: Mass for the Earth*

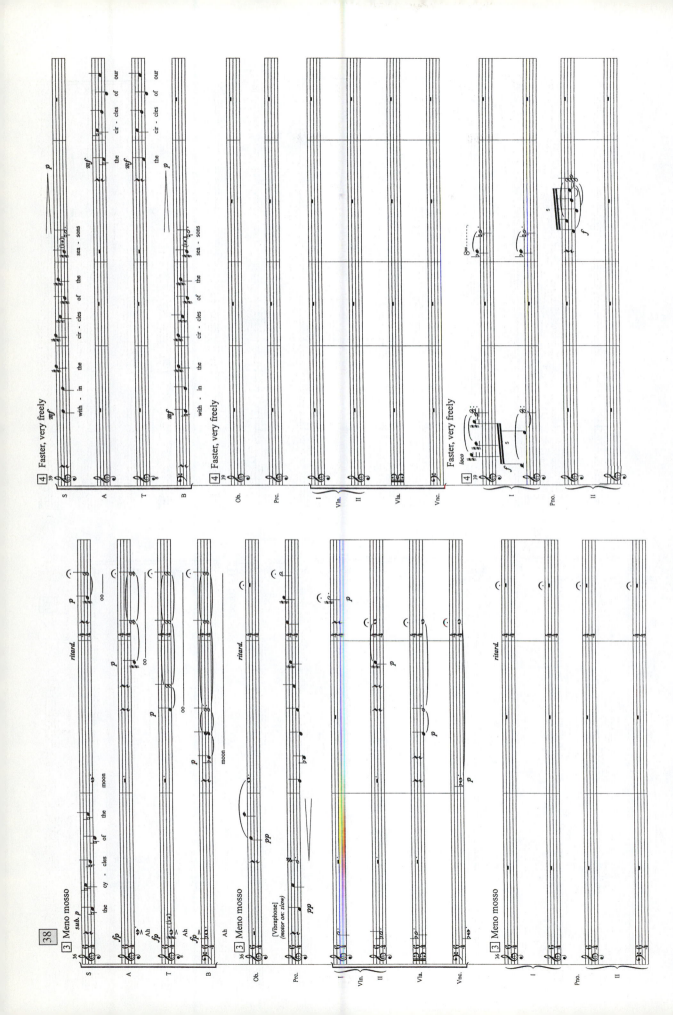

No. 184 Larsen: *Missa Gaia: Mass for the Earth*

No. 184 Larsen: *Missa Gaia: Mass for the Earth*

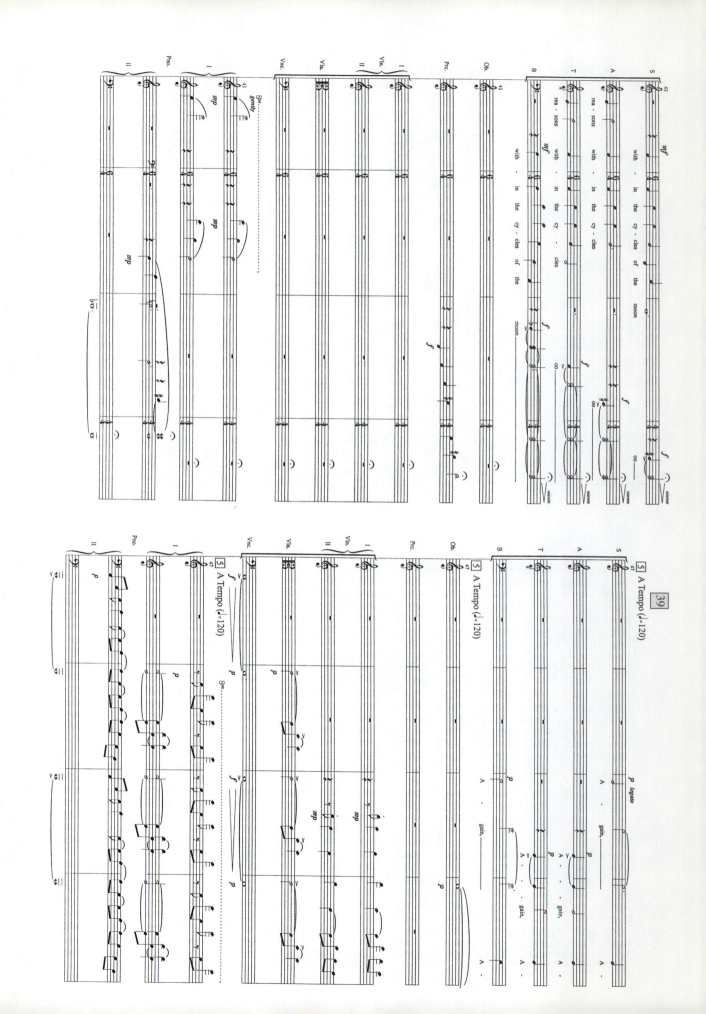

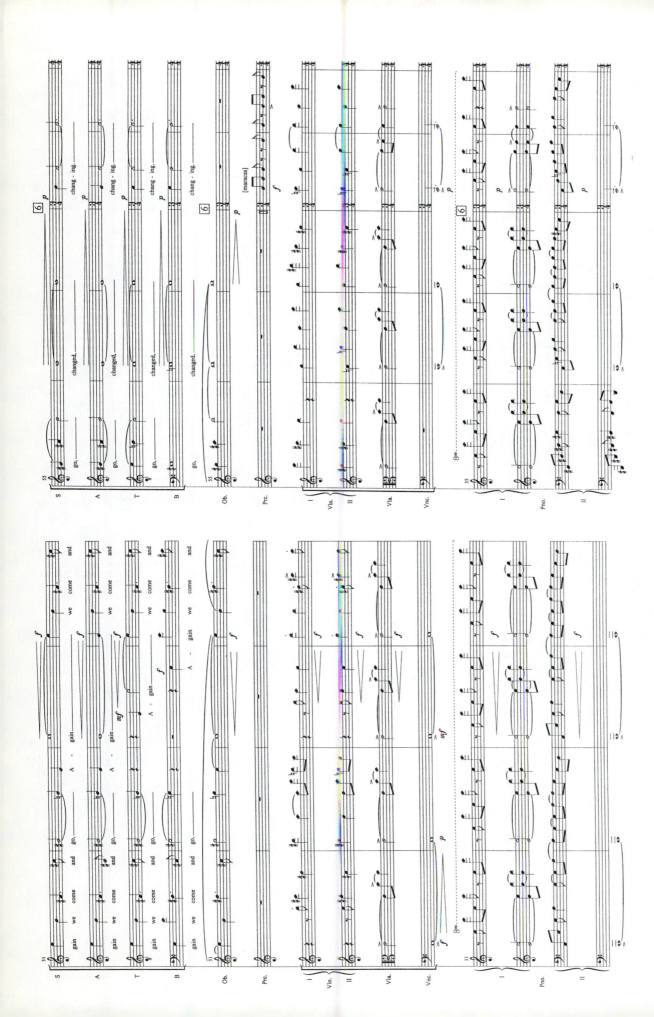

No. 184 Larsen: *Missa Gaia: Mass for the Earth*

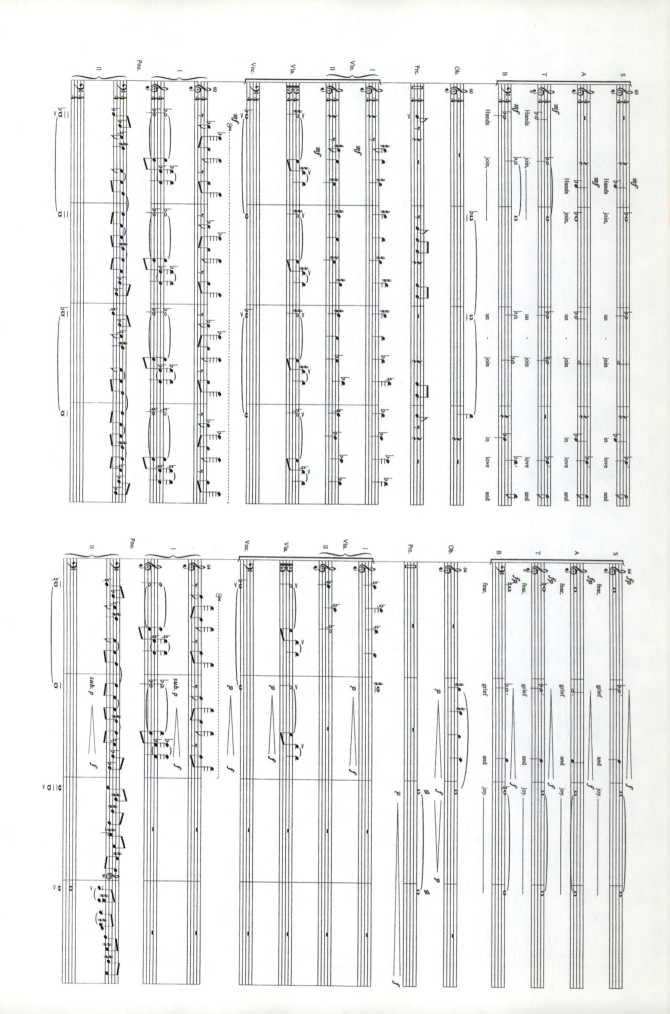

No. 184 Larsen: Missa Gaia: Mass for the Earth

79
S
A
T
B
each giv-ing in-to each, in-to all. on-ly mus-ic keeps us here:
pp warmly
Ob.
Prc.
Vln. I
Vln. II
Vla.
Vnc.
Pno. I
Pno. II
9
86
poco accel.
ritard.
held,
held.
oth-ers held,
oth-ers held.
all the oth-ers held,
all the oth-ers held.
each by all the oth-ers held,
each by all the oth-ers held.
dolce
loco

No. 184 Larsen: *Missa Gaia: Mass for the Earth*

S
A
T
B
Ob.
Prc.
Vln.
I
II
Vla.
Vnc.
Pno.
100
11
104
8va
turn in pairs, we turn in pairs, that join - ing, join - ing
pairs, we turn in pairs, pairs, join - ing
turn in pairs, we turn in pairs, that join - ing, join - ing
pairs, we turn in pairs join - ing
each to all a - gain, we turn in
each to all a - gain,
each to all a - gain, we turn in
each to all a - gain,
ff
p
mf
mp
pp

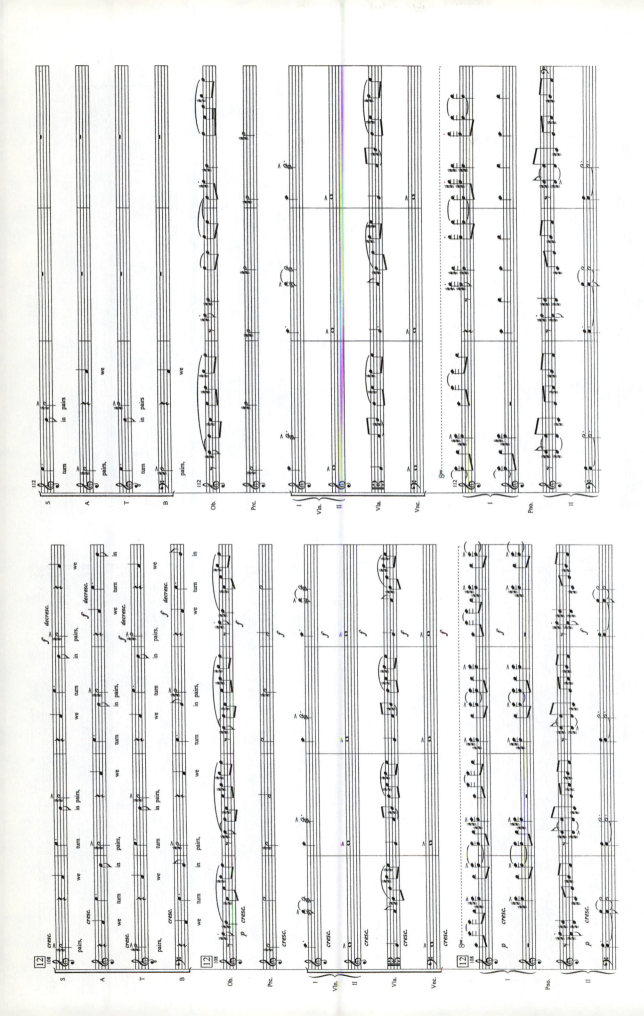

No. 184 Larsen: *Missa Gaia: Mass for the Earth*

No. 184 Larsen: *Missa Gaia: Mass for the Earth*

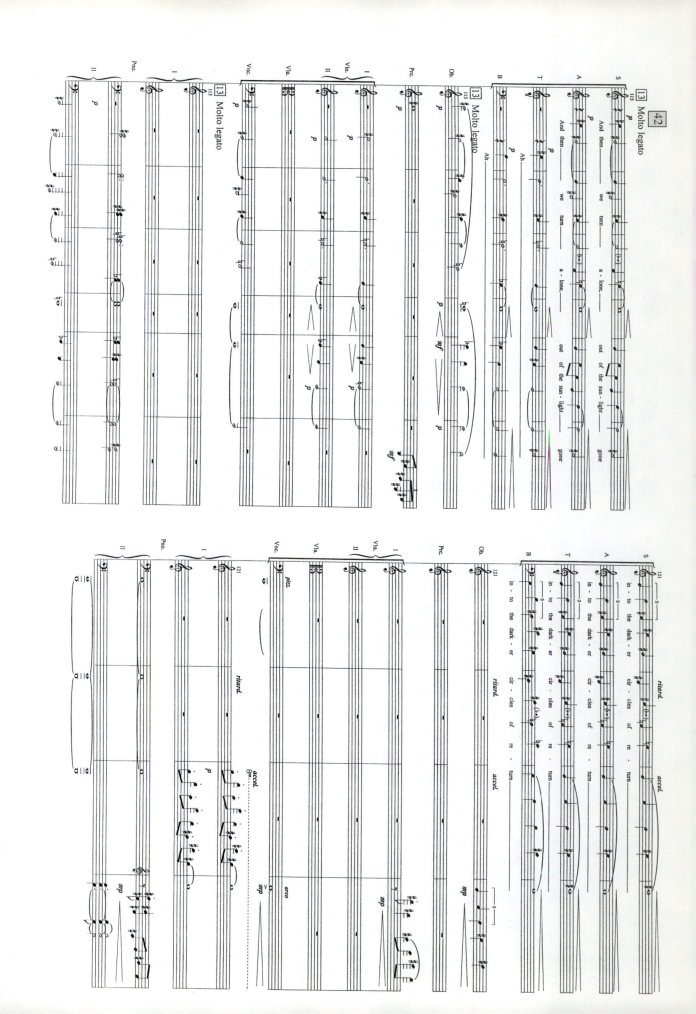

Libby Larsen's *Missa Gaia* (1992) evokes the traditions of the Mass in its movements headings of Introit, Kyrie, Gloria, Credo, Agnus Dei/Sanctus, and Benediction. But the texts of these individual movements are not liturgical; they draw instead on a variety of sources that address the relationship of human beings to the earth (*gaia* is the ancient Greek word for the earth). The text to the Introit ("Within the Circle of Our Lives") is by the American poet Wendell Berry (b. 1934), whose work often touches on issues of the environment. Larsen (b. 1950) uses the image of circles in nature as the central trope of the *Missa gaia*. Much of the work's melodic material uses ascending and descending fifths and fourths that suggest movement through the circle of fifths and whose contours outline rising and falling motions of various kinds. Like much postmodern music, the *Missa gaia* is decidedly tonal, yet not in the conventional triadic sense. The harmonies are dominated by unisons, octaves, fourths and open fifths: melodic and harmonic thirds appear only occasionally and stand out as a result.

No. 184 Larsen: *Missa Gaia: Mass for the Earth*

CREDITS

592

594